GLOBAL INVESTING

A HANDBOOK FOR SOPHISTICATED INVESTORS

GLOBAL INVESTING

A HANDBOOK FOR SOPHISTICATED INVESTORS

SUMNER N. LEVINE, editor

Nortech Associates
and
State University of New York
Stony Brook, NY

 HarperBusiness

A Division of HarperCollins*Publishers*

HarperCollins books may be purchased for educational, business, or sales promotional use. For information, please call or write: Special Markets Department, HarperCollins Publishers, Inc., 10 East 53rd Street, New York, NY 10022. Telephone: (212) 207-7528; Fax: (212) 207-7222.

This publication is designed to provide accurate and authoritative information in regard to the subject matter covered. It is sold with the understanding that neither the author nor the publisher is engaged in rendering legal, accounting, or other professional service. If legal advice or other expert assistance is required, the services of a competent professional person should be sought.

From a Declaration of Principles jointly adopted by a Committee of the American Bar Association and a Committee of Publishers.

FIRST EDITION

Library of Congress Cataloging in Publication Data
Levine, Sumner N.
    Global investing : a handbook for sophisticated investors / Sumner
N. Levine.
       p.   cm.
    Includes index.
    ISBN 0-88730-498-2
    1. Investments, Foreign. 2. Portfolio management. I. Title.
HG4538.L39   1992
332.6'73–dc20
                                     92-0236

92 93 94 95 96 PS/RRD 10 9 8 7 6 5 4 3 2 1

CONTENTS

Preface

In recent years there has been a growing interest in global investment opportunities. This book is intended to provide a broad overview of the subject. Initial chapters offer a detailed discussion of international asset allocation. As explained therein, optimal global allocation is intended to provide the best return for a given risk level, or less risk for a given return.

Going global, however, introduces a number of new uncertainties into investment decision making. Foremost among these are fluctuations in the exchange rate and problems arising from political instability. These issues are explored in Parts II and III. The chapters that follow deal with fixed-income investing (Part IV) and the management and monitoring of international portfolios (Part V).

Evaluation of global opportunities requires timely investment information about foreign companies and economies. Part VI provides helpful sources of such information. Chapter 16, on analyzing international financial statements, is intended to guide investors who must deal with unfamiliar accounting and reporting practices. Investing in emerging markets is discussed in Part VII, while Part VIII provides a guide to the world's securities exchanges.

Finally, I want to express my gratitude to the many outstanding contributors who made this book possible.

Sumner N. Levine

CONTRIBUTORS

Robert D. Arnott joined First Quadrant Corporation in 1988 as its president and chief investment officer. He is a member of the editorial board of the *Journal of Portfolio Management* and coedited the book *Asset Allocation* with Frank J. Fabozzi. Before coming to First Quadrant, Mr. Arnott was a vice president and strategist at Salomon Brothers Inc.

W. Scott Bauman, professor of finance at Northern Illinois University, was formerly the executive director of the Institute of Chartered Financial Analysts and the Research Foundation of the I.C.F.A. He has also been a professor at the University of Virginia Darden Graduate School of Business Administration.

Gary L. Bergstrom is president of Acadian Asset Management, Inc., which he founded in 1977. In 1978 Acadian entered into a joint venture with the State Street Bank and Trust Company to design, structure, and implement the State Street International Index Fund, as well as State Street's active country selection strategy. Mr. Bergstrom started and managed the Putnam International Fund in the early and middle 1970s.

John F. O. Bilson is the president of TCC Futures Management and a senior vice president of the Chicago Corporation. Prior to joining the Chicago Corporation in 1987, Mr. Bilson was an associate professor of international economics at the University of Chicago Graduate School of Business from 1978 to 1986. In 1986, Mr. Bilson also established BetaSoft Management, a commodity trading advisor.

Fischer Black is a partner in the trading and arbitrage division of Goldman, Sachs & Co. Before joining Goldman Sachs, he was a professor of finance at MIT's Sloan School of Management and at the University of Chicago. Dr. Black developed, with Myron Scholes, the Black-Scholes option pricing formula.

Richard C. Carr is a managing partner of Brinson Partners, Inc., where he is responsible for all aspects of the management of international assets. He is also a member of the firm's senior management team that develops and coordinates overall business and investment strategy. Mr. Carr joined First Chicago Corporation in 1964 and established First Chicago's international investment office in London in 1972. His investment team launched an international equity portfolio for U.S. retirement plans in 1974, one of the first in the industry, and two international fixed-income portfolios in 1980.

Matthew J. Celebuski is a senior vice president in global structured products at Deutsche Bank Capital Corporation in Frankfurt, Germany. He oversees trading and risk management of derivative asset structures for Deutsche Bank AG, including such products as OTC options, derivative arbitrage, listed warrants, and customized private placements. Prior to joining Deutsche Bank, Mr. Celebuski was first vice president and head of structured products at PaineWebber Inc. in New York.

Frederick D. S. Choi is a research professor of accounting and international business at New York University's Stern School of Business. He served as chairman of NYU's Area of Accounting, Taxation and Business Law from 1983 to 1986 and is former director of the Vincent C. Ross Institute of Accounting Research. His textbook, *International Accounting* with G. Mueller, was recently awarded the Wildman Gold Medal by the American Accounting Association. Professor Choi is editor-in-chief of a new specialist journal entitled the *Journal of International Financial Management and Accounting*.

William D. Coplin is a professor of political science and director of the Public Affairs Program at Syracuse University's Maxwell School. In 1979, Dr. Coplin and Dr. Michael K. O'Leary developed and became directors of the Political Risk Services (PRS) Division of Frost & Sullivan. In February 1989, International Business Communications (holdings) plc, acquired Political Risk Services from Frost & Sullivan. Dr. Coplin is a founding director of the Association of Political Risk Analysts (APRA).

Edwin J. Elton is Nomura Professor of Finance at the Leonard N. Stern School of Business of New York University. He was formerly coeditor of the *Journal of Finance*. He has been a member of the board of directors of the American Finance Association and an associate editor of *Management Science*. He is the author of *Modern Portfolio Theory and Investment Analysis* with Dr. Martin J. Gruber.

Ronald D. Frashure is the vice president of Acadian Asset Management. Previously he served as a portfolio manager at Putnam Investment Company, where he later became the firm's director of asset allocation.

Martin J. Gruber is the chairman of the Department of Finance and Nomura Professor of Finance at the Leonard N. Stern School of Business at New York University. He is the author of *Modern Portfolio Theory and Investment Analysis* with Dr. Edwin J. Elton. He was formerly coeditor of the *Journal of Finance* and Department Editor for Finance of *Management Science*. He is currently an associate editor of the *Journal of Banking and Finance* and the *Journal of Accounting, Auditing and Finance*.

Janice C. Harding is with Frank Russell International, where she is responsible for client strategy projects and is instrumental in the development of new products, including the International Equity Profile and Salomon-Russell International Indexes.

Roy D. Henriksson is the senior vice president of product development at Kidder, Peabody & Co. Previously, he was a vice president of asset allocation at Salomon Brothers Inc., where he was a member of the Asset Allocation Committee. He has also served as a professor in the Graduate School of Business at the University of California at Berkeley.

Joanne M. Hill is the managing director in charge of the Derivative Products Research Group and a member of the Management Group for Equity Derivatives and Foreign Exchange Trading and Sales within Capital Markets at PaineWebber. Prior to joining PaineWebber, she was the director of research in the Financial Futures Department of Kidder, Peabody & Co. and the director of new product development at Brown, Brothers, Harriman and Co. She is a director of the Financial Management Association and serves on the board of the Futures Industry Institute, the board of Financial Analysts Foundation, the editorial board of the *Journal of Portfolio Management,* and the Financial Products Advisory Committee of the CFTC.

John J. Kilgannon is a vice president within the Derivative Products Research Group of Capital Markets at PaineWebber. Prior to joining PaineWebber, he was a systems coordinator within the investment banking division of Goldman Sachs and a programmer analyst in the information systems area of Brown, Brothers, Harriman and Co.

Donald R. Lessard is a professor of international management at MIT's Sloan School of Management. His research and teaching interests include international aspects of corporate finance; corporate strategy and organization, especially as it interacts with financial product and factor markets; and financing of less-developed countries, especially Latin America. Dr. Lessard's recent publications include *Managing the Globalization of Business* (STOA-Editoriale Scientifica); *Capital Flight: The Problem and Policy Responses* and *Financial Intermediation Beyond the Debt Crisis* (both written with John Williamson and published by the Institute for International Economics); and *International Financial Management* (John Wiley).

Sumner N. Levine is the director of Nortech Associates, and a professor emeritus at the State University of New York at Stony Brook. He is also the editor of the annual *Business One Irwin Business and Investment Almanac,* and numerous other publications.

Geoffrey H. Moore is the director of the Center for International Business Cycle Research, Graduate School of Business, Columbia University and director emeritus of the National Bureau of Economic Research. He was a commissioner of labor statistics at the U.S. Department of Labor from 1969 to 1973. In addition, he has taught at New York University and Columbia University's Hoover Institute.

Alfred C. Morley is currently president of Morley Co. Previously he served as president and chief executive officer of the Institute of Chartered Financial Analysts.

Michael K. O'Leary is a professor of political science at the Maxwell School of Syracuse University, where he has served as the director of the International Relations Program. Prior to joining the Syracuse faculty, Dr. O'Leary taught at Dartmouth College, the University of Southern California, and Princeton University. In conjunction with Dr. William D. Coplin, he developed Political Risk Services, a division of International Business Communications.

Gideon Pell is a senior manager in the New York Financial Services Practice of KPMG Peat Marwick, serving clients in the stockbrokerage, investment banking, and asset management markets. Peat Marwick is the U.S. arm of KPMG, one of the world's pre-eminent professional services organizations. KPMG provides accounting, auditing, tax, and management consulting services through a network of more than 700 offices in almost 120 countries, with a total staff numbering over 75,000. KPMG is the leading firm of accountants and consultants in virtually every major financial center around the world.

Michael R. Rosenberg is the manager of the International Fixed-Income Research Department at Merrill Lynch Capital Markets. Prior to joining Merrill Lynch, he worked as the director of international bond management for Prudential Insurance Company of America.

Theodore S. Roman is a senior vice president in the equity derivative products group at Nomura Securities International, Inc., where he is responsible for marketing equity derivative products. Mr. Roman joined Nomura from Goldman Sachs, where he was a vice president in the equities division. Before joining Goldman Sachs, Mr. Roman was a manager in the New York office of Price Waterhouse.

Joseph R. Schmuckler is a senior vice president with Nomura Securities International, Inc. responsible for the firm's equity derivative products operations. Prior to joining Nomura, Mr. Schmuckler was with Kidder, Peabody & Co., where his responsibilities included the development and management of Kidder's derivatives operations within the Financial Futures and Options Group.

Jayant S. Tata is a securities markets advisor at International Finance Corporation (IFC), where he has also been a division manager in the Capital Markets Department. Prior to joining IFC, Mr. Tata was a trustee at Batterymarch Financial Management, responsible for managing the firm's emerging markets funds.

Kie Ann Wong is professor and head of the Department of Finance and Banking in the Faculty of Business Administration at the National University of Singapore.

PART

I

GLOBAL ASSET ALLOCATION AND ANALYSIS

Risks and Returns from International Investments*

Donald R. Lessard
Sloan School of Management
Massachusetts Institute
of Technology
Cambridge, MA

Unlike many innovations in investment management, international diversification has appeal to individuals with a wide range of investment perspectives. To disciples of modern portfolio theory, it is a logical extension of the arguments for holding passive, well-diversified domestic portfolios. To active managers who seek to outguess other market participants, it is a new frontier where insightful analysis is likely to result in superior performance.

The basic arguments in favor of international diversification have not changed in 15 years. Today, however, it is much harder to ignore opportunities outside the United States—the U.S. equity market now represents less than one-third of world equity market capitalization instead of the more than 60 percent level in the mid sixties, and many perceived obstacles to international investment have turned out to be illusory, reflecting little more than the limited experience of U.S. managers and investors with foreign markets. While the U.S. experience base in international equity investment has clearly increased, the proportion of U.S. portfolios allocated to foreign equities remains under 5 percent.

The potential advantage of international diversification is a better ratio of reward to risk than that of a purely domestic portfolio—a higher expected return for a given level of risk or a lower level of risk

* This chapter is a revision and update of that appearing in *The Financial Analysts' Handbook*, 2nd edition, edited by Sumner Levine. Homewood, IL: Business One Irwin, 1988.

for a given return. While it is possible that this advantage can be gained by consistently investing in one or a few foreign markets that outperform the U.S. market on a risk-adjusted basis, it is more likely to follow from the fact that the returns from common stocks in various countries do not move in lockstep and thus the risk-return combinations available with internationally diversified portfolio are likely to be superior to those of the individual stock markets.

There is now extensive evidence that the co-movement of returns across countries is low enough that international diversification results in a considerably improved risk-return mix, and internationally diversified funds consistently rank near the top in this regard. The question is no longer whether investors should commit a substantial proportion of their assets abroad, but whether this commitment should remain in the 5 percent to 10 percent range or should approach the 50 percent level implied by market capitalizations.

Although most outright obstacles to international investment have diminished in recent years, investors may be justified in maintaining some degree of "home country bias" in their portfolio holdings for several reasons. The traditional perceived obstacles to international investment include concern over currency risks and political risks; perceived limitations in the size, depth, and efficiency of foreign markets; and difficulties in obtaining information on foreign securities.

Financial theory and investor experience show that currency risk should not be an obstacle to foreign investment but, at most, a reason for hedging. If there are limits to the size, depth, or efficiency of foreign markets, which does not appear to be the case for major non-U.S. markets at least, these limits will affect both foreign and domestic investors and therefore do not necessarily discourage international diversification. With regard to the availability of information, the boom in international money management suggests that information is available to all comers at a competitive price. Nevertheless, domestic investors often face more favorable treatment on distributed income, especially when domestic and cross-border withholding taxes are taken into account. This chapter first reviews the evidence regarding the advantages of international diversification. It then examines various perceived drawbacks.

The Potential Advantages of International Diversification

The concept underlying international diversification is the same one that applies to diversification along any other dimension: Whenever the returns of different assets are not subject to exactly the same risks, the risk of a diversified portfolio of these assets will be lower than the risk of the typical individual security.

The proportion of the risk of individual investments that is diversifiable depends on the degree of correlation among the returns on these assets. Within the United States, the degree of synchronization or correlation between returns on shares of individual firms and a broad-based market index is typically around .5. This means that, on average, the undiversifiable or systematic risk of a security is 50 percent of its total risk. In general, the proportion of the systematic risk of securities in other countries is higher than in the United States. This reflects the fact that these countries typically have less diverse industrial bases than the United States and, in some cases, more volatile political environments. This is particularly true for less-developed countries, which have much less room for risk reduction through domestic diversification (see Figure 1.1).

When diversification is extended across national boundaries, a substantial proportion of the systematic risk within each country can be eliminated. Figure 1.1 shows this by comparing the risk reduction obtainable through diversification within the United States to that obtainable through international diversification, where portfolio risk drops to 33 percent of that of the typical stock, one-third less than the U.S. figure.

The reason for this additional risk reduction is that returns on diversified single-country portfolios display considerable independence. Many of the factors affecting share values are essentially domestic. For instance, nations differ in the evolution of tax laws, monetary policies, and general political climate. Further, various national economies tend to be concentrated in particular industries, so international investment is a form of cross-industry diversification as well. Even factors that influence the

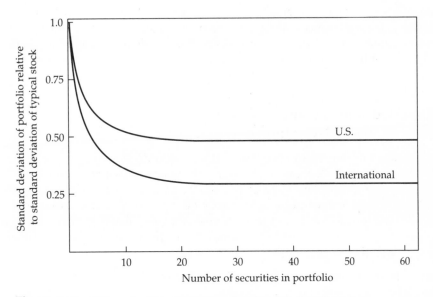

Figure 1.1. Risk reduction through national and international diversification.

(Source: B. H. Solnik, "Why Not Diversify Internationally Rather than Domestically?" *The Financial Analysis Journal* [July–August 1974]: pp 48–54.)

Table 1.1.   Correlation of Major World Equity Markets with the United States

Country	1959–63	1964–68	1969–73	1973–74	1975–79	1980–85	1986–90
France	.45	.02	.20	.37	.32	.45	.48
Germany	.48	.12	.41	.52	.38	.35	.39
Japan	.02	.07	.42	.39	.36	.26	.27
Netherlands	.67	.60	.54	.37	.50	.33	.67
Switzerland	.52	.35	.49	.49	.45	.47	.55
United Kingdom	.29	.19	.41	.08	.34	.34	.68

All returns measured in U.S. dollars, based on stock market data reported by Morgan Stanley, *Capital International Perspective* (Geneva, Switzerland). Computations for 1986–1990 courtesy Acadian Financial Research.

entire world economy, such as oil shocks, can affect individual economies differently.

The disparities among nations can be seen in the correlations between returns on the stock markets of six major countries and the United States for different periods of time through 1990, as reported in Table 1.1.

Because low correlations among countries are key to diversification gains, an important question is whether markets are moving more closely together over time.[1] It is well recognized that in recent years the major nations of the world have become more interdependent, both politically and economically. The 1987 crash, which cut across most markets, brought a sense that correlations among markets had increased substantially. In fact, during the short period surrounding the crash, correlations were markedly higher, but it is hard to discern an upward trend during the longer period, 1985–1990.

Expected Returns and Gains from International Diversification

Although the degree of correlation among countries indicates the extent to which risk can be reduced through international diversification, it does not provide a complete view of the advantages of international diversification because it does not reveal exactly how domestic and internationally diversified portfolios compare in terms of risk-adjusted returns. Such a comparison requires knowledge about the expected returns in each market as well as the correlations among them.

Historical Returns as a Guide to the Future

The past performance of foreign markets suggests the best of both worlds—lower risk and higher returns. Table 1.2 shows that realized

[1] See, for example, Roll (1988).

Table 1.2. Realized Total Rate of
Return in U.S. Dollars (percent per
year compounded)

	12/1969 to 12/1990
Japan	19.1
Netherlands	15.3
United Kingdom	13.5
France	12.4
Germany	12.2
Switzerland	11.6
United States	10.0

Source: Morgan Stanley, *Capital International Perspective* (Geneva, Switzerland). All returns include reinvestment of estimated dividends and are adjusted to U.S. dollars at current exchange rates.

total returns on most foreign markets have outstripped U.S. returns over the last two decades. Research findings for the United States and other markets, however, show that past returns (unless perhaps for very long periods) provide little information on future returns.

Further, at least part of the performance of foreign markets can be traced to circumstances that are unlikely to be repeated—the postwar economic recovery of Europe; its subsequent boom resulting from the formation of the Common Market; and the economic phenomenon of Japan, propelled in part by a major increase in the degree of world economic integration. Structural shifts of this magnitude are unlikely to recur in the near future for mature industrialized countries, although Singapore and Hong Kong provided similar returns in the late 1970s and other emerging markets such as Mexico and Brazil may do so in the 1990s. Nonetheless, analysis of fundamental economic conditions in various countries provides a helpful point of departure in considering the growth of overall activity, corporate profits, and hence, share values. Savings rates and rates of capital formation in many countries, for example, continue to outstrip those of the United States. The key question from an investor's perspective, though, is to what extent these anticipated outcomes are capitalized in share values and at what rate they are capitalized; that is, the expected rate of return given normal expectations of future economic outcomes.

A second way to assess likely future returns is to compute the future returns that appear to be impounded in share valuations in various countries. While in principle a complete dividend discount model, which not only takes into account valuation in relation to current earnings but also growth prospects, is required for this approach, some insight is

Table 1.3.   Price-Cash Earnings Ratios for Major World Stock
Markets

Country	1974–1978[a]	December 1985	December 1990
Singapore	10.0	12.3	10.4
Hong Kong	8.8	15.4	8.5
Italy	6.5	5.5	2.4
Japan	6.6	9.0	10.6
Australia	5.5	7.2	6.5
Canada	5.0	. 7.0	7.1
United Kingdom	4.6	6.8	6.6
United States	5.9	6.9	7.3
Belgium	4.1	3.8	4.3
Germany	3.8	6.0	3.9
Spain	6.2	2.9	3.6
Sweden	3.1	6.0	5.4
France	2.8	4.3	4.6
Netherlands	3.1	3.3	5.0

a. Average of year-end ratios.

Source: Morgan Stanley, *Capital International Perspective*, (Geneva, Switzerland, January 1975–January 1979, 1986, 1990).

provided by the current price-cash earnings multiplier[2]—a crude measure
of the market capitalization rate. These ratios, shown in Table 1.3, suggest
that unless investors in general expect poorer economic performance from
countries other than the United States, expected returns abroad are as
high as or higher than those for the United States. Of the major countries,
only Japan has a substantially higher ratio, and it is now recognized that
this ratio is biased upward from its true level by 25 percent to 30 percent
because of the extensive pattern of cross-holdings, which are reflected in
share values but not in earnings.[3]

Equilibrium Return Approaches

An alternative approach to estimating expected returns is to consider what
returns would have to be (relative to one another) to cause investors in
the aggregate to hold all securities in market value proportions. This is
the logic of the capital asset pricing model for which William Sharpe was
awarded a Nobel prize, and it is applicable internationally as well as within
a single country. The big issue in an international context is whether national markets are viewed as part of an integrated global market or as
separate, segmented markets.

[2] Cash earnings are defined by Capital International as reported earnings plus depreciation.
[3] On this point, see McDonald (1989) and French and Poterba (1989).

If various national markets are completely isolated from one another, returns will be based solely on a domestic risk-return trade-off that reflects the total riskiness of a national portfolio and the risk preferences of domestic investors. In contrast, if capital markets are integrated into a single market, all securities will be priced in terms of their undiversifiable (β) risk from a world perspective.

One can argue that whether markets are segmented or integrated, international diversification is desirable, although the degree of benefit differs. If securities are priced according to their domestic systematic risk, internationally diversified investors will earn risk premiums for risks that they can partially diversify! If national markets are integrated, they will lose if they hold a solely domestic portfolio since they will be bearing some risks for which they earn no risk premium. If, however, markets are segmented by barriers or taxes on cross-border investment, then some of these benefits will be offset and the ideal portfolio for investors will depend on their domiciles. In the extreme case, with very high barriers or costs to foreign investment, investors will do best to hold only home assets.

Principal national markets are unlikely to be either completely segmented or completely integrated. There are substantial international investment flows, and many shares are cross-listed on various exchanges. This fact would appear to ensure comparative valuation from both national and international perspectives. Yet total integration does not appear to occur, because of the home country bias in the portfolio holdings of virtually all investors. Most likely, prices are determined in a relatively complex fashion because of the obstacles to international capital flows and the differences in preferences and perceptions by domestic and international investors toward what to them are either local or foreign securities.

Obstacles to International Investment

Currency Risk

The prime motivation of diversifying a portfolio internationally is to improve the reward-to-risk trade-off by taking advantage of the relatively low correlation among returns on assets of different countries. However, since international investment implies investing in assets that provide returns in currencies whose values may fluctuate relative to the dollar, it involves taking foreign exchange risks. A key question facing the investor, then, is whether these exchange risks are so large as to offset the benefits of international diversification. A related question is what, if any, special strategies should be followed to reduce the impact of foreign exchange risk.

Foreign exchange risk is a special type of risk that affects investors differentially and hence does not fit into a normal reward-to-risk framework. Further, since foreign holdings can be separated into two components— a hedged position in the foreign security, which represents a bet on the risk premium, and a position in the foreign currency—investors should offset the currency position by hedging.

Perold and Shulman (1990) explore this point in some detail, arguing that little is to be gained from bearing foreign exchange risk since it should not (and does not) command a risk premium. Jorion (1990) comes to a similar conclusion. The appropriate treatment of exchange risk depends on its nature—whether it is a risk that affects all investors equally or only certain investors—and its magnitude compared to other equity market risks. To understand the nature and importance of currency risk, one must take into account how exchange rates are related to returns on securities in relatively efficient markets. If security markets function reasonably well, anticipated movements in exchange rates will be reflected in both interest rates and security prices. There will be uncertainty about these future currency values, but this uncertainty can, to a large extent, be avoided by hedging; that is, borrowing or entering into a forward currency contract.

Of course, even if anticipated changes in the exchange rate are fully reflected in interest rates and stock prices, after-the-fact deviations from anticipated rates may have a significant impact on the relative performance of national stock markets.

Managing Currency Risks

If a manager decides against bearing the risks of fluctuations in a particular currency, several routes are open. It is possible to hedge by borrowing in the currency in question in the same amount as the market value of the equity investment at that time or by entering into forward contracts for an equal amount. Either of these steps will offset the majority of the currency exposure of the equity portfolio.

The expected cost of hedging in the case of borrowing is the difference between the interest differential of the two currencies and the expected percentage change in the exchange rate. The cost of hedging in the case of forward contracts is the difference between the forward discount or premium and the expected percentage change in the exchange rate. Barring controls on capital flows or access to forward markets, these two costs will be identical through interest rate parity. The cost of hedging is often incorrectly defined as the interest differential itself or the forward discount or premium, with no consideration of the expected change in exchange rates. This incorrect definition often leads to statements that hedging is "prohibitively expensive" and rests on the implicit assumption that foreign exchange markets are inefficient and do not reflect anticipations regarding a currency's future. Hedging is occasionally expensive, but substantial research shows that its cost ranges from 0.1 percent to 0.5 percent per year for most major countries.

In addition to hedging currency risks, an active manager may occasionally wish to take a position in a currency to take advantage of a forecast of currency movements that differs from the general market expectation. Again, the alternatives include taking a money market position; that is, borrowing or lending, buying or selling forward exchange, or buying or selling stock. It should be clear, however, that buying shares in a particular country to take advantage of an expected currency appreciation involves assuming substantial additional uncertainty, because equity returns are even more volatile than currency changes. If the forecast is limited solely to a currency movement, taking an equity position is an unreasonable strategy. By the same logic, selling equities to avoid a currency risk is also unreasonable. Forward contracts or borrowing and lending allow the manager to deal with exchange risk much more specifically.

Political or Sovereign Risk

Political, or sovereign, risk is viewed by many as a major obstacle to international investment. Clearly, political factors play a major role in determining how attractive a country is for investment. Countries viewed as likely candidates for internal political upheaval or even a gradual erosion of private capital will be unattractive to all investors, foreign and domestic alike; as a result, securities of these countries should be priced accordingly, and little new private real investment will take place. The general question of the impact of political risk on international investment strategies can be broken down into three specific questions:

1. Are political risks properly reflected in securities prices?
2. Do these risks differ from the perspectives of foreign and domestic investors?
3. If so, what does this imply about international investment strategies?

There has been little research into any of these questions. Most research on political or sovereign risk focuses on the conflict between host governments and firms with direct investment or on the risk associated with bank loans to developing countries rather than on portfolio investment.

In judging whether political risks are properly reflected in prices, the only evidence is that relating to the overall efficiency of markets. The evidence suggests that information is rapidly reflected in major markets and that realized returns in general bear a reasonable relationship to the risks taken.

The key consideration is that local as well as foreign investors are typically affected by these risks. There is no reason to believe that local investors will be systematically optimistic about their country's future. When political risks increase significantly, such investors will attempt to diversify out of the home market as rapidly as foreigners. As a result, prices will fall until someone will be satisfied to hold the securities of a risky country.

Political risks are principally domestic phenomena that can be substantially diversified away internationally. As a result they will loom much larger to the domestic investor whose portfolio is concentrated in home assets. Accordingly, domestic shares might well be more attractive to foreign than domestic investors in periods of high perceived political risk.

Limited Size and Depth of Foreign Markets

A traditional objection to international diversification that no longer has merit, if it ever had, is that the practical scope of foreign investing is limited. In the early 1960s the U.S. securities markets represented over two-thirds of world market value. In the 1990s the proportions are reversed. Foreign markets have come of age. Figures 1.2 and 1.3 illustrate the growth of these markets since 1966 in terms of capitalization and turnover. The growth of the capitalization of foreign markets is especially striking— increasing from 24 percent of the world total in 1966 to 56 percent in 1985. Undoubtedly, there are many foreign stocks whose total capitalization and turnover are too limited for them to be of interest to most U.S. institutional investors, but this does not rule out international diversification in general.

For some markets—particularly the Japanese and German—market capitalizations may be a misleading indicator of an issue's marketability, because a large proportion of the shares may be owned by banks, holding companies, or other concerns. These considerations do not, however, imply that these markets are less attractive to foreign institutional investors than to local investors. In fact, just the opposite may be the case. Domestic investors who depend primarily on their own market for liquidity and diversification are likely to be more constrained by these limitations than international investors who, through diversification, can virtually eliminate the nonmarket risk unique to individual companies even if they hold only a small number of shares in each market. They also need not rely on any single market for liquidity and, as a result, can take a longer view

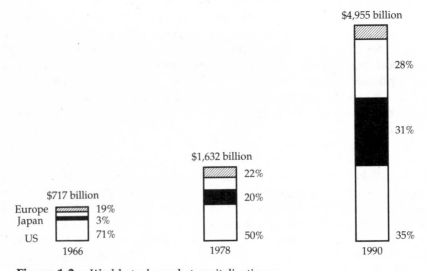

Figure 1.2. World stock market capitalizations.

(Source: Morgan Stanley, *Capital International Perspective* [Geneva, Switzerland].)

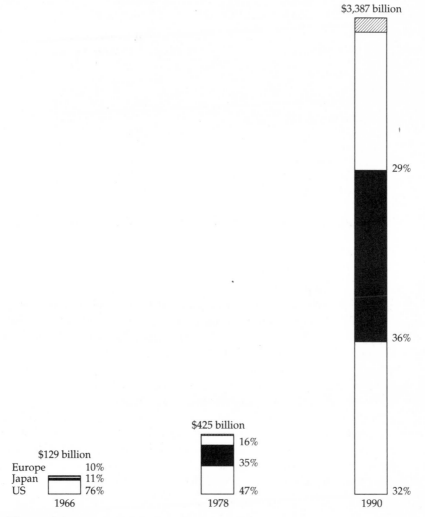

Figure 1.3. World share turnover.

(Source: Morgan Stanley, *Capital International Perspective* [Geneva, Switzerland].)

in regard to each market and security, even though they wish to realize profits within a reasonable period in each market and currency.

The constraints on diversification within a single market become apparent when one considers the degree of concentration within various markets. As shown in Table 1.4, a small number of shares account for a major portion of the value of all shares in most smaller markets, such as Belgium, Netherlands, and Switzerland, as well as in Germany.[4]

[4] Roll (1990) shows that the concentration of national indexes is a significant determinant of their volatility.

Table 1.4.   **Stock Market Concentration Ratios (1990)**

Exchange	Percentage of total equity capitalization by 10 largest stocks
Netherlands	77.2
Belgium	52.7
Switzerland	50.4
Germany (all exchanges)	39.4
Italy	39.2
France	26.6
United Kingdom	25.4
Japan	18.7
United States	15.4

Source: Morgan Stanley, *Capital International Perspective* (Geneva, Switzerland).

Considering that 30 or more issues in about equal proportions are necessary to diversify away most of the specific (nonmarket) risk within a single national market, even a moderate-sized domestic fund will find it difficult to achieve a high degree of diversification. Consequently, domestic investors in such markets will want to hold foreign assets, and a substantial proportion of the shares of the dominant companies should be held by foreigners even if the systematic risk component of returns in the local economy is closely related to the world market index.

Since all shares must be held by someone, investors must be induced to accept the limitations imposed by the thinness and concentration of particular markets. Many of these limitations will be more severe for domestic than for international investors and, if anything, should be a motivation for, rather than an obstacle to, international investment.

Relative Efficiency of Foreign Markets

Market efficiency has sometimes been interpreted in an extreme fashion to imply that "prices are always right." More recently, theoretical and empirical work by academics has resulted in a more balanced view in which absolute efficiency is being replaced by relative efficiency. While there is considerable difference of opinion on the absolute efficiency of a market— whether the level of security prices is "right"—there is very strong agreement on their relative efficiency—whether comparable securities are priced similarly.

Most evidence on market efficiency falls into one of three categories:

1. Direct tests of the randomness of stock price changes
2. Analyses of the relationship between realized returns and risk
3. Tests of the actual performance achieved by professional managers

Tests of the Randomness of Stock Price Changes.   Tests of the random walk hypothesis were first conducted on U.S. securities markets, but extensive studies have now been performed for most other major markets, as well as for a large proportion of the emerging markets. In a survey of more than 280 studies of the efficiency of capital markets in 14 European countries, Hawawini (1984) identifies 112 studies that deal with weak-form efficiency. In reviewing these studies, he concludes:

> When returns are measured over intervals longer than a week, the Random Walk Model ("RWM") cannot be rejected and there is no evidence that mechanical trading rules can be applied to earn abnormal returns net of transactions costs.

An alternative test of weak-form efficiency—whether specific mechanical trading rules yield excess returns—has been applied to European as well as U.S. markets. Hawawini (1984) reports on 18 such studies and finds that only three involving daily data reject weak-form efficiency. He views this as confirming the weak-form efficiency of European markets:

> In general, European equity markets, regardless of their size, are weak-form efficient, even when price changes are measured over daily differencing intervals.[5]

Much recent work in the United States and abroad has focused on certain persistent anomalies in the form of departures from the random walk hypothesis. Among the most extensively studied anomalies are the so-called Friday and January effects, persistent patterns of lower or higher returns on particular days of the week or months of the year. In a recent study, Jaffe and Westerfield (1989) examine the Monday effect for a variety of countries and find similar departures from the RWM in the United States, the United Kingdom, Japan, Canada, and Australia. Similarly, Roll (1990) documents a significant Monday effect for virtually all major markets. Researchers have performed extensive tests of the major European markets, and these same tests have recently been extended to the major Asian markets. The studies find that price changes show greater serial correlation in foreign markets than in the U.S. market. The magnitude of these departures from randomness is, however, typically insufficient to yield gains from trading strategies based on past prices.

Tests of the Risk-Return Trade-off.   More complex tests of market efficiency based on price behavior seek to determine whether the average holding period returns (dividend yields plus capital gains resulting from price changes) on individual shares or portfolios of shares over time are what they should be given the risk of the security in question. Such tests are substantially more difficult than tests of the RWM since they involve a joint

---

[5] Hawawini (1984, p. 60).

hypothesis of market efficiency and of a particular equilibrium relationship between risk and return.

The most widely accepted and tested model of the equilibrium relationship between risk and return is the capital asset pricing model (CAPM), which states that the holding period return on the shares of a particular firm should depend only on its systematic or market risk and not on its specific risk. Although there are many variants of this model, the results of such tests are by and large not substantially different when applied to U.S. and other major equity markets. Hawawini (1984, pp. 89–93) summarizes 31 such studies for eight European markets and concludes that their results are basically similar to those for the United States in a variety of respects: the beta coefficients of individual stocks (the sensitivity of individual stocks to movements in the home country market index) are relatively stable, averaging close to 1.0, and are explained by fundamental information regarding leverage; unsystematic risk in general does not contribute to the pricing of assets; and so on, as one would expect in a well-functioning market.

Solnik (1988) and others have noted that whereas it is a fairly straightforward matter to determine how efficient individual markets are in a risk-reward sense, it is much more difficult to establish whether individual national markets are priced properly in relation to one another. The primary source of this difficulty is that for a variety of reasons, including discriminatory taxation, legal restrictions, transaction costs, and psychological barriers (discussed later), international markets appear to be "weakly segmented"; that is, most shares in each country are held by investors domiciled in that country, and these investors have the primary influence on pricing.

Tests for Superior Performance.   The measurement of performance is considerably more complex in an international setting than within a single national market. To be valid, tests of performance must compare portfolio results with benchmark results for the same universe of securities. If a study shows that domestically managed funds outperform the market index, care must be taken to ensure that their performance does not reflect foreign holdings or domestic securities not included in the benchmark index. Taking this into account, there appear to be no credible studies that show consistently superior performance by managed funds in any major foreign market. Cumby and Glen (1990), for example, find that individually and collectively the performance of professional international asset managers closely matches that of broad international indexes, suggesting that the risk-return trade-offs that determine valuation in each market are roughly in line with one another.

In summary, studies suggest that foreign markets can generally be considered efficient in the sense that prices adjust rapidly to new information and relationships between risk and return are consistent with those predicted by capital market theory. Whether they are efficient to the extent that most professional managers are unable consistently to outperform appropriate market benchmarks remains an open question. The results available, however, suggest that this ability is, at best, uncommon.

Taxes, Restrictions on Ownership, and Other Institutional Obstacles

From time to time several institutional obstacles have made international investing costly, undesirable, or, in some cases, impossible. They include formal barriers to international transactions, such as exchange controls that do not allow investors in one country to invest overseas or limit overseas investment to a fixed pool, such as those that were imposed in the United Kingdom through 1981; double taxation of portfolio income for certain investors in particular countries; and restrictions on ownership of securities or on the exercise of control rights according to the nationality of the investor. Gultekin, Gultekin, and Penati (1989) tested for the impact of capital controls on the integration of the U.S. and Japanese stock markets using a multifactor model. They found clear differences in the pricing of the various factors before 1981 but no significant differences in their pricing thereafter. They concluded that government controls were a major source of market segmentation but that with their disappearance the pricing of equities has become much more common across these two countries.

If there are barriers to cross-border investment, investors with different legal domiciles or tax situations will want to hold different portfolios. It is, however, difficult to determine how much such optimal portfolios should differ from the world market portfolio. The extent of this divergence would depend how the effect of the obstacles balances against the gains from more complete diversification. Cooper and Kaplanis (1986) derive explicit estimates of the size of cross-border barriers that would be required to justify partial or full home bias in investing. To hold only home assets, for example, U.S. investors would have to face a 3 percent per annum penalty for cross-border investing. However, 1 to 1.5 percent would justify the actual degree of home bias.

Obstacles to foreign investments may also include informal barriers such as the difficulty of obtaining information about a market, differences in reporting practices that make international comparisons difficult, and, perhaps most important, tradition. Many managers resist stepping into uncharted territory and may thus overestimate the risks associated with foreign investment.

Obstacles to International Investment: In Conclusion

When examined closely, many alleged obstacles to international investment are less serious than commonly thought. This does not mean that there are no difficulties, but it does appear that the advantages of diversification, when properly pursued, outweigh the drawbacks.

Regarding the major specific areas of concern, currency risks apparently do not significantly reduce the gains from broadly based diversification. There is little reason to believe that political risks are systematically ignored by local investors or that they weigh more heavily on foreign investors. Finally, major foreign markets are not as narrow or inefficient as sometimes perceived. Given the significant risk reduction advantages of international diversification, therefore, international investment should be viewed as the rule rather than the exception.

REFERENCES AND FURTHER READING

Correlations of Returns and Gains from International Diversification

Bergstrom, G., D. R. Lessard, J. K. Koeneman, and M. J. Siegel. (1986). "International Securities Markets." In *Handbook of Financial Markets,* ed. F. J. Fabozzi and F. G. Zarb, 2nd ed. Homewood, Ill.: Dow Jones-Irwin, pp. 208–246.

Cholerton, K., P. Pieraerts, and B. H. Solnik. (1986). "Why Invest in Foreign Currency Bonds?" *Journal of Portfolio Management* 12(4) (Summer): 4–8.

Eun, E., and B. Resnick. (1984). "Estimating the Correlation Structure of International Share Prices." *Journal of Finance* 39(5) (December): 1311–24.

Grinold, R., A. Rudd, and D. Stefak. (1989). "Global Factors: Fact or Fictions?" *Journal of Portfolio Management* (Fall): 79–88.

Jacquillat, B., and B. H. Solnik. (1978). "Multinationals Are Poor Tools for International Diversification," *Journal of Portfolio Management* 4(2) (Winter): 8–12.

Lessard, D. R. (1976). "World, Country, and Industry Relationships in Equity Returns: Implications for Risk Reduction through International Diversification." *Financial Analysis Journal* (January-February): 2–8.

Roll, R. W. (1988). "The International Crash of 1987." *Financial Analysts Journal* (September–October): 19–35.

———. (1990). "Industrial Structure and the Comparative Behavior of International Stock Market Indexes." Working paper, UCLA (June).

Senschak, A., and W. Beedles. (1980). "Is International Diversification Desirable?" *Journal of Portfolio Management* 6(2) (Winter): 49–57.

Solnik, B. (1988) *International Investments,* Addison-Wesley, Reading, MA.

Solnik, B. H. (1974). "Why Not Diversify Internationally Rather than Domestically?" *Financial Analysts Journal* 30(4) (July–August): 48–54.

Solnik, B. H., and B. Noetzlin. (1982). "Optimal International Asset Allocation." *Journal of Portfolio Management* 9(1) (Fall): 11–21.

Pricing of Securities in an International Context

Adler, M., and B. Dumas. (1983). "International Portfolio Choice and Corporate Finance: A Synthesis." *Journal of Finance* 38(3) (June): 925–984.

Black, F. (1974). "International Capital Market Equilibrium with Investment Barriers." *Journal of Financial Economics* 1(4): 339–352.

Cooper, I. A., and E. Kaplanis. (1986). "Costs to Crossborder Investment and International Equity Market Equilibrium." In *Recent Advance in Corporate Finance,* ed. J. Edwards et al. Cambridge, U.K.: Cambridge University Press.

Errunza, V., and E. Losq. (1985). "International Asset Pricing under Mild Segmentation: Theory and Test." *Journal of Finance* 40(1) (March): 105–24.

Gultekin, M., B. Gultekin, and A. Penati. (1989). "Capital Controls and International Capital Market Segmentation: The Evidence from the Japanese and American Stock Markets." *Journal of Finance* 44 (September): 849–69.

Harvey, C. R. (1991). "The World Price of Covariance Risk." *Journal of Finance* (March): 111-157.

Hietala, P. T. (1989). "Asset Pricing in Partially Segmented Markets: Evidence from the Finnish Market." *Journal of Finance,* 44 (July): 697–718.

Jorion, P., and E. Schwartz. (1986). "Integration versus Segmentation in the Canadian Stock Market." *Journal of Finance* (July): 603–614.

Kester, W. C., and T. Luehrman. (1990). "The Price of Risk in the United States and Japan." Working paper, Boston, MA: Harvard Business School.

Solnik, B. H. (1974). "Equilibrium in an International Capital Market under Uncertainty." *Journal of Economic Theory* 8(4) (August): 500–524.

Stulz, R. M. (1981). "On the Effects of Barriers to International Investment." *Journal of Finance* (September): 923–34.

———. (1981). "A Model of International Asset Pricing." *Journal of Financial Economics* (December): 383–406.

Wheatley, S. (1988). "Some Tests of International Equity Integration." *Journal of Financial Economics* 21(2) (September): 177–212.

On Currency Risks

Adler, M., and B. Dumas. (1983). "International Portfolio Choice and Corporate Finance: A Synthesis." *Journal of Finance* (June): 925–984.

——— and D. Simon. (1986). "Exchange Risk Surprises in International Portfolios." *Journal of Portfolio Management* 2(12) (Winter): 44–53.

Black, F. (1990). "Equilibrium Exchange Rate Hedging." *Journal of Finance* (July): 899–907.

Cholerton, K., P. Pieraerts, and B. H. Solnik. (1986). "Why Invest in Foreign Currency Bonds?" *Journal of Portfolio Management* 12(4) (Summer): 4–8.

Jorion, P. (1990). "The Pricing of Exchange Rate Risk in the Stock Market." Working paper, Columbia University (June).

Perold, A., and E. Shulman. (1990). "The Free Lunch in Currency Hedging: Implications for Investment Policy and Performance Standards." *Financial Analysts Journal* 44 (May–June): 45–50.

The Efficiency of Foreign Markets

Hawawini, G. A. (1984). *European Equity Markets: Price Behavior and Efficiency.* Monograph of the Salomon Brothers Center for Study of Financial Institutions. New York: New York University.

Jaffe, J. F., and R. Westerfield. (1989). "A Twist on the Monday Effect in Stock Prices: Evidence for the U.S. and Foreign Stock Markets." *Journal of Banking and Finance*, 13: 641–50.

LeRoy, S. (1989). "Capital Market Efficiency: An Update." *Economic Review, Federal Reserve Bank of San Francisco* (Spring): 29–40.

Solnik, B. H. (1973). "A Note on the Validity of the Random Walk for European Stock Prices." *Journal of Finance* (December): 1151–1160.

On Valuation Comparisons across Countries

Aron, P. (1989). *Japanese P/E Multiples: The Tradition Continues*. Daiwa Securities America, Inc., NTIS, 35.

French, K., and J. Poterba. (1989). "Are Japanese Stock Prices Too High?" NBER Working Paper, Cambridge, MA: National Bureau of Economic Research.

McDonald, J. G. (1989). "The Mochai Effect: Japanese Corporate Cross Holdings." *Journal of Portfolio Management* 16(1)(Fall): 90–94.

On the Performance of Internationally Diversified Portfolios

Brinson, G. P., and N. Fachler. (1985). "Measuring Non-U.S. Equity Portfolio Performance." *Journal of Portfolio Management* 11(3) (Spring): 73–76.

Corner, D. C., and D. C. Stafford. (1977). *Open-End Investment Funds in the EEC and Switzerland*. Boulder, CO: Westview Press.

Cumby, Robert E., and Jack D. Glen. (1990). "Evaluating the Performance of International Mutual Funds." *Journal of Finance*, 45 (June): 497–522.

Farber, A. L. (1975). "Performance of Internationally Diversified Mutual Funds." In *International Capital Markets*, ed. E. J. Elton and M. H. Gruber. New York: American Elsevier.

2

International Diversification

Edwin J. Elton
Martin J. Gruber
Leonard N. Stern School of Business,
New York University

Portfolio managers in France, Germany, and England routinely invest a large fraction of their funds in securities that are traded in other countries. Foreign securities are found less frequently in the portfolios of U.S. investors and, when present, usually involve a relatively small proportion of the portfolio. Is this provincialism on the part of U.S. investors or are there sound economic reasons for their actions? In this chapter we attempt to present sufficient evidence for the readers to decide for themselves.

In the first section of this chapter we examine the market value of equities and debt worldwide. It turns out that no country comprises most of the world's wealth. Given the great number of opportunities worldwide, we discuss whether international diversification is a sensible strategy for investors. To analyze this question, we first show how returns on foreign assets are computed. The reasonableness of international diversification depends on the correlation coefficient across markets, the risk of each market, and the returns in each market. This is the subject of the next section of the chapter. One of the major sources of risk in international investment are changes in exchange rates. The impact of exchange risk on international diversification and the possibility of eliminating part of the risk through hedging is examined next. The next two sections of this chapter examine the key role of return expectations in determining the benefits of international diversification. Break-even returns are derived and evidence is presented from actively managed international portfolios. After

Source: *Modern Portfolio Theory and Investment Analysis*, Edwin J. Elton and Martin J. Gruber, fourth edition. New York: John Wiley & Sons, Inc.

discussing the reasonableness of international diversification, we focus on active and passive strategies for international investment.

The World Portfolio

In discussing the size of capital markets it is interesting to employ the concept of a world portfolio. The world portfolio represents the total market value of all stocks (or bonds) that an investor would own if he or she bought the total of all marketable stocks on all the major stock exchanges in the world. Table 2.1 shows the percentage that each nation's equity securities represented of the world portfolio in 1989. In this year, the largest equity markets were Japan, which represented 39% of the world total, whereas the next largest was the United States, which represented 30.3% of the total. All of the major European countries combined accounted for only 25.2% of the world equity market.[1] Table 2.2 shows similar percentages for the various bond markets in 1988. The U.S. bond market represented 46% of the world value and Japan's bond market was 22% of

Table 2.1. Comparative Sizes of World Equity Markets, 1989[a]

Area or country	Dollar value in billions	Percentage of total
Europe	$1,533	25.2%
United Kingdom	495	8.1
West Germany	224	3.7
Switzerland	177	2.9
France	188	3.1
Netherlands	92	1.5
Sweden	88	1.4
Italy	94	1.5
Spain	63	1.0
Belgium	39	0.6
Pacific area	$2,536	41.7%
Japan	2,366	38.9
Australia	83	1.4
Singapore	36	0.6
Hong Kong	41	0.7
North America	$2,008	33.0%
United States	1,846	30.3
Canada	162	2.7
World	$6,077	100.0%

Source: Morgan Stanley, *Capital International Perspective*, (Geneva, Switzerland) January 1990.

a. Column sums may not equal totals because of rounding error.

Table 2.2. Size of Major Bond Markets at
Year-End, 1988[a]

Bond market	Total publicly issued	Percentage of public issues in major markets
U.S. dollar	$4,517.0	46.3%
Japanese yen	2,161.0	22.1
Deutsche mark	753.5	7.7
Italian lira	534.3	5.5
U.K. sterling	344.4	3.5
French franc	332.4	3.4
Canadian dollar	245.3	2.5
Belgian franc	187.8	1.9
Danish krone	159.7	1.6
Swedish krona	157.0	1.6
Swiss franc	156.3	1.6
Dutch guilder	133.5	1.4
Australian dollar	81.6	0.8
Total	$9,763.8	100.0%

Source: Salomon Brothers.

a. Nominal value outstanding, billions of U.S. dollars
equivalent.

world value. In this case the major European markets accounted for 29% of the world bond portfolio. Even for U.S. investors a large part of the investment opportunities lie outside the domestic market. For investors from any other country the opportunities (in terms of market value of countries) outside the home country are much greater than those within the country of domicile. Thus for all investors a large part of the world's wealth lies outside the investor's home country. International assets could be duplicates of those found in the home country, in which case they do not offer new opportunities, or they could represent opportunities not duplicated in the home country. Which of these possibilities holds needs to be analyzed in order to determine whether international diversification should be an important part of each investor's portfolio. To examine this question we need to analyze the correlation between markets and the risk and return of each market. But before we do this we must first examine how to calculate returns on foreign investments.

Calculating the Return on Foreign Investments

The return on a foreign investment is affected by the return on the asset within its own market and the change in the exchange rate between the security's own currency and the currency of the purchaser's home country. Thus the return on a foreign investment can be quite different than simply the return in the asset's own market and, in fact, can differ according to the domicile of the purchaser. From the viewpoint of an American investor, it is convenient to express foreign currency as costing so many dollars.[2] Thus it is convenient to express an exchange rate of 2 marks to the dollar, as 1 mark costs $.50. Assume the following information:

	1	2	
Time	Cost of 1 mark	Value of German shares	Value in dollars (1 × 2)
0	$.50	40 DM	.50 × 40 = $20
1	$.40	45 DM	.40 × 45 = $18

Further assume there are no cash flows on German shares. In this case the return to the German investor expressed in the home currency (marks) is

$$(1 + R_H) = \frac{45}{40} \quad \text{or} \quad R_H = .125 \text{ or } 12.5\%$$

However, the return to the U.S. investor is

$$(1 + R_{US}) = \frac{.40 \times 45}{.50 \times 40} = \frac{18}{20} \quad \text{or} \quad R_{US} = -.10 \text{ or } -10\%$$

The German investor received a positive return, whereas the U.S. investor lost money because marks were worth less at time one than at time zero. It is convenient to divide the return to the American investor into a component due to return in the home or German market and the return due to exchange gains or losses. Letting R_x be the exchange return we have

$$(1 + R_{US}) = (1 + R_x)(1 + R_H)$$

$$1 + R_x = \frac{.40}{.50} = 1 - .20 \quad \text{or} \quad R_x = -.20$$

$$1 + R_H = \frac{45}{40} = 1 + .125 \quad \text{or} \quad R_H = .125$$

$$(1 + R_{US}) = (1 - .20)(1 + .125) = -.90 \quad \text{or} \quad R_{US} = -.10$$

Thus the 12 1/2% gain on the German investment was more than offset by the 20% loss on the change in the value of the mark. Restating the preceding equation

$$(1 + R_{US}) = (1 + R_x)(1 + R_H)$$

Simplifying

$$R_{US} = R_x + R_H + R_x R_H$$

In the example

$$-.10 = -.20 + .125 + (-.20) \times (.125)$$
$$= -.20 + .125 - .025$$

The last term (the cross-product term) will be much smaller than the other two terms, so that return to the U.S. investor is approximately the return of the security in its home market plus the exchange gain or loss. Using this approximation, we have the following expressions for expected return and standard deviation of return on a foreign security.

Expected return

$$\bar{R}_{US} = \bar{R}_x + \bar{R}_H$$

Standard deviation of return

$$\sigma_{US}^2 = [\sigma_x^2 + \sigma_H^2 + 2\sigma_{Hx}]^{1/2}$$

As will be very clear when we examine real data, the standard deviation of the return on foreign securities (σ_{US}) is much less than the sum of the standard deviation of the return on the security in its home country (σ_H) plus the standard deviation of the exchange gains and losses (σ_x). This relationship results from two factors. First, there is very low correlation between exchange gains (or losses) and returns in a country (and therefore the last term σ_{Hx} is close to zero). Second, squaring the standard deviations, adding them, and then taking the square root of the sum is less than adding them directly. To see this, let

$$\sigma_x = .10$$
$$\sigma_H = .15$$
$$\rho_{Hx} = 0 \quad \text{(to make the covariance zero)}$$

then

$$\sigma_{US}^2 = .10^2 + .15^2$$

and

$$\sigma_{US} = 0.18$$

Thus the standard deviation of the return expressed in dollars is considerably less than the sum of the standard deviation of the exchange gains and losses and the standard deviation of the return on the security in its home currency. The reader should be conscious of this difference in the tables that follow.

Having developed some preliminary relationships it is useful to examine some actual data on risk and return.

The Risk of Foreign Securities

Table 2.3 presents the correlation between the equity markets of several countries for the period 1980–1988. These correlation coefficients have been computed using monthly returns on market indices. The indices are computed by Morgan Stanley Capital International. They are market-weighted indexes with each stock's proportion in the index determined by its market value divided by the aggregate market value of all stocks. The indices include securities representing approximately 60 percent of the aggregate market value of each country. All returns were converted to U.S. dollars at prevailing exchange rates before correlations were calculated. Thus, Table 2.3 presents the correlation from the viewpoint of a U.S. investor. These are very low correlation coefficients relative to those found within a do-

Table 2.3. Correlations among Stock Indexes Measured in U.S. Dollars

	Australia	Austria	Belgium	Canada	Denmark	France	Germany
Australia							
Austria	0.135						
Belgium	0.351	0.469					
Canada	0.632	0.208	0.372				
Denmark	0.280	0.180	0.422	0.357			
France	0.357	0.492	0.670	0.417	0.374		
Germany	0.321	0.568	0.605	0.338	0.376	0.587	
Hong Kong	0.460	0.185	0.263	0.359	0.206	0.222	0.307
Italy	0.246	0.221	0.391	0.309	0.306	0.475	0.301
Japan	0.291	0.157	0.449	0.278	0.336	0.455	0.345
Mexico	0.302	0.050	0.150	0.099	−0.088	0.082	0.157
Netherlands	0.412	0.380	0.605	0.602	0.447	0.586	0.656
Norway	0.521	0.280	0.592	0.506	0.406	0.572	0.495
Sweden	0.388	0.261	0.369	0.383	0.228	0.374	0.387
Switzerland	0.452	0.556	0.666	0.516	0.466	0.629	0.794
United Kingdom	0.550	0.274	0.544	0.647	0.362	0.533	0.440
United States	0.476	0.171	0.410	0.726	0.369	0.458	0.399

mestic market. The average correlation coefficient between a pair of U.S. common stocks is about .40, and the correlation between U.S. indices is much higher. For example, the correlation between the S & P index of 425 large stocks and the rest of the stocks on the New York Stock Exchange for 1980–1988 is .97. The correlation between a market-weighted portfolio of the 1000 largest stocks in the U.S. market and a market-weighted portfolio of the next 2000 largest stocks for 1980–1988 is .92. Finally, the correlation coefficient between two 100-security portfolios drawn at random from the New York Stock Exchange is on the order of 0.95. The numbers in the table are much smaller than this, with the average correlation being .38.

The correlations between international indices are roughly the same as the correlation between two securities in the United States and less than the correlation between two securities in most other markets. The correlations shown in Table 2.3 are very similar to those found in other studies. Thus Table 2.3 is representative of typical correlation coefficients. For example, Solnik [48] studied the 15-year period 1971–1986 and found an average correlation of .35 between countries. Similarly, Kaplanis and Schaefer [30], studying the period February 1978 to June 1987, found an average correlation of .32. Finally, Eun and Resnick [17], studying the period 1973–1982, found an average correlation of .41.

Hong Kong	Italy	Japan	Mexico	Netherlands	Norway	Sweden	Switzerland	United Kingdom
0.331								
0.173	0.402							
0.227	0.072	0.062						
0.467	0.359	0.379	0.214					
0.405	0.213	0.283	0.247	0.646				
0.354	0.358	0.258	0.217	0.424	0.467			
0.361	0.308	0.375	0.114	0.705	0.614	0.504		
0.475	0.375	0.349	0.198	0.667	0.560	0.457	0.556	
0.318	0.240	0.247	0.147	0.638	0.537	0.398	0.542	0.564

Table 2.4.   Correlations among Bond Indexes Measured in U.S. Dollars

	Canada	France	Germany	Japan	Netherlands	Switzerland	United Kingdom
Canada							
France	0.447						
Germany	0.469	0.917					
Japan	0.475	0.704	0.721				
Netherlands	0.480	0.920	0.976	0.730			
Switzerland	0.479	0.834	0.917	0.736	0.925		
United Kingdom	0.515	0.572	0.612	0.575	0.608	0.585	
United States	0.677	0.386	0.475	0.434	0.444	0.491	0.415

Although the number of studies is much more limited, preliminary results suggest that similar conclusions hold for bonds. Table 2.4 shows the correlation between the Salomon Brothers long-term bond indices of eight countries for the years 1980–1988. These indices are value-weighted indices of the major issues in each country. Once again the correlations are very low relative to the correlations of two intracountry indices or bond portfolios. The average correlation between countries shown in Table 2.4 is .63. In contrast, Kaplanis and Schaefer [30] show an average correlation between countries of .43 for long-term bond indices in their sample period, and Chollerton, Pieraerts, and Solnik [13] find .43. This can be contrasted with the correlation between two typical American bond mutual funds of .94 and the correlation between the U.S. government and corporate bond index of .98.

Finally, Table 2.5 shows correlation coefficients for short-term bonds, in particular, three-month debt. The average correlation for the same eight

Table 2.5.   Correlations for Three-month Bond Indexes Measured in U.S. Dollars

	Canada	France	Germany	Japan	Netherlands	Switzerland	United Kingdom
Canada							
France	0.321						
Germany	0.311	0.952					
Japan	0.223	0.662	0.637				
Netherlands	0.320	0.955	0.991	0.643			
Switzerland	0.321	0.883	0.929	0.676	0.933		
United Kingdom	0.392	0.626	0.633	0.520	0.666	0.639	
United States	0.164	−0.254	−0.220	−0.164	−0.228	−0.180	−0.197

countries shown in Table 2.4 is .44. The low correlation across markets for stocks, bonds, and T-bills is the strongest evidence in favor of international diversification. The low correlation suggests that international diversification could reduce the risk on an investor's portfolio.

Risk depends not only on correlation coefficients but also on the standard deviation of return. Table 2.6 shows the standard deviation of return for an investment in the common equity indices, the long-term bond indices and the short-term bond indices discussed earlier. It should be emphasized once again that the standard deviation is calculated on market indices and is therefore a measure of risk for a well-diversified portfolio, consisting only of securities traded within the country under examination.

As shown in the last section, there are two sources of risks. The return on an investment in foreign securities varies because of variation of security prices within the securities home market and because of exchange gains and losses.

The column headed "Domestic Risk" shows the standard deviation of return when returns are calculated in the indexes' own currency. Thus the standard deviation of 19.77 for Germany is the standard deviation when returns on German stocks are calculated in marks. The second source of risk is exchange risk. Exchange risk arises because the exchange rate between the mark and dollar changes over time, affecting the return to a U.S. investor on an investment in German securities. The variability of the exchange rate for each currency converted to dollars is shown in the column titled "Exchange Risk." As discussed in the last section, the exchange risk and the within country risk are relatively independent and standard deviations are not additive. Thus total risk to the U.S. investor is much less than the sum of exchange risk and within country risk. For example, the standard deviation of German stocks in marks is 19.77 percent. The standard deviation of changes in the mark dollar exchange rate is 12.76 percent. However, the risk of German stocks in dollars when both fluctuations are taken into account is 22.99 percent. It should be emphasized that the variability of exchange rates is calculated by examining the variability of each currency in dollars. Thus the total risk is measured from a U.S. investor's point of view.

As shown in Table 2.6 over the 1980–1988 time period, the standard deviation of an index of the U.S. equity market was less than the standard deviation of most other market indexes when each market was stated in its own currency. When the effect of exchange risk is taken into account, the higher risk of foreign markets was even more pronounced. These results are not atypical. Solnik [48], Kaplanis and Schaefer [30], and Eun and Resnick [17] find the same results for different periods. For long-term bonds, however, the standard deviation of the U.S. bond index is among the highest when each index is stated in its own currency. When returns are adjusted for changes in exchange rates and all returns are expressed in dollars, the risk for the U.S. bond index is much lower than for any

Table 2.6.   Risk for U.S. Investors 1980–1988

	Domestic risk	Exchange risk	Total risk
Stocks			
Australia	27.19	10.85	31.41
Austria	19.65	12.58	23.05
Belgium	20.18	13.45	24.17
Canada	21.02	4.71	23.46
Denmark	19.35	12.29	20.89
France	21.61	12.37	25.27
Germany	19.77	12.76	22.99
Hong Kong	36.70	6.52	39.25
Italy	29.46	11.60	29.45
Japan	17.47	13.02	22.84
Mexico	48.07	35.53	60.30
Netherlands	20.37	12.51	21.26
Norway	28.43	10.27	30.39
Sweden	24.19	10.49	24.68
Switzerland	16.39	13.94	20.31
United Kingdom	20.47	12.18	23.55
United States	17.30	—	17.30
Value-weighted index (non-U.S.)			17.91
Equal-weighted index (non-U.S.)	15.03	8.83	17.26
Bonds			
Canada	7.28	4.71	9.51
France	5.17	12.37	14.19
Germany	6.95	12.76	16.43
Japan	8.91	13.02	17.16
Netherlands	4.91	12.51	14.58
Switzerland	5.37	13.94	16.70
United Kingdom	8.51	12.18	16.39
United States	8.27	—	8.27
Value-weighted index (non-U.S.)			14.05
Equal-weighted index (non-U.S.)	5.0	9.98	12.92
Three-month securities			
Canada	1.96	4.71	4.75
France	2.31	12.37	12.39
Germany	4.06	12.76	12.72
Japan	4.68	13.02	12.96
Netherlands	1.90	12.51	12.59
Switzerland	2.30	13.94	14.18
United Kingdom	3.54	12.18	12.27
United States	1.04	—	1.04
Value-weighted index (non-U.S.)			9.82
Equal-weighted index (non-U.S.)	1.52	9.98	10.10

foreign index. This illustrates the importance of exchange rate fluctuations on returns and risk. Finally, for short-term bonds the effect of exchange rates is even more dramatic. The exchange rate risk is by far the largest component of total risk. When the standard deviation is calculated for a U.S. investor, the standard deviation of U.S. T-bills is much less than the standard deviation for non-U.S. investments. For the case of T-bills and perhaps bonds, although the relatively low correlation strongly suggests that international diversification pays, the higher standard deviation suggests it may not.

Table 2.7 shows the combination of a value-weighted index of non-U.S. markets and the corresponding U.S. index. The numbers in the table are standard deviations of this combination when various percentages are invested in the international portfolio. When considering equities the minimum risk is achieved with 53 percent in the U.S. portfolio and 47 percent in the market-weighted world portfolio (excluding U.S. securities), and total risk is reduced by 12 percent compared with exclusive investment in the U.S. market. The risk reduction for long-term bonds is much less dramatic because the relative risk of a non-U.S. market-weighted international bond portfolio is much higher and the correlation slightly higher. Nevertheless a slight risk reduction is achieved. Finally, for T-bills some international diversification lowers risk (slightly less than 1 percent). Because of exchange risk the standard deviation of a value-weighted non-U.S. international short-term bond portfolio is dramatically higher than

Table 2.7. Risk from Placing X Percent in a World Index[a]

X percent in world index	Value-weighted index		
	Stocks	Long-term bonds	T-bills
0	17.30	8.27	1.04
10	16.52	8.23	1.20
20	15.90	8.38	1.96
30	15.46	8.69	2.88
40	15.22	9.16	3.84
50	15.18	9.76	4.82
60	15.36	10.48	5.81
70	15.73	11.28	6.81
80	16.29	12.15	7.81
90	17.03	13.07	8.81
100	17.91	14.05	9.82

a. Excluding U.S. securities and the rest in U.S. index.

the standard deviation of U.S. T-bills. In this time period, however, the correlation of U.S. T-bills and a value-weighted index of foreign T-bills was −.22.[3] Thus, even with the high standard deviation, a modest amount of international diversification lowered risk.

These results were derived using data from 1980–1988. An interesting question to analyze is whether the results are unique to the period examined or if we can safely generalize them. The conclusions depend on the correlation between the world portfolio and the U.S. index and the standard deviation of each index. As discussed earlier, the correlations used in this analysis are very similar to the correlations other researchers have found in other periods. The variability of return for foreign markets during this period is higher than the variability of return that most other researchers have found.

Thus the risk reduction shown in Table 2.7 would hold if data from other periods were used and the results are likely to be robust across periods. Furthermore, for stocks, rather substantial errors in selecting the optimal mix could be made and risk would still be reduced. Therefore, using data from a prior period to decide on a mixture of an international and domestic portfolio would likely result in a less risky portfolio than pure domestic investment. For long-term bonds and T-bills, the risk reduction via international diversification is so small that errors in determining the risk-minimizing mix of international and domestic portfolios could easily result in a portfolio more risky than the domestic one held alone.

Returns from International Diversification

The decade of the 1980s was an especially favorable time for foreign markets relative to U.S. markets. Table 2.8 shows the average annual returns from January 1980 to December 1988 on several international markets. The "Exchange Gain" column is the difference between the return in the assets home country and the assets return in the United States.[4] The average non-U.S. equity index had a return of 22.23 percent in its home country compared with 16.12 percent for the U.S. market. Even with an exchange loss averaging −3.73 percent, when converted to dollars the average non-U.S. equity index returned 18.5 percent. When a market-weighted international index excluding the United States was used, the results were even more dramatic with a return of 23.04 percent. This high return is primarily due to Japan. Japan comprises a very large percentage of the non-U.S. value-weighted index. Converted to dollars, the Japanese index returned 30.28 percent per year. Thus, because of the high Japanese return in this period, a non-U.S. value-weighted international index outperformed an equally weighted index.

The column in Table 2.8 that presents returns in U.S. dollars shows only four countries had returns substantially below the United States. Thus, almost any internationally diversified equity portfolio would have

Table 2.8. Return to U.S. Investors 1980–1988 (Percent per annum)

	Own country	Effect of exchange gain or loss	To U.S. investor
Stocks			
Australia	20.97	−4.69	16.37
Austria	10.80	+2.02	12.82
Belgium	23.93	−0.98	22.95
Canada	12.46	−0.77	11.69
Denmark	17.91	−1.47	16.44
France	19.39	−2.83	16.56
Germany	12.56	+3.03	15.59
Hong Kong	24.86	−4.69	20.17
Italy	30.98	−4.73	26.25
Japan	20.66	+9.62	30.28
Mexico	63.81	−50.35	13.64
Netherlands	19.92	+.94	20.86
Norway	13.12	−2.42	10.70
Sweden	31.43	−4.31	27.12
Switzerland	9.36	+3.37	12.73
United Kingdom	23.57	−1.70	21.87
United States	16.12		16.12
Value-weighted index (non-U.S.)			23.04
Equal-weighted index (non-U.S.)	22.23	−3.73	18.50
Bonds			
Canada	12.32	−1.14	11.18
France	12.69	−2.84	9.85
Germany	7.44	+3.47	10.91
Japan	9.56	+9.55	19.11
Netherlands	10.20	+1.69	11.89
Switzerland	5.75	+3.93	9.68
United Kingdom	14.13	−1.35	12.78
United States	12.05	—	12.05
Value-weighted index (non-U.S.)			15.19
Equal-weighted index (non-U.S.)	10.30	+1.90	12.20
Three-month securities			
Canada	11.73	−1.23	10.50
France	13.69	−2.98	10.71
Germany	5.84	+3.10	8.94
Japan	7.04	+9.21	16.25
Netherlands	7.75	+1.54	9.29
Switzerland	5.36	+3.67	9.03
United Kingdom	12.26	−1.62	10.64
United States	10.93	—	10.93
Value-weighted index (non-U.S.)			10.46
Equal-weighted index (non-U.S.)	9.10	+1.67	10.77

had a higher return than the U.S. market index over this period. During this period international diversification had the advantage of not only lowering risk, but it also resulted in higher average returns.

The results for long-term bonds are not as clear. The equally weighted portfolio of country return indexes (excluding the United States) did slightly better than the U.S. market index. Part of this was due to an almost 2 percent exchange gain. Once again the value-weighted portfolio performed better. As with equities, this was due primarily to the performance of Japanese bonds. In yen, Japanese bonds returned about 9.6 percent, but over this period, the dollar value of the yen also increased by 9.5 percent, resulting in a 19.1 percent return to U.S. investors. A fair number of countries underperformed in the U.S. bond market. Thus many international portfolios would also have underperformed a portfolio of U.S. bonds.

For three-month T-bills the return on both the equally weighted and value-weighted index was less than the return on U.S. T-bills. Given the higher risk discussed earlier, it would be unlikely that an international portfolio would have been superior. A U.S. index offered both lower risk and higher return.

Although these results are appropriate for the period discussed, it is useful to examine other periods. Solnik [48] studied equity indexes for 17 countries for the years 1971–1985. For all but two countries the return on the foreign index expressed in dollars was greater than the return on the U.S. equity index. The exchange gain from holding foreign equities added only .2 percent on average to this return. For long and short bonds only, Canada and the United Kingdom had a lower return when return was expressed in U.S. dollars. For bonds, however, a major factor contributing to the return being above the U.S. return was exchange gains. Thus, although the decade of the 1980s was a favorable period for returns in non-U.S. markets, it was not a unique period.

For portfolio decisions, estimates of future values of mean return, standard deviation, and correlation coefficients are needed. The correlation coefficients between international markets have been very low historically relative to intracountry correlations. As Europe integrates its markets and as all countries move toward greater integration, these coefficients are likely to rise.[5] However, they are still likely to be low relative to intracountry correlation. For example, the correlation coefficient between countries whose economies are relatively highly integrated, such as Canada and the United States, the Benelux countries, or the Scandinavian countries, is still much lower than the intracountry correlation coefficients. Thus international diversification is likely to continue to lead to risk reduction in the foreseeable future. However, we know of no economic reason to argue that returns will be higher internationally as they have been in the recent past for U.S. investors. Furthermore, for investors in many countries besides the United States, historic returns on international portfolios have been less than returns on domestic portfolios.

The Effect of Exchange Risk

In the first section we showed how the return on a foreign investment could be split into the return in the security's home market and the return from changes in exchange rates. In each of the prior tables we separated out the effect of changes in the exchange rate on return and risk. The column entitled "Exchange Return or Exchange Risk" calculated the effect of converting all currencies into dollars. Obviously if we were presenting the same tables from a French or Norwegian point of view, the "Exchange Rate Expected Return" and "Risk" columns would be different, because they would contain results as if all currencies were converted to francs (for the French person) or kroner (for the Norwegian). Because francs and kroner have not fluctuated perfectly with the dollar, these columns would be different. Thus the country of domicile affects the expected returns and risk (including correlation coefficients) from international diversification.

Table 2.9 illustrates this by computing expected return and risk from the U.S. investor's point of view (which is a repeat of prior tables) and from the French point of view. The numbers are clearly quite different. It is possible to protect partially against exchange rate fluctuations. An investor can enter into a contract for future delivery of a currency; for example, an American investor purchasing German securities could simultaneously agree to convert marks into dollars at a future date and at a known rate. If the investor knew exactly what the security would be worth at the

Table 2.9.   The Effect of Country of Domicile on Mean Return and Risk

Country	Mean Return		Variance	
	Francs	Dollars	Francs	Dollars
Australia	19.3	16.4	32.2	31.4
Austria	15.7	12.8	20.3	23.0
Belgium	25.9	23.0	21.5	24.2
Canada	14.6	11.7	24.8	23.5
Denmark	19.3	16.4	20.1	20.9
France	19.5	16.6	21.5	25.3
Germany	18.5	15.6	20.8	23.0
Hong Kong	23.1	20.2	40.8	39.3
Italy	29.2	26.3	29.5	29.5
Japan	33.2	30.3	22.0	22.8
Mexico	16.5	13.6	62.2	60.3
Netherlands	23.8	20.9	21.0	21.3
Norway	13.6	10.7	29.2	30.4
Sweden	30.0	27.1	25.7	24.7
Switzerland	15.6	12.7	17.2	20.3
United Kingdom	24.8	21.9	23.1	23.6
United States	19.0	16.1	21.0	17.3

end of the period, he or she would be completely protected against rate fluctuations by agreeing to switch an amount of marks exactly equal to the value of the investment. However, given that, in general, the end-of-period value of the investment is random, the best the investor can do is protect against a particular outcome (e.g., its expected value).[6]

As shown earlier, the standard deviation of foreign investments is increased as a result of exchange risk. If exchange risk was completely hedged, then the "Domestic Risk" column in Table 2.6 would be the relevant column used to measure risk. In all cases except Italy, entries in the domestic column are substantially less than the column titled "Total Risk." This is especially true for long- and short-term bonds. Although we will not present the tables, the correlation coefficients are somewhat lower when we calculate the correlation between returns assuming exchange risk is fully hedged away. Exchange movement increases the correlation among countries' returns. The average correlation coefficient between two countries is .31, assuming exchange risk is hedged away for the countries shown in Table 2.3. This contrasts with .38 when exchange risk is fully borne. Similarly, Kaplanis and Schaefer [30] found an average correlation of .37 when including the effect of exchange risk and .32 when exchange risk was fully hedged. Thus risk in international portfolios is considerably reduced if exchange risk is hedged away. The effect on expected return is less clear. Table 2.8 shows that during the 1980–1988 period, exchange movements caused losses to U.S. investors for most countries. The same table in the 1970s would have shown mostly gains. Also, the loss to the U.S. investor is the gain to the foreign investor, so that a different table would hold if we expressed returns in, for example, Swiss francs. Thus the effect of eliminating exchange gains or losses on expected return varies from country to country and period to period.

One way to determine whether international diversification will be a useful strategy in the future is to analyze how low returns in foreign countries would have to be for an investor not to gain via international diversification.

Return Expectations and Portfolio Performance

Most of the literature on domestic and international diversification tells us that history is a much better guide in forecasting risk than it is in forecasting returns. If we accept the historical data on risk as indicative of the future, for any assumed return on the U.S. market we can solve for the minimum return that must be offered by any foreign market to make it an attractive investment from the U.S. standpoint.

We did this under two assumptions: that the U.S. market would return 12 percent and that it would return 16 percent. These numbers were selected because 16 percent is approximately the return for the U.S. equity market in the 1980s and 12 percent is roughly the historical long-term

**Table 2.10. Minimum Returns on Foreign
Markets Necessary for International
Diversification to be Justified**

United States	12 percent	16 percent
Australia	11.32	14.78
Austria	8.14	9.05
Belgium	9.86	12.16
Canada	11.92	15.86
Denmark	9.23	11.01
France	10.34	13.02
Germany	9.65	11.77
Hong Kong	10.61	13.49
Italy	9.04	10.68
Japan	8.63	9.93
Mexico	9.56	11.61
Netherlands	10.92	10.62
Norway	11.72	15.49
Sweden	9.84	12.11
Switzerland	10.18	12.73
United Kingdom	10.84	13.91
Value-weighted index	9.53	11.55

return on U.S. equities. The calculations used the correlation coefficients shown in Table 2.3 and the standard deviations shown in Table 2.6, and a risk-free rate of 7 percent. These numbers are shown in Table 2.10. The basic formula to determine these numbers is as follows:

Hold non-U.S. securities as long as[7]

$$\frac{\overline{R}_N - R_F}{\sigma_N} > \frac{\overline{R}_{US} - R_F}{\sigma_{US}} \rho_{N,US} \tag{2.1}$$

where

$\overline{R}_N$ is the expected return on the non-U.S. securities
$\overline{R}_{US}$ is the expected return on the U.S. securities
σ_N is the standard deviation of the non-U.S. securities
σ_{US} is the standard deviation of U.S. securities
$\rho_{N,US}$ is the correlation between U.S. securities and non-U.S. securities
R_F is the risk-free rate of interest

Although this equation is written from a U.S. investor's point of view, a similar equation holds for investors in any country considering foreign investment. The reader would simply redefine the symbols presently sub-scripted US to the country of interest.

Note in Table 2.10 that the return required on a foreign investment is for most markets considerably less than the return on the U.S. invest-ment. For an assumed U.S. expected return of 12 percent, Austrian se-curities would have to have an expected return of less than 8.14 percent for it not to pay to invest in Austrian securities at all. The other extreme is, of course, Canada. Since Canadian securities are so highly correlated with U.S. securities, diversification into Canadian securities is less advan-tageous for a U.S. investor. Thus Canadian securities must have a return almost as high as U.S. securities for diversification to pay.

If we rearrange the expression 2.1, we have

Hold non-U.S. securities as long as

$$\overline{R}_N - R_F > [(\overline{R}_{US} - R_F)]\left[\frac{\sigma_N \rho_{N,US}}{\sigma_{US}}\right] \qquad (2.2)$$

As long as the expression in the last bracket is less than one, foreign secur-ities should be held even with expected returns lower than those found in the domestic market. For all the countries examined, the expression in the last bracket was less than one so the expected return on non-U.S. securities could be less than U.S. securities and international diversification would still pay. Thus, for the period studied, expected returns in non-U.S. coun-tries could have been considerably less than in the U.S. and international diversification would still have paid.

All the entries in Table 2.10 with the exception of those in the last row showed the minimum expected return when one country was added to the U.S. portfolio. Thus the portfolio was composed of two countries' securities. The last row shows the expected return on a value-weighted index necessary to justify adding it to U.S. securities. Although not the lowest return, it is considerably less than most countries' return considered separately. If the expected return on U.S. securities is 16 percent, a value-weighted portfolio should be added if its expected return is greater than 11.55 percent. This is a general result. Portfolios of securities from many countries will be less risky than portfolios of a single country's securities. Examining Equation 2.2 shows that for a given correlation, the lower the standard deviation the lower the expected return on a foreign portfolio can be and still have international diversification pay.

We argued in the first section that international diversification lowers risk. In this section we have shown that returns in foreign markets would have to be much lower than returns in the domestic market or international diversification pays. What is foreign to one investor is domestic to another, however. Are there any circumstances where international diversification does not pay for investors of every country?

To understand this issue, consider the U.S. and U.K. markets and refer to Table 2.10. This table shows that if the return in the U.K. market is not less than 13.91 when returns in the U.S. market are 16 percent, a U.S. investor should purchase some U.K. securities. Furthermore, it is easy to show that if a U.K. investor believed expected returns in the U.K. would be less than in the United States, then the U.K. investor should purchase U.S. stocks. If investors in the two markets agree on expected returns, we have one of three situations: both gain from diversification, the U.S. investor gains, or the U.K. investor gains. In all three cases, however, at least one investor should diversify internationally. If the investors do not agree on returns in the two markets, then it is possible that neither the U.S. investor nor the U.K. investor will benefit from international diversification. For example, assume U.S. investors believe that U.K. markets have an expected return of 5 percent, whereas U.S. markets would have an expected return of 10 percent. Further assume that U.K. investors believe U.K. markets have an expected return of 10 percent, whereas U.S. markets have an expected return of 5 percent. Under this set of expected returns neither U.S. nor U.K. investors would wish to diversify internationally. Are there any circumstances in which investors in all countries could rationally believe that returns are higher in their country relative to the rest of the world? The answer is *yes!*

If governments tax foreign investments at rates very different from domestic investments, then the pattern just discussed would be possible for after-tax returns. Differential taxation has occurred in the past, continues to occur today, and will likely persist into the future.[8] Second, many countries impose a withholding tax on dividends. Taxable investors may receive a domestic credit for the foreign tax withheld and thus not have lowered returns. However, for nontaxable investors (or for a nontaxable part of an investor's portfolio, such as pension assets), the withholding is a cost that lowers the return of foreign investment. A third situation that could cause foreign investments to have a lower return than domestic investments for all investors is if there are differential transaction costs for domestic and foreign purchases. This could occur if there was difficulty in purchasing foreign securities or currency controls existed. For example, there may be restrictions in converting domestic to foreign currency that could affect returns. The exchange of currency A for B might take place at an official rate that is higher than the free market rate, and there might be an expectation of a later reversal. A fourth situation that can result in investors in all countries having an expectation of higher returns from domestic investments relative to foreign, is a danger of a government restricting the ability of foreigners to withdraw funds. Governments can and do place such restrictions on foreigners, and this can reduce returns to foreigners. The considerations just discussed are real and can affect the returns from international diversification.

Before leaving this section, one other issue needs to be discussed. It has been suggested that investors could confine themselves to a national market and receive most of the benefits of international diversification by purchasing stocks in multinational corporations. Jacquillat and Solnik [26] have tested this for the American investor. They found that stock prices of multinational firms do not seem to be affected by foreign factors and behave much like the stocks of domestic firms. The American investor cannot gain much of the advantage of international diversification by investing in the securities of the multinational firm.

Other Evidence on Internationally Diversified Portfolios

In prior sections we have presented the considerations that are important in deciding on the reasonableness of international diversification. Obviously, we feel that the type of analysis we have presented is the relevant way to analyze the problem. However, several studies analyze the reasonableness of international diversification by examining the characteristics of international portfolios selecting using historical data. The most common approach attempts to show the advantages of international diversification by forming an optimal portfolio of international and domestic securities using historical data and comparing the return to an exclusively domestically held portfolio over the same time period. It should not surprise the reader that knowing the exact values of mean returns, variance, and covariances for international markets allows construction of portfolios that dominate investment exclusively in the domestic portfolio. A variant of this analysis presents the efficient frontier using historical data with and without international securities and "shows" that adding international securities improves the efficient frontier.

In recent years several studies have been undertaken that do not assume perfect forecasting ability but rather follow procedures that an investor could actually follow. Both Jorion [29] and Grauer and Hakansson [20] use historical return data on foreign security markets to form expectations about correlations, standard deviations, and mean returns. They then form portfolios and examine performance in subsequent periods. Since during the time of their studies, foreign markets (especially Japan) outperformed U.S. markets, the resulting portfolios generally dominated investment in only U.S. markets on both return and risk dimensions. These studies are very useful and provide additional evidence in favor of international diversification.

The real test of international diversification is the performance of actual internationally diversified portfolios compared with the performance of purely domestic portfolios. Unfortunately, there is not a great deal of evidence on this subject.

McDonald [42] examined the performance of French mutual funds. French funds, in general, hold a substantial part of their portfolio in foreign securities, primarily U.S. securities. From our previous discussion of international markets one would expect that a large part of the variability of French mutual fund returns would be unrelated to movements of the French stock market and this is, in fact, the case. Table 2.11 shows the results for McDonald's sample of seven funds. These are low numbers. Large diversified portfolios such as mutual funds usually have 90 percent or more of their variance explained by movements in the market index. The low relationship has to be a result of international diversification.[9] The promise of an internationally diversified portfolio having a substantially lower correlation with the domestic market seems to hold.

The period of McDonald's study was a period in which the U.S. market had a higher rate of return than the French market. Thus, it should not be surprising that the internationally diversified mutual funds also outperformed the French market. In this period they did about 30 percent better. U.S. markets did not have to outperform French markets for the internationally diversified funds to have been superior. Even if the U.S. market had a lower return and securities had been selected randomly, the funds would have been good purchases given their low risk.[10]

A recent study of U.S. internationally diversified funds was undertaken by Eun, Kolodny, and Resnick [16]. They studied five funds that held only non-U.S. securities. These funds are of interest because from a U.S. investor's point of view they represent a vehicle that would allow international diversification. Table 2.12 presents evidence on the characteristics of these funds. As shown in Table 2.12, investment for the five funds was fairly evenly split between Europe and Asia.

The major promise of international diversification is the low correlation between domestic securities and foreign securities. For these five funds the promise was met. For the 10-year period 1977–1986, the average proportion of the total variability explained by the S & P index for the five international funds was .45, and for the 5-year period 1982–1986, the average was .25.

Table 2.11. Proportion of Variance Explained by Market Movements

Fund	Percentage explained
1	62
2	51
3	36
4	34
5	51
6	58
7	17
Average	44.1

Table 2.12. Performance of International Funds

	Composition[a]		1977–1986[b]				1982–1986			
	Asia	Europe	Mean return monthly	Standard deviation	β	Percent of variation explained by market	Mean return monthly	Standard deviation	β	Percent of variation explained by market
Kemper	51%	48%	1.14	4.29	0.69	0.47	1.76	4.52	0.44	0.17
Keystone	60%	40%	1.46	4.23	0.50	0.26	1.47	4.59	0.58	0.29
Scudder	34%	58%					1.88	4.30	0.46	0.21
T Rowe Price	43%	57%					1.95	4.66	0.47	0.19
United	58%	30%	1.41	3.86	0.71	0.61	1.76	3.43	0.51	0.40
Ave			1.34	4.13	0.63	0.45	1.76	4.30	0.49	0.25
MNC[c]			1.34	4.38	0.98	0.90	1.85	4.59	1.04	0.94
S&P			1.17	4.25	1.0	1.0	1.60	4.26	1.0	1.0
MSCI[d]			1.46	3.80	0.70	0.61	2.04	4.01	0.68	0.53

a. The percentages don't add up to one. The remainder is non-U.S. North and South American.

b. β and percentage of variation explained by market are calculated with respect to S&P index.

c. Index of U.S. multinational corporations.

d. Morgan Stanley Capital international index of non-U.S. equity markets.

Source: Eun, Kolodny, and Resnick (forthcoming). The authors studied 15 funds. The funds in the table are the noncountry funds with only foreign investment.

Numbers this low would never be found for a U.S. mutual fund investing primarily in common stock. Rather, the average would be above .90. This is strong evidence that the extensive analysis discussed earlier concerning low correlation among countries can be reflected in actual performance of international mutual funds. Similarly, the column entitled "Beta" shows the responsiveness of international funds to a change in the S & P index. The beta for the common stock portion of a fund invested in U.S. securities would be close to one. In 1977–1986 the average beta of the international funds was .63. In 1982–1986 the average beta was .49. This is additional evidence that international funds are less sensitive than domestic funds to movements in the U.S. market.

As shown in Table 2.6, the U.S. market is less risky than other national markets from a U.S. perspective. Given the low correlation between non-U.S. markets, however, the relative riskiness of U.S. portfolios and an internationally diversified portfolio is less clear. The average standard deviation of the five funds over the 10-year period was less than the S & P index: in the five-year period it was slightly more. This evidence would suggest that the higher risk of individual countries relative to U.S. markets was balanced by low correlation between countries to produce a portfolio with risk comparable to a U.S. portfolio.

In both the five- and ten-year periods, the average return for international funds was greater than that of U.S. portfolios as represented by the S & P index. In both periods the performance of international funds was less than the non-U.S. Morgan Stanley capital world index (MSCI), which is not surprising. During this time period, foreign markets outperformed the United States, with Japan leading the way. International funds underinvested in Japan relative to the Morgan Stanley index. Because Japan had the greatest return, it is easy to understand why international funds underperformed the Morgan Stanley index.

The risk structure between various countries has been studied for 20 years, and the results of low correlation among international markets relative to intra-country portfolios have been consistently found. Thus the risk characteristics of international funds that have been found in the past are likely to be found in the future. It is hard, however, to develop a convincing economic case that the U.S. market will underperform other markets in the future as it did in the last five or ten years. Thus, once again, we believe the relevant way to utilize mutual fund data to examine the reasonableness of international diversification is to examine the proportions to invest in the United States and an international portfolio at various levels of assumed differences between returns in the United States and returns in other countries. Table 2.13 shows the optimal investment proportions for a portfolio of the S & P index and the average international funds shown in Table 2.12. The data for 1977–1986 international mutual funds show that international diversification pays as long as the return on the international portfolio is no less than 2 percent below the return on the S & P index.

Table 2.13.   Investment Proportions

Return on international portfolio	1977–1986 data on optimal proportions		1982–1986 data on optimal proportions	
	United States	International	United States	International
+2%			40	60
+1%	35	65	45	55
Same as S&P	47	53	51	49
−1%	69	31	57	43
−2%	100	0	64	36
−3%			71	29
−4%			78	22
−5%			87	13
−6%			96	4
−6.2%			100	0

Using the data on the average international fund for the period 1982–1986 shows that international diversification pays as long as the return on the international fund is no lower than 6.2 percent below the S & P index.[11] Only by explicitly defining required differentials can rational decisions be made on investing in international mutual funds.

Models for Managing International Portfolios

Prior sections present analysis that suggests that a portfolio of international equities should be a part of an optimum portfolio. Furthermore, examining the performance of international funds shows that the analysis is confirmed by actual performance. The conclusions were less clear for international bond funds.

The obvious strategy for an investor deciding to diversify internationally but not wishing to determine how to construct an international portfolio is to hold an international index fund. The parallel to holding a domestic index fund is to hold a value-weighted portfolio of international securities. The Morgan Stanley Capital International Index excluding the United States is a value-weighted index, and an investment matching this index would be a value-weighted index fund.[12] The rationale for holding an index fund is much weaker internationally than domestically. If expected return is related to a market index and if securities are in equilibrium, then bearing nonmarket or unique risk does not result in additional compensation. The way to eliminate nonmarket risk is to hold an index fund. Thus the investment implication of believing that markets are in equilibrium and that the CAPM determines expected returns is to hold an index fund. Even an investor who believes that securities are out of equilibrium but does not profess to know which securities give a positive or negative nonequilibrium return (has no forecasting ability) should hold the index fund. In this case, bearing nonmarket risk on average does not improve expected return because the investor on average selects securities with zero nonmarket return. Thus the investor should eliminate non-market risk by holding an index fund. If there was good evidence that individual securities' expected returns were determined by an international CAPM, and if a value-weighted index was the fact or affecting expected returns, a parallel argument could be presented for holding an international value-weighted index fund. However, the evidence in favor of any international model determining expected return is weak to nonexistent. For example, Table 2.14 shows how much of the return on each country's securities is explained by the international index, the country's own index, the industry the security belongs to, the change in currency values, and the joint effect of all four factors combined. Note that the percent explained by all indexes is not very different from the percent explained by the securities' relationship with the domestic index. Thus adding the other influences does not increase the explanatory power significantly. This implies that there

Table 2.14.   The Relation of World, Industrial, Currency and Domestic Factors to the Return of a Stock

Locality	Percentage of Returns Explained by Various Factors				All four factors
	World	Industrial	Currency	Domestic	
Switzerland	0.18	0.17	0.00	0.38	0.39
West Germany	0.08	0.10	0.00	0.41	0.42
Australia	0.24	0.26	0.01	0.72	0.72
Belgium	0.07	0.08	0.00	0.42	0.43
Canada	0.27	0.24	0.07	0.45	0.48
Spain	0.22	0.03	0.00	0.45	0.45
United States	0.26	0.47	0.01	0.35	0.55
France	0.13	0.08	0.01	0.45	0.60
United Kingdom	0.20	0.17	0.01	0.53	0.55
Hong Kong	0.06	0.25	0.17	0.79	0.81
Italy	0.05	0.03	0.00	0.35	0.35
Japan	0.09	0.16	0.01	0.26	0.33
Norway	0.17	0.28	0.00	0.84	0.85
Netherlands	0.12	0.07	0.01	0.34	0.31
Singapore	0.16	0.15	0.02	0.32	0.33
Sweden	0.19	0.06	0.01	0.42	0.43
All countries	0.18	0.23	0.01	0.42	0.46

Source: Modified from Bruno Solnik. Reprinted with permission.

is no major factor explaining the return on securities traded in different countries. Rather, a security's return is explained primarily by changes in the domestic market. Although this might be interpreted as evidence that one index fund should be held for each country, it casts doubt on holding country portfolios in market proportions.

A second argument against holding a non-U.S. international value-weighted index is the percentage represented by one country, Japan, which represents approximately 60 percent of the non-U.S. value-weighted index. Unless one believes Japan will continue to have abnormally high return, it is hard to justify this percentage. For diversification or risk arguments, it is clearly inappropriate.

The authors have listened to a number of presentations suggesting other weighting schemes, such as trade or GNP or total wealth of the country. Until we develop an explicit international equilibrium model, none of these choices has an economic justification.

Until there is good evidence supporting an international CAPM that partitions risk into that part that results in higher expected return and that part that is unique, it is appropriate for an investor without an ability to forecast expected returns to minimize total risk. The risk structure is reasonably predictable through time. The low correlation on average among country portfolios, and the pattern of relatively high correlation among countries with close economic links (such as the United States and Canada) is likely to continue in the future. Both Jorion [29] and Eun and Resnick [17] have examined the stability of the correlation structure and have found predictability. Thus the past correlation matrices can be used to predict the future. Similarly, Jorion [29] has shown that standard deviations are predictable, and thus a low-risk international portfolio can be developed.

If one wishes to develop an active international portfolio, then many of the same considerations are involved as are present in developing an active domestic portfolio. However, international investment adds two elements to the investment process not present in pure domestic investment— country selection and exchange exposure.[13]

The decision concerning how much to invest in each country depends on the factors discussed earlier, namely, intercountry correlation, the variance of return for each country's securities, and the expected return in each country. There is good evidence that the past standard deviations and correlations are useful in predicting the future. However, there has been very little research concerning the estimation of expected return for various countries. Some researchers such as Grauer and Hakansson [20] have used past return to predict the future; past return has not been shown to be strongly related to future return, however.[14] Other possibilities have been suggested in prior chapters. For example, any of the index models that relate return to economic variables could potentially be used to forecast returns. Methods are available on how to estimate the coefficients

of an index model. Once these are estimated, there is a relationship between expected return and economic variables. For example, one model
could be

Expected return on equities
$$= 4 + 2 \text{ (Growth in GNP)} - \text{(Change in inflation)}$$

As the equation is written, there is no time subscript on the economic
variables. If the equation for expected return on equities as a function of
the growth in GNP in the prior period and change in inflation in the prior
period, the forecasting is straightforward. Current values for change in
GNP and change in inflation are substituted in the equation, and next
period's expected return is estimated. If the equation for expected return
on equities is a function of the contemporaneous change in GNP and
inflation, the forecasting task is switched from forecasting expected return
to forecasting economic variables, which may be an easier task. Forecasts
of these variables may well be available. Thus using an index model with
economic variables may help in estimating returns in various markets.

The infinite constant growth model states that

$$\text{Expected return} = \frac{\text{Dividend}}{\text{Price}} + \text{Growth}$$

Estimates of the next period's dividend could be obtained by estimating
earnings and estimating the proportion of earnings paid out as dividends
(the payout ratio). The payout ratio for a country portfolio is very stable
over time, and forecasts of earnings are widely available and at an economy
level quite accurate. Estimates of growth rates in earnings are also widely
available internationally. Thus valuation models offer a feasible way to
estimate expected returns.[15]

One of the few studies to examine some alternative ways of estimating
expected return is Arnott and Henriksson [8]. They forecast the relative
performance of each country's stocks compared to the country's bonds on
the basis of current risk premiums and economic variables. They define
the risk premium as the difference in expected return between common
equity and bonds. They measure expected return on bonds by using the
yield to maturity. They measure expected return on equity by calculating
the earnings divided by price. Comparing this measure with the valuation
model just presented shows that growth should be added and differences
in payout taken into account. These differences, as well as differences in
accounting conventions across countries and the impact of this on earnings, could affect risk premium comparisons across countries. They recognize these influences, and instead of using risk premiums directly, they
use risk premiums relative to past risk premiums. Their forecast equation

states that future performance is related to current risk premiums divided by average risk premiums in the past. In equation form this is

Future returns on equities relative to debt = Constant + Constant
(Current risk premium/Average risk premium prior two years)

They find for many countries that this equation is a useful predictor and that for some countries it can be improved by adding other macroeconomic variables, such as prediction of trade and production statistics. This model could be used to estimate which countries have higher expected future returns on equities by using current bond yields as expected returns for bonds, and the preceding equation to estimate the difference between bond and equity returns. Clearly, further testing of all these models is necessary. However, they are suggestive of the type of analysis that can be done in active international asset allocation

The second new consideration that international investment introduces is exchange risk. As discussed earlier, entering into futures contracts can reduce the variability due to the exchange risk. Considering only risk, this is useful. Entering into futures contracts can also affect expected return, however. The return on a futures contract should be related to differences in interest rates between the two countries. Thus entering into a futures contract could lower expected returns. Furthermore, the investor may have some beliefs about changes in exchange rates different from those contained in market prices.[16] In this case the sacrifice in expected return may lead the investor to choose not to eliminate exchange risk.

Finally, Black [10] has shown that taking some exchange risk can increase expected return. Thus exchange rate exposure involves a risk-return tradeoff.

Conclusion

In this chapter we have discussed the evidence in support of international diversification. The evidence that international diversification reduces risk is uniform and extensive. Given the low risk, international diversification is justified even if expected returns are less internationally than domestically. Unless there are mechanisms such as taxes or currency restrictions that substantially reduce the return on foreign investment relative to domestic investment, international diversification has to be profitable for investors of some countries, and possibly all.

Notes

1. Japan has a large number of companies with substantial equity holdings of other companies. The result of companies having a portion of their assets invested in stock of other companies is to overstate the market value of the assets, because

the same assets are valued in the company that owns them and in companies that own its shares. Estimates of Japanese cross holdings are between 50% and 60%, which is much greater than other countries. Thus these tables very much overstate the value of the Japanese assets. European countries are the next largest in cross holdings. Thus European values are somewhat overstated, although not nearly to the extent of Japan.

2. Foreign currency exchange rates can be quoted in two ways. If an exchange rate is stated as the amount of dollars per unit of foreign currency, the exchange rate is quoted in direct (or American) terms. If the exchange rate is given as the amount of foreign currency per dollar, the quote is in indirect (or foreign) terms. The form of quotes differs across markets. In the interbank market indirect quotes are used, whereas direct quotes are the norm in futures and options markets.

3. Note that this correlation of $-.22$ differs from the average correlation of 0.44 discussed earlier. The negative number arises in this case because (as the reader can see by examining Table 2.5), the correlation between American T-bills and non-U.S. T-bills is negative, whereas the correlation between the T-bills of other countries with each other is positive.

4. From Section Two of this chapter, the expected return to a U.S. investor is not the sum of exchange gains and losses and the return in the investor's home country. Thus column two is not the exchange return.

5. In particular, exchange rates between European currencies will be fixed. Although European currencies will continue to fluctuate with the U.S. currency, any advantage in diversifying across currencies will be eliminated. Note, however, that they are currently fixed within narrow limits so that the change will not be significant.

6. Procedures exist for changing the hedge through time in order to eliminate most of the exchange risk. See Kaplanis and Schaefer (30).

7. See Chapter 3 of this text for derivations.

8. A government's ability to enforce payment of taxes may be lower on foreign than domestic securities. Tax cheating could mitigate tax rate differentials.

9. French mutual funds in this period were required to hold at least 30% of their assets in bonds. Although this lowers total risk, it should not substantially affect the percent explained by the market.

10. McDonald attributes the higher return to superior selection of French securities. It is impossible to say why it occurred.

11. One consideration an investor in international portfolio needs to consider is that there is some evidence that international managers underperform domestic managers. At a number of conferences the authors have listened to industry speakers who specialize in evaluating international portfolios. They estimate a U.S. manager of a portfolio of foreign securities (such as Japanese) underperforms the foreign (Japanese) manager. The estimates we have heard range from 2 percent to 4 percent. The underperformance may well hold. Estimates of the exact amount should be treated with some skepticism.

12. Although the Morgan Stanley index is the most widely used index, differences by country in the cross holdings of securities (one company owning shares in another) means that its weighting is very different than an index using the value of a country's equity assets. Japan in particular is very much overweighted.

13. Technically the amount to invest in any security should depend on securities selected in other countries. Thus our treatment of first selecting each portfolio within a country and then doing country selection is nonoptimal. However, it captures much of practice. Furthermore, as shown in Table 2.15, intercountry factors are relatively unimportant in determining each securities' return so this assumption may be a simplification that improves performance.
14. See Arnott and Henriksson [8], for example.
15. Testing of the accuracy of forecasts produced by these models is unavailable, so all we can do is to suggest types of analysis; we cannot report results.
16. Levich [37] and [38] has shown that some forecasters are able to predict exchange rate movements.

References and Further Reading

1. Adler, Michael. "The Cost of Capital and Valuation of a Two-Country Firm." *Journal of Finance*, **29**, No. 1 (March 1974) pp. 119–132.
2. Adler, Michael, and Reuven Horesh. "The Relationship Among Equity Markets: Comment on [3]." *Journal of Finance*, **29**, No. 4 (Sept. 1974) pp. 1131–1137.
3. Adler, Michael, and Bernard Dumas. "International Portfolio Choice and Corporate Finance: A Synthesis." *Journal of Finance*, **38**, No. 3 (June 1983) pp. 925–984.
4. Agmon, Tamir. "The Relations Among Equity Markets: A Study of Share Price Co-Movements in the United States, United Kingdom, Germany and Japan." *Journal of Finance*, **28**, No. 3 (June 1972) pp. 839–855.
5. ———. "Country Risk: The Significance of the Country Factor for Share-Price Movements in the United Kingdom, Germany, and Japan." *Journal of Business*, **46**, No. 1 (Jan. 1973) pp. 24–32.
6. ———. "Reply to [2]." *Journal of Finance*, **29**, No. 4 (Sept. 1974) pp. 1318–1319.
7. Agmon, Tamir, and Donald Lessard. "Investor Recognition of Corporate International Diversification." *Journal of Finance, 32*, No. 4 (Sept. 1977) pp. 1049–1055.
8. Arnott, A., and N. Henriksson. "A Disciplined Approach to Global Asset Allocation." *Financial Analyst Journal* (March–April 1989) pp. 17–28.
9. Black, F. "International Capital Market Equilibrium with Investment Barriers." *Journal of Financial Economics*, **1**, No. 4 (Dec. 1974) pp. 337–352.
10. ———. "Equilibrium Exchange Rate Hedging." NBER Working Paper, No. 2947 (April 1989).
11. Branch, Ben. "Common Stock Performance and Inflation: An International Comparison." *Journal of Business*, **47**, No. 1 (Jan. 1973) pp. 48–52.
12. Cho, Chinhyung D., Cheol S. Eun, and Lemma Senbet. "International Arbitrage Pricing Theory: An Empirical Investigation." *Journal of Finance*, **41**, No. 2 (June 1986) pp. 313–329.
13. Chollerton, Kenneth, Pierre Pieraerts, and Bruno Solnik. "Why Invest in Foreign Currency Bonds?" *Journal of Portfolio Management* (Summer 1986) pp. 4–8.
14. Cumby, Robert, and Jack Glen. "Evaluating the Performance of International Mutual Funds." *Journal of Finance* (1990).
15. Elton, Edwin J., Martin J. Gruber, and Joel Rentzler. "Professionally Managed, Publicly Traded Commodity Funds." *The Journal of Business*, **60**, No. 2 (April 1987) pp. 175–199.

16. Eun, Cheol, Richard Kolodny, and Bruce Resnick. "U.S. Based International Mutual Funds: a Performance Evaluation." Forthcoming in *Journal of Portfolio Management*.

17. Eun, Cheol, and Bruce Resnick. "Exchange Rate Uncertainty, Forward Contracts and International Portfolio Selection." *Journal of Finance* (March 1989).

18. Farber, Andre L. "Performance of Internationally Diversified Mutual Funds," in Elton and Gruber, *International Capital Markets*. (Amsterdam: North-Holland, 1975).

19. Fatemi, Ali M. "Shareholder Benefits from Corporate International Diversification." *The Journal of Finance*, **39**, No. 5 (Dec. 1984) pp. 1325–1344.

20. Grauer, R., and Nils Hakansson. "Gains from Internation Diversification: 1968–85 Returns on Portfolios of Stocks and Bonds." *Journal of Finance* (July 1987) pp. 721–738.

21. Grauer, F., R. Litzenberger, and R. Stehle. "Sharing Rules and Equilibrium in an International Capital Market Under Uncertainty." *Journal of Financial Economics*, **3**, No. 3 (June 1976) pp. 233–256.

22. Grubel, Herbert. "Internally Diversified Portfolios: Welfare Gains and Capital Flows." *American Economic Review*, **58**, No. 5, Part 1 (Dec. 1968) pp. 1299–1314.

23. Grubel, G. Herbert, and Kenneth Fadner. "The Interdependence of International Equity Markets." *Journal of Finance*, **26**, No. 1 (Mach 1971) pp. 89–94.

24. Gultekin, N. Bulent. "Stock Market Returns and Inflation: Evidence from Other Countries." *Journal of Finance*, **38**, No. 1 (March 1983) pp. 49–68.

25. Guy, J. "The Performance of the British Investment Trust Industry." *Journal of Finance* (May 1978) pp. 443–455.

26. Jacquillat, Bertrand, and Bruno Solnik. "Multi-Nationals Are Poor Tools for Diversification." *Journal of Portfolio Management* (Winter 1978) pp. 8–12.

27. Joy, Maurice, Don Panton, Frank Reilly, and Stanley Martin. "Co-Movements of International Equity Markets." *The Financial Review* (1976) pp. 1–20.

28. Ibbotson, Roger, Lawrence Siegal, and Kathryn Love. "World Wealth: Market Values and Returns." *Journal of Portfolio Management* (Fall 1985) pp. 4–23.

29. Jorion, Philippe. "International Diversification with Estimation Risk." *Journal of Business* (July 1958) pp. 259–278.

30. Kaplanis, C. E., and Steve Schaefer. "Exchange Risk and International Diversification in Bond and Equity Portfolios." Unpublished manuscript. London Business School.

31. Lessard, Donald. "World, Country, and Industry Relationships in Equity Returns: Implications for Risk Reduction Through International Diversification." *Financial Analysts Journal*, **32**, No. 1 (Jan./Feb. 1976) pp. 32–38.

32. ———. "International Portfolio Diversification: A Multivariate Analysis for a Group of Latin American Countries." *Journal of Finance*, **28**, No. 3 (June 1973) pp. 619–633.

33. ———. "World, National and Industry Factors in Equity Returns." *Journal of Finance*, **26**, No. 2 (May 1974) pp. 379–391.

34. ———. "The Structure of Returns and Gains from International Diversification: A Multivariate Approach," in Elton and Gruber, *International Capital Markets*. (Amsterdam: North-Holland, 1975).

35. Levich, Richard, and Jacob Frenkel. "Covered Interest Arbitrage: Unexplored Profits?" *Journal of Political Economy* (April 1975) pp. 325–338.

36. ——. "Transaction Costs and Interest Arbitrage: Tranquil versus Turbulent Periods." *Journal of Political Economy* (Dec. 1977) pp. 1209–1286.

37. Levich, Richard. "On the Efficiency of Markets for Foreign Exchange," in Frenkel and Dornbusch, *International Economic Policy: Theory and Evidence.* (Baltimore, MD: Johns Hopkins Press, 1970).

38. ——. "The Efficiency of Markets for Foreign Exchange: A Review and Extension," in Lessard, *International Financial Management: Theory and Application.* (New York: Warren, Gorham and Lamont, 1979).

39. Levy, Haim, and Marshall Sarnat. "International Diversification of Investment Portfolios." *American Economic Review,* **60,** No. 4 (Sept. 1970) pp. 668–675.

40. ——. "Devaluation Risk and the Portfolio Analysis of International Investment," in Elton and Gruber, *International Capital Markets.* (Amsterdam: North-Holland, 1975).

41. Makin, John. "Portfolio Theory and the Problem of Foreign Exchange Risk." *Journal of Finance,* **33,** No. 2 (May 1978) pp. 517–534.

42. McDonald, John. "French Mutual Fund Performance: Evaluation of Internationally-Diversified Portfolios." *Journal of Finance,* **28,** No. 5 (Dec. 1973) pp. 1161–1180.

43. Panton, Don, Parker Lessig, and Maurice Joy. "Co-Movement of International Equity Markets: A Taxonomic Approach." *Journal of Financial and Quantitative Analysis,* **11,** No. 3 (Sept. 1976) pp. 415–432.

44. Ripley, Duncan. "Systematic Elements in the Linkage of National Stock Market Indices." *Review of Economics and Statistics,* **55,** No. 3 (Aug. 1973) pp. 356–361.

45. Robicher, Alexander, and Mark Eaker. "Foreign Exchange Hedging and the Capital Asset Pricing Model." *Journal of Finance,* **33,** No. 3 (June 1978) pp. 1011–1018.

46. Severn, Alan. "Investor Evaluation of Foreign and Domestic Risk." *Journal of Finance,* **29,** No. 2 (May 1974) pp. 545–550.

47. Sharma, J. L., and Robert Kennedy. "A Comparative Analysis of Stock Price Behavior on the Bombay, London, and New York Stock Exchanges." *Journal of Financial and Quantitative Analysis,* **12,** No. 3 (Sept. 1977) pp. 391–413.

48. Solnik, Bruno. *International Investments.* (Reading, MA: Addison-Wesley, 1988).

49. ——. "The Advantages of Domestic and International Diversification," in Elton and Gruber, *International Capital Markets.* (Amsterdam: North-Holland, 1975).

50. ——. "Why Not Diversify Internationally?" *Financial Analysts Journal,* **20,** No. 4 (July/Aug. 1974) pp. 48–54.

51. ——. "The International Pricing of Risk: An Empirical Investigation of the World Capital Market Structure." *Journal of Finance,* **29,** No. 2 (May 1974) pp. 365–378.

52. ——. "An Equilibrium Model of the International Capital Market." *Journal of Economic Theory,* **8,** No. 4 (Aug. 1974) pp. 500–524.

53. ——. "An International Market Model of Security Price Behavior." *Journal of Financial and Quantitative Analysis,* **9,** No. 4 (Sept. 1974) pp. 537–554.

54. ——. "Testing International Asset Pricing: Some Pessimistic Views." *Journal of Finance,* **32,** No. 2 (May 1977) pp. 503–512.

55. Solnik, Bruno, and A. deFreitas. "International Factors of Stock Price Behavior." CESA Working Paper (Feb. 1986).

56. Solnik, Bruno, and B. Noetzlin. "Optimal International Asset Allocation." *Journal of Portfolio Management* (Fall 1982) pp. 11–21.
57. Stehle, Richard. "An Empirical Test of the Alternative Hypotheses of National and International Pricing of Risky Assets." *Journal of Finance,* **12**, No. 2 (May 1977) pp. 493–502.
58. Subrahmanyam, Marti. "On the Optimality of International Capital Market Integration." *Journal of Financial Economics,* **2**, No. 1 (March 1975) pp. 3–28.
59. ———. "International Capital Markets, Equilibrium, and Investor Welfare with Unequal Interest Rates," in Elton and Gruber, *International Capital Markets.* (Amsterdam: North-Holland, 1975).

CHAPTER

3

Quantitative Aspects of Global Investing

Sumner N. Levine
Nortech Associates
Setauket, NY
and
State University of New York
Stony Brook, NY

This chapter summarizes some of the more widely employed relationships for analyzing global investments. In the following we consider, in order, the factors affecting the return on foreign investments, portfolio optimization, and the parity-exchange rate relationships.

Notation

h or f	used to designate *home* or *foreign* quantities
$e(t)$	spot exchange rate at time t expressed as units of home currency per unit of foreign currency
$f(t)$	forward exchange rate for time t
$i(t)$	nominal interest rate for holding period of duration t
I	inflation rate
$\ell(t)$	real interest rate
$P_{h(f)}(t)$	price of an investment asset in home (or foreign) currency at time t
$\overline{R}_i$	expected rate of return for the ith investment
$\overline{R}_p$	expected return of the portfolio
X_i	fraction of the total investment in the ith asset
R_F	risk-free rate of return
σ_i^2	variance of the ith portfolio
γ	$\dfrac{\overline{R}_p - R_F}{\sigma^2}$
Z_i	$X_i\gamma$

Return on Foreign Investments

Estimating the return on foreign investments requires consideration of (1) exchange rate fluctuations; (2) foreign taxes on capital gains, dividends, and interest rates; and (3) transaction costs.

Exchange rate fluctuations are a major source of uncertainty. If a foreign security is purchased at a price $P_f(o)$ and sold at time t a price $P_f(t)$, and pays d_f, then in terms of the investor's *home* currency, the return over t is:

$$R_h = \frac{P_f(t)e(t) - P_f(o)e(o) + d_f e(t)}{P_f(o)e(o)}$$

where $e(t)$ is the exchange rate at the designated time t. The above can be expressed as:

$$R_h + 1 = [(1 + R_g) + R_d](1 + R_e)$$

where

$$R_g = \frac{\Delta P_f(t)}{P_f(o)}$$

$$R_d = \frac{d_f}{P_f(o)}$$

$$R_e = \frac{\Delta e(t)}{e(o)}$$

$$\Delta e(t) = e(t) - e(o)$$

Note that R_g and R_d are expressed in terms of foreign currency.

As an example, consider the following for a six-month period: $R_g = 15\%$; $R_d = 5\%$; and $R_e = -10\%$. Then:

$$R_h = [(1.15) + .05][.9] - 1$$
$$= 1.08 - 1 = 8\%$$

The imposition of foreign investment taxes and transaction costs serves to reduce returns. However, the adverse effects of foreign taxes may be offset by various credits and adjustments. Neglecting the latter, the inclusion of foreign taxes and transaction costs in the expression for return gives the result:

$$R_h + 1 = [R_g(1 - t_g) + R_d(1 - t_d) + 1](1 + R_e) - R_c$$

where t_g is the foreign tax rate on capital gains
t_d is the foreign tax rate on dividends (interest)
R_c is the transaction costs expressed as a fraction of the initial investment, where costs and investment are given in the foreign currency.

Asset Allocation Theory

The objective of asset allocation is to structure an investment portfolio to provide the greatest return for a given risk or, alternatively, to achieve a given return for the least risk.

The analysis is carried out by optimizing an appropriate objective function that is subject to possible constraints. In the following, we consider two different approaches to the allocation problem. In the first, the objective function to be maximized is the ratio of the excess portfolio return (i.e., return in excess of the riskless rate) to the portfolio standard deviation. In the second approach, the objective function to be minimized is the portfolio variance subject to a specified portfolio return.

Optimizing the Return-Risk Ratio

The objective function, z, in this case is given by:

$$z = \frac{\overline{R}_P - R_F}{\sigma_P}$$

which is to be minimized. In the previously given notation,

$$\overline{R}_P = \sum_{i=1}^{N} X_i \overline{R}_i$$

and

$$\overline{R}_P - R_F = \sum_{i=1}^{N} X_i(\overline{R}_i - R_F)$$

since $\Sigma X_i = 1$. Also,

$$\sigma_P^2 = \sum_{i=1}^{N} \sum_{j=1}^{N} X_i X_j \sigma_{ij}$$

or

$$\sigma_P^2 = \sum_{i=1}^{N} X_i^2 \sigma_i^2 + \sum_{i=1}^{N} \sum_{\substack{j=1 \\ j \neq i}}^{N} X_i X_j \sigma_{ij}$$

Here σ_{ij} is the covariance of assets i and j (say, a U.S. stock portfolio and a European portfolio).

With the notation,

$$\phi = \sum \sigma_{ij} X_i X_j \equiv \sigma_P^2$$

the objective function can be written

$$z = \frac{\sum(\overline{R}_i - R_F)}{\phi^{1/2}}$$

The objective function is optimized by setting the first partial derivative of z with respect to each X_i equal to zero:

$$\frac{dz}{dx_i} = \frac{(\overline{R}_i - R_F)}{\phi^{1/2}} - \frac{1}{2}\frac{\sum(\overline{R}_i - R_F)X_i}{\phi^{3/2}}\left[2\sigma_i^2 X_i + 2\sum_{\substack{j \\ j \neq i}} \sigma_{ij}X_j\right] = 0$$

Eliminating $\phi^{1/2}$ and introducing

$$Z_i = \gamma X_i$$
$$\gamma = \frac{R_P - R_F}{\sigma_P^2}$$

the above optimizing expressions can be written

$$\overline{R}_1 - R_F = Z_1\sigma_1^2 + Z_2\sigma_{12} + Z_3\sigma_{13} + \cdots + Z_N\sigma_{1N}$$
$$\overline{R}_2 - R_F = Z_1\sigma_{12} + Z_2\sigma_2^2 + Z_3\sigma_{23} + \cdots + Z_N\sigma_{2N}$$
$$\overline{R}_3 - R_F = Z_1\sigma_{13} + Z_2\sigma_{23} + Z_3\sigma_3^2 + \cdots + Z_N\sigma_{3N}$$
$$\vdots$$
$$\overline{R}_N - R_F = Z_1\sigma_{1N} + Z_2\sigma_{2N} + Z_3\sigma_{3N} + \cdots + Z_N\sigma_N^2$$

Note that from the definition of Z

$$X_k = Z_k \bigg/ \sum_{i=1}^{N} Z_i$$

We therefore have

$$\sum_{k=1}^{N} X_k = 1$$

A number of computer programs are available for solving systems of linear equations such as those shown above.

As a simple application of the above results, we consider the conditions on the returns and variances that justify including foreign investments in a portfolio. Let the parameters of the portfolio of home company stocks be designated by the subscript h, and those of the foreign portfolio by the subscript f. Then

$$Z_h \sigma_h^2 + Z_f \sigma_{hf} = \overline{R}_h - R_F$$
$$Z_h \sigma_{hf} + Z_f \sigma_f^2 = \overline{R}_f - R_F$$

Solving, we find that

$$Z_h = \frac{(\overline{R}_h - R_F)\sigma_f^2 - (\overline{R}_f - R_F)\sigma h_f}{\sigma_h^2 \sigma_f^2 - \sigma_{hf}^2}$$

$$Z_f = \frac{(\overline{R}_f - R_F)\sigma_h^2 - (\overline{R}_h - R_F)\sigma_{hf}}{\sigma_h^2 \sigma_f^2 - \sigma_{hf}^2}$$

The inclusion of foreign equities in a combined portfolio implies that

$$Z_f > 0$$

or

$$\overline{R}_f - R_F > (\overline{R}_h - R_F)\frac{\sigma_{hf}}{\sigma_h^2}$$

The above can also be written in terms of the correlation coefficient,

$$\rho_{hf} = \frac{\sigma_{hf}}{\sigma_h \sigma_f}$$

$$\frac{\overline{R}_f - R_F}{\sigma_f} > \frac{(\overline{R}_h - R_F)}{\sigma_h}\rho_{hf}$$

This is the result given in Chapter 2 of this book.

Consider two weakly correlated index portfolios, one foreign and the other home, with:

$$\overline{R}_h = 12\%$$
$$\overline{R}_f = 10\%$$
$$R_F = 7\%$$
$$\sigma_{hf} = .03$$
$$\sigma_h = .3$$

Since

$$\frac{(\overline{R}_h - R_F)}{\sigma_h^2}\sigma_{hf} = \frac{(.12 - .07)}{(.3)^2} \times .03$$

$$= .0167$$

and

$$(R_f - R_F) = (.1 - .07) = .03$$

then according to the above criteria, the portfolio should include foreign securities, even though its expected return is less than that of a portfolio of home-based equities.

Minimizing the Portfolio Variance

A second approach to optimizing a portfolio is to minimize the portfolio variance subject to achieving a target portfolio return E^*. Thus,

$$\text{minimize } \sigma_P^2$$
$$\text{subject to}$$
$$\sum \overline{R}_i X_i = E^*$$
$$\sum X_i = 1$$

Introducing Lagrangian multipliers, λ_i and λ_2, the objective function to be minimized is

$$z = \sum_{i,j} X_i X_j \sigma_{ij} + \lambda_2 \left(\sum_i X_i \overline{R}_i - E^* \right) + \lambda_1 \left(\sum_i X_i - 1 \right)$$

Setting the first derivatives with respect to X_i equal to zero and using the constraints, it is easy to show that the linear system of equations in $n + 2$ unknowns to be solved is the following:

$$2X_1 \sigma_1^2 + 2X_2 \sigma_{12} + \cdots + 2X_n \sigma_{1n} + \lambda_2 \overline{R}_1 + \lambda_1 = 0$$

$$2X_1 \sigma_{12} + 2X_2 \sigma_2^2 + \cdots + 2X_n \sigma_{2n} + \lambda_2 \overline{R}_2 + \lambda_1 = 0$$

$$\vdots$$

$$2X_n \sigma_{1n} + 2X_2 \sigma_{2n}^2 + \cdots + 2X_n \sigma_n^2 + \lambda_2 \overline{R}_n + \lambda_1 = 0$$

$$X_1 + X_2 + \cdots + X_n = 1$$

$$\overline{R}_1 X_1 + \overline{R}_2 X_2 + \cdots + R_n X_n = E^*$$

Exchange Rates and Parity Concepts

In this final section, we derive expressions for exchange rates based on purchasing power parity (PPP) and interest rate parity (IRP). It is assumed that goods and currency can move freely between countries and that all relevant information is available to market participants. In such a world-wide market, the exchange prices between tradable goods should be the same at equilibrium. Equalization occurs as the result of a tendency on the part of participants to buy low-priced goods and avoid high-priced items, assuming equal quality. Similarly, capital tends to move into countries with high interest rates and out of those with low rates, other things being equal. At equilibrium, rates tend to be equalized.

Equalization of the price of tradable goods implies

$$e(t)P_f(t) = P_h(t)$$

where e is the exchange rate (units of home currency per unit of foreign currency). It is convenient to refer prices to a base year so that the above may be written

$$\frac{e(t)P_f(t)}{e(o)P_f(o)} = \frac{P_h(t)}{P_h(o)}$$

where $P(o)$ and $e(o)$ refer to the prices and exchange rate of the base year. If I is the inflation rate, then

$$P_h(t) = P_h(o)(1 + I_h)$$
$$P_f(t) = P_f(o)(1 + I_f)$$

for home and foreign prices. Hence,

$$\frac{e(t)}{e(o)} = \frac{1 + I_h}{1 + I_f}$$

Or, on subtracting unity from each side of the above,

$$\frac{e(t) - e(o)}{e(o)} = \frac{I_h - I_f}{1 + I_f}$$

As an example of the application of the last expression, consider the case of an inflation rate of 8 percent in the home economy and 12 percent in the foreign economy. Then

$$\frac{e(t) - e(o)}{e(o)} = \frac{.08 - .12}{1.12} = -.036$$

so that the exchange rate may be expected, according to PPP, to decrease by 3.6 percent.

As discussed in the references to this chapter, studies on price indexes indicate that departures from PPP can be substantial over both short and long time periods. The deviations have been attributed to trade restrictions, lack of mobility of certain goods (land, buildings, educational facilities, etc.), and variation from country to country in the relative importance of items in the price index.

We note in passing that the relation between the nominal interest rate (i) and the real interest rate (ℓ) is

$$(1 + i) = (1 + \ell)(1 + I)$$

or

$$\ell = \frac{1 + i}{1 + I} - 1$$

Thus, if nominal rates are 8 percent and inflation 4 percent,

$$\ell = \frac{1.08}{1.04} - 1 = 3.8\%$$

We next consider the interest parity approach to exchange rates. Parity requires that the return to foreign investment equal the return to home investment.

Suppose that P_h home currency units are exchanged for foreign currency at the spot rate $e(o)$ and that the amount is then invested at an interest rate $i_f(t)$ over a time t. As a hedge, a forward contract that provides for a conversion rate $f(t)$ (home currency units per foreign currency units) is purchased on the home currency. On converting back to home currency at time t, the return from the foreign investment will be

$$P_h(t) = \frac{f(t)}{e(o)} P_h(o)[1 + i_f(t)]$$

If instead the same principal had been invested in the home currency, the return would have been

$$P_h(t) = P_h(o)[1 + i_h(t)]$$

Interest parity requires that both returns be equal, so that

$$\frac{f(t)}{e(o)} = \frac{1 + i_h}{1 + i_f}$$

or

$$\frac{f(t) - e(o)}{e(o)} = \frac{i_h - i_f}{1 + i_f}$$

The forward annualized discount (or premium) rate d is defined by

$$d = \frac{f(t) - e(o)}{e(o)} \times \frac{12}{t}$$

where t is duration of the forward contract.

As an example, let the 90-day interest rate in the United States be 7 percent per year and the comparable rate in Japan be 4 percent. If the spot rate on the yen is $.00420, what are the 90-day forward rate and the discount, assuming interest rate parity? The solutions are

$$f(90) = .00420 \frac{1 + .07/4}{1 + .04/4} = \$.00423$$

$$d = \frac{.00423 - .00420}{.00420} \times \frac{12}{3} = .02857$$

Hence, the forward contract should be at a premium relative to the spot price.

Though the relation does not hold exactly, the evidence for interest rate parity is more convincing than that for PPP.

REFERENCES

Aliber, R. Z., and B. R. Bruce. *Global Portfolios*. Homewood, IL: Business One Irwin, 1991.

Eitmon, K. E., and A. I. Stonehill. *Multinational Business Finance*. Reading, MA: Addison-Wesley, 1989.

Elton, E. J., and M. J. Gruber. *Modern Portfolio Theory and Investment Analysis*. New York: John Wiley, 1991.

Francis, J. C., and S. H. Archer. *Portfolio Analysis*. Englewood Cliffs, NJ: Prentice Hall, 1979.

Grabbe, J. O. *International Financial Markets*. New York: Elsevier, 1986.

Levi, M. D. *International Finance*. New York: McGraw-Hill, 1990.

Rodriguez, R. M., and E. E. Carter. *International Financial Management*. Englewood Cliffs, NJ: Prentice Hall, 1989.

Shapiro, A. C. *Multinational Financial Management*. Boston: Allyn and Bacon, 1989.

Solnik, B. *International Investments*. Reading, MA: Addison-Wesley, 1989.

A Disciplined Approach to Global Asset Allocation

Robert D. Arnott
First Quadrant Corp.
Morristown, NJ

Roy D. Henriksson
Kidder Peabody
New York

Objective measures of prospective market "returns" can provide valuable guidance for asset allocation by revealing the relative market outlook for various asset classes. Much of this information is provided by the market. We know the yield for cash equivalents; we know the yield to maturity for bonds; and we can estimate the approximate earnings yield or dividend discount model return for equities. These measures have been used with great success to profit from the relative performance of stocks, bonds, and cash in the United States.[1] The use of a disciplined approach for including other information, such as the recent inflation rate and economic experience, may provide additional insight.

Does a disciplined approach to active asset allocation lend itself to export? Can the methods developed for the allocation of assets in the United States be applied in overseas markets? The answer to both these questions is yes. Our preliminary empirical results suggest that the same tools that have proved so profitable in the United States may also have value in the international arena. If a global strategy for asset allocation is difficult, it is only because the most profitable strategy is to focus on the least comfortable asset class.

Fundamentals in Asset Allocation

Pricing in any market aggregates the judgments of all the participants in that market. Basing a measure of future asset class returns on current

Source: *Financial Analysts Journal,* Association for Investment Management and Research, March–April 1989.

indications of relative opportunity capitalizes on this information. The assumption underlying such a model is that financial markets demand differential return premiums for different asset classes.

The sophisticated investor faces a critical and ongoing asset allocation question: In the prevailing market environment, which assets merit emphasis? The natural tendency is to choose the comfortable answer, the answer that minimizes anxiety. However, the comfortable answer is rarely the profitable answer. How many managers were aggressively cutting equity holdings in early 1973 or mid-1987? How many managers were doing the opposite in late 1974 or mid-1982?

A disciplined approach to asset allocation may provide a basis for confidently resisting the comfortable consensus when pursuit of a contrarian strategy would be most rewarding. One such approach in essence involves letting the market provide measures of future returns. The asset allocation decision is based primarily on the relative attractiveness of returns from various asset classes and will change only as their relative return prospects change.

Unlocking Market Outlook

This disciplined approach to asset allocation rests on four assumptions:

- Prospective long-term returns for various asset classes can be estimated. We know the yield on cash; we know the yield to maturity on long bonds; and the capital markets provide some crude but objective measures of long-term return prospects in equities in the form of earnings yields, dividend yields, or consensus-based dividend discount models.
- These returns are based on current market prices. They reflect the view of all market participants regarding the relative attractiveness of asset classes. If calculated equity returns are high relative to bond returns, for example, the market is implicitly demanding a substantial equity risk premium, which suggests that investors are uneasy about equities.
- These relative returns tend to exhibit a normal or "equilibrium" level.
- When prospective future returns, as measured against investment alternatives, stray from this normal equilibrium, market forces pull them back into line, creating an asset allocation profit mechanism.

Even if we disregard the third and fourth assumptions, and assume no equilibrating mechanism in the markets, an ojective approach to asset allocation can still work. If the objective measure of long-term equity return prospects rises relative to other asset classes by 100 basis points, then the investor will expect to earn 100 basis points of excess return over the long run, even if there is no tendency to move back towards an equilibrium condition.

Nonetheless, the equilibrating mechanism is the source of the impressive profits achieved in recent years by active asset allocation disciplines. Suppose, for example, that the equity risk premium is 100 basis points too high relative to long bonds. Then either long bond yields should rise by 100 basis points or stock earnings yields should fall by 100 basis points to restore the equilibrium relationship. This would imply a price move in either stocks or bonds that amounts to many times the 100-basis-point disequilibrium (because it would take a *price* move far larger than 100 basis points to shift either the earnings yield or the bond yield by a full 100 basis points). In other words, an equilibrating mechanism is not essential to the success of active asset allocation, but it is a key mechanism for providing the considerable profits an active asset allocation process is capable of delivering.

Why Do Conventional Global Comparisons Fail?

One of the most common global allocation errors stems from the assumption that equity value measures (such as dividend yields or price/earnings ratios) can be directly compared across global boundaries. No one makes such assumptions about bonds or cash. The reasons why such comparisons fail in the bond markets may tell us something about the error in assuming comparability of equity valuation measures.

Bond yield differences are explained by equilibrium theory in the context of long-term inflation rates and currency shifts. Ten-year government bonds in one country may offer a yield of 10 percent, while the corresponding yield in another country is 5 percent. This makes perfect sense, *if* the currency in the high-yield country erodes by 5 percent per year vis-à-vis the currency in the low-yield country. Such a differential would result in a 40 percent currency depreciation over the course of a decade. Currency moves of this magnitude over a decade are so commonplace as to be routine. In other words, no serious economist would suggest that international interest rate differences run contrary to equilibrium theory.

The same holds true for dividend discount model rates of return. A dividend discount model rate of return of 15 percent for one country and 10 percent for another can be fully justified in the face of a long-term *expectation* of 5 percent annual currency divergence. The investor in the low-return country, seeking to capture the superior performance offered by the high-return country, would forfeit the performance differential through currency depreciation. If the investor were to seek protection against this currency erosion by hedging in the foreign exchange markets, the foreign exchange forward markets would similarly be priced to take away the rate of return differential.

P/E Ratio Differences

Price/earnings ratios have historically tended to be closely correlated with dividend discount model rates of return. So the above argument can be readily applied to P/E comparisons. If $100 buys $5 per year of earnings in one country and $10 per year of earnings in another, nothing in equilibrium theory suggests that this P/E difference should be inappropriate. Suppose the high-P/E country exhibits currency appreciation vis-à-vis the low-P/E country. Then the book value, the sales, and the currency-adjusted earnings of the companies in the low-P/E country would all diminish when measured in the currency of the high-P/E country.

In short, the common argument that countries with low P/E ratios, low price-to-cash-flow ratios, or low price-to-book-value ratios are inherently more attractive investment opportunities than their high-multiple counterparts is theoretically flawed. No such argument can be made consistent with equilibrium theory.

In looking at P/E ratios, factors other than currency risk cloud the picture when one country is compared with another.

- Accounting principles differ across countries.
- Growth opportunities differ across countries.
- Different countries face different economic risks.
- Differences in political environments will influence investors' perceptions of future cash flows.

All these considerations, and other lesser considerations, could justify large differences in earnings yields, *even in the absence of currency considerations.*

Comparing Equity Markets

We can observe empirically that low-multiple countries have a slight tendency to offer higher return prospects than high-multiple countries. This may be expected even if there is not a corresponding difference in interest rates.

Suppose two countries have the same interest rates, but different P/E ratios. Under this circumstance, any currency-based justification for the relative P/E ratios could be readily arbitraged in the currency markets. With no difference in interest rates, currency futures would be priced at or near current exchange rates. In this example, any difference in P/E multiples would have to be explained in the context of either greater growth prospects or higher risks for one country versus the other. Differences in equilibrium-expected returns, in the absence of market barriers, should result from differences in risks.

Because P/E ratios *should* differ across countries, the best way to compare equity markets in different countries is first to measure the equity risk premium in each country, then to compare equity risk premiums across countries. Even here, we encounter a potential pitfall. Because different growth rates, accounting standards, or political/economic climates can justify different P/E ratios, equity risk premiums cannot be compared directly with one another. The *equilibrium* relation between earnings yield and bond or cash yield (hence the normal equity risk premium) in one country may be higher or lower than that in another country.

This leads to the final step in the comparative analysis: If we measure the equity risk premium in any particular country, and compare that equity risk premium with the "normal" equity risk premium for that country, we can then measure the *abnormal equity risk premium*. This abnormal equity risk premium indicates the extent to which an equity market offers rewards in excess of (or below) its normal reward opportunities. In essence, this tells us how far the markets *within* a country have strayed from equilibrium. These abnormal risk premiums, which measure disequilibriums within a country, *can* be directly compared across country boundaries.

Asset Allocation versus Currency Selection

The framework outlined above makes no naive assumptions about normal relationships between different countries' P/E ratios. It makes no assumptions that are inconsistent with equilibrium theory. Furthermore, and importantly, it *disaggregates the currency forecast from the asset class forecast*. In so doing, it presents the investor with an array of fully hedged investment alternatives. Its forecasts are consistent with the currency expectations implicit in the markets and can be supplemented with independent forecasts of currency returns.

The disaggregation of asset class expectations and currency expectations is important because it achieves two often contradictory objectives: It broadens the set of investment alternatives while simplifying the discipline for evaluating those alternatives. If asset class decisions are made based on fully hedged (local-currency) return expectations, we wind up with a model that yields approximate equivalency between cash equivalents around the globe, because the forward markets are largely driven by this arbitrage. Figure 4.1 illustrates this graphically.

This structure leads to direct comparability of the asset classes and to variance/covariance measures that are independent of the "home currency." The currency decision can then be made separately, based on whether the incremental return associated with an attractive currency would justify the incremental risk associated with lifting the hedge.

Hedging vs. Not Hedging

This view of the capital markets very clearly suggests that the currency decision and the asset allocation decision can and should be made

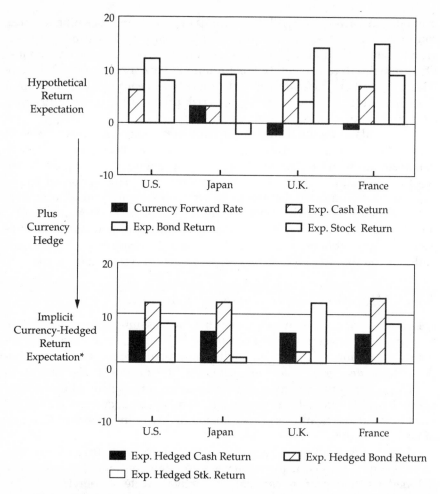

Figure 4.1. Effects of Hedging

independently. It is worth asking whether history supports this view. Tables 4.1 and 4.2 summarize the historical returns and volatilities of international equities. We should note that historical returns tend to be poor
indicators of future returns; historical volatility does better, but is still im-
precise as an indicator of future volatility. The individual numbers are thus
not very meaningful, but the general pattern of the results is.

Clearly, over the three years ended June 1987, a hedged strategy
sharply impaired the performance of a global portfolio. The reason is clear:
The dollar fell relative to other world currencies far more than the forward
rates used for hedging would have suggested. The results over a longer
horizon are somewhat more encouraging. It would seem that the dollar

Table 4.1. Total Returns of International Equities[a]

	1-Year		3-Year		5-Year		10-Year	
	Unhedged	Hedged	Unhedged	Hedged	Unhedged	Hedged	Unhedged	Hedged
France	32.9	13.5	51.9	33.3	40.6	33.4	24.4	20.3
Germany	16.6	(1.1)	46.5	30.7	35.4	31.4	18.3	19.2
Italy	22.4	NA	68.3	NA	43.0	NA	27.6	NA
Japan	76.3	59.5	64.2	42.7	48.6	36.5	29.2	24.9
U.K.	52.4	40.5	46.2	34.8	32.6	32.9	24.3	23.4
U.S.	23.8	23.8	30.3	30.3	27.2	27.2	16.2	16.2
World	43.4	35.0	42.2	34.0	34.1	31.1	20.5	19.9

a. All periods end 6/87; data from Frank Russell International.

Table 4.2.   Volatilities of International Equities[a]

	3-Year		5-Year		10-Year	
	Unhedged	Hedged	Unhedged	Hedged	Unhedged	Hedged
France	30.2	24.8	24.9	20.6	28.1	21.9
Germany	24.9	20.5	22.7	18.2	21.7	15.7
Italy	41.4	35.7	37.8	32.6	36.4	33.4
Japan	23.9	15.3	26.5	16.2	24.2	15.0
U.K.	21.0	15.8	20.8	15.0	21.7	6.4
U.S.	15.6	15.6	15.3	15.3	14.8	4.8
World	13.2	10.9	13.9	11.3	14.7	1.8

a. All periods end 6/87; data from Frank Russell International.

out-paced forward rate expectations early in the past decade by nearly as much as it underperformed in the past three years.

Without a hedge, the U.S. market is less volatile than any other market around the world. But the correlations between the world markets are low enough that the volatility of the world market, even on an unhedged basis, is slightly below that of the United States, whether we are looking at a three-year, five-year or ten-year span. By hedging, we expose ourselves only to the volatility of each market in local-currency terms; we do not subject ourselves to the coupling of market and currency risk. The hedged results are striking: Over any historical time span, most individual world markets (with the exception of Italy) exhibited only slightly more volatility than the U.S. market.

Because world markets are not highly correlated, the hedged world portfolio consistently exhibited some 20 percent less volatility than the unhedged world portfolio. When compared with a simple U.S. equity investment, the hedged world portfolio was 20 percent to 30 percent less volatile. This holds true even though the U.S. market represented a large portion (35 percent to 60 percent) of the world market!

The Cost of Not Hedging

Table 4.3 gives some indication of the cost of risk. Suppose we believed that all world markets offered an expected return of 12 percnt. Then an investment solely in the U.S. market, with an average volatility of 15 percent, might be expected to deliver 10.9 percent on a compound geometric return basis. (If we assumed a higher standard deviation in the wake of October 1987, the cost of volatility would, of course, be even greater.) Use of a global hedged portfolio could reduce that risk by 20 percent, so that the geometric return rises by 40 basis points, to 11.3 percent.

Table 4.3.   The Penalty of Risk

Average Return (%)	Standard Deviation (%)	Geometric Return (%)
12	10	11.5
12	12	11.3
12	15	10.9
12	20	10.0
12	25	8.9

This increase in return does not rely on any assumptions regarding active management or the ability to select countries or markets, but simply on currency hedging. Currency hedging on the forward markets is very inexpensive; its very real rewards far outweigh its cost. Furthermore, if the asset allocation disciplines described in this article are effective in selecting the better-performing world markets, then the rewards of hedged international investing can be greater still.

We would not advocate automatic use of a currency hedge. If an investor believes that a certain foreign currency will perform much better than its forward rates, then a hedge is not necessarily desirable. In the absence of a confident view of foreign currency strength, however, a currency hedge not only reduces the risk of global investing significantly, but in so doing actually improves long-term returns. In fact, the appropriate "no-forecast" allocation for investors will probably be fully hedged, because the two-sided nature of the currency market makes it unlikely that the normal expected return from being unhedged is sufficiently positive to justify bearing the additional risk.

Empirical Results: Stage I

The expected return on bonds can be represented by yield to maturity, and that on cash by cash yield. Equity valuation presents a more difficult problem; ideally, equity valuation calls for a measure of the net present value of future cash flows. Among the equity valuation measures readily available for the international markets, normalized earnings yields have proved to be the most consistent indicator of stock performance.[2] In calculating total returns for equity, it is necessary to add a measure of sustainable growth; the addition of economic variables to the regressions indirectly accomplishes this.

None of these measures differs conceptually from those now widely used in similar models in the United States. In general, remarkably few changes are required to adjust the model for use in other countries.

At this stage, we make the assumption that objective measures of *prospective* relative return should be positively correlated with subsequent *actual* relative returns. Is the equity risk premium vis-à-vis bonds (stock earnings yield minus bond yield) positively correlated with subsequent stock-versus-bond relative performance? Is the equity risk premium versus cash (stock earnings yield minus cash yield) positively correlated with the subsequent performance of stocks versus cash? Is the bond maturity premium (bond yield minus cash yield) positively correlated with subsequent bond-versus-cash relative performance? If so, then a "Stage I" asset allocation model will work.

In all the tests, monthly observations were used and the predictive variables were sufficiently lagged to ensure that the inputs were actually available prior to the period over which the corresponding realized returns were measured. While the results should be viewed as preliminary, given the length of the time periods used in the tests, the results are encouraging in that they support the results from actual money under management in the United States.[3]

Market-Implicit Rates of Return

Tables 4.4, 4.5, and 4.6 show the univariate regression coefficients for Stage I asset allocation for 15 different countries. In each instance, we are

Table 4.4.   Stock Earnings Yield Minus Bond Yield

	Coefficient of Regression with Subsequent Asset Class Relative Performance		
	Stock-Bond	Stock-Cash	Bond-Cash
Australia	−0.23	−0.76	−0.53
Austria	1.09	0.98	−0.11
Belgium	0.24	0.19	−0.05
Canada	0.33	0.28	−0.05
Denmark	0.05	−0.18	−0.23*
France	0.16	−0.05	−0.21**
Germany	0.46	0.29	−0.16
Italy	0.04	−0.05	−0.10**
Japan	1.39	1.36	−0.03
Netherlands	1.64**	0.97**	−0.67*
Spain	2.90**	2.79**	−0.11
Sweden	0.79	0.44	−0.34
Switzerland	0.86*	0.88*	0.02
U.K.	1.36**	0.80	−0.54
U.S.	0.36	0.10	−0.26
Average	0.76**	0.54	−0.22**

*Significant at a 95% confidence level.

**Significant at a 99% confidence level.

testing the relation between objective measures of the prospective return difference between any two asset classes and the subsequent realized return differences over a one-month horizon.

It may be helpful to focus on a single country. In Table 4.4, the equity risk premium is measured vis-à-vis bonds. This gives us an objective measure of the relative attractiveness of stocks and bonds, which is regressed against the subsequent excess return of stocks over bonds. The result for Japan is a coefficient of 1.39. Thus, every 100-basis-point difference between the Japanese stock market earnings yield and the Japanese 10-year bond yield translates into an average 139-basis-point difference in the relative performance of stocks versus bonds over the subsequent month.

This might seem counterintuitive on the surface. How can a 100-basis-point difference in yields translate into *more than* 100 basis points in subsequent one-month performance? The answer is found in the leverage inherent in the capital markets. Suppose that the average earnings yield in Japan during the period covered by this test was 4 percent and the average 10-year bond yield 8 percent. A 100-basis-point rally in stocks would depress the earnings yield by only four basis points (from 4.00 to 3.96 percent). A 100-basis-point rise in the bonds would depress bond yields

Table 4.5.   Stock Earnings Yield Minus Cash Yield

	Coefficient of Regression with Subsequent Asset Class Relative Performance		
	Stock-Bond	**Stock-Cash**	**Bond-Cash**
Australia	−0.30	−0.32	−0.03
Austria	0.25	0.42	0.16*
Belgium	0.11	0.18*	0.07*
Canada	0.17	0.22	0.05
Denmark	0.03	0.01	−0.03
France	0.45*	0.95**	0.40**
Germany	0.27	0.35*	0.08
Italy	0.12	0.32	0.20**
Japan	1.77	1.64	−0.13
Netherlands	0.60**	0.61**	0.01
Spain	0.68	0.72	0.04
Sweden	0.43	0.24	−0.18
Switzerland	0.16	0.28	0.12**
U.K.	0.34	0.14	−0.18
U.S.	0.30*	0.37**	0.07
Average	0.36**	0.41**	0.04

*Significant at a 95% confidence level.

**Significant at a 99% confidence level.

Table 4.6.   Bond Yield Minus Cash Yield

	Coefficient of Regression with Subsequent Asset Class Relative Performance		
	Stock-Bond	**Stock-Cash**	**Bond-Cash**
Australia	−0.47	−0.44	0.03
Austria	0.08	0.43	0.36**
Belgium	0.12	0.23*	0.12**
Canada	−0.02	0.25	0.28*
Denmark	−0.16	0.24	−0.26*
France	0.20	0.54**	0.34**
Germany	0.19	0.42*	0.22**
Italy	0.04	0.28*	0.24**
Japan	0.72	−0.8*	−0.09
Netherlands	0.26	0.53**	0.27
Spain	−0.48	−0.34	0.14
Sweden	−0.01	0.00	0.01
Switzerland	−0.02	0.14	0.16**
U.K.	−0.04	−0.12	−0.06
U.S.	0.22**	0.52**	0.30*
Average	−0.05	0.12	0.17**

*Significant at a 95% confidence level.
**Significant at a 99% confidence level.

by only about 12 basis points (from 8.00 to about 7.88 percent). In other words, a 139-basis-point relative performance difference in a single month, stemming from a 100-basis-point stock-bond disequilibrium, could result from either a 5.6-basis-point change in stock earnings yield or a 16.7-basis-point change in bond yields.

The striking finding in Table 4.4 is that disequilibrium in the measure of stock earnings yield versus bond yield works as a predictor of stock-bond relative returns in 14 of the 15 countries tested (four of them with statistical significance). The link between the stock-bond disequilibrium measure and subsequent stock-bond relative performance is a strong one: On average, every 100 basis points of measured disequilibrium translates into 76 basis points of subsequent one-month relative performance. The variable is also powerful in suggesting future bond behavior: In 14 of the 15 countries tested, an abnormally high equity risk premium is associated with adverse bond market performance in the subsequent month.

Table 4.5 suggests that the equity-versus-cash risk premium (stock earnings yield minus cash yield) is a good indicator of stock excess returns vis-à-vis cash in 14 of the 15 countries tested. The stock-cash risk premium is also indicative of stock-versus-bond relative performance in 14 of the 15 countries tested.

Finally, Table 4.6 suggests that the slope of the bond market yield curve is a powerful indicator of subsequent bond performance relative to cash. If the yield curve is unusually steep (bond yields high relative to cash yields), fixed income returns are likely to do well in the future. This relationship is statistically significant in over half the countries tested. We also find that a steep yield curve bodes well for stock market excess returns, as measured against cash.

The implications of these three tests are relatively straightforward: Market-implicit rates of return matter. A high equity risk premium suggests investor aversion to equities; investors with the courage to bear equity risk will be rewarded. A high bond market maturity premium suggests investor aversion to interest rate risk; the investor willing to bear that risk will reap rewards.

A Changing Equilibrium: Stage II

The previous results depend on an investment framework in which the equilibrium risk-return tradeoff remains stationary. Recent studies of capital market behavior suggest that equilibrium relationships between asset classes can change.[4] The obvious question is whether it makes sense to explore a structure in which disequilibrium measures are based on recent equilibriums.

Tables 4.7, 4.8, and 4.9 are based on a short-term definition of equilibrium. In these tables, instead of comparing objective risk premiums with a long-term definition of the equilibrium relationships, we compare risk premiums with their most recent 24-month averages. The risk premium at the beginning of January 1987, for example, is compared with the average stock-versus-bond risk premium (stock earnings yield minus bond yield) over the two years 1985 and 1986. Any difference is viewed as a disequilibrium and suggests relative opportunities between stocks and bonds.

As Table 4.7 shows, this approach actually worked better than the Stage I approach for most countries. Instead of four stock-bond relationships achieving statistical significance, five do. Also, the average coefficient comparing this short-term disequilibrium measure with the subsequent relative performance rises from 0.76 to 0.95, a 25 percent improvement. We observe the same kind of pattern for stock-cash disequilibriums and for bond-cash disequilibriums.

Real Interest Rates

We have observed that the trend in real interest rates, defined as Treasury-bill yields minus 12-month CPI inflation, has been a powerful factor in U.S. capital markets.[5] The results in Table 4.10 reaffirm that relationship. They

Table 4.7.   24-Month Trend in Stock Earnings Yield Minus Bond Yield

	Coefficient of Regression with Subsequent Asset Class Relative Performance		
	Stock-Bond	**Stock-Cash**	**Bond-Cash**
Australia	−0.48	−0.70	−0.22
Austria	0.11	0.24	0.13
Belgium	0.36	0.28	−0.09
Canada	0.44	0.75*	0.31*
Denmark	0.08	0.13	0.05
France	1.18*	1.57**	0.38*
Germany	0.66	0.92*	0.26
Italy	0.14	0.47	0.33**
Japan	4.16*	3.16	−0.16
Netherlands	1.32**	1.00**	−0.23
Spain	2.58**	2.42*	0.16
Sweden	1.00	0.78	−0.23
Switzerland	0.96	1.39*	0.43**
U.K.	1.22*	0.82	−0.34
U.S.	0.49	0.84**	0.35
Average	0.95**	0.94**	−0.01

*Significant at a 95% confidence level.
**Significant at a 99% confidence level.

Table 4.8.   24-Month Trend in Stock Earnings Yield Minus Cash Yield

	Coefficient of Regression with Subsequent Asset Class Relative Performance		
	Stock-Bond	**Stock-Cash**	**Bond-Cash**
Australia	−0.26	−0.26	0.00
Austria	−0.20	0.00	0.19**
Belgium	0.08	0.14	0.05
Canada	0.11	0.30	0.20*
Denmark	0.04	0.33*	0.29*
France	1.28	1.61*	0.34**
Germany	0.32*	0.50**	0.18*
Italy	−0.04	0.18	0.22**
Japan	2.11	1.90	−0.22
Netherlands	1.55**	0.62**	0.07
Spain	3.07*	2.97*	−0.10
Sweden	0.22	0.61	−0.08
Switzerland	0.24	0.41*	0.17**
U.K.	0.16	0.06	−0.07
U.S.	0.39*	0.61**	0.22
Average	0.47*	0.60**	0.10

*Significant at a 95% confidence level.
**Significant at a 99% confidence level.

Table 4.9. 24-Month Trend in Bond Yield Minus Cash Yield

	Coefficient of Regression with Subsequent Asset Class Relative Performance		
	Stock-Bond	Stock-Cash	Bond-Cash
Australia	−0.38	−0.34	0.05
Austria	−0.54	−0.14	0.40**
Belgium	0.01	0.10	0.08**
Canada	−0.05	0.19	0.24
Denmark	−0.02	0.24	0.26*
France	−0.04	0.28	0.32**
Germany	0.27	0.45*	0.19*
Italy	−0.12	−0.04	0.08
Japan	0.30	0.64	0.34
Netherlands	0.37	0.60**	0.23
Spain	−0.60	−0.50	0.10
Sweden	0.63	0.69	0.06
Switzerland	0.21	0.41	0.20**
U.K.	−0.10	−0.11	−0.01
U.S.	0.40*	0.60**	0.20*
Average	0.02	0.20	0.18**

*Significant at a 95% confidence level.
**Significant at a 99% confidence level.

Table 4.10. 24-Month Trend in Real Cash Yield

	Coefficient of Regression with Subsequent Asset Class Relative Performance		
	Stock-Bond	Stock-Cash	Bond-Cash
Australia	−0.21	−0.11	0.01
Austria	0.69	0.47	−0.22
Belgium	0.00	−0.03	−0.03
Canada	−0.18	−0.16	0.01
Denmark	0.08	−0.01	−0.09
France	0.03	−0.08	−0.11
Germany	−0.40*	0.54**	−0.14
Italy	−0.03	0.02	0.04
Japan	−0.76	−0.35	0.40
Netherlands	−0.42**	−0.46**	−0.04
Spain	−0.88	−0.86	0.02
Sweden	−0.29	−0.01	0.28
Switzerland	0.01	0.00	−0.01
U.K.	−0.16	0.16	0.35
U.S.	−0.50**	−0.43**	0.07
Average	−0.20	−0.16	0.04

*Significant at a 95% confidence level.
**Significant at a 99% confidence level.

suggest that a rise in real interest rates in the United States induces a flight of money out of stocks. Every 100-basis-point rise in real interest rates translates into a 50-basis-point one-month performance penalty for stocks versus bonds! The result is significant at a 1 percent level.

When we broaden this research to the global arena, however, we find that the relationship is not consistent around the globe. It is significant in only three countries (but highly significant in those three)—namely, the United States, Germany, and the Netherlands. Outside of those countries, the relationship is spotty and inconsistent at best. In short, CPI inflation appears to have only limited merit in active asset allocation decisions in the global arena.

Does this mean that the United States, German and Netherlands results are spurious, the result of luck? Or does it mean that these three countries are unique, perhaps because the investment community in each of the three countries focuses close attention on CPI inflation? Statistical tools cannot answer these questions. Relationships that are inconsistent, which do not stand up to a broader evaluation, might be viewed with skepticism. We would lean towards ignoring models, such as the trend in real yields, that exhibit only intermittent statistical significance.

The Influence of the Macroeconomy: Stage III

Capital markets do not exist in a vacuum. Asset values do not rise and fall of their own accord. Rather, they reflect the investment community's views of future macroeconomic prospects. In an investment world where the judgments of millions of investors shape market prices, it might seem reasonable to assume efficiency, to assume that the macroeconomy cannot provide useful information that is not already reflected in consensus prices. The historical evidence does not necessarily support this view.

Several macroeconomic factors appear to have significant bearing on the subsequent performance of various assets. We explored (1) stock return variance; (2) rate of change in retail sales; (3) rate of change in producer prices; (4) levels of unemployment; and (5) rate of change in unit labor costs. We tested each of these variables, using a regression analysis in which the data were appropriately lagged to reflect reporting delays (which differ from country to country). The results were surprising.

Stock return variance, measured as the volatility of stock market performance over the prior six months, has been shown to be a powerful indicator of future stock market performance in the United States.[6] Of course, higher volatility should require a higher expected return as compensation for the higher risks faced by an investor. This in itself should offer favorable oppotunities for investors whose tolerance for risk is greater than that of the aggregate market. As a predictor for asset class returns, prior return volatility appears to have merit in 11 of the 13 countries tested, as Table 4.11 shows.

Table 4.11. Stock Return Variance

	Coefficient of Regression with Subsequent Asset Class Relative Performance		
	Stock-Bond	Stock-Cash	Bond-Cash
Australia	−0.33	0.77	1.01
Belgium	0.65*	0.88**	0.23**
Canada	2.00*	2.48**	0.47
Denmark	0.14	0.60	0.46
France	−0.47	−0.84	−0.37
Germany	0.22	0.44	0.22
Italy	0.36	0.37	0.02
Japan	1.00	1.13	0.13
Netherlands	0.73	1.04	0.32
Sweden	2.40	2.88*	0.48
Switzerland	0.25	0.28	0.04
U.K.	−0.18	−0.25	−0.11
U.S.	1.27*	1.83**	0.56
Average	0.62*	0.89**	0.27**

*Significant at a 95% confidence level.
**Significant at a 99% confidence level.

Stock volatility also appears to be useful as a predictor of bond market performance. When stock volatility rose, not only did stocks subsequently perform better, but bonds did, too. It is beyond the scope of this article to delve deeply into the reasons behind this relationship, but two possibilities come to mind. It may reflect the positive correlation between bond and stock returns. Alternatively, it may arise because heightened volatility in one asset breeds general investor uncertainty, leading to a demand for superior rewards in all risky assets. Nonetheless, we should note that the bond results were not significant in any country other than Belgium.

On the surface, it might seem that the rate of change in retail sales is a useful indicator of accelerating or decelerating economic activity; hence it may indicate improving or eroding equity prospects. Unfortunately, the evidence in Table 4.12 suggests that retail sales are fully discounted in security prices. There are six statistically significant relationships, but no consistent directional pattern. Retail sales are significantly positively related to German stock performance and significantly negatively related to British equity performance. These are not results that would earn the confidence of any sensible investor.

By contrast, the results for producer prices are remarkable in their consistency. While the results presented in Table 4.10 suggested that real

Table 4.12.   Percentage Change in Retail Sales

	Coefficient of Regression with Subsequent Asset Class Relative Performance		
	Stock-Bond	**Stock-Cash**	**Bond-Cash**
Australia	0.00	0.02	0.01
Belgium	0.02	0.02	0.00
Canada	0.14	−0.09	−0.23
Denmark	0.04	0.07	0.03
France	0.04	−0.05	−0.09
Germany	0.34*	0.37**	0.03
Italy	0.00	0.00	0.00
Japan	0.34	0.12	−0.23
Netherlands	0.02	0.05	0.03
Sweden	−0.01	−0.05	−0.03
Switzerland	0.07**	0.07*	0.00
U.K.	−0.62	−0.77*	−0.14
U.S.	0.31	−0.09	−0.39*
Average	0.05*	−0.03	−0.08

*Significant at a 95% confidence level.
**Significant at a 99% confidence level.

yields, based on a CPI definition of inflation, are of limited value, inflation as measured in producer prices turns out to be consistently useful. As Table 4.13 shows, in *every single country* tested, an acceleration in PPI inflation translates into an erosion in bond performance relative to cash. In 6 of the 13 countries, the relationship is statistically significant, and in 5 of the 13 countries, it is significant at the 1 percent level.

Acceleration in PPI inflation also has a bearing on stock market performance. Here we find a relatively consistent pattern in which accelerating PPI inflation depresses subsequent stock market performance vis-à-vis cash. Five of 13 relationships are statistically significant, and each of the significant relationships is negative.

Table 4.14 gives the results of a test of unemployment. A rise in unemployment is associated with better subsequent rewards for both stocks and bonds. While the relationship is slightly more consistent in bonds than in stocks (in bonds it fails only in Canada, whereas in stocks it fails in three countries), all the statistically significant relationships point to stronger capital market performance in the wake of high unemployment than low.

Finally, Table 4.15 examines the effects of unit labor costs, which may reflect both employment and compensation levels. Here we find an even more consistent relationship. Rising unit labor costs hurt stock market

Table 4.13. Percentage Change in Producer Price Index

	Coefficient of Regression with Subsequent Asset Class Relative Performance		
	Stock-Bond	**Stock-Cash**	**Bond-Cash**
Australia	0.13	0.08	−0.06
Belgium	−0.43	−0.55*	−0.12*
Canada	2.34	1.43	−0.91
Denmark	0.60	0.13	−0.47
France	−0.14	−0.34	−0.20**
Germany	−0.98	−1.91**	−0.92**
Italy	−0.02	−0.75	−0.73**
Japan	0.46	0.45	−0.01
Netherlands	−0.62	−0.87*	−0.25
Sweden	−0.90	−1.36	−0.46
Switzerland	−1.45**	−1.81**	−0.35**
U.K.	0.17	−0.60	0.78
U.S.	−0.18	−1.08**	0.90**
Average	−0.08	−0.55	−0.47**

*Significant at a 95% confidence level.
**Significant at a 99% confidence level.

Table 4.14. Unemployment

	Coefficient of Regression with Subsequent Asset Class Relative Performance		
	Stock-Bond	**Stock-Cash**	**Bond-Cash**
Australia	−0.96	−0.16	0.80
Belgium	0.15*	0.23**	0.08**
Canada	−0.11	−0.24	−0.13
Denmark	−0.42*	−0.07	0.36
France	0.46	0.96*	0.49*
Germany	0.26**	0.39**	0.12*
Japan	0.05	0.06	0.02
Netherlands	0.12	0.21	0.09
Switzerland	1.92	2.09	0.16
U.K.	0.02	0.23	0.22
U.S.	0.33	0.69**	0.35
Average	0.17	0.40	0.23**

*Significant at a 95% confidence level.
**Significant at a 99% confidence level.

Table 4.15.   Percentage Change in Unit Labor Costs

	Coefficient of Regression with Subsequent Asset Class Relative Performance		
	Stock-Bond	Stock-Cash	Bond-Cash
Belgium	−0.40	−0.51	−0.11
Canada	−0.08	−0.06	0.02
Denmark	0.37	−0.30	−0.67
France	−1.18	−2.03	−0.84
Germany	−0.31**	−0.30	0.01
Italy	−0.23	−0.40	−0.17*
Netherlands	−0.46	−1.16	−0.70
Sweden	0.09	−0.04	−0.13
U.K.	0.47	−0.02	−0.54
U.S.	0.06	−0.44	−0.50
Average	−0.17	−0.53**	−0.36*

*Significant at a 95% confidence level.
**Significant at a 99% confidence level.

performance in all ten countries where this statistic is available. Bonds are hurt by rising unit labor costs in all but one country (Canada).

Conclusion

The relationships that have proved useful for asset allocation strategies in the United States may also hold true for international markets. While statistical significance was not always found, the persistence of relationships from one country to another is grounds for ample encouragement. The evidence suggests that a disciplined approach to global investment management is not only intuitively appealing, it is likely to add value.

Notes

1. See J. Ernine and R. Henriksson, "Asset Allocation and Options," *Journal of Portfolio Management* (Fall 1987).
2. See R. D. Arnott and E. H. Sorensen, "The Equity Risk Premium and Stock Market Performance." (New York: Salomon Brothers Inc, July 1987).
3. The data cover various time spans. For most countries, the data covered December 1982 through February 1987, but for Australia, Austria, Japan, Spain, Sweden, and the U.K., data began on September 1979 or July 1981.

4. See R. D. Arnott and J. N. von Germeten, "Systemic Asset Allocation," *Financial Analysts Journal* (November/December 1983), and Arnott, "The Pension Sponsor's View of Asset Allocation," *Financial Analysts Journal* (September/October 1985).
5. See Arnott and von Germeten, "Systematic Asset Allocation," op. cit.
6. See R. D. Arnott, "Risk and Reward—An Intriguing Tool," (New York: Salomon Brothers Inc, April 6, 1987).

RISK AND ECONOMIC ANALYSIS

CHAPTER

5

Political Risk Analysis for Global Investing*

William D. Coplin
Michael K. O'Leary
Public Affairs Program,
Maxwell School,
Syracuse University
Directors Political Risk Services,
a division of IBC USA (Publications) Inc.

Introduction

Global investors are learning the importance of foreign and domestic political conditions in shaping both risks and opportunities. Unfortunately, the complexity and subjectivity of political analysis, coupled with a lack of valid, relevant, and up-to-date information, make it very difficult to integrate political analysis into the process of making investment decisions.

The impact of a political event cannot be easily quantified and is sometimes volatile. In most cases, the political status quo continues, but massive alterations can occur very quickly. Although about 85 percent of the governments in power at the beginning of 1991 will remain so in mid-1992, governments that have been in power for decades can vanish overnight, as we have seen in Eastern Europe and the former Soviet Union. Yet even a significant change in government may not alter the policies affecting the investment climate. Conversely, the continuation of a regime does not necessarily result in a continuation of business policies.

* This chapter is based on material provided in *A Business Guide to Political Risk for International Decisions* (Syracuse, New York: Political Risk Services, 1991).

Faced with this complexity, what are global investors to do? Certainly, they should not rely on:

1. The news media, which tend to hype the extremes
2. Banks, governments, and members of the business community, who assume the status quo will continue (if the particular organization favors the country, it will paint a rosy picture; otherwise, the forecast will be gloomy)
3. So-called individual experts, whether within or outside the investment community, because they usually have some axe to grind

Rather, global investors should rely on systematic political risk analysis. Such an analysis must be based on multiple expert sources who have no vested political or economic interest in the outcome of the events and conditions they are forecasting. The analysis must also be unencumbered by the jargon peculiar to academics or the ideologies of politicians disguised as objective analysts. Continuous monitoring is also necessary to gain perspective on the political and economic conditions within specific countries and to compare and contrast conditions across a large number of countries.

Two basic analytical questions confront the global investor. First, what political conditions are likely in one or more countries? Second, what effect will those conditions have on global investment decisions? In the first question, we are primarily concerned with who will govern the country, what political influences will shape decisions of individuals within the government, and whether or not the government will be able to limit political violence against itself and the society. The second question is even more complex. Since each investment decision is situation-specific, the impacts of general political and economic trends may vary with the economic sector, the specific company, and the duration of the investment.

A systematic approach to political risk analysis can yield a framework that allows comparison across countries and can integrate a complex set of factors to facilitate a general judgment. With such a rigorous framework in hand, the investor can then consider implications for the specific investment.

This chapter presents a framework that we initially developed in the 1970s while assisting the Central Intelligence Agency and the State Department of the U.S. government in improving their ability to make political forecasts. We began to develop the approach more fully for international business beginning in 1979. At that time, we established a forecasting service under Frost & Sullivan, Inc. of New York, which sold the division to IBC of London in February 1989. Under our editorial direction, the service continues to provide political and economic analysis to more than 1,000 clients a year in 85 countries throughout the world. The principles of this framework can be applied in a variety of contexts and adapted to the interests and capabilities of the users.

This chapter is divided into four sections. The first presents our interpretation of political risk analysis, that is, the factors we consider when assessing the climate for investment in a given country. The second describes the sources of background data used to compile our country reports. The third outlines the recruitment, assessment, and systematic analytical procedures used by country specialists. The fourth presents the Prince Model, the political forecasting mode that we use in compiling our reports and can easily be used in forecasting any political event.

Political Risk Factors

Four types of political risk factors must be examined in assessing the climate for investment in any given country. They are:

- Regime change: A change in key government personnel through normal electoral or authorized political processes, or through illegal means.
- Political turmoil: General levels of politically inspired violence, including violent strikes, demonstrations, riots, terrorist activities, guerrilla actions, or civil war.
- Government policy: Decisions with respect to fiscal and monetary policies, trade restrictions, or foreign investment regulations.
- External events: Other countries' actions that affect the country of concern.

Of these four factors, government policy has the most frequent and pervasive effects. The regime of any given country changes infrequently, as we have already noted. Moreover, changes in regime often lead neither to more political violence nor to radically different domestic or foreign policies. Political violence occurs rarely, except in countries where it is endemic, such as Peru and some South Asian countries. In these places, investors and businesses have already protected themselves against political violence. In countries where it occurs sporadically, such as Egypt and Morocco, it is repressed quickly and effectively. External events can have extremely far-reaching consequences, especially if the United States becomes involved, but they are also infrequent.

There are, of course, exceptions to the general rule that government policy is the greatest source of political risk to the investment climate rather than regime change, political violence, and external events. The fall of the shah of Iran resulted in large losses for foreign corporations operating in Iran. Political violence in Eastern Europe opened those economies to Western business, while the student rebellions and the subsequent crackdown in June 1989 dampened investment opportunity in China. Economic sanctions, such as those against South Africa during the 1980s and against Iraq after its invasion of Kuwait, have had a significant effect on investment opportunity in those two countries.

However, governmental policy can greatly affect the business environment. We have developed a letter-grade system that places countries in the categories of A, B, C, or D for financial transfer risks and direct investment risks.

Financial Transfer Risk

The term *transfer* in our risk summaries refers to the risk from financial transfer, nonconvertibility from the local currency to the desired foreign currency, and the transfer of foreign currency out of the country. The transfer could be for the payment of exports, repatriation of profits or capital, or any other business purpose. Risk ratings, expressed as letter grades, are used in both 18-month and 5-year periods. Countries are rated for financial transfer risk according to a scale ranging from A+ for the least risky to D− for the most risky.

The "A" countries: No exchange controls, repatriation restrictions, or other barriers to financial transfer; little likelihood that controls will increase in the forecast period.

The "B" countries: Modest or sporadic delays in financial transfers; a reasonable chance that delays will be high in the forecast period.

The "C" countries: Modest to heavy delays, or even blockage, of financial transfers; a reasonable chance that barriers will increase, and little chance that they will decrease within the forecast period.

The "D" countries: Heavy exchange controls and long delays for the transfer of currency; little chance that conditions will improve within the forecast period.

Direct Investment Risk Ratings

The term *investment* refers to the risks to foreign investment in wholly owned subsidiaries, joint ventures, and other forms of direct ownership of assets in a country. Risk ratings, expressed as letter grades, are used in both 18-month and 5-year periods. Countries are rated for direct investment risk according to a scale ranging from A+ for the least risky to D− for the most risky.

The "A" countries: Few restrictions on equity ownership in most industries; few controls on local operations, the repatriation of funds, or foreign exchange; taxation policy that does not discriminate between foreign and domestic business; little likelihood that restrictions will increase and little threat from political turmoil.

The "B" countries: Some threat to equity ownership, frequently in the form of a requirement for partial ownership by nationals; restrictions on local operations, particularly regarding local procurement; few restrictions on repatriation, but some exchange controls possible; some threat to business from political turmoil, and a possibility that restrictions and turmoil may increase.

The "C" countries: Considerable restrictions on equity ownership, including a requirement that nationals hold a majority percentage; considerable restriction on local operations, repatriation, and foreign exchange; some taxation discrimination possible; political turmoil may be a serious threat; a good chance that restrictions and turmoil will remain high or increase during the forecast period.

The "D" countries: Considerable restriction on equity ownership, including a prohibition against equity ownership by foreigners; substantial regulation of local operations, repatriation, and foreign exchange; taxation discrimination; political turmoil may present a serious threat to business operations; a good chance that restrictions and turmoil will remain high or increase during the forecast period.

Sources of Background Data

In compiling a country report, one must collect essential political, social, and economic information. We will first describe our overall strategy for gathering information, then outline some specific problems we have faced and the solutions we have developed. We will close this section by defining the variables used and describing the sources of our information.

The Sources

Our basic source of all political, economic, and social background is our own country specialists. The U.S. Department of State and Department of Commerce provide additional information through personal contacts. Foreign embassies located in Washington are used very selectively. For economic data, our primary source is the International Monetary Fund's monthly publication, *International Financial Statistics* (IFS), the most reliable, comprehensive, and timely source available for making comparisons between countries. Our research and editorial staff also rely on U.S. government publications for limited, mostly historical, references. Newspaper clippings, magazine stories, and electronic clipping services help monitor day-to-day events that may necessitate changes in our Fact Sheets.

Our Network   A team of country risk experts covers each country. We select our specialists on the basis of a track record of objective and accurate research on a country. At least once a year, country team members fully review and revise their country's Fact Sheet. Many team members have access to classified host government data, which they can share on a confidential basis. They contribute information on recent social trends, such as population growth. Country team members cross-check all information, and each member may add information or make corrections. This process is especially important for East European and Middle Eastern countries, for which information regarding unemployment, wages, and debt service is rarely available from the usual sources.

Direct Contact   We have given considerable effort to developing and maintaining personal sources of information within the departments of State and Commerce. In the case of either agency, the task is to find the person who possesses a given piece of information.

In the State Department, this might be a country desk officer, an intelligence analyst, or an officer in the regional Bureau of Economic Policy. Depending on the information sought and the willingness of the particular officer, State Department sources may be able to provide unpublished estimates from government or international agencies, reasons for discrepancies in reported figures, or recent figures received from U.S. government sources. The best contacts in the State Department are well informed on the statistics of their countries and on the political reality behind those statistics. They can also offer sophisticated insight in interpreting figures about a country. The problem is finding and maintaining such contacts amid the frequent rotation of State Department officials from one job to another.

Country desk officers in the Department of Commerce have the advantage of being more likely to stay in their jobs for longer periods of time. However, their range of knowledge tends to be more restricted, as they usually specialize in market conditions within a country. Furthermore, since most Commerce Department officers cover several countries, they lack perspective on the total economic situation of every country. Occasionally they have information from a forthcoming issue of *Foreign Economic Trends*.

Few officers at either Commerce or State have an extensive background in international economics, making it difficult to obtain help concerning technical questions. Few, for example, can distinguish one definition of international debt from another. Also, since most officers rely on figures the embassies mail to them, the timeliness of their data is limited.

Embassy Officials   In most cases, U.S. government sources have more timely information from American embassies abroad than the foreign embassies have about their own countries. The type of information most frequently obtained from an embassy relates to questions about election law, the constitution, or the distribution of legislative seats among political parties.

The International Monetary Fund (IMF)   The IMF publication *International Financial Statistics* (IFS) is especially valuable for its consistency in tracking historical trends. Any breaks in trend data or changes in the definition or source of information are noted for each country.

For most countries we cover, IFS is used to calculate nominal gross domestic product (GDP), GDP per capita, real GDP growth, inflation, exports, imports, and current account balance. IFS cannot be used for some countries because they are not members of the IMF. In these cases, we must consult supplementary sources, primarily from U.S. government agencies. The departments of Commerce and State are particularly helpful.

Government Publications   *Background Notes*, published by the U.S. Department of State, contains information on political, social, and economic conditions in a particular country. While useful for historical information, most issues are three or four years old.

The Commerce Department's *Foreign Economic Trends* (FET) contains reports on most countries and is used to fill information gaps, especially when an economic indicator is missing from IFS or a country is not an IMF member. Unemployment, wage, and debt service data are often available in FET, but the publication has several shortcomings. First, comparisons between countries are virtually impossible; country studies follow the idiosyncrasies of their writers, U.S. embassy personnel. A second problem is timeliness; two-year delays on key economic figures are not uncommon. The FETs suffer from low priority and uneven efforts in gathering the information, as well as wide variations in the ability and willingness of host governments to provide the necessary information.

The Press   Cabinet reorganizations, elections, the dissolution of a legislature, or newly released economic indicators are often the subject of news articles in American or foreign daily publications. The *New York Times*, *Wall Street Journal*, and *Financial Times* are checked daily for political and economic news. Regional publications, such as *Middle East Economic Digest* and *Far Eastern Economic Review*, also assist in tracking economic and political trends. We keep all articles relevant to each country for several years so that our research staff can cross-check information from the country's team of specialists.

The Problems

In compiling the information for the Fact Sheets, we often find that the goals of consistency, accuracy, and timeliness are difficult to achieve simultaneously. Conflicting information from official government sources is one of the most widespread frustrations in gathering data. Whether a country's trade balance is reported as a deficit or surplus may depend on which ministry furnishes the figures. The method of compiling of trade statistics is not consistent within national governments, let alone among international agencies.

Political Meddling   Inconsistencies and inaccuracies have many sources, including incompetence and the manipulation of figures for political reasons. Among developing countries, for example, inflated population figures are common. However, even the highly documented industrialized countries are not immune to such problems. *The Economist* (September 3,

1983) pointed out an accounting error in reports from the United Kingdom: In late August 1983, the Central Statistical Office announced that the country's international trade account figures for 1982 showed a surplus of approximately $7 billion. A week later, the same ministry reported that an extra $2.6 billion in net income had been "found," making the actual current account surplus closer to $10 billion. The error was quickly corrected, but not before the value of the pound had dropped in response to the $7 billion figure.

Changes in Reporting   Sometimes a report forsakes consistency so that the data mirrors what other financial publications have reported. In an October 1983 publication, we reported that Mexico's inflation rate in 1982 was 98.8 percent, a figure also reported in other major financial publications, even though the actual rate in the 1982 calendar year was about 60 percent, according to the IMF. The problem was that the 98.8 percent figure reflected the change in Mexico's consumer price index from December 1981 to December 1982, rather than for January to December 1982. We decided to publish the 98.8 percent figure, even though it was not consistent with usual reporting practices, because readers would be puzzled by the 60 percent figure, since the *New York Times*, the *Wall Street Journal*, and other publications were using the higher figure. Thus, the problem here was not a question of defining the figure, but rather of defining the year.

Overcoming Problems

Reporting economic, political, and social indicators poses a variety of problems. Over the years, we have tried to overcome these problems by developing standard methods of providing a predictable format for information that is easy to use, particularly in making comparisons between countries. Early on, we decided to publish all economic statistics in U.S. dollars. We have also devised procedures for filling data gaps with reliable information and for providing up-to-date statistics when only past figures are available from our normal sources.

Currency Conversion   In order for country data to be comparable, nominal figures must be reported in a single currency. Like most international publishers, we use the U.S. dollar as the comparative figure, converting at the average yearly exchange rate. This causes problems in converting national currencies to U.S. dollars. For instance, in a time of major devaluation, a country may have economic growth and high inflation, yet still show a declining GDP in U.S. dollars. The currency conversion problem could be resolved by reporting all nominal indicators in national currency, but those figures would have little meaning for most readers, and country comparisons would be impossible. The nominal indicators may not accurately reflect how well a country performed during a given year, but for consistency's sake, we report all data in U.S. dollars.

Comparability of Data   The lack of data that can be compared makes it difficult to monitor economic, political, and social conditions. It would be convenient if all governments had the same definitions of national income, if all governments calculated both GDP and GNP for both calendar and fiscal years, and if Eastern European nations released statistics comparable with those of the rest of the world. Such is not the case, however, so every effort is made to get numbers that are as accurate, current, and consistent as possible. Problems in gathering data occur daily, and they are dealt with by making compromises. If the only nominal data available is for a fiscal year, rather than a calendar year, we use it and note the difference.

In reporting the current year's figures (and, for some countries, the previous year's figures), estimates are made from published data, country team members, and other sources. If figures are unavailable from data sources, estimates are made using linear regression based on related variables. For example, if the export and current account figures are available for a country but the import figures are missing, an estimate of the imports might be made using exports, current account, and past trends of imports as the independent variables. The actual variables used to make an estimate for a particular country depend on how closely figures are correlated for that country over the previous five years.

Our standard reporting varies for certain countries that do not report data in the same form as others:

- Eastern Bloc countries not members of the IMF: Trade figures include only hard currency trade with the West.
- Yugoslavia: In order to make our figures consistent with those of the IMF, gross material product is reported in place of gross domestic product.

Figures for social indicators such as population, infant deaths, and urban population present another problem. Although these figures are reported in standard international sources for many of the countries we monitor, the coverage is not universal, and it is almost always several years old. Our policy is to present estimates of social data for the year preceding the year of publication. In many cases, this requires projecting past trends up to the year reported. However, sometimes developments in the country make it clear that straight-line projections will produce inaccurate estimates. We then consult our country specialists, demographers, or other specialists to make revised estimates that account for particular developments in a given country.

Terminology

The following definitions of the terms used as variables in our calculations coincide with the most common data sources. When a description includes more than one source, the major source of information is indicated with an asterisk. "Data files" refers to information files maintained by our research staff—primarily news sources and the reports of our country specialists.

Background

Capital: The designated seat of government of the country (*World Almanac*)

Population: A mid-year estimate of the total number of people living in the country (*International Financial Statistics*, Data files)

Area: The total area of the country in square kilometers (*Statesman's Yearbook*)

Official Language: The designated language(s) of the government for official use (**Statesman's Yearbook*, *World Almanac*)

Constitution: The date of promulgation of the country's current constitution (**Statesman's Yearbook*, *Background Notes*)

Head of State: The formal leader of the country, with the year he or she came to power (**Chiefs of State and Cabinet Members of Foreign Governments*, *World Almanac*)

Head of Government: The administrative leader of the government, with the year he or she came to power (**Chiefs of State and Cabinet Members of Foreign Governments*, *World Almanac*)

Officials: A listing of major government officials and their posts, with priority given to the following: Deputy Prime Minister, Agriculture, Commerce, Defense, Development, Energy, Finance, Foreign Affairs, Industry, Interior, Labor, Mining, Planning, Security, and Trade (**Chiefs of State and Cabinet Members of Foreign Governments*, Data files)

Administrative Subdivisions: The number and type of administrative districts in the country (**Statesman's Yearbook*, *World Almanac*, *Defense and Foreign Affairs Handbook*)

Legislature: The types of national legislative bodies and the distribution of seats among the major political parties (**Data files*, *Defense and Foreign Affairs Handbook*)

Elections: The election schedule and terms of office, as well as the date of the last and next scheduled elections for national offices (Data files)

Status of the Press: The freedom accorded to the news media to report and editorialize (*Country Reports on Human Rights Practice*)

Sectors of Government Participation: The areas of the economy in which the government exercises control or ownership (Data files)

Currency Exchange System: A description of currency exchange characteristics (**International Financial Statistics*, Data files)

Exchange Rate: The value of the currency in relation to the U.S. dollar on the most recent date available; the dollar is reported in relation to the deutsche mark (Data files)

Economic Indicators
Domestic

Gross Domestic Product (GDP): The value of the total final output of goods and services produced by the country's economy during a period of one year, regardless of its allocation to domestic or foreign factors (*International Financial Statistics, Foreign Economic Trends, OECD Economic Surveys*, Data files) NOTE: For a few countries, gross domestic product cannot be reported; we substitute either gross national product (GNP) or gross material product (GMP)

Per Capita GDP: The ratio of GDP to population (*International Financial Statistics, Foreign Economic Trends, OECD Economic Surveys*, Data files)

Real Growth Rate: The annual percentage change in real GDP, adjusted for the inflation rate (*International Financial Statistics, Foreign Economic Trends, Caribbean and Central American Databook, Economic and Social Progress in Latin America, OECD Economic Surveys*, Data files)

Inflation: The annual percentage change in a consumer price index (*International Financial Statistics, Foreign Economic Trends, Caribbean and Central American Databook, Economic and Social Progress in Latin America, OECD Economic Surveys*, Data files)

Capital Investment: The value of gross fixed capital formation (*International Financial Statistics*)

Budget Balance: The difference between (a) revenue and applicable grants received and (b) expenditure and lending, minus repayments (includes foreign lending) (*International Financial Statistics*)

Change in Real Wages: The annual percentage change in real (inflation-adjusted) wages (*International Financial Statistics, Foreign Economic Trends*, Data files)

Unemployment Rate: The average percentage of the labor force without work during the period cited (*Foreign Economic Trends, OECD Economic Outlook, Caribbean and Central American Databook, Economic and Social Progress in Latin America*, Data files)

International

Debt Service Ratio: The sum of interest and principal repayments on external public and publicly guaranteed debt (unless otherwise noted) as a percentage of exports of goods and services (*Data files, Annual Report World Bank, Caribbean and Central American Databook, Economic and Social Progress in Latin American, Foreign Economic Trends*)

Current Account: The balance of payments on goods and services and all transfer payments, defined as the difference between (a) exports of goods and services, plus inflows of unrequited official and private transfers, and (b) imports of goods and services, plus unrequited transfers to the rest of the world (*International Financial Statistics, Foreign Economic Trends, OECD Economic Surveys,* Data files)

Exports: The value of merchandise exports, measured free-on-board (f.o.b.) (*International Financial Statistics, Foreign Economic Trends,* Data files)

Imports: The value of merchandise imports, measured free-on-board (f.o.b.) (*International Financial Statistics, Foreign Economic Trends,* Data files)

Currency Changes: The annual percentage changes in the national currency value in relation to the U.S. dollar (*International Financial Statistics*)

Principal Exports: A list of the country's primary exports and its main export partners (*Defense and Foreign Affairs Handbook, World Almanac, Handbook of Economic Statistics,* Data files)

Principal Imports: A list of the country's primary imports and its main import partners (*Defense and Foreign Affairs Handbook, World Almanac, Handbook of Economic Statistics,* Data files)

Social Indicators
Energy

Per Capita Consumption: The amount of energy consumed per person in the equivalent of kilograms of oil (*World Development Report*)

Imports as a Percent of Exports: The ratio of the value of fuel imports to the value of total merchandise exports (*World Development Report, International Financial Statistics*)

Population

Annual Growth Rate: The average annual percentage change in population over the last decade (*World Development Report*)

Infant Deaths per 1,000: The number of deaths of children under one year of age per 1,000 live births in a calendar year (*World Development Report*)

Persons Under 15: The percentage of the population aged 0 to 14 years, inclusive (*World Almanac*)

Urban Population: The percentage of the population living in urban areas (*World Development Report*)

Literacy: The percentage of persons aged 15 and over who can read and write (*World Development Report, World Almanac,* Data files)

Work Force Distribution

Agriculture: The percentage of the work force employed in agricultural production (*World Development Report, Handbook of Economic Statistics*)

Industry and Commerce: The percentage of the work force employed in industrial production and commerce (*World Development Report, Handbook of Economic Statistics*)

Services: The percentage of the work force employed in service-oriented production (*World Development Report, Handbook of Economic Statistics*)

Unions: The percent of the work force that is organized independent of the government (Data files)

Other

Ethnic Groups: Groups with which significant percentages of the population identify themselves (*World Almanac, Background Notes*)

Languages: Languages spoken by significant percentages of the population (*World Almanac, Background Notes*)

Religions: The religious preferences of significant percentages of the population (*World Almanac, Background Notes*)

BIBLIOGRAPHY OF DATA SOURCES

Annual Report. Washington, DC: The World Bank, Annual.

Annual Report on Exchange Arrangements and Exchange Restrictions. Washington, DC: International Monetary Fund, Annual

Background Notes on countries of the world. Washington, DC: U.S. State Department.

Caribbean and Central American Databook. Washington, DC: Caribbean and Central American Action, Annual.

Chiefs of State and Cabinet Members of Foreign Governments. Springfield, VA: National Technical Information Service, Monthly.

Country Reports on Human Rights Practices. Washington, DC: U.S. Congress House Committee on Foreign Affairs and Senate Committee on Foreign Relations, Annual.

Defense and Foreign Affairs Handbook. Washington, DC: Defense and Foreign Affairs, Ltd., Annual.

Economic and Social Progress in Latin America. Washington, DC: Inter-American Development Bank, Annual.

Foreign Economic Trends. Washington, DC: U.S. Department of Commerce, Periodical.

Handbook of Economic Statistics. Washington, DC: Central Intelligence Agency, Annual.

International Financial Statistics. Washington, DC: International Monetary Fund, Monthly.

OECD Economic Outlook. Paris: Organization for Economic Cooperation and Development, Periodical.

OECD Economic Surveys. Paris: Organization for Economic Cooperation and Development, Annual.

Risk Assessment. Arlington, VA: International Division, Business Risks International, Inc., Weekly.

The Statesman's Yearbook. John Paxton, ed. New York: St. Martin's Press, Annual.

The World Almanac and Book of Facts. New York: Newspaper Enterprise Association, Annual.

World Development Report. Washington, DC: The World Bank, Annual.

Country Specialists

Overview

A team of country specialists, carefully selected for their professional expertise, prepares each Country Report. The team members draw upon their experience as academic researchers, as consultants to government and business, as government specialists, or as analysts who serve multinational banks, trade associations, and manufacturers.

Every country study is compiled from information provided by a team of country specialists. Each team member provides independent estimates, which are combined into the report forecasts. The quality of the forecasts depends on both the abilities of the specialists who participate in the study and the effectiveness of the questionnaire procedures employed to obtain a systematic analysis.

A detailed 40-page questionnaire elicits a systematic analysis from each team member. Some members write the draft, while others update, revise, and review the initial analysis. The structure of the questionnaire not only yields specific information that ensures the necessary analysis, but also allows for easy and methodical comparisons between team members.

Criteria for Selecting Experts

We require our experts to be more than mere information-gatherers and reporters. The collection and presentation of raw information is easy; it is much more difficult to piece together information to forecast political events and assess their impact on international business. Thus, we devote considerable time to the process of locating quality specialists.

The most important criterion for the selection of country specialists is the ability to analyze the politics of the country. We seek individuals who have demonstrated their analytical abilities through publication, reputation in the field, professional background, and graduate training. We further test new specialists by having them complete an analysis of an existing report. We continuously assess current specialists by maintaining a record of their analyses.

We are also concerned with the information base of the specialist. We heavily weigh the length of time a specialist has lived in the country. We also look at the quality of a specialist's governmental and non-governmental contacts. The information provided in response to the 40-page questionnaire also reveals the specialist's factual knowledge. The specialists' particular areas of expertise will vary. Some have more detailed knowledge about general political conditions, others about business and economics. We make sure the team of specialists for each country has an adequate and balanced background.

The political perspectives of the specialists are also important. We seek specialists who have an objective viewpoint. Since no political analyst is completely objective, the criterion is the ability to consider all the factors relating to a political forecast and to present the evidence clearly. We avoid individuals who are associated with any group or institution that might affect their viewpoints. Most individuals who are associated with local institutions, who are nationals of the country being studied, who work for businesses with a heavy stake in the country, or who are active in a political organization are likely to be strongly biased. Our use of such individuals is therefore highly selective. We prefer to use those who have a professional commitment to the serious study of the country.

Our insistence on an analysis and a forecasting approach to the study of each country minimizes the extent to which we obtain information in great detail about day-to-day political issues and routine procedures for doing business in a country. We assume that our clients already have access to such information, either from their own people in the field or from other sources. Our clients have indicated their need for the analytical attitude of the professional dedicated to studying the political forces in a country and predicting those events of most importance to foreign business.

We have access to the perspectives of persons with a direct stake in the country. Members of the host government, other governments, business officials, lobbyists, and local political figures frequently react to our country studies. Their views are not incorporated directly into the study, but are shared with members of our country team.

Identification and Recruitment

We have several avenues for the continual recruitment of new country specialists. We identify potential new country specialists on the basis of their published works or speeches, or on the recommendation of established members of our network. Occasionally prospective specialists approach us.

By regularly monitoring and evaluating lists of new books and articles, we identify potential country specialists. The authors of publications showing high analytical content are contacted and asked to complete a brief questionnaire. Contracts are then offered to specialists who demonstrate the requisite interest and competence. A similar procedure is used for speakers at professional conferences and seminars. We attend such meetings in order to meet and observe potential specialists for the country teams.

A recommendation from our established network of country experts is the second important method used (sometimes in conjunction with the first) to identify potential new members. Since those in the network have already demonstrated their competence, their opinions are highly valued. Individuals named independently by several of our experts are contacted, and their published work is evaluated. As our network has grown and strengthened, this method has become the most important source for identifying country specialists, particularly those not in academia. On several occasions, our clients have also made useful recommendations. In addition to country specialists, we have selected a Senior Adviser for each world region, as well as one responsible for international finance and economics. The members of this advisory group have played an increasingly important role in identifying and recruiting new country specialists.

About five percent of the country specialists in our network made the initial contact themselves. We receive several inquiries a week from potential specialists offering their services to us. When we receive an inquiry, we check references, assess publications, and ask whether any of our existing specialists have information about the applicant. While the majority are not qualified, those who appear to fit our needs are given further consideration.

Eliciting the Forecast

The procedure for acquiring forecasts and analyses from our country specialists is the most important factor in maintaining the high standards of our products and services. The procedures we have established to maintain this system also contribute to the quality of the analysis. We have developed an efficient set of questions to solicit specific information in a way that not only ensures that the country specialist is capable of performing the required analysis, but also allows for easy and systematic comparisons among the various responses.

The Country Report questionnaire, given to writers and reviewers, asks for the same information in different forms. For example, the questionnaire asks the specialist for a prediction of regime stability in three different ways:

1. By marking a closed-choice scale, as illustrated below:

"Check the box above the number that best represents your estimate of the PROBABILITY THAT THE MOST LIKELY REGIME WILL BE IN POWER 18 MONTHS FROM NOW."

0 1	2 3	4 5 6	7 8	9 10
Very Unlikely	Unlikely	Uncertain	Likely	Very Likely

2. By completing a Prince Chart (described later), which asks the expert to identify major political actors and estimate their relative influence on the stability of the regime
3. By writing a one-page analysis presenting the reasons behind the forecast

Having the country specialists state their views in these three different formats encourages a precise and well-reasoned analysis, since any inconsistencies in the alternative forms of response will be readily apparent. This procedure also standardizes the responses used to prepare a single Country Report. We can quickly compare the choices expressed by each specialist on each scale, as well as variations in the attitude and power assigned to actors on the Prince Charts (see the next section of this chapter), then easily determine any differences expressed in the brief written statement. In addition, having a standardized format removes the confusion over terms that frequently hinders the integration of political analysis.

A Track Record for Each Specialist

Because our country specialists work on a free-lance basis, we are highly selective about retaining country team members. We do not continue working with someone who fails to provide the balanced and well-informed analysis we need. We periodically assess the consistency between each specialist's forecasts and the course of events within the country. We are careful to determine why a country specialist's views proved correct or incorrect and keep only those whose analysis seems reasonable in retrospect.

This does not mean that we stop using a country specialist who produces a single incorrect forecast, for a sound analysis may have reasonably discounted the events that unfolded. Nevertheless, we maintain a success record for each of our specialists, which we use when putting together country teams for updating Country Reports. To prepare for such revisions, we also require the writer to make a retrospective analysis of the previous year's forecasts.

The Prince Political Forecasting System

The Prince Model

This section describes the "Prince Model," the basis of all our forecasts for international business. This unique feature of our Country Reports is the framework that supports the conduct of a systematic and uniform political analysis. This framework is used to generate probability scores for the most likely regime, turmoil, and restrictions on international investment and trade. Our clients can use this model to conduct their own analyses in order to supplement and complement our forecasts.

Table 5.1. Prince Chart for Regime Stability in the Dominican Republic, October 1987

Actor	Orientation	Certainty	Power		Salience	Prince Score
Armed Forces	+	4 ×	4 ×		3 =	+48
Cuba	−	4 ×	1 ×		3 =	−12
Dominican Liberation Party (PLD)	−	5 ×	2 ×		4 =	−40
Dominican Revolutionary Party (PRD)	−	5 ×	2 ×		5 =	−50
International Financial Community	+	2 ×	4 ×		3 =	+24
Labor	+	3 ×	2 ×		3 =	+18
Radical Left	−	5 ×	1 ×		5 =	−25
Reformist Party (PR)	+	5 ×	4 ×		5 =	+100
Roman Catholic Church	+	3 ×	3 ×		3 =	+27
Rural Workers	+	2 ×	2 ×		4 =	+16
United States	+	5 ×	5 ×		4 =	+100
University Students	−	3 ×	2 ×		4 =	−24
PROBABILITY						69%

TOTAL POSITIVE SCORES: 333
TOTAL OF ALL SCORES: 484
PROBABILITY: 333/484 = 70% (rounded to the nearest multiple of five)

Data for the Prince Model

Actors and Their Positions   In using the Prince Model, the first step is to survey the team of expert analysts (at least three for each country). Each team member answers a questionnaire that includes several "Prince Charts," which are used to record the positions of major political actors on a particular risk factor that could affect international business in the country. The sample Prince Chart in Table 5.1 is the chart for regime stability in the Dominican Republic, giving the consensus of the country team that produced the October 1987 report.

In completing the charts, the experts must first identify at least 7 actors that are able to influence each risk factor during the next 18 months. These actors may be individuals, groups, or ministries within the government or opponents of the government, as well as individuals or groups within the society as a whole such as business, unions, or ethnic organizations. Actors may also include foreign individuals, foreign governments, or institutions, such as the International Monetary Fund. The experts then estimate the position of each actor listed, according to four categories:

Orientation: The general attitude of the actor, classified into one of three categories: supports (+), neutral (N), or opposes (−).

Certainty: The firmness of the actor's orientation. For group actors, certainty is a function of the extent to which there is consensus of support or opposition among the membership. Certainty is measured on a scale ranging from 1 (little or no certainty) to 5 (extremely high certainty). The firmness of a neutral actor's orientation is not taken into account in computing the Prince Score for that actor.

Power: The degree to which the actor can exert influence, directly or indirectly, in support of or in opposition to a particular risk factor, relative to all other actors. An actor's power can have a variety of bases, and the exercise of power takes many forms. Power may be based on such factors as group size, wealth, physical resources, institutional authority, prestige, and political skill. Power is measured on a scale ranging from 1 (little or no power) to 5 (extremely high power).

Salience: The importance attached to supporting or opposing the risk factor, relative to all other concerns facing that actor. Salience is measured on a scale ranging from 1 (little or no importance) to 5 (extremely high importance).

Analysis of Table 5.1   The major supporters of the regime, the Reformist Party (PR) and the United States, have positive Prince Scores of 100. The major opponents of the regime are the Dominican Revolutionary Party (PRD), with a Prince Score of −50; the Dominican Liberation Party (PLD), with a Prince Score of −40; and the Radical Left, with a Prince Score of −25.

Constructing the Prince Model   Political Risk Services analyzes the Prince Charts obtained from each of the team members. If they differ significantly on an actor's position, the directors seek additional information. After reaching a clear consensus among the experts, the individual charts are combined into a single set of estimates, from which four Prince Charts are developed. The Prince Maps in the 85 Country Reports are labeled "Support/Opposition" (illustrated in Figure 5.1).

Risk Categories   Based on the country specialists' analysis, we estimate each actor's position relative to four specific risk factors during the 18-month forecast period: (1) the stability of the most likely regime; (2) the likelihood of turmoil; (3) future restrictions on international investment; and (4) future restrictions on trade. Each actor is assigned a total score in the appropriate Prince Charts.

Application of the Prince Model   The Prince Model is applied in several ways throughout our Country Reports. The probability of the most likely regime in the 18-month forecast appears in the Executive Summary and in the section on Regime Stability in each report. The first page(s) of the Political

Actors section summarizes the actors' influence by presenting all Prince Scores for the four risk categories. The remainder of this section includes descriptions for most, if not all, of the actors listed on the summary page.

The Total Picture   At the bottom of each column on the summary is a range of probability based on the calculations of the Prince Model. This range of percentages can be interpreted as the likelihood of occurrence for that risk category. The closer the number is to 100%, the greater the likelihood. The Prince Chart for each risk category is graphically presented as a Support/Opposition Chart. The appropriate charts for Turmoil, International Investment Restrictions, and Restrictions on Trade appear in those perspective sections of each Country Report.

Understanding Individual Positions   The larger an actor's positive score, the more important and supportive it is for the topic being predicted; the higher the negative score, the stronger and more important its opposition. Numbers contained in parentheses indicate the potential influence of neutral actors. All scores are derived from the Prince Model. For the summary page, Prince Scores of +125 and −125 are converted to +100 and −100 respectively.

This scoring system enables you to scan the configuration of actors in the political system in the four forecast categories. Actors with negative scores on turmoil, international investment restrictions, and restrictions on trade are generally supportive of international business. Actors with positive scores on those three factors are generally hostile (or threatening) toward international business.

Calculation of Prince Scores and Probabilities

A "Prince Score" is the product of the firmness of the actor's orientation (certainty), the player's ability to influence the outcome (power), and the importance of the specific risk factor to the actor (salience). Support is indicated by a positive (+) sign next to the score, and opposition is expressed by a negative (−) sign.

Probability Calculation   As illustrated previously, the Prince Chart numbers provide the basis for a formal estimate of the probability of occurrence. The probability is defined as the numerator, which is the sum of all *positive* Prince Scores and one-half the value of each neutral score, divided by the denominator, which is the sum of *all* scores, regardless of sign (i.e., the absolute value of all scores). Refer to the sample Prince Chart in Table 5.1 to follow the steps in determining Prince Scores and probabilities.

Determining Individual Prince Scores   The Prince Score for each actor having a positive or negative orientation is obtained by multiplying certainty times power times salience. The resulting product has the sign of the player's orientation—positive if the player supports, negative if the player opposes. For a neutral player, certainty has no relevance; therefore, the Prince Score becomes the product of power times salience.

Neutral Players   If a player is neutral, one-half of that player's Prince Score is added to the numerator, and the full value of the Prince Score is added to the denominator. The addition of only half the neutral actor's score to the numerator is based on the assumption of an even chance that the actor will eventually either support or oppose the action.

An Example   The scores from the sample Prince Chart in Table 5.1 were used to calculate the probability in the Dominican Republic example. The total weight of the actors in the political system was 484, the denominator in the probability equation. The numerator was the sum of the positive actor scores, 333. The quotient, representing the probability of the regime remaining in power for the next 18 months following October 1987, was 70%. The same method can be used for any political decision.

Placing the Players   The Support/Opposition Charts in each Country Report that evolve from the Prince Charts represent a consensus of the experts' estimates, which also produce the actor scores on the political actors' summary page of a Country Report. Four Support/Opposition Charts illustrate the relative support and opposition of the actors for each risk factor: regime stability (as related to the most likely 18-month regime), turmoil, restrictions on international investment, and restrictions on trade. This visual display presents an overall picture of probable changes concerning the factor.

Relative Positions   On the charts, each actor is placed along the vertical axis according to whether the certainty of its support for, neutrality toward, or opposition to the risk factor in question, and along the horizontal axis according to its importance in determining the outcome as measured by its power (ability to influence change). Thus, the position of the actors in relation to the two axes indicates their roles in determining the forecasts of regime stability, turmoil, and restrictions on international investment and trade.

Upper Right: Actors located in the upper right corner exert the maximum weight in support of the risk factor.

Lower Right: Actors in the lower right corner of the chart exert the maximum weight against the risk factor.

The Middle: Actors located in the middle of the vertical axis are either undecided or likely to shift positions.

Upper Left: Actors located in the upper left are strong supporters of the action but carry little weight in determining the outcome.

Lower Left: Actors found in the lower left corner are opponents with little influence.

Analyzing Support and Opposition

The political analysis underlying Political Risk Services' forecasts can best be understood by examining the Support/Opposition Chart in Figure 5.1

Most likely regime: Balaguer

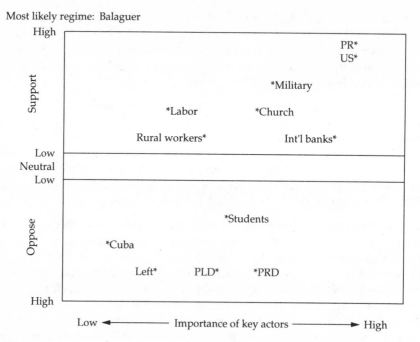

Figure 5.1.   Support/Opposition Chart for the Dominican Republic

in conjunction with the narrative analysis provided for each estimate. The following narrative that accompanies this chart describes the factors underlying the positions and the importance of the actors, possible coalition changes, other actors that may become important, and the impact of the changes on international business.

This Support/Opposition Chart is based on the Prince Chart for the Dominican Republic shown in Table 5.1. Numerically and graphically, the two charts show significant differences among the actors in the Dominican Republic concerning regime stability. One extreme position is that of the Reformist Party, located in the upper right corner of the Support/Opposition Chart, not only adamantly in support of the most likely 18-month regime, but also having the capability to exert maximum weight to support that orientation. A different extreme position is that of Cuba, located in the lower left corner of the Support/Opposition Chart, opposed to the regime, yet with little ability to bring about change.

The Prince Concept

The Prince Model was designed by the directors, William D. Coplin and Michael K. O'Leary. Since its first application in 1969, Coplin and O'Leary have developed and expanded its uses. The most recent publication describing the use of the Prince Model is *Power Persuasion* (Reading, Mass: Addison-Wesley, Inc., 1985).

Development of the Model   The Prince Model, a general political forecasting model that can be applied to any collective action, has evolved over many years. It is useful in a wide variety of political situations and is one of the few approaches to political forecasting that is both systematic and relevant to decision-makers. The Prince Model provides a means for rigorous analysis, yielding calculations that are used to forecast the probability of specific political outcomes. At the same time, it incorporates the invaluable and unique expertise of specialists who draw on their own qualitative and subjective knowledge about a given country to supply information for the model and to adjust the resulting calculations.

Versatility of the Model   *Power Persuasion*, using the term "power persuasion" instead of "Prince," illustrates how to use the system to achieve personal and business goals in a corporate setting. The range of applicability for the Prince Model can be widened to include general forecasting of any of the numerous collective actions that shape the political risks facing multinational corporations.

Other Applications   Coplin and O'Leary have also applied the Prince Model to areas other than political risk analysis. In 1972, they assisted the Intelligence and Research Bureau of the U.S. Department of State in forecasting the probability of a successful agreement between North and South Korea concerning an agenda of outstanding issues. They assisted the U.S. Army Corps of Engineers in estimating the likelihood of decisions affecting wetlands regulatory policy in the mid-1970s. They also aided the Central Intelligence Agency in estimating the probable position of 52 countries on various issues at the 1979 World Administrative Radio Conference. Several local government agencies have also used the model to forecast political events.

The following is a list of other publications by William D. Coplin and Michael K. O'Leary describing diverse methods of applying the Prince Model during the course of its development.

Policy Profiling Army Corps Decisions. Syracuse, NY: Syracuse Research Corporation, 1979.

Urban Forestry Programs: Analysis and Recommendations. Syracuse, NY: Syracuse Research Corporation, 1979.

"Testing Two Methods of Short Term Forecasting of Political Violence," *Technological Forecasting and Social Change*, 14(2) (1979), Published by American Elsevier Publishing Co., New York.

The 1979 World Administrative Radio Conference. *Briefing Manual for Issue Analysis.* Syracuse, NY: Syracuse Research Corporation, 1978.

Towards the Improvement of Foreign Service Reporting. Washington, D.C.: U.S. Government Printing Office, 1975. Based on a report to the (Murphy) Commission to Study the Organization of the Government in the Conduct of Foreign Policy.

Quantitative Techniques in Foreign Policy Forecasting and Analysis, (New York: Praeger, 1975).

"Quest for relevance: Quantitative International Relations Research and Government Foreign Affairs Analysis," *International Studies Quarterly*, 18 (June 1974).

"The PRINCE Concepts and the Study of Foreign Policy," *The Sage International Yearbook of Foreign Policy Studies*. Patrick McGowan, ed. Beverly Hills, CA: Sage Publications, 1974.

Everyman's PRINCE: A Guide to Understanding Your Political Problems, rev. ed. North Scituate, MA: Duxbury Publishing Company, 1976.

CHAPTER

6

International Business Cycles

Geoffrey H. Moore
*Center for International
Business Cycle Research
Columbia University
New York*

Business cycles in the major industrial countries have a powerful influence on the volume of capital investment and the terms on which such investments are made. In this chapter, we examine the chronologies of business cycles in a number of countries, consider the extent to which they synchronize across countries, look at the behavior of stock prices and interest rates in relation to the business cycles, and note what other factors throw light on the direction and magnitude of future swings in business cycles and capital markets.

The Center for International Business Cycle Research at Columbia University's Graduate School of Business has identified the highs and lows in growth cycles in 11 countries since the 1940s or 1950s. A "growth cycle" is a particular form of business cycle, representing the fluctuation that remains in broad measures of production, employment, income, and trade *after* the long-run growth trends in those measures have been removed. Periods of expansion in the growth cycle, therefore, represent periods when the growth of aggregate economic activity is faster than the long-run growth rate, while growth cycle contractions are periods when growth is slower than the long-run trend rate, or possibly negative. Table 6.1 shows the monthly peak and trough dates in the growth cycles of the 11 countries.

It should be noted in using this table that a growth cycle is defined differently from the way business cycles are usually identified in the United States. The National Bureau of Economic Research bases its business cycle dates on the same types of measures of aggregate economic activity as we use for growth cycles, but without removing the long-run trends. This means that the NBER business cycle peaks usually come later than the

Table 6.1.   Growth Cycle Peak and Trough Dates, 11 Countries, 1948–89 (Revised December 1990)[a]

Peak or Trough	North America		Europe				Pacific Region	
	United States	Canada	United Kingdom	West Germany	France	Italy	Japan	Australia
P	7/48							
T	10/49	5/50						
P	3/51	4/51	3/51	2/51				4/51
T	7/52	12/51	8/52					11/52
P	3/53	3/53					12/53	
T	8/54	10/54		2/54			6/55	
P	2/57	11/56	12/55	10/55	8/57	10/56	5/57	8/55
T	4/58	8/58	11/58	4/59	8/59	7/59	1/59	1/58
P	2/60	10/59						8/60
T	2/61	3/61						9/61
P	5/62	3/62	3/61	2/61			1/62	
T	10/64	5/63	2/63	2/63			1/63	
P					2/64	9/63	7/64	
T					6/65	3/65	2/66	
P	6/66	3/66	2/66	5/65	6/66			4/65
T	10/67	2/68	8/67	8/67	5/68			1/68
P	3/69	2/69	6/69	5/70	11/69	8/69	6/70	5/70
T	11/70	12/70	2/72	12/71	11/71	9/72	1/72	3/72
P	3/73	2/74	6/73	8/73	5/74	4/74	11/73	2/74
T	3/75	10/75	8/75	5/75	6/75	5/75	3/75	10/75
P		5/76				12/76		8/76
T		12/77				10/77		10/77
P	12/78	10/79	6/79	2/80	8/79	2/80	2/80	
T		5/80			8/81*			
P		6/81			3/83*			6/81
T	12/82	11/82	6/83	7/83	1/85*	4/83*	6/83	5/83
P	6/84*	11/85*				6/85*	5/85*	11/85
T	1/87*	11/86*				8/88*	5/87*	3/87
P	2/89*							6/89*

Pacific Region						10 Countries excl. U.S.	G-7 Countries	11 Countries
Taiwan, R.O.C.	South Korea	New Zealand	North America	Europe	Pacific			
			10/49					
			4/51					
			7/52					
			3/53					
			8/54					
			2/57	5/57		5/57	3/57	3/57
			4/58	3/59	1/59	2/59	5/58	5/58
			2/60				2/60	2/60
			2/61				2/61	4/61
			4/62	3/61	3/61	3/61	2/62	2/62
6/63			11/63	2/63	1/63	2/63	2/63	2/63
					9/64			
					3/66	2/64		
4/65		6/66	3/66	3/66			6/66	3/66
8/67	9/66	4/68	10/67	5/68		5/68	10/67	10/67
11/68	10/69	7/70	8/69	4/70	6/70	6/70	10/69	10/69
1/71	3/72	11/72	11/70	2/72	1/72	2/72	11/71	11/71
12/73	10/73	2/74	11/73	11/73	10/73	11/73	11/73	11/73
2/75	6/75	3/75	5/75	8/75	2/75	8/75	5/75	5/75
6/76		12/76						
7/77		2/78						
8/78	2/79	1/80	12/78	11/79	2/80	2/80	2/80	2/80
	10/80	11/80	6/80					
		7/81	7/81					
10/82	2/84	5/83	12/82		5/83	5/83	12/82	2/83
5/84*		8/84	6/84	6/84	5/85	5/85	5/85	5/85
8/85*	10/85		1/87		5/87	5/87	5/87	5/87

a. The chronologies for groups of countries are based on composite indexes of output, income, employment, and trade, weighted by each country's GNP in 1980, expressed in U.S. dollars. The chronologies begin at different dates because appropriate data are not available earlier. Since the chronologies are not updated frequently, the absence of a recent date does not necessarily mean that a turn has not occurred. G-7 countries group includes United States, Canada, United Kingdom, West Germany, France, Italy, and Japan.

*Based on trend-adjusted coincident index.

Source: For the United States through 1982, National Bureau of Economic Research. For other countries, Center for International Business Cycle Research.

growth cycle peaks, and the troughs occasionally come earlier, as a result of the upward trend. In addition, some growth cycle downswings are not matched by business cycle downswings because the long-run trend kept the economy moving up, albeit at a slow pace. For example, in 1984–87 the United States showed a growth cycle downswing but no business cycle recession.

The growth cycle concept is particularly useful for international comparisons. For example, West Germany and Japan in the 1950s and 1960s grew so rapidly that no declines in the level of economic activity could be observed, but they did have slowdowns in growth at about the same time that the United States and other countries experienced economic declines. The growth cycle procedure makes it possible to compare them. Many of the developing countries have been in a similar position in recent years. For further discussion see Mintz (1970) and Klein and Moore (1985).

A glance at Table 6.1 reveals that the growth cycle peak and trough dates are similar in many countries. For example, every one of the eleven countries reached a peak in 1973 or 1974 and a trough in 1975. The consensus is also shown in the dates for the groups of countries on the right side of the table. This is one way of demonstrating that an international economic cycle does exist, since cycles can be identified in broad measures of economic activity covering groups of countries as well as individual countries. Financial markets, of course, reflect both these global pressures and the differences that develop among individual countries.

Another way to observe the global dimension of business cycles and its causes and consequences is to count the number of countries that are experiencing growth or decline at any given time. Leading and coincident indexes of economic activity for each of the 11 countries in Table 6.1 are available monthly, and their growth rates indicate whether an expansion or contraction is in progress. The percentage of countries exhibiting expansion is called a diffusion index, since it shows how widespread expansion is across countries. Figure 6.1 and Table 6.2 show these diffusion indexes for recent years, and Table 6.3 shows how they have been related to the severity of business cycle recessions in the United States since 1957. The relationship probably runs in both directions: Sharp recessions in the United States shrink U.S. imports, hence leading to recessions abroad, while widespread recessions in the other countries lead to sharp reductions in U.S. exports.

Table 6.2 also shows that the development of international recessions and recoveries can usually be observed earlier in the movements of leading indicators than in those of coincident indicators. For example, the leading diffusion index began dropping sharply in the autumn of 1989, whereas the coincident index did not fall sharply until the summer of 1990. This difference is another fundamental characteristic of international economic cycles, observed over many years in many countries, as illustrated in Table 6.4.

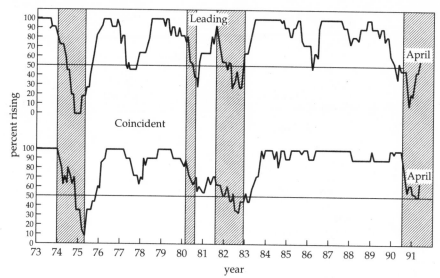

Shaded areas represent periods of recession in the U.S. economy. The diffusion indexes show what proportion of the eleven countries have rising leading or coincident indexes, based on whether the current month's index is higher or lower than the preceding 12-month average. The countries are: United States, Canada, United Kingdom, West Germany, France, Italy, Japan, Australia, Taiwan, South Korea, and New Zealand.

Figure 6.1. Leading and Coincident Diffusion Indexes, 11 Countries

The list of indicators shown in Table 6.4 was selected in 1966 on the basis of studies of the U.S. economy. We found that the list could be duplicated quite well in other industrialized countries, especially since the 1950s or 1960s. When the cyclical turns in each indicator were compared with the growth cycle turns, we found that the indicators classified as leaders in the United States generally performed as leaders in other countries, while those that were laggers in the United States were usually laggers in other countries. This trend is indicated by the predominance of minus signs, representing leads, in the upper section of Table 6.4 and plus signs, representing lags, in the lower section. Stock price indexes, for example, lead in ten of the eleven countries (Taiwan is the exception), whereas interest rates lag. The cumulative results for all countries are listed in the right-hand column of the table, where it is clear that the U.S. experience has proven to be a reliable guide to the leading and lagging indicators elsewhere. Even the length of the leads and lags are correlated to some degree. It is evident that the economic relationships that generate growth cycles operate similarly in market economies wherever they are located.

These results justify the development and use of composite indexes of leading, coincident, and lagging indicators as a basis for comparing many

---

Table 6.2.   Leading and Coincident Diffusion Indexes, 11 Countries

	Percent Rising		
	Leading	Coincident	Leading and Coincident
1989			
July	77	91	84
Aug.	82	91	86
Sep.	82	91	86
Oct.	68	91	80
Nov.	64	100	82
Dec.	55	100	77
1990			
Jan.	55	96	75
Feb.	46	100	73
Mar.	36	100	68
Apr.	55	100	77
May	46	100	73
June	46	86r	66r
July	46	82	64
Aug.	46	73	59
Sep.	27	55	41
Oct.	9	64r	36r
Nov.	23	64r	43r
Dec.	18	55r	36r
1991			
Jan.	36	55r	45r
Feb.	46r	50(10)	48(21)r
Mar.	46r	50(10)r	48(21)r
Apr.	57(7)	67(6)	62(13)

Note: Numbers in parentheses are the number of indexes included when not all are available. When the growth rate is 0.0, the index is counted as 1/2 rising. r = revised.

Source: Center for International Business Cycle Research, June 1991.

---

countries. They may be used for forecasting growth cycles in general, or in particular sectors of the economy. Leading indexes help detect recessions or recoveries at an early stage, and their growth rates provide advance information about the severity of recessions or the vigor of recoveries (see Moore, 1983, 1990). The growth rates in recent years of leading and coincident indexes for the United States and for ten other countries taken

Table 6.3. Severity and International Scope of U.S. Recessions

Recession Dates		Percent Change in Real GNP (from High to Low)	Lowest Percent of Leading and Coincident Indexes Rising, 11 Countries	
Peak	Trough		Percent	Date
8/57	4/58	−3.5	46	11/57
4/60	2/61	−1.0	62	2/61
12/69	11/70	−1.1	55	7/70
11/73	3/75	−4.3	14	2/75
1/80	7/80	−2.3	41	8/80
7/81	11/82	−3.4	32	8/82
Averages:				
3 Mild Recessions ('60, '69, '80)		−1.5	53	
3 Sharp Recessions ('57, '73, '81)		−3.7	31	
6 Recessions		−2.6	42	

Correlation between severity and international scope (cols. 3 and 4): RSQ = .79.
Source: Center for International Business Cycle Research, November 1990.

as a group are shown in Figure 6.2. The movements in the leading indexes generally precede those in the coincident by a few months. The greater severity of the growth cycle recession in 1980–1982, as compared to 1984–1987, shows up clearly in both the leading and coincident indexes in both the United States and the other ten countries. Moreover, one can see that the United States has usually gotten into and out of recessions before the "group of ten." Since the indexes are comparable across countries both in terms of economic content and method of construction, some of the statistical problems that plague comparisons of this sort are avoided.

The leading indexes have been found to be applicable to the forecasting of not only recessions and recoveries, but also exports, inflation, gold prices, bond yields, and stock prices. Many of these applications have taken the form of signaling systems, whereby the attainment of a certain previously defined growth rate in the leading index produces a signal either to buy or to sell. For example, we have constructed "long leading indexes" for the period from 1969–1989 for the United States, United

Table 6.4. Lead/Lag Record of Individual Indicators at Growth Cycle Turns, 11 Countries

Indicator: U.S. Classification and Title[a]	United States	Canada	United Kingdom	West Germany	France
Part A. Median Lead (−) or Lag (+), in Months, at Growth Cycle Peaks					
Leading Indicators					
Average workweek, mfg	−3	−3	0	−8	−4
New unemployment claims[b]	−1	−1	NA	+2	−41
New orders, consumer goods[c]	−2	−2	NA	NA	−11
Formation of business enterprises	−11	NA	−8	−8	NA
Contracts and orders, plant and equipment[c]	+1	+3	−3	−6	NA
Building permits, housing	−6	−3	−11	−10	−9
Change in business inventories[c]	0	0	−4	−4	+2
Industrial materials price change	−8	−2	+3	−5	−2
Stock price index	−4	−3	−5	−6	−3
Profits[c]	−4	−5	−4	−8	NA
Ratio, price to labor cost	−8	+1	−14	−9	−4
Change in consumer debt[c]	−6	−2	−16	−21	NA
Median	−4	−2	−5	−6	−4
Coincident Indicators					
Nonfarm employment	+1	+2	+2	+3	+6
Unemployment rate[b]	0	+1	+1	+3	0
Gross national product[c]	0	0	−13	0	−1
Industrial production	+3	0	0	0	0
Personal income[c]	−1	+1	−4	−6	NA
Manufacturing and trade sales[c]	−1	−2	−3	−3	−2
Median	0	0	−2	0	0
Lagging Indicators					
Long duration unemployment[b]	+6	+1	+6	NA	NA
Plant and equipment investment[c]	+5	+4	+5	−2	NA
Business inventories[c]	+6	+9	+10	+15	+8
Productivity change, nonfarm[b]	+11	+15	+8	+11	NA
Business loans outstanding[c]	+6	+3	+4	NA	NA
Interest rates, business loans	+7	+5	+5	+2	+6
Median	+6	+4	+6	+6	+7

Italy	Japan	Australia	Taiwan[d]	South Korea[e]	New Zealand	All Countries
0	−4	−2	−8	−7	0	−3
NA	NA	NA	NA	NA	NA	−1
−8	NA	NA	+6	NA	0	−2
−4	−10	−8	NA	NA	NA	−8
NA	−5	−2	NA	−1	0	−2
−2	−12	−5	−3	NA	+2	−6
NA	−1	NA	NA	NA	−6	−1
0	−4	−5	NA	NA	−3	−3
−6	−8	−7	0	−6	−7	−6
NA	−10	−2	NA	NA	NA	−4
+2	−2	−14	NA	NA	0	−4
NA	−9	−10	NA	NA	−3	−9
−5	−6	−5	−4	−2	0	−4
+6	+2	+3	+1	+5	+9	+3
+1	0	+1	+3	−6	0	+1
+1	−5	0	−10	+2	0	0
0	0	0	0	+2	NA	0
NA	−9	−3	−4	NA	−4	−4
−1	−8	−2	+2	0	0	−2
+1	−2	0	−1	+2	0	0
NA	NA	+7	NA	NA	NA	+6
NA	0	+2	+6	NA	NA	+4
+6	+4	+8	+24	NA	NA	+8
NA	+8	+12	+10	NA	NA	+11
NA	−6	+8	+5	NA	NA	+4
+3	+7	+3	+7	NA	NA	+5
+4	+4	+8	+7	NA	NA	+6

NA = no indicator available.

a. The series available for each country are sometimes only roughly equivalent in content to the U.S. series. In some cases two series are used to match the U.S. series, and the median includes all observations for both series. The periods covered vary for each indicator and each country, but all are within the years 1948–1987.

b. Inverted.

c. In constant prices.

d. Additional leading indicators for Taiwan and medians at peaks and troughs are: exports[c], −9, −3; money supply[c], −4, −4. Additional coincident indicators are: freight traffic, 0, −4; bank clearings[c], −4, −8.

e. Additional leading indicators for South Korea are: accession rate, −1, −5; letter of credit arrivals[c], −2, −8; inventories to shipments[b], −1, −3.

Indicator: U.S. Classification and Title[a]	United States	Canada	United Kingdom	West Germany	France
Part B. Median Lead (−) or Lag (+), in Months, at Growth Cycle Troughs					
Leading Indicators					
Average workweek, mfg	−2	−5	−2	−1	−3
New unemployment claims[b]	−5	−2	NA	−3	NA
New orders, consumer goods[c]	−2	0	NA	NA	−12
Formation of business enterprises	−1	NA	−10	−4	NA
Contracts and orders, plant and equipment[c]	−5	0	−1	0	NA
Building permits, housing	−9	−9	−10	+2	−7
Change in business inventories[c]	−2	0	−6	−1	+1
Industrial materials price change	−4	−4	+3	+1	−1
Profits[c]	−4	−6	−8	−8	−9
Stock price index	−2	−2	−3	−12	NA
Ratio, price to labor cost	−7	0	−9	−6	−3
Change in consumer debt[c]	−4	−11	−15	−18	NA
Median	−4	−2	−7	−3	−5
Coincident Indicators					
Nonfarm employment	+1	0	+2	+6	+7
Unemployment rate[b]	+1	+2	+1	0	+1
Gross national product[c]	−1	−1	0	0	−4
Industrial production	0	0	0	0	−3
Personal income[c]	0	0	−3	+6	NA
Manufacturing and trade sales[c]	0	0	−1	0	0
Median	0	0	0	0	0
Lagging Indicators					
Long duration unemployment[b]	+4	+2	+3	NA	NA
Plant and equipment investment[c]	+7	+6	+8	0	NA
Business inventories[c]	+6	+8	+6	+16	+4
Productivity change, nonfarm[b]	+10	+8	+12	+3	NA
Business loans outstanding[c]	+6	+3	+6	NA	NA
Interest rates, business loans	+11	+5	−1	+18	+8
Median	+6	+6	+6	+10	+6

Italy	Japan	Australia	Taiwan[d]	South Korea[e]	New Zealand	All Countries
+4	−4	−4	−12	−10	+3	−3
NA	NA	NA	NA	NA	NA	−3
−9	NA	NA	−13	NA	−3	−6
−7	−14	−8	NA	NA	NA	−8
NA	0	0	NA	−2	−4	0
−2	−6	−7	−7	NA	−2	−7
NA	−4	NA	NA	NA	−2	−2
+1	−7	+1	NA	NA	+3	+1
−8	−4	−4	0	−1	−10	−6
NA	−10	−2	NA	NA	NA	−2
+1	−2	−9	NA	NA	+5	−3
NA	−6	−6	NA	NA	−6	−6
−8	−5	−4	−6	−4	−2	−4
+8	+2	+4	0	+7	0	+2
+7	+2	0	0	0	0	+1
−1	−2	0	0	+2	+2	0
0	0	0	0	0	NA	0
NA	+1	+1	+1	NA	+3	+1
−7	−1	−2	−4	0	−4	−1
0	0	0	0	0	0	0
NA	NA	+5	NA	NA	NA	+4
NA	+4	+6	+6	NA	NA	+6
+5	+5	+16	+19	NA	NA	+6
NA	+8	+16	+8	NA	NA	+8
NA	0	−7	−6	NA	NA	+2
+9	+18	+16	+15	NA	NA	+11
+7	+5	+11	+8	NA	NA	+6

NA = no indicator available.

a. The series available for each country are sometimes only roughly equivalent in content to the U.S. series. In some cases two series are used to match the U.S. series, and the median includes all observations for both series. The periods covered vary for each indicator and each country, but all are within the years 1948–1987.

b. Inverted.

c. In constant prices.

d. Additional leading indicators for Taiwan and medians at peaks and troughs are: exports[c], −9, −3; money supply[c], −4, −4. Additional coincident indicators are: freight traffic, 0, −4; bank clearings[c], −4, −8.

e. Additional leading indicators for South Korea are: accession rate, −1, −5; letter of credit arrivals[c], −2, −8; inventories to shipments[b], −1, −3.

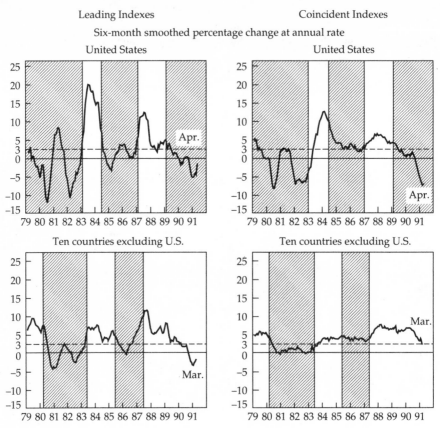

Leading Indexes   Coincident Indexes

Six-month smoothed percentage change at annual rate

Shaded areas are growth cycle recessions. See table 6.1 for dates.

Arrows indicate rate of change, 1976-1986, in the index and real GNP. The ten countries are Canada, United Kingdom, West Germany, France, Italy, Japan, Australia, Taiwan (R.O.C.), Korea (R.O.K.), and New Zealand.

Figure 6.2. Growth Rates in Leading and Coincident Indexes, 11 Countries, 1979–1991 (Source: Center for International Business Cycle Research)

Kingdom, West Germany, Japan, and Australia, using leading indicators that in the United States have average leads of at least 12 months at peaks and 6 months at troughs. That gives them an edge on stock prices, which typically have shorter leads. We found that a market-timing strategy based on signals from the long leading indexes, with subsequent switching between stocks and short-term interest-bearing securities would have produced both a higher and a more stable rate of return than a buy-and-hold strategy for the period (Boehm and Moore, 1990):

Investment Strategy	Average Annual Rate of Return	Standard Deviation of Rates of Return
Switching between stocks and bills according to signals	14.4%	13.5%
Buying and holding stocks	13.3%	19.3%

This example illustrates the practical benefits that can be derived from the study and analysis of international business cycles. Other examples that include the use of growth rate signals to pick up major changes in inflation rates and interest rates are given in the references listed below.

REFERENCES

Boehm, Ernst A., and Geoffrey H. Moore. (1990). *Financial Market Forecasts and Rates of Return based on Leading Index Signals,* Tenth Annual International Symposium on Forecasting, Delphi, Greece. For current information on this signal system see the monthly report, *Leading Indicator Global Market Timing System,* published by the Foundation for International Business Cycle Research, 475 Riverside Drive, New York, NY.

Klein, Philip A., and Geoffrey H. Moore. (1985). *Monitoring Growth Cycles in Market-Oriented Countries.* Cambridge, MA: Ballinger.

Lahiri, Kajal, and Geoffrey H. Moore. (1991). *Leading Economic Indicators: New Approaches and Forecasting Records.* New York: Cambridge University Press.

Mintz, Ilse. (1970). *Dating Postwar Business Cycles: Methods and their Application to Western Germany, 1950-67.* National Bureau of Economic Research, Occasional Paper 107.

Moore, Geoffrey H. (1983). *Business Cycles, Inflation and Forecasting.* 2nd ed. Cambridge, MA: Ballinger.

Moore, Geoffrey H. (1990). *Leading Indicators for the 1990's.* Homewood, IL: Dow Jones-Irwin.

Moore, Geoffrey H., and John P. Cullity. (1990). *Growth Cycle Signals as Inflation Indicators for Major Industrial Nations.* 19th CIRET Conference, Osaka, Japan.

CURRENCY HEDGING

7

Hedging Currency Risk

John F. O. Bilson
The Chicago Corporation
Chicago, IL

Introduction

This chapter is addressed to investment managers who must decide whether to hedge the currency exposure of an investment made in a foreign bond or equity market. Ten years ago, a relatively small number of managers in the United States were confronted with this problem. At that time, the fraction of U.S. institutional investments denominated in foreign currencies was small enough that the problem of foreign currency risk could safely be ignored. Several recent developments have drastically changed this situation

The most pervasive of these developments is the growth of global investment strategies. Equity managers were among the first to recognize that global markets offered size and diversification prospects that could be utilized to improve the performance of a domestically resident portfolio. International bond managers then realized that the breakdown of the Bretton Woods System of fixed exchange rates created differences in yields on bonds denominated in different currencies. The development of international short term money market funds during the past year marks the beginning of the final phase of global diversification. As managers move from equities and long bonds to short-term multicurrency strategies, the currency component comes to represent a growing fraction of the variance of the return on the investment, thus increasing the importance of foreign currency risk management.

Another development which has increased the importance of managing currency risk is the recognition that currency movements do not have a neutral influence on returns. Under the classic neutrality conditions of a floating exchange rate system, each country had an inflation rate that was determined by its monetary policy relative to its real growth rate. This inflation rate was embedded in the country's interest rates and in the long-term nominal appreciation of its stock market. The appreciation or depreciation of the country's exchange rate, relative to the currency of a trading partner, depended on whether its inflation rate was higher or lower than the inflation rate of the trading partner. Thus, the decision to hedge or not to hedge had little effect on the return on the investment.

However, the classical neutrality conditions have not held under the post-Bretton Woods System of flexible exchange rates. Foreign exchange rates have fluctuated over ranges too large to conceivably be attributed to differences in inflation rates. Interest rate differentials have also varied widely in response to domestic monetary policies. As a result, the currency factor has become a dominant component of the dollar-based return from international investments. For example, Adler and Simon (1990, p. 125) report that currency factors account for approximately 70 percent of the weekly return for dollar-resident investors in both the German and Japanese equity markets for the period from November 1979 to December 1982.

As the importance of currency exposure has increased, so has the variety of possible hedge mechanisms. Traditionally, managers who decided to hedge currency exposure would do so either by purchasing forward contracts or by borrowing in the local market to finance the investment. Modern managers have a wide range of additional hedging instruments at their disposal, including futures, options, collars, caps, and other derivative products. Currency hedging is also expanding into multicurrency strategies. A U.S. investor in Spain, for example, might hedge the currency risk of an investment with Deutsche mark financing, since the volatility in the peseta-mark cross is small relative to the volatility in the dollar-mark rate, and since German interest rates are substantially lower than Spanish rates.

A final development that has bearing on our discussion is the growing recognition of the possibility of forecasting the ex-post return on foreign currencies. In the absence of forecasting ability, the currency hedge decision is reduced to a static hedge/no hedge framework in which the main motivating factor is the client's attitude toward risk. Once forecasting ability is acknowledged, a manager has the capability to introduce a dynamic strategy in which the proportion of the exposure to be hedged varies over time in response to price dynamics and interest rates.

A complete discussion of all of these issues is certainly beyond the ability of the author. Therefore, I intend to provide an approach to the problem of currency hedging based upon my own research and experience in the markets. While this approach will certainly differ from those offered by other practitioners, some common themes will emerge. To the greatest extent possible, I will refer to other research in the area without attempting a comprehensive and critical review.

In the first section, I will briefly review the hedge/no hedge debate, demonstrating that the debate can be reduced to a discussion of two important issues: the efficiency of the foreign exchange market and the exposure of assets to fluctuations in foreign exchange rates. In the next two sections, the efficiency issue will be addressed by surveying the literature relating to the two main departures from market efficiency: the failure of forward premiums/discounts to forecast changes in exchange rates and the apparent success of technical trading models specializing in foreign exchange trading. In the next section, I will combine these two departures from market efficiency in a mean-variance portfolio optimization. This approach will be found to be most useful as an addition to an existing portfolio of equity and fixed-income instruments. In the final section, I will demonstrate how options can be used to more closely monitor the risks associated with cross-currency investments.

The Hedge/No Hedge Debate[1]

An asset is considered to be exposed to foreign currency fluctuations if its return is predictably related to the return on the foreign currency. In making this determination, it is useful to distinguish between real and nominal assets for the cases of both anticipated and unanticipated changes in foreign currency values. A real asset—a factory, farm, building, or piece of equipment—is a physical entity whose local currency price will vary according to both the supply/demand conditions in its local market and the local inflation rate. A nominal asset—a local bank note, deposit, or bond—has a fixed nominal value in the local currency.

Under the twin neutrality conditions of purchasing power parity and interest rate parity, neither real nor nominal assets will be exposed to anticipated changes in exchange rates. If local monetary conditions call for a stable 10 percent rate of depreciation against the dollar, and this rate of depreciation is widely anticipated, then local interest rates should be 10 percent above dollar rates and local prices should be increasing at a rate 10 percent greater than the dollar rate of inflation. At the same time, the local currency will be trading at a discount in the forward market of 10 percent. Under these circumstances, the return on an investment in either equities or bonds will not be affected by the decision to hedge the currency exposure.

The situation is somewhat different regarding an unanticipated change in the exchange rate. Suppose, for example, that a government announces a completely unanticipated 10 percent devaluation of its currency relative to the dollar. Again, under the assumption of purchasing power parity, local currency prices would have to rise by 10 percent in order to preserve the parity. Consequently, holders of real assets would find that the local currency inflation offsets the effect of the devaluation, leaving the dollar value unaffected. This is generally not the case with nominal assets, whose "price" is fixed in the local currency. Even if all of the classical neutrality conditions hold, no mechanism will protect holders of nominal assets from an unanticipated change in the exchange rate. (Though of limited practical use, there are two exceptions to this rule. First, when bond yields anticipate a devaluation, the actual event may lead to an appreciation in local currency bond prices when the event actually takes place. Second, if changes in exchange rates are predictably negatively autocorrelated, as in the famous Dornbusch (1976) overshooting model, the foreign currency value of local assets may subsequently appreciate while simultaneously bearing a lower yield.)

All of this suggests that hedging is of greater importance to fixed-income managers than to equity managers. The historical evidence tends to support this view. Gadkari and Spindel (1990) examined international fixed-income and equity portfolios from December 1977 to December 1988. They found that hedging reduced the volatility of a non-U.S. bond portfolio from 13.9 percent to 6.1 percent on an annualized basis. On the other hand, the volatility of a non-U.S.-based equity portfolio was only reduced from 17.4 percent to 13.4 percent. Over the entire period, hedging had a minimal effect on average returns in both cases. As Rosenberg (1990) forcefully states, the empirical evidence only demonstrates that hedging of international fixed-income portfolios would have been beneficial over the past decade. There is no presumption that such benefits will continue in the future.

The hedge/no hedge decision becomes much more difficult when the classical neutrality conditions break down. With the decline in the importance of Keynesian monetary activist policies, real factors have come to play a greater role as a determinant of movements in exchange rates. This policy change has crucial implications for the hedging decision. It has already been stated that a neutral expansion in the money supply will create offsetting movements in exchange rates and local prices, leaving foreign investors unharmed. However, consider a real factor, such as an unanticipated recession in the foreign country. The recession will typically be associated with both a decline in local equity prices and a depreciation of the exchange rate, so that foreign investors lose on both fronts. Yet, if the local bond market responds to a recession with falling yields, fixed-income investors will be partially protected against adverse exchange rate movements by rising bond prices. In this case, equity managers may find that their foreign exchange exposure exceeds that of fixed-income managers.[2]

For the U.S.-based investment, the hedge/no hedge decision should rest not only upon considerations like average return and absolute risk, but also upon correlations with the U.S. market. In the asset allocation approach to the question, the investigator attempts to find the optimal portfolio of hedged and unhedged instruments. The following example is taken from Jorion (1990) and is based on data from January 1978 to December 1988. The asset classes are: (1) the S&P 500 Index, for U.S. stocks; (2) The Salomon Brothers U.S. Government Bond Index, for U.S. bonds; (3) The Morgan Stanley Capital International EAFE Index, for foreign stocks; and (4) The Salomon Brothers Nondollar Bond Index, for foreign bonds. The two foreign indexes are calculated in both unhedged and hedged dollar-based returns. As a first step, Jorion computes the average return and standard deviation for each index over the entire sample period.

	Average Return	Standard Deviation
U.S. stocks	15.8%	16.5%
U.S. bonds	9.7%	11.2%
Foreign stocks (unhedged)	22.9%	17.2%
Foreign bonds (unhedged)	12.6%	13.7%
Foreign stocks (hedged)	20.9%	13.1%
Foreign bonds (hedged)	11.3%	6.8%

Source: Jorion (1990).

These results support the findings reported earlier by Gadkari and Spindell. Both hedged/unhedged foreign stocks and bonds outperformed their U.S. counterparts. However, the unhedged portfolios were typically riskier than their U.S. counterparts while the hedged portfolios typically carried less risk.

On the basis of these numbers, Jorion estimates mean-variance efficient portfolios. Over the entire period, he finds that the best portfolio consists of 9 percent unhedged foreign bonds, 62 percent hedged foreign stocks, and 29 percent hedged foreign bonds. Somewhat surprisingly, neither U.S. stocks nor U.S. bonds enter into the optimal portfolio! As Jorion himself has demonstrated elsewhere, Jorion (1985), these results tell us more about the inadequacy of mean-variance portfolio optimization techniques than about the hedge/no hedge decision. Based on past estimates of mean and variance, the optimizer merely states what would have been the best portfolio over the sample period. Since investors at the time could not have known the full sample statistics, they would not have been able to produce these portfolios during the sample period. For investors to-day, the use of these optimal portfolio procedures requires the substantial leap of faith of believing that sample averages from the past are unbiased indicators of future performance.

To illustrate this point, Jorion divides his sample into three periods: the weak dollar period of 1978–1980, the strong dollar period of 1981–1984, and the weak dollar period of 1985–1988. As one would expect, the optimal portfolio is strongly biased toward unhedged investments during periods of dollar weakness and toward hedged investments during periods of dollar strength. One way to examine the in-sample bias of these techniques is to take the opposite extreme. In the following example, we assume that the investor uses the 1978–1980 weighting over the period from 1981–1984 and the 1981–1984 weighting for the period from 1985–1988. We examine the performance of the optimal portfolios relative to the U.S. standards.

	U.S. Stocks	U.S. Bonds	Optimal
1981–1984	11.2%	6.0%	17.4%
1985–1988	18.3%	13.2%	12.0%

Source: Jorion (1990).

The optimal portfolio outperformed the U.S. markets in the first period but lagged in the second period. Thus, to suggest that any manager can significantly outperform the market through the utilization of simple averages and standard deviations is to excessively blaspheme the gods of the efficient markets. We can summarize this debate by concluding that although hedging clearly does significantly reduce the risks of international fixed-income investments, we expect that over the long term, this reduction will be associated with a reduction in the average return on these assets.

One other conclusion of this discussion is that investors should hedge when the dollar is strong, but not when the dollar is weak. We now turn to the issue of forecasting dollar strength and weakness. In the next section, I shall discuss forecasting models that rely primarily upon interest rate differentials. In the following section, I will review technical approaches to market forecasting.

Yields and Currency Appreciation[3]

What determines the level of interest rates? In a closed economy, interest rates are primarily determined by monetary policy, real growth, and inflationary expectations. In a purely open, risk-free, system, differences in nominal interest rates primarily reflect the expected rate of appreciation or depreciation of the exchange rate. Currency risk makes the existing system of floating exchange rates a hybrid of the open and closed systems.

Any forecasting model that uses international yield differentials to predict currency appreciation must be founded upon the interest rate parity relationship, which describes the risk-free arbitrage relationship between deposits denominated in different currencies. A U.S. resident investor holding a one-month Eurocurrency deposit will receive $(1 + i)$, where i is the interest rate, at the end of the investment period. In order to invest in a foreign currency-denominated deposit, the investor must first convert the dollars to the foreign currency at the initial spot rate, S. The foreign currency deposit will then return $(1 + i^*)$, where i^* is the foreign interest rate, at the end of the investment period. In order to eliminate currency exposure, the prospective amount must be sold in the forward exchange market at the current forward exchange rate, F. Since both investments now promise a set return in dollars, the return will be the same for the two investments. This leads to the arbitrage condition:

$$1 + i = \frac{F}{S}(1 + i^*) \tag{7-1}$$

This "forward parity" condition is often formulated as:

$$i = i^* + \frac{F - S}{S} + \frac{(F - S)}{S}i^* \tag{7-2}$$

The third interaction term in this expression is insignificant at short maturities. Ignoring this term, the expression states that the U.S. interest rate is equal to the foreign interest rate plus the forward premium or discount on the currency. In Modigliani-Miller terms, the yield on the dollar will equal the yield on the foreign currency plus the "locked in" capital gain.

The forward parity condition provides another link between yields and exchange rates. In a world of risk-neutral investors, the forward price of a currency equals the market expectation of the future spot rate, as expressed in equation (7-3):

$$F_t = E(S_{t+1}) \tag{7-3}$$

where subscripts have been added to represent the values at the beginning and end of the period. Combining (7-2) and (7-3) and again ignoring the interaction term, we arrive at:

$$i_t - i_t^* = (E(S_{t+1}) - S_t)/S_t \tag{7-4}$$

According to (7-4), international differences in short-term interest rates purely reflect the market's anticipation of currency appreciation or depreciation. High-yielding currencies will depreciate on average against low-yielding currencies.

This view of the world is difficult to reconcile with some widespread beliefs based on the circumstantial evidence on the workings of international financial markets. Central bankers often point to the fact that flexible exchange rates increase their ability to control monetary policy through relatively autonomous variation in interest rates. Market commentators in financial journals often write that a currency is being supported by higher interest rates. Finally, markets almost inevitably respond to increases in central bank discount rates by bidding the local currency. While it is not impossible to reconcile these beliefs within an efficient market framework, a growing body of statistical evidence casts doubt upon the validity of the forward parity as a forecasting model. (See, for example, Hodrick [1987] for an excellent recent review.)

The forward parity model is based on the theory that if the market sets the forward rate as an unbiased forecast of the future spot rate, and if the market is efficient, then the forward premium should be an unbiased forecast of the subsequently observed actual rate of appreciation. As an alternative, one might argue that exchange rates actually evolve as a random walk, rendering the forward rate irrelevant as a forecasting tool. This alternative "forward parity neutrality" theory suggests that the best forecast of the future spot rate is the current spot rate. The forecast of the future spot rate is given by equation (7-5):

$$S_{t+1} = b_1 S_t + b_2 F_t + u_t \qquad (7\text{-}5)$$

where u_t is the forecast error.

If the forward parity model is correct, the coefficient b_2 will not be significantly different from unity and b_1 will not be significantly different from zero. For estimation purposes, it is useful to restrict the two regression coefficients to sum to unity and to divide through the equation by the current forward rate in order to reduce heteroscedasticity. This leads to:

$$\frac{S_{t+1} - F_t}{F_t} = b_1 \frac{F_t - S_t}{F_t} + \frac{u_t}{F_t} \qquad (7\text{-}6)$$

We shall refer to the dependent variable in this regression as the realized return on a forward currency position. If Q_t is the quantity of foreign currency purchased or sold in the forward market, then $(S_{t+1} - F_t)Q_t$ is the realized profit or loss on the position. Multiplying and dividing by the forward rate leads to $[(S_{t+1} - F_t)/F_t] \times (F_t Q_t)$. The second part of this expression is the dollar value of the forward position. The profit or loss is then equal to the realized return times the dollar position. The success of the strategy obviously depends on the ability of the right hand side variables to forecast the realized return. If the forward parity neutrality theory is correct, the forward premium or discount will not forecast the realized return.

We now examine the forecasting ability of equation (7-6) for the three major exchange rates against the U.S. dollar and for the mark-yen cross rate. The regressions are based on monthly observations from April 1975 to April 1991 using New York interbank spot rates and one-month forward rates inferred from one-month Eurocurrency deposit rates at the New York close. For estimation purposes, we also include a constant in the regression with coefficient b_0. The equations have been estimated by ordinary least squares.

	b_0	b_1	Standard Error (S.E.)	R^2
British pound	−.0064	−3.3119	.034	.068
	(2.01)	(3.74)		
Deutsche mark	.0076	−3.0119	.034	.023
	(1.70)	(2.16)		
Japanese yen	.0099	−3.1221	.035	.051
	(2.83)	(3.22)		
mark-yen	−.0014	−3.6545	.030	.039
	(0.65)	(2.79)		

(*t*-statistics in parentheses beneath the coefficients)

These regressions tell a remarkably similar story. The b_1 coefficients all have a value of approximately −3, and all are statistically significant at the 1 percent level. The non-technical interpretation of these results is that the ex-post return on a currency is, on average, equal to three times the interest rate differential. Thus, if one month Euro-sterling rates are 12 percent, and one-month dollar rates are 6 percent, then the return on borrowing dollars and investing in sterling is approximately 18 percent on an annualized basis. This ex-post return can be decomposed into the 6 percent interest rate differential and a 12 percent anticipated appreciation of sterling. If the monthly standard deviation is 3 percent, then the annualized standard deviation is 10.39 percent. Consequently, the two-standard-deviation range for the strategy may be estimated to be from −2.78 percent to 38.78 percent. This analysis requires, of course, the crucial assumption that the historical relationships will continue into the future. While there is no theoretical basis for making this assumption, the evidence of a relationship between international differences in yields and the ex-post realized return on forward currency positions has been known for over a decade. Hence, though the results should not be considered as infallible, international fund managers should not ignore interest rates in formulating their hedging strategies.

There is, in fact, growing evidence that managers are using the interest rate–exchange rate relationship to enhance portfolio performance. Equity managers with positions in European markets are increasingly using low-yielding currencies like marks and Swiss francs to hedge positions in high-yielding currencies. On a more direct level, international money market funds have improved yields by investing in high-yielding currencies like pesetas, sterling, and kronor, while simultaneously hedging the dollar exposure with marks and Swiss francs. The economic consequence of this behaviour is a tendency for convergence among yields. In 1982, it was not uncommon to observe yield differentials ranging from 8 percent (France) to 12 percent (Italy, Denmark) on long European bonds relative to long German bonds. By 1990, these differentials had been reduced to approximately 2 percent. This convergence can also be observed in the major currencies.

If the interest rate game has run its course, traders using technical rules continue to find profitable opportunities in the currency markets. In the next section, I will outline what I believe to be the basic philosophy of technical trading and will then apply the analysis to the currency hedging debate.

Technical Analysis in the Currency Markets

The term *technical analysis* is used to denote an approach to markets that relies solely on information generated by the market itself. This information set typically includes prices (open, high, low, close), volume, open interest, and, more recently, implied volatility. In this section, I will not attempt to review the wide variety of technical models that have been applied to the currency markets (see Taylor, 1990) but I will attempt to explain in a general way why these models tend to "work" despite the typical failure of regression approaches to the market.

The most successful of the technical models have been the trend-following ones, including filter rule studies (Alexander [1961], Sweeny [1986, 1988]), channel rules, and moving average cross over models. Taylor examines the performance of these and other trading rules and finds that these models did produce statistically significant trading profits during the floating rate period.

Rather than attempt to develop a sophisticated model of trend determination, we shall work with an extremely simple concept, the rate of appreciation or depreciation over the past three months. This concept is problematic from a trading perspective because the trend is influenced as much by today's change as by the change three months ago. While this difficulty precludes implementation on a daily basis, it is not an important consideration for our monthly model.

Having defined the trend, let us again take the case of the three major exchange rates against the U.S. dollar and the mark-yen cross rate to examine how a regression-based model tests the hypothesis that trend is a statistically significant factor in determining the actual return on a foreign currency. A natural approach would be to run the following regression:

$$(S_{t+1} - F_t)/F_t = b_0 + b_1(F_t - F_{t-3})/F_{t-3} + u_t \qquad (7\text{-}7)$$

where the dependent variable is the realized return and the independent variable is the three-month trend. The results of these regressions are disappointing.

	b_0	b_1	Standard Error (S.E.)	R^2
British pound	.0012	.0352	.035	.003
	(0.49)	(0.86)		
Deutsche mark	−.0007	.0384	.035	.004
	(0.29)	(0.91)		
Japanese yen	.0013	.0521	.036	.008
	(0.51)	(1.29)		
mark-yen	−.0017	.0687	.030	.014
	(0.77)	(1.69)		

(*t*-statistics in parentheses)

The dismal R^2 and *t*-statistics could certainly lead a regression analyst to conclude that exchange rates evolve as a random walk and that "technical" studies purporting to prove otherwise must be based upon flawed methodology.

For the technical analyst, however, the problematic outcome is rooted in the regression analysis, which posits a linear relationship between the past trend and the future actual return. In effect, the regression model assumes that the expected return is proportional to the past trend. In contrast, technical models assume that the relationship between past trends and future returns is nonlinear. One of the oldest technical models is the moving average cross over system. In this system, the analyst plots the differences between moving averages of short and long duration. When the short is above the long, the trend is determined to be up, generating a buy signal. Under the key assumption of nonlinearity, the buy signal is influenced purely by the sign of the difference between the two moving averages, regardless of the size. A similar point can be made about channel and filter rule systems. These systems each contain a neutral, nontrending zone from which the price must break out before a signal is given, though such signal is, once again, only a function of the sign.

In order to understand the importance of the nonlinearity, we begin by dividing the trend of the currency exchange rates into standard deviation "blocks." The standard deviation of the quarterly trend is approximately 6 percent. Consequently, we refer to the normalized trend as the trend/.06. For example, the zero block includes all observations between −0.25 and +0.25 standard deviations and the two-standard-deviation block includes all observations greater than 1.75 standard deviations. We then relate the normalized trend to the realized rate of return over the next month. The results are presented in Figure 7.1. Clearly there is a predictable tendency for currencies to trend (i.e., for the past trend and the realized return to be positively correlated) in the range from .5 to 1.5 standard deviations. Furthermore, the nature of the correlation is not proportional to the normalized trend, as the average realized return is approximately the same over the .5 to 1.5 range. There is no predictable correlation for a zero trend,

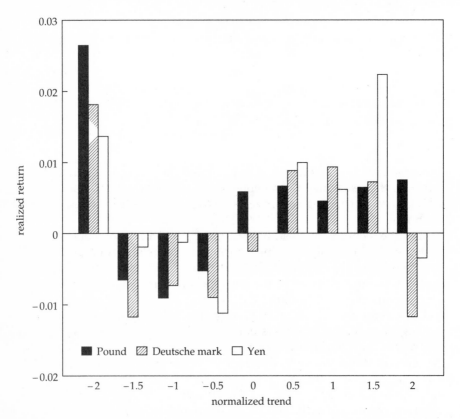

Figure 7.1.   Past Trends and Future Returns

but trends greater than 1.75 standard deviations in absolute value appear to be generally negatively correlated.

A more formal test of the pattern of correlation may be conducted using dummy variables. Each block is represented by a unit dummy variable. We then estimate the relationship between the realized return and the past trend for all of the currencies using Zellner's seemingly unrelated regression technique. To improve the efficiency of the estimates, we assume that the regression coefficient on each dummy variable is the same for each currency.

Trend (T)	Coefficient	t-statistic
T < −1.75	1.16	1.62
−1.75 < T < −1.25	−0.31	0.64
−1.25 < T < −0.75	−0.69	1.80
−0.75 < T < −0.25	−0.80	2.50
−0.25 < T < +0.25	−0.14	0.42
+0.25 < T < +0.75	+0.97	3.08
+0.75 < T+ < 1.25	+0.81	2.19
+1.25 < T < +1.75	+0.95	2.07
T > 1.75	−0.26	0.52

In this table, the coefficients represent the average monthly percentage return when the trend is in the block. For example, when a currency has fallen by more than 1.75 standard deviations over the past three months, it has experienced a positive rate of return of 1.16 percent in the subsequent month.

It is instructive to relate these results to the evolution of the technical trading rules. The early trend-following models simply assumed that trends would continue. As in Model 1, these can be represented by a dummy variable which takes the value of −1 if the trend is negative and +1 if the trend is positive. The filter and channel rule models eliminated some of the noise around the zero trend level by specifying a minimum trend before a position is taken. As in Model 2, these can be represented by a dummy variable taking the value of −1 if the trend is less than −.25 standard deviations and +1 if the trend exceeds .25 standard deviations. Finally, the most recent technical models also take account of "over-bought" and "over-sold" situations. As in Model 3, these can be represented by adding additional dummy variables when the trend is less than −1.75 standard deviations or when it exceeds 1.75 standard deviations. Estimation of these restricted models for the three major currencies leads to the following results.

Model 1: $Return = .0550 + .4995 \ Trend1$
(0.25)   (3.84)

Model 2: $Return = .0545 + .7210 \ Trend2$
(0.25)   (4.93)

Model 3: $Return = .0976 + .8156 \ Trend3 + .5427 \ Trend4$
(0.45)   (5.54)   (1.36)

(t-statistics in parentheses)

In these equations, the *Trend* variables represent the dummy variables of the linear regression in Equation (7-7). These results demonstrate that there has been a predictable pattern of serial correlation in exchange rate which has not been captured by linear regression models.

While dummy variable regression is a useful technique for describing the pattern of serial correlation, its implementation in practice encounters serious difficulties. The problem is that the dummy variable model, like any buy/sell system, requires large discrete changes in position when a certain price is reached. Price instability around entry and exit points can create substantial losses that are not related to price trends. For this reason, we prefer to create a continuous function which smooths the entry and exit into the market. In the next section of the paper, I will introduce one variant of a continuous function for this purpose and then examine its performance using a mean-variance portfolio optimization procedure.

Expected Returns and Portfolio Optimization

In the preceding sections, I have demonstrated that yield differentials and trends play an important role in predicting the ex-post returns on currencies during the floating rate period. While forecasting ability is important, it does not by itself give a manager any insight into the return-risk trade-off implied by the strategy. I will address the issue of this trade-off in this section of the paper, first summarizing the previous results in a single forecasting approach, then incorporating this forecasting equation into a mean-variance portfolio optimization model to evaluate the risk-return trade-off.

We can summarize our discussion of forecasting with the continuous combined regression function:

$$y = b_1 X1 + b_2 X2 + b_3 X3 + u \qquad (7\text{-}8)$$

where

$$y = \frac{(S_{t+1} - F_t)}{F_t}$$

$$X1 = \frac{(F_t - S_t)}{F_t} \text{ is the yield indicator}$$

$X2 = (F_t - F_{t-3})/F_{t-3}$ is the trend indicator

$$X3 = X2 \exp \frac{-\text{abs}(X2)}{\text{std}(X2)}$$

The third variable, which we shall refer to as the discounted trend, accounts for the nonlinear pattern of serial correlation by discounting large trend values. As we shall see, incorporating the discounted trend allows the model to capture the pattern of nonlinearity described in the dummy variable regressions.

Let us estimate the function model described in equation (7-8) to the monthly data from April 1975 to April 1991 for the three major currencies against the dollar. We will restrict the coefficients to be the same for each currency and estimate the system using Zellner's seemingly unrelated regression procedure, obtaining, with the t-statistics in parentheses, results:

$$y = -1.0041\ X1 - 0.0939\ X2 + 0.6009 X3$$
$$\quad\ (3.03)\qquad (2.66)\qquad (5.10) \tag{7-9}$$

All of the coefficients are significantly different from zero at the 1 percent level. It is interesting to note that the coefficient on the yield variable has declined from -3 in the single variable regressions to -1 in the combined regression. This result is apparently due to the positive correlation between the trend and yield indicators.

The pattern of serial correlation estimated by the continuous function model is described in Figure 7.2. The block function described in the previous section is included for comparative purposes. The expected return attributed to trend rises rapidly to around .7 percent per month (8.73 percent annualized) and then declines towards zero at a trend of approximately 12 percent (2 standard deviations). It is clear from the diagram that the continuous function avoids the discrete changes in expected return that would result from the use of the block function.

We next examine the forecasting ability of the continuous function model. Let $E(y)$ denote the fitted value from the regression described in equation (7-9):

Pound	$y = -.1071 + 1.0948E(y)$
	$\quad\ (0.41)\qquad (3.26)$
	S.E. $= .034\ R^2 = .052$
	significance level $= .001$
Deutsche mark	$y = .2436\ + 1.2637E(y)$
	$\quad\ (0.94)\qquad (3.64)$
	S.E. $= .034\ R^2 = .065$
	significance level $= .0003$
Yen	$y = .5911\ + 1.4089E(y)$
	$\quad\ (2.23)\qquad (4.23)$
	S.E. $= .034\ R^2 = .085$
	significance level $= .00003$

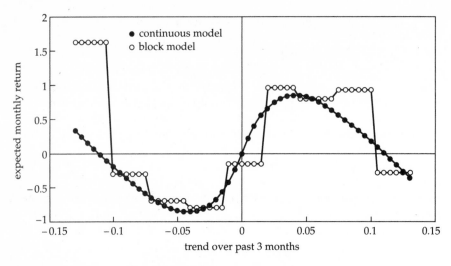

Figure 7.2. Trend-related Expected Returns

These results demonstrate that the expected returns are a statistically significant indicator of actual returns and that the expected return accounts for between 5 percent and 8 percent of the monthly variation in the ex-post realized returns on the currency. Two questions inevitably arise at this point. The first relates to the value of simulated performance figures and the fact that the statistics were calculated over the full sample period. I have addressed this issue in a previous paper (Bilson, 1990) by first estimating the model over the period from April 1975 to December 1983 and then testing over the period from January 1984 to December 1988. The model's performance was shown to be robust to out of sample testing, providing unbiased forecasts of post-sample profitability. The second question relates to the economic and financial implications of the results of the continuous function combined regressions: what sort of returns are implied by these regressions and how can these results be used to formulate a trading strategy? I will answer this second question in two parts. In previous papers, I have advocated the use of mean-variance optimization procedures to cross the bridge from statistical analysis to program implementation. I will briefly present this analysis again, point out some deficiencies with the mean-variance approach, and suggest an alternative which may be more attractive to portfolio managers.

The mean-variance approach begins with the specification of the investor's objective function. One approach well-suited to the incorporation of the regression results is:

$$E(U) = q'E(y) - \left(\frac{1}{2g}\right)q'Vq \qquad (7\text{-}10)$$

where q is an $(n \times 1)$ vector whose typical element is the dollar value of the position taken in a particular currency, V is the $(n \times n)$ covariance matrix of the forecast errors, and g is a scalar representing the investor's degree of risk aversion. If we set g equal to 10 percent of the investor's capital results to create a risk-return trade-off similar to that of the S&P 500 Index, then $q'E(y)$ is the expected profit on the position and $q'Vq$ is the anticipated variance of profit.

Maximizing $E(U)$ with respect to q and setting the resulting first order conditions equal to zero results in the following expression for the currency positions:

$$q = gV^{-1}E(y) \qquad (7\text{-}11)$$

In the following analysis, we estimate the position vectors for the three major currencies against the U.S. dollar and evaluate the performance of the simulated currency strategy of the mean-variance approach. We begin by calculating the compound annualized return for each year in the sample in Table 7.1. The strategy was profitable in 15 out of 17 years. The average return was 29.29 percent, which was 4.35 standard deviations above zero. These returns are gross trading returns which neither include interest on the base capital nor account for commissions, slippage, or management and incentive fees. As Figure 7.3 indicates, there are three distinct periods in the performance history:

		Average	Std. Dev.	*t*-statistic
Period 1	1975–1977	11.08%	9.54%	1.16
Period 2	1978–1981	69.09%	19.98%	3.45
Period 3	1982–1991	18.69%	14.61%	1.27

It is clear from these statistics that the 1978–1981 period offered exceptional opportunities for the type of program described in this paper. The activities of Jimmy Carter in the White House and Paul Volcker at the Federal Reserve during this period created a combination of interest rate and exchange rate instability that is unlikely to be repeated in the near future. For this reason, we shall restrict the evaluation of the mean-variance currency strategy to the 1982–1991 period. The currency program over this period had an average annual compound return of 18.69 percent, with an annual standard deviation of 14.61 percent. Over the period of a year, the program predicts a two-standard-deviation range of returns from -10.53 percent to 47.91 percent. The actual one-year range during the same period was -14.49 percent to 55.95 percent.

Table 7.1. Simulated Returns by Year

Year	Simulated Return
1975 (9 months)	16.9 %
1976	13.25%
1977	41.71%
1978	75.76%
1979	98.98%
1980	53.44%
1981	22.50%
1982	24.88%
1983	24.88%
1984	1.59%
1985	20.57%
1986	−2.25%
1987	20.47%
1988	22.08%
1989	10.36%
1990	55.95%
1991 (4 months)	−3.07%

How does this performance compare with other risky investments? As our standard of comparison, we will use the S&P 500 Index with reinvestment of dividends. This index had the following performance characteristics over the sample period:

		Average	Std. Dev.	*t*-statistic
Period 1	1975–1977	15.44%	16.04%	0.96
Period 3	1982–1991	17.79%	17.13%	1.03

Relative to the S&P 500 Index, during the 1982–1991 period, the currency program had a slightly higher rate of return and a slightly lower risk. The differences are so slight, however, that the two assets should be classified in the same risk return class. In Figure 7.4, the performances of the two investments are plotted. The most obvious characteristic of the figure is the low, perhaps even negative, degree of correlation exhibited by the returns on the two investments. During the stock market boom from 1985 to 1987, the returns on the currency program were negligible. However, during the stock market crash of 24 percent between October and January 1987, the currency program appreciated by 20 percent. Similarly,

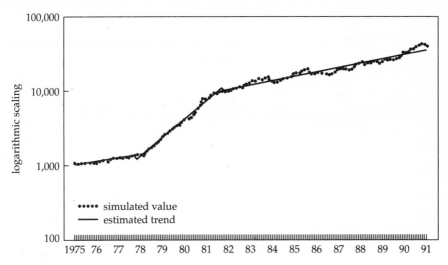

Figure 7.3.   Simulated Value of $1,000 Initial Investment

during the stock market decline of 20 percent between July and November 1990, the currency program appreciated by 21 percent.

While this pattern of negative correlation may appear to be coinciden-tal, it may also be the result of the increasing integration of the world's asset markets. Exchange rates and interest rates are valid indicators of the relative performance of the world's major economies, so it is likely

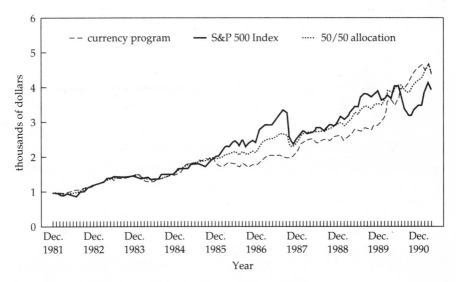

Figure 7.4.   Simulated Value of $1,000 Initial Investment

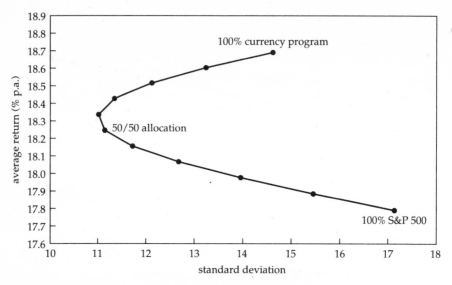

Figure 7.5. Efficient Frontier Analysis

that movements in exchange rates will be correlated with movements in national stock markets.

The implications for the U.S. resident of diversifying into foreign currencies is described in Figure 7.5 which plots the efficient frontier resulting from combinations of the two investments. Over the 1982–1991 period, the S&P 500 Index had an annualized standard deviation of approximately 17 percent. By allocating capital away from the index and into the currency program, this measure of risk was reduced to approximately 11 percent. For example, a 50/50 combination of the two investments resulted in an average return of 18.25 percent and a standard deviation of 11.13 percent. The implications of this reduction in risk are substantial; on a twelve-month basis, the largest loss on the S&P 500 Index was approximately 18 percent, while the largest loss on the combined program was only 5.47 percent.

Hedging on a Currency by Currency Basis

In the portfolio optimization approach, the program simultaneously chooses long and short positions in each currency. While this approach results in the best risk-return trade-off, it may not be entirely appropriate as a hedge mechanism. In most hedging situations, the fundamental asset—be it bond, equity, or cash denominated in a foreign currency—is taken as given, reducing the hedge decision to a determination of the fraction of the foreign currency exposure to be hedged in the foreign market. In this section, we shall modify the previously introduced dynamic hedging approach to apply to such a hedging decision.

In this analysis, the fundamental asset will be one-month Eurocurrency deposits denominated in sterling, marks, and yen. Because these deposits are short-term, they are most strongly influenced by currency changes. From a dollar-based perspective, the return on a foreign bank deposit may be written as:

$$\$\text{Return} = \frac{S_{t+1} - S_t}{S_t} + i_t^* + \frac{S_{t+1} - S_t}{S_t} i_t^* \tag{7-12}$$

The first term in this expression is the percentage change in the exchange rate over the holding period, the second term is the yield on the foreign deposit, and the third term is an interaction term representing the effect of the exchange rate on the dollar value of the interest payment. Since the interest rate is determined at the beginning of the period, the main source of variation in equation (7-12) is the variation in the exchange rate. Thus, the return is proportional to the change in the exchange rate, and the bank deposit is fully exposed to currency fluctuations.

The regression model introduced in the previous section provides a forecast of the expected return on a forward contract over a one-month horizon. The largest value of this expected return is about 1 percent per month, or a compounded annual rate of 12.68 percent per annum. In order to use the model as a hedging instrument, we express the expected return during each period as a fraction of its maximum value.

$$\text{Hedge Ratio} = \frac{E(R)}{.01} \tag{7-13}$$

Since the underlying position is long, we also restrict the hedge ratio to a negative value. In other words, when the model forecasts a positive return from holding the currency, the hedge ratio will be zero. The actual return on the hedge is now equal to:

$$\text{Hedge Return} = \frac{S_{t+1} - F_t}{S_t} HR \tag{7-14}$$

If the hedge ratio, HR, is equal to -1, indicating a complete hedge, then the total return on the investment would be equal to the one-month Euro-deposit rate.

As a first step in the hedging analysis, we examine the average return and the standard deviation of the return on the deposits for the three major currencies over the period from April 1975 to April 1991. In each case, implementing the hedging strategy resulted in an improvement in the average annual rate of return and a reduction in risk. On average, the hedging strategy increased the average return by 42.43 percent and decreased the standard deviation by 22.61 percent.

	Average	Std. Dev.
British pound		
unhedged	11.26%	12.16%
hedged	14.42%	10.32%
Deutsche mark		
unhedged	9.13%	12.10%
hedged	15.20%	8.52%
Japanese yen		
unhedged	12.47%	12.39%
hedged	19.05%	9.53%

For a portfolio manager, the reduction in risk depends not only on the absolute risk, as measured by the standard deviation, but also on the correlation between the returns. If correlations are low, then the portfolio of currency positions will typically have a lower risk than the individual assets. As the following table demonstrates, hedging also tends to reduce the correlations between the returns.

	Unhedged	Hedged
pound-mark	.7361	.4861
pound-yen	.5897	.4273
mark-yen	.7271	.4879

In order to examine the overall impact of hedging on an international short-term portfolio, we compare the performance of two mean-variance optimal portfolios, one unhedged and one hedged. The optimal weights are based on the historical average returns and the historical covariance matrix. For the unhedged portfolio, the optimal portfolio consists of a 50/50 weighting of sterling and yen deposits. The mark is allocated a zero weight because unhedged Deutsche mark deposits have had a lower average return than sterling or yen deposits, and because the mark is highly correlated with sterling and yen. For the hedged portfolio, the optimal weighting is 20 percent sterling, 30 percent marks, and 50 percent yen. The performance characteristics of the two portfolios are described below.

	Average Return	Standard Deviation	Ratio
Unhedged	12.31%	11.50%	1.07
Hedged	16.44%	7.88%	2.08

These statistics suggest that the addition of the dynamic hedging strategy almost doubles the risk-return trade-off relative to the unhedged strategy. The hedged portfolio also has superior risk-return characteristics relative to the S&P 500 Index and the mean-variance model discussed in the previous section. In part, this is due to the fact that the hedged strategy includes the interest yield on the funds committed but it also indicates that not a lot is lost by ignoring the correlations between the various currencies. The simulated value of a $1,000 initial investment is plotted in Figure 7.6. Over the nine-year period, a $1,000 investment in the unhedged program would have grown to $2,703, while the same investment in the dynamic hedging program would have grown to $4,025. The dynamic hedging program would also have experienced lower drawdowns: the largest loss over twelve months for the unhedged program was 12.46 percent, whereas the hedged program's worst twelve-month period resulted in a positive return of 2.92 percent.

It is also possible to improve the hedging strategy by trading on a single currency basis. The trading function depicted in Figure 7.2 can be considered as a variant of the portfolio insurance hedging rule. In the portfolio insurance literature, the client is often thought of as the purchaser of a put on the underlying asset. Using Black-Scholes option theory, the trader attempts to replicate the performance of the put by dynamically purchasing and selling quantities of the underlying asset (or, more normally, forward or futures contracts on the underlying asset). As the experience of October 1987 demonstrated, this strategy can be difficult to implement

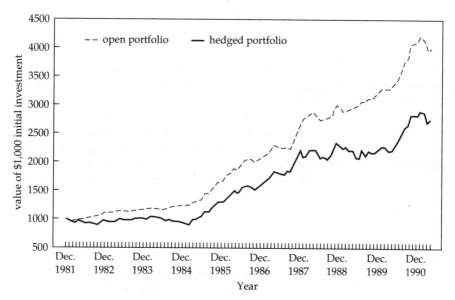

Figure 7.6.   Open and Hedged Bank Deposits

when market conditions are extremely volatile. These types of problems also apply to the trading system described in this paper. Large movements, particularly overnight, could result in actual positions that are relatively far from the positions specified in the program.

The trader can increase the "fit" between the actual and desired positions through the use of options. I will explain this process using data for the British pound for July, 1990. In the beginning of July, spot sterling was at 1.7476, relative to a value of 1.5904 three months before, and sterling one-month deposit rates were 5.86 percent above U.S. rates. Both factors, upward trend and high yield, suggest that long positions in sterling should have been profitable. However, the trend of 9.43 percent corresponds to 1.5 standard deviations. If sterling were to rally another 4 cents to 1.7876, an overbought condition would emerge, and the program would begin to take profits on the position. The following table shows the relationship between movements in the spot price and the recommended position, as measured in thousands of U.S dollars for a US$1,000,000 account.

Spot	Desired Position	Delta 1.80 Call	Delta 1.70 Put	Delta Position
1.7076	$929	.105	−.443	$939
1.7276	$790	.165	−.337	$786
1.7376	$715	.201	−.288	$710
1.7476	$637	.242	−.244	$633
1.7576	$556	.287	−.203	$554
1.7676	$475	.334	−.167	$476
1.7876	$310	.436	−.108	$323

The column entitled "Desired Position" describes the relationship between the price of sterling and the position recommended by the trading function. It is clear that the program is in the downward sloping part of the curve in the positive quadrant in Figure 7.2. The second and third columns provide estimates of the theoretical options deltas for the 1.80 Call and the 1.70 Put. The options deltas vary with price as the options move from being in the money to out of the money. This relationship between delta and price can be used to implement the dynamic hedging strategy. The overall position can be written as:

$$\text{Pos}(p) = \text{Pos}_f + (D_{Cp} \times \text{Pos}_C) + (D_{Pp} \times \text{Pos}_P) + U(\text{Pos}) \qquad (7\text{-}15)$$

where

Pos_p = Desired position related to price p

Pos_f = Position in forward or futures contracts

$$
\begin{aligned}
D_{Cp} &= \text{Call delta related to price } p \\
\text{Pos}_C &= \text{Position in calls} \\
D_{Pp} &= \text{Put delta related to price } p \\
\text{Pos}_P &= \text{Position in puts} \\
U(\text{Pos}) &= \text{Forecast tracking error}
\end{aligned}
$$

Equation (7-15) may be considered as a regression relationship. Assuming that the objective is to minimize the sum of squared tracking errors, ordinary least squares may be used to estimate the positions as a function of the deltas. Estimating this regression with the above data results in the following position vector: Forwards $680, Calls −$1,173, and Puts −$875. Multiplying these positions by the deltas yields the delta of the position, given in the last column of the table. It is clear that the use of options allows the program to track the desired position over a fairly wide variation in price. This feature represents another advantage from dealing in individual currencies that is not possible with the mean-variance optimization procedure.

Conclusion

This paper has discussed a number of methods for estimating and hedging currency exposure. Although the techniques have worked well over the period from 1975 to the present, there is no theoretical justification for assuming that the performance will continue into the future. Indeed, theory would suggest that if market participants utilize these techniques, then the advantage gained from them should gradually erode. There is already considerable evidence that erosion has taken place in the case of strategies based on yield differentials. The growing presence of technically based commodity funds in the currency markets could likewise lead to a deterioration of technically based performance. Due to these concerns, the procedures discussed herein should not be considered as a guide to the future performance of the strategies.

Notes

1. For a detailed discussion of this debate, see Thomas (1990), chapters 1 to 12. Most of my discussion in this section is based on my interpretation of the results offered by the contributors to the Thomas book.
2. See Adler and Dumas (1983) and Adler and Simon (1990).
3. There is a very large and growing body of research on the topics discussed in this section. For a review, see Hodrick (1987, chapters 3, 4). The approach that I am taking had its origins in Bilson (1981). For a critical review of this approach, see Hodrick and Srivastava (1984).
4. Fink and Feduniak (1988) provide a useful review of technical approaches to trading strategies. Taylor (1990) compares a number of different strategies.

REFERENCES

Alexander, S. S. "Price Movements in Speculative Markets: Trends or Random Walks?" *Industrial Management Review*, 2 (1961) pp. 7–26.

Adler, M., and D. Simon. "Exchange Risk Surprises in International Portfolios." *Journal of Portfolio Management*, 4 (1986) p. 44–53.

Bilson, John F. O. "The 'Speculative Efficiency' Hypothesis." *Journal of Business*, 54 (1981) pp. 435–452.

Bilson, John F. O. "Technical Currency Trading," in Lee Thomas, ed., *The Currency Hedging Debate*. (IFR, 1990) pp. 257–270.

Dornbusch, R. "Expectations and Exchange Rate Dynamics." *Journal of Political Economy* (December 1976) pp. 1161–74.

Fink, R. E., and R. B. Feduniak. *Futures Trading: Concepts and Strategies*. (New York: New York Institute of Finance, 1988).

Gadkari, V., and M. Spindel. "Currency Hedging and International Diversification—Implications of a World Reserve Currency Effect." *Journal of International Securities Markets*, 4 (1990).

Hodrick, R. J. *The Empirical Evidence on the Efficiency of Forward and Futures Foreign Exchange Markets*. (Harwood Academic Publishers, 1987).

Hodrick, R. J., and S. Srivastava. "An Investigation of Risk and Return in Forward Foreign Exchange." *Journal of International Money and Finance*, 3 (1984) pp. 1–29.

Jorion, P. "International Portfolio Diversification with Estimation Risk." *Journal of Business* (July 1985) pp. 259–278.

Jorion, P. "Asset Allocation with Hedged and Unhedged Foreign Stocks and Bonds," in Lee Thomas, ed., *The Currency Hedging Debate*. (IFR, 1990) pp. 41–50.

Rosenberg, M. R. "Why There Is No Free Lunch in Currency Hedging," in Lee Thomas, ed., *The Currency Hedging Debate* (IFR, 1990) pp. 83–93.

Sweeney, R. J. "Beating the Foreign Exchange Market." *Journal of Finance*, 41 (1986) pp. 163–182.

Sweeney, R. J. "Some New Filter Rule Tests: Methods and Results." *Journal of Financial and Quantitative Analysis*, 23 (1988) pp. 285–300.

Taylor, S. J. "Profitable Currency Futures Trading: A Comparison of Technical and Time-Series Trading Rules," in Lee Thomas, ed., *The Currency Hedging Debate*. (IFR, 1990) pp. 203–240.

Thomas, Lee, ed. *The Currency Hedging Debate*. (IFR, 1990).

8

Managing Currency Exposures in International Portfolios

Matthew J. Celebuski*
Joanne M. Hill
John J. Kilgannon
Derivative Products Research,
Paine Webber Incorporated
New York

Most investors have treated currency exposure and international investment decisions in a linked fashion. In fact, much of the favorable return to U.S. investors in foreign assets has come from their implicit holdings of foreign currencies in a world where the dollar was losing relative value. But the recent reversal in the value of the U.S. dollar, the strong 1988 performance of foreign equity markets in local-currency terms, and the availability of sophisticated hedging approaches raise some questions about the proper way to manage currency exposure.

This article discusses the current arguments for and against currency hedging in the contexts of risk minimization and forecasting. We also compare three different currency hedging techniques—*full hedging, minimum-variance hedging*, and *option-based hedging*—and compare the relative advantages of two forms of option-based hedging—the individual currency approach and the total currency portfolio approach. Finally, we look at two methods of creating a synthetic option on a portfolio currency exposure.

The Rationale for a Hedging Posture

If currencies are treated as a separate asset class, indicators of local market performance, including valuation and technical measures, can be analyzed

* Currently at Deutsche Bank, Frankfurt, Germany.

Source: *Financial Analysts Journal*, Association for Investment Management and Research, January-February, 1990.

independently of currency movements. In addition, a full hedge of currency exposure can reduce the volatility of foreign equity returns by 15 percent to 40 percent.[1] A decision *not* to hedge would seem to be warranted only if the returns from currency exposure could be forecast with some accuracy.

The problem with forecasting is that currency expectations are driven primarily by foreign interest rate differentials, which are already reflected in forward exchange rates. Thus currency positions cannot in general be expected to return anything in excess of the returns implied by forward exchange rates. Of course, there are investors who believe they have access to forecasts that are superior to the consensus forecasts implied by forward rates. Many investors, for example, feel that currency movements exhibit highly cyclical patterns, which make them amenable to forecasting with technical systems or time-series techniques. For those investors, full hedging may seem to be more an opportunity to forgo returns than to reduce risk.

Another case for stepping away from a fully hedged position lies in the definition of risk to the investor. Investment portfolios are presumably established to supply funds for the future consumption needs of the investor or, in the case of a pension fund, the beneficiaries. Consider an investment portfolio set up to provide for the purchase of a typical basket of consumption goods in the country in which the investor is located at some time in the future. This basket of goods will have some components—automobiles and electric appliances, for example—that are produced abroad either in whole or in part. Hedging currency exposure would decrease the portfolio's volatility, but it could actually introduce risk in terms of a mismatch between changes in the value of the hedged portfolio and changes in the present value of the basket of goods the investment position is expected to fund.

The appropriate approach to currency hedging therefore depends on the composition of the consumption basket the investment portfolio is expected to fund and on the correlation between potential investments and the value of that basket. In the extreme case in which all goods are provided by a local economy unaffected by global economic developments, the portfolio would be invested internationally for diversification purposes, but its currency exposures would be fully hedged. In the other extreme case, in which the investor purchases all goods and services externally, the tastes of the investor would dictate the portfolio's currency exposures, which would be managed separately from the underlying international investment portfolio.

In both cases, currency exposure is treated as a separate asset class. The difference lies in the proportion of the exposure that should be hedged. Fischer Black has developed a universal hedging formula, consistent with the equilibrium Capital Asset Pricing Model, which indicates that the proportion of currency exposure that should be hedged depends on the expected excess (above risk-free) return on the world market portfolio, the volatility of the world market portfolio, and exchange rate volatility averaged across all investors and all countries.[2] Based on recent historical data, Black's model indicates that the proportion hedged will range from 30 percent to 77 percent, depending on expected returns to the world market portfolio. Unfortunately, the solution from this model is too dependent on the measurement of world market returns and volatilities and does not deal effectively with the differences in the sensitivities of international investors' consumption baskets to currency movements.

A final complexity in deciding on an appropriate currency exposure is the link between security and currency returns. The prospects for the stocks of companies domiciled abroad are linked to the prospects for that country's currency. Most equity markets appreciate as their local currencies rise in value. Relative currency values are simultaneously determined with local interest rates, which in turn affect the prices of domestic financial assets. A U.S. investor's position in a Japanese stock, even if fully hedged, will be influenced by changes in the value of the yen to the extent that the Japanese firm is dependent on foreign markets or foreign components. Only if every firm completely hedges the currency exposure arising from its assets and liabilities will these effects be totally eliminated.[3]

What is an investor to do? The first thing is to realize that there is no general right or wrong answer to the question of how much should be hedged. The answer depends on the ability to forecast currency movements, the nature of the liabilities (consumption baskets) to be funded by the investment portfolio, and volatilities and correlations across currencies and between currencies and other foreign assets.

To some extent, it is possible to separate currency exposure management from the selection of international investments and to evaluate the performance of each task separately. With the use of futures, options, and forward markets, currency exposure can be controlled independently of the stock and bond exposure in a given country. Separate benchmarks, hedged and unhedged, can be used for performance attribution purposes. But the delineation of a policy for managing currency exposure requires careful thought and study, especially when investors have large components of international investments.

Currency Risk Management

The owner of a portfolio denominated in foreign currencies must consider two types of risk: (1) the contribution of each asset to the portfolio's risk in local currency terms and (2) the contribution of the currency risk associated with the asset to the portfolio's volatility. Of course, these two risk components are not unrelated. Changes in the value of an underlying asset will also change the amount of the portfolio's currency exposure. Thus, management of currency risk is a dynamic process. The size of the hedge must be adjusted as the amount of exposure to each currency changes with fluctuations in the values of the assets.

There are numerous instruments that could be used to manage currency exposure, including futures, forwards, and options. In practice, however, the vehicles for managing asset risk outside of the United States are limited. In many cases, investors choose from a relatively small set of currencies and derivatives deemed to be liquid enough for risk management purposes.[4] The sources of currency volatility in the portfolio will determine the makeup of the basket used to hedge currency exposure.

Three Techniques

Currency hedging techniques can be broken down into three distinct categories: (1) full hedging; (2) minimum-variance, or regression, hedging; and (3) downside, or option-based, hedging. Each technique has its own distinctive characteristics, and the selection of a particular technique depends upon one's investment objectives.

Full hedging attempts to strip away completely the currency risk component of the portfolio and to attain a risk-return profile identical to that of a local-currency investor. This is accomplished through the sale of forward contracts in an amount exactly equal to the foreign currency exposure.

Because currency exposure changes with changes in asset value, an investor using full hedging will become under- or over-hedged with a rise or fall in asset values. To maintain an ideal hedge, the forward contract position would have to be continuously rebalanced. In practice, however, frequent rebalancing becomes expensive, and investors accept a certain amount of deviation from the ideal full hedge.

Full hedging is relatively easy to implement. Furthermore, it allows the investor to isolate local market bets from currency bets. But a fully hedged portfolio does not benefit from favorable currency movements. Nor does a full hedge take into account correlations across currencies and between currencies and their associated assets.

Minimum-variance, or regression, *hedging* attempts to find an optimal hedge ratio based on relative volatilities of an historical correlations between assets and the currencies in which they are denominated. Whereas full hedging approaches the currency hedging problem without considering the impact of currency movements on asset prices, minimum-variance hedging combines the effects of asset risk and currency risk in deriving the proper hedge ratio.

If Japanese equities and the Japanese yen tend to be positively correlated, for example, then the optimal hedge ratio will be greater than one. That is, the portfolio will be hedged not only against changes in the yen, but also against changes in the value of the Japanese asset due to changes in the yen.

It is important to identify the fundamental difference between the objectives of full hedging and minimum-variance hedging. *Full hedging* attempts to neutralize the currency component of overall risk. *Minimum-variance* hedging attempts to minimize the overall risk of holding an asset denominated in a foreign currency. It provides a framework for managing both asset and currency risk. It is also relatively easy to implement, once an optimal hedge ratio has been found. However, *minimum-variance* hedging depends upon accurate forecasts of asset and currency volatilities and their correlations.

Downside or *option-based hedging* is essentially a form of insurance against *un*favorable currency movements. Many investors are attracted to option-based currency hedging strategies because they retain exposure to favorable currency movements. An increase in the value of the currencies in which the assets are denominated can yield sizable profits.

An option-based hedging strategy can be implemented in three ways: (1) the purchase of put options on individual currencies; (2) the purchase of put options on a basket of the currencies; or (3) the purchase of put options on the total base-currency value of the portfolio (in effect hedging the local asset value in concert with the currency fluctuations). The options may be purchased in the over-the-counter market or created synthetically. Options on individual currencies may also be available on exchanges.

The first two methods of option-based hedging, like full hedging, separate the currency hedging decision from the asset selection decision. The first method hedges each currency separately, while the second hedges a basket of currencies. The basket approach can result in a dramatic reduction in the cost of protection relative to hedging each currency position independently. The third method, like minimum-variance hedging, focuses on the total risk of the portfolio, incorporating the risks of both assets and currencies and their cross-correlations.

The advantages of each type of protection are fairly clear. The differences between them and the costs involved are not as straightforward.

Individual Options vs. Portfolio Options

To protect against adverse movements in currencies while allowing for positive gains from currency appreciation, the portfolio manager may want to hedge exposures with put options. Individual currency options are available on exchanges or in the over-the-counter market. An option on a portfolio of currencies would have to be tailored to the individual portfolio; it would not be available on an exchange and would have to be created synthetically or customized in the OTC option market.

The value of an option on an individual currency will depend on the volatility of the currency and its weight in the portfolio. The value of an option on a basket of currencies will depend on the currencies' volatilities and weights and also on the correlations between the currencies. Below we show how the expected payoffs of individual options differ from those of portfolio options.

Payoffs of Individual Currency Options

Figure 8.1 illustrates the increase or decrease in the dollar value of yen and sterling. The axes represent the hypothetical effects of sterling and yen changes on a $1,000 portfolio consisting of $500 positions in each currency. If the yen increases by 1 percent, a $500 portfolio in yen increases by $5. If sterling increases by 1 percent, $500 worth of sterling also increases by $5 (point **a**). If both decrease by 1 percent, the portfolio value in dollars falls $10 (point **b**).[5]

At-the-money options on the individual currencies pay off in three of the four quadrants of Figure 8.1. The yen pays off in quadrants I and II, while sterling pays off in quadrants II and III. Both options pay off in quadrant II, and neither pays in quadrant IV. In three-quarters of the possibilities, the individual currency options have a positive intrinsic value. Options on individual currencies can be used to protect against adverse movements in *any* currency.

Figure 8.2 illustrates the three-dimensional payoffs of the individual at-the-money yen and sterling options. In quadrant II, both options have

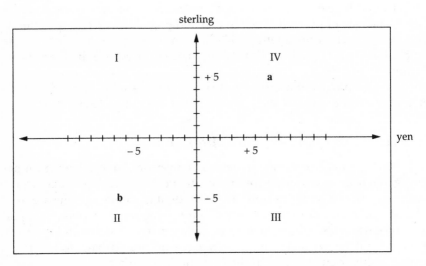

Figure 8.1. Currency Changes and Individual Currency Options

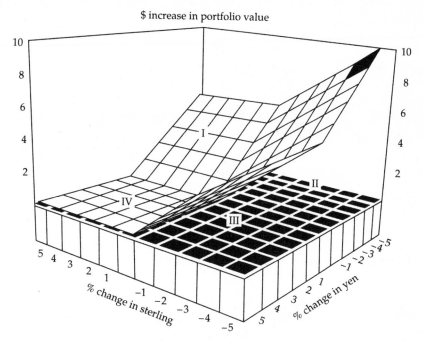

Figure 8.2. Payoffs of Options on Individual Currencies

positive intrinsic values. This is the payoff produced when portfolio currency risks are protected with individual currency options.

Payoffs of Portfolio Options

An option on the portfolio of currencies pays off when the dollar value of the portfolio falls below $1,000. If the yen decreases by $5 and sterling increases by $5, for example, the net portfolio change is zero. When the combined dollar value of the yen and sterling positions falls below $1,000, however, the portfolio option will pay off.

Figure 8.3 illustrates the payoff of a portfolio option in the case of a two-currency portfolio. The option pays off in half of quadrants I and III and all of quadrant II. No individual asset is insured; rather, the combination of assets is insured. Figure 8.4 shows the payoff of an option on the portfolio in three-dimensional space.

Figure 8.5 illustrates the excess, or net, payoff of individual currency options versus a portfolio option. Excess payoffs occur in quadrants I and III. Excess payoffs to the individual currency options occur when one currency position decreases in value more than the other currency increases.

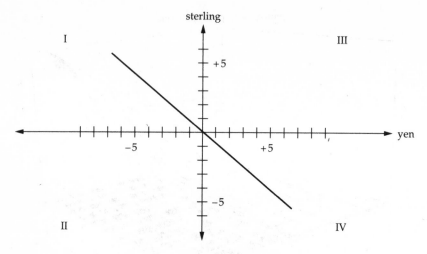

Figure 8.3. Currency Changes and Portfolio Option

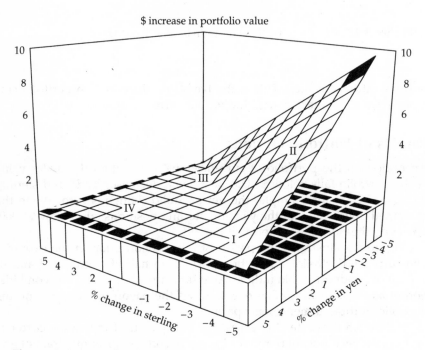

Figure 8.4. Payoffs of Portfolio Option

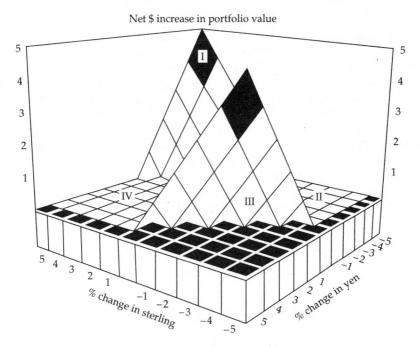

Figure 8.5.   Excess Payoffs to Individual Options vs. Portfolio Option

Replicating a Currency Portfolio Option

Replicating an option on a currency portfolio is similar to replicating an option on an index. The only difference is that currencies have no expected return—just standard deviation, or volatility. The relevant volatility for a U.S. investor is the currency portfolio's volatility in terms of U.S. dollars. This is a function of the individual currency volatilities, the correlations between currencies, and the currencies' weights in the portfolio. The relevant risk-free rate (for the U.S. investor) is the U.S. interest rate to expiration of the option, while the relevant foreign rate is a weighted average of foreign interest rates.

The most straightforward way to create a put option on a currency portfolio is to use the delta from an option model to create a short position in the currency portfolio. Delta gives the change in the currency portfolio for changes in the underlying currencies. Forwards or futures on each individual currency are then sold short according to the base-currency (U.S. dollar) value of the currency position multiplied by the currency portfolio's delta. For slight moves in the currencies, the resulting short portfolio will match the payoffs to a put option on the portfolio.

One could, alternatively, start by examining the individual currencies and determining the proportion of portfolio variance contributed by each in order to arrive at a hedge ratio for each currency. This approach has an advantage over the portfolio delta method. Suppose, for example, that a portfolio has equal exposures to three currencies, and that two of the currencies are perfectly negatively correlated. That is, when the dollar value of one currency increases, the dollar value of the other decreases by the same amount. Under the portfolio delta approach, an option on the currency portfolio would consist of short positions in all three currencies, even though the exposure would really only be to one currency. It would be more efficient to transact only in the currency that is not perfectly negatively correlated with another currency.

Consider a portfolio of three currencies named a, b, and c. The dollar volatility of the portfolio is a function of the volatility of each currency, the currencies' weights in the portfolio and their correlations. Assume each currency has a volatility, σ, of 0.09, so that $\sigma_a = \sigma_b = \sigma_c = 0.09$. Each currency has the same weight, w, in the portfolio, so that $w_a = w_b = w_c = \frac{1}{3}$. Finally, the correlation between currency a and currency b, ρ_{ab} is -1, while currency c is completely uncorrelated with currencies a and b, so $\rho_{ac} = \rho_{bc} = 0$.

The variance of any currency j within a portfolio of n assets is:

$$\sigma_j^2 w_j^2 + \sum_{\substack{i=1 \\ i \neq j}}^{n} \sigma_j \sigma_i w_i w_j \rho_{ij}$$

The weighted sum of all the variances equals the variance of the portfolio. In our abc portfolio, currencies a and b have zero effect on the variance of the portfolio because they are perfectly negatively correlated with each other and because they have the same weight. The only currency that affects the variance of the portfolio is currency c. The variance of currency c in the portfolio is 0.0009, and this is also the total variance of the three-currency portfolio:

$$\text{portfolio variance} = \sum_{i=1}^{n} \sigma_i^2 w_i^2$$

$$+ \sum_{j=1}^{n} \sum_{\substack{i=1 \\ i \neq j}}^{n} \sigma_j \sigma_i w_i w_j \rho_{ij}$$

$$\sigma^2 = 0.0027 - 0.0018 = 0.0009.$$

An option on the total portfolio can be created by trading in those currencies that affect the portfolio, by the amount they affect the portfolio. For the abc portfolio, currencies a and b do not affect the portfolio at all, because their movements relative to one another are offsetting. Currency c does affect the volatility of the portfolio and should therefore be hedged.

The volatility used in the option price is the variance explained by currency c.

In this application, the strike price of each individual currency option is a function of (1) the portfolio value in the base currency; (2) the forward portfolio value in the base currency; and (3) the forward exchange rate between each currency and the base currency. The forward portfolio value is determined as follows:

$$\text{Forward portfolio value} = \text{Current portfolio value}$$

$$\times \sum_{i=1}^{n} (w_i) \frac{\text{Forward exchange rate}_i}{\text{Spot exchange rate}_i}$$

Suppose the forward exchange rate for each currency is such that the forward portfolio value is 95 percent of its current value. In that case, the strike price for the total portfolio, in order to be at the money, would have to be 5.26 percent above the portfolio's forward value (100/95). The strike price for each currency should therefore also be 5.26 percent above the forward exchange rate of that currency:

$$\text{Currency strike price} = \frac{\text{Portfolio strike value}}{\text{Forward portfolio value}} \times \frac{\text{Currency forward}}{\text{Exchange rate}}$$

The strike price of the option on each currency will thus change as the currency's forward exchange rate changes. In a dynamic hedging program, then, forward or futures positions must be adjusted to different strike prices for each option.

Option-based hedging approaches conducted at the portfolio level are sensitive to the variances and covariances of the currencies within the portfolio. As the composition of the portfolio changes, adjustments must be made to the individual hedge ratios. Furthermore, the reliability of a portfolio approach depends on the ability to forecast currency correlations. Underestimating correlations results in underhedging of the portfolio, which exposes the portfolio to a greater degree of currency risk. Overestimating correlations can increase the cost of hedging beyond the necessary level.

Notes

1. See A. F. Perold and E. Shulman, "The Free Lunch in Currency Hedging: Implications for Investment Policy and Performance Standards," *Financial Analysts*

Journal (May/June 1988), and R. A. Arnott and R. D. Henriksson, "A Disciplined Approach to Global Asset Allocation," *Financial Analysts Journal* (March/April 1989).

2. F. Black, "Universal Hedging: Optimizing Currency Risk and Reward in International Equity Portfolios," *Financial Analysts Journal* (July/August 1989).

3. For a discussion of the relations between currencies, interest rates, and asset returns, see B. Solnik, "Optimal Currency Hedge Ratios: The Influence of the Interest Rate Differential," (Paper presented at Pacific Basin Finance Conference, Taipei, Taiwan, March 1989).

4. We do not address issues associated with the selection of this optimal mix.

5. The perpendicular positioning of the axes is consistent with zero correlation between the two currencies.

Universal Hedging: Optimizing Currency Risk and Reward in International Equity Portfolios

Fischer Black
Goldman, Sachs & Co.
New York

In a world where everyone can hedge against changes in the value of real exchange rates (the relative values of domestic and foreign goods), and where no barriers limit international investment, there is a universal constant that gives the optimal hedge ratio—the fraction of your foreign investments you should hedge. The formula for this optimal hedge ratio depends on just three inputs:

- the expected return on the world market portfolio
- the volatility of the world market portfolio
- average exchange rate volatility

The formula in turn yields three rules:

- Hedge your foreign equities.
- Hedge equities equally for all countries.
- Don't hedge 100 percent of your foreign equities.

This formula applies to every investor who holds foreign securities. It applies equally to a U.S. investor holding Japanese assets, a Japanese investor holding British assets, and a British investor holding U.S. assets. That's why we call this method *universal hedging*.

Source: *Financial Analysts Journal*, Association for Investment Management and Research, July-August, 1989.

Why Hedge at All?

You may consider hedging a "zero-sum game." After all, if U.S. investors hedge their Japanese investments, and Japanese investors hedge their U.S. investments, then when U.S. investors gain on their hedges, Japanese investors lose, and vice versa. But even though one side always wins and the other side always loses, hedging *reduces risk* for both sides.

More often than not, when performance is measured in local currency, U.S. investors gain on their hedging when their portfolios do badly, and Japanese investors gain on their hedging when their portfolios do badly. The gains from hedging are similar to the gains from international diversification. Because it reduces risk for both sides, currency hedging provides a "free lunch."

Why Not Hedge *All*?

If investors in all countries can reduce risk through currency hedging, why shouldn't they hedge 100 percent of their foreign investments? Why hedge less?

The answer contains our most interesting finding. When they have different consumption baskets, investors in different countries can all add to their expected returns by taking some currency risk in their portfolios.

To see how this can be, imagine an extremely simple case where the exchange rate between two countries is now 1:1 but will change over the next year to either 2:1 or 1:2 with equal probability. Call the consumption goods in one country *apples* and those in the other *oranges.*

Imagine that the world market portfolio contains equal amounts of apples and oranges. To the apple consumer, holding oranges is risky. To the orange consumer, holding apples is risky.

The apple consumer could choose to hold only apples, and thus bear no risk at all. Likewise, the orange consumer could decide to hold only oranges. But, surprisingly enough, each will gain in expected return by trading an apple and an orange. At year-end, an orange will be worth either two apples or 0.5 apples. Its expected value is 1.25 apples. Similarly, an apple will have an expected value of 1.25 oranges. So each consumer will gain from the swap.

This isn't a mathematical trick. In fact, it's sometimes called *Siegel's paradox.*[1] It's real, and it means that investors generally want to hedge less than 100 percent of their foreign investments.

To understand Siegel's paradox, consider historical exchange rate data for Deutsche marks and U.S. dollars. Table 9.1 shows the quarterly percentage changes in the exchange rates and their averages. Note that, in each period and for the average, the gain for one currency exceeds the loss for the other currency.

Table 9.1. Siegel's Paradox

Quarter	Start-of-Quarter Exchange Rates		Percentage Changes in Exchange Rates	
	mark / dollar	dollar / mark	mark / dollar	dollar / mark
1Q84	2.75	.362	−5.58	5.90
2Q84	2.60	.384	7.18	−6.69
3Q84	2.79	.358	9.64	−8.79
4Q84	3.06	.326	3.66	−3.52
1Q85	3.17	.315	−1.83	1.84
2Q85	3.11	.321	−2.25	2.30
3Q85	3.04	.328	−13.04	15.01
4Q85	2.64	.377	−7.59	8.21
1Q86	2.44	.408	−4.46	4.67
2Q86	2.33	.427	−6.80	7.29
3Q86	2.17	.459	−7.16	7.73
4Q86	2.02	.494	−5.19	5.46
1Q87	1.91	.521	−5.11	5.41
2Q87	1.81	.549	0.49	−0.49
3Q87	1.82	.547	1.09	−1.08
4Q87	1.84	.541	−14.00	16.28
1Q88	1.58	.629	4.29	−4.12
2Q88	1.65	.603	9.83	−8.95
3Q88	1.82	.549	2.27	−2.22
4Q88	1.86	.537	−4.88	5.12
Average			−1.97	2.47

Why *Universal* Hedging?

Why is the optimal hedge ratio identical for investors everywhere? The answer lies in how exchange rates reach equilibrium.

Models of international equilibrium generally assume that the typical investor in any country consumes a single good or basket of goods.[2] The investor wants to maximize expected return and minimize risk, measuring expected return and risk in terms of his own consumption good.

Given the risk-reducing and return-enhancing properties of international diversification, an investor will want to hold an internationally diversified portfolio of equities. Given no barriers to international investment, every investor will hold a share of a fully diversified portfolio of world equities. And, in the absence of government participation, some investor must lend when another investor borrows, and some investor must go long a currency when another goes short.

Whatever the given levels of market volatility, exchange rate volatilities, correlations between exchange rates, and correlations between exchange rates and stock, in equilibrium prices will adjust until everyone is willing to hold all stocks and until someone is willing to take the other side of every exchange rate contract.

Suppose, for example, that we know the return on a portfolio in one currency, and we know the change in the exchange rate between that currency and another currency. We can thus derive the portfolio return in the other currency. We can write down an equation relating expected returns and exchange rate volatilities from the points of view of two investors in the two different currencies.

Suppose that Investor A finds a high correlation between the returns on his stocks in another country and the corresponding exchange rate change. He will probably want to hedge in order to reduce his portfolio risk. But suppose an Investor B in that other country would increase his own portfolio's risk by taking the other side of A's hedge. Investor A may be so anxious to hedge that he will be willing to pay B to take the other side. As a result, the exchange rate contract will be priced so that the hedge reduces A's expected return but increases B's.

In equilibrium, both investors will hedge. Investor A will hedge to reduce risk, while Investor B will hedge to increase expected return. But they will hedge equally, in proportion to their stock holdings.

The Universal Hedging Formula

By extending the above analysis to investors in all possible pairs of countries, we find that the proportion that each investor wants to hedge depends on three averages: the average across countries of the expected excess return on the world market portfolio; the average across countries of the volatility of the world market portfolio; and the average across all pairs of countries of exchange rate volatility. These averages become inputs for the universal hedging formula:[3]

$$\frac{\mu_m - \sigma_m^2}{\mu_m - \frac{1}{2}\sigma_e^2}$$

where μ_m = the average across investors of the expected excess return (return above each investor's riskless rate) on the world market portfolio (which contains stocks from all major countries in proportion to each country's market value)

σ_m = the average across investors of the volatility of the world market portfolio (where variances, rather than standard deviation, are averaged)

σ_e = the average exchange rate volatility (averaged variances) across all pairs of countries

Neither expected changes in exchange rates nor correlations between exchange rate changes and stock returns or other exchange rate changes affect optimal hedge ratios. In equilibrium, the expected changes and the correlations cancel one another, so they do not appear in the universal hedging formula.

In the same way, the Black-Scholes option formula includes neither the underlying stock's expected return nor its beta. In equilibrium, they cancel one another.

The Capital Asset Pricing Model is similar. The optimal portfolio for any one investor could depend on the expected returns and volatilities of all available assets. In equilibrium, however, the optimal portfolio for any investor is a mix of the market portfolio with borrowing or lending. The expected returns and volatilities cancel one another (except for the market as a whole), so they do not affect the investor's optimal holdings.

Inputs for the Formula

Historical data and judgment are used to create inputs for the formula. Tables 9.2 through 9.8 give some historical data that may be helpful.

Table 9.2 lists weights that can be applied to different countries in estimating the three averages. Japan, the United States, and the United Kingdom carry the most weight.

Tables 9.3 to 9.5 contain statistics for 1986–1988, and Tables 9.6 to 9.8 contain statistics for 1981–1985. These subperiods give an indication of how statistics change from one sample period to another.

When averaging exchange rate volatilities over pairs of countries, we include the volatility of a country's exchange rate with itself. Those volatilities are always zero; they run diagonally through Tables 9.3 and 9.6. This means that the average exchange rate volatilities shown in Tables 9.5 and 9.8 are lower than the averages of the positive numbers in Tables 9.3 and 9.6.

The excess returns in Tables 9.4 and 9.7 are averages for the world market return in each country's currency, minus that country's riskless interest rate. The average excess returns differ between countries because of differences in exchange rate movements.

The excess returns are *not* national market returns. For example, the Japanese market did better than the U.S. market in 1987, but the world market portfolio did better relative to interest rates in the U.S. than in Japan.

Because exchange rate volatility contributes to average stock market volatility, $\sigma_m{}^2$ should be greater than $\frac{1}{2}\sigma_e{}^2$. Exchange rate volatility also

Table 9.2. Capitalizations and Capitalization Weights

	Domestic Companies Listed on the Major Stock Exchange as of 31 December 1987*		Companies in the FT-Actuaries World Indices™ as of 31 December 1987[†]	
	Capitalization (U.S. $ billions)	Weight (%)	Capitalization (U.S. $ billions)	Weight (%)
Japan	2700.0	40.00	2100.0	41.00
U.S.	2100.0	31.00	1800.0	34.00
U.K.	680.0	10.00	560.0	11.00
Canada	220.0	3.20	110.0	2.10
Germany	220.0	3.20	160.0	3.10
France	160.0	2.30	100.0	2.00
Australia	140.0	2.00	64.0	1.20
Switzerland	130.0	1.90	58.0	1.10
Italy	120.0	1.80	85.0	1.60
Netherlands	87.0	1.30	66.0	1.30
Sweden	70.0	1.00	17.0	0.32
Hong Kong	54.0	0.79	38.0	0.72
Belgium	42.0	0.61	29.0	0.56
Denmark	20.0	0.30	11.0	0.20
Singapore	18.0	0.26	6.2	0.12
New Zealand	16.0	0.23	7.4	0.14
Norway	12.0	0.17	2.2	0.042
Austria	7.9	0.12	3.9	0.074
Total	6800.0	100.00	5300.0	100.00

*From "Activities and Statistics: 1987 Report" by Federation Internationale des Bourses de Valeurs (page 16).

[†]The FT-Actuaries World Indices™ are jointly compiled by The Financial Times Limited, Goldman, Sachs & Co., and County NatWest/Wood Mackenzie in conjunction with the Institute of Actuaries and the Faculty of Actuaries. This table excludes Finland, Ireland, Malaysia, Mexico, South Africa, and Spain.

contributes to the average return on the world market, so μ_m should be greater than $\frac{1}{2}\sigma_e^2$, too.

An Example

Tables 9.5 and 9.8 suggest one way to create inputs for the formula. The average excess return on the world market was 3 percent in the earlier period and 11 percent in the later period. We may thus estimate a future excess return of 8 percent.

The volatility of the world market was higher in the later period, but that included the crash, so we may want to use the 15 percent volatility from the earlier period. The average exchange rate volatility of 10 percent in the earlier period may also be a better estimate of the future than the more recent 8 percent.

This reasoning leads to the following possible values for the inputs:

$$\mu_m = 8\%$$
$$\sigma_m = 15\%$$
$$\sigma_i = 10\%$$

Given these inputs, the formula tells us that 77 percent of holdings should be hedged:

$$\frac{0.08 - 0.15^2}{0.08 - \frac{1}{2}(0.10)^2} = 0.77$$

To compare the results of using different inputs, we can use the historical averages from both the earlier and later periods:

$$\mu_m = 3\% \text{ or } 11\%$$
$$\sigma_m = 15\% \text{ or } 18\%$$
$$\sigma_e = 10\% \text{ or } 8\%$$

With the historical averages from the earlier period as inputs, the fraction hedged comes to 30 percent:

$$\frac{0.03 - 0.15^2}{0.03 - \frac{1}{2}(0.10)^2} = 0.30$$

Using averages from the later period gives a fraction hedged of 73 percent:

$$\frac{0.11 - 0.18^2}{0.11 - \frac{1}{2}(0.08)^2} = 0.73$$

Generally, straight historical averages vary too much to serve as useful inputs for the formula. Estimates of long-run average values are better.

Optimization

The universal hedging formula assumes that you put into the formula your opinions about what investors around the world expect for the future. If your own views on stock markets and on exchange rates are the same as those you attribute to investors generally, then you can use the formula as it is.

Table 9.3.   Exchange Rate Volatilities, 1986–1988

	Japan	U.S.	U.K.	Canada	Germany	France	Australia	Switzer-land
Japan	0	11	9	12	7	7	14	7
U.S.	11	0	11	5	11	11	11	12
U.K.	9	10	0	11	8	8	14	9
Canada	12	5	11	0	12	11	12	13
Germany	7	11	8	12	0	3	15	4
France	7	11	8	11	2	0	14	5
Australia	14	11	14	12	14	14	0	15
Switzerland	7	12	9	13	4	5	15	0
Italy	8	10	8	11	3	3	14	5
Netherlands	7	11	8	11	2	3	14	5
Sweden	7	8	7	9	5	5	12	7
Hong Kong	11	4	11	6	11	11	11	12
Belgium	9	11	9	12	6	6	14	8
Denmark	8	11	8	11	4	4	14	6
Singapore	10	6	10	8	10	10	12	11
New Zealand	17	15	16	15	17	17	14	18
Norway	9	10	9	10	7	7	13	9
Austria	8	11	9	12	5	5	15	7

Source: The FT-Actuaries World Indices^{TM} database.

If your views differ from those of the consensus, you may want to incorporate them using optimization methods. Starting with expected returns and covariances for the stock markets and exchange rates, you would find the mix that maximizes the expected portfolio return for a given level of volatility.

The optimization approach is fully consistent with the universal hedging approach. When you put the expectations of investors around the world into the optimization approach, you will find that the optimal currency hedge for any foreign investment will be given by the universal hedging formula.

A Note on the Currency Hedge

The formula assumes that investors hedge real (inflation-adjusted) exchange rate changes, not changes due to inflation differentials between countries. To the extent that currency changes are the result of changes in inflation, the formula is only an approximation.

Italy	Nether-lands	Sweden	Hong Kong	Belgium	Denmark	Singa-pore	New Zealand	Norway	Austria
8	7	7	11	9	8	10	17	9	8
10	11	8	4	11	11	6	15	10	11
8	8	7	11	9	8	10	16	9	9
11	11	9	6	12	11	8	15	10	12
3	2	5	11	6	4	10	17	8	5
3	3	5	11	6	4	10	17	7	5
14	14	12	11	14	14	12	14	14	14
5	5	7	12	8	6	11	18	9	7
0	3	5	11	6	4	10	17	7	5
3	0	5	11	6	4	10	17	7	5
5	5	0	8	6	4	8	16	6	5
10	11	8	0	11	11	5	14	10	11
6	6	6	11	0	6	10	17	8	6
4	4	4	11	6	0	10	17	7	5
10	10	8	5	10	10	0	15	10	10
17	17	15	14	17	17	15	0	16	17
7	7	5	10	8	7	10	16	0	7
5	5	5	11	6	5	10	17	8	0

In other words, currency hedging only approximates real exchange rate hedging. But most changes in currency values, at least in countries with moderate inflation rates, are due to changes in real exchange rates. Thus currency hedging will normally be a good approximation to real exchange rate hedging.

In constructing a hedging basket, it may be desirable to substitute highly liquid currencies for less liquid ones. This can best be done by building a currency hedge basket that closely tracks the basket based on the universal hedging formula. When there is tracking error, the fraction hedged should be reduced.

In practice, then, hedging may be done using a basket of a few of the most liquid currencies and using a fraction somewhat smaller than the one the formula suggests.

The formula also assumes that the real exchange rate between two countries is defined as the relative value of domestic and foreign goods. Domestic goods are those consumed at home, not those produced at home. Imports thus count as domestic goods. Foreign goods are those goods consumed abroad, not those produced abroad.

Table 9.4.   World Market Excess Returns and Return
Volatilities in Different Currencies, 1986–1988

Currency	Excess Return			Return Volatility		
	1986	1987	1988	1986	1987	1988
Japan	8	−12	21	14	26	15
U.S.	29	12	14	13	25	11
U.K.	23	−14	16	14	26	15
Canada	26	4	5	14	24	11
Germany	8	−5	30	15	27	14
France	11	−7	27	14	26	14
Australia	23	−2	−6	19	25	14
Switzerland	8	−8	36	15	27	15
Italy	2	−6	23	15	27	14
Netherlands	8	−7	30	15	27	14
Sweden	16	−6	19	13	25	13
Hong Kong	30	13	17	13	25	11
Belgium	7	−8	28	15	27	14
Denmark	8	−10	26	15	27	14
Singapore	36	6	16	12	25	12
New Zealand	15	−22	13	20	29	14
Norway	19	−11	15	14	26	12
Austria	7	−6	30	15	27	14

Source: The FT-Actuaries World Indices^{TM} database.

Table 9.5.   World Average Values, 1986–1988

	Excess Return	Return Volatility	Exchange Rate Volatility
1986	17	14	9
1987	−3	26	8
1988	18	13	8
1986–88	11	18	8

Table 9.6. Exchange Rate Volatilities, 1981–1985

	Japan	U.S.	U.K.	Canada	Germany	France	Australia	Switzerland	Italy	Netherlands
Japan	0	12	13	11	10	10	12	11	9	10
U.S.	11	0	12	4	12	13	11	13	10	12
U.K.	12	13	0	12	10	11	14	12	11	10
Canada	11	4	11	0	11	12	10	12	10	11
Germany	10	12	10	12	0	5	13	7	5	2
France	10	13	11	12	4	0	12	8	5	5
Australia	12	10	13	10	12	12	0	13	11	12
Switzerland	11	14	12	13	7	8	14	0	8	7
Italy	9	10	11	10	5	5	12	8	0	5
Netherlands	10	12	10	11	2	5	12	7	5	0

Source: The FT-Actuaries World Indices™ database.

Table 9.7. World Market Excess Returns and Return Volatilities in Different Currencies, 1981–1985

Currency	Excess Return	Return Volatility
Japan	3	17
U.S.	−1	13
U.K.	10	16
Canada	2	13
Germany	8	15
France	7	16
Australia	7	18
Switzerland	9	16
Italy	4	15
Netherlands	8	15

Table 9.8. World Average Values, 1981–1985

Excess Return	Return Volatility	Exchange Rate Volatility
3	15	10

Currency changes should be examined to see if they track real exchange rate changes so defined. When the currency rate changes between two countries differ from *real* exchange rate changes, the hedging done in that currency can be modified or omitted.

If everyone in the world eventually consumes the same mix of goods and services, and prices of goods and services are the same everywhere, hedging will no longer help.

Applying the Formula to Other Types of Portfolios

How can you use the formula if you don't have a fully diversified international portfolio, or if foreign equities are only a small part of your portfolio? The answer depends on why you have a small amount in foreign equities. You may be:

(1) wary of foreign exchange risk
(2) wary of foreign equity risk, even if it is optimally hedged
(3) wary of foreign exchange risk and foreign equity risk, in equal measure

In case (1), you should hedge more than the formula suggests. In case (2), you should hedge less than the formula suggests. In case (3), it probably makes sense to apply the formula as given to the foreign equities you hold.

If the barriers to foreign investment are small, you should gain by investing more abroad and by continuing to hedge the optimal fraction of your foreign equities.

Foreign Bonds

What if your portfolio contains foreign bonds as well as foreign stocks?

The approach that led to the universal hedging formula for stocks suggests 100 percent hedging for foreign bonds. A portfolio of foreign bonds that is hedged with short-term forward contracts still has foreign interest rate risk, as well as the expected return that goes with that risk.

Any foreign bonds you hold unhedged can be counted as part of your total exposure to foreign currency risk. The less you hedge your foreign bonds, the more you will want to hedge your foreign stocks.

At times, you may want to hold unhedged foreign bonds because you believe that the exchange rate will move in your favor in the near future. In the long run, though, you will want to hedge your foreign bonds even more than your foreign equities.

Conclusion

The formula's results may be thought of as a base case. When you have special views on the prospects for a certain currency, or when a currency's forward market is illiquid, you can adjust the hedging positions that the formula suggests.

When you deviate from the formula because you think a particular currency is overpriced or underpriced, you can plan to bring your position back to normal as the currency returns to normal. You may even want to use options, so that your effective hedge changes automatically as the currency price changes.

Notes

1. J. J. Siegel, "Risk, Interest Rates, and the Forward Exchange," *Quarterly Journal of Economics* (May 1972).
2. See, for example, B. H. Solnik, "An Equilibrium Model of the International Capital Market," *Journal of Economic Theory* (August 1974); F. L. A. Grauer, R. H. Litzenberger, and R. E. Stehle, "Sharing Rules and Equilibrium in an International Capital Market Under Uncertainty," *Journal of Financial Economics* (June

1976); P. Sercu, "A Generalization of the International Asset Pricing Model," *Revue de l'Association Francaise de Finance* (June 1980); and R. Stulz, "A Model of International Asset Pricing," *Journal of Financial Economics* (December 1981).
3. The derivation of the formula is described in detail in F. Black, "Equilibrium Exchange Rate Hedging," National Bureau of Economic Research Working Paper No. 2947 (April 1989).

PART

IV

FIXED-INCOME INVESTING

Implementing the Global Fixed-Income Process— Strategic Mix, Management Styles, and Performance Measurement*

Michael R. Rosenberg
*International Fixed-Income
Research,
Merrill Lynch
New York*

The greatest challenge in international bond portfolio management is to know how to exploit opportunities when they arise. The real gains from international bond management have come from active management, not from passive management. The international bond manager must constantly look for ways to seize the opportunities and avoid the pitfalls. The trick is to seize the opportunities, avoid the pitfalls, but still get home by 6 o'clock—something that is often hard to do.

Opportunities and Risks in Nondollar Fixed-Income Investment

The kinds of opportunities available in the international bond markets are illustrated in Figure 10.1. This figure shows the average difference in performance between the best- and worst-performance markets from 1975 to 1985. On average, there is a 35 percentage point difference between the

* Source: From *International Bonds and Currencies,* by permission of the Association for Investment Management and Research, Charlottesville, Virginia, and the author, 1985, pp. 66–71.

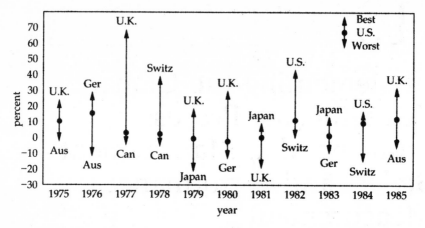

Figure 10.1. Opportunities from Active Management of Global Bond Portfolios—Total Returns (Percent) in U.S. Dollar Terms (Source: Merrill Lynch Capital Markets)

best and worst performing markets per year, so the trick is to overweight the strong performing markets and underweight the weak performing markets year by year. Of course, that is easier said than done! In this figure the heavy dot is the U.S. bond market performance. On average, the spread between the U.S. performance and the best-performing market is a full 12 percentage points. So if a U.S. investor committed funds to nondollar bonds on a piecemeal basis, accurately picking the best-performing market could significantly increase return over that of a pure U.S. portfolio.

The problem in international investing, and the greatest source of risk, is exchange rate fluctuation. Currency changes can be very beneficial in terms of providing significant incremental return, but it also can hurt as well, as shown in Figure 10.2. The solid black bar is the local currency return, the open bar is the contribution that currency changes make to total return, and the solid line is the total return performance. In the 1970s, strong local market returns and strong currency gains gave large total returns in U.S. dollar terms from fixed-income investments abroad. But in the 1980s, in spite of very decent gains in local market returns in the foreign bond markets, currencies made a negative contribution and kept returns low. Only in 1985, for the first time in six years, has currency given a positive contribution.

The standard deviation of returns in the U.S. and foreign bond markets is shown in Table 10.1. While international investment opportunities are frequently emphasized, there are great risks as well. A U.S. bond portfolio can be quite volatile; the annualized standard deviation of monthly returns averaged around 9.5 percent in the U.S. Treasury market during the 1973–1984 period. The foreign bond markets' standard deviation of returns in local currency terms was only 4.8 percent

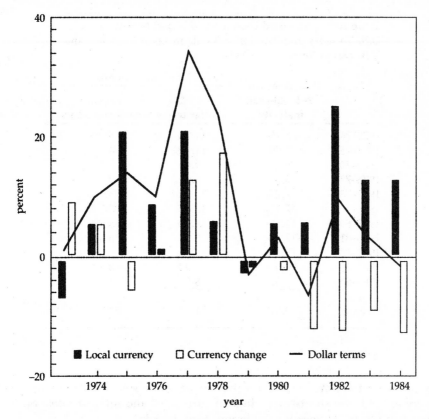

Figure 10.2. Foreign Bond Market Performance: Contribution of Local Currency Return and Currency Changes to Total Return in Dollar Terms (Source: Merrill Lynch Capital Markets)

in the last 10 years, implying half as much volatility as the U.S. bond market. But when translated into dollar terms—because that is what a dollar-based investor has to do—foreign bonds are actually quite a bit more volatile than a U.S. Treasury portfolio. In fact, there are going to be many times when management finds itself caught out on a limb, and then the issue really is whether or not it has the staying power to absorb hits when they occur or recognizes the right time to bail out.

Implementing the Global Fixed-Income Investment Process

Getting Started: Setting Up an International Bond Portfolio

Setting up an international bond portfolio has several steps. First, determine the financial objectives. Are they to maximize return, to minimize risk, or to reach some kind of middle ground, trying to maximize returns subject to some kind of predetermined risk constraint? The second step is

Table 10.1.   **Standard Deviation of Monthly Returns on U.S. Treasury and Nondollar Bonds in Local Currency and U.S. Dollar Terms, 1973–1984**

	U.S. Treasuries 7- to 10-year maturity	Non-dollar bonds	
		% Dollar terms	Local currency terms
1973–74	5.7%	14.7%	5.0%
1974–75	7.0%	11.1%	4.8%
1975–76	5.4%	9.4%	3.3%
1976–77	4.2%	6.0%	3.1%
1977–78	3.2%	11.8%	3.3%
1978–79	7.1%	13.6%	3.2%
1979–80	14.4%	14.0%	5.9%
1980–81	17.3%	15.9%	6.4%
1981–82	13.9%	13.1%	5.4%
1982–83	9.0%	9.3%	3.7%
1983–84	8.5%	8.0%	2.9%
Average	9.5%	11.5%	4.8%

to decide on the time horizon for the investment decisions. Are you going to try to catch the short-run swings in currencies and interest rates, or are you going to try to capture the longer-term trends?

Once these basic objectives are determined, the next consideration is what kind of instruments and currency exposure to commit to the portfolio. This should be done by setting up a delegation-of-authority list. The principal issue is identifying the credits that are going to be allowed in the portfolio. A highly risk-averse fund will only buy government bonds or supranational and sovereign issues. A less risk-averse fund may consider single A, double A, and triple A corporates, while more aggressive funds may not have any constraints on the kinds of bonds held in the portfolio.

Selecting a global custodian is extremely important when buying and selling government securities abroad. The custodian will settle and hold these securities. Without a good custodian, you will find you are spending considerable time trying to locate where your money and your securities are and in handling failed trades.

Finally, it is very important to establish proper portfolio management guidelines. Table 10.2 shows the kinds of portfolio management guidelines one would want to implement for a hypothetical global bond fund for the purposes of providing ample latitude for active management and at the same time insuring adequate diversification. In such guidelines

Table 10.2. Merrill Lynch International Fixed-Income Research Guidelines for Structuring a Global Bond Portfolio

Currency bloc	Minimum position	Fundamentally ←bearish→	Normal	Fundamentally ←bullish→	Maximum position
U.S. dollar*	25%		50%		75%
German mark**	10		20		60
Japanese yen	10		20		60
British pound	5		10		55

*Includes Canadian dollar market.
**Includes Dutch guilder, Swiss franc, French franc, and ECU markets.

it is important to assign minimum, normal, and maximum positions to any single currency bloc. For instance, the holder of a truly global fund might not want to move lower than 25 percent in dollars, and at the same time might not want to be more than 75 percent in dollars to insure some diversification in the other markets. The 25 percent to 75 percent spread gives ample latitude to overweight the dollar or underweight the dollar depending on the outlook for currencies and interest rates.

Total Return Analysis

International bond portfolio management lends itself much more to a top-down than a bottom-up approach. Given your assessment of currencies and interest rates, it is necessary to establish a ranking according to the total return outlook. Calculating the total returns in local currency terms and translating them into a single base currency such as the U.S. dollar is fairly straightforward. This is illustrated in Table 10.3. The total return— one plus the dollar return—is equal to one plus the local currency return times one plus the currency gain or loss. However, people often get this equation wrong. The reason is evident in the second equation, which puts it more simply. The dollar return is equal to a local currency term plus the currency return plus a cross-product term. The tendency is to ignore that cross-product term. Sometimes it is small enough to ignore, but at other times it can be quite large. For example, if a currency is expected to go up 5 percent and the local market will return 10 percent, some people conclude that there will be a 15 percent total return in dollar terms in that particular market. Actually, the total return turns out to be 15.5 percent. The greater the gain in the currency or the greater the return in the local market, the greater the impact that cross-product term has on a calculation of the total return.

Table 10.3. Total Return Analysis

- Top/down assessment of total return outcomes.
- Ranking markets according to projected total return performance.

$$(1 + R\$) = (1 + LC) \times (1 + \$)$$

or

$$R\$ = LC + \$ + (\$ \times LC)$$

where

$R\$ =$ total return in dollar terms

$LC =$ local currency return

$\$ =$ currency gain or loss

Example

$$LC = 10\%$$
$$\$ = 5\%$$
$$R\$ = 15.5\%$$

$$(1 + R\$) = (1 + LC) \times (1 + \$)$$
$$(1 + R\$) = (1 + .10) \times (1.05)$$
$$(1 + R\$) = 1.155$$
$$R\$ = 15.5\%$$

Global Bond Portfolio Strategy

In trying to assess the outlook for currencies and interest rates in all of the markets, it is necessary to establish a ranking process. First, total returns must be calculated along the yield curve in all the relevant markets. In the example in Figure 10.3, the longer-term market is expected to outperform the shorter end of the market in local currency terms. Assuming also that the currency is going to appreciate, in dollar terms the total return curve is almost, but not quite, a parallel shift upward of the local currency return curve. Such calculations of returns in dollars along the yield curve must be done for all the different markets before beginning a ranking process.

Figure 10.4 illustrates a simple exercise in ranking markets. Assume that foreign bond market No. 1 is expected to have a strong currency, while foreign bond market No. 2 is expected to have a weak currency. Interest rates in all markets are expected to fall, and therefore it is a very simple matter to overweight foreign bond market No. 1, underweight foreign bond market No. 2, and normally weight the U.S. bond market. But it is often not this simple and straightforward.

Suppose that in the case of foreign bond market No. 1, the underlying currency is expected to appreciate and interest rates are expected to rise. In

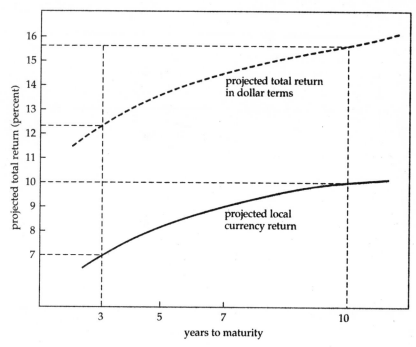

Figure 10.3. Calculating Total Returns on Foreign Bonds (Source: Merrill Lynch Capital Markets)

such a case, the short end of foreign bond market No. 1 will outperform the long end. In foreign bond market No. 2, assume the currency is expected to weaken but interest rates are falling, so the long end of foreign bond market No. 2 is outperforming the short end. As shown in **Figure 10.5, this** gives a situation where even though there is a weak currency in foreign bond market No. 2, the long end is going to do quite well because of a strong local market. The opposite case occurs in foreign bond market No. 1, as the impact of a strong currency is partially offset by the poorly performing market, making the returns highest at the short end. So, a portfolio manager would want to overweight the short end of foreign bond market No. 1, overweight the long end of foreign bond market No. 2, and underweight the U.S. market.

Judgements about performance in the different markets must be implemented within the context of the parameters set for managing portfolio risk. For those markets projected to perform the best, you would hold somewhere between a normal and maximum position. For those markets expected to perform poorly, you would hold a position somewhere between a minimum and a normal position. A confirmation from technical analysis can be particularly helpful. If the technical view confirms a fundamentally bullish view, then close to a maximum position in that market

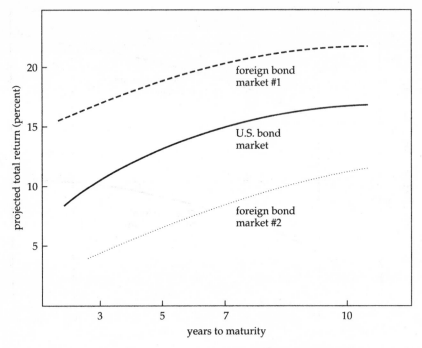

Figure 10.4. Hypothetical Projected Total Returns in Dollar Terms on U.S. and Foreign Bonds (Source: Merrill Lynch Capital Markets)

would be indicated. If a fundamentally bullish view is not supported by the technical view, then the market should not be overweighted, and the same is true if you are fundamentally bearish on a market but the technical side looks bullish. It is wise to try to integrate both fundamental and technical analysis in the portfolio management decision process.

In designing global bond portfolio strategy, it is important to assess where you are before you can really make a decision as to where you want to head. You should have at least a weekly security evaluation report to review what kind of credits you own, what the current price is versus the purchase price, and how that position stands relative to the entire portfolio. Finally, compiling a table similar to Table 10.4, which appears as a regular feature of our weekly review at Merrill Lynch, would be beneficial. This table outlines, in a fairly detailed manner that can be compared against your benchmark, where you stand in terms of currency exposure, cash-bond exposure, maturity exposure, and sector exposure.

In this example, which shows Merrill Lynch's recent view, we were recommending overweighting nondollar bonds. We were recommending 35 percent dollars and a much bigger exposure in Deutsche marks and sterling. But with G-5 and the big drop in the dollar, we now believe that

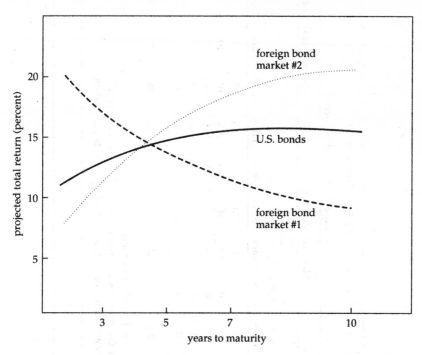

Figure 10.5. Hypothetical Projected Total Returns in Dollar Terms on U.S. and Foreign Bonds (Source: Merrill Lynch Capital Markets)

profit-taking is warranted. At this point in time the risks probably are that the dollar could stage a comeback sometime in 1986. For this reason we would rather have a neutral stance at the current time, holding a 50 percent weight in the dollar market. At the end of 1985, we have been recommending a fully invested position in U.S. bonds, with no cash—but recommending all cash in the yen market, all cash in the sterling market, and all cash in "other," which is the Australia/New Zealand market. This takes advantage of the fact that yield curves in all of the markets are inverted. We see little prospect of interest rates coming down immediately in those markets. It may look as though we are inordinately defensive here, but we are simply taking advantage of the inverted yield curves. We feel that the world bond market rally is now four years along, and we are fairly defensive in terms of maturity exposure. In fact, we recently made a recommendation to cut even the long position of the U.S. market from that 10 percent down to zero and moved it into the 7- to 10-year area.

In conclusion, international bonds offer tremendous opportunities, but they also offer a great deal of risk. An international bond portfolio based on carefully established guidelines and an active management of those risks will help you stay on top.

Table 10.4. Guidelines for Structuring a Global Bond Portfolio Recommended Asset Mix (Percent Breakdown)

Currency bloc	Currency decision		Market decision			Composition of bond portfolio								
						Maturity structure						Sector breakdown		
	Net currency position	Currency hedge	Gross currency position	Cash equivalent	Bonds	1–3 Years	3–5 Years	5–7 Years	7–10 Years	10–15 Years	Long	Govt.	Euro.	Foreign
U.S. dollars*	50	+10	40	0	40	0	0	20	10	0	10	25	5	10
Deutsche mark**	10	−10	20	0	20	0	0	10	10	NA	NA	10	10	0
Yen	20	0	20	20	0	0	0	0	0	NA	NA	0	0	0
STG	10	0	10	10	0	0	0	0	0	0	0	0	0	0
Other†	10	0	10	10	0	0	0	0	0	0	0	0	0	0
Total	100	0	100	40	60	0	0	30	20	0	10	35	15	10

Key: + Buy currency forward
 − Sell currency forward
 NA Not applicable

* Includes U.S. and Canadian markets
** Includes West German, Dutch, Swiss, French, and ECU markets
† Includes Australia, New Zealand, and other selected bond markets

Source: Merrill Lynch Capital Markets.

11

International Bonds and Currencies: Risks and Returns

Richard C. Carr, CFA
Brinson Partners, Inc.
Chicago, IL

Introduction

International bonds form a very large asset class with distinctly different investment characteristics from U.S. bonds. The addition of international bonds to a U.S. portfolio (or a domestic portfolio from any country) improves diversification by lowering the volatility of the total portfolio and also offers a wider set of opportunities for enhancing return.

The foreign currency exposure associated with international bonds (or any form of international investment) has an important impact on the return, risk, and covariance relationships of the asset class. Currencies are not a separate asset class but, rather, are a dimension of international bond investing that must be recognized and managed.

Size of Markets

The size of international bond markets is shown in Figure 11.1 in the context of the market capitalization and composition of global securities markets. At the end of 1990, the total (preliminary) in U.S. dollar terms for all the securities markets available to U.S. investors was $22.4 trillion. Nondollar bonds were 28.1 percent of the total, or $6.3 trillion. U.S. domestic bonds and international dollar-denominated bonds were a smaller proportion of the total, 25.1 percent, or $5.62 trillion. Aggregate non-U.S. equity markets, at 24.5 percent, occupied a larger share of the total global securities markets than did U.S. equities at 14.8 percent. The combination of nondollar bonds and international equities constituted 52.6 percent of

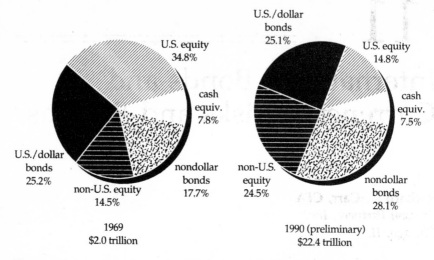

Figure 11.1. Global Securities Markets (Source: Brinson Partners, Inc.)

the total global securities markets at the end of 1990. Markets outside the United States represented more than half of the opportunities available to investors!

Figure 11.1 also shows the size and composition of the $2.0 trillion 1969 global securities markets. At that time, nondollar bonds formed 17.7 percent of the total. The subsequent growth in the relative size of the non-dollar bond markets is due to the increase in deficit financing outside the United States, particularly in Japan (U.S. dollar bonds remained roughly constant in proportionate terms), and the rise in the value of foreign currencies relative to the U.S. dollar.

Government bond markets make up approximately 80 percent of the market value of bond markets outside the United States. The composition by country of one major nondollar government bond index at the end of 1990 is shown in Table 11.1. Japan had 36.3 percent of the total, followed by Germany, which accounted for 18.4 percent of the total. As with international equities, the Japanese market is the largest foreign market available to U.S. investors. Because smaller countries either do not have bond markets or their bond markets lack adequate liquidity, the benchmark indices contain fewer bond than equity markets.

For this chapter, nondollar bond markets refer to fixed-income obligations that are denominated in currencies other than the U.S. dollar. The return, risk, and covariance data are constructed from government bonds in major countries outside the United States. Nondollar bonds issued by corporate organizations are relatively unimportant or, in many countries, relatively illiquid.

Table 11.1. Nondollar Government Bond Markets as
of 12/31/90

Markets	% Total	Avg. Maturity (Years)	Avg. Duration (Years)
Japan	36.3	6.7	5.1
Germany	18.4	5.6	4.3
France	12.6	6.5	4.2
U.K.	12.3	8.7	5.1
Netherlands	7.9	5.7	4.3
Canada	7.7	8.3	4.8
Denmark	2.8	4.9	3.7
Australia	1.5	5.0	3.5
Switzerland	0.5	6.3	5.0
	100.0		

Source: Salomon Brothers.

Investing from the United States

Investing in non-U.S. bond markets is a fairly recent experience for U.S. institutions and individuals. For institutions, policies governing such investment were not developed until the early 1980s, once success of international equity investing, begun on a sustained basis after the 1974 elimination of the Interest Equalization Tax had become apparent. Yet, in 1990, allocations to international bond markets remained a relatively small part of institutional investments. According to InterSec Research Corporation, international fixed-income mandates from U.S. tax-exempt institutions totaled only $19 billion at the end of 1990, or 20 percent of the aggregate $93 billion invested by U.S. institutions outside their home market. The other $74 billion was invested in the international equity markets. Even the total of $93 billion represented only 4 percent of the aggregate market value of U.S. private and public pension funds. Nondollar bonds comprise more than a fourth of the global securities markets, yet U.S. pension plans have invested less than 1 percent of their assets in this asset class.

Individuals have more difficulty investing directly into other bond markets and, therefore, are more likely to use international and global mutual funds. At the end of 1990 a number of open-end mutual funds and closed-end funds were investing into non-U.S. fixed-income markets for U.S. investors, but again, the aggregate size was relatively small.

Historical Returns

The dollar returns from investing in the aggregate of all nondollar bond markets as compared to U.S. bonds are shown in Figure 11.2. In the period beginning December 31, 1969 and ending December 31, 1990, nondollar bonds provided a return to U.S. investors of 11.46 percent per year, while U.S. bonds provided a return of 9.59 percent per year. The return histories are presented in terms of wealth indices which begin on December 31, 1969.

Consistent data on returns from international bonds are not available for periods earlier than the 1970s. Prior to that time there are indices available for larger bond markets, such as the United Kingdom and Canada, but not for all the markets, and those that do exist are not constructed consistently. Some studies of bond markets have linked aggregate interest rates from the Organization for Economic Cooperation and Development or International Monetary Fund data with assumptions about maturities, but such constructed data is fraught with problems. Although not as plentiful as for the U.S. markets, the historical data that are available can be analyzed to reveal the characteristics of non-U.S. bond markets.

Table 11.2 places the returns from international bonds in the context of returns from other asset classes available to U.S. investors. While nondollar bonds have generated a higher return than U.S. bonds, international equity

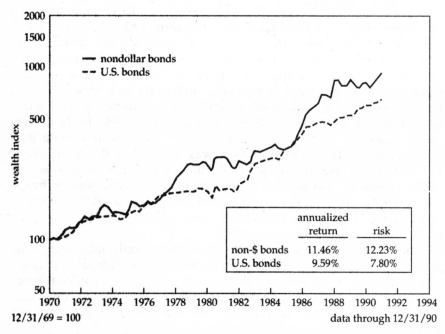

Figure 11.2. Nondollar Bonds vs. U.S. Bonds (Source: Brinson Partners, Inc.)

Table 11.2.   Global Securities Markets Performance
Characteristics, 12/31/69–12/31/90

	Annualized Return (%)	Standard Deviation (%)[a]
Equities		
U.S. equity	10.55	19.22
Non-U.S. equity	13.08	20.33
Fixed-Income Securities		
U.S. bonds	9.59	7.80
Nondollar bonds	11.46	12.23
International dollar bonds	10.05	6.35
Cash equivalents (U.S.)	7.60	1.26
Global Securities Markets Index	11.32	13.21
Inflation (CPIU)	6.24	1.73

a. Annualized standard deviation of quarterly logarithmic returns.

(Source: Brinson Partners, Inc.)

returns have been even higher, as one might expect. International equities had a return of 13.08 percent per year, compared to 11.46 percent from nondollar bonds. International dollar bonds usually sell at a higher yield than comparable domestic U.S. bonds. Accordingly, the annualized return from international dollar bonds over this time period was 10.05 percent versus 9.59 percent from U.S. domestic bonds. International dollar bonds comprise a market capitalization weighted average of dollar-denominated Eurobonds and yankee bonds (respectively, dollar bonds issued outside the United States, and those issued by non-U.S. organizations into the United States). They also offer exposure to a wider set of credits from a number of countries, although international dollar bond returns are highly correlated with the returns from U.S. domestic bonds.

Historical Risks

The higher dollar returns obtained from investing in nondollar bonds have been accompanied by higher volatility. Figure 11.2 shows that the volatility of dollar returns from nondollar bonds throughout the period was 12.23 percent, while U.S. bonds experienced a lower volatility of 7.80 percent. Figure 11.3 illustrates the history of volatility of returns from nondollar bonds and U.S. bonds over the period, expressed in terms of rolling five-year trailing standard deviations. Although the five-year volatilities have varied, especially with the change in U.S. monetary policy in the early

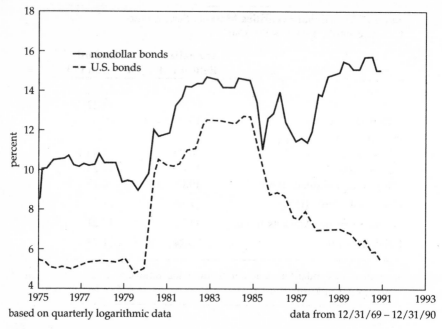

Figure 11.3. Nondollar Bonds and U.S. Bonds (in U.S. Dollar Terms), Five-year Trailing Standard Deviation (Source: Brinson Partners, Inc.)

1980s, the historical risks of U.S. bonds have been consistently less than those of nondollar bonds.

In Table 11.2, the risks of nondollar bonds are compared with the risks of the other global securities markets during the period December 31, 1969 to December 31, 1990. The higher historical volatilities are associated with higher returns and asset classes that are considered to have more fundamental risk. Notice, however, that the historical volatility of international equities does not differ greatly from that of U.S. equities, whereas the historical volatility of U.S. bonds is significantly less than that of nondollar bonds, as already discussed.

Historical Correlations

Asset allocation policies and analyses are established by considering three investment characteristics: returns, risks, and the correlations of returns. We have seen that historical returns and volatilities from nondollar bonds have been greater than those of U.S. bonds. The third element, the correlation of returns between asset classes, is a critical component of the rationale for investing in bond markets outside the United States.

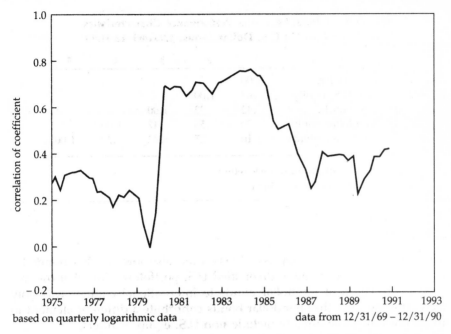

based on quarterly logarithmic data   data from 12/31/69 – 12/31/90

Figure 11.4. Nondollar Bonds and U.S. Bonds, Five-year Trailing Correlation
(Source: Brinson Partners, Inc.)

The surprisingly low correlation of returns from U.S. and nondollar bonds is graphically presented in Figure 11.4. During the period December 31, 1969 to December 31, 1990, the correlations over rolling five-year time periods ranged below 0.10 and above 0.70 and was 0.47 over the entire period. This low correlation of returns occurred despite the greater integration of financial markets, the increasing degree of cross-border investing, and the trend of companies, industries, and investors to have a more global perspective and behavior. The historical evidence indicates diversification in utilizing nondollar bonds in a U.S.-based portfolio. Why is diversification an advantage? Because a portfolio diversified among asset classes with low cross-correlations produces a higher return per unit of risk than a nondiversified portfolio. Moreover, no trend toward higher correlations between U.S. bonds and the aggregate of nondollar bonds is apparent. Differences remain between markets in the movement of inflation rates; the pattern and timing of economic cycles; fiscal and monetary policies; political, social, and cultural characteristics; and other factors that affect interest rates. These differences create opportunities for investors in non-U.S. bond markets to improve diversification and enhance returns.

The correlation of returns between nondollar bonds and other asset classes beside U.S. bonds is shown in Table 11.3 in the form of a matrix.

Table 11.3.   **Global Securities Performance Characteristics**
Correlation Matrix in U.S. Dollar Terms, 12/31/69–12/31/90*

		1	2	3	4	5
1.	U.S. equity	1.00				
2.	Non-U.S. equity	.67	1.00			
3.	U.S. bonds	.42	.32	1.00		
4.	Nondollar bonds	.20	.58	.47	1.00	
5.	Cash equivalents	−.10	−.25	−.02	−.29	1.00

*Based on quarterly logarithmic returns.
(Source: Brinson Partners, Inc.)

The correlations with other asset classes are also low, so that nondollar bonds offer an advantage to diversified U.S. portfolios. Note that the historical correlation of nondollar bonds to international equities was only 0.58. This signifies that nondollar bonds contribute a different element to those portfolios that already include non-U.S. equity markets.

The Effect of Diversification

In the past, the addition of nondollar bonds to a U.S. bond portfolio has added to returns and reduced volatility. Figure 11.5 shows the impact of diversification on return and risk over the period December 31, 1969 to December 31, 1990. The first point on the bow-shaped curve at the lower left of the chart represents the return and risk from investing 100 percent of the portfolio in U.S. bonds. Each subsequent point on the curve illustrates the return and risk of 2.5 percent changes in the portfolio (e.g., the second point has 97.5 percent in U.S. bonds and 2.5 percent in nondollar bonds). The last point on the curve at the upper right of the figure represents the results of a portfolio invested 100 percent in nondollar bonds. For this time period, including greater proportions of nondollar bonds in a domestic bond portfolio increased return and simultaneously decreased volatility, up to a point where relatively large commitments to nondollar bonds also increased volatility. The reduction in volatility occurred, despite the higher risk of nondollar bonds, as a result of the low correlation of returns between the two asset classes. For higher proportions of nondollar bonds, the greater volatility outweighed the low correlation.

The role of nondollar bonds in a broader portfolio that is diversified across both global equity and bond markets is depicted in Figure 11.6, which plots the annual return and risk for non-U.S. equities, U.S. equities, nondollar bonds, U.S. bonds, cash, and the Global Securities

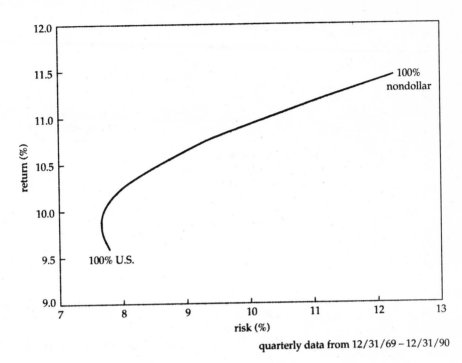

Figure 11.5. The Effects of Diversification, Salomon BIG Bond Index and Nondollar Bond Index in U.S. Dollars (Source: Brinson Partners, Inc.)

Markets Index during the 1969–1990 time period. The Global Securities Markets Index combines all of the asset classes in fixed proportions, which are shown in Figure 11.7. The aggregate proportions are similar to those of a typical U.S. pension fund (67% equities, 28% bonds, 5% cash equivalents), but the Index includes non-U.S. elements in a mix designed to optimize the risk-return characteristics (it is not market-capitalization weighted). The Global Securities Market Index had a return somewhat greater than that of U.S. equities alone, with significantly less volatility. The interaction of returns from the global asset classes and their low covariance produced a superior performance over this time period. Another way to examine this interaction is to create similar equity/fixed-income portfolios separately for U.S. assets and for global assets. As shown in Figure 11.8, an 80/20 mix of U.S. equities and U.S. bonds was inferior (less return at same volatility) to a mix of 60% U.S. equities, 20% non-U.S. equities, 15% U.S. bonds, and 5% nondollar bonds. Similarly, the Global Securities Index had risk-return outcomes superior to a traditional 60/40 U.S. stock and bond mix.

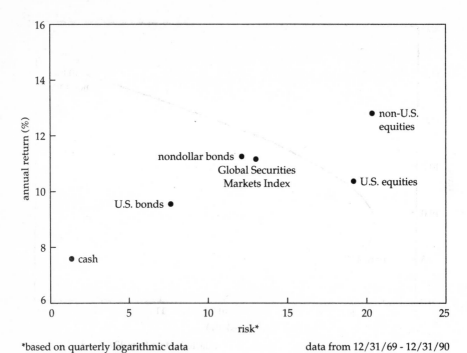

*based on quarterly logarithmic data   data from 12/31/69 - 12/31/90

Figure 11.6.   The Investment Playing Field: Historical Performance
Characteristics (Source: Brinson Partners, Inc.)

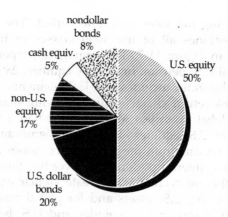

Figure 11.7.   Global Securities
Markets Index (Source: Brinson
Partners, Inc.)

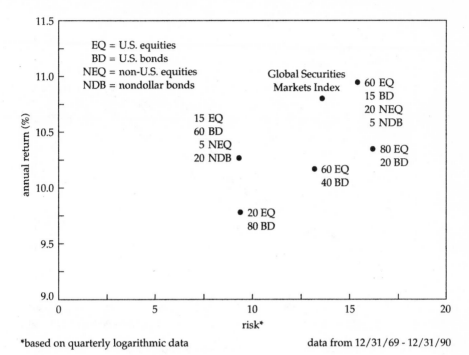

Figure 11.8. U.S. and Global Asset Mixes, Historical Performance Characteristics in U.S. Dollars (Source: Brinson Partners, Inc.)

Role of Currency

The previous analyses centered on the risks and correlations associated with dollar-adjusted returns from nondollar bond markets. The dollar-adjusted returns are a combination of the returns from the local markets and the translation of foreign currencies into U.S. dollars. The next analysis explores the role currency translation played in generating the historical performance characteristics of nondollar bonds.

Figure 11.9 compares three measurements of returns from nondollar bonds from December 31, 1974 through December 31, 1990: dollar-adjusted, local currency, and hedged into U.S. dollars. Return data from this period begins at the introduction of floating exchange rates since earlier historical data would be less relevant. Dollar-adjusted returns convert local market returns into U.S. dollars using the foreign exchange rate at the moment of each return; local currency returns are those recorded in the local markets, before conversion into U.S. dollars; hedged returns convert local market returns into U.S. dollar returns at forward exchange rates locked in by selling the foreign currencies into U.S. dollars at three-month intervals. Since the U.S. dollar depreciated on average during this

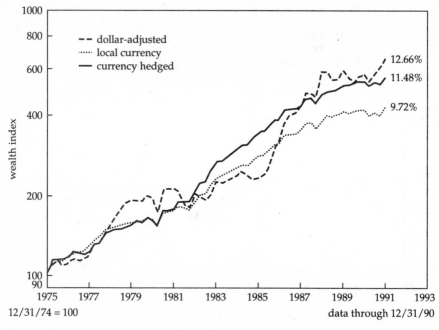

Figure 11.9.   Nondollar Bonds in Local Currency and Dollar-Adjusted Terms
(Source: Brinson Partners, Inc.)

period, dollar-adjusted returns were higher than local currency returns, 12.66 percent per year versus 9.72 percent. Hedged returns were
closer to dollar-adjusted returns, 12.66 percent versus 11.48 percent.
The volatilities of the returns, however, were quite different. The pattern of accumulation of the wealth indices shows that local currency
and hedged returns were relatively stable, while dollar-adjusted returns
were far more volatile.

The element of currency translation can add to or subtract from local
market returns over any given time period. The data for the period in
Figure 11.9 indicates that currency translation enhanced returns (dollar-
adjusted returns were higher than local market returns), but also increased
volatility.

On the other hand, currency plays a positive role if one considers
the correlation of returns in local and dollar-adjusted terms. Figure 11.10
describes the rolling five-year correlations between returns of U.S. bonds
and nondollar bonds from 1974–1990 in both local currency terms and
U.S. dollar terms. The distinctly lower correlations in U.S. dollar terms
implies that one function of currency is to weaken the relationship between
nondollar and U.S. bonds. In other words, foreign exchange translation
increases volatility of returns to U.S. investors, but decreases correlations
with other asset classes.

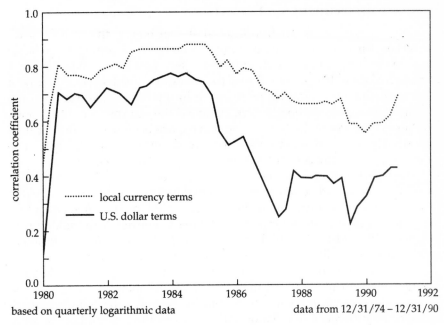

Figure 11.10. U.S. Bonds and Nondollar Bonds, Five-year Trailing Correlation (Source: Brinson Partners, Inc.)

Note also the absence of any tendency for correlations to rise, even in local currency terms. The disparate movement of currencies vis-à-vis the U.S. dollar enhances the opportunities for diversification outside the U.S., but even in local market terms significant differences in the pattern of returns remain.

The returns in local currency terms are interesting as a point of reference, but they are not directly relevant to the U.S. investor. Since only a local investor can obtain local market returns, the U.S. investor (or any international investor) must translate gains or losses from local markets into a base currency. The base currency of the U.S. investor is the U.S. dollar, with returns translated either at current exchange rates or by hedging into the U.S. dollar. For example, the yield on U.K. government bonds has often been higher than the yield on U.S. government bonds. The U.S. investor who is tempted by that higher current yield must either incur the risk of converting British pounds into U.S. dollars when coupon payments are received and the portfolio is priced, or hedge British pounds into U.S. dollars over the investment time horizon. The impact of hedging on returns, as will be discussed later, is a function of the differences in short-term interest rates between the two countries. The higher interest rates that determine the price of the currency hedge will often offset higher bond yields.

Expected Investment Characteristics

In analyzing the characteristics of international bonds, the history of returns is useful as a departure point but should not be accepted as a reliable guide to the future, particularly since this asset class has a limited amount of historical data. It is essential that the investor consider whether any of the critical characteristics will be different in the future. For example, the returns from nondollar bonds have exceeded the returns from U.S. bonds over longer time periods, though the reverse has been true in shorter time periods. The investor must decide if there is any fundamental reason to expect superior returns in the future.

The return from a bond is composed of a real return on cash equivalents in the local market, a risk premium that induces the investor to switch from money-market instruments into longer-dated instruments, and a premium that compensates for *expected* inflation. Countries with high rates of inflation will tend to have high interest rates, while countries with lower rates of inflation will tend to have lower interest rates.

The change in the value of a currency relative to the U.S. dollar is a critical element for the U.S. investor. There are many reasons why exchange rates vary in the short term, but in the longer term an important factor is the difference in inflation rates between the U.S. and other countries. Countries with inflation rates that are high relative to other countries would be expected to experience long-term currency depreciation against those currencies, thus offsetting higher interest rates. This is a simple theory of exchange rate determination, but it illustrates the influence of inflation on both currency changes and interest rates. Over time, assuming similar maturities, durations, risk premiums, and credit quality, the returns to a dollar-based investor from non-U.S. bond markets should be similar to the returns from the U.S. bond market.

Although it is reasonable to expect similar long-term returns from U.S. and nondollar bonds, it is unlikely that the risks of nondollar bonds will diminish in the future. Exchange rate volatility, the primary cause of incremental volatility, will continue to be high. Furthermore, there is no reason to think that local markets' risks will decline. In fact, future volatility may increase in several bond markets that were less volatile than the U.S. bond market over the period (see Table 11.7), such as Japan and Germany. Some of those markets, in particular Japan, are experiencing greater deregulation and internationalization. Such loosening of control is usually accompanied by greater volatility, at least in the near term. Inflation rates are tending toward convergence across most countries, which should lead to more similar volatilities and risk premiums, in contrast to the variation of what was observed in the past.

A change in the correlation of returns between bond markets is also unlikely, though there could be greater integration within regional blocs like Europe. Correlations between the U.S. and the aggregate non-U.S. markets were earlier shown not to have a tendency to rise.

Table 11.4. Long-Term Asset Class
Equilibrium Returns for U.S. Dollar-Based
Investor

Asset Class	Equilibrium Return* (%)	Risk (%)
1. U.S. equity	11.20	17.5
2. Non-U.S. equity	10.76	17.0
3. U.S. bonds	7.90	8.0
4. Nondollar bonds	7.88	12.5
5. Cash equivalents	6.08	1.5

* Assuming 4% U.S. inflation.
Source: Brinson Partners, Inc.

Table 11.4 shows a set of integrated equilibrium returns and risks for the major asset classes available to the U.S. investor. These long-term forecasts are independent of economic and market cycles. Nondollar bonds are expected to generate returns very similar to those of U.S. bonds. The volatility of nondollar bonds, including exchange rate effects, should continue to be greater than that of U.S. bonds.

Table 11.5 extends the forecasts to the correlations between returns from major asset classes. Under these assumptions, the correlations of returns between nondollar bonds and other asset classes will continue to be low.

Table 11.5. Long-Term Asset Class Equilibrium Returns
Correlation Forecasts*

	1	2	3	4	5
1. U.S. equity	1.00				
2. Non-U.S. equity	.60	1.00			
3. U.S. bonds	.45	.25	1.00		
4. Nondollar bonds	.25	.60	.10	1.00	
5. Cash equivalents	−.10	−.15	−.10	−.05	1.00

* Annualized returns.
Source: Brinson Partners, Inc.

Hedged vs. Unhedged Policies

The higher volatility of nondollar bonds has led to the development of several means of attempting to reduce the currency-induced risk element in risk. Some investors have adopted fully hedged (currency) policies, or benchmarks, in order to reduce risk. A fully hedged policy (active managers are usually allowed to "unhedge" in order to hold non-U.S. currencies when they are expected to rise against the dollar) is said to reduce volatility without decreasing return since, over long periods of time, currency change is offset by interest rate differentials. Proponents of fully hedged policies view currency as a negative investment characteristic, adding risk without increasing return, that should be eliminated by normally hedging all other currencies into the U.S. dollar. In fact, fully hedged policies possess both advantages and disadvantages. Since objectives and constraints vary among investors, there can be no universally applicable conclusion on this issue.

An important consequence of a fully hedged portfolio is a loss of diversification. We saw earlier that the element of currency translation increased volatility but simultaneously decreased correlations with other asset classes. The loss of diversification occurs because the fully hedged investor creates, in effect, a synthetic U.S. cash instrument within the nondollar bond portfolio. Due to the arbitrage in the forward foreign exchange markets, the true yields on hedged nondollar bonds should be similar to the yields on comparable U.S. bonds. The diversification advantage a fully-hedged portfolio does have lies in the participation in the variation of local market returns.

Another aspect to consider is the impact of hedged bonds on the total portfolio rather than only the international bond segment. Figure 11.11 compares the reduction in forecast risk of an unhedged global bond portfolio to a hedged global bond portfolio. The two lines show the change in forecast risk as increments of nondollar bonds are added to a portfolio that is initially invested entirely in U.S. bonds. For the unhedged portfolio, as seen earlier in this chapter, the addition of moderate proportions of nondollar bonds reduces risk. However, risk ultimately rises with the very significant use of nondollar bonds. For the hedged portfolio, risk decreases along most of the curve, until 30 percent or less of the portfolio is composed of U.S. bonds. At lower proportions of international diversification, unhedged and fully hedged portfolios differ little in risk reduction. For example, investing 10 percent of an unhedged bond portfolio into the aggregate of non-U.S. markets reduces risk only 8 basis points from that of the same portfolio when hedged.

The argument for hedged portfolios focuses on the assets of the investor rather than the liabilities. Figure 11.12 illustrates asset volatility and returns for hedged and unhedged global securities portfolios over the period 1974–1988. The risk-return dimensions of the U.S. and hedged

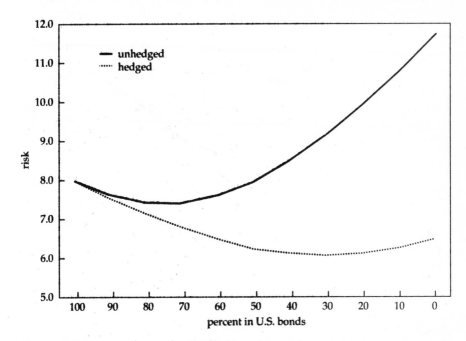

Figure 11.11. Forecast Risk of Global Bond Portfolios, Hedged vs. Unhedged (Source: Brinson Partners, Inc.)

international portfolio are clearly superior to the same dimensions for the U.S. and unhedged international portfolio.

Some investors, particularly pension plan sponsors, may want to consider liabilities as well as assets. Figure 11.13 shows that the unhedged portfolio is superior to the hedged portfolio for the surplus of a pension fund. A hedged policy no longer seems to have a clear advantage because hedged assets and liabilities have a lower correlation than unhedged assets and liabilities. Figure 11.13 examines an historical efficient frontier in covering the same period as Figure 11.12, but this time for assets less the simulated liabilities of the active members of a pension plan. Assuming a static company, work force, and age distribution, the active liabilities were grown at the inflation rate at the end of each quarter and then discounted back using historical yield curves. The process was repeated quarterly to show how the liabilities would have changed as the asset markets changed.

Another consideration in hedged bond portfolios is the cost that arises from spreads in the foreign exchange market and market impact. Estimates of this cost vary according to the analyst and the length of the hedge period (monthly rollovers would be more expensive than annual rollovers), but

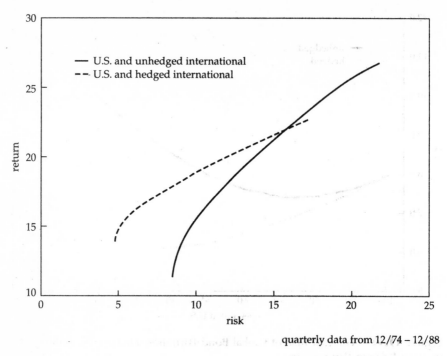

Figure 11.12.   Historical Efficient Frontiers: Assets Only (Source: Brinson Partners, Inc.)

are generally cited at between 20 and 40 basis points per year. The need to sell or buy securities in the portfolio when the matured hedge contract results in a loss or gain also affects the cost of hedging. For example, a fully hedged portfolio would experience losses as contracts are rolled over during a period of U.S. dollar weakness; securities would have to be liquidated to raise cash to settle the contracts. The sale (or purchase during a period of dollar strength) adds an additional cost. In addition, hedges must be adjusted to fit the complete portfolio during periods of sharp market movements.

Individual Markets

So far, nondollar bonds have been discussed in terms of their aggregate investment characteristics. In reality, this asset class contains a number of fixed-income markets, each with different investment characteristics. Table 11.6 presents the returns from the major bond markets over the period December 31, 1974 to December 31, 1990 in both local currency and U.S. dollar terms. The Japanese bond market recorded the highest performance in U.S. dollar terms, with a return of 14.6 percent per year, while the

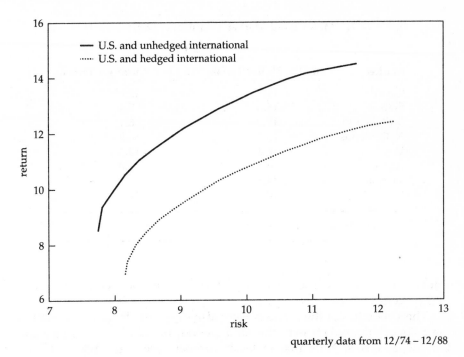

Figure 11.13. Historical Efficient Frontiers: Assets Less Active Liability (Source: Brinson Partners, Inc.)

Table 11.6. Major Bond Market Returns, 12/31/74–12/31/90

Market	Average Annualized Return (%)	
	In U.S. Dollar Terms	In Local Currency Terms
Canada	9.0	10.0
France	10.1	11.0
Switzerland	10.2	5.6
Netherlands	10.6	8.0
U.K.	12.9	14.3
Japan	14.6	9.0
Germany	11.2	7.9
U.S.	10.4	10.4

(Source: Brinson Partners, Inc.)

Table 11.7.   **Major Bond Market Volatilities, 12/31/74–12/31/90**

Market	Risk (%) In U.S. Dollar Terms	In Local Currency Terms
Canada	14.9	12.8
France	15.3	7.4
Switzerland	17.0	6.1
Netherlands	15.2	6.2
U.K.	18.4	12.3
Japan	16.8	7.0
Germany	14.8	5.1
U.S.	10.4	10.4

(Source: Brinson Partners, Inc.)

United Kingdom had the greatest performance in local currency terms, 14.3 percent per year.

The volatilities of the markets were also different. Table 11.7 describes the risks of the markets over the same period, in both local currency and U.S. dollar terms. Note that in local currency terms, the high inflation countries such as the United Kingdom and Canada experienced the greatest fluctuations in returns, and many of the markets were considerably less volatile than the U.S. bond market. As explained earlier, future differences are unlikely to be as great.

The most interesting aspect of the returns from individual markets is the low correlations between the non-U.S. markets. The nondollar bond markets in the aggregate are not closely related to the U.S. market, and

Table 11.8.   **Bond Correlation Matrix in U.S. Dollar Terms, 12/31/74–12/31/90**

Market	1	2	3	4	5	6	7	8
Canada	1.00							
France	0.33	1.00						
Switzerland	0.43	0.71	1.00					
Netherlands	0.42	0.82	0.83	1.00				
U.K.	0.39	0.46	0.48	0.50	1.00			
Japan	0.40	0.64	0.76	0.69	0.52	1.00		
Germany	0.41	0.82	0.87	0.96	0.49	0.72	1.00	
U.S.	0.89	0.36	0.45	0.48	0.31	0.37	0.47	1.00

(Source: Brinson Partners, Inc.)

Table 11.9. Bond Market Performance: Highest
and Lowest U.S. Dollar Returns

Year		Best		Worst
			Return (%)	
	Best		**Worst**	
1981	5.4	Japan	−18.0	U.K.
1982	35.8	Canada	1.2	Switzerland
1983	12.6	Japan	−8.6	Netherlands
1984	14.3	U.S.	−14.6	Switzerland
1985	52.8	France	−12.5	Australia
1986	40.1	Japan	14.8	U.K.
1987	46.6	U.K.	1.9	U.S.
1988	28.8	Australia	−12.6	Switzerland
1989	16.2	Canada	−14.3	Japan
1990	30.9	U.K.	7.7	Canada

Notes: Australian bonds included from 1985, Danish bonds
from March 31, 1989.

(Source: Brinson Parnters, Inc.)

the individual markets are seldom closely related to each other. Table 11.8 shows the correlation of returns between the various markets, over the 1974–1990 period. Although the correlation between the major markets is low, a high correlation exists between markets in the same geographic or economic bloc (e.g., Germany and the Netherlands). This additional diversification advantage serves as an argument for evaluating nondollar bonds on a disaggregated basis rather than as a bloc.

Table 11.9 lists the best- and worst-performing bond markets from the perspective of a U.S. investor for each year from 1981 to 1990. In only one year was the U.S. the best performing bond market, providing additional justification for investing into international bond markets to enhance return.

The optimization of nondollar bonds with U.S. bonds was previously calculated with aggregated data in Figure 11.5. In Figure 11.14, the optimization exercise is repeated, this time with the nondollar bond markets considered individually vis-à-vis the United States. The dashed line shows the change in the risk and return of various U.S. and aggregate nondollar bond combinations, similar to those in Figure 11.5. This is referred to as partial optimization. The solid line in Figure 11.14, for the period 1974–1990, demonstrates the risk-return for combinations of the U.S. bond market and available individual bond markets. This is referred to as full optimization. Investing in individual markets rather than in the pre-aggregated bloc of markets is clearly advantageous. The full optimization efficient frontier has a higher return at any given level of risk and a lower risk at any given level of return. This advantage stems from the

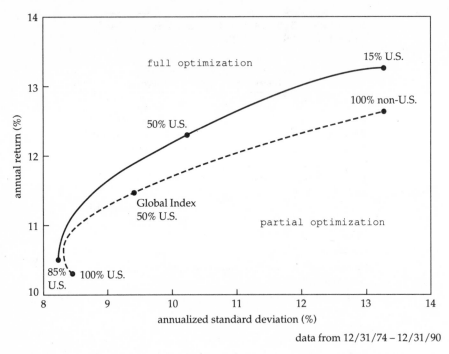

Figure 11.14.   Global Bonds, in U.S. Dollars (Source: Brinson Partners, Inc.)

failure of pre-aggregated calculations to incorporate correlations between individual nondollar markets and U.S. markets.

Management of International Bond Portfolios

The management of international bonds involves decisions on several dimensions of a portfolio: market exposure, currency exposure, interest rate sensitivity within markets, quality/sector exposure, and issue selection.

The exposure to individual nondollar bond markets, the exclusion or inclusion of markets from an available universe, and the weighting of markets relative to a benchmark index cannot be done in isolation from evaluations of currency exposure. Because there are several techniques for estimating the return from markets. A market must not be judged solely by expected return in local currency terms. The gain or loss that results from the necessary conversion of local currency returns into the investor's base currency is inescapable. Consider the case of bonds or fixed-income obligations in countries that have suffered from extremely high inflation, such as Mexico or Brazil. The high yields and returns are usually offset by corresponding currency depreciation. The currency could be hedged, but the impact would be very negative (because of the large yield differential), making even those hedged returns unattractive. A global investor would be biased toward high-yield, high-inflation countries if simple maximization of local market return was the objective. Similarly, performance attribution systems that measure local currency returns separately can give very misleading results.

Local market evaluations cannot be independent of currency considerations. Investors from outside a country must either accept exchange rate risk or hedge the currency into their own base currency. Consider again the case of U.K. government bonds which had a semiannual yield of 11.07 percent at the end of 1990. Three-month interest rates in the United Kingdom were then 14.03 percent, compared to 7.50 percent in the United States. The pound sterling at the end of 1990 was traded at $1.93. A U.S. investor faced the choice of investing in U.K. bonds on an unhedged basis, which carried the risk of sterling depreciation against the dollar (the pound sterling was then considered to be overvalued against the dollar in fundamental terms—prices of equivalent goods were much cheaper in the United States) or hedging the pound sterling into the U.S. dollar. That hedge would have an adverse outcome because short-term interest rates (most hedges are for shorter-term periods of less than a year and are therefore priced from short-term money market instruments) were much higher in the United Kingdom. The impact of the hedge would be -6.53 percent per annum for three months (7.50 percent in the U.S. less 14.03 percent in the U.K.), thus reducing the attraction of U.K. bonds.

Interest rate sensitivity is usually managed within each market rather than across markets. Since no "global interest rate" exists, an average maturity or duration has no relevance for an international bond portfolio. Managers often base duration strategies within each market on anticipated changes in interest rates. Duration strategies can vary considerably relative to the benchmark in each market. Thus, interest rates can be declining in Australia while rising in Germany.

Quality and sector management of international bonds is usually not as complex as for domestic U.S. bonds. Government, government agency, or supranational obligations are usually the only sectors available in practice to large institutional investors. Credit quality is therefore normally quite high, with little real opportunity for less traditional instruments such as mortgage pass-throughs and the like. However, the Eurobond market, denominated in several currencies, does represent an alternative to government bonds traded in local markets. The nondollar Eurobonds are generally high-quality credits.

Issue selection also has less importance in international bond management. Most issues are government; the choices are between government obligations that will achieve duration and yield curve targets. Switching between issues is of minimal benefit because bid-ask spreads are wider (a higher cost to trading). The more critical determinants of performance are strategic decisions as to market exposure, currency exposure, and duration.

Benchmarks

The first consistent benchmark for international bond market analysis and management was provided by Salomon Brothers in 1981. The Salomon Brothers World Bond Index was a market-capitalization weighted index of the aggregate of major bond markets, including the United States. The series included both the aggregate nondollar bond markets and each individual market. The index was largely government bonds but also contained Eurobonds, all of which had maturities of five years or more. Historical data was provided on market returns back to 1977.

In 1986, Salomon Brothers launched a World Government Bond Index that included all bonds with maturities of one year or more, in order to be consistent with domestic U.S. bond indices. This index consisted only of government bonds (the U.S. segment of the world index is entirely treasuries), and historical data began with December 1984.

It is important to note that most statistical analyses of returns use the five-year maturity series because it has a longer history and because volatilities are greater than those associated with an index of maturities of one year or more. This chapter uses data on returns from the Salomon indices with maturities of five years or more for most of the period. Forecast risk is based on maturities of one year or more for both U.S. and nondollar bonds. The Salomon Brothers indices are the most commonly used benchmarks for international bonds. A fully hedged set of indices is also available, consistent with the unhedged indices, as are indices measured in any major base currency. In 1989, J. P. Morgan Securities, Inc. created a set of world bond indices that included other large bond markets like Spain and Italy. These indices focus more on traded bonds and have different versions that highlight very liquid bonds.

The world and non-U.S. bond (and equity) indices are market-capitalization weighted, consistent with the construction of domestic single asset class indices. Yet the case for constructing indices across markets on a capitalization-weighted basis is not strong. Although markets that are efficient and integrated can be treated in that statistical manner, in reality, considerable barriers to a free flow of capital across markets remain. Taxation, regulation, custom, and lack of information continue to inhibit cross-market efficiency.

A logical alternative to market-capitalization weighted benchmarks are "normal" benchmarks with fixed policy weights based on the equilibrium investment characteristics of each market and the investor's risk tolerance. An analogy with asset allocation policies in the United States may help to make this point clear. In the United States, the typical pension fund guideline of 60 percent stocks and 40 percent bonds is not based upon market size. If capitalization was the determinant of policy weighting, U.S. pension funds would be heavily invested in tax-exempt bonds and real estate. Why then use market size outside the home market as a policy guideline? Shouldn't markets be considered on the basis of return, risk, and covariance rather than size?

An optimal policy benchmark derived from investment characteristics must also be set relative to the allocation in the United States. For example, optimization of non-U.S. markets without any consideration of the United States would lead to a relatively high allocation to Canada, a market that normally does not have as much currency volatility relative to the U.S. dollar as other markets. But when the United States is included within an optimization program, the calculated optimal portfolio has a much lower weighting in Canada. Thus, the normal or optimal benchmark is conditional on the ultimate global allocation to the U.S. bond market. Allocation must be considered within a global framework. The risks and returns of international bonds and currencies cannot be evaluated in isolation from U.S. markets.

Mandates

International bond managers usually operate with either non-U.S. or global bond mandates. The non-U.S. mandate normally prohibits investments into U.S. bonds, though it often permits hedging into the U.S. dollar. The global mandate allows the manager to shift funds to and from the United States, sometimes within predetermined ranges. The suitability of a particular mandate is usually a function of who should or can control the asset allocation decision. Under a non-U.S. mandate, the client determines the initial U.S./non-U.S. allocation which subsequently either remains fixed or is strategically/tactically changed by the client. Within a global mandate, this asset allocation decision is delegated to the investment manager. The global mandate has less investment risk and offers a wider range of opportunities from which to add value. However, it does carry the possibility of losing diversification benefits should the active manager allocate all or most of the portfolio to the U.S. market.

Withholding Taxes

The withholding tax imposed on interest and dividends at source by host governments can reduce returns from international bond markets. The potential delay in receipt of tax reclaims caused by the withholding tax also affects the timing of returns. Details are shown in Table 11.10. Eurobonds are not subject to withholding taxes, but they are usually not as liquid as domestically issued bonds. The differences across markets should be considered in any comparative analysis.

Table 11.10.   Withholding Taxes to U.S. Residents on Domestically Issued Bonds

	Percent of Coupon Payment	Percent Reclaimable	Net Percent of Coupon*
Japan	20	10% reclaimable by U.S. tax-exempt funds	10
United Kingdom**	25	25% reclaimable by U.S.	0 or 25
Germany	0	–	–
Netherlands	0	–	–
Switzerland	35	30% reclaimable	5
France***	0	–	–
Canada	0	–	–
Australia	10	10% reclaimable by U.S. tax-exempt	0 or 10

*In some cases, U.S. residents may be able of offset these net foreign withholding taxes against their federal U.S. income taxes.

**Certain government bonds issued in the United Kingdom are free of withholding taxes to non-U.K. residents, irrespective of the investors domestic tax status in his own country.

***Nonresidents must file declaration of nonresident status.

(Source: Brinson Partners, Inc.)

MANAGING THE GLOBAL PORTFOLIO

12

Setting and Implementing Global Investment Objectives

Ronald D. Frashure
Gary L. Bergstrom
Acadian Asset
Management, Inc.
Boston, MA

Introduction

Setting overall investment objectives is the most critical task for a fund sponsor, especially one operating on a global scale. As noted by Charles Ellis, the sponsor of institutional funds must establish sensible investment policies for achieving specified, realistic investment objectives. An appropriate and timely change of relatively modest magnitude in the asset allocation decision can, for example, produce an improvement in total investment return significantly greater than that produced by the well-known "beat the market syndrome," as Ellis puts it.[1]

We will begin by addressing the strategic issue of setting investment objectives for a global equity diversification program from the perspective of a fund sponsor in the United States, the point of view most likely to be taken by readers. We will also provide additional perspectives from the frame of reference of investors based in key countries outside the United States. We will touch on the investment styles and methods available to implement desired investment objectives. Next, we will discuss the essential issue of selecting appropriate index benchmarks and criteria for performance measurement, so that the fund sponsor can judge whether critical objectives are being met through the ongoing portfolio implementation process. Finally, we will explore the merits of a systematic global tactical asset allocation approach employing a very broad array of asset classes across the world's major liquid and potentially investable capital markets.

Critical Issues

Fund sponsors frequently ask about strategies for setting objectives to attain the optimal structuring of a global equity diversification program. These questions are prompted, we believe, by the awareness of most sponsors who already are investing globally that they are not yet attaining the full return enhancement and risk reduction benefits from their allocations to foreign equities that an optimal structure might achieve. Other fund sponsors just beginning to diversify into international investments obviously want to avoid repeating mistakes which others have made and implement the most advanced possible program.

We now briefly outline from a sponsor's perspective the critical issues in setting objectives for and structuring a program of diversification into international equities. As we see it, the most important issues confronting a fund sponsor in implementing a program of global equity diversification are currently as follows:

1. How much of the fund's overall assets should be allocated to non-U.S. equities?
2. Should the allocation to non-U.S. equities be invested actively or passively, or both?
3. What specific investment styles or methods should be selected for implementation and in what proportions?
4. What performance benchmarks should be utilized?
5. Should currency risk be hedged or unhedged? If it is to be hedged, should this be done passively or actively? Alternatively, should the fund sponsor overlay a different currency strategy on top of the equity managers' currency exposure?
6. Should a global asset allocation view that considers other markets in addition to world equity markets be taken?

The best answers to these questions obviously depend on the fund sponsor's individual risk and return objectives and the desired attributes of the fund. Thus the responses are likely to be highly individualistic to the specific fund sponsor. However, we will make some general comments which can help arrive at reasonable answers.

The Optimal Allocation to International Equities

We will assume that the fund sponsor has already determined an appropriate strategic policy regarding the overall asset allocation to publicly traded equities in the context of the aggregate fund. We assume that the sponsor has set policy ranges for allocations to other asset classes (such as fixed-income securities or real estate). Hopefully, all of this has been done in a systematic fashion, taking into account the likely return and risk characteristics of different asset mixes and their impacts on the fund and its sponsor over time.

The return enhancement and risk reduction benefits of adopting a truly global perspective on equity investing were laid out a decade and a half ago by Bergstrom, who presented both the theoretical arguments in terms of Markowitz's seminal contributions to the understanding of portfolio diversification as well as actual empirical results available at that time.[2] In 1977, Bergstrom and Frashure advanced similar arguments from the point of view of U.S. pension funds, concluding that U.S.-based fund sponsors were likely to receive significant benefits from global portfolio diversification.[3]

Updated empirical evidence indicates that for U.S.-based fund sponsors, a substantial allocation to international equities has, in fact, greatly reduced risk or portfolio variability over long-term periods while simultaneously increasing the achieved rate of return. Figure 12.1 shows in risk-return terms the impact of adding international stocks, as represented by the Morgan Stanley Capital International Europe, Australia, Far East (EAFE) Index of non-U.S. equities, to a U.S. stock portfolio (proxied by the S&P 500) in varying proportions over the 1970–1990 period. As can be seen, holding approximately half of the aggregate stock portfolio in international equities has been the lowest-risk allocation for a U.S. fund sponsor. In addition, increased allocations to international stocks significantly raised portfolio returns.

Almost all U.S. fund sponsors have invested well below the optimum risk reduction level of allocation to non-U.S. equities in their aggregate portfolios. However, many are now increasing allocations significantly, suggesting greater acceptance of a global investment perspective. Based on a survey by Greenwich Associates (as reported in the *Wall Street Journal*[4]), corporate pension funds in the United States are projected to reach an allocation of 9.5 percent of their total assets to foreign stocks by 1993, while public employee funds expect to have 5.7 percent of their portfolios in foreign stocks. These results are displayed in Table 12.1. The percentages of total equities invested in foreign stocks in 1993 would thus be 17.2 percent for corporate funds and 12.4 percent for public funds.

We now shift the frame of reference to investors based in Japan and the United Kingdom, increasingly investing on a global scale along with U.S.-based funds. Figure 12.2 shows the risk-return curve for global equity diversification over the last two decades from a Japanese perspective. Figure 12.3 shows analogous data from a U.K. vantage point. Interestingly, in both cases the risk-minimizing asset allocation has consisted of about half the aggregate portfolio invested in domestic equities, and half in world equities outside the domestic market.

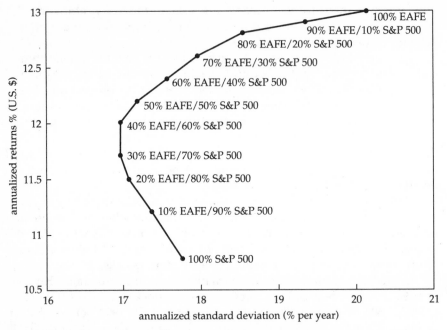

Figure 12.1. International Equity Diversification, Return Versus Risk, 1970–1990

The risk reduction attributes of global equity diversification have been derived from:

- Moderate correlations of foreign equity market returns with those from domestic stocks.
- Roughly similar return volatilities for domestic equities and aggregate global equities outside the home market.

Hunter and Coggin recently examined updated empirical evidence on the risk reduction effect of global diversification for U.S. fund sponsors. They demonstrate, based on data for the 1970–1986 period, that international equity diversification could have reduced investment risk (defined by variance of return) to about 56 percent of the level achieved using only national diversification. The authors conclude: "Hence, while there is a limit on international diversification benefit, the potential gain is sizable indeed."[5]

Before we turn to the key aspect of possible future return enhancement arising from global equity diversification, we should consider several important issues:

- Whether a U.S.-based investor looks toward the Pacific Rim or toward Europe, the dynamics of real economic growth seem to favor foreign

Table 12.1. Shifting Investments of U.S. Pension Funds

Investment	Percentage of portfolio invested				Percent Change 1990–1993
	1988	1989	1990	1993*	
Corporate Funds					
U.S. stocks	45.3	46.1	46.1	45.7	−8.6
Foreign stocks	4.0	4.8	5.6	9.5	69.6
Bonds total	27.4	28.8	27.3	25.9	−5.1
GICs**	7.0	5.9	7.1	6.6	−7.0
Real estate	4.6	5.8	5.2	5.4	3.8
Cash and other	11.6	8.7	8.7	6.9	−20.6
Public Funds					
U.S. stocks	39.5	39.8	36.9	40.3	9.2
Foreign stocks	1.3	2.7	3.2	5.7	78.1
Bonds total	45.4	43.6	44.3	39.3	−11.2
GICs**	0.6	0.8	0.5	0.4	−20.0
Real estate	3.9	4.7	4.3	4.7	9.3
Cash and other	9.3	8.3	10.8	9.7	−10.2

*Estimated.
**Guaranteed Investment Contracts.
Source: Greenwich Associates.

economies over the long pull (the next five to ten years or more). Many economists currently believe that the sustainable real growth rate of the U.S. domestic economy without major inflationary pressure will be about 2.75 percent annually. However, economic growth rates, the ultimate engine behind equity returns, will be much higher in the Pacific Basin. Although Japan, the world's second largest economy, will probably moderate (compared to its past trends) to a 4 percent to 4.5 percent annual real growth rate between now and the year 2000, the Pacific "tigers," such as Singapore, Malaysia, Hong Kong, South Korea, and Thailand, will probably continue to register real annual growth rates averaging 6 percent to 8 percent. This growth could even be exceeded by some of the more rapid "sprinters" among the Pacific economies.

• The growth dynamics of Western Europe have also changed as a result of the moves toward closer economic integration, coupled with the more recent trend toward free market economies in Eastern Europe. The Organization for Economic Cooperation and Development (OECD) and other forecasters project that Europe may grow half a percentage point or more faster in annual real terms than the United

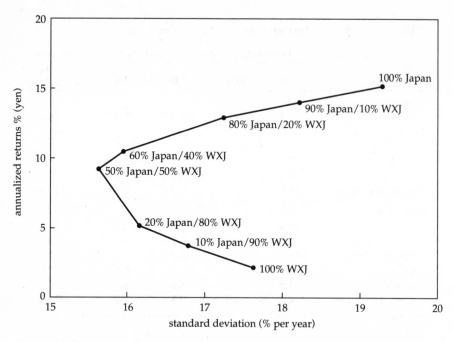

Figure 12.2. Efficient frontier for Japan/world except Japan (WXJ), December 31, 1969 to December 31, 1989

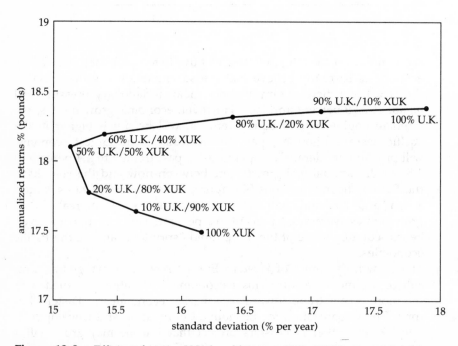

Figure 12.3. Efficient frontier U.K./world except U.K. (XUK), December 31, 1969 to December 31, 1989

States over the next 5 years due to the macroeconomic benefits of achieving a common market across 12 nations with a population of 320 million. Again, higher real growth should be a driver of higher equity returns.

- In a broad conceptual view, a long-term convergence of global economic development levels in a world with relatively free capital flows should tend to accelerate growth in regions with relatively low labor costs and high returns to invested capital. Equity returns in these regions may be higher than those in more mature economies. Examples of such developments include the surge of foreign investment in Spain, where labor costs remain low compared to most of Europe; the "hollowing-out" of some Japanese industries, which are building manufacturing facilities in lower-cost areas such as Thailand, Malaysia, and the Philippines; and the rapid growth of *maquiladora* plants in Mexico along the U.S. border.
- A tangible "work ethic" and drive to achieve is an important cultural factor in many of the Pacific economies. Although hard to quantify (except in variables such as savings rates), it is nonetheless likely to be a critical element in the long-term returns from equity investment in the region.
- If a global fund sponsor looks at the individual country and security level in the Pacific Basin, the ongoing massive infrastructure building in Japan presents many specific investment opportunities. In their national plans, the Japanese are expected to spend some 1,000 trillion yen (or about 7 trillion dollars) through the year 2000 to upgrade virtually every aspect of their physical structure.
- If we turn again to Europe, the economic integration dynamics of "Europe 1992" are creating many specific investment opportunities in addition to the broad impetus which higher economic growth is giving to equity returns overall.

Active or Passive Management for International Equities?

After an appropriate policy range for the international equity allocation has been set, the issue of active versus passive management must be confronted by fund sponsors in defining their global investment objectives and developing an implementation plan. Past performance has shown that conventional active management of international equities has resulted in performances that have consistently fallen considerably short of passive benchmark indices over most relevant time periods.

This substantial performance shortfall has been pervasive. It is not simply a result of having been underweighted in Japan, as is frequently claimed by managers. Rather, careful return attribution studies from leading investment consulting firms show that the failure to add value has extended widely across countries. Across the full range of major markets, median stock selection results have fallen short of benchmark indices.

Primarily because of concerns regarding value-added and the consistency achieved by conventional active management, many fund sponsors are increasingly utilizing passive index-matching strategies to implement their international equity diversification programs. Despite the current popularity of passive strategies, arguments for active management approaches should be considered along with those for indexing. Key issues supporting this view are as follows:

1. Emulating a capitalization-weighted index in a passive strategy results in a high weighting currently in a single country that is not necessarily tied to fundamental valuation factors—50 percent in Japan if one indexes relative to the Morgan Stanley Capital International (MSCI) benchmark for Europe, Australia, and the Far East (EAFE) or the Financial Times-Actuaries Europe and Pacific Basin Index. Other countries may also be held at weightings that are not necessarily optimal.
2. Aside from the country weighting issue, the popularity of EAFE-emulation indexing has caused many of the individual stocks in the index to be pushed to price levels at which their fundamental valuation may be unattractive. In this respect, Richard Grinold and John Freeman of BARRA, the investment consulting firm, have charted the returns due solely to MSCI index membership in Japan, showing an advantage of approximately 2.6 percent per year since international indexing accelerated in popularity in the mid-1980s.[6] These trends are unlikely to continue indefinitely when they are contrary to fundamental valuation considerations.
3. Analytical tools for predicting and controlling risk in global equity portfolios have improved immensely in the last several years. These tools now allow a portfolio manager to construct portfolios for clients that can potentially add tangible value with only a modest and predictable risk of deviation from the chosen benchmark index. Specific techniques that can now be employed for risk control include sophisticated, fundamentally oriented risk models and arbitrage pricing theory-based risk models, as well as portfolio optimization.
4. Careful and disciplined managers have seen a dramatic decline in transaction costs in most equity markets since international indexing surged in popularity around 1985. This decline significantly raises the effectiveness and potential value-added of carefully designed and implemented active management strategies.

In evaluating active managers, fund sponsors should focus on the underlying sources of value-added. As noted in a recent commentary from the BARRA organization, the critical sources of added value are *skill* and *breadth*. In this framework, skill represents the correlation of forecasts for country or stock returns with actual subsequently realized returns, and breadth represents the number of assets (markets and securities) covered by those forecasts.

Sponsors should thus ask potential active managers questions such as the following to evaluate their ability to add value and justify management fees:

- Does the manager have convincing empirical evidence of forecasting skill, supported by proof of significant correlations between forecast returns for country markets and individual securities versus actual returns?
- Does the manager employ the most advanced valuation and risk-control techniques possible?
- Does the manager focus on relevant information in portfolio construction and carefully avoid making incidental bets?
- Is the manager applying whatever skills he seems to possess across a sufficiently broad range of markets and securities to enhance the likelihood of success?

Selecting Investment Styles and Methods to Implement Global Investment Objectives

After the fund sponsor has reached the critical decisions regarding global asset allocation goals and the appropriate use of active management versus passive indexing, the next key issue to be resolved is the specific investment approaches to be pursued in global equity management.

Traditionally many fund sponsors in the United States have attempted to achieve a diversification by "style" in selecting domestic equity managers. Some common style categories for domestic managers include value, growth, small-capitalization, and sector rotator.

Defining appropriate benchmarks, or "normal portfolios," for different domestic styles to see whether managers are adding any value can pose certain technical and organizational difficulties. These same issues must also be confronted in the global investment arena. However, much greater complexity arises when we look at global investment styles and methods because of the increased number of variables to be considered across many different markets and currencies.

We will attempt to lay out some possible frameworks for classifying global investment styles and methods. This will be followed by some brief comments regarding which approaches to classification may be most useful and practical for a fund sponsor interested in adding value through a global diversification program.

Geographical Mandates

One obvious way to categorize international managers is by geographical classifications. Table 12.2 lists the most common geographical mandates or investment assignments given to managers.

Table 12.2.   Geographic Classification for International Mandates

Global
• includes U.S.
• typically focuses on established markets

EAFE mandate
• Focuses on markets in MSCI EAFE Index or principal alternatives, such as FT-A or Salomon-Russell indices

Regional

Country-specific

New or emerging markets

A *global* mandate is traditionally defined to include the U.S. equity market and usually Canada, as well as the established markets of Europe and the Pacific Basin. This is one of the broadest assignments which can be given and one in which a manager who has good predictive ability across all major markets can add the most value. The principal drawback of the global mandate is that the fund sponsor may wish to retain control over the asset allocation decision, especially if the international equity diversification program is at an early stage and the non-U.S. allocation is small.

An *EAFE mandate* refers to an assignment to invest in those established markets that make up the Morgan Stanley Capital International Index for Europe, Australia, and the Far East (EAFE) or an alternative benchmark which the fund sponsor may have chosen. Other major index benchmarks for international mandates include the Financial Times-Actuaries Euro-Pacific Index and the Salomon-Russell Europe-Asia Index. These alternatives all now cover approximately the same twenty developed markets.

Typical examples of *regional* assignments for an investment manager would be to invest in Europe only or exclusively in the Pacific Basin, either with or without Japan. A manager with a more narrowly defined role might use a *country-specific* mandate, such as limiting investments to Japan only or the United Kingdom only.

Finally, a distinct category of geographical mandates focuses on *emerging* markets, which are typically not included in the major capitalization-weighted benchmarks such as EAFE, the FT-A indexes, or Salomon-Russell indexes.

A fund sponsor must consider several important issues when assigning geographical mandates to managers. The first is straightforward: The more narrowly the manager's role is defined, the more asset allocation responsibility is shifted to the fund sponsor. If a fund sponsor is not comfortable in calling the shots for geographical allocations on an ongoing

Table 12.3. The Fundamental Law of Active Management

Value-added $= Mc^2$

Where M is the breadth of the strategy, and c is the manager's skill in forecasting exceptional returns.

---

basis or does not have access to the information and disciplined decision-making tools required to do so effectively, less restrictive mandates for managers are probably preferable.

Another major issue in assigning geographical mandates to active international equity managers is the manager's skill in predicting rates of return across different markets. If a manager can document reasonably good predictive ability over a number of markets, then a wide investment mandate will potentially increase the value-added above the benchmark produced by the manager. To illustrate the magnitude of this relationship between value-added and scope of mandate, let us consider what Richard Grinold of the investment consulting firm BARRA calls "the fundamental law of active management" (shown in Table 12.3).[7]

This relationship (which has a certain similarity to another famous formula from physics!) shows that the value an active manager can add for the fund sponsor varies directly with the number of assets or markets from which he or she can choose and is proportional to the square of his or her forecasting ability. The proof of the formula is given in detail in Grinold's article. For our purposes, we can think of M as how often a manager plays (number of times per year) and c as a measure of how well he plays.

One can infer from this formula that the value a manager can potentially add increases as the "playing field" is broadened. Skill in predicting exceptional returns has an even more powerful effect on value-added. Doubling the skill level quadruples the added value. Thus, fund sponsors considering geographical mandates for active managers should seek concrete evidence of a manager's ability to predict above-index returns on a consistent basis within the region or regions of interest.

Style Classifications for International Equity Management

Within geographical assignments, international equity managers can be classified along another axis according to investment style. Some possible style classifications for *active* international equity managers are shown in Table 12.4. As just noted, there are a number of possible ways of looking at or categorizing active managers. Of course, there exists another style category of *passive* management or index-emulation which is a separate area of discussion and which we have touched on.

Table 12.4. Possible Style Classifications for Active International Equity Managers

Top-down country allocator (also country selection)
- Without currency bets
- With active currency bets

Fundamental

Growth

Value

Currency-driven

Derivative strategies

Multi-factor

Top-down country allocator is a distinct and important active style. Country allocation or country selection managers use a top-down valuation process to actively pick country markets in which to invest. Stock selections are often made by matching or tracking the country index for the selected markets.

A country selection approach can be implemented with or without active currency bets. A manager with predictive ability for currency returns might value the individual countries in local currency terms and add active currency management as a separate part of the investment process. Currency is so important as a component of global equity investing that we will address this topic separately.

Another style classification for active international equity management is *fundamental-oriented* managers. These managers typically have a bottom-up orientation and engage in traditional security analysis, considering such variables as balance sheet and income statement ratios.

Growth management is a common style classification from domestic equity management that some have tried to carry over into the international arena. However, growth investing is not as easy to define for foreign equity management, partly because of the complexities and differences in financial accounting across national borders that greatly reduce the usefulness of some earnings growth measures normally used for U.S. stocks.

Value investing internationally is more clear-cut and analogous to the same style in U.S. equity management. Some value measures widely used in the domestic market, such as low price/earnings, low price/book, and low price/sales ratios, are used by major investment consulting firms to define this style category of international equity managers.

Currency-driven is yet another classification that some managers use. Their portfolio actions are driven more by currency predictions than by other factors.

A *derivative strategies* style classification is likely to be encountered more frequently as the breadth and liquidity of foreign stock index futures and options markets increase. Managers in this category use derivative instruments such as futures and options to implement their portfolio decisions at least in part.

Now that we have defined the classifications, we must investigate the more important question of how a fund sponsor can effectively use such a schema to help set up an international equity diversification program.

Return attribution studies by the leading investment consulting firms show that most active international equity managers who have added value have done so through country selection. Clearly, managers in this style classification must be able to document some predictive accuracy for the returns from country markets in order to add value with this strategy.

Fund sponsors can learn much from historical evidence about the fundamental, growth, and value styles. In the domestic market, the evidence shows that a single style has often gone out of favor for extended periods of time. For example, Figure 12.4, based on data from BARRA, shows the pattern of cumulative returns from the growth factor alone in the U.S. market over the period since January 1973. As can be seen by looking at periods when the return line is declining, growth has sometimes been out of favor for periods of several years. For comparison, Figure 12.5 shows a similar analysis of the returns to growth for Japanese equities since January 1977.

To help in evaluating whether value can be employed as a helpful and distinct style classification by fund sponsors, Figure 12.6 and Figure 12.7 show the return patterns from price/earnings and price/book value, two widely used value attributes, since January 1975 in the four largest international equity markets. The exhibits show the differences in annualized returns for the high and low quintiles (equally weighted) based on these attributes for the four markets, rebalanced at the beginning of each year. Figure 12.8 and Figure 12.9, based again on data from BARRA, show the returns from BARRA's composite value factors for the Japanese and U.K. markets, respectively. As can be seen, value measures have been relevant to style classification. For additional information on the historical performance of value measures and other stock return anomalies outside of the United States see Bergstrom, Frashure, and Chisholm.[8]

Another approach to style classifications for international managers is to consider the full range of styles and methods or anomalies that have proven useful in the domestic market. Table 12.5 shows data from a comprehensive study of a large number of these style factors or anomalies in the U.S. stock market done by Jacobs and Levy analyzing the 1978–1986

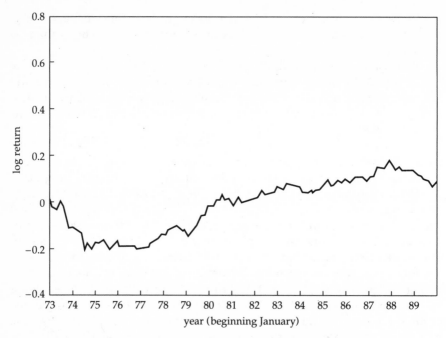

Figure 12.4. Cumulative Growth Factor Returns for Domestic Equities (Source: BARRA)

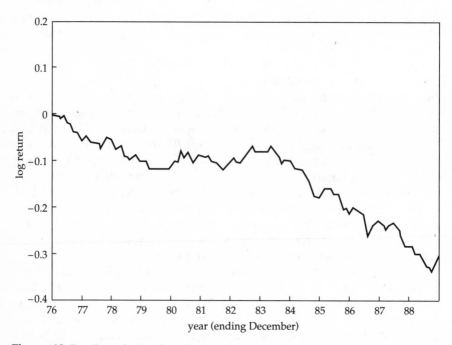

Figure 12.5. Cumulative Growth Factor Returns for Japanese Equities (Source: BARRA)

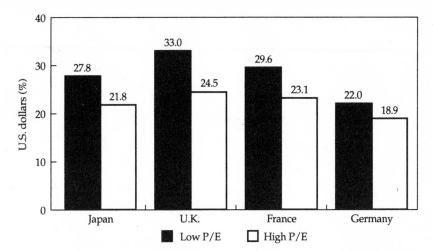

Figure 12.6. Stock Selection: The Low P/E Effect in Four Major Markets, December 31, 1974 to December 31, 1990

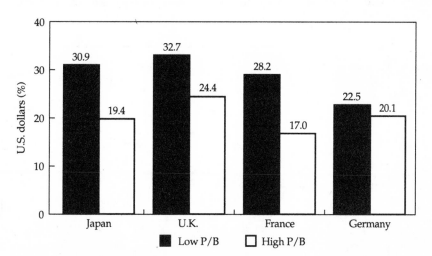

Figure 12.7. Stock Selection: The Low P/B Effect in Four Major Markets, December 31, 1974 to December 31, 1990

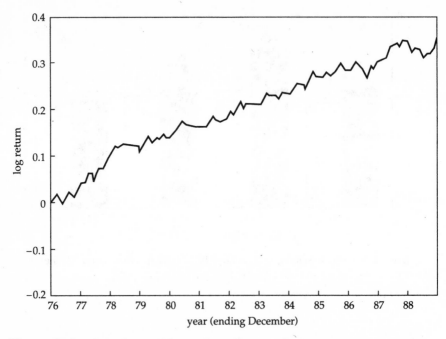

Figure 12.8.   Cumulative Value-to-Price Measure for Japanese Equity Market
(Source: BARRA)

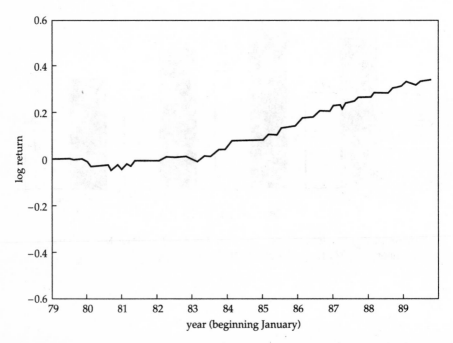

Figure 12.9.   Cumulative Value-to-Price Measure for U.K. Equity Market
(Source: BARRA)

Table 12.5. Style Factors in Domestic Equity Market

Style Factor	Monthly Excess Return (%)	Statistical Significance
Low P/E	0.46	Very High
Small size	0.12	Very High
Analyst neglect	0.10	High
Sales/price	...	Very High
Trend in earnings estimates		
One-month	0.51	Very High
Two-month	0.28	Very High
Three-month	0.19	Very High
Earnings surprise (one-month)	0.48	Very High
Earnings "torpedo"	−0.10	Very High
Return reversal ("oversold" rebound)		
One-month	1.08	Very High
Two-month	0.37	Very High

Source: Bruce I. Jacobs and Kenneth N. Levy, "Disentangling Equity Return Regularities: New Insights and Investment Opportunities," *Financial Analysts Journal* (May–June 1986) p. 25.

period.[9] As can be seen, the style factors that have been useful in U.S. stock selection are diverse. Some are representative of the value style, such as low P/E or sales/price; some are growth-related, such as trends in security analysts' earnings estimates; and some are not easy to classify, such as return reversals or the tendency of stocks which have been "oversold" to subsequently rebound.

This style diversity suggests that a *multi-factor* approach might be a useful and productive way to look at equity managers. Major investment consulting firms now frequently use such classification schemas in working with fund sponsors to establish an effective mix of active investment managers.

Capitalization Size Mandates for International Equity Management

Capitalization size has clearly been a relevant style factor in the domestic equity market. Figure 12.10 illustrates its relevance as a style classification factor to international markets as well from 1975 forward.

At this juncture, logical capitalization style categories for international managers would be large-capitalization, intermediate-capitalization, and small-capitalization. Some managers may integrate small- and intermediate-capitalization into combined strategies; others may concentrate on very small stocks (such as the bottom decile by capitalization size).

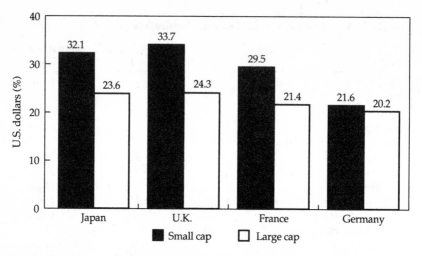

Figure 12.10.   Stock selection: the small-stock effect in four major markets, December 31, 1974 to December 31, 1990

A special case of the small-capitalization investment style would be emerging market managers, which we discussed earlier under geographical mandates. The nature of most companies in these markets renders emerging market managers essentially the same as small-capitalization managers in a specialized sector.

Choice of a Performance Benchmark

The benchmark selected by the fund sponsor for performance measurement is a very important issue in setting global investment objectives, since it will have a major impact on the future pattern of risk and return. As with domestic portfolios, the benchmark is considered the normal portfolio for active managers against which value-added from deviations would typically be measured.

Currently, the most widely used benchmarks for international equity performance measurement are capitalization-weighted indexes of the major world equity markets, such as the Morgan Stanley Capital International EAFE Index; the Salomon-Frank Russell (SFR) Europe-Asia Index; and the Financial Times-Actuaries (FT-A) Index for Europe and the Pacific Basin. Conceptually, the calculation and use of these indexes in international markets is similar to the utilization of a capitalization-weighted index such as the S&P 500 in the U.S. stock market.

In recent years, primarily due to concerns about the valuation level of the Japanese equity market and the relatively high weighting of Japan in the capitalization-weighted benchmarks, alternatives to EAFE, the SFR

Index, and the FT-A Index have been proposed. One of the initial premises motivating the search for additional benchmarks has perhaps been the supposed overvaluation of the Japanese stock market. This issue should be critically examined before moving to alternative benchmarks. Fund sponsors should consider the accounting issues affecting the reported earnings for Japanese companies, as well as the factors bearing on the market capitalization rate (or price/earnings ratio) applied to these earnings.

In addition, it should be recognized that the cross-holdings effect significantly overstates the weight of Japan in capitalization-weighted indexes. The *mochiai* effect, which refers to the cross-holding of stocks by publicly traded companies including financial institutions, is widespread in Japan. Japan, however, is not alone in this practice; significant cross-holdings also occur in Germany and other European equity markets.

Jack McDonald, professor of finance at Stanford University, has published the most complete study of this phenomenon to date.

McDonald estimated that, as of 1987, the double counting from the *mochiai* effect accounts for *at least* 24 percent of Japan's total reported market capitalization.[10] Therefore, we should conservatively multiply the reported Japanese market capitalization of $1,817 billion in the Morgan Stanley EAFE Index (as of June 30, 1990) by 76 percent to get an adjusted market capitalization estimate of $1,381 billion. After this adjustment, the Japanese weight in the MSCI EAFE Index drops significantly to 41 percent from the 48 percent reported recently.

One of the most frequently proposed alternatives to the major capitalization-weighted benchmarks for international equity performance is an index tied to countries' gross domestic products, or GDP weights. While a GDP-weighted index does have the effect of significantly reducing the weighting in Japan, there are valid reasons why a country's GDP weighting is not directly proportional to its equity market capitalization:

- The rate of future growth of a nation's economy and corporate profits has a critical bearing on the capitalization rate (or P/E ratio) applied to the earnings stream of companies in that country. These growth rates will, it is expected, vary considerably, depending on an economy's stage of development, savings rate, prospects for future productivity increases, and many other factors.
- Corporate profitability (the ratio of corporate profits to GDP) varies significantly from country to country.
- Many large firms that account for sizable portions of countries' economic output are not traded in the public equity markets (such as many government-owned telecommunications firms in Europe).
- Financial reporting practices differ markedly across countries, so that reported P/E levels for world equity markets can be misleading unless properly restated to a common set of accounting standards.

- The expected future rates of inflation and real interest rates, which are considerably different across countries, directly affect the capitalization rate of corporate profits.
- Local market volatility or return variability also has a direct impact on the rate at which future corporate earnings are likely to be capitalized.

Should a client wish to pursue a GDP-weighted benchmark, modifying the GDP weights to better reflect countries' future economic growth prospects might result in a superior benchmark. Such a growth-enhanced GDP benchmark has been developed and discussed by Frashure.[11]

It might be useful for a fund sponsor to step back and carefully assess the objectives for an international equity performance benchmark before choosing one. One clear objective would be to help appraise active investment managers' skills in obtaining the best results (in terms of both return and risk) from the opportunity set of investable securities available to them.

Another key objective is tied to the ultimate goal of the fund sponsor, which typically is to maximize long-term real wealth for the ultimate beneficiaries of the fund—retirees in the case of a pension plan, a university or foundation and its resources in the case of an endowment fund, or private individuals within a commingled trust. The fund sponsor may wish to consider articulating an investment objective of a minimal *real* rate of long-term return to be sought by the investment manager along with superior *relative* returns versus the benchmark index selected.

Currency Issues in Setting Global Investment Objectives

From a U.S. fund sponsor's perspective, even though exchange rates have not played a dominant role in producing the long-term higher returns achieved by foreign stocks vis-à-vis domestic equities, they can be an important component of returns over the short- to intermediate-term. Variations in currency exchange rates in individual markets are also a source of return variability.

As they establish their global investment objectives, fund sponsors should consider and probably adopt an explicit policy toward the management of currency risk in their international equity portfolios. Alternatives include accepting this risk in the context of total portfolio variability or adopting a policy of passive or active currency hedging (which in turn could employ a fully hedged or partially hedged benchmark). Unfortunately, the issues confronting fund sponsors in defining such a policy are not clear-cut, and there is no one simple answer that is likely to be appropriate for the individual needs of all fund sponsors. (For an earlier discussion of some of the issues see Bergstrom, et al.[12])

The major considerations to be addressed in developing a reasoned policy on currency issues are the empirical evidence evaluating the effect of different currency risk management approaches on risk and return characteristics of international equity portfolios during the period of floating exchange rates, and the intermediate- and long-term outlook for the U.S. dollar's exchange value.

The Empirical Evidence for Currency Management Approaches

Figure 12.11 shows the results over a recent 12-year time frame (including most of the modern period of floating exchange rates) that would have been achieved from different passive currency hedging strategies applied to an EAFE equity portfolio. The empirical evidence over this period demonstrates that the risk (as expressed by return variability) of an international equity portfolio could have been reduced almost one-fifth by a fully hedged currency position. However, U.S. dollar returns for a fully hedged position were about 1.5 percent per year lower than unhedged returns. It should be noted that these results were highly time-specific. In other words, outcomes, as might be expected, were extremely variable over shorter time intervals, depending on whether a period of U.S. dollar strength or weakness occurred.

These results logically suggest different currency mandates that might be assigned to managers (Table 12.6). An unhedged mandate could be most appropriate if the fund sponsor is not as concerned about shorter- or

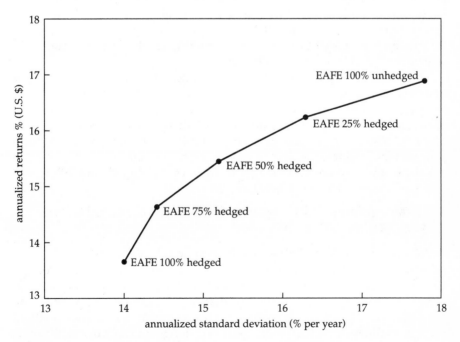

Figure 12.11. MSCI EAFE Index Risk-return Profile, 1977–1990

Table 12.6. Possible Currency Mandates for International Equity Managers

I. No hedge

  • Unhedged benchmark and portfolio

II. Fully or partially hedged

   Passive implementation

  • Portfolio compared to hedged benchmark index

  • May use "basket" approach instead of hedging all currencies

   Active implementation

  • Currency management with positive and negative bets

  • Aggressive or defensive implementation

  • Appropriate only if manager has predictive ability

---

intermediate-term portfolio return variability, or if the long-term outlook for the dollar is considered bearish (that is, the dollar is believed more likely to decline in exchange rate). Another key consideration is the total percentage allocation to international equities that the fund sponsor is planning. Studies by First Chicago and others covering the past ten years have shown that an investment in foreign equities does not benefit significantly from hedging until the international equity allocation exceeds a threshold level of about 25 percent. Below that level, the historical loss in return has offset the reduction in risk.

In addition to passive currency hedging, another possible currency mandate would be, of course, to make active currency bets. Opportunistic hedging could be implemented to aggressively enhance returns or used as a defensive strategy when dollar strength is expected. An active currency management strategy has one critical requirement from the fund sponsor's perspective. As in the case of active country or stock selection decisions, the investment manager must have developed compelling evidence of some consistent predictive ability.

The Intermediate- and Long-term Outlook for the U.S. Dollar's Exchange Value

There will undoubtedly be periods from time to time when the U.S. dollar will rise in exchange value versus a trade-weighted basket of foreign currencies. Some respected economists who specialize in international economies have expounded the case that, in a longer-term view of five to ten years, the U.S. dollar is more likely to be lower in its trade-weighted average exchange rate than it is now. Thus, long-run exchange rate trends could well be a positive enhancement to U.S. dollar-stated returns from international equities over an extended time frame for U.S.-based global fund sponsors.

The basic elements underlying such views on the long-range situation of the dollar are as follows:

- The very large trade deficits accumulated by the United States in the 1980s caused America's debt to the rest of the world to rise to over $700 billion, underscoring the nation's recently acquired status as the world's largest debtor. While some have argued that U.S. direct investment overseas is understated, economists who track the figures closely point out that this is offset by a possibly greater understatement of U.S. external obligations arising from unrecorded capital flows into the country. All incoming capital flows, whether recorded or not, create future obligations to pay interest, dividends, or rent to entities outside the United States of course.

- The United States is continuing to accumulate external debt at a significant pace, as indicated by trade and current account deficits that were recently running at annual rates of close to $100 billion.

- The already existing debt level and trends in external deficits together point to an accumulation of U.S. external obligations approaching $1 trillion by the mid-1990s, unless the trade and current account deficits can be reduced sharply and kept down on a sustained basis.

- Annual debt service for the United States in the mid-1990s could thus run at a rate of $60 billion to $80 billion, depending on the level of interest rates and other key factors at the time and how far the dollar drops in the interim period.

- The United States will have an urgent need by the mid-1990s to service its obligations from ongoing *current* economic transactions with the rest of the world. In other words, the current U.S. trade deficit probably needs to swing to a significant trade surplus. If the trade gap is merely eliminated and the annual interest rate on external debt around the time frame of the mid-1990s (say 8% to 9%) is higher than the *nominal* growth rate in U.S. GNP at the time (say 7% to 8%—2.5% to 3% real and 4.5% to 5% inflation), then the external debt/GNP ratio for the United States would still be rising inexorably. This situation would likely be unsustainable, since foreign holders of U.S. dollar-stated obligations would lose confidence at some point in American economic policy, precipitating a flight from the currency.

- To prevent such a crisis of confidence, or conceivably in reaction to recurrent crises over the next few years, the dollar will apparently have to decline further in exchange value to allow a reduction in the trade imbalance to a sustainable equilibrium level or even to produce a surplus to offset debt service. The evidence so far indicates that the decline in the dollar's exchange rate has not yet had a sufficient impact on the trade imbalance. Thus over the long run, a further secular decline in the exchange value of the dollar seems necessary, a process that would add to long-term returns stated in U.S. dollars from foreign equities for American fund sponsors. However, the dollar will periodically rise in exchange rate even in the context of what may be a long-term downtrend.

Additional Considerations

A policy towards currency risk management should be set by global fund sponsors with the following additional considerations in mind:

- *The confidence level of the fund sponsor or the fund's investment managers in forecasting short- and intermediate-term foreign currency movements versus the U.S. dollar.* If active currency management is to be pursued, the frameworks for predicting exchange rate movements should have strong grounding in economic principles and empirical market behavior, as well as demonstrated sufficient predictive ability to add value in the presence of transaction costs.
- *The role of international equities in the fund sponsor's overall portfolio and the different risk profiles of hedged and unhedged foreign equities (in terms of both return volatilities and correlations with U.S. equities).* If risk diversification is a significant factor in holding international equities, the somewhat higher historical correlation of hedged foreign stocks to the U.S. market (versus an unhedged portfolio) should be considered.
- *The proportion of the fund sponsor's total portfolio represented by international equities and the fund's tolerance of variability in dollar-stated rates of return from the foreign stock allocation.* This represents the impact of portfolio variability in financial terms on the organization. As noted previously, once international equities exceed about 25 percent of total portfolio value, variability due to foreign exchange movements typically becomes more significant.
- *The relevant time horizon of the fund sponsor's analysis of risk-return tradeoffs.*
- *The method of implementation of a hedged or partially hedged approach:*

  - Establishment of an appropriate benchmark index. This should include consideration of possibly dysfunctional effects on equity or bond managers, such as interference with their normal strategy implementations.
  - Implementation by individual managers, either on a discretionary basis (for example, unhedged to 100% hedged) or specified at a fixed, passive policy level (such as 50% hedged at all times).
  - Implementation internally by the fund sponsor, which obviously requires selection of appropriate hedging tools and procedures.
  - Hiring of a separate, specialized, currency overlay manager.
  - Accounting, legal, and administrative considerations related to currency hedging.

To summarize, in setting global investment objectives, currency issues should be addressed explicitly, according to the individual situation of each fund sponsor. The fund sponsor's investment managers and consultants may be able to provide advice on these issues, helping the sponsor to reach an informed policy decision.

A Comprehensive Tactical Approach to Implementing Global Investment Objectives

So far in this chapter, we have focused on setting and implementing global investment objectives from the perspective of U.S.-based fund sponsors, with an emphasis on issues relating to their global equity diversification. But in the future there may be no reason to define the focus so narrowly.

Currently, the commonly accepted global equity indexes contain some twenty major investable equity markets, not including emerging markets. However, the opportunity set of potential liquid capital markets for a global fund sponsor could include a much larger range of investment alternatives. If one were to include not only the major equity markets, but also global bond markets that have adequate liquidity for significant positions, the important world currencies, and cash or short-term investment markets in these same countries, the potential opportunity set of liquid capital markets could contain 40 different asset alternatives.

As noted earlier, the relation between the value-added from active management, the breadth of a strategy, and a manager's predictive ability is that the potential value is a function of the strategy's breadth used and the square of the information coefficient, or predictive accuracy of the investment manager. Thus, by increasing the number of global asset alternatives included in a strategy, the potential value-added can be increased significantly if the manager's ability to predict excess returns is meaningful across the different asset classes. There is increasing evidence that broadly based global tactical asset allocation approaches can be designed and implemented to add significant value for fund sponsors. The merits of such approaches should be considered as the fund sponsor sets global investment objectives.

A well-designed global tactical asset allocation approach might have the following attributes:

- Multiple predictive factors for forecasting asset class returns.
- Forecasting approaches based upon plausible causal relationships.
- Rigorous historical testing with extensive databases.
- Use of findings about U.S. capital markets.
- Forecasting models tailored to individual markets.
- Predictive accuracy well above required levels.

Table 12.7.   Potential Performance Gains from Broadly
Based Global Asset Allocation Framework

Year	Percent Gain	
	MSCI World Index	Global Strategy
1984	4.7	7.3
1985	40.6	38.6
1986	41.9	55.2
1987	16.2	29.9
1988	23.3	26.7
1989	16.6	15.1
1990	−17.0	−6.6
Annual Return	16.4%	22.3%
Standard Deviation	18.8%	17.0%

Design of a global tactical asset allocation approach should be based on the fundamental factors driving asset class returns. Some of the predictive measures which might be considered would include:

• Market valuation levels
• Risk premium measures
• Business/economic cycle data
• Interest rates/monetary policy
• Market sentiment/investor confidence

There is some evidence that a global tactical asset allocation strategy could be designed with the preceding points in mind to yield significant added value, compared to the outcome of an unmanaged global equity benchmark, with risk levels below those of the benchmark. Table 12.7 depicts the results from such a strategy, based on the use of a full array of global asset classes as discussed earlier.

Conclusion

Carefully setting strategic global investment objectives is the most critical issue confronting a major fund sponsor today. Value-added implementation of these objectives and appropriate tactical asset allocation decisions are also crucial in attaining the best long-range results for the fund sponsor. The most advantageous solutions to these issues are individual and should be tailored to the specific requirements of the fund sponsor. Nevertheless, we have suggested some general guidelines that might be helpful to fund sponsors seeking to implement a thoughtful, truly global approach to investing.

Notes

1. Charles D. Ellis, "Setting Investment Objectives," *Investment Manager's Handbook,* Sumner N. Levine, ed. (Homewood, IL: Dow Jones-Irwin, 1980) pp. 61–62.

2. Gary L. Bergstrom, "A New Route to Higher Returns and Lower Risks," *Journal of Portfolio Management* (Fall 1975) pp. 30–38.

3. Gary L. Bergstrom and Ronald D. Frashure, "Setting Investment Policy for Pension Funds," *Sloan Management Review,* Massachusetts Institute of Technology, 18:3 (Spring 1977) pp. 1–16.

4. James A. White, "Pension Funds Speak: Foreign Stocks In, Property Out," *Wall Street Journal* (January 3, 1991) p. C1.

5. John E. Hunter and T. Daniel Coggin, "An Analysis of the Diversification Benefit from International Equity Investment," *Journal of Portfolio Management* (Fall 1990) pp. 33–36.

6. Richard Grinold and John Freeman, "The S&P 500 Anomaly," *Investment Management Review* (May–June 1988) 35–44.

7. Richard C. Grinold, "The Fundamental Law of Active Management," *Journal of Portfolio Management* (Spring 1989) pp. 30–37.

8. Gary L. Bergstrom, Ronald D. Frashure, John R. Chisholm, "Stock Return Anomalies in Non-U.S. Markets," in *Global Portfolios* (Homewood, IL: Dow Jones-Irwin, 1991) pp. 241–253.

9. Bruce I. Jacobs and Kenneth N. Levy, "Disentangling Equity Return Regularities: New Insights and Investment Opportunities," *Financial Analysts Journal,* (May–June 1986) pp. 18–43.

10. Jack McDonald, "The Mochiai Effect: Japanese Corporate Cross-Holdings," *Journal of Portfolio Management* (Fall 1989) pp. 90–94.

11. Ronald D. Frashure, "International Fine-Tuning," *Pensions & Investment Age* (September 9, 1988) p. 27.

12. Gary L. Bergstrom, "International Securities Markets," *Handbook of Financial Markets: Securities, Options and Futures* (Homewood, IL: Dow-Jones-Irwin, 1986) pp. 208–248.

13

Monitoring and Evaluating International Managers

Janice C. Harding
Frank Russell Company
Tacoma, WA

Introduction

As the benefits of international equity investing have become widely known, pension assets invested in this asset class have grown tremendously, from about $8 billion in 1980 to more than $90 billion by the end of 1990. Indications are that the trend will continue. Whether managed externally or internally, actively or indexed, those assets must be invested by someone. The purpose of this chapter is to review the theory, practice, and tools available to help the investor evaluate and monitor international equity managers.

Is International Equity a Different Beast?

> *Where so'er I turn my view,*
> *all is strange yet nothing new.*
>
> *Samuel Johnson*

The decision by a liability-related investor to move beyond U.S. Treasury bills or bonds indicates a willingness to take on risk in order to improve return. In the terminology of modern portfolio theory, the investor wants to move to a higher return position on the efficient frontier. Active fixed income, real estate, U.S. equity, non-U.S. equity, and venture capital are all alternative asset classes that, in the right combinations, can move the investor to any desired point on the efficient frontier, matching the investor's tolerance for risk with the highest expected return portfolio.

What each of the alternative asset classes has in common is that the investor must select one or more managers, active or passive, internal or external, from a universe of managers who are competing for the investor's assets. Once selected, managers must be monitored to assure that they continue to provide the quality product for which they were chosen.

Most investors already have in place such a process for evaluating and monitoring their U.S. equity managers. Is the nature of the international portfolio so different that it requires a different process?

The answer is yes—and no. The investor's existing process of evaluating and monitoring U.S. equity managers can likely form the foundation for the process applied to international portfolio managers. However, the complexities involved with multiple markets and currencies create additional areas of the manager's investment process to explore and evaluate, necessitating the use of special "tools" to monitor the performance and characteristics of the international portfolio.

The Manager Research Process

The purpose of manager research is to identify the more skillful risk takers among a broad universe of managers in a specific investment style. To accomplish this goal, the researcher (hereafter called the investor) must use a number of qualitative and quantitative tools, each designed to explore a specific facet of the complex business of investment management.

It is important to emphasize that manager research is a discovery process and should not be confrontational or antagonistic. The investor's task is to elicit sufficient information to select the best managers to carry out a particular investment strategy. The manager's task, which may at times conflict with that of the investor, is to present his or her investment approach in the best light to win the appointment. Occasionally during the search and selection process, a manager will withdraw from contention, feeling that his or her investment approach is not what the investor is looking for, but that is not typical.

It is critical that the research process discriminate by investment style of the manager, otherwise managers could be compared to the wrong peer group, leading to incorrect conclusions about their skill and their role in an investment strategy. We will discuss investment styles as they pertain to the international arena further in this and the following sections.

International Portfolio Manager Research: The Qualitative Aspects

Although the investment process is ultimately expressed in terms of returns and dollars gained or lost, it is still a people business. Investment decisions are made by people, computer models are built and interpreted by people, and the manager selection decision is often influenced by the "chemistry" between people.

The qualitative side of manager research focuses on those aspects of the investment process that most affect people, their ability to carry out the investment process, and their level of satisfaction with their firm. There is no "right" way for a firm to orient itself on qualitative issues. A small firm with individual ownership will be just the right environment for one professional, while a niche in a big firm will better suit someone else. The goal in qualitative manager research is to understand the individuals involved and how the structure of the firm helps or hinders their individual goals and the investment process.

Following is a discussion of important qualitative aspects of a firm for an investor to consider as part of the evaluation process. There is no formula for scoring responses, but taking them all together, the investor should feel either more or less comfortable about placing assets with the firm.

Organizational Issues

Financial Stability.   Sufficient capitalization or sponsorship is important to assure financial stability through downturns in the markets, when asset-based fee income is reduced.

Ownership.   The international investment community has been experiencing, since the mid-1980s, what the U.S. investment community went through in the 1960s. With the dramatic increase in assets being targeted for the international area, firms have begun to bid up the salaries and perks for experienced international investment professionals. One of the best inducements for attracting talented people is to offer ownership in the firm. The attraction of ownership is so compelling that professionals often leave the "comfort" of larger, more secure organizations to set up firms on their own. While other aspects of a firm—such as salary or a profit sharing plan—might compensate for lack of ownership opportunity, the existence of that opportunity helps to assure continuity of the professional staff.

Salary.   In this area, research generally focuses on (1) compensation relative to industry standards, (2) the role of salary as compensation in the firm versus equity participation, and (3) incentives to reward effort and success.

Opportunities for Advancement.   The tradeoff between large and small firms is particularly evident in the assessment of opportunities for advancement. Small firms may offer participation in the growth of the company, but junior professionals might not have the opportunities for advancement in small firms that they would find in larger companies.

Leadership and Succession.   Leadership roles are difficult to fill in any organization. In investment management shops, it is vital to have a strong leader who balances the role of arbitrator with that of primary decision-maker, understands how to delegate effectively, and grooms a successor to allow for an orderly transition.

Communication. Firms with regional offices face a number of communication problems. When those offices are in different countries, the difficulties are even greater: Time zone differences, cultural differences, mail or transmission problems, and a general lack of camaraderie are all exacerbated by distance. International firms with multiple offices should recognize and have clearly defined methods for dealing with the problems caused by long-distance communication.

Even central, single-location offices can have communication problems. The investor/researcher should look for signs that formal lines of communication are logical and supported by all levels of the organization.

Investment Process Issues

Investment Philosophy. The firm should have a clear and articulated investment philosophy. Its statement about its philosophy should capture its belief about the marketplace and identify its place within the market environment. A firm might, for example, believe that individual markets are efficient and that value can only be added by the country-weighting decision. Another firm might believe that there are inefficiencies within markets that can be exploited through research. In the first case, the investor would expect to see an investment process that indexed or focused on larger capitalization stocks within the countries and focused on country-level factors to guide the weighting decision. In the second case, the investor would expect to find a larger research staff and would explore the staff's research techniques. Regardless of the belief, in either case the investment process should logically support it.

Style Description. What the investor wants to capture here is how the firm describes its investment approach. In the quantitative analysis section, we will discuss how to determine if the firm actually invests the way it has described, but first we want an understanding of the differences between various approaches.

Certain phrases regarding investment approaches have become common among investment managers but may mean different things to different people. Rather than assume a common definition, the investor/researcher should press for a more thorough description of the approach. Some commonly-used terminology:

- *Top down:* This is usually used to describe an approach that focuses on the country level. Top-down managers typically try to add value through the country-weighting decision or through timing between markets. They analyze macroeconomic data (interest rate environment, currency implications, trade balances, inventory data, etc.) to anticipate which countries will have the better performing stock markets over the next period. Top-down managers tend to hold portfolios of larger capitalization stocks to facilitate liquidity and minimize trading costs. While there are significant exceptions, most managers who follow a top-down approach invest portfolios that are neutral to the market in terms of P/E, dividend, and economic sector weights.

- *Bottom up:* Managers who focus on security selection are often described as bottom up. (Here we are concerned only with fundamental or quantitatively assisted managers, not model-driven managers, which are dealt with separately.) Fundamental, bottom-up managers generally have larger research staffs, make frequent company visits, and are conversant on the underlying financials of their stocks. Quantitatively assisted managers use models to support security selection, screening for certain characteristics such as size or P/E. They typically have smaller staffs, rely on databases rather than direct company research, and are more indifferent to the actual names in the portfolio.
- *Price-Driven:* Managers in this group are frequently referred to as *value managers*. While there are differences in how organizations define value, a security's current market price is usually the critical variable. Since no one purports to seek *over*valued securities, the term "value manager" is overused and misleading. "Price-Driven" captures the focus on current price without the emotional overtones of "value."
- *Market-Oriented:* These managers do not evidence a *strong* preference for the types of companies emphasized in Price-Driven or Earnings Growth managers' portfolios. They select from the broad market and may remain market-neutral or display a slight tilt toward one of the other styles. Managers often dislike the Market-Oriented description, fearing that it makes their product sound bland or easily replaced by an index alternative.
- *Earnings Growth:* Managers in this category devote their efforts to identifying companies with above-average Earnings Growth prospects. They are typically more willing to "pay up" for the superior growth rate/profitability they anticipate and often accept lower dividends and pay higher P/E multiples for the securities they hold.
- *Small-Capitalization:* As the name implies, these managers focus on the smaller capitalization end of the market. They may have a style bias to the portfolio as well (i.e., Price-Driven), but the most distinguishing characteristic of their portfolios is the smallness of their holdings.

Accountability for Investment Decisions.   Who in the organization decides how much risk should be taken at what level? Who decides (a) country allocation, (b) currency exposure, (c) which stocks to buy/sell? If accountability is spread among several people, is there an internal process for measuring the impact of decisions at the appropriate level? For example, a firm that describes itself as top down with an Earnings Growth emphasis may have a committee or individual to determine country allocations and country-level managers who invest the allocation they are given. Such a firm should have a way of measuring the impact of the country decision separate from the stock decision.

Style and the International Portfolio Manager. The styles just described were originally developed to make distinctions among U.S. equity managers. Some research firms have further differentiated U.S. managers by sub-styles, trying to refine expectations about the manager's portfolio and correctly identify the universe for appropriate comparison. Are these styles or substyles appropriate for characterizing international portfolio managers?

In an unpublished study by Frank Russell Company, managers' returns were analyzed to determine if there was quantitative support for style groupings similar to those used in the United States. The study concluded that the returns of Price-Driven managers were different than those of other managers, and the difference was statistically significant. However, the quantitative analysis could not differentiate between Market-Oriented and Earnings Growth managers, with only a few exceptions. Furthermore, it was observed that although the coefficient of determination (R^2) of international managers to the Morgan Stanley Capital International (MSCI) Europe, Australia, Far East (EAFE) Index was *lower* than that of U.S. managers to the S&P 500 Index, the correlations *between* international managers were *higher*, on average, than between U.S. managers.

This suggests that style is a less important factor in evaluating international managers than it is in the United States, with the exception of Price-Driven managers. It has been suggested that international managers have relatively short performance histories and that over time more distinguishable styles may emerge, but currently only two broad categories of international styles appear to be useful—Price-Driven and Market/Growth.

The reasons for caring about how a manager describes his or her investment style are twofold. First, from an investment-strategy point of view, the investor with more than one international manager will want to diversify by style, and the manager's self-description will assist in meeting that goal. Second, and more importantly in terms of evaluating the manager, the manager's self-description of style provides the investor with a basis for determining if the investment process is consistent. For example, the typical Price-Driven manager has low turnover. If a manager describes his or her style as Price-Driven but has high turnover, the process may not be consistent with the style. Likewise, a manager who claims to focus on growth opportunities should have a process for measuring the current and expected growth estimates of the companies researched.

International Portfolio Manager Research: The Quantitative Aspects

Regardless of whether managers describe their process as top down, bottom up, Price-Driven, or Earnings Growth, at the end of the day they must buy a portfolio of stocks. The characteristics of that portfolio will tell the investor much about the consistency between the investment philosophy and the investment process. More importantly, if the characteristics of the invested portfolio are consistent over time, the investor has a more reliable basis for diversifying among managers than managers' self-descriptions alone.

Performance-Related Issues

Return.   Of the 46 managers who were in the top half of the Russell Non-U.S. Equity Universe in 1986, only 23 were also in the top half in 1987. Only 10 of those 23 remained in the top half in 1988, five in 1989, and by the end of 1990, only two managers had stayed in the top half of the universe for each of the five years (see Figure 13.1). As every manager's prospectus says, "Past performance is no guarantee of future performance."

An analysis of returns might indicate to the investor those managers to avoid (i.e., the consistent underperformers) but will be of limited use in identifying those firms that could be expected to provide competitive returns in the future.

Risk.   Performance is comprised of two factors, return and risk (standard deviation). While past returns are no guarantee of future returns, past standard deviations are generally reliable forecasts of future risk levels. By reviewing both the return and risk history of managers, the investor can better assess the likely level of volatility and the manager's past ability to compensate for that risk.

Attribution.   The international portfolio manager's return is comprised of at least four elements: currency exposure, country exposure, equity

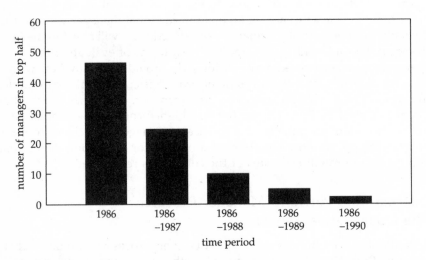

Figure 13.1.   Managers in the Top Half of the Russell Non-U.S. Equity Universe, 1986–1990

selection, and non-equity exposure. Even though the actual return might not be reliable in forecasting future returns, the *source* of the return should be consistent with the manager's investment philosophy. A manager who professes to be top down and macroeconomically oriented, for example, should add value in country selection and use of non-equity investments. A Price-Driven manager would be expected to add value primarily in stock selection and secondarily in country selection.

It is important that the attribution system separate currency from the other contributors to return. Currency introduces noise into the other factors and can lead to incorrect assessments of managers' skills if not analyzed independently. Depending on how the investor views the role of currency (discussed near the end of this chapter), the currency impact might be ignored, seen as a source of return for which the manager should be judged, or managed separately through an overlay program.

Portfolio Characteristics

A pivotal element of manager research is portfolio analysis. In this process, the investor looks at summary statistics and individual holdings for (1) confirmation of the investment process (e.g., the Price-Driven manager has a low P/E or P/B); (2) portfolio concentration levels by categories such as country, currency, and stock, to assess where the risks are taken in the portfolio; and (3) continuity of portfolio strategies (characteristics) over time. To conduct this type of analysis, the investor needs a reliable, broad database and a report creating key summary statistics on the portfolio.

The biggest obstacle to evaluating and monitoring the invested portfolios of international managers has been the lack of reliable data on international stocks. Different reporting requirements and standards, accounting procedures, and lack of a dominant information source have slowed the adaptation to the international environment of some of the "tools" available for analyzing U.S. managers. As the data situation improves, so do the analytical tools available to the investor looking outside the U.S.

Russell's International Equity Profile (IEP) is one analytical tool that has proven useful in monitoring and evaluating the portfolio characteristics of non-U.S. managers. This type of report or analysis begins with stock-level information, company names, and shares held, then accesses a database of company-specific information, including country of issue, economic sector, capitalization, and P/E. Individual stock characteristics are aggregated to totals for each country and for the whole portfolio, and in a multi-manager strategy, for the composite of all managers. Portfolios are compared to the index the investor chooses: MSCI EAFE, Salomon-Russell Broad Market Index Ex-U.S. (BMI), or regional versions of these.

Country Bets. It is important to capture the country allocation of each manager's portfolio, showing the allocation in the investor's base currency, the percent each country represents in the total portfolio, and the percent of the allocation invested in the equity market (an important figure, as most non-U.S. managers have the discretion to hold cash). Some measure of the size of a manager's country allocations relative to the benchmark index will yield insights into the country bets over time. To measure this factor, Russell calculates a country deviation measure using the square of the sum of the squares of the weighting difference between the portfolio and the index (see Table 13.1). In most instances, it approximates the percent of the portfolio invested differently than the index.

A score of 1.00 in Table 13.2 indicates that the portfolio, on average, was neutral to the index in each country in which the manager had invested. A score below 1.00 indicates a smaller capitalization bias relative to the index, while a score above 1.00 indicates that the manager tends to concentrate on larger capitalization stocks than the index.

Economic Sector Bets.   Just as managers may make country bets away from the benchmark allocations, they may likewise make industry bets within countries. The sector deviation measure captures the size of those bets using the same methodology as the country deviation measure (see Table 13.2).

Market Capitalization.   Managers may vary significantly in the market capitalization tiers in which they invest, both at the individual stock level and in the aggregate. Such differences in market capitalization emphasis may account for significant performance differentials over short and long time periods. A measure of the market capitalization distribution for the total portfolio and at the individual country level is helpful in reviewing a manager's capitalization niche.

In this analysis, market-relative data may be particularly useful when making intermarket comparisons, as varying market capitalization across countries distorts the absolute data. In the international markets, capitalization size is a relative concept. What would be a larger company in Italy might be a medium-sized company when compared to a broad index. A medium to smaller Japanese company might look very large compared to the average French company. Consequently, the absolute capitalization size of a portfolio tends to be dominated by the amount invested in the countries with the largest companies (e.g., a measure of how much is in Japan) rather than revealing the manager's capitalization preference within countries. To get around that problem, market capitalization may be measured on a weighted market-relative basis. The investor should also use an adjustment factor to dilute the effect of outliers on average statistics (it only takes a tiny holding in NTT to make the total portfolio look large cap).

Valuation.   Key valuation summary statistics, such as P/E and Price/Book, are vital in reviewing a manager's valuation orientation. Once again, market-relative data is the most useful, as it prevents intermarket valuation variability from clouding the analytical process.

Table 13.1. Russel International Equity Profile: Sample IEP Composite, March 1991

Currency: U.S. Dollar in Millions
Indexes in Billions

Total Portfolio Country	Manager A XYZ Corporation 50.0 Dollar	Tot%	Eq%	Manager B XYZ Corporation 50.0 Dollar	Tot%	Eq%	Manager C XYZ Corporation 50.0 Dollar	Tot%	Eq%	Composite 150.0 Dollar	Tot%	Eq%	MSCI EAFE 3315.3 Dollar	Tot%	Eq%	S-R BMI EX-US 3341.9 Dollar	Tot%	Eq%
Australia	4.1	8.1	99.0	3.8	7.5	89.9	1.1	2.2	98.2	9.0	6.0	95.0	79.5	2.4	100.0	62.0	1.9	100.0
Austria	0.0	0.0	0.0	0.3	0.6	99.9				0.3	0.2	99.6	15.5	0.5	90.3	8.3	0.2	88.6
Belgium	3.2	6.5	96.5	3.2	6.4	94.2				6.4	4.3	95.4	38.8	1.2	100.0	26.1	0.8	100.0
Canada				0.8	1.5	97.9	4.6	9.3	100.0	5.4	3.6	99.7				133.2	4.0	99.7
Chile				0.1	0.2	100.0				0.1	0.1	100.0						
Denmark	0.0	0.0	0.0	0.1	0.1	100.0				0.1	0.1	86.1	24.9	0.8	97.0	22.8	0.7	96.3
Finland				0.6	1.1	67.8				0.6	0.4	67.8	13.2	0.4	99.0	2.0	0.1	93.3
France	5.1	10.3	92.5	3.6	7.3	96.1	0.9	1.8	99.3	9.6	6.4	94.5	179.7	5.4	100.0	143.9	4.3	99.8
Germany	0.0	0.1	0.0	4.3	8.7	91.0	5.3	10.5	90.2	9.6	6.4	90.2	194.9	5.9	97.0	188.4	5.6	95.5
Hong Kong	0.0	0.0	0.0	2.9	5.8	81.0	2.8	5.6	98.9	5.7	3.8	89.7	54.5	1.6	100.0	46.5	1.4	99.9
Hungary				0.1	0.2	100.0				0.1	0.1	100.0						
Ireland				0.2	0.4	97.9				0.2	0.1	97.9				7.2	0.2	100.0
Italy	3.9	7.8	95.4	2.3	4.5	92.1	0.4	0.8	100.0	6.6	4.4	94.5	78.9	2.4	95.8	73.1	2.2	96.7
Japan	25.4	50.8	98.8	3.4	6.8	97.2	14.6	29.3	99.5	43.4	28.9	99.5	1679.5	50.7	100.0	1622.9	48.6	100.0
Luxembourg	0.2	0.3	100.0							0.2	0.1	100.0				0.8	0.0	100.0
Malaysia	0.0	0.1	94.8				1.0	2.0	98.9	1.0	0.7	98.9	15.2	0.5	100.0	16.3	0.5	100.0
Netherlands	0.0	0.0	0.0	4.7	9.5	83.0	1.1	2.1	100.0	5.8	3.9	86.0	88.5	2.7	100.0	93.4	2.8	100.0
New Zealand	0.0	0.0	0.0	1.0	1.9	99.2	1.5	2.9	99.7	2.5	1.7	99.4	6.1	0.2	100.0	5.6	0.2	100.0
Norway	0.0	0.0	0.0	0.1	0.3	99.5				0.1	0.1	89.0	14.6	0.4	100.0	7.8	0.2	100.0
Singapore	0.0	0.1	0.0	0.2	0.4	99.4	1.5	2.9	99.8	1.7	1.1	97.6	25.0	0.8	100.0	19.1	0.6	100.0
South Africa	0.0	0.0	0.0							0.0	0.0	0.0						
Spain	4.3	8.5	90.4	2.6	5.3	99.6	0.1	0.2	100.0	7.0	4.7	94.0	66.0	2.0	100.0	53.3	1.6	100.0
Sweden	0.0	0.0	0.0	0.4	0.8	100.0	1.8	3.6	100.0	2.2	1.5	100.4	57.5	1.7	100.0	29.4	0.9	100.0
Switzerland	0.0	0.0	0.0	1.2	2.4	99.9	2.8	5.6	99.9	4.0	2.7	100.3	106.8	3.2	100.0	78.2	2.3	99.8
United Kingdom	3.7	7.3	133.3	13.3	26.7	97.3	9.8	19.7	99.7	26.8	17.9	103.1	576.2	17.4	100.0	701.4	21.0	100.0
United States	0.1	0.1	0.0	0.8	1.6	0.0	0.7	1.4	0.0	1.6	1.1	0.0						
Country Deviation	17.8			46.6			25.2			23.1			0.0			6.1		

255

Table 13.2.   Russel International Equity Profile: Sample IEP Composite, March 1991

Currency: U.S. Dollar in Millions Indexes in Billions		Manager A XYZ Corporation		Manager B XYZ Corporation	
Total Portfolio		50.0		50.0	
Equity		49.9	99.8%	45.9	91.8%
Cash Equivalents		0.0	0.1	2.5	5.0
Fixed Income		0.0	0.0	0.7	1.3
Other		0.1	0.1	0.9	1.9
Size of Companies —	**No. Holdings/%**				
Large	10.51 & Above	24.0	1.74%	30.0	17.4%
Med/Large	3.30–10.51	58.0	24.9	57.0	30.8
Medium	1.12–3.30	88.0	34.4	57.0	30.6
Med/Small	0.35–1.12	63.0	18.3	28.0	9.7
Small	0.35 & Below	22.0	5.0	22.0	8.1
Unclassified		2.0	0.1	9.0	3.5
Market Cap — $ Wtd Average (Bil)		7.8		6.0	
Market Cap — Nlog (Bil)		3.0		2.9	
Market Cap — Nlog Mkt Ret (% Incl)		0.49	99.6%	0.68	94.5%
Portfolio Characteristics—Val/% Incl					
P/E Ratio Mkt Relative		0.92	92.3%	0.71	82.4%
P/E Ratio (Ex-Negative)		16.0	92.6	8.3	83.6
Dividend Yield		2.6	90.9	4.9	84.3
Economic Sectors—No. Holdings/%					
Technology		10.0	4.1%	11.0	4.5%
Health Care		10.0	3.2	4.0	0.8
Consumer Discretionary		29.0	9.1	17.0	7.5
Consumer Staples		19.0	5.9	6.0	3.2
Integrated Oils		8.0	3.9	7.0	4.6
Other Energy		3.0	0.7	1.0	0.4
Materials and Processing		58.0	18.8	52.0	24.6
Producer Durables		22.0	8.2	12.0	6.1
Autos and Transportation		21.0	7.1	20.0	10.2
Financial Services		42.0	23.9	36.0	17.2
Utilities		16.0	8.8	16.0	10.3
Other		19.0	6.5	21.0	10.7
Stock Concentration					
Sector Deviation		4.8		14.9	
Number of Holdings		257.0		203.0	
Ten Largest Holdings			11.9%		18.0%

Manager C XYZ Corporation		Composite		MSCI EAFE		S-R BMI EX-US	
50.0		150.0		3315.3		3341.9	
48.6	97.2%	144.4	96.2%	3303.8	99.7%	3328.2	99.6%
1.2	2.5	3.8	2.5	0.0	0.0	0.0	0.0
0.1	0.2	0.8	0.5	11.5	0.3	13.4	0.4
0.1	0.1	1.1	0.7	0.0	0.0	0.4	0.0
14.0	21.9%	48.0	18.9%	74.0	41.2%	90.0	34.1%
27.0	33.5	115.0	29.7	216.0	33.4	305.0	28.6
19.0	18.6	144.0	27.9	343.0	19.4	743.0	21.5
18.0	17.2	96.0	15.2	281.0	5.1	1277.0	12.3
8.0	3.4	50.0	5.5	125.0	0.7	745.0	3.0
5.0	5.3	16.0	2.9	9.0	0.2	36.0	0.5
6.7		6.9		13.8		11.8	
3.6		3.2		7.6		5.2	
0.74	85.2%	0.61	93.1%	1.00	99.8%	0.69	95.3%
1.26	83.0%	0.92	86.0%	1.00	96.5%	1.03	91.0%
18.0	91.8	13.0	89.5	18.3	96.5	18.6	94.6
2.4	90.1	3.2	88.5	2.3	96.5	2.5	96.0
5.0	6.9%	20.0	5.1%	40.0	4.9%	146.0	4.3%
8.0	10.9	20.0	5.0	55.0	5.3	130.0	4.3
14.0	13.4	51.0	10.0	141.0	10.9	441.0	11.0
2.0	1.4	24.0	3.5	75.0	6.0	179.0	6.1
0.0	0.0	11.0	2.8	14.0	3.9	32.0	4.0
0.0	0.0	4.0	0.4	17.0	0.5	60.0	0.9
15.0	16.2	110.0	19.8	256.0	16.5	776.0	15.9
8.0	9.7	33.0	8.0	102.0	8.0	310.0	7.8
5.0	4.4	40.0	7.2	81.0	8.1	229.0	7.0
19.0	21.2	81.0	20.8	148.0	24.7	471.0	27.5
5.0	6.1	28.0	8.3	38.0	6.7	102.0	6.0
10.0	9.8	49.0	9.0	81.0	4.4	320.0	5.2
11.7		7.7		0.0		3.5	
91.0		471.0		1048.0		3196.0	
	28.3%		10.4%		13.7%		10.1%

Different conventions for consolidating and reporting earnings and accounting practices make it very difficult to compare P/E ratios across countries. For example, a portfolio with a P/E of 30 would be a very high P/E portfolio in Germany but would represent a low P/E portfolio in Japan. To avoid direct cross-country comparisons the P/E is measured on a weighted market-relative basis. The P/E of the manager's German portfolio is measured against the P/E for the German component of this benchmark index and weighted into the manager's market-relative P/E by his or her weight in Germany. Likewise, each country is measured relative to that country's index until the manager's total portfolio is accounted for.

Portfolio Characteristic Universe Comparisons

Knowledge of the characteristics of a manager's portfolio relative to the benchmark index is important in the evaluation and monitoring process but is even more useful when analyzed relative to other managers' portfolios. Such analysis should focus on key characteristics and allow for both manager- and index-relative comparisons. The resulting information is particularly useful for ensuring adequate diversification when constructing a multi-manager strategy. Even when the investor is selecting a single international manager, it is important to understand any deliberate *and* residual bets contained in the portfolio.

Ideally, such analysis should capture the characteristics of both the current portfolio and the portfolio over time. In monitoring international managers, it is important to identify persistent portfolio characteristics and not base decisions on the portfolio as it looks at a single point in time. Figures 13.2 to 13.5 show how three managers with different investment approaches evidence their portfolio characteristics over time.

Benchmark Selection

A benchmark should be the neutral (i.e., unbiased) representation of the universe of securities from which a rational investor could be expected to select portfolio holdings. It should reflect the passive portfolio alternative, which an active manager must seek to outperform through skill and judgment. Selection of an appropriate benchmark is critical in evaluating international portfolio managers. Benchmark misspecification can lead to dissatisfaction with a manager's performance and frustration of both the manager and the investor.

Since it was established in 1969, the most widely used international benchmark has been the Morgan Stanley Capital International (MSCI) Europe, Australia, Far East (EAFE) Index. It is a sampled index of 1,048 companies in 19 countries. The MSCI EAFE Index has a large capitalization bias relative to virtually all non-U.S. equity managers.

Over the past several years, alternative indexes have been developed. The FT-Actuaries Index is also a sampled index, but it is comprised of significantly more issues, including smaller companies. The Salomon-Russell

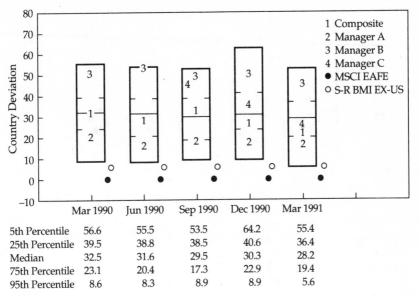

	Mar 1990	Jun 1990	Sep 1990	Dec 1990	Mar 1991
5th Percentile	56.6	55.5	53.5	64.2	55.4
25th Percentile	39.5	38.8	38.5	40.6	36.4
Median	32.5	31.6	29.5	30.3	28.2
75th Percentile	23.1	20.4	17.3	22.9	19.4
95th Percentile	8.6	8.3	8.9	8.9	5.6

Figure 13.2. Non-U.S. Equity Portfolios: Country Deviation, Sample IEP Composite

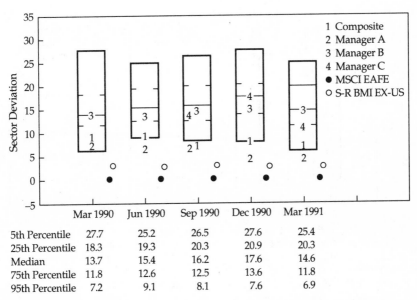

	Mar 1990	Jun 1990	Sep 1990	Dec 1990	Mar 1991
5th Percentile	27.7	25.2	26.5	27.6	25.4
25th Percentile	18.3	19.3	20.3	20.9	20.3
Median	13.7	15.4	16.2	17.6	14.6
75th Percentile	11.8	12.6	12.5	13.6	11.8
95th Percentile	7.2	9.1	8.1	7.6	6.9

Figure 13.3. Non-U.S. Equity Portfolios: Sector Deviation, Sample IEP Composite

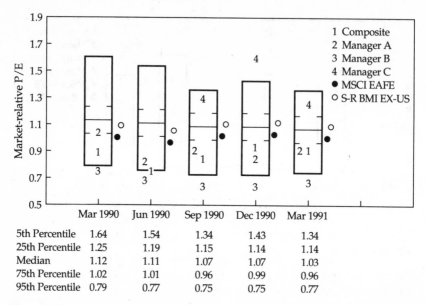

	Mar 1990	Jun 1990	Sep 1990	Dec 1990	Mar 1991
5th Percentile	1.64	1.54	1.34	1.43	1.34
25th Percentile	1.25	1.19	1.15	1.14	1.14
Median	1.12	1.11	1.07	1.07	1.03
75th Percentile	1.02	1.01	0.96	0.99	0.96
95th Percentile	0.79	0.77	0.75	0.75	0.77

Figure 13.4.   Non-U.S. Equity Portfolios: Market-Relative P/E, Sample IEP Composite

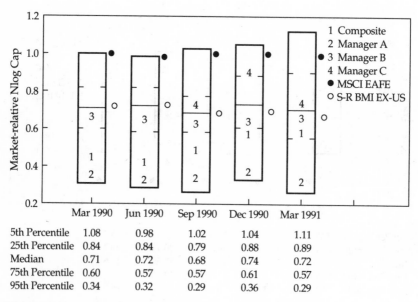

	Mar 1990	Jun 1990	Sep 1990	Dec 1990	Mar 1991
5th Percentile	1.08	0.98	1.02	1.04	1.11
25th Percentile	0.84	0.84	0.79	0.88	0.89
Median	0.71	0.72	0.68	0.74	0.72
75th Percentile	0.60	0.57	0.57	0.61	0.57
95th Percentile	0.34	0.32	0.29	0.36	0.29

Figure 13.5.   Non-U.S. Equity Portfolios: Market-Relative Nlog Cap, Sample IEP Composite

Broad Market Index Ex-US (BMI) is not sampled but includes all companies with available capitalization over US$100 million. Like the FT-A Index, the BMI includes representation of the smaller company sector.

It is beyond the scope of this chapter to examine each of these alternative indexes in detail, but the investor should be aware that there are several alternative benchmarks available. Selection of the benchmark should be determined by the investor's own objectives.

Currency Managers: New Players in the International Arena

Although currency exposure has long been part of international investing, it has only recently begun to get specific attention. It is not uncommon for currency to be a major component of annual gain or loss in an international portfolio, yet it has often been treated as a residual decision by managers.

The role of currency management depends on the individual objectives of each international program. Academics and practitioners generally accept that, over a long time horizon (perhaps more than 20 years), the net return from currency is expected to be zero. However, in the shorter term, the returns to investors holding securities denominated in foreign currencies are composed of two elements: the return of each security in local currency plus the impact of each security's currency exposure. One action investors can take to avoid the uncertainty of that currency impact is hedging (a hedge is an agreement between two parties to exchange currencies at a specified rate and time in the future). Alternatively, the investor may elect to manage currency exposure by hiring an active currency manager. Any decision to employ either a passive hedging program or active currency management should begin with a discussion of objectives.

Active Currency Management

Traditional currency managers have tended to fall into one of two camps: fundamental and technical. Some try to combine elements of both, but one usually predominates. What they have in common is that they attempt to add value by anticipating currency moves and being on the right side of those moves, usually by using the forward contract market. A new style of currency management has recently come on the scene as well. Building on the concepts of portfolio insurance, dynamic currency strategies use forward contracts, futures, or currency options to structure currency exposure such that the portfolio has limited downside risk but participates (albeit with some cost) in any upside movement.

Fundamental Approaches. Fundamental approaches focus on aspects of the economy that appear to most strongly influence currency exchange rates, such as trade balances, current accounts, money supply, and inflation rates. Currency managers expect to add value by correctly forecasting changes in these fundamentals and their affects on exchange rates.

Managers using a fundamental approach tend to have a relatively long time horizon, so that positions in currencies may be taken for six months or longer.

Many of the more traditional investment firms use this fundamental approach in valuing currencies and deciding when to hedge. Most firms also monitor at least some technical information, but it is the fundamental information that drives their decisions.

In evaluating fundamental currency managers, the investor should determine the extent of the resources available to the manager. Fundamental managers require extensive factual information on a number of economic variables. The process for bringing such information together into a cohesive approach to the currency market should be logical, well-articulated, and supported by the organizational structure.

Technical Approaches.   Technical currency managers tend to rely heavily on cycle and momentum analysis. They review charts to discover patterns that may indicate future currency moves and analyze recent currency levels to determine the timing of changes in their exposure. Most technical currency managers have models that generate "signals" to buy or sell a currency. Depending on the sensitivity or aggressiveness of the model, those signals could be as short as intraday or set at levels where they could be expected to occur only several times a year. In general, technical models call for more trading than fundamental approaches.

Technical managers should have sufficient computer support to facilitate the frequent updating of information as markets move throughout the day. In-house programming ability is a plus, as reliance on commercial software should provide no edge relative to others.

Dynamic Currency Approaches.   Managers using dynamic approaches don't attempt to anticipate exchange rate fluctuation. They use currency forward contracts, futures, or options (options are often the preferred instrument) to set a floor on losses while allowing participation in gains. Since the world didn't learn about portfolio insurance programs in general until 1987, the total costs and final payoff can be estimated but not guaranteed.

For all three approaches, the trading desk is critical to the success of the operation. The firm should have sufficient traders to cover the market at all times, and information should flow easily to and from the trading desk.

Monitoring and Evaluating Currency Managers

Monitoring currency managers is particularly difficult because each currency management assignment is unique. The most common use of currency managers, outside the commodity pool area (which is not discussed here), is as an overlay to underlying international equity managers. An investor who has confidence in the country selection and stock selection skills of an international manager, but who is less confident about the

of measuring investment performance. In spite of considerable debate about both the method of measurement and the benchmark upon which it should be based, relative performance has become the accepted method and the S&P 500 Index the accepted benchmark. The periodic relative performance results calculated by the pension consultants demonstrate that over long periods of time active managers have difficulty consistently outperforming the S&P 500 Index. Moreover, the concept of relative performance has gained favor over absolute performance, the previously accepted performance standard. This change to relative performance standards, combined with the fee structure extant for active managers, has led to the creation of indexation as an alternative equity investment strategy. Although considered as a mainstream strategy today, indexation was considered revolutionary when it was first introduced.

With the advent of indexation came the need to execute large numbers of transactions at closing prices. Fortunately for the index vendors, the reduction in trading costs that resulted from the elimination of fixed commissions made it possible to efficiently carry out these orders. Brokers developed trading techniques and systems to manage the execution of a large number of transactions. In the beginning, these index-related transactions generally involved the investment of cash into indexed portfolios. Later, the transactions involved swaps from active portfolios into indexed portfolios, swaps between active portfolios, and investment of cash into active portfolios.

At first, package trades could only be executed in the cash market using manual techniques. However, in the early 1980s the listing of futures on the S&P 500 Index on the Chicago Mercantile Exchange and the development of electronic trading systems on the New York Stock Exchange dramatically changed this situation. The first event greatly expanded the tools and strategies available to the package trader, and the second altered the process by which orders were executed. With the listing of index futures, package traders had, for the first time, a choice of instruments when executing orders. With the creation of electronic trading systems, package traders had efficient systems for executing orders. The success of the S&P 500 Index futures contract has led to the listing of other index derivatives in the United States. These include index options, options on index futures, index warrants, and index participation notes. A list of the more widely traded contracts is presented in Table 14.1.

Package trading in the United States took another step forward in the 1980s with the creation of structured products. Like listed derivatives, these products offered the package trader another avenue for implementing investment decisions. From a practical standpoint, structured products generally include over-the-counter options, synthetic futures, synthetic index funds, bonds with embedded options, swaps, and forwards. For reference to the evolution of package trading in the United States, see Figure 14.1.

Table 14.1.   Chronology of Selected Index Derivatives Listed in the
United States

Date Listed	Contract	Exchange
24 February 1982	Value Line Stock Index futures	Kansas City Board of Trade
21 April 1982	Standard & Poor's 500 Composite Stock Price Index futures	Chicago Mercantile Exchange
6 May 1982	NYSE Composite Index futures	New York Futures Exchange, Inc.
28 January 1983	NYSE Composite Index options on futures	New York Futures Exchange, Inc.
28 January 1983	Standard & Poor's 100 Composite Stock Price Index options on futures	Chicago Mercantile Exchange
11 March 1983	Standard & Poor's 500 Composite Stock Price Index options	Chicago Board Options Exchange
29 April 1983	Major Market Index options	American Stock Exchange
1 July 1983	Standard & Poor's 500 Composite Price Index options	Chicago Board Options Exchange
23 September 1983	NYSE Composite Index options	New York Stock Exchange, Inc.
6 August 1985	Major Market Index futures	Chicago Board of Trade
21 May 1991	Standard & Poor's 500 Composite Stock Price Stock Index growth notes	New York Stock Exchange, Inc.

Evolution of International Package Trading

The evolution of package trading in the United States served as a blueprint
for the evolution of international package trading. Just as the passage of
ERISA and the elimination of fixed commissions marked the beginning of
a new era in domestic investing, the demonstrated benefits of international
diversification and the reduction of barriers to international investing ush-
ered in a new era in international investing. The barrier reductions, which
made international diversification possible, include the reduction or elimination of exchange controls, the reduction or elimination of transaction
taxes, the reduction or elimination of fixed commissions, the admissions
of foreign brokerage firms to domestic equity and commodity exchanges,
the listing of index derivatives (see Table 14.2), and the implementation

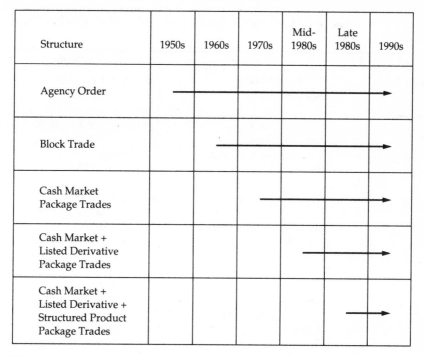

Structure	1950s	1960s	1970s	Mid-1980s	Late 1980s	1990s
Agency Order						
Block Trade						
Cash Market Package Trades						
Cash Market + Listed Derivative Package Trades						
Cash Market + Listed Derivative + Structured Product Package Trades						

Figure 14.1.   Evolution of Package Trading in the United States

of efficient settlement systems. For comparison with the United States, a graphical summary of evolution of international package trading is presented in Figure 14.2.

Uses of International Package Trading

As a general principal, international package trading is used to implement strategic investment decisions efficiently, including investment in, divestiture of, or rebalancing of international index funds, or international quantitative funds; swaps between countries; swaps between economic sectors or industries, either within a country or between countries; allocation shifts between asset classes, either within a country or between countries; allocation shifts between industries, either within a country or between countries; and shifts between managers. In these transactions, one or more of the following complicating issues exist: multiple positions, multiple classes of equities, multiple restrictions on nonresident ownership, multiple market structures, multiple settlement procedures, multiple currencies, multiple trading practices, multiple trading cost structures, and multiple hedging structures. In comparison, the only complicating issues that exist in domestic package trading are multiple positions

Table 14.2.   Chronology of Selected Index Derivatives Listed in the Four Largest Non-U.S. Markets*

Date Listed	Contract	Exchange
3 May 1984	FT-SE 100 Share Index futures	London International Financial Futures Exchange
3 May 1984	FT-SE 100 Share Index options	London Traded Options Market
3 September 1986	Nikkei Stock Average futures	Singapore International Monetary Exchange
10 August 1988	CAC-40 Stock Index futures	Marché à Terme International de France
3 September 1988	Nikkei Stock Average futures	Osaka Securities Exchange
3 September 1988	Tokyo Stock Price Index futures	Tokyo Stock Exchange
9 November 1988	CAC-40 Stock Index options	Marché des Options Nègociables de Paris
12 June 1989	Nikkei Stock Average options	Osaka Securities Exchange
17 August 1989	Option 25 Index options	Nagoya Stock Exchange
20 October 1989	Tokyo Stock Price Index options	Tokyo Stock Exchange
1 February 1990	Euro FT-SE 100 Share Index options	London Traded Options Market
9 November 1990	Swiss Market Index futures	Swiss Options and Financial Futures Exchange
23 November 1990	Deutsche Aktienindex futures	Deutsche Terminboerse

*In addition to index derivatives on country indices, index derivatives on Europe excluding United Kingdom and Europe in its entirety are soon to be listed.

and multiple hedging structures. The package trading approach has the purpose of establishing a trade structure in which these complicating issues are efficiently managed.

Advantages of International Package Trading

International package trading has several advantages over traditional approaches to the execution of international buy and sell orders. These

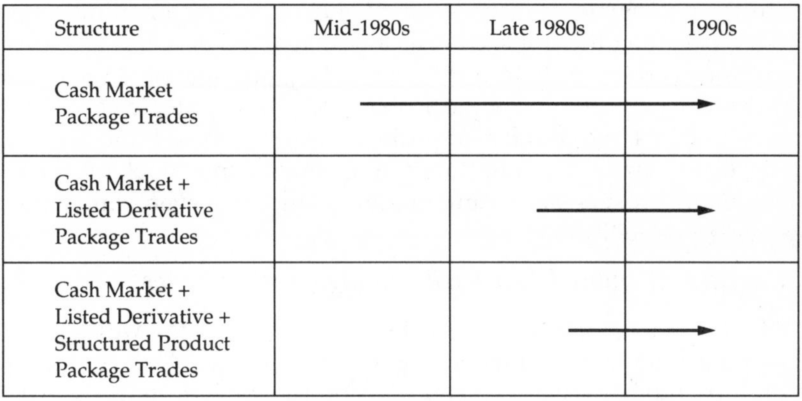

Structure	Mid-1980s	Late 1980s	1990s
Cash Market Package Trades			
Cash Market + Listed Derivative Package Trades			
Cash Market + Listed Derivative + Structured Product Package Trades			

Figure 14.2. Evolution of International Package Trading

advantages include control of position and currency risk, availability of package trading counterparties, availability of index level risk management vehicles, management of transaction costs, and control of operational risk. Let us look at each of these in greater detail.

Control of Position Risk

In a domestic package trade, the number of positions to be executed rarely exceeds 500 and is considerably smaller in general. In an international package trade, however, the number of positions to be executed can exceed 1000. Moreover, if the trade involves the setup or liquidation of an international index fund, as many as 20 markets located in 5 time zones can be involved. Without executing the trade as a package, coordination and control of so many positions is virtually impossible.

Control of Currency Risk

A domestic package trade is conducted in only one currency, while an international package trade involves as many as twenty currencies. Because the purchase of international equities creates both currency and equity risk, it is desirable to coordinate the currency and equity transactions. Although not required, it is common for the same broker to execute the equity trades and the currency trades.

Availability of Package Trading Counterparties

In all trading situations, whether domestic or international, the best execution occurs when a natural counterparty to the trade is found. In the case of international equities, the counterparty is particularly important since international equities generally trade with larger bid-ask spreads and smaller sizes than do U.S. equities. Extending this concept from the stock level to the package level increases the value of finding a natural counterparty. By executing the transaction as a package, the broker is able to look for a counterparty with both a complementary investment strategy and a complementary opinion on a particular stock. If a strategic counterparty can be found, a large number of positions can be crossed and significant cost savings realized. Trading the same positions on a stock-by-stock basis with many brokers significantly reduces, and may even eliminate, this cost-saving possibility.

Availability of Index Level Risk Management Vehicles

In 1984, futures contracts on the FT-SE 100 Share Index were listed on the London International Financial Futures Exchange. This contract was not the first index derivative listed outside the United States, but it did represent the first index derivative covering a major non-U.S. market. Today, index derivatives cover almost every major market of North America, Europe, and the Pacific Basin. Because liquid hedging vehicles now exist on a portfolio level basis, trading international equities as a package permits the use of risk management vehicles which may not exist at an individual stock level. With the idea of hedging in mind, it is useful to look at the correlation among indexes in various countries, particularly between those indexes upon which index derivatives are based and those upon which performance measurement is based. The correlation between the major indexes in the United States is presented in Table 14.3. Because the construction policies for many of these indexes differ significantly, the correlations between them is relatively low, with the exception of the correlation between the S&P 500 and the U.S. components of the two widely recognized global indexes: the Morgan Stanley Capital International Indexes and the FT-Actuaries World Indexes. This is in contrast with the high correlations between the major indexes in each of the four largest capital markets outside the United States presented in Table 14.4. With the exception of the Nikkei Stock Average in Japan, which is a price-weighted index, the indexes upon which index derivatives are based are closely correlated with both the other local indexes for the country and the global indexes.

Management of Transaction Costs

Transaction costs consist of four components: taxes, commissions, market impact, and opportunity costs.

Taxes represent levies imposed by local authorities on securities and commodities transactions. Examples of these include the sales tax of 30 basis points charged to sellers of exchange-traded Japanese equities and the stamp duty of 50 basis points charged to purchasers of exchange-traded U.K. equities. The levies imposed on securities and commodities transactions vary from country to country in both amount and transaction side charged. Such a cost structure differs significantly

Table 14.3.   Correlation Between Major Indexes in the United States

	Value Line	NYSE	S&P 500	OEX	MMI	MSCI	FT-A
Value Line	1.000	–	–	–	–	–	–
NYSE	0.927	1.000	–	–	–	–	–
S&P 500	0.912	0.997	1.000	–	–	–	–
OEX	0.892	0.990	0.993	1.000	–	–	–
MMI	0.834	0.966	0.980	0.984	1.000	–	–
MSCI	0.898	0.996	0.998	0.993	0.978	1.000	–
FT-A	0.915	0.999	0.998	0.991	0.971	0.999	1.000

Value Line: Value Line Stock Index

NYSE: NYSE Composite Index

S&P 500: Standard & Poor's 500 Composite Stock Price Index

OEX: Standard & Poor's 100 Composite Stock Price Index

MMI: Major Market Index

MSCI: Morgan Stanley Capital International Indexes

FT-A: FT-Actuaries World Index

from the one within the United States, where virtually no transfer or sales taxes are imposed on securities or commodities transactions. However, the trend in international markets over the last six years has been to either reduce or eliminate these levies.

Commissions represent the charges made by brokers for their execution services. In the mid-1980s virtually all brokerage commissions outside the United States were based on fixed schedules. Today, most brokerage commissions are negotiable between buyer and seller, with the most notable exception being Japan, where a fixed commission schedule is still in place. Even in Japan, however, there has been a downward revision of the fixed commission schedule.

Market impact refers to the price movement, either above the offer or below the bid, that results from the execution of an order to buy or to sell securities. Because of the relatively wider spreads and smaller sizes at which international securities trade, relative to U.S. securities, this cost must be carefully assessed in deciding on the appropriate transaction structure. Data constraints make market impact the most difficult cost to measure.

Opportunity cost refers to the profit or loss that results from a delay in putting a strategy into place. It is generally calculated by subtracting the actual execution value of the portfolio from the value of the portfolio on the day the strategy is decided. In the case of a purchase transaction, a positive difference represents opportunity cost, meaning the actual

Table 14.4.   Correlation Between Major Indexes for the Four Largest Non-U.S. Markets

Japan

	TOPIX	Nikkei	MSCI	FT-A
TOPIX	1.000	–	–	–
Nikkei	0.967	1.000	–	–
MSCI	0.991	0.949	1.000	–
FT-A	0.995	0.957	0.999	1.000

United Kingdom

	All Share	FT-SE 100	MSCI	FT-A
All Share	1.000	–	–	–
FT-SE 100	0.984	1.000	–	–
MSCI	0.990	0.998	1.000	–
FT-A	0.996	0.993	0.997	1.000

Germany

	FAZ	DAX	MSCI	FT-A
FAZ	1.000	–	–	–
DAX	0.995	1.000	–	–
MSCI	0.999	0.997	1.000	–
FT-A	0.998	0.998	0.998	1.000

France

	CAC	CAC-40	MSCI	FT-A
CAC	1.000	–	–	–
CAC-40	0.967	1.000	–	–
MSCI	0.987	0.990	1.000	–
FT-A	0.989	0.985	0.998	1.000

TOPIX: Tokyo Stock Price Index

Nikkei: Nikkei Stock Average

All Share: FT-SE All Share Index

FT-SE 100: FT-SE 100 Stock Index

FAZ: Frankfurter Allgemeine Zeitung Index

DAX: Deutscher Aktien Index

CAC: CAC General Index

CAC-40: CAC-40 Stock Index

MSCI: Morgan Stanley Capital International Indexes

FT-A: FT-Actuaries World Indexes

purchase value of the portfolio exceeded the benchmark value, while a negative difference represents opportunity profit. In the case of a sell transaction, a positive difference represents opportunity profit and a negative difference represents opportunity cost. Uncertainty of opportunity cost can be eliminated, at a price, through the transaction structuring process. Generally, there is a trade-off between commissions, or spread, and opportunity cost. The greater the opportunity cost transferred to the broker, the greater the commission or spread.

Transaction costs are classified in two ways: those that can be determined before the trade and, therefore, can be included explicitly in the transaction structuring process; and those that are determined after the trade and, therefore, are incorporated in the post-trade analysis and in the transaction structuring process for subsequent trades. Transaction costs can be summarized as follows:

Transaction Cost	Accuracy of Determination	
	Pre-Trade	Post-Trade
Taxes	High	High
Commissions	Low–High	High
Market Impact	Low–Medium	Low–Medium
Opportunity Cost	Not Determinable	High

Taxes are readily determinable since they are established by local authorities and the basis for their calculation is a matter of public record. Commissions, on the other hand, are slightly more complex. In the case of an agency trade, they are known precisely. In the case of other structures, they may be determined only after the trade or they may be bundled with other costs. Market impact is perhaps the most difficult to determine. Before the trade, its determination depends on an estimate of the extent to which a portfolio can be traded within the bid-ask spread or the extent to which index derivatives can be used. After the fact, its determination depends on the selection of a benchmark as well as detailed data on executions. In the international markets, the lack of real-time data in certain markets hampers this process. Finally, opportunity costs by definition cannot be determined before the transaction but can be precisely determined after the fact.

Control of Operational Risk

Operational risk involves issues of clearing, settlement, portfolio administration and cash flow management. Unlike a domestic package trade, in which there is only one clearing and settlement system, one class of equity (with some minor exceptions), and one currency, an international package trade involves multiple clearing and settlement systems, multiple

classes of equity (some of which are wholly or partially restricted to resident ownership), multiple currencies, and complex cash flow issues. For
example, a sale of French equities that settles at the end of a month may
not generate cash flow in time to pay for the purchase of Japanese equities
that settles in three business days. The use of a package trade allows these
issues to be managed in a coordinated way not readily possible when executing individual buy and sell orders. For reference, a comparison of the
clearing and settlement procedures in the world's five largest markets is
presented in Tables 14.5, 14.5A, and 14.5B.

The Transaction-Structuring Process

An international package trade begins with a review of the available investment research and a decision to invest in international equities. The
investment decision is followed by a style allocation decision that is either
passive, quantitative, or active management of the assets or a combination
of these styles. The relatively straightforward passive decision involves the
selection of a benchmark index and an implementation strategy. There are
three generally accepted global indices—the Morgan Stanley Capital International Indices, the FT-Actuaries World Indices, and the Salomon-Russell
Global Indices—and two generally accepted implementation strategies—
full replication and statistical replication using either optimization or sampling. The quantitative decision involves more choices. These include, but
are not limited to, active/passive country selection, active/passive industry
selection, yield tilts, capitalization tilts, and fundamental ratio tilts. The
active decision involves the selection of securities based on balance sheet
and income statement analysis as well as on industry and macroeconomic
factors. A top-down approach, a bottom-up approach, or a combination
of the two can be used. Moreover, the portfolio selected may represent
value stocks or growth stocks. Once the equity mix has been formulated
and the stocks selected, a transaction structure must be determined.

For the purposes of an example, let us assume that the investment
is from cash; therefore, no crossing opportunities exist. The transaction-
structuring process begins with the analysis of five factors and ends with
the selection of a transaction structure. The five factors are the client requirements, portfolio characteristics, the market's condition at the time of
the structuring, the availability of hedging vehicles, and the existence of
coincident transactions. The analyses of client requirements and portfolio
characteristics are supplied by the client. The analyses of market conditions, available hedging vehicles, and coincident transactions are generally
supplied by the broker, although the client may have significant input. Although, in theory, the number of possible structures is unlimited. There
are four widely used structures: agency, incentive agency, risk-disclosed,
and risk-undisclosed. We will analyze the five factors cited above and the
four general transaction structures, and then we will put the two together.

Table 14.5. Clearing and Settlement Procedures in the World's Five Largest Markets

Country	Equities	Futures	Options on Futures	Options
United States	T + 5	T + 1	T + 1	T + 1
Japan	T + 3	T + 2[1] T + 3[2]	N/A	T + 2[1] T + 3[2]
United Kingdom	See Table 14.5A	T + 1	N/A	T + 1
Germany	T + 3	T + 1	N/A	T + 1
France	See Table 14.5B	T + 1	N/A	T + 1

[1] Settlement of initiating transaction.

[2] Settlement of liquidating transaction.

Let us turn to the client's requirements first. Clients generally divide their requirements into two types; risk and administrative efficiency. Risk requirements refer to the question of whether the client wants to retain, share, or transfer risk. In this instance, risk is not defined as the variability of returns around a mean, but rather as the possibility that an absolute loss of principle will occur in a sell transaction or that excessively high prices will be paid in a buy transaction. This risk is generated from two sources: market impact and opportunity costs. The second requirement, administrative efficiency, refers to the time, effort, and actual cost that a client must incur in monitoring a transaction.

Let us look at risk first. Unlike a single stock decision, a decision which results in an international package trade generally takes considerable institutional resources to effect. The process often results in the selection of a particular day for execution, and the determination of the associated portfolio value on that day as the start date for the new strategy. Finally, the strategy selected often requires trading at fixed prices. The degree to which a client needs to lock in prices serves as the basis for risk transfer. The components of risk, market impact, and opportunity cost can be separately analyzed after the transaction but not before. As such, they are often grouped together in setting a transaction structure.

The other client requirement, administrative efficiency, refers to the time, effort, and actual cost that a client must incur in monitoring and settling a transaction. Because there are a substantial number of administrative issues involved in executing an international package trade, the issue of administrative efficiency is exceptionally important. Unlike the United States, where the execution of trades, the reporting of information, and the generation of tickets are all accomplished electronically, trading in the international markets is often a manual process. Moreover, when executing an international package trade,

Table 14.5A. Settlement Schedule for U.K. Equities, 1991

Number	Account letter	New time dealings	First day of dealings	Option declaration day	Last day of dealings	Account day	Number of dealing days if exceptional
1	A	Dec 6	Dec 10	Dec 27	Dec 28	Jan 7 †	13*
2	B	Dec 27	Dec 31	Jan 10	Jan 11	Jan 21	9
3	C	Jan 10	Jan 14	Jan 24	Jan 25	Feb 4	
4	D	Jan 24	Jan 28	Feb 7	Feb 8	Feb 18	
5	E	Feb 7	Feb 11	Feb 21	Feb 22	Mar 4	
6	F	Feb 21	Feb 25	Mar 7	Mar 8	Mar 18	
7	G	Mar 7	Mar 11	Mar 27	Mar 28	Apr 8 †	14*
8	H	Mar 27	Apr 2	Apr 11	Apr 12	Apr 22	9
9	I	Apr 11	Apr 15	Apr 25	Apr 26	May 7 (Tue) †	
10	J	Apr 25	Apr 29	May 16	May 17	May 28 (Tue) †	14*
11	K	May 16	May 20	May 30	May 31	Jun 10	9
12	L	May 30	Jun 3	Jun 13	Jun 14	Jun 24	
13	M	Jun 13	Jun 17	Jun 27	Jun 28	Jul 8	
14	N	Jun 27	Jul 1	Jul 11	Jul 12	Jul 22	
15	O	Jul 11	Jul 15	Jul 25	Jul 26	Aug 5	
16	P	Jul 25	Jul 29	Aug 8	Aug 9	Aug 19	
17	Q	Aug 8	Aug 12	Aug 29	Aug 30	Sep 9	14*
18	R	Aug 29	Sep 2	Sep 12	Sep 13	Sep 23	
19	S	Sep 12	Sep 16	Sep 26	Sep 27	Oct 7	
20	T	Sep 26	Sep 30	Oct 10	Oct 11	Oct 21	
21	U	Oct 10	Oct 14	Oct 24	Oct 25	Nov 4	
22	V	Oct 24	Oct 28	Nov 7	Nov 8	Nov 18	
23	W	Nov 7	Nov 11	Nov 21	Nov 22	Dec 2	
24	X	Nov 21	Nov 25	Dec 5	Dec 6	Dec 16	
1991/92							
1	A	Dec 5	Dec 9	Dec 23 ††	Dec 27	Jan 6 †	13*
2	B	Dec 24	Dec 30	Jan 9	Jan 10	Jan 20	9

* 3-week account.   † nonstandard settlement period.   †† nonstandard option declaration day.

Table 14.5B. Settlement Schedule for French Equities, 1991

Month	Expiration day holder of straddles make their decision to exercise or not	1st day liquidation day end of account	2nd day Carry-over day (first day of new account)	Operation between brokerage firms	Cash Settlement*
January	January 22	January 23	January 24	January 29	January 31
February	February 19	February 20	February 21	February 26	February 28
March	March 19	March 20	March 21	March 26	March 28
April	April 19	April 22	April 23	April 26	April 30
May	May 22	May 23	May 24	May 29	May 31
June	June 20	June 21	June 24	June 28	June 28
July	July 23	July 24	July 25	July 31	July 31
August	August 22	August 23	August 26	August 30	August 30
September	September 20	September 23	September 24	September 30	September 30
October	October 23	October 24	October 25	October 31	October 31
November	November 21	November 22	November 25	November 29	November 29
December	December 20	December 23	December 24	December 31	December 31

* As of June 1, 1991, following the start of the RELIT system, settlement and delivery will be simultaneous.

there are generally as many settlement procedures and currencies as there are countries.

The second element which drives the trade-structuring process is analysis of the portfolio to be traded. Different portfolios have different levels of risk. Generally speaking, the less risky the portfolio, the lower the need to incur the cost of transferring risk from the client to the broker. Many factors go into assessing the risk of a portfolio, including the number of names, value, number of shares, industry concentration, liquidity, spread, and correlation with available hedging vehicles. In the United States, where information is readily available, accurate, and easy to assemble at reasonable cost, portfolios can be accurately analyzed. Since foreign data possess few of these attributes, assessing the risk of an international portfolio requires considerable experience. Taken together, the portfolio characteristics cited should give the broker sufficient insight into the difficulty or ease with which positions can be traded and the degree to which natural counterparties can be found. An example of a typical international package trading inquiry sheet is seen in Table 14.6.

In summary, the requirement to transfer risk, as determined by the client, as well as the potential extent of the risk, as determined by the broker, forms one half of the transaction-structuring equation. The second half is supplied by the market.

The third factor to consider is market condition. Although past market performance cannot be used to predict future short-term market performance, conditions in the market place affect the transaction-structuring decision. For example, if recent volume has been low and spreads have widened, the risk of a two-sided restructuring would be higher than if volume were high and spreads were narrow. Similarly, if markets have traded through recent highs and futures are trading at mispriced levels, the risk of a buy transaction would be higher than if markets were trading within a narrow range and futures were trading at fair value.

The fourth factor is the availability of hedging vehicles. When international package trading started in the mid-1980s this was not an important consideration. However, over the past six years the number of index derivatives listed on non-U.S. markets has expanded dramatically. In addition, these instruments have also become more liquid, such that the index hedging and index-based transaction strategies developed for domestic package trading can now be used for international package trading as well. These strategies include the synthetic index structures, basis trades, swaps, and structured products that have been common in the U.S. market.

The final issue involves coincident transactions. Such transactions may be complementary to, or in conflict with, the planned transaction.

Together, these factors and negotiations with the client should result in the establishment of an optimal transaction. A graphic representation of this process is presented in Figure 14.3.

Let us now turn to the final step in the process of putting together an international package trade—structuring the specific transaction. Before we do this, however, it is necessary to review the general classes of structures. These are agency, incentive agency, risk-disclosed, and risk-undisclosed. The unifying concept behind these structures is the extent to which execution risk is transferred from the client to the broker. At one end of the risk spectrum is the agency structure, at the other is the risk-undisclosed structure. In an agency transaction, all market impact and opportunity costs remain with the client. In essence, the client is renting the broker's skill in finding natural counterparties to the trade, while often using index derivatives, and administering the international operational aspects of the trade. Of all the structures, the agency structure carries the lowest total cost. However, this cost cannot be determined until after the trade has been executed. In an agency structure, no principal positions are taken by the broker without the express permission of the client.

The second structure is an incentive agency trade, in which some of the market impact and opportunity costs are transferred to the broker. This transfer is accomplished by establishing a benchmark against which the executions will be measured and a sharing arrangement under which the de facto performance versus the benchmark will be split in the form of negotiated commissions. The sharing arrangement generally calls for commissions to be increased in the case of profits, with a ceiling representing a multiple of the agency rate, and reduced in the case of losses, with a floor of zero. The benchmark is established through negotiation between broker and client based on an analysis of the five factors previously cited. After the benchmark has been set, the broker executes the orders. As part of the transaction-structuring process, a time limit is generally set for completion of the trade.

The third type of structure is a risk-disclosed trade. In this transaction the names of the stocks in the portfolios to be purchased or sold are disclosed to the broker prior to the time that the risk is transferred. These transactions are generally bid for or offered on a competitive basis. To protect both the winning broker and the client, only the characteristics of the portfolios to be purchased or sold are disclosed at the time competitive bids or offers are solicited. Only the winning broker is shown the actual portfolios to be traded.

As a practical matter, the entire process of competitive tender and portfolio execution generally takes place during one or two trading days. At the end of the first day, the risk is transferred to the broker, who then has the responsibility of selling long positions or covering short positions within the negotiated spread. To the extent that this is accomplished, a profit will result; if not, a loss will result.

For the purpose of establishing portfolio values at which risk is transferred, certain pricing mechanisms have been adopted. These conventions apply not only to risk-disclosed transactions but also to risk-undisclosed

---

Table 14.6.   Sample International Package Trading Inquiry

A. Date of inquiry:
B. Client:
C. Expected date of transaction:
D. Description of transaction:
   1. Number of clients:
   2. Summary of portfolio characteristics:

	Buy	Sell	Total
Names			
Shares			
Value ($ millions)			

   3. Portfolio characteristics by client:

	Client 1	Client 2
Names		
Shares		
Value ($ millions)		

   4. Portfolio risk characteristics:
     a. Benchmark:
     b. Annual tracking error vs. benchmark:
     c. R^2:
     d. Beta:
     e. Yield: Benchmark: _____ Portfolio: _____
     f. Average capitalization: Benchmark: _____ Portfolio: _____
   5. Liquidity analysis:
     a. Details of liquid positions:

Market	Liquidity Percentage	Shares	Value

     b. Analysis of illiquid positions:

	Shares		Value	
	Number	%	Dollars	%
Illiquid positions				
Liquid positions				

(*continued*)

Table 14.6. (*Continued*)

6. Share prices and spread analysis:
   a. Average share price:
   b. Estimated weighted average bid-ask spread:
7. Analysis of stocks by market:

Shares	No.	NYSE	AMEX	PBN	MSE	PCSE	OTC	TSEM	TSE

E. Bidding structure:
   1. Competition:
   2. Type:
   3. Pricing:
F. Trading structure:

G. Settlement of differences:

H. Other issues:

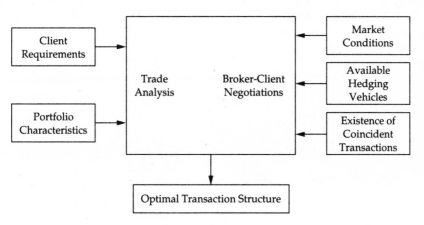

Figure 14.3. The Transaction-Structuring Process

Table 14.7. Generally Accepted Pricing Mechanisms for International Package Trades

Country	Pricing Mechanism
United States	Last sale on the primary market for listed securities and the average of the inside bid-ask spread at 4:00 P.M. for over-the-counter securities.
Japan	Last sale as reported on Quick.
United Kingdom	Mid-point price at 17:00 as reported on TOPIC.
All other major markets	Last sale as reported on Reuters.

transactions. Moreover, they are often used to set the benchmark values for incentive agency programs. These mechanisms are set forth in Table 14.7.

The final type of structure is the risk-undisclosed trade, in which the client only discloses the characteristics of the portfolio to be executed prior to the transfer of risk. For these transactions the client has decided that the cost of transferring risk to the broker is appropriate. Unlike the risk-disclosed structure, the portfolio is disclosed to the winning broker only after the risk has been transferred. However, the winning broker is generally notified that he or she has won prior to the closing of the markets involved. Depending on the characteristics of the portfolio and the availability and pricing of hedging vehicles, the broker will decide whether or not to establish a hedge. A comparison of the risk trade-off for the four structures described above is presented in Figure 14.4.

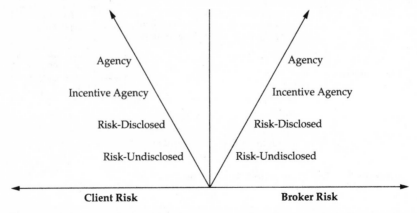

Figure 14.4. Risk Summary of International Package Trading Transaction Structures

Putting the Pieces Together

Finally, let us put these pieces together by comparing the nominal commission, market impact, and opportunity cost for the four transaction structures:

		Transaction Structure		
	Agency	Incentive Agency	Risk-Disclosed	Risk-Undisclosed
Nominal Commission	Low	Low	Low to Medium	High
Market Impact	Indeterminate	Indeterminate	Partly Determinate	Determinate
Opportunity Cost	Indeterminate	Indeterminate	None	Determinate

As is suggested, the various transaction structures contain a trade-off between certainty and cost. The higher the certainty to the client, the greater are the pre-trade determinable costs. There is no right answer as to which transaction should be selected in any given circumstance. Two different clients with the same portfolio may select different structures depending on their desire to maintain, transfer, or share risk. Similarly, two clients with the same risk profile may select different transaction structures based on the current market conditions or coincident transactions. It is the

Table 14.8.   Broker Evaluation Checklist

	Score	
	Highest	Lowest
Portfolio trading	5 . . . 4 . . . 3 . . . 2 . . . 1	
Portfolio hedging	5 . . . 4 . . . 3 . . . 2 . . . 1	
Distribution	5 . . . 4 . . . 3 . . . 2 . . . 1	
Foreign exchange trading	5 . . . 4 . . . 3 . . . 2 . . . 1	
Information management	5 . . . 4 . . . 3 . . . 2 . . . 1	
Clearance and settlement	5 . . . 4 . . . 3 . . . 2 . . . 1	
Post-transaction analysis	5 . . . 4 . . . 3 . . . 2 . . . 1	
Transaction experience	5 . . . 4 . . . 3 . . . 2 . . . 1	

Raw Score: _____   Weighted Score: _____

goal of the broker and the client to develop together the most appropriate structure. It is often necessary for the client to carefully evaluate the ability of the broker to work on his or her behalf. Some suggested credentials are listed in Table 14.8.

As one can appreciate, setting up the potential transaction structure is both an art and a science. It is an art in that the ultimate decision to transact is determined by an individual portfolio manager's utility, timing, and desires. It is a science only to the extent that these rules and procedures can offer some additional structure to that decision-making process.

RESEARCHING GLOBAL INVESTMENTS

Information Sources
for International Investors

Sumner N. Levine
Nortech Associates
Setauket, NY
and
State University of New York
Stony Brook, NY

Information is the raw material for investment research. The present chapter summarizes some of the more widely used information sourcesd available in on-line, compact disk, or published form. The first section discusses information sources which focus on the economic, financial, and political characteristics of countries and regions, while the second section of the chapter gives company and industry sources. A final section briefly summarizes (for the benefit of the uninitiated) some of the major on-line vendors.

One of the problems with the generally available sources discussed below is their lack of timeliness. Often the information is weeks or even months old, and according to the efficient-market gospel, has been discounted by the market. Consequently, other resources such as trade shows, personal contacts, and site visits are often helpful.

The sheer amount of available on-line and published information also presents problems. A malady sometimes called hyperinformation paralysis is not unknown. A suggested remedy is to determine as precisely as possible what information is relevant and where it can best be located before undertaking a search.

Publications and Databases about Countries and Regions

Some of the best sources of current and historical financial information about countries and regions are the publications of international agencies such as the World Bank, the International Monetary Fund (IMF), the

Organization for Economic Cooperation and Development (OECD), and the United Nations. Because of the impressive outpouring of information, both published and machine-readable, it is recommended that current catalogues listing publications be obtained from each of the international agencies. A selection of some of the more helpful publications and machine readable databases follows.

World Bank

Headquarters
  1818 H Street, N.W.
  Washington, DC 20433
  U.S.A.

European Office
  66, avenue d'Iena
  75116 Paris, France

Tokyo Office
  Kokusai Building
  1-1, Marunouchi 3-chome
  Chiyoda-ku, Tokyo 100, Japan

Among the many titles, the author has found the following to be of value:

Emerging Stock Markets Factbook. Published annually by the Capital Markets Department of the International Finance Corporation. Provides time series of fundamental stock market data on the leading securities markets in developing countries.

Trends in Developing Economies. Published annually. Provides detailed tables of economic and financial data for nearly 100 of the member countries of the World Bank, together with textual discussion of problems and issues faced by each country.

International Monetary Fund

International Monetary Fund
  700 19th Street, N.W.
  Washington, DC 20431
  U.S.A.

The main publications of general interest to investment analysts are the following:

International Financial Statistics, published monthly, and the associated *Yearbook*. These provide comprehensive country-by-country data relating to major economic aggregates used in the analysis of economic developments and generally include data on a country's exchange rates, international liquidity, money and banking, interest rates, production, prices, international transactions, government accounts, national accounts, and population growth.

World Economic Outlook. Published twice a year, it offers a comprehensive view of the international economic situation, together with a great deal of data.

Other serial publications include:

Balance of Payment Statistics
Direction of Trade Statistics
Government Finance Yearbook

All of the above are also available in machine-readable form.

Organization for Economic Cooperation and Development (OECD)

France
  OECD Publication Service
  2, rue Andre-Pascal
  75775 Paris Cedex 16, France

Austria-Germany-Switzerland
  OECD Publications and Information Centre
  Schedestrasse-7
  D-W5300 BONN 1, Germany

Japan
  OECD Publications and Information Centre
  Landic Akasaka Building
  2-3-4 Akasaka, Minato-ku
  Tokyo 107, Japan

United Kingdom
  HMS Bookstore
  49 High Holborn
  London WCIV, U.K.

United States of America
  OECD Publications and Information Centre
  2001 L Street, N.W., Suite 700
  Washington, DC 20036-4095 U.S.A.

The focus of OECD information is on the more advanced countries, which include Australia, Austria, Belgium, Canada, Denmark, Finland, France, Germany, Greece, Iceland, Ireland, Italy, Japan, Luxembourg, the Netherlands, Norway, Portugal, Spain, Sweden, Switzerland, Turkey, the United Kingdom, and the United States.

It is evident from this list that the bulk of most international portfolios will be in the securities of the OECD countries.

In addition to publications, much data is also provided in machine-readable form. The following are of particular interest:

OECD Economic Outlook. Surveys the latest economic developments in the OECD area and assesses policies and future prospects, making use of an internationally-consistent set of quantitative forecasts. It includes analysis and projections of real growth, evolution of domestic demand, costs and prices, employment and productivity, unemployment, foreign trade, developments in major groups of non-OECD countries, international financial developments, and much more. It is published twice a year.

Main Economic Indicators. This monthly publication is designed to provide a picture of the most recent changes in the economies of OECD countries and a collection of international statistics on the economic developments affecting the OECD area in the past few years. The indicators selected cover national accounts, industrial production, deliveries, stocks and orders, construction, internal trade, labor, prices, domestic and foreign finance, interest rates, trade and payments, and business surveys.

The OECD Observer. Articles on the most important issues dealt with by OECD: economic growth, labor markets, social policy, demography, education, industry, agriculture, services, energy, financial markets, trade, fiscal policy, public sector, environment, science and technology, multinational enterprises, research and development, regulation, transport, the OECD and developing world. A subscription to the *OECD Observer* also covers *OECD in Figures,* its annual supplement, which accompanies the June/July issue. *OECD in Figures* contains statistics on the member countries drawn from the publications and databases of the organization. Published in pocket format, it offers information on all subjects covered in the *OECD Observer* as well as on a range of others, including national product, national accounts, and money. It is a bimonthly publication.

OECD Economic Surveys. These surveys on economic developments in each of the member countries and Yugoslavia provide a detailed analysis of recent developments in demand, production, employment, prices and wages, conditions in the money and capital markets, and developments in the balance of payments. They include short-term forecasts as well as analyses of economic issues that are of special relevance to the country's economic policies at the time of the annual review. Considerable attention is paid to reviewing the progress of structural reform in the markets for goods and services, labor and capital, as well as in the public sector. About 17 to 19 surveys are published per year.

Financial Market Trends. Provides an assessment of trends and prospects in the international and major domestic financial markets of the OECD area. Each issue includes a comprehensive commentary, statistics, and charts on current developments in international bank lending, Eurobonds, and traditional foreign bond issues, and a review of monetary and financial trends in major OECD member countries. Analyses, statistics, and charts of current developments are regularly supplemented by special features dealing with financial matters of topical interest or with developments over the longer term in specific sectors of the international market or major domestic financial markets. It is published three times per year.

United Nations

United Nations
  Sales Dept. 401
  New York, NY 10017
  USA

United Nations
  Sales Section
  Palais des Nations
  1211 Geneva 10 Switzerland

The U.N. publishes a large number of reports, many of which are available in machine-readable form. A sampling of relevant publications are described below.

Statistical Yearbook. Statistical data for more than 270 countries/territories on population, agriculture, manufacturing, construction, transport, commodity import/export trade, balance of payments, national income, education, and culture. It is presented on an internationally comparable basis using overall world summary tables and data by country.

Economic Bulletin for Asia and the Pacific. Articles on topics such as development planning, energy supply, trade between developing countries and socialist countries of Eastern Europe, economics and sociology of alternative energy sources, and individual country reports on economic performance and prospects.

Economic Survey of Europe. Provides analysis and insight with an annual, thorough, review of the European economy, including an in-depth, and up-to-date study of developments in Eastern Europe and the USSR.

Economic Survey of Latin America and the Caribbean. This in-depth survey covers both a regional overview and individual country analysis of economic conditions, and quantifies trends in production and employment, supply and demand for goods and services, prices and wages, external debt and inflation.

U.S. Government Sources

U.S. State Department country desk officers and Department of Commerce International Trade Administration desk officers are sometimes very helpful in providing political background and commercial information. Consult the agency phone directories to contact the right desk officer. Commerce provides several informative publications:

Business America: The Magazine of International Trade. A biweekly publication of ITA designed especially for American exporters who want to grow and American businesses ready to enter the world of exporting. It contains country-by-country marketing reports, economic analyses, worldwide trade leads, advance notice of planned exhibitions of U.S. products worldwide, and success stories of selected American business firms in the field of exporting.

Foreign Economic Trends (FET). Present business and economic developments and the latest economic indicators for almost 100 countries. They are prepared on an annual or semiannual basis by the U.S. Foreign Service. More than 100 reports are issued each year.

Overseas Business Reports (OBR). Current and detailed marketing information, trade outlooks, statistics, regulations, and marketing profiles for most countries.

The Central Intelligence Agency puts out the annual *World Fact Book*, which provides succinct background sketches on over 330 countries. For agency phone directories and other publications, contact:

Superintendent of Documents
 U.S. Government Printing Office
 Washington, DC 20402

Regional Development Organizations

Regional organizations publish a great deal of information often of value to the analyst. Here are some important organizations and samples of their publications. Obtaining publication catalogues put out by these organizations is well worthwhile.

Asian Development Bank

Asian Development Bank
  PO Box 789
  1099 Manila
  Philippines

The Bank is an organization of 47 member countries that promotes economic progress in the region. Publications include:

Asian Development Bank Review. This biannual provides in-depth studies of the region.
Key Indicators of Developing Member Countries. Provides statistics and an annual summary of the area.

European Community (EC)

Office for Official Publications of the European   UNIPUB
  Communities   4611-F Assembly Drive
  2, rue Mercier   Lanham, MD 20706 U.S.A.
  L-2985 Luxembourg

The European Community has offices in many major cities throughout the world. Among the many publications are:

The Statistical Year Book. Annual.
Eurostatistics. Monthly.
Bulletin of the European Communities. A monthly covering political, financial, social developments.

Private Sector Organizations

Several private companies with international affiliations publish reports and newsletters that assess the current business and political situation in various countries.

Business International

International Reports
  215 Park Avenue South
  New York, NY 10002 U.S.A.

This organization is the U.S. distributor of the reports issued by the London-based Economist Intelligence Unit. Publications include:

International Country Risk Guide (ICRG). Identifies the countries where significant changes are occurring and tells what to look for in new legislation, interest rates, debt restructuring, exchange rates, and other factors that affect risk in six regions—Western Europe, Latin America, the Caribbean, Asia and the Pacific, the Middle East and Africa, and the centrally planned economies. Each country is rated separately by political, economic, and financial risk; these ratings are then combined to form a single composite rating for each country.

International Reports. A weekly publication that provides in-depth economic, financial, and political coverage for countries throughout the world.

Country Reports. Evaluate growth prospects for over 165 countries around the world. Every quarter *Country Reports* provides business-oriented analyses of the latest economic and political indicators. In addition to four *Country Reports* for each nation, subscribers receive an annual *Country Profile*, providing a summary of the country's politics, society, economy, and industry. Reports are sold for individual countries.

Frost and Sullivan

Frost and Sullivan
106 Fulton Street
New York, NY 10038 U.S.A.

This organization publishes a number of in-depth reports focusing on international technology developments. Frost and Sullivan provides a *Political Risk Letter*, which discusses political and economic trends affecting business and investments. The letter is also available on-line through Newsnet.

Public Affairs Information Service (PAIS)

Public Affairs Information Service
521 W. 43rd Street
New York, NY 10036 U.S.A.

PAIS indexes articles on business, economics, and social issues appearing in hundreds of periodicals and other publications. The major publications are the *PAIS Bulletin*, issued twice monthly, which emphasizes English language articles; and the *PAIS Foreign Language Index*, published quarterly. The latter provides English language references to publications in foreign languages. PAIS publications are also available on-line through Dialog.

Predicasts Inc.

Predicasts Inc.
  200 University Research Circle
  1101 Cedar Avenue
  Cleveland, OH 44106 U.S.A.

Predicasts is one of the world's largest database and indexing organizations. The *Predicasts F & S Index International* provides country, company, and industry information on non-U.S. countries and organizations. Many of the Predicasts' databases are available on-line via Dialog as discussed in the On-line Database section of this chapter.

Leading Financial Newspapers

To keep current with developments at the world's major financial centers—New York, London, Tokyo, and Frankfurt—the following English language publications are very helpful:

Wall Street Journal
  200 Liberty Street
  New York, NY 10281 U.S.A.

The paper also publishes Asian and European editions.

Financial Times
  102 Clerkenwell Road
  London ECIM 55A England

In the U.S., the *Financial Times* is located at:

14 East 60th Street
New York, NY 10022 U.S.A.

The *Financial Times* has offices in other major financial centers.

Nihon Keizai Shimbun Inc.
  9-5 Otemachi 1-chome
  Chiyoda-ku
  Tokyo 100-66 Japan

The *Nikkei Weekly* is the English language publication of this major Japanese news service. To subscribe contact:

Nihon Keizai Shimbun America, Inc.
  1221 Avenue of the Americas
  New York, NY 10020 U.S.A.

Frankfurter Allgemeine Zeitung
Hellerhofstrasse 2-4, D-6000
Frankfurt-am-Main
Germany

German Brief is an English language weekly published by the same newspaper. To subscribe contact:

European Business Publications Inc.
P.O. Box 891
Darien, CT 06820 U.S.A.

Foreign National Financial Press

Reading the local financial press is a must for the analyst specializing in a specific region or country. Following are listed some of the leading financial newspapers and other periodicals listed by country. Unless stated otherwise, the indicated item is in the local language.

AUSTRALIA
Australian Financial Times
P.O. Box 506
Sidney GP02001, Australia

AUSTRIA
Weiner Zeitung (daily)
Osterreichisches Staatsdruckerei,
Rennweg 16
A-1037 Vienna, Austria

BELGIUM
L'Echo de la Bourse (daily)
131 Rue de Birmingham
B-1070 Brussels, Belgium

BRAZIL
Gazeta Mercantil (daily)
Rue Major Quendinho 90
01.050 San Paulo, Brazil

CANADA
The Financial Post (daily)
333 King Street
Toronto, Ontario M5A4N2
Canada

DENMARK
Finanstidende (weekly)
Store Kannikestraede 16, DK-1169
Copenhagen, Denmark

FRANCE
Les Echos (daily)
37 Avenue des Champs Elysées
F-75381 Paris Cedex 8, France

GERMANY
Handelsblatt (daily)
Kreuzstrasse 21, Postfach 1102
D-4000 Dusseldorf, Germany

INDONESIA
The Indonesian Times (daily, in English)
Jalan Letjen Parman Kav. 72, Box 224,
Slipi
Jakarta, Indonesia

ITALY
Il Globo (daily)
Piazza Indipendenza 11/B, 00185
Rome, Italy

JAPAN
Nihon Keizai Shimbun, Inc. (daily)
9-5 Otemachi 1-chome, Chiyoda-ku
Tokyo 100-66, Japan

MALAYSIA
Malaysian Business (bimonthly, in English)
22 Jolan Liku, 59100
Kuala, Malaysia

MEXICO
El Financiero
Lago Bolsena 176
Mexico D.F. 11320

THE NETHERLANDS
Economische Dagblad (daily)
Koopmansstraat 9
2288 BC Rijkswijk, The Netherlands

NORWAY
Dagbladet (daily)
Akersgata 49
Oslo 1, Norway

PHILIPPINES
Business Day (weekdays, in English)
807 Epifanio de los Santos Avenue
Quezon City, Philippines

PORTUGAL
O Comércio do Porto (daily)
Avenida dos Aliados 107
4000 Oporto, Portugal

SINGAPORE
Singapore Business (monthly, in English)
Times Center
1 New Industrial Road
Singapore

SOUTH KOREA
Korea News Review (weekly)
C.P.O. Box 2147
Seoul, South Korea

SPAIN
Actualidad Economica (weekly)
Punto Editorial, S.A.
Recoletos 1, 7
Madrid 1, Spain

SWEDEN
Svenska Dagbladet (daily)
Ralambsvagen 7
S-10517 Stockholm, Sweden

SWITZERLAND
Neue Zurcher Zeitung (daily)
Falkenstrasse 11
Postfach 215
CH-8021 Zurich, Switzerland

TAIWAN
China Post (daily, in English)
8 Fu Shun Street
Taipei, Taiwan

THAILAND
Bangkok Post (daily, in English)
U-Chuliang Building
968 Rama IV Road
Bangkok 10500, Thailand

UNITED KINGDOM
Financial Times (daily)
102 Clerkenwell Road
London ECIM 55A, U.K.

in the U.S.:
14 East 60th Street
New York, NY 10022 U.S.A.

Regional Directories

Unless otherwise indicated, the following are available from:

Gale Research Inc.
835 Penobscot Building
Detroit, MI 48226 U.S.A.

Directory of European Industrial and Trade Associations. Covers about 6,000 industrial and trade associations, including national associations for all countries of Europe (except Great Britain and Ireland) and appropriate regional associations of national significance.

Directory of British Associations and Associations in Ireland. Covers 7,000 national organizations based in England, Wales, Scotland, and Ireland.

Whitakers Almanack. Detailed reporting of current events and social, political, and economic developments in Great Britain. Published by J. Whitaker & Sons, London.

Directory of European Professional and Learned Societies. This directory provides thorough coverage of European-based professional and learned associations, together with scientific and technical societies.

European Directory of Marketing Information Sources. Sources of marketing information for European countries, including libraries, research companies, government publications, trade associations, and journals, with details on the type of information they offer.

The European Directory of Consumer Goods Manufacturers. This practical directory gives you access to key information on 6,000 European-based manufacturers of consumer goods.

Major Financial Institutions of Continental Europe. Provides essential data on more than 1,000 leading financial institutions in the countries of Western Europe. Banks, investment firms, insurance/leasing companies, and other institutions are profiled.

European Technical Consultancies. European-based technical consulting services ranging from market surveys to product development and project management. Information on 800 firms and organizations offering services to industries ranging from aerospace to telecommunications.

European Research Centres. Profiles more than 17,000 scientific, technological, agricultural, and medical laboratories and departments in 31 major countries of eastern and western Europe.

European Sources of Scientific and Technical Information. Covering a wide range of scientific and technical fields for both western and eastern Europe, this directory includes information on patents and standards offices, national offices of information, and scientific and technical organizations all arranged by country under 22 science subjects.

The Europa World Year Book. Revised annually, contains background information, statistical data, and directories of businesses and institutions for every country. Each entry contains comprehensive data on the country's political, diplomatic, and judicial systems. A separate section provides full descriptions of 1,500 international organizations. Published by Europa Publications, London.

Canadian Almanac and Directory. Contains four sections: Canadian Directory, Almanac Information, Canadian Information and Statistics, and Canadian Law Firms and Lawyers. Directory sections provide full names and addresses of a wide range of social, political, and economic organizations and companies. Published by Almanac and Directory Publishing Co., Toronto, Canada.

Japan Trade Directory. Furnishes the latest available information on 2,900 Japanese companies that import or export products and services. Detailed company profiles provide financial data, corporate structure, full information on trade contacts, and the company's interests in importing and exporting. Published by Japanese External Trade Organization (JETRO).

Complete Directory of Japan. Covers the political, economic, commercial, educational, and cultural spheres of Japanese society. Published by the International Culture Institute.

Far East and Australasia. This standard reference gives expert, informed essays on topics of concern to the region as a whole, details on international and regional organizations active there, and surveys and directories for each nation and territory. Signed articles cover the physical and social geography, recent history, and economy for each country. Published by Europa Publications, London.

Pacific Research Centres. Provides details on 3,500 research centers located in Japan, the People's Republic of China, and other countries of the western Pacific region.

General References

International Accounting Summaries. Authored by the firm of Coopers & Lybrand, it provides an in-depth comparison of accounting practices in 24 major countries. Published annually by:

John Wiley
605 Third Avenue
New York, NY 10157 U.S.A.

The Handbook of World Stock and Commodity Exchanges. This comprehensive volume provides specifics on trading practices for most worldwide exchanges. Topics included are listings of principal offices, history, structure, trading hours, number of listed shares, settling and clearing procedures, commission rates, taxation, investor protection, and much more. Available from:

Basil Blackwell Ltd.
108 Cowley Road
Oxford OX 41 JF
United Kingdom

Basil Blackwell, Inc.
3 Cambridge Center
Cambridge, MA 02142 U.S.A.

Telephone directories of foreign cities can be ordered from:

World Wide Directories
P.O. Box 5977
St. Louis, MO 63134 U.S.A.

Foreign Trade and Professional Directories

The following are available through:

Gale Research Inc.
835 Penobscot Building
Detroit, MI 48225-9948 U.S.A.

International Directories in Print (IDIP). Gives detailed information that is useful for global marketing and research projects. This directory covers a wide range of directories from over 100 countries. These directories are excellent sources of information and lists for numerous worldwide groups and industries.

Directories in Print. This directory is a source of information on nationally significant directories published in the United States and Canada.

Newsletters in Print. This reference provides detailed entries for over 10,000 sources of authoritative information on a wide range of high-interest topics.

International Directory of Business Information Agencies and Services. This directory of agencies and services covers live sources of business information located outside the United States. Covering 23 countries, the directory is arranged by country, and within each country by type of agency or service. Included are names, addresses, telephone/telex numbers, contact persons, and descriptions for more than 3,000 chambers of commerce, foreign trade-promoting organizations, government organizations, independent organizations, research organizations, sources of statistical information, and business libraries. Published by Europa.

Computer-Readable Databases. Descriptions of more than 5,000 publicly available databases, including on-line and transactional databases, CD-ROM databases, electronic bulletin boards, off-line files available for batch processing, and databases on magnetic tape and diskette.

Information Industry Directory. This reference enables users to contact nearly 4,600 producers and vendors of electronic information and related services.

Encyclopedia of Associations. Features detailed entries describing over 22,000 active associations, organizations, clubs, and other nonprofit membership groups in virtually every field of human endeavor.

International Organizations. Lists over 10,300 international organizations, including over 4,000 national organizations of countries other than the United States. This work gives organizations with international memberships, binational organizations, and national organizations in more than 180 countries of the world. Also available on CD-ROM and on-line via Dialog.

International Research Centers Directory. Over 6,600 entries provide details on research facilities of all types, including government, university, and private research firms, in 145 countries (excluding the United States).

Gale International Directory of Publications. Country-by-country coverage of more than 4,800 newspapers and general interest magazines published in over 100 countries, gives access to periodicals internationally.

Trade Shows Worldwide. Contains detailed entries for more than 5,000 scheduled exhibitions, trade shows, association conventions, and similar events. Approximately one-third of the listed shows are based outside the United States and Canada.

Directory of Special Libraries and Information Centers. Gives details on the specialized collections of books, periodicals, databases, and other information sources maintained. In addition to coverage of the United States and Canada, there are listings of major special libraries in over 80 countries.

Standard Periodical Directory. Includes 65,000 periodicals published in the United States and Canada. Listings of periodicals published worldwide, including newsletters, magazines, journals, and conference reports. Includes publisher, address and telephone number, periodical title, subtitle, alternate and former title, subscription price, circulation, abstracts, indexes, and book reviews. Available from:

R.R. Bowker
  245 West 17 Street
  New York, NY 10011 U.S.A.

Trade Directories of the World. Contact:

Croner Publications Inc.
  34 Jericho Turnpike
  Jericho, NY 11753 U.S.A.

Company Information Sources: Computer Readable Databases

Listed below are several of the more helpful on-line and compact disk databases that provide information about companies and industries. Often these databases are also available on CD-ROM and in published format.

Disclosure

Disclosure, Inc.
  5161 River Road
  Bethesda, MD 20826 U.S.A.

Available on-line, compact disks, and in printed form, Disclosure data provides access to the financial reports of several thousand international companies. Disclosure recently teamed up with Worldscope (see below) to expand its services. Disclosure is available on Dow Jones News/Retrieval and Dialog. A sample printout is shown in Exhibit 15.1.

Extel/Global Vantage

Standard & Poor's Compustat Services, Inc.
  1221 Avenue of the Americas
  New York, NY 10020 U.S.A.

Extel Financial Limited
  Fitzroy House
  13-17 Epworth Street
  London EC2A 4DL
  United Kingdom

A product of London-based Extel and Standard and Poor's, the database provides financial information on international companies. Data is derived from annual shareholder reports, 10K reports for U.S. companies, stock exchanges, and direct contacts. The database consists of three files:

Financial File
- Over 200 data items from shareholders' reports and other company filings.
- Historical data (not restated)
- Six-year history at product introduction
- Income statement models reflecting intracountry presentation
- Balance Sheet
- Flow of funds statements where appropriate
- Supplementary income statement and balance sheet items
- Company, country, period, and currency identifiers
- Key links to other files within the database and to other SPCS and Extel Financial databases outside this product

Issue File
- Monthly prices, dividends, shares traded, annual earnings per share (EPS), shares used to calculate EPS, shares outstanding, and issued capital
- Six-year history at product introduction
- High, low, and close prices from primary local exchanges
- Common stock issues
- Index markers on appropriate issues
- Issue, country, period, exchange, index, and currency identifiers
- Key links to other files within the database and to other SPCS and Extel Financial databases outside this product

Currency File
- Translation rate at month end
- Monthly average translation rate based on daily rates
- 12-month moving average translation rate
- Complete translation rate matrix for 16 designated currencies
- Translation rate matrix relative to the U.S. dollar, British pound, Japanese yen, and Swiss franc for an additional 39 currencies
- Six-year history at product introduction

Extel also publishes *Card Service*, which provides detailed financial information and news items about thousands of international companies.

In addition, Extel's on-line international bond service, EX BOND, provides information on thousands of international bonds.

Institutional Brokers Estimate System (I/B/E/S)

Lynch, Jones, and Ryan
345 Hudson Street
New York, NY 10014 U.S.A.

I/B/E/S is a financial information service that provides worldwide earnings forecast information for nearly all publicly traded corporations followed by security analysts. This database is a comprehensive source of annual earnings-per-share projections, quarterly and long-term growth rate forecasts.

EPS estimate data is obtained from thousands of analysts working for the world's investment firms who voluntarily contribute their estimates to I/B/E/S. The items included in a representative report are shown in Exhibit 15.2.

Investext

Thomson Financial Networks
  11 Farnsworth Street
  Boston, MA 02210 U.S.A.

Investext provides research reports produced by security analysts at leading investment banks, brokerage houses, and other research firms stationed throughout the world. This service is available on Dow Jones News/Retrieval, Dialog, and other vendors. Searches may be done by company, industry, or product type. Investext will also monitor developments in specified companies.

Moody's International Databases

Moody's Investors Service
  99 Church Street
  New York, NY 10007 U.S.A.

Moody's International Corporate News Report is available on-line through Dialog. Also available on compact disk is comprehensive data on over 5,000 non-U.S. companies. The compact disks are updated quarterly. Companies can be accessed by name and by country. As with many other compact disk databases, it is possible to manipulate the data to provide various comparisons and screens. The compact disks also permit accessing, by means of Dialog, Moody's on-line International News Reports, thereby providing timeliness to the service.

Categories of information on the compact disks are: incorporation, principal business, management, mergers and acquisitions, subsidiaries, head office address and telephone, data on long-term debt and capital stock highlighting (includes Moody's rating and debt provisions), dividends, transfer agent and registrar, news reports, and up to seven years of financial statements featuring income accounts and balance sheets.

Predicasts

Predicasts
  1101 Cedar Avenue
  Cleveland, OH 44106 U.S.A.

Predicasts
  8-10 Denman Street
  London WIV 7RF
  United Kingdom

Predicasts is a large on-line source of business information which makes available the contents of over 2,000 international business and trade publications. Predicast's databases are available on Dialog. Two are of particular value to analysts following specific industries:

Infomat International Business. Database provides English language abstracts of business news articles appearing in over 500 international newspapers and journals. Helpful in following developments in specific industries.

PTS Promt. Database is a multi-industry source providing international coverage of companies, products, and markets. It comprises abstracts and full text from over 1,000 of the world's important business publications, including trade journals, newsletters, financial newspapers, analysts reports, and others.

Worldscope

Wright Investors' Service
P.O. Box 428
Bridgeport, CT 06601 U.S.A.

Worldscope provides company financial data, both in published and CD formats. On-line access is available on the Dow Jones News/Retrieval Service. The database covers over 4,500 companies in 25 countries. Recently the company has entered into a joint venture with Disclosure for the distribution of financial information.

A listing of data items provided by Worldscope is given in Exhibit 15.3.

Directories and Reference Books Focusing on Companies

Major Companies of Europe. Published by Graham and Trotman of London, this set of three books provides information about the world's major companies. Included is material on a company's finances, personnel, structure, products, profitability, and key decision-makers and executives. Available separately are: Volume 1, *Major Companies of the Continental European Economic Community*; Volume 2, *Major Companies of the United Kingdom*; Volume 3, *Major Companies of Western Europe Outside the European Economic Community*. Also published by Graham and Trotman are: *Major Companies of the Arab World* and *Major Companies of the Far East* (in 3 volumes: Volume 1, Southeast Asia; Volume 2, East Asia; Volume 3, Australia and New Zealand).

Medium Companies of Europe. Contains information on more than 7,000 emerging companies in the European business, finance, and industry. Volume 1 covers the Continental European Economic Community (EEC); Volume 2, the United Kingdom; and Volume 3, the non-EEC countries.

The titles mentioned above are available in the United States through:

Gale Research
835 Penobscot Building
Detroit, MI 48226 U.S.A.

International Directory of Corporate Affiliation. Gives essential facts on the worldwide connections of some 30,000 major international corporations, both American- and foreign-owned. Contact:

Macmillan Directory
860 Third Avenue
New York, NY 10022 U.S.A.

The Hambro Company Guide. Published quarterly by Hemmington Scott Publishing Limited, it provides data on over 2,000 companies listed on the U.K. stock market. Included is information on five-year profit-and-loss balance sheet figures, head and registered office addresses with telephone and facsimile numbers, capital structure, gearing and return on capital, market capitalization ratios, advisers, board members, and share price performance.

The Hambro Corporate Register. Published semiannually by Hemmington Scott, this is a directory of the "who's who" of corporate Britain. Included are the range of company activities, head office locations, executive and nonexecutive directors, executives' names and titles, extensive biographical details, and share capital.

The two Hambro volumes listed are available in the United States through:

Monitor Publishing Company
104 Fifth Avenue
New York, NY 10011 U.S.A.

The Japan Company Handbooks. Published quarterly by Toyokeizai Inc. *The Japan Company Handbook, First Section* covers the leading Blue Chip Japanese companies listed on Japan's major stock exchange. *The Japan Company Handbook, Second Section* focuses on Japan's younger growth companies. The books are cross-referenced and categorized by industry. The information contained in these volumes includes corporate names; business descriptions; headquarters' addresses; telephone, facsimile, and telex numbers; short- and long-term outlooks; senior officers' names and titles; shareholders' equities; major stockholders; and overseas offices and subsidiaries. Also included are financial analyses and historical data on revenues, assets, sales breakdowns, profits, stock prices, dividends, liabilities, working capital, and other financial data.

The Japan Company Handbooks are distributed by:

Monitor Publishing Company
104 Fifth Avenue
New York, NY 10011 U.S.A.

Major Companies of the Far East. A two-volume set that provides up-to-date information on nearly 4,500 major companies. Covered are the company's finances, personnel, structure, products and profitability. Available from:

Gale Research
835 Penobscot Building
Detroit, MI 48226 U.S.A.

Moody's International Manuals. Published annually, these manuals give an in-depth account of company history, financials, stock, and debt. Covers over 5,000 non-U.S.-based companies. Material is updated twice a week by newsletters. The same information is also available on compact disks (see section on Company Information Sources). Contact:

Moody's Investor Service
99 Church Street
New York, NY 10007 U.S.A.

Survey of Major Database Vendors

An overview of some of the major database vendors of interest to the analyst is given here. While the analyst should be familiar with the more important databases, searching these in a cost- and time-efficient way presents a formidable challenge. Unless the analyst is very familiar with the database vendor, the job is best left to services which specialize in on-line searches. Many of these are listed in *Encyclopedia of Information Systems and Services,* published by:

Gale Research Company
835 Penobscot Building
Detroit, MI 48226 U.S.A.

The key to success with the use of such services (and searches in general) is formulating the task in as precise a manner as possible.

Dialog

Dialog Information Service
3460 Hillview Avenue
Palo Alto, CA 97304 U.S.A.

Dialog provides access to over 380 databases and ranks among the largest information vendor in the world. Representative databases are listed below by category information. For details, consult the Dialog Database Catalogue.

Asian topics
- Asian-Pacific (provides news of the Pacific Rim)
- Japan Economic Newswire (compiled by Kyodo News International)
- Japan Technology

European Business
- D & B—International Dun's Market Identifiers
- ICC British Company Directory
- Hoppenstedt Directory of German Companies

International Financial Services
- Investext®
- Moody's® Corporate News—International

International News
- Financial Times Full Text
- PTS Newsletter Database
- Trade & Industry ASAP
- Reuters

Dow Jones News/Retrieval

Dow Jones News/Retrieval
P.O. Box 300
Princeton, NJ 08543 U.S.A.

This well-known on-line service provides access to several databases of interest to the international investor.

Worldscope. Financial profiles and stock performance data on more than 4,500 major companies from 25 countries.

Dow Jones News. Stories from the Dow Jones News Service wire and selected, condensed stories from *The Wall Street Journal* and *Barron's*. As recent as 90 seconds and as far back as 90 days. Searched easily by company, industry, or category.

Dow Jones International News. Up-to-the-minute international business news from Dow Jones' international newswires, the *Wall Street Journal*, the *Wall Street Journal Europe*, and the *Asian Wall Street Journal*.

Japan Economic Daily. Same-day coverage of major Japanese business, financial, and political news from the Kyodo News Service in Japan.

News/Retrieval World Report. Continuously updated national and international news from the Associated Press, Dow Jones News Service, and broadcast media.

Corporate Canada Online. Canadian business news and the financial and market information on more than 2,200 public, private, and Crown Canadian Companies from Info Globe, publishers of Canada's national newspaper, the *Globe and Mail*.

Investext. Full text of more than 20,000 research reports from top brokers, investment bankers, and other analysts, covering more than 4,000 U.S. and Canadian companies and 52 industries and including historical, current, and forecasted marketing and financial information.

Nikkei Economic Database Bank System (NEEDS)

Nihon Keizai Shimbun Co.
 9-5 Otemachi 1-chome, Chiyoda-ku
 Tokyo 100
 Japan

 In the U.S.:

Nihon Keizai Shimbun
 1221 Avenue of the Americas
 New York, NY 10020 U.S.A.

Nihon Keizai Shimbun is the largest financial publisher and financial database company in Japan. The NEEDS databases provide extensive news coverage from the *Japan Economic Journal, Japan Times,* and other major sources, price quotations on Japanese securities, earnings estimates, and financial data on all quoted Japanese companies. An Asian Profile database provides background data on companies in China, Korea, Hong Kong, Singapore, Malaysia, Thailand, Indonesia, and the Philippines.

Reuters

Reuters Ltd.   *Reuters Information Service*
 85 Fleet Street   60 Broadway
 London EC4P 4AJ   New York, NY 10006 U.S.A.
 United Kingdom

Reuters is among the world's largest news and information organizations. On-line services include the following:

Textline. One of the world's leading business information databases. News and comment from more than 1,000 international newspapers, magazines, journals, and newswires has been stored on Textline since 1980.

Newsline. Gives current international business-related news headlines taken overnight from a wide range of U.K. national and regional newspapers and a selection of European papers.

Dataline. Provides a five-year history of financial statements on over 3,000 international manufacturing companies. The information is presented in a standardized, structured format and comprises income statements, financing tables, balance sheets, and accounting ratios.

Accountline. Contains the full text of the annual reports of a wide range of U.K. companies in the original unadjusted format. Search facilities enable you to select an entire report or specify a particular section of a report or a series of reports within an industry sector.

Country Reports. This service is a database of breaking economic, political, and general news, combined with a 90-day back file. It also includes updated economic indicators and in-depth country profiles. Data from Reuters' global network of over 1,000 journalists is available for 190 countries and territories.

Company Newsyear. Provides fast and easy access to 365 days of equity market news on over 20,000 quoted companies worldwide. Company news items are taken from more than 1,000 international newspapers, magazines, journals, and newswires.

Sample Corporate Record

```
BANG & OLUFSEN A/S
P. BANGS VEJ 15
STRUER    DENMARK
POSTAL BOX: NA

TELEPHONE 07-851122
COMPANY NUMBER: 0167878
SHORT NAME: NA

STOCK EXCHANGE: COPENHAGEN DENMARK

SIC CODES:
340  FABRICATED METAL PRODUCTS
350  MACHINERY, EXCEPT ELECTRICAL
360  ELECTRIC & ELECTRONIC EQUIPMENT
760  MISCELLANEOUS REPAIR SERVICES

OUTSTANDING SHARES:   1,125,250
EMPLOYEES:    2,545

ORIGINAL CURRENCY: DANISH KRONE
EXCHANGE RATE: 0.13

FISCAL YEAR END: 05/31
LATEST ANNUAL FINANCIAL DATE: 05/31/89

AUDITOR: REVISIONSFIRMAET SEIER-PETERSEN
AUDITOR'S ADDRESS:
STRUER
DENMARK

AUDITOR'S REPORT: APPROVED
```

```
                    FIVE YEAR SUMMARY
DATE            SALES ($000)  NET INCOME       EPS
1989             272,844         3,042        2.70
1988             254,241        -1,352       -1.20
1987             247,273         5,239          NA
1986             232,427         3,146          NA
1985             208,013        -1,638          NA
GROWTH RATE         7.75       -71.25       -81.25
```

```
COMMENTS: 1984;-THE SHARE CAPITAL INCREASED BY KR.25 MILLION.   1988;1987/1988 WAS A
DISAPPOINTING YEAR FOR BANG & OLUFSEN.THE RESULT AFTER TAX FOR THE 1987/1988 FINANCIAL
YEAR WAS A LOSS OF KR.10 MILLION, COMPARED TO LAST YEAR PROFIT OF KR.40 MILLION.THE
EFFECTS OF THE OCTOBER 1987 CRISIS WERE IMMEDIATELY FELT IN THE MARKET SECTOR TO WHICH
BANG & OLUFSEN PRODUCTS ARE TARGETED.
```

```
COMPANY OFFICIALS (NAME/TITLE):
LANGEBAEK , S./ CHAIRMAN MANAGING BOARD
OLUFSEN , P.S./ VICE-CHAIRMAN MANAGING BOARD
BANG , J./ MEMBER MANAGING BOARD
HAVERSEN, G./ MEMBER MANAGING BOARD
HJELT, P./ MEMBER MANAGING BOARD
```

Exhibit 15.1.   Representative Database Elements Provided by Disclosure/ Worldscope

```
                      ANNUAL ASSETS (000$)
FISCAL YEAR ENDING      05/31/89      05/31/88      05/31/87
CASH                       4,082         4,043         3,822
MRKTABLE SECURITIES           NA            NA            NA
TOTAL LIQUID ASSETS        4,082         4,043         3,822
RECEIVABLES               45,188        40,599        37,505
NOTES RECEIVABLE              NA            NA         3,458
OTH CUR AST & PPD EX       6,877         7,046         2,496
TOTAL CURRENT ASSETS      52,065        47,645        43,459
RAW MAT. & FIN GOODS      53,599        50,778        59,449
WORK IN PROGRESS           8,268         5,655         5,980
ADVANCE TO SUPPLIERS          NA            NA            NA
PPD EXP - INVENTORY           NA            NA            NA
OTHER INVENTORY               NA            NA            NA
TOTAL INVENTORIES         61,867        56,433        65,429
LAND & BUILDINGS          29,783        20,956        19,214
PLANT & EQUIPMENT         27,690        27,937        24,167
INVEST & ADV TO SUBS         377            NA            NA
LOANS GIVEN                   NA           377           286
DEP & OTH FIX ASSETS          NA         4,381         4,433
TOTAL FIXED ASSETS        57,850        53,651        48,100
TREASURY STOCK                NA            NA            NA
ADVANCES TO PARTNERS          NA            NA            NA
PATENTS & TRADEMARKS          NA            NA            NA
DEFERRED CHARGES              NA            NA            NA
OTHER ASSETS                  NA            NA            NA
TOTAL MISC. ASSETS            NA            NA            NA
TOTAL ASSETS             175,864       161,772       160,810

                    ANNUAL LIABILITIES (000$)
FISCAL YEAR ENDING      05/31/89      05/31/88      05/31/87
ACCOUNTS PAYABLE          23,530        15,444        17,485
INCOME TAXES               1,833           793         2,340
NOTES PAYABLE             39,507            NA            NA
CUR PORT CAP LEASES       22,347        62,127        27,144
DIVIDENDS PAYABLE          1,612            NA         1,300
ACCRUED EXPENSES           3,068           637        30,953
OTHER CURRENT LIAB            NA            NA            NA
TOTAL CURRENT LIAB        91,897        79,001        79,222
CONVERTIBLE DEBT              NA            NA            NA
MORTGAGES                 16,315        17,485            NA
LONG TERM DEBT             5,837         8,606        23,114
PENSION FUND               2,600           143            NA
DEFERRED TAXES             1,560         1,547         3,315
NON-CUR CAP LEASES            NA            NA            NA
TOTAL LONG TERM LIAB      26,312        27,781        26,429
SUBORDINATED LOANS            NA            NA            NA
OTHER LOANS                   NA            NA            NA
TOTAL LOANS                   NA            NA            NA
ALLOWANCE RESERVE          2,171         1,846         1,729
OTHER RESERVES                NA            NA            NA
OTHER LIABILITIES          2,171         1,846         1,729
TOTAL LIABILITIES        120,380       108,628       107,380
COMMON & PREF STOCK       16,120        16,120        13,000
RETAINED EARNINGS         24,869        19,409        21,476
EXTRAORD RESERVES         11,466        15,496        17,290
REVAL OF FIXED ASSET       3,029         2,119         1,664
SHAREHOLDER EQUITY        55,484        53,144        53,430
TOT LIAB & NET WORTH     175,864       161,772       160,810
```

Exhibit 15.1.   (*continued*)

```
                    ANNUAL INCOME (000$)
FISCAL YEAR ENDING       05/31/89      05/31/88      05/31/87
SALES                    272,844       254,241       247,273
RETURNS & CREDITS             NA            NA            NA
NET SALES                272,844       254,241       247,273
COST OF GOODS            102,726        70,668        63,089
GROSS PROFIT             170,118       183,573       184,184
EMPLOYEE WAGES            62,062        59,657        60,450
GENERAL EXPENSES          88,049        81,692        74,932
PROVISIONS                  -819          -234            NA
SELLING & ADMIN EXP      149,292       141,115       135,382
INC BEF DEP & AMORT       20,826        42,458        48,802
INTEREST EXPENSE           4,901         7,683         7,371
DEPRECIATION & AMORT      11,453        10,855         9,412
TOTAL INT & DEPREC.       16,354        18,538        16,783
NET INC BEF EX ITEMS       4,472        23,920        32,019
EXTRAORDINARY INCOME         156            NA            NA
EXTRAORDINARY EXPENS          NA        26,052        24,115
TOTAL EXTRAORD ITEMS         156       -26,052       -24,115
INCOME BEFORE TAX          4,628        -2,132         7,904
TAXES                      1,586          -780         2,665
NET INCOME                 3,042        -1,352         5,239


                  SELECTED FINANCIAL DATA
FISCAL YEAR ENDING       05/31/89      05/31/88      05/31/87
SALES                    272,844       254,241       247,273
SHAREHOLDER EQUITY        55,484        53,144        53,430
QUICK RATIO                 0.61          0.65          0.59
CURRENT RATIO               1.28          1.36          1.42
NET INCOME/SH EQUITY        5.72          2.53         10.41
NET INCOME/NET SALES        1.11          0.53          2.12
CASHFLOW                  14,495         9,503        14,651
NET INCOME                 3,042        -1,352         5,239
WORKING CAPITAL           26,117        29,120        33,488
AVG REAS CREDIT TERM          60            58            55
```

March, 1990

*Note: This is a representation of the database elements found in each corporate record.
Actual records will contain a full five-year statement rather than the three years of
annual data shown above. Financial data may also be searched and displayed in the original
currency.*

Exhibit 15.1. *(continued)*

JUNE 16, 1989

LYNCH, JONES & RYAN MARKETING SAMPLE I/B/E/S DETAIL REPORT

ABBOTT LABS   ABT US$ ACTUAL 12/88   3.33   4QTR 3/89   3.45   DIV 1.40   GRTH 18.8   STAB 0.9   YIELD 2.5   BETA 1.05

BROKER	ANALYST	-QUARTER- EST EARNS 6/89	CURRENT EST EARNS 12/88	CURRENT EST DATE 1989	PRIOR EST EARNS 4QTR	PRIOR EST DATE	CURRENT EST EARNS 1990	CURRENT EST DATE	PRIOR EST EARNS	PRIOR EST DATE	GROWTH FORE-CAST	EARNINGS UPDATE REVIEW
SHEARSON LEHMAN	M WILLARD	0.96	3.90	10/13	4.00	08/09	4.50	03/01	NA		NA	06/13/89
FOURTEEN RESEARC	J ANDERSON	NA	3.85	08/16	3.75	04/13	NA		NA		15.0	06/12/89
GRUNTAL & CO	J TRACHTMAN	NA	3.85	04/05	3.75	08/25	NA		NA		NA	05/24/89
JANNEY MONTGOMER	M MARTORELLI	NA	3.85	11/23	3.80	08/18	4.40	06/12	NA		18.0	06/12/89
INTERSTATE/ULANE	M YOST	NA	3.85	02/23	NA		4.45	03/15	NA		NA	06/05/89
EDWARD D. JONES	M FINN	NA	3.85	03/01	NA		NA		NA		NA	06/13/89
SALOMON BROS	L SCHWARTZ	NA	3.85	02/23	3.90	08/04	4.45	04/19	4.52	02/23	16.0	06/02/89
MORGAN STANLEY	A SEBULSKY	0.95	3.85	11/16	3.95	04/21	4.40	01/25	4.40		12.0	06/14/89
DEAN WITTER REYN	R GOLDMAN	0.95	3.85	04/27	3.80	01/16	4.45	05/17	4.40	01/16	15.0	06/07/89
DONALDSON LUFKIN	K BLAIR	NA	3.85	06/08	3.80	03/30	4.45	03/30	NA		16.0	06/13/89
DREXEL BURNHAM	P SIDOTI	0.95	3.85	06/14	3.90	10/13	4.45	06/14	4.35	12/29	16.0	06/14/89
DUFF & PHELPS	J FULLER	NA	3.85	11/03	3.90	05/11	4.40	04/19	NA		15.0	06/13/89
FIRST BOSTON	R STERN	NA	3.85	10/19	3.90	10/13	4.40	03/15	NA		17.0	05/09/89
SMITH BARNEY	J FRANCE	0.95	3.85	07/27	3.80	04/20	4.45	04/19	NA		14.7	06/13/89
THOMSON MCKINNON	G SASIC	NA	3.85	06/01	4.00	01/26	4.75	01/26	NA		NA	06/07/89
WOOD GUNDY U.S.	W SAMMON	NA	3.85	01/10	3.80	12/08	4.55	04/13	NA		NA	06/08/89
MERRILL LYNCH	L OLWELL	0.94	3.82	10/17	3.90	04/27	4.35	02/15	NA		15.0	06/08/89
H.G. WELLINGTON		NA	3.80	05/24	NA		4.50	05/24	NA		NA	05/31/89
OHIO COMPANY	R SABA	NA	3.80	03/22	3.90	12/27	4.40	04/27	NA		NA	05/15/89
PRU-BACHE SECUR.	R ESQUIVEL	0.94	3.80	03/09	3.90	01/26	4.40	05/11	NA		15.0	06/08/89
FIRST MANHATTAN	G WRIGHT	NA	3.80	05/17	3.75	04/27	4.30	05/17	4.25	04/27	16.0	05/24/89
ARGUS RESEARCH	J NOBLE	NA	3.80	05/06	3.90	12/01	4.70	06/06	NA		20.0	06/12/89
BLUNT ELLIS & LO	J HOLMES	0.90	3.80	03/09	3.65	03/29	4.35	04/05	NA		NA	06/13/89
ADVEST	L WEBB	NA	3.75	06/08	3.80	12/28	NA		NA		NA	06/08/89
STANDARD & POORS	H SAFTLAS	0.93	3.75	02/09	3.70	01/17	NA		NA		NA	06/06/89
NAIVE FORECAST		NA	3.96	05/18	3.95	04/20	4.70	05/18	4.69	04/20	NA	05/18/89
BUYSIDE MEAN (5/ 2/ 4)		NA	3.86	06/15	3.85	05/18	4.47	06/15	4.55	05/18	14.5	

	EST	UP	DOWN	MEAN	CHANGE		HIGH	LOW	MEDIAN	CHANGE	STD DEV
6&89Q	13	0	0	0.94	-0.01		0.96	0.90	0.94	-0.01	0.02
9&89Q	4	1	0	0.90	-0.01		0.96	0.88	0.89	0.00	0.04
1989	34	1	0	3.83	-0.01		3.90	3.70	3.85	0.00	0.04
1990	29	1	0	4.43	-0.02		4.75	4.25	4.45	0.05	0.11
GROWTH	21			15.5%	-0.1%		20.0%	12.0%	15.0%	0.0%	1.67

P/E   14.9   12.9

------ QUARTERLY EPS ------
	12/88	09/88	06/88
	0.99	0.88	0.76
PRICE 03/89	0.88		0.82
RANGE HIGH 06/14	57.000	09/88 CHG	-3.875
	61.000	LOW	43.000
REL 1.10	VOL 303.3	SHS	223.97

I/B/E/S ANALYST ESTIMATE DETAIL REPORT

DEFINITIONS OF DATA ITEMS

SECTION I — SPECIFIC ESTIMATES OF EACH BROKER AND ANALYST
BROKER: - The Brokerage or research firm providing the reported forecasts.
ANALYST: - The Securities Analyst who's forecasts are reported here.
QUARTER EST. EARNS: - The Earnings Estimate for the current Quarter. The earnings forecast made by each analyst for the current quarter or the past quarter if the company hasn't reported earnings yet. The date of the quarter in question is stated just below the heading.

CURRENT EST. EARNS
(fiscal year): - Current Estimated Earnings for the date specified. The most recent earnings forecast for the fiscal year specified.

CURRENT EST. DATE
(fiscal year): - The date the earnings forecast was actually entered into I/B/E/S.
PRIOR EST. EARNS
(fiscal year): - The Prior Earnings Estimate. This forecast, combined with the Current Est., gives the user the trend of each analyst's forecast.

PRIOR EST. DATE
(fiscal year): - The date the earnings forecast was actually entered into I/B/E/S.
EARNINGS UPDATE
REVIEW: - The date that the respective earnings forecast was last verified with the contributor. For example, an estimate might have been made six months ago (see Est. Date) and not have been changed. The Earnings Update Review is the user's assurance that I/B/E/S data is continuously reviewed and updated.

GROWTH FORECAST: - Each analyst's forecast for annual growth over the next 5 years.

SECTION II — BASIC INFORMATION
DIL: - The Dilution factor of each company. If the company's earnings are reported on a diluted basis, a "D" follows the dilution factor.
ACTUAL (fiscal year:) - The last reported annual earnings for the company. The date in parentheses is the fiscal year end of the reported figure.
4 QTR: - The sum of earnings for each of the past 4 Quarters.
DIV: - The current Indicated Annual Dividend. The indicated annual Dividend is usually 4 times the last recorded, quarterly dividend.
GRTH: - 5 Year Earnings Per Share Growth. The average annual growth rate of each company's earnings over the past five years. Five Year Earnings Per Share Growth is calculated by the Least Squares method using the last 20 quarters of reported last four quarter earnings.
STAB: - 5 Year Earnings per Share Stability. Earnings Stability measures the consistency of earnings per share over the prior twenty quarters. Have earnings grown at a steady pace or has growth been erratic? The lower the number, the more uniform growth has been. Combined with the adjacent Earnings Growth data the user is presented with a multi-dimensional view of earnings growth over the past five years. Earnings Stability is calculated as the mean of the differences between actual earnings per share and a calculated trend line earnings per share for the past five years. (20 quarters) expressed as a percentage of trend line earnings per share.

Exhibit 15.2. *(continued)*

DEFINITIONS OF DATA ITEMS (continued)

SECTION II - BASIC INFORMATION (continued)

YIELD:
- The Indicated Annual Dividend paid as a percentage of current stock price.

BETA:
- Beta measures sensitivity of price movement relative to a norm, in this case, to the S&P 500. Beta tells you the average movement in each stock's price when the S&P 500 moved up or down. It indicates the degree to which each stock moves with or against the market. For example, a beta greater than 1 means that the stock in question is expected to move in the same direction as the S&P 500 and with a greater relative change in price. A beta below 1 indicates expected price movement in the same direction but with a lesser relative change in price. The beta included here is the three year weekly price beta.

NAIVE FORECAST:
- Naive Forecast represents the extension of the company's historical 5 year growth rate (GRTH) into the next two Fiscal Years.

BUYSIDE MEAN:
- "Buyside Mean" is the consensus of I/B/E/S buyside institutions. The numbers in parentheses represent the number of Fiscal Year 1, Fiscal Year 2 and Long Term Growth forecasts, respectively.

SECTION III I/B/E/S SUMMARY DATA

EST.:
- The total number of brokers making estimates for each company for each fiscal period and the number of estimates revised "up" or "down" from the preceding month.

MEAN:
- The arithmetic average of all estimates: "change" is the arithmetic change from last month.

HIGH-LOW:
- The range of estimates from all brokers covering a particular company.

MEDIAN:
- The middle point in the series of reported estimates; "change" is the arithmetic change from last month.

STD DEV:
- Standard Deviation (in dollars & cents for earnings and percent for long term growth) indicates the range within which approximately two thirds of the estimates fall.

P/E:
- Price Earnings Ratio, is calculated from current price and the mean estimate for each year.
- The actual, reported earnings for each of the last 4 fiscal Quarters.

QUARTERLY:
SECTION IV PRICE STATISTICS

PRICE:
- Price when report was printed and change in price from last month.

RANGE:
- High-Low price range on an extended year basis.

REL:
- Price relative showing how well (or poorly) the stock has performed, as compared to the performance of the S&P 500 over a twenty-five (25) week period.

VOL:
- The median volume per trading day over the latest 10 week period, shown in thousands of shares.

SHS:
- Shares outstanding, shown in millions.

List of Currency Codes

Argentina	AUSTR	Germany	DM	Japan	YEN	South Africa RAND	Taiwan NT$
Australia	A$	Hong Kong	HK$	Korea	WON	Spain %	Thailand BAHT
Austria	SCH	Ireland	IPT	Malaysia	M$	Sweden SKR	United Kingdom PENCE
Belgium	BFR	Itlay	LIT	Netherlands	FLOR	Switzerland SFR	United States US$
Canada	$C					New Zealand NZ$	
Denmark	DKR					Norway NKR	
Finland	FMR					Philippines PESO	
France	FFR					Singapore S$	

U = ESTIMATE CONVERTED FROM CANADIAN TO US DOLLARS
C = ESTIMATE CONVERTED FROM US TO CANADIAN DOLLARS

Footnotes:
   D = ALL DATA FOR THIS COMPANY IS ON A DILUTED BASIS
   J = PRIMARY OR DILUTED ESTIMATE ADJUSTED TO PROVIDE COMPARABILITY
   $C = ALL DATA FOR THIS COMPANY IN CANADIAN DOLLARS

Exhibit 15.2. *(continued)*

SIEMENS AG

GERMANY
ELECTRICAL

Fiscal Year End: September 30	1990	1989	1988	1987	1986	1985
Financial Statement Data						

(Millions of Deutsche Mark)

	1990	1989	1988	1987	1986	1985
Income Statement						
Net Sales	A63,185	A61,128	A59,374	51,431	47,023	54,616
Depreciation, Deple. & Amort.	3,975	4,057	3,715	3,467	3,390	2,598
Operating Income	-3,451	-2,803	-2,332	-1,378	-2,560	-1,068
Interest Expense	B1,490	B1,383	B1,034	B893	B786	B664
Pretax Income	2,823	2,788	2,475	2,598	2,703	3,592
Net Income	1,547	1,473	1,317	1,217	1,455	1,502
Balance Sheet - Assets						
Cash & Short Term Investments	19,345	21,232	24,016	23,039	21,730	20,540
Receivables - Net	13,688	13,659	10,431	10,008	9,923	9,454
Inventories	C21,527	19,794	19,726	23,336	23,745	17,763
Total Current Assets	D58,368	D58,827	D58,076	D59,600	D58,243	D53,574
Net Property,Plant & Equipment	14,456	13,901	13,623	13,419	12,372	8,019
Total Assets	DE78,661	D77,295	D75,425	D76,392	D73,874	D63,171
Balance Sheet - Liabilities						
Total Current Liabilities	25,847	21,969	25,954	30,693	37,781	35,831
Long Term Debt	1,588	1,817	1,937	2,015	2,576	1,306
Preferred Stock	F	F	F	F	F	F
Common Equity	D016,766	D017,841	D16,853	D15,521	D14,918	D13,120
Liabilities & Equity	78,661	77,295	75,425	76,392	73,874	63,171
Sources & Uses of Funds						
From Operations	6,765	7,072	6,812	5,923	7,224	6,856
L.T. External Financing - Net	H-2,228	H-67	493	H-663	H2,212	H694
Dividends	622	538	534	575	571	442
Capital Expenditures	4,391	7,872	5,210	4,750	5,275	3,702
Change in Working Capital	-4,337	4,736	3,215	-362	-2,604	927
International Business						
Foreign Assets	n.a.	n.a.	n.a.	n.a.	n.a.	n.a.
Foreign Sales	K23,681	K29,397	K24,948	K22,677	K20,662	K25,545
Foreign Income	n.a.	n.a.	n.a.	n.a.	n.a.	n.a.
Supplementary Data						
Employees	373,000	365,000	353,000	359,000	359,000	334,000
R & D Expense	6,980	6,900	6,468	6,211	5,401	4,799
Common Shares (millions)	M52	M50	M49	M49	M48	M48
Financial Ratios and Growth Rates						
Profitability						
Operating Margin	-5.5%	-4.6%	-3.9%	-2.7%	-5.4%	-2.0%
Effective Tax Rate	40.9%	43.4%	43.8%	50.9%	45.5%	59.1%
Net Margin	2.4%	2.4%	2.2%	2.4%	3.1%	2.8%
Return on Assets	3.3%	3.2%	2.6%	2.4%	3.0%	3.3%
Return on Equity	8.7%	8.7%	8.5%	8.2%	11.1%	13.1%
Cash Flow/Sales	10.7%	11.6%	11.5%	11.5%	15.4%	12.6%
Sales Per Employee (000)	169.4	167.5	168.2	143.3	131.0	163.5
Asset Utilization						
Total Assets Turnover	0.8x	0.8x	0.8x	0.7x	0.6x	0.9x
Assets per Employee (000)	210.9	211.8	213.7	212.8	205.8	189.1
Capital Exp./Fixed Assets	11.3%	21.5%	15.3%	14.8%	18.2%	n.c.
Accum. Dep./Fixed Assets	62.8%	62.0%	60.1%	58.3%	57.4%	n.c.
Liquidity						
Current Ratio	2.3x	2.7x	2.2x	1.9x	1.5x	1.5x
Quick Ratio	1.3x	1.6x	1.3x	1.1x	0.8x	0.8x
Leverage						
Common Equity/Assets	21.3%	23.1%	22.3%	20.3%	20.2%	20.8%
L.T. Debt/Total Capital	8.3%	8.9%	9.9%	10.6%	14.1%	8.5%
EBIT/Fixed Charges	2.9x	3.0x	3.3x	3.8x	4.3x	4.5x
Oper. Cash/Fixed Charges	4.5x	5.0x	6.5x	6.5x	9.0x	6.7x
Growth						
Net Sales	3.4%	3.0%	15.4%	9.4%	-13.9%	19.2%
Operating Income	n.c.	n.c.	n.c.	n.c.	n.c.	n.c.
Total Assets	1.8%	2.5%	-1.3%	3.4%	16.9%	3.2%
Earnings per Shr (fis year basis)	0.2%	10.0%	7.4%	-17.5%	-3.8%	39.4%
Div per Shr (fis year basis)	4.0%	13.6%	0.0%	-8.3%	0.0%	25.7%
Book Val per Shr (fis year basis)	-10.3%	4.1%	7.7%	2.7%	12.9%	11.6%
Per Share Data and Investment Ratios						

(Fiscal year end basis)

	1990	1989	1988	1987	1986	1985
Earnings per Share	L29.65	L29.59	KL26.91	L25.06	L30.35	L31.56
Dividends per Share	13.00	12.50	11.00	11.00	J12.00	J12.00
Book Value per Share	321.43	358.44	344.33	319.65	311.13	275.67
Market Price per Share	514.60	596.00	472.70	659.50	670.50	605.50
Total Return	-11.5%	28.7%	-26.7%	0.0%	10.7%	48.2%
Price/Earnings Ratio	17.4x	20.1x	17.6x	26.3x	22.1x	19.2x
Price/Book Value Ratio	1.6x	1.7x	1.4x	2.1x	2.2x	2.2x
Dividend Yield	2.5%	2.1%	2.3%	1.7%	1.8%	2.0%
Dividend Payout	43.8%	42.2%	40.9%	43.9%	39.5%	38.0%

Notes: (A): ACQ'D NIXDORF COMPUTER AG & 5 OTHER COS IN 90, 3 COS IN 89, SEVERAL ACTIVITIES OF BENDIX GROUP IN 88; (B): SIMILAR CHARGES INCLUDED; (C): BEFORE ADJUSTMENT FOR PREPAYMENTS ON WORK IN PROGRESS WHICH HAS BEEN TREATED AS A LIABILITY; (D): ADJUSTED TO EXCLUDE TREASURY STOCK; (E): ADJUSTED TO EXCLUDE UNAPPROPRIATED NET LOSS; (F): INCLUDED IN COMMON EQUITY; (G): INCL 46.2 MIL OF PREF STOCK WHICH SHARES IN PROFITS OF CO; (H): MAY REFLECT CHANGES DUE TO ACQUISITIONS AND ACCOUNTING POLICIES; (J): ALL ITEMS ADJUSTED FOR STOCK SPLITS OR DIVIDENDS 18:17 RIGHTS ISS (4.8% DIV) IN 85; (K): INCLUDES THE EFFECTS OF A CHANGE IN ACCOUNTING POLICIES OR TAX LAWS - ADOPTED NEW ACCOUNTING PRINCIPLES LAW FOR 4TH & 7TH EEC DIRECTIVES IN 88, EARNS IMPACT UNSPECIFIED; (L): EARNINGS PER SHARE ESTIMATED USING NET INCOME AFTER PREFERRED DIVIDEND DIVIDED BY THE NUMBER OF SHARES OUSTANDING AT THE YEAR END; (M): EQUIVALENT NUMBER OF SHARES BASED ON PAR VALUE; (N): INCLUDES EXPORT SALES WHICH CANNOT BE SUBTRACTED OUT.

Information is obtained from sources believed reliable, but accuracy and completeness are not guaranteed.

DISCLOSURE/WORLDSCOPE ● *Industrial Company Profiles* GER-123 7/91

General Information

Chairman, Board of Management
  K. KASKE
Chief Financial Officer
  K-H. BAUMANN
Chairman, Supervisory Board
  H. NAERGER
Vice-Chairman, Supervisory Board
  R. MOOSHAMMER

Address:
  POSTFACH 103
  WITTELSBACHERPLATZ 2
  D-8000 MUENCHEN 2
  GERMANY
Telephone: (089) 2340
Exchange: FRA DUS AMS BRU
Business:
  ENERGY SYSTEMS & INSTALLATIONS
  ACCTD FOR 48% OF 90 REVS; INFOTECH
  SYSTEMS, 18%; TELECOM & SECURITY,
  18% & OTHER, 16%

Selected Data in U.S. Dollars ($Mil) At 1990 Fiscal Year End

Market Capitalization	17,108
Common Equity	10,686
Total Assets	50,135
Sales	40,271
Net Income	986

5 Year Annual Growth Rates

Net Sales	+3.0%
Net Income	+0.8%
Total Assets	+4.5%
Employees	+2.2%
Earnings per Share	-1.2%
Dividends per Share	+1.6%
Book Value per Share	+3.1%

Financial Ratios 5 Year Average

Operating Margin	-4.4%
Net Margin	2.5%
Return on Assets	2.9%
Return on Equity	9.0%
Reinvestment Rate	5.2%
Price/Earnings Ratio	20.6x
Price/Book Value Ratio	1.8x
Dividend Yield	2.0%
Dividend Payout	42.0%

Accounting Practices

Acct. Standards: Local standards with some EEC guidelines
Acct. for Goodwill: Not disclosed
Consol. Practices: Consolidation for significant subsidiaries, others are on an equity basis
Contingent Liab.: Guarantees or warranties, litigation and leases
Deferred Taxes: No, taxes paid as incurred
Deprec. Method: Mixed depreciation methods
Discretionary Reserves: Used
EPS Numerator: No EPS reported by the company
Fin. Stat. Cost Basis: Historical cost entirely
Foreign Curr. Gain/Loss: Taken to income statement
Funds Definition: Partial cash flow statement
Inventory Cost Method: Mixed
Marketable Securities: Lower of cost or market
Minority Interest: Before bottom line in income statement and incl'd in shareholders' equity in balance sheet
Treas. Stock Gain/Loss: Not disclosed

Exhibit 15.3. Disclosure/ Worldscope Report

16

Analyzing International Financial Statements*

Frederick D. S. Choi
Leonard N. Stern School of Business
New York University
New York

Introduction

The 1990s promise to be an exciting decade for the world of international investing. The dramatic developments occurring in Eastern Europe on both political and economic fronts, as well as the renewed commitment to integrate Western Europe's financial markets, are expanding the regional opportunity set for both direct and portfolio investors. Indeed, the globalization of the world's financial markets, which has been spurred by the continued deregulation of national capital markets, the growing international market for corporate control, enhanced global competition, and a deepening of financial technology due to advances in computer and telecommunication technologies, is accelerating crossborder commercial, financial, and investment transactions. A principle effect of globalization has been a significant increase in the number of markets in which companies such as General Electric, Siemens, or Hitachi can source their long-term financing needs. Likewise, investment fund managers can often find superior investment returns in trading the securities of foreign entities listed on home exchanges or traded in offshore markets.

These fast-breaking developments in the world of international business and finance have significant implications for financial analysts. As business and financial decisions are premised to a large extent on data contained in a reporting entity's financial accounts, proper understanding

---

*This discussion draws on the author's chapter appearing in *International Accounting*, 2nd. ed., with G. G. Mueller, Englewood Cliffs, NJ: Prentice Hall, Inc., 1992.

of the underlying information set is crucial to proper interpretation and analysis. This analysis includes evaluating foreign subsidiary performance, appraising potential joint venture partners and acquisition targets, assessing competitor strengths and weaknesses, determining the credit worthiness of foreign borrowers and commercial customers, and profiling the risk and return dimensions of foreign security investments.

This chapter examines some of the problems that executives and investors can expect to encounter when analyzing foreign financial statements. These problems differ in terms of their relative magnitude and degree of tractability. Methods used to cope with such differences are identified and illustrated where possible.

Language and Terminology

Financial analysts who have spent most of their professional lives pouring over domestic accounts will experience quite a jolt when they attempt to read the financial statements of a company such as Germany's Krupp Stahl or France's Hachette, which are expressed in the respective country's national idiom. While an increasing number of companies are adopting English as the international business language when communicating with foreign readers, many do not.

Then too, accounting terminology differences can easily confuse. Thus, the term *stock* is automatically associated in a North American context with shares of ownership, whereas it is typically associated with merchandise inventory in Commonwealth countries. Other examples include *turnover* (sales revenue), *debtors* and *creditors* (accounts receivable and payable), and *provisions* (contra-asset accounts, appropriations of retained earnings, or estimated liabilities).

A logical alternative for coping with language differences is the development of multilingual capabilities on the part of the analyst. Most Swiss investors, for example, are fluent in at least four languages—English, French, German, and Italian. Most Brazilians are comfortable with English, Portuguese, and Spanish. Reliance on language translation is another alternative. Language translation could entail: (1) the use of accounting lexicons to translate foreign language account titles and terms into English or other languages,[1] (2) the use of professional translators to translate key account titles and terms when lexicons covering a given language are not available, (3) reliance on investment advisory services with in-house foreign language capabilities, or (4) the use of foreign nationals as members of the research effort. Whether language translations are personally undertaken or delegated to others, caution must still be exercised. Cursory translations can often lead to message distortions. As an example, consider the

---

[1] For example, the *Lexique UEC* facilitates Danish, Dutch, English, German, Italian, Portuguese, and Spanish translations.

word *current*. When translated into the Japanese language, the Japanese word equivalent is similar to *present*. While these two words appear to convey the same meaning, such may not be the case when they are used in an asset valuation context. Thus, valuing off-balance sheet interest rate swap obligations at *current value* does not necessarily connote the same measurement yardstick as *present value*. The former normally implies a market valuation concept; the latter a discounted cash flow measure. Each could yield a very different measurement.

Statement Format

Table 16.1 contains the balance sheet of AECI, a major industrial group in South Africa. To an analyst used to seeing financial statements presented in the account form, this presentation understandably evokes some initial discomfort. In the account form, assets are listed on the left or on the top, in decreasing order of maturity. Liabilities are listed on the right or immediately following assets, in increasing order of maturity. Designed to afford readers a glimpse of the liquidity position of the firm, this practice is not as prevalent in many European and Commonwealth countries.

Account classifications often vary quite considerably in international reporting. In the United States, analysts are used to seeing multiple step income statements that break out important expense categories, such as cost of sales. In countries such as Germany, analysts must often impute cost of sales, as expenses tend to be disclosed by type rather than function (i.e., wages are aggregated whether they relate to production or distribution). Whereas treasury stock is treated as a reduction in shareholders' equity in the United States, it is often classified as an asset in Italy, Korea, and Portugal; and whereas the time frame distinguishing a current and noncurrent liability is typically a year in the United States, the cutoff point is commonly four years in Germany. An analyst who is unmindful of such classification differences can err when comparing current ratios between the two countries.

Owing to harmonization efforts at the international level, as well as a growing participation by reporting entities in global capital markets, financial statement formats are beginning to converge. For example, the European Community's Fourth Directive now prescribes a limited number of statement formats in an attempt to reduce the diversity of formats that have heretofore characterized European financial reporting practices. Exhibit 16.1 illustrates recommended formats for the balance sheet and income statement. Essentially two variations are permitted, a horizontal and a vertical format, for both the balance sheet and income statement. In the latter case, expenses can either be classified by type or purpose.

While efforts of the European Community will probably influence statement formats of reporting entities outside of Europe, variations are

Table 16.1. AECI's Balance Sheet as of December 31, 1990

Company R millions			Notes	Group R millions	
1989	1990		**Notes**	1990	1989
		Capital employed			
1 065	1 040	Ordinary shareholders' interest		1 331	1 311
228	228	Capital	7	228	228
32	26	Non-distributable reserve	8	25	30
805	786	Distributable reserve	8	1 078	1 053
6	6	Preference capital	7	6	6
		Outside shareholders' interest in subsidiaries		36	36
1 071	1 046	**Total shareholders' interest**		1 373	1 353
117	199	**Deferred taxation**	9	205	119
315	309	**Long term borrowings**	10	331	334
1 503	1 554			1 909	1 806
		Employment of capital			
936	992	**Fixed assets**	11	1 143	1 058
155	188	**Investments**	12	260	225
(31)	(63)	**Subsidiaries**	13	13	16
443	437	**Net current assets**		493	507
1 647	1 611	Current assets		1 819	1 804
866	845	Stocks	14	965	948
731	764	Accounts receivable	15	852	799
50	2	Liquid funds	16	2	57
1 204	1 174	Current liabilities		1 326	1 297
594	622	Accounts payable		700	647
264	421	Short term borrowings	17	460	289
258	43	Taxation		78	273
88	88	Dividend declared	5	88	88
1 503	1 554			1 909	1 806

likely to remain. In such cases statement readers must reclassify accounting formats to the benchmark that is being used as a standard of comparison. Another coping mechanism is to utilize standardized computer financial databases, described later in this chapter, that provide data in terms of a common reporting format. Even here, however, analysts must be aware of limitations in classifications, since the data services themselves may not have access to sufficient information to place all companies covered on a uniform reporting basis.

LAYOUT OF THE BALANCE SHEET -- HORIZONTAL FORMAT
(as prescribed by article 9 of the directive)

ASSETS

A SUBSCRIBED CAPITAL UNPAID (or if only called-up capital shown under share capital then any amounts called but not paid)

B FORMATION EXPENSES (although law may provide for this to be shown as the first item under 'Intangible assets')

C FIXED ASSETS
(I) Intangible assets
 1 Cost of research and development
 2 Patents, licences and trade marks
 3 Goodwill
 4 Payments on account

(II) Tangible assets
 1 Land and buildings
 2 Plant and machinery
 3 Other fixtures and fittings, tools and equipment
 4 Payments on account and tangible assets in course of construction

(III) Financial assets
 1 Shares in affiliates
 2 Loans to affiliates
 3 Participating interests
 4 Loans to participating interests
 5 Investments held as fixed assets
 6 Other loans
 7 Own shares

D CURRENT ASSETS
(I) Stocks
 1 Raw materials and consumables
 2 Work in progress
 3 Finished goods and goods for resale
 4 Payments on account

(II) Debtors
due and payable in: more than one year / one year or less
 1 Trade debtors
 2 Owed by affiliates
 3 Owed by participating interests
 4 Other debtors
 5 Subscribed capital called but not paid (unless under A-Assets)
 6 Prepayments and accrued income (unless under E-Assets)

(III) Investments
 1 Shares in affiliates
 2 Own shares
 3 Other investments

(IV) Cash at bank and in hand

E PREPAYMENTS AND ACCRUED INCOME (unless under D.II.6-Assets)

F LOSS FOR THE FINANCIAL YEAR (unless under A.VI-Liabilities)

LIABILITIES

A CAPITAL AND RESERVES
(I) Subscribed capital (or called-up capital)
(II) Share premium account
(III) Revaluation reserve
(IV) Reserves
 1 Legal reserve
 2 For own shares
 3 Required by articles of association
 4 Other reserves
(V) Profit or loss brought forward
(VI) Profit or loss for the financial year (unless under F-Assets or E-Liabilities)

B PROVISIONS FOR LIABILITIES AND CHARGES
 1 Provisions for pensions and similar obligations
 2 Provisions for taxation
 3 Other provisions

C CREDITORS
due and payable in: more than one year / one year or less
 1 Debenture loans (showing convertible loans separately)
 2 Owed to credit institutions
 3 Payments on account of orders
 4 Trade creditors
 5 Bills payable
 6 Owed to affiliates
 7 Owed to participating interests
 8 Other including tax and social security
 9 Accruals and deferred income (unless under D-Liabilities)

D ACCRUALS AND DEFERRED INCOME (unless under C.9-Liabilities)

E PROFIT FOR THE FINANCIAL YEAR (unless under A.VI-Liabilities)

Source: European 4th Directive

Exhibit 16.1. EC Fourth Directive Financial Statement Formats (a) Layout of the Balance Sheet—Horizontal Format

LAYOUT OF THE BALANCE SHEET – VERTICAL FORMAT
(as prescribed by article 10 of the directive)

A SUBSCRIBED CAPITAL UNPAID
(or if only called-up capital shown under share capital then any amounts called but not paid)   x

B FORMATION EXPENSES
(national law may provide for this to be shown as the first item under "intangible assets".)   x

C FIXED ASSETS
(I) Intangible assets   x
    1 Costs of research and development   x
    2 Patents, licences and trade marks   x
    3 Goodwill   x
    4 Payments on account   —

(II) Tangible assets   x
    1 Land and buildings   x
    2 Plant and machinery   x
    3 Other fixtures and fittings, tools and equipment   x
    4 Payments on account and tangible assets in course of construction   x   —

(III) Financial assets   x
    1 Shares in affiliates   x
    2 Loans to affiliates   x
    3 Participating interests   x
    4 Loans to participating interests   x
    5 Investments held as fixed assets   x
    6 Other loans   x
    7 Own shares   x   —

D CURRENT ASSETS
(I) Stocks
    1 Raw materials and consumables   x
    2 Work in progress   x
    3 Finished goods and goods for resale   x
    4 Payments on account   x   —

(II) Debtors   *due and payable in:* more than one year / one year or less
    1 Trade debtors   x
    2 Owed by affiliates   x
    3 Owed by participating interests   x
    4 Other debtors   x
    5 Subscribed capital called but not paid (if not in A)   x   x
    6 Prepayments and accrued income (if not in E)   x   x
    —   —

(III) Investments
    1 Shares in affiliates   x
    2 Own shares   x
    3 Other investments   x   —

(IV) Cash at bank and in hand   x

E PREPAYMENTS AND ACCRUED INCOME
(not required if shown under D.II.6)   x

F CREDITORS
Due and payable in one year or less   (x)
    1 Debenture loans (showing convertible loans separately)   (x)
    2 Owed to credit institutions   (x)
    3 Payments on account of orders   (x)
    4 Trade creditors   (x)
    5 Bills payable   (x)
    6 Owed to affiliates   (x)
    7 Owed to participating interests   (x)
    8 Other including tax and social security   (x)
    9 Accruals and deferred income (if not in K)   (x)   —

G NET CURRENT ASSETS/LIABILITIES   x
(i.e. current assets plus prepayments and accrued income less liabilities due in one year or less and the current portion of accruals and deferred income)

H TOTAL ASSETS LESS CURRENT LIABILITIES   x

I CREDITORS
Due and payable in more than one year   (x)
    1 Debenture loans (showing convertible loans separately)   (x)
    2 Owed to credit institutions   (x)
    3 Payments on account of orders   (x)
    4 Trade creditors   (x)
    5 Bills payable   (x)
    6 Owed to affiliates   (x)
    7 Owed to participating interests   (x)
    8 Other including tax and social security   (x)
    9 Accruals and deferred income (if not in K)   (x)   —

J PROVISIONS FOR LIABILITIES AND CHARGES   (x)
    1 Provisions for pensions and similar obligations   (x)
    2 Provisions for taxation   (x)
    3 Other provisions   (x)   —

K ACCRUALS AND DEFERRED INCOME   (x)
(if not shown under F9 or I9 but otherwise current portion to be deducted in calculating G)

L CAPITAL AND RESERVES   x
(I) Subscribed capital (or called-up capital)   x
(II) Share premium account   x
(III) Revaluation reserve   x
(IV) Reserves   x
    1 Legal reserve   x
    2 For own shares   x
    3 Required by articles of association   x
    4 Other reserves   x   —
(V) Profit or loss brought forward   x
(VI) Profit or loss for the financial year   x   —

Exhibit 16.1. (b) Layout of the Balance Sheet—Vertical Format

LAYOUT OF THE PROFIT AND LOSS ACCOUNT – HORIZONTAL (TYPE OF EXPENDITURE) FORMAT 3

(as prescribed by article 24 of the directive)

A   CHARGES

*1	Reduction in stocks of finished goods and in work in progress	x
*2	(a) Raw materials and consumables	x
	(b) Other external charges	x
3	Staff costs	
	(a) Wages and salaries	x
	(b) Social security costs (pension costs to be indicated separately)	x
4	(a) Value adjustments in respect of formation expenses and of tangible and intangible fixed assets	x
	(b) Value adjustments in respect of current assets, to the extent that they exceed the amount of value adjustments which are normal in the undertaking concerned	x
5	Other operating charges	x
6	Value adjustments in respect of financial assets and of investments held as current assets	x
7	Interest payable and similar charges, showing separately that concerning affiliates	x
8	Tax on profit or loss on ordinary activities	x
9	Profit on ordinary activities after taxation (carried down)	x
		=
9	Loss on ordinary activities after taxation (brought down)	x
10	Extraordinary charges	x
11	Tax on extraordinary profit or loss	x
12	Other taxes not shown under the above items	x
13	Profit for the financial year	x
		=

B   INCOME

*1	Net turnover	
*2	Increase in stocks of finished goods and in work in progress	
*3	Work performed by the undertaking for its own purposes and capitalised	
*4	Other operating income	
5	Income from participating interests (income from affiliates to be disclosed separately)	
6	Income from other investments and loans forming part of the fixed assets, showing separately that derived from affiliates	
7	Other interest receivable and similar income, showing separately that derived from affiliates	
8	Loss on ordinary activities after taxation (carried down)	
8	Profit on ordinary activities after taxation (brought down)	
9	Extraordinary income	
10	Loss for the financial year	

* Small and medium companies may be allowed to combine these items under one item called "Gross profit or loss" (article 27). Small companies may be exempted from publishing, but not from preparing, a profit and loss account (article 47(2)).

Exhibit 16.1.   (c) Layout of the Profit and Loss Account—Horizontal (Type of Expenditure) Format[a]

[a] A similar format is permitted where expenditures are classified by nature of expenditure.

LAYOUT OF THE PROFIT AND LOSS ACCOUNT–
VERTICAL (PURPOSE OF EXPENDITURE) FORMAT
(as prescribed by article 25 of the directive)

*1	Net turnover			x
*2	Cost of sales (including value adjustments)			(x)
				—
*3	Gross profit or loss			x
4	Distribution costs (including value adjustments)			(x)
5	Administrative expenses (including value adjustments)			(x)
*6	Other operating income			x
7	Income from participating interests (income from affiliates to be disclosed separately)			x
8	Income from other investments and loans forming part of the fixed assets, showing separately that derived from affiliates			x
9	Other interest receivable and similar income, showing separately that derived from affiliates			x
10	Value adjustments in respect of financial assets and of investments held as current assets			(x)
11	Interest payable and similar charges, showing separately those concerning affiliates			(x)
12	Tax on profit or loss on ordinary activities			(x)
				—
13	Profit or loss on ordinary activities after taxation			x
14	Extraordinary income		x	
15	Extraordinary charges		(x)	
			—	
16	Extraordinary profit or loss		x	
17	Tax on extraordinary profit or loss		(x)	x
			—	
18	Other taxes not shown under the above items			(x)
				—
19	Profit or loss for the financial year			x
				=

* Small and medium companies may be allowed to combine items 1 to 3 and 6 under one item called "Gross profit or loss" (article 27). Small companies may be exempted from publishing, but not from preparing, a profit and loss account.

Exhibit 16.1. (d) Layout of the Profit and Loss Account—Vertical (Purpose of Expenditure) Format[a]

[a] A similar format is permitted by type of expenditure

Reporting Currency

As a convenience to foreign readers, reporting companies in some countries, notably Japan, will translate their financial statements to the reporting currency of the reader's country of domicile. Exhibit 16.2 illustrates a recent income statement of Japan's Kao Corporation. Foreign readers are provided with two sets of comparative figures, one in Japanese yen, the other in U.S. dollars. The exchange rate that is used is the year-end rate and simply involves multiplying all statement items by a constant.

Kao Corporation and Consolidated Subsidiaries

CONSOLIDATED STATEMENTS OF INCOME

Years ended March 31, 1990 and 1989

	Millions of yen		Thousands of U.S. dollars (Note 2)	
	1990	1989	1990	1989
Net sales	¥620,429	¥572,182	$3,926,766	$3,621,405
Cost of sales	312,919	294,745	1,980,500	1,865,475
Gross profit	307,510	277,437	1,946,266	1,755,930
Selling, general and administrative expenses	263,987	236,036	1,670,804	1,493,898
Operating income	43,523	41,401	275,462	262,032
Other (income) expenses:				
Interest and dividend income	(2,925)	(3,564)	(18,513)	(22,557)
Interest expense	4,203	3,420	26,601	21,646
Net foreign currency exchange gain	(1,091)	(234)	(6,905)	(1,481)
Other, net (Note 9)	3,110	3,982	19,684	25,202
	3,297	3,604	20,867	22,810
Income before income taxes, equity items and other	40,226	37,797	254,595	239,222
Income taxes (Note 3):				
Current	20,255	22,667	128,196	143,462
Deferred	1,365	(854)	8,639	(5,405)
	21,620	21,813	136,835	138,057
Equity items:				
Minority interests in earnings of consolidated subsidiaries	(178)	(267)	(1,127)	(1,690)
Equity in earnings of nonconsolidated subsidiaries and affiliates	434	740	2,747	4,684
Other:				
Amortization of differences between investment cost and net equity upon acquisitions	54	21	342	133
Adjustments on translation of financial statements of consolidated overseas subsidiaries	(1,106)	1,059	(7,000)	6,702
Net income	¥ 17,810	¥ 17,537	$ 112,722	$ 110,994
	Yen		U.S. dollars (Note 2)	
Net income per share	¥35.02	¥35.08	$0.22	$0.22

See notes to consolidated financial statements.

Exhibit 16.2. Income Statement for KAO Corporation

Convenience translations like those provided by the Japanese tend, however, to be the exception, as the vast majority of companies denominate their financial accounts in their national currency. Readers may conduct their analysis in foreign currency or utilize a convenience translation methodology similar to that employed by Kao Corporation. Those adopting the former approach have little cause for concern since financial ratios that transform nominal (interval) measurements to percentage relationships are independent of the currency of denomination. A debt-to-equity ratio computed from a French balance sheet expressed in francs is no different from a debt-to-equity ratio computed from the same financial statements translated into dollars using a consistent convenience translation rate (e.g., the year-end exchange rate).

Analysts preferring to work with convenience translations, however, must be careful when analyzing time series data. Use of convenience rates to translate foreign currency amounts can distort underlying trends owing to changes in exchange rates over time. To illustrate, consider the following revenue pattern for Reckitt and Coleman during the last three years:

	1988	1989	1990
Net sales (£ millions)	£1,394	£1,566	£1,764

Convenience translations using year-end exchange for 1988, 1989 and 1990 would yield the following year-to-year percentage changes in terms of U.S. dollar equivalents: 1990/1989, −.1%; 1991/1990, 35.1%; 1991/1989, 34.9%. This contrasts with the trend percentages in sterling owing to changes in the relation between sterling and the dollar during the period in question, as shown in Table 16.2.

The foregoing problem can be remedied by scaling prior year data for exchange rate differentials between years. Alternatively, data expressed in sterling can be translated to dollars using a single base-year's rate as a benchmark. In the foregoing example, the benchmark rate could be either that prevailing as of the first year in the time series or that of the most recent year in the time series. Use of a base-year rate will yield a trend analysis consistent with that in British pounds. This result is illustrated in Table 16.2.

Owing to problems caused by exchange rate changes over time, analysis of trend data in local currency is advocated. For those preferring translated data, use of the most recent year's exchange rate is convenient since this rate provides a reference point that spans the time of the decision. An exception is advised when examining time series data that have been adjusted for inflation. If foreign currency balances are

Table 16.2. Trend Analysis with Base-Year Exchange Rate

	Sales Revenue			Percent change		
	1988	1989	1990	89/88	90/89	90/88
Pounds	£1,394	£1,566	£1,764	12.3%	12.6%	26.5%
Dollars						
Using 1988 base-year rate	$2,509	$2,819	$3,175	12.3%	12.6%	26.5%
Using 1990 base-year rate	$2,676	$3,007	$3,387	12.3%	12.6%	26.5%

expressed in base-year purchasing power equivalents, then year-end exchange rates associated with the given base-year purchasing power equivalents should be used. As an example, if net sales were expressed in base year purchasing power, where the base-year is 1988, the 1988 exchange rate should be used. Use of the 1990 exchange rate could produce a "double-dip" effect in the translated numbers.

Exchange rate changes and existing foreign currency translation procedures can produce an additional aberration for analysts examining the accounts of multinational companies with extensive foreign operations. Consolidated financial statements provide readers with a view of a multinational company's total operations, both foreign and domestic, in terms of the reporting currency. Unfortunately, it is not always clear whether reported sources and uses of funds appearing in a firm's statement of changes in financial position (funds statement) reflect underlying operational decisions or simply the effects of exchange rate changes that are an integral part of the consolidation process.

To illustrate, the translated statement of earnings, financial position, and changes in financial position for the French affiliate of a Canadian-based multinational company appears in Table 16.3. The company utilizes cash as its concept of funds and employs the current rate translation method because it defines the franc as its functional currency for consolidation purposes.

An analyst looking at the translated funds statement would surmise that funds for the period being reported were derived from profitable operations, the issuance of long-term debt, and foreign currency translation gains. Funds were, in turn, used to purchase fixed assets.

Because translation adjustments are simply the result of a restatement process, the components appearing in the funds statement contain, in reality, a mixture of translation effects and actual cash flows. Thus, an analyst must find out what portion of the $3,168,000 increase in long-term debt is actually the result of a financing transaction as opposed to changes in exchange rates. Similar considerations apply to the $5,390,000 increase in fixed assets.

Assume that the translated statements appearing in Table 16.3 are based on the French franc balances appearing in Table 16.4 and that the relevant exchange rate information is as stated.

A comparison of funds flows in francs versus Canadian dollars yields some striking contrasts. Whereas long-term debt appears as a source of cash in Canadian dollars, it is neither a source nor a use in francs. Similarly, the use of cash to acquire fixed assets from a Canadian dollar perspective turns out to be a pure translation phenomenon.

Further analysis suggests that fixed assets did not change during the period. The year-end balance should have been the beginning book value, C$17,000,000 (F170,000,000), less depreciation of C$1,110,000 (F10,000,000)

Table 16.3.   Financial Statements of a French Subsidiary (in thousands of Canadian dollars)

Balance Sheet

	December 31	
	19X2	**19X3**
Assets (000s)		
Cash	$ 4,800	$ 7,980
Net fixed assets	17,000	21,280
Total assets	$21,800	$29,260
Liabilities and Owners' Equity		
Can. dollar payable	$ 1,000	$ 1,000
Long-term franc debt	9,600	12,768
Capital stock	7,636	7,636
Retained earnings	3,564	4,060
Translation adjustment	—	3,796
Total liabilities and owners' equity	$21,800	$29,260

19X3 Income Statement (000s)

Sales		$ 2,664
Expenses:		
Operating costs	$ 1,332	
Depreciation	1,110	
Foreign exchange gain	(278)	2,164
Net income		$ 500

Funds Statement (000s)

Sources:		
Net income	$ 500	
Depreciation	1,110	
Increase in LT debt	3,168	
Translation adjustment	3,796	$ 8,574
Uses:		
Increase in fixed assets		5,390
Net increase in cash		$ 3,180

Table 16.4. Local Currency Statements of a French Affiliate

Balance Sheet

	December 31	
	19X2	19X3
Assets (000s)		
Cash	F 48,000	F 60,000
Net fixed assets	170,000	160,000
Total assets	F218,000	F220,000
Liabilities and Owners' Equity		
Can. dollar payable	F 10,000	F 7,500
Long-term franc debt	96,000	96,000
Capital stock	92,000	92,000
Retained earnings	20,000	24,500
Total liabilities and owners' equity	F218,000	F220,000

Funds Statement (000s)

Sources:	
Net income	F 4,500
Depreciation	10,000
Less franc foreign exchange gain	(2,500)
Uses:	
None	—
Net increase in cash	F12,000

Relevant Exchange Rates

December 31, 19X2	F1 = C$0.100
Average during 19X3	F1 = C$0.111
December 31, 19X3	F1 = C$0.133

or C$15,890,000. The actual ending balance was C$21,280,000, suggesting that the entire increase in fixing assets (C$21,280,000 − C$15,890,000) was due to an exchange rate effect. A similar analysis reveals that there was no change in French franc long-term debt during the year either. The entire increase in long-term debt in Canadian dollars is solely due to a translation adjustment. These and additional translation effects related to the French subsidiary's working capital accounts are summarized below:

Cash	C$ 1,848,000
Fixed assets	5,390,000
Intercompany payable	(276,000)
Long-term debt	(3,168,000)
Aggregate translation adjustment	C$ 3,794,000

As can be seen, the sum of all the translation adjustments appearing above are equal to the aggregate translation adjustment appearing in the owners' equity section of the translated balance sheet. An analyst who analyzes a funds statement that identifies translation adjustments as a source or use of funds should be alerted to the need to isolate the influence of exchange rate changes from the reporting entity's financing and investing activities.

Information Disclosure

Corporate financial disclosure practices for international companies have improved over time. Institutional pressures from market regulators are one motivating force. For example, the International Organization of Securities Commissions, whose membership includes securities administrators from nearly 50 countries, has become a strong advocate of the worldwide harmonization of disclosure standards to enhance the efficiency of the capital-raising process. Efforts are also underway to encourage the international development of continuing disclosure documents. Other organizations that are working toward improved international corporate disclosure practices include the International Accounting Standards Committee, the European Community, and the Organization for Economic Cooperation and Development.

At the same time, market forces are proving effective in encouraging reporting entities to voluntarily increase the amount of information provided. Competition for low-cost capital is one major contributing force. Examples of disclosures intended to facilitate international statement analysis include convenience translations, special supplements, limited restatements, and primary-secondary disclosures.

Convenience translations include language translations to the national idiom of major national user groups. Many Dutch, German, Swedish, and Swiss companies regularly publish their annual reports in as many as six foreign language editions. As was illustrated for Kao Corporation, many companies also translate monetary amounts to the currency of the readers' country of domicile. As another example, Corporacion Nacional del Cobre presents its annual report in twin columns, with Spanish text and peso amounts in one column and English text and dollars in another. However, readers of such statements should not be lulled into assuming that the accounting principles underlying the convenience translations have been translated as well. Such is seldom the case.

Another accommodation to foreign readers takes the form of information supplements designed to explain the particular accounting standards and practices constituting the basis for their reporting. Many reporting entities in Sweden regularly insert in their annual reports an information booklet entitled *Key to Understanding Swedish Financial Statements*. An example of this supplementary disclosure document for Alfa Laval appears in Exhibit 16.3.

A basic premise underlying supplementary disclosures such as that illustrated in Exhibit 16.3 is that investors possess the expertise to make the necessary reconciliations. Some firms go a step further and reconcile reported statistics to a basis that is familiar to foreign readers. Exhibit 16.4 provides one such partial restatement, in which domestic earnings numbers of Sweden's Volvo are reconciled to the measurement framework of the U.S. reader. In doing so, the major measurement principles accounting for differences are highlighted. The major drawback to this kind of disclosure is its partial nature.

Some companies, such as Italy's Montedison, attempt to remedy the drawback of partial restatements by preparing financial accounts that are based on U.S. accounting standards. Many large Japanese multinationals even provide two sets of financial statements. *Primary* statements, aimed at local investors, are based on Japanese accounting and reporting norms. *Secondary* statements, aimed at U.S. analysts, are translated to the English language, expressed in dollar equivalents, translated to U.S. generally accepted accounting principles (GAAP), and contain an audit report prepared by a major U.S. auditing firm. Secondary statements represent, perhaps, the ultimate accommodation to foreign readers, but despite their appeal, readers must remember that financial reporting standards are environmentally based, and that national reporting environments can differ significantly. Hence, readers must be certain that convenience translations do not distort original messages.

Although progress has been made in international reporting, disclosure levels still vary considerably both between and within countries. Interviews with large institutional investors in Frankfurt, London, New

α ALFA-LAVAL

1990 CONCISE KEY TO UNDERSTANDING SWEDISH FINANCIAL STATEMENTS

General background
The underlying principles on which Swedish financial statements are based are the universally accepted ones of historical cost, accrual accounting – i.e. matching income and expense on a correct inter-period allocation basis – and conservatism – recognizing a loss risk as soon as it is measurable but not taking credit for income items until actually earned. Certain exceptions from the consistent application of these principles are described below.

Apart from differences from generally accepted international accounting principles due to Swedish law and the single biggest factor in distorting Swedish financial statements is the unique stranglehold which Swedish tax law and practice have on the country's accounting and reporting practices. The fiscal legislators have carried to the extreme the basic rule of Swedish taxation that taxable income is principally based on book income. This has been extended to a requirement that taxpayers who wish to claim several of the more important tax incentives available in Sweden must record charges in their books equivalent to the gross (i.e. pretax) amount of these incentives.

Swedish financial statements are further complicated by the effect of two significant differences from U.S., and U.K., practice: the absence of deferred tax accounting and the balance sheet classification of the accumulated gross amount of the tax incentives as a separate item ("Untaxed reserves") between liabilities and shareholders' equity.

Consolidation principles
The great majority of Swedish consolidations are prepared using the purchase accounting method. Pooling is met in a few cases. The purchase accounting procedures applied in Sweden are comparable to those used in the U.S. and the U.K. Special features to be noted are:
1. Normally the only balance sheet items to be revalued are fixed assets (usually property, plant and equipment), portfolio investments and long-term liabilities, usually pension provisions.
2. Untaxed reserves (such as inventory reserves, reserves for future investments, etc) in an acquired subsidiary's books (at the time of acquisition), less deferred tax thereon, are treated as part of the acquired equity.
3. Any resultant goodwill arising on consolidation has to be amortized over a maximum of ten years. Some Swedish companies have started using longer periods.

Equity accounting
Accounting for a company's share in the undistributed earnings of an associated company (i.e. a 20 – 25 up to 50 % holding) is not dealt with in the Swedish accounting or company legislation. According to a draft recommendation from FAR equity accounting may only be applied in consolidated financial statements, and the equity in an associated company's undistributed earnings must be classified as non-distributable consolidated equity. Equity accounting may not be applied in parent company or single company financial statements; in these cases a form of note disclosure on the face of the income statement is proposed.

Property, plant and equipment
These assets are normally stated at original cost, but the Companies Act allows them to be revalued, subject to certain restrictions. Land and buildings, for instance, may not be written up to more than their tax assessment value (which normally would not exceed 75 % of their current market value).

Other assets may not be revalued to more than their current value to the business. The amount by which depreciable assets are written up must be written off over the remaining life of the assets and the unamortized amount of such revaluations disclosed in the financial statements.

The amount of a fixed asset revaluation can either be used to provide for required writedowns of other fixed assets, or to finance a bonus issue of capital stock, or be transferred to a revaluation reserve (in the equity section of the balance sheet) which can later be used for either of the preceding two purposes.

Depreciation
Swedish companies show depreciation charges at two levels in their income statements, in arriving at operating income and as a transfer to/from special reserves.

The charge to operating income is normally computed on a straight line basis over the estimated useful lives of the various classes of asset.

The difference between the charge to operating income and the total amount claimed for tax purposes (which as described above has to be recorded in the books) is shown as a transfer to from untaxed reserves.

Swedish tax depreciation on buildings and land improvements is generally broadly in line with normal straightline useful life original cost depreciation, but in the case of machinery and equipment the methods allowed for tax purposes in effect permit such assets to be written off over five years. In addition to the annual depreciation charges under the tax regulations companies can also utilize reserves for future investments to achieve significant accelerated depreciation benefits.

Income taxes payable
The accounting principles on which taxes payable are reported are rarely disclosed and only a minority, albeit growing, disclose the reasons for abnormal effective tax rates. These usually include investment allowances, the effect of double taxation treaties on foreign earnings, deduction for dividends on new capital stock issues and other similar "permanent" differences. Another item which is rarely disclosed is the amount of unutilized tax loss carry forwards, and the effect of their subsequent utilization.

The reported tax charge includes, as well as income tax, the amount of any profit-sharing and temporary profits tax payable.

The current income tax rate is reduced to 40 % for companies with accounting years ending December 31, 1989 or later. Rates for appropriations to untaxed reserves are reduced for these companies.

Deferred income taxes
Swedish law and practice do not recognize deferred tax accounting except in the case of untaxed reserves in acquired subsidiaries (see "Consolidation principles"). This results in Swedish financial statements being totally silent on the existence of considerable deferred tax liabilities relating to the untaxed reserves to be found in practically every balance sheet. Swedish readers are naturally aware of the situation and automatically make the necessary adjustments in their head (usually using a 50 % tax rate which should now be reduced to 40–46 % or possibly 30 %) as they read the statements.

Untaxed reserves
The main types of untaxed reserves, apart from additional depreciation, are:
• *Inventory reserves* have existed for many years as a means whereby manufacturing industry could defer taxes and/or even out taxable income.
• *Payroll reserves* extend the same sort of possibility to labour-intensive companies with little or no inventory.
• *Reserves for future investments* are in effect advance additional depreciation in respect of unspecified fixed assets yet to be acquired.
• *Compulsory investment reserves* were introduced as a means of mopping up excess corporate liquidity through the related compulsory deposits. These reserves can be used in the same way as reserves for future investments.
• *Development reserves* are compulsory appropriations of pre-tax profits. They can be used for employee training or research and development purposes.
• *"Blocked accounts with the Bank of Sweden"* which frequently appear as a separate item between current assets and fixed assets relate to compulsory non-interest bearing deposits associated with reserves for future investments and development reserves.

Earnings per share
There is no legal requirement to disclose earnings per share, but the great majority of Swedish listed companies do in fact present this information.

The most commonly used starting point for computing earnings per share is to apply a standard tax rate (usually 50 % which should now be 40 – 46 % or possibly 30 %) to the reported figure of earnings before special adjustments and taxes.

Adjustments
Swedish financial statements can be basically adjusted to reflect U.S. accounting principles as follows:
• Increase reported net income by 54 % of the year's transfers to untaxed reserves, and
• Increase reported shareholders' equity by 54 % of untaxed reserves in the balance sheet

46 % of each of these items represents deferred taxes.

Exhibit 16.3. Supplemental Information

29 **Generally Accepted Accounting Principles in the United States (U.S. GAAP)**

The consolidated financial statements of AB Volvo and its subsidiaries have been prepared in accordance with accounting principles generally accepted in Sweden. These accounting principles differ in certain significant respects from accounting principles generally accepted in the United States (U.S. GAAP). The approximate net loss in accordance with U.S. GAAP for 1990 amounted to 23 (gain 5,400) compared with a net loss in accordance with Swedish accounting principles of 1,020 (gain 4,787). The estimated net loss per share in accordance with U.S. GAAP amounted to SEK 0.30 (gain 69.60), while the loss per share in accordance with Swedish accounting principles was SEK 13.10 (gain 61.70). The difference in 1990 amounted to SEK 12.80 and was due primarily to differences in accounting for tooling costs and income taxes.

Application of U.S. GAAP would have the following approximate effect on Consolidated net income and Shareholders' equity of the Group:

Net income (loss)

	1990	1989
Net income (loss) in accordance with Swedish accounting principles	(1,020)	4,787
Items increasing (decreasing) reported income:		
Income taxes (Note A)	58	(474)
Tooling costs (Note B)	718	492
Interest costs (Note C)	140	72
Business combinations (Note D)	(50)	512
Foreign currency translation (Note E)	(51)	57
Leasing (Note F)	41	(361)
Other (Note G)	141	315
Net increase in net income	997	613
Approximate net income (loss) in accordance with U.S. GAAP	(23)	5,400
Approximate net income (loss) per share in accordance with U.S. GAAP, SEK	(0.30)	69.60
Weighted average number of shares outstanding (in thousands)	77,605	77,605

Shareholders' equity

	1990	1989
Shareholders' equity in accordance with Swedish accounting principles	35,291	37,639
Items increasing (decreasing) reported shareholders' equity:		
Income taxes (Note A)	(7,133)	(7,318)
Tooling costs (Note B)	2,706	1,990
Interest costs (Note C)	391	251
Business combinations (Note D)	196	246
Leasing (Note F)	(278)	(294)
Other (Note G)	257	66
Net decrease in shareholders' equity	(3,861)	(5,059)
Approximate shareholders' equity in accordance with U.S. GAAP	31,430	32,580

Explanation of U.S. GAAP differences

A. Income taxes
Under U.S. GAAP (APB 11), deferred taxes are provided for timing differences, based on tax rates in effect when such timing differences originate. Such deferred tax liabilities are not adjusted for subsequent changes in statutory tax rates. Volvo accounts for deferred taxes under the liability method using current statutory tax rates. During 1990, the reversal of timing differences resulted in a decrease of tax expense of 964 for U.S. GAAP as compared with a decrease of 423 in Volvo's consolidated income statement.

Under U.S. GAAP, the tax effects of certain transactions which directly affect shareholders' equity are removed from income and included in equity.

This adjustment also includes the tax effect of other U.S. GAAP adjustments.

B. Tooling costs
Volvo generally expenses tooling costs as incurred. Industry practice in the United States is to capitalize all significant tooling costs. Accordingly, for U.S. GAAP purposes, tooling costs are capitalized and amortized over a period not exceeding 5 years.

C. Interest costs
In accordance with Swedish accounting practice, Volvo does not capitalize interest costs incurred in connection with financing the construction of property, plant and equipment. Under U.S. GAAP, such interest costs are capitalized.

D. Business combinations
The method of accounting for certain acquisitions is different for Swedish reporting and U.S. GAAP, particularly as it relates to the recognition and amortization of excess values and accounting for the tax benefits related to utilization of loss carryforwards of purchased subsidiaries.

E. Foreign currency translation
Volvo recognizes the effects of all foreign exchange gains and losses caused by fluctuations in exchange rates in income in the period such fluctuations occur. In accordance with U.S. GAAP, under certain circumstances, borrowings denominated in foreign currencies may be designated and effectively function as a hedge of a net investment in a foreign subsidiary. Transaction gains and losses, net of related income taxes, attributable to such foreign currency transactions may be excluded from the determination of net income and directly included in shareholders' equity.

F. Leasing
Certain leasing transactions are reported differently in accordance with Volvo's accounting principles and in accordance with U.S. GAAP. The differences mainly relate to sale-leaseback transactions and the leasing of certain assets.

G. Other
Includes adjustments pertaining to pension costs, gain on sale of securities as well as minority interests in U.S. GAAP adjustments.

Exhibit 16.4. Partial Restatements (Source: Volvo)

York, Tokyo, and Zurich reveal the following areas where international disclosure practices are considered most wanting: segmental information, methods of asset valuation, foreign operations disclosures, frequency and completeness of interim information, description of capital expenditures, hidden reserves, and off-balance sheet items.

Company visitations and attendance at corporate road shows are commonly used methods to secure added information. Coping sometimes takes the form of assigning firms into investment versus speculative grades. Sometimes firms providing adequate disclosures are classified as investment grade and firms that are less forthcoming as speculative grade. Some investors engage in active stock selection when information disclosures are satisfactory. When such is not the case, they adopt a passive investment strategy involving a mutual fund approach to foreign investing. Here emphasis is placed on industry and macro considerations rather than firm-specific information.

Accounting Principles Differences

Aside from questions of disclosure, a major hurdle facing foreign analysts is the need to analyze company statistics that have been prepared according to an unfamiliar set of accounting measurement rules. Owing to the diversity that characterizes national accounting measurements internationally, differences in reported profitability between two reporting entities located in two different countries may be due as much to differences in national accounting principles as they are to differences in the underlying economics. Exhibit 16.5 provides an overview of accounting conventions adopted by accounting rule makers in various countries around the world. Given the diversity that characterizes accounting standards around the world, the application of local benchmarks to evaluate accounting-based financial ratios generated in one national environment to a company whose financial statements are prepared under another national measurement framework could lead to misunderstanding and misinterpretation.

Do international accounting differences actually affect investor decisions? In what is probably one of the first studies to marshall empirical evidence on this important question, Choi and Levich conducted in-depth interviews with institutional investors, corporate issuers, investment underwriters, market regulators, and international ratings agencies around the world.[2] More than half of the investors interviewed felt that international accounting differences hindered the measurement of their

---

[2] F. D. S. Choi and R. M. Levich, *The Capital Market Effects of International Accounting Diversity*, Homewood, Illinois: Dow Jones-Irwin, 1990.

	United States	Japan	United Kingdom	France	Germany	Netherlands	Switzerland	Canada	Italy	Brazil
Capitalization of Research and Development Costs	Not Allowed	Allowed in certain circumstances	Allowed in certain circumstances	Allowed in certain circumstances	Not Allowed	Allowed in certain circumstances	Allowed in certain circumstances	Allowed in certain circumstances	Allowed in certain circumstances	Allowed in certain circumstances
Fixed Assets Revaluations Stated at Amount in Excess of Cost	Not Allowed	Not Allowed	Allowed	Allowed	Not Allowed	Allowed in certain circumstances	Not allowed	Not allowed	Allowed in certain circumstances	Allowed
Inventory Valuation Using LIFO	Allowed	Allowed	Allowed but rarely done	Not allowed	Allowed in certain circumstances	Allowed	Allowed	Allowed	Allowed	Allowed but rarely done
Finance Leases Capitalized	Required	Allowed in certain circumstances	Required	Not allowed	Allowed in certain circumstances	Required	Allowed	Required	Not allowed	Not allowed
Pension Expense Accrued During Period of Service	Required	Allowed	Required	Allowed	Required	Required	Allowed	Required	Allowed	Allowed
Book and Tax Timing Differences Presented on the Balance Sheet as Deferred Tax	Required	Allowed in certain circumstances	Allowed	Allowed in certain circumstances	Allowed but rarely done	Required	Allowed	Allowed	Allowed but rarely done	Allowed
Current Rate Method Used for Foreign Currency Translation	Required	Allowed in certain circumstances	Required	Allowed	Allowed	Required	Required	Allowed in certain circumstances	Required	Required
Pooling Method Used for Mergers	Required in certain circumstances	Allowed in certain circumstances	Allowed in certain circumstances	Not allowed	Allowed in certain circumstances	Allowed but rarely done	Allowed but rarely done	Allowed but rarely done	Not allowed	Allowed but rarely done
Equity Method Used for 20–50% Ownership	Required	Required	Required	Allowed in certain circumstances	Allowed	Required	Required	Required	Allowed	Required

Exhibit 16.5. Summary of Principal Accounting Differences Around the World (Source: Peller & Schwitter, 1991)

decision variables and ultimately affected their investment decisions. Capital market effects ranged from the geographic location of their foreign investments to the types of companies or securities they invested in and to the valuation of foreign securities. Methods of coping with international accounting differences varied. Some investors coped by comparing rates of change in a company's performance over time. Others relied on variables less sensitive to corporate accounting treatments such as using a discounted dividend model as a basis for investment picks, as opposed to a discounted earnings framework. Reliance on cash flow data is a variant of this approach. Adoption of a top-down approach to foreign investing can also be considered a coping mechanism. In this investment approach, assets are allocated by country according to macroeconomic variables and then by funds invested in a diversified portfolio of securities within each country. A significant number of investors coped by restating foreign accounting numbers to the reporting principles of the investor's country or to a set of internationally recognized measurement rules. It should be noted that restatement was not always sufficient to entirely remove problems caused by accounting differences. This suggests that extant restatement algorithms may not be optimal, are not being applied effectively perhaps owing to insufficient firm disclosure, or are incapable of producing meaningful information. Some investors therefore preferred to rely on original accounting statements and a well-developed knowledge of foreign accounting practices and local financial market conditions. Investors who have developed multiple accounting principles capabilities (MPCers), while small in number, reported no decision problems or capital market effects associated with accounting diversity.

Readers of international financial statements thus face a choice. They can attempt to restate foreign accounts to a measurement framework with which they are more familiar, or they can become MPCers and develop a facility for using and interpreting original accounting data. Each choice has benefits and costs.

Given that GAAP restatements are an accepted method of coping with accounting diversity, we next offer a simplified case example of how one might go about effecting GAAP restatements. Year-end financial statements for a hypothetical Japanese company, Hondo Enterprises, are contained in Table 16.5. To facilitate comparison with a U.S. counterpart, the statements of Hondo will be restated to U.S. GAAP.

Upon examination of the notes to Hondo Enterprise's statements, the following adjustments would be advised:

1. Inventories would be adjusted to reflect differences in costing methods. This would entail an increase in inventories and a decrease in cost of sales of ¥594,000.

Table 16.5. Hondo Enterprises, Year-end Financial Statements and Related Notes (¥ 000s)

Balance Sheet

Assets

Cash	¥ 373,500
Accounts receivable, net	1,530,000
Marketable securities	135,000
Inventory	1,170,000
Investments	450,000
Plant and equipment, net	841,500
Goodwill	—
Total	¥4,500,000

Liabilities & Owners' Equity

Short-term payables	¥ 495,000
Short-term debt	1,575,000
Deferred taxes	—
Other current liabilities	270,000
Long-term debt	1,560,000
Reserves	270,000
Capital Stock	225,000
Retained earnings	105,000
Total	¥4,500,000

Income Statement

Sales	¥4,200,000
Operating expenses:	
Cost of sales including depreciation	2,360,000
Selling and administrative	300,000
Other operating	342,600
Goodwill amortization	—

Income before taxes	113,400
Income taxes	71,400
Income after taxes	42,000
Equity in earnings of unconsolidated subs	—
Net income	¥42,000

Notes:

1. The balance sheet and income statement are prepared in accordance with the Japanese Commercial Code and related regulations.

2. Investments in subsidiaries and affiliated companies are stated at cost.

3. Inventories are stated at average cost. Ending inventories restated to a FIFO basis would have been ¥594,000,000 higher.

4. Plant and equipment are carried at cost. Depreciation, with minor exceptions, is computed by the sum-of-the-years-digits method.

5. Operating expenses include lease rental payments of ¥120,000,000. The average term of the lease contracts is five years. All leases transfer ownership to the lessor at the end of the lease term. Assume that a U.S. counterpart's cost of capital is estimated to be 8 percent.

6. A translation gain of ¥60,000,000 relating to consolidation of foreign operations with a negative exposure is being deferred under long-term debt.

7. Purchased goodwill amounted to ¥36,000,000 for the year and is included under Other Operating Expenses. Under U.S. GAAP, it would have been amortized to expense over a ten-year period.

8. Hondo Enterprises is allowed to set up "special purpose" reserves (i.e., government-sanctioned charges against earnings) equal to a certain percentage of total export revenues. This year's charge (included in Other Operating Expenses) was ¥79,200,000. Similarly, this year's addition to Hondo's general purpose reserves totaled ¥92,400,000.

9. Deferred taxes are not provided in Japan for book-tax differences.

10. The ¥/$ exchange rate at year-end was ¥138 = $1.

11. Hondo Enterprise's marginal income tax rate is 35 percent.

12. The U.S. counterpart against which Hondo Enterprises is being compared bases its financial on U.S. GAAP. Inventories are carried at FIFO cost, plant and equipment is depreciated in straight-line fashion, and foreign operations are consolidated with those of the U.S. parent using the temporal method of translation.

337

2. The difference between depreciation methods would yield an adjustment to cost of sales and net plant and equipment of ¥140,250. The depreciation differential for the preceding year would be ¥420,750. Based on a marginal tax rate of 35 percent, the ¥420,750 increase in reported earnings would give rise to ¥147,264 in deferred taxes with the balance being credited to retained earnings.
3. Under U.S. GAAP, the lease transaction would be capitalized. Discounting the stream of ¥120,000,000 periodic rental payments at 8 percent for five years yields a present value attributable to both a leased asset and a lease obligation of ¥478,800,000. Based on this amount, the annual lease payment can be desegregated into an interest component of ¥38,304,000 and a reduction of the lease obligation of ¥81,696,000. Straight-line depreciation of the leased asset would yield an expense of ¥95,760,000.
4. The translation gain would be backed out from long-term debt and taken to income per Financial Accounting Standard No. 52.
5. Goodwill amortization expense is overstated by ¥32,400,000. A correcting adjustment would recognize an asset and a reduction in an operating expense.
6. Discretionary reserves are not permitted in the United States. Hence, the special purpose and general purpose reserves would be backed out and taken to income.
7. The foregoing adjustments would cause Honda Enterprise's restated earnings to increase by ¥984,186,000 of which ¥60,000,000 relating to the translation gain would not be recognized for tax purposes. This would yield a tax expense of ¥114,822,000, deferred taxes of ¥21,000,000, and a balance of ¥323,466,000 payable to the tax authorities.

If accounting measurement rules were the only difference among countries, then straightforward transformation of the figures would be sufficient to enable accounting reports—assuming sufficient data were available to the user to make the desired adjustments—to be universally understood and interpreted unambiguously. Unfortunately, countries also reflect substantial economic and cultural differences that often preclude identical interpretations of accounting figures, even if they were generated using the same measurement standards. If national environmental differences are substantial, simple restatement of foreign accounting numbers incorporating GAAP differences may not be sufficient for proper analysis.

Foreign Information Sources

A key ingredient to informed decisions is financial data. In a country such as the United States, sources of information on reporting entities abound. Even though parallels to U.S. information sources can be found with increasing frequency in more and more countries, U.S. investors often find it difficult to access foreign information sources. As investor interest in foreign security investments continues to mount, information services that specialize in providing financial profiles of foreign companies promise to remedy this situation. A recent survey of information sources around the world bears this out. Table 16.6 lists some of the major services that currently provide financial statistics on international companies and includes the type of financial data supplied, language used, frequency of information updates, number of reporting companies covered, and data format.

To provide a better perspective on the kinds of information that are currently being supplied, we briefly describe the offerings of three leading data services that provide international coverage.

In the previous section, two contrasting approaches were identified with respect to coping with differences in accounting systems. The first involved restating foreign accounting data to a measurement framework considered more relevant to the decision maker. In most cases this framework would be that restatement to the reporting framework of the user's home country; though in some others it might mean restatement to an international or proprietary framework. The second involved adoption of a local perspective for analyzing foreign financial data (i.e., development of an MPC capability). Consistent with a top-down investment strategy,[3] this approach avoids cross-country comparisons. The first two databases described here are consistent with the first approach; the second consistent with either the MPC or restatement approaches.

Euroequities. Euroequities is a microcomputer financial database providing information on European listed companies, both industrial and financial. The information service covers approximately 1,000 companies in 15 European countries as follows:

Austria	13	Netherlands	87
Belgium	26	Norway	26
Denmark	26	Portugal	25
Finland	22	Spain	73
France	131	Sweden	37
Germany	132	Switzerland	53
Italy	89	United Kingdom	264
Luxembourg	1		

The data set covers 56 variables including 16 balance sheet-, 16 income statement-, and 12 security-related data since 1981 and has been restated to fit into a standard format that takes into account national accounting dif-

---

[3] A "top-down" investment approach to stock investments involves allocating investment funds across countries on the basis of macroeconomic variables and then diversifying in a portfolio of stocks within a country.

Table 16.6. International Data Bases

Information Service	Publisher	Information Type	Language	Frequency of Update	No. of Companies	Format
Agrodata	Institute Agro Mediteranean	Selected Acs.	French	Annual	120	Hard Copy
Association of Int'l Bond Dealers	Data Resources	Eurobond Price and Yield Quotes	English	Daily	N.P.*	Online
Bankers Almanac & Yearbook	Thomas Skinner Directories	B/S & I/S Acs.	English	Annual	N.P.	Hard Copy
Bankstat	Bankers Trust Global Operating & Information Service	B/S & I/S Acs, Ratios	English	Daily	1,400	Data Tape
World Companies Electronics File	Ben Electronics	Sales, Income, Cap. Exp. Shares Prices	English	Annual	1,500	Hard Copy
Capital Int'l Perspective	Capital Int'l Perspective, SA	Full B/S & I/S, Stock Data	English	Quarterly	1,600	Hard Copy
Chemfacts (Country)	Chemical Data Services	Selected Data	English	Annual	N.P.	Datatape
Compmark	Citishare	Pub. Priv. B/S & I/S Acs.	English	Quarterly	44,000	Online
Global Vantage	Standard & Poor's Compusint Services, Inc.	Full B/S & I/S, Stock Data	English	Monthly	6,000	Datatape
Eurabank	Sleigh Corporation	Bank Annual Report Data	English	Weekly	3,500	Online
European Elect. Co. File	Benn Electronics Publications Ltd.	Leading Fin. Indicators	English/ French	Annual	100	Annual
Examiner	Extel Financial	Share Price Data	English	Daily	N.P.	Online
Euro Equities		B/S & I/S Acs., Ratios, Share Price Data	English	Bi-weekly	1,100	Online

Name	Provider	Content	Language	Frequency	Number	Format
Exbond	Securities Int'l	Eurobond Price and Issue Date	English	Daily	N.A.**	Online
Financial Leaders	Japan Export Magazine	Complete B/S & I/S Acs.	English	Annual	250	Hard Copy
Exshare	Extel Computing	Share Price Data	English	Daily	100,000	Online
Exstat	Extel Financial	B/S & I/S Data	English	Annual	3,500	Online
Financial Times	Ins. Oil & Gas	Summarized B/S & I/S Acs.	English	Annual	3,500	Hard Copy
Financial Times Share Index	Financial Times Business Info.	Share Data Index	English	Daily	N.P.	Online
Financial Times World Accounting	Financial Times Bus. Info. Ltd.	Rating Quality of Annual Reports	English	4 years	175	Hard Copy
Forbes Annual Directory	Forbes, Inc.	Selected Financial Statistics	English	Annual	800	Hard Copy/Online
Fortune World Business Directory	Fortune, Inc.	Selected B/S & I/S Acs.	English	Annual	500	Hard Copy
Global Report	Citibank, N.A.	Financial Data Stock Quotes	English	Daily	10,000	Online
Industry Groups	Dodwell Marketing	Selected Accounts	English	Annual	2,900	Hard Copy
Dataline Securities Database	Faxon Company	U.S.-Canadian Share Prices	English	Daily	N.P.	
Datastream	Datastream Int'l	B/S & I/S Acs., Share Prices	English	Continuous	800	Online
IBES Summary Statistics	Lynch, Jones, & Ryan	Earnings Forecasts	English	Weekly	7,000	Online

ICAP Financial Dir. of Greek Cos.	ICAP Hellas SA	Selected B/S & I/S Acs.	Greek English	Annual	10,700	Hard Copy
International Corp. Scoreboard	Business Week	Selected B/S & I/S	English	Annual	1,000	Hard Copy
International Securities Database	Extel Computing	Month-End Price	English	Monthly	70,000	Online
INVESTEXT	Business Research Corp.	Full B/S & I/S Acs. & Share Prices	English	Continuous	5,000	Online
LeNouvel Economiste 5000	Nouvelle Economiste	Selected B/S & I/S Acs.	French	Annual	5,000	Hard Copy
Major Companies of Europe	Graham & Trotman	Sales, Profits, Dividends	English	Annual	5,500	Online
Mining Journal Quarterly Review	Mining Journal	Inv. Full B/S & I/S Acs.	English	Annual	15 Min. 38 Min.	Hard Copy
Moody's Corporate News-International	Moody's Investor Service	Selected Financial Data	English	Semi-Annual	5,000	Online
Morgan Stanley Capital Int'l Indices	Data Resources	Nat'l Stock Indexes	English	Daily	N.A.	Online
Polk's World Bank Directory	R.L. Polk & Co.	Selected B/S Acs.	English	Annual	N.P.	Hard Copy
Railway Directory Yearbook	IPC Transport	Selected B/S Acs.	English	Annual	N.P.	Hard Copy
Rand McNally Int'l Bankers Directory	Rand McNally	Selected Fin. B/S Acs. Statistics	English	Semi-Annual	125,000	Hard Copy
Scan Times 1000	Scicon Ltd. Times Book	Share Price Data Selected B/S & I/S Acs.	English English	Daily Annual	30,000 1,000	Online Hard Copy
Worldscope	Wright Investors Service	Selected B/S & I/S	English	Quarterly	3,000	Hard Copy

Source: Choi, 1989.

ferences. Manuals are provided containing country-by-country guidelines for the conversion of published company accounts into the Euroequities standard format. Forecast data for two years are provided by 13 banks or brokerage firms from each of the major markets covered in the database.

The data is available via floppy diskettes, enables the user to upload proprietary data, and is fully compatible with Lotus 123. Historical and forecast data are updated twice each month via diskettes and includes new companies added to the database, newly published historical data, changes in forecasts, and price and market data updates.

Worldscope Profiles. Similar in nature to Euroequities, Worldscope financial data are available in both loose-leaf and computer-readable format. It covers over 3,000 industrial companies and over 1,000 financial and service companies, including the United States. In the loose-leaf service, single-page financial summaries are provided for each firm, giving a six-year financial history and a variety of accounting and financial statistics. An attempt is made to adjust the data for national accounting differences. A summary of the accounting principles used by each firm is provided, as well as industry and country averages of basic accounting and financial measures.

Global Vantage. A product of Standard & Poor's Compustat Services, Inc., Global Vantage is a computer-readable library comprising fundamental financial, market-related, and currency translation rate information for 6,000 industrial/commercial companies from 24 major world markets. A financial services file now provides comparable information for 730 financial institutions from the same 24 country set. The following data items are currently provided for both the industrial/commercial and financial services files since 1982:

	Industrial/ Commercial File	Financial Services File
Assets	34	126
Liabilities	37	66
Equity	17	29
Income statement	56	116
Funds statement	27	—
Descriptive (including accounting standards used)	51	51
Stock data	13	13
Foreign exchange rate	3	3

Information for each company is reported in its functional currency using standardized definitions, extensive notation, and a currency capability to allow analysts to make adjustments for cross-border analyses. However, Global Vantage does not adjust financial data for accounting differences. Instead, it provides information on relevant accounting standards, data definitions, and available firm-specific disclosures to enable the user to make whatever adjustments are deemed necessary or desirable for cross-country comparisons. Hence, the data provided are compatible with either an MPC or restatement approach to foreign investing.

The information is currently available on magnetic tape and on CD-ROM.

Summary

Investors in international securities face a number of hurdles when attempting to read and understand the financial accounts of the investee companies. These obstacles relate to differences in language and accounting terminology, statement format, currency of denomination, extent of disclosure, accounting measurement standards, and information availability.

Some of these hurdles are more easily overcome than others. As the appetite for foreign equities within the world's investment community grows, the information base to support international investments improves. The last section of this chapter identified a growing number of information services that provide financial information on foreign companies. More and more of the information is being made available in the English language, utilizes a standard account format, and employs uniform terminology. Since investors appear divided on whether restated or original foreign data is the best approach to be used in analyses, information services are likely to cater to each of these preferences. Some will attempt to restate foreign accounting data to a common frame of reference such as Worldscope Profiles. Others, such as Standard & Poor's Global Vantage, will adopt an events approach in reporting unadulterated accounting numbers accompanied by sufficient information to provide financial analysts the option of restating foreign accounts from one set of accounting standards to another if they so desire. Until empirical studies confirm the superiority of one investment approach over the other, the latter posture appears to be a sound course of action.

REFERENCES

Aaron, P. "Japanese P/E Multiples: The Tradition Continues." Daiwa Securities America, Report #35, October 23, 1989.

American Institute of Certified Public Accountants. *Professional Accounting in Foreign Countries Series*. New York: AICPA, 1987–90.

Choi, F. D. S. "International Data Sources for Empirical Research in Financial Management." *Financial Management* (Summer 1988) pp. 80–98.

Choi, F. D. S., and R. M. Levich. *The Capital Market Effects of International Accounting Diversity*. Homewood, IL: Dow Jones-Irwin, 1990.

Choi, F. D. S., H. Hino, S. K. Min, S. O. Nam, J. Ujiie, and A. I. Stonehill. "Analyzing Foreign Financial Statements: The Use and Misuse of International Ratio Analysis." *Journal of International Business Studies* (Spring/ Summer 1983) pp. 113–131.

Choi, F. D. S., and K. Hiramatsu, eds. *Accounting and Financial Reporting in Japan.* Berkshire, England: Van Nostrand Reinhold, 1987.

Choi, F. D. S., and G. G. Mueller. *International Accounting.* 2nd ed. Englewood Cliffs, N.J.: Prentice Hall, Inc., forthcoming.

Choi, F. D. S., and A. Sondhi. "SFAS 52 and the Funds Statement." *Corporate Accounting* (Spring 1984) pp. 46–56.

Coopers & Lybrand. *1991 International Accounting Summaries: A Guide for Interpretation and Comparison.* New York: John Wiley & Sons, 1991.

Nobes, C., and R. Parker, eds. *Comparative International Accounting.* 2nd ed. London: Philip Allen Pub., Ltd., 1985.

Orsini, L., J. McAllister, and R. Parikh. *World Accounting.* New York: Matthew Bender & Co., 1990.

Peller, P. R., and F. J. Schwitter. "A Summary of Accounting Principle Differences Around the World." *Handbook of International Accounting.* F. D. S. Choi, ed. New York: John Wiley & Sons, 1991.

Peat, Marwick, Mitchell & Co. "Annual Accounts of Companies—Directive 4." *EEC Company Law Series—Part 1.* Nottingham, England: PM&M, 1981.

Saudagaran, S. M., and M. B. Solomon. "Worldwide Regulatory Disclosure Requirements." *Handbook of International Accounting.* F. D. S. Choi, ed. New York: John Wiley & Sons, 1991.

Schieneman, G. S. "Japanese P/E Ratios II: Myth and Reality." Prudential Bache Securities, March 30, 1989.

Smith, Roy C. "Integration of World Financial Markets—Past, Present and Future." *Handbook of International Accounting.* F. D. S. Choi, ed. New York: John Wiley & Sons, 1991.

Spicer & Oppenheim. *The Spicer & Oppenheim Guide to Financial Statements Around the World.* F. D. S. Choi, ed. New York: John Wiley & Sons, 1989.

Todd, R., and R. Sherman. "International Financial Statement Analysis." *Handbook of International Accounting.* F. D. S. Choi, ed. New York: John Wiley & Sons, 1991.

Tonkin, D. J., ed. *World Survey of Published Accounts.* London: Lafferty Publications, 1989.

UBS Philips & Drew. *Understanding European Financial Statements.* Basel: Union Bank of Switzerland, June 1987, pp. 4–5.

Wyatt, A. R. "International Accounting Standards and Organizations: Quo Vadis?" *Handbook of International Accounting.* F. D. S. Choi, ed. New York: John Wiley & Sons, 1991.

Training and Regulation of Security Analysts: An International Perspective

Alfred C. Morley, CFA
*Former President
and Senior Advisor,
Association for Investment
Management and Research
(comprising the Financial
Analysts Federation and the
Institute of Chartered
Financial Analysts)
Charlottesville, VA*

Estimates indicate that the market value of global investment securities totals on the order of 25 trillion dollars, divided approximately 40 percent in common stocks, another 40 percent in fixed income instruments, and the remaining 20 percent in cash equivalents, equity real estate, venture capital, and other marketable asset classes. The comparable figure 20 years ago is believed to have been less than 5 trillion dollars. There has been not only sharp growth in total global investable assets (a consequence, among other factors, of the issuance of new securities, increasing earnings and asset values, and higher valuation of those earnings and assets), but also increasing dispersion of those assets among more and more countries around the world. For example, using only global common stock market capitalizations, studies show that although the United States, Japan, Germany, and the United Kingdom together accounted for close to 90 percent of the total in 1970, their share has subsequently dropped to around 75 percent. Accounting for the growth from roughly 10 percent to 25 percent in the "all other" category during this time span has been the significant and continuing development of capital markets in other global areas, particularly in such Asian countries as Korea, Taiwan, Hong Kong, Singapore, Indonesia, Malaysia, and Thailand. This is not to overlook positive trends in other regions of the world such as the smaller European Community countries, Mexico, and some parts of South America. Still to come are possible benefits from the shift to market-driven economies in Eastern Europe, and perhaps in due course, in China and Russia. Global security markets are, indeed, huge in size, and promise to become even larger and more geographically diverse.

With the growing aggregate size of global capital markets, and within the aggregate increasing diversification in terms of both number of asset classes and geographical locations, world investors will have broader opportunities of investment choice in construction and management of portfolios. This will translate into greater competition between and within individual capital markets in attracting and retaining investor commitments. It seems inevitable that, over the longer term, those capital markets that provide investors the highest level of service, as measured by quantity and more particularly quality, will enhance their competitive position. Service in this context involves an array of factors, among which are maintenance of fair and orderly markets; efficient execution and settlement procedures; full and timely disclosure of corporate financial information; innovative and comprehensive analysis of internal and external influences impacting security values, and effective dissemination thereof; and establishment of sound portfolio management policies and practices. In short, global investors likely will be attracted to those capital markets in which they have confidence that high levels of professional and ethical standards are being practiced and will shy away from markets where they have doubts about such practices.

More and more global capital markets are recognizing the merits of strengthening their professional and ethical standards of practice in order to retain or enhance their competitive standing. A leading role in the accomplishment of this objective has been assigned to established and new investment professional organizations composed of security analysts, portfolio managers, and others involved in various aspects of the investment decision-making process. Worldwide membership in such organizations exceeds 35,000 persons and continues to grow at a comparatively rapid rate.

The major world investment professional organizations are the Asian Securities' Analysts Council (ASAC), the European Federation of Financial Analysts Societies (EFFAS), and the Association for Investment Management and Research (AIMR), comprising the Financial Analysts Federation (FAF) and the Institute of Chartered Financial Analysts (ICFA), headquartered in North America. Within each of these three groups are numerous constituent societies, both established and newly formed. Smaller in membership than ASAC, EFFAS, or AIMR are the Investment Society of Southern Africa and ABAMEC in Brazil, though both countries are experiencing ongoing development of capital markets and the associated professionalism of security analysts, portfolio managers, and others in the investment community. Each of the five foregoing groups has delegate representation on the International Coordinating Committee (ICC), which meets periodically to discuss common interests, including the enhancement of global market efficiency and the effective allocation of capital worldwide through appropriate generation and dissemination of investment information; the promotion of high ethical and professional standards of practice on a worldwide basis; and establishment of common accounting standards at the global level.

ASAC

ASAC, established in 1979 as an international cooperative organization for security analysts in Asia and Oceania, now comprises 11 member societies located in Australia, Hong Kong, India, Indonesia, Japan, Korea, Malaysia, New Zealand, Singapore, Taipei, and Thailand. Membership in these societies exceeds 8400 persons affiliated with a diverse list of investment organizations in the respective communities. ASAC is not organized in a formal federation structure as in the case of EFFAS in Europe and AIMR in North America, but rather conducts its activities through cooperative efforts among all of the societies. An ASAC conference is held each year, giving attendees the opportunity to share views and learn of investment developments in the various countries. ASAC has sponsored the preparation and publication of *Securities Markets in Asia and Oceania*, a book that fully describes the characteristics and regulation of security markets in each of the countries of the region. An ASAC directory providing information on activities of the societies is published annually.

Formalized training and qualification programs for security analysts, portfolio managers, and other investment professionals are conducted, in varying degrees, by the ASAC societies in Australia, India, Japan, Korea, and New Zealand. Such programs have been recently or are soon to be inaugurated in Indonesia, Malaysia, and Thailand and are under consideration in the remaining countries.

Among the more established and sizable programs is the one sponsored by the Security Analysts Association of Japan (SAAJ). This organization offers a study and examination course covering the subjects of security analysis and portfolio management, economics, financial accounting, and financial statement analysis at Level I; and security analysis and portfolio management, economics, and financial accounting and analysis at Level II. Those candidates who pass the examinations and meet experience and other qualifications are awarded the Chartered Member of the Security Analysts Association of Japan (CMA) designation. Some 3,000 members have attained CMA status, and more than 10,000 candidates currently are enrolled at Level I and over 2,000 at Level II.

The CMA curriculum is continually enhanced to reflect the dynamics of the body of knowledge applicable to the investment process. In recent years, such enhancement has also reflected cooperative efforts between the SAAJ and the Institute of Chartered Financial Analysts (ICFA) whereby the curriculum has been modified to the extent that a CMA wishing to pursue the Chartered Financial Analyst (CFA) designation will be granted waivers from taking the CFA Level I and Level II examinations, and therefore needs to pass only the CFA level III test to be awarded that designation. Such an arrangement is also in place with the Society of Investment Analysts (SIA) in London, and in both cases, provides the opportunity for CFAs to earn the designation awarded by the organizations in London and Tokyo through the successful completion of a limited examination.

In collaboration with the ICFA, the Institute of Chartered Financial Analysts of India (ICFAI) was organized in 1985 to offer a study and examination program to qualified persons in India that covers not only various aspects of investment management, but also financial services and corporate finance. Well over 10,000 candidates have entered the program, specifically designed to address issues pertinent to the economy in India, and the first graduates were awarded the CFAI designation in 1990.

Representatives from investment and governmental groups in Indonesia, Malaysia, and Thailand have recently initiated major planning to develop training and qualification programs for security analysts and portfolio managers in their respective communities, in all three cases using a dual track approach. One track will be in the English language using the established CFA Study and Examination Program, the successful completion of which will lead to the award of the CFA designation by the ICFA. The other track will be in the language of the country and based on a curriculum modeled after that of the Level I and Level II CFA courses, plus a module pertaining to local regulations and customs. Successful completion of the latter will lead to the award of a designation from the sponsoring organization, in most cases the security analysts association of the country.

Among other ASAC countries, the Securities Institute of Australia offers two formal educational courses, a post-graduate diploma course and an open-entry certificate course; the Hong Kong Society of Security Analysts is considering an examination program, as is the Security Analysts Association in Taipei; the Korea Securities Analysts Association provides a six-month training course to improve investment research capabilities and awards a certificate to successful candidates; and the New Zealand Society of Investment Analysts has established a course in financial analysis in association with a university, and those candidates who complete the program and meet other requirements receive an Investment Analysts Certificate.

The Singapore Society of Financial Analysts strongly endorses training and qualification of professionals in the investment community, primarily via participation in the ICFA program. Nearly 80 Singaporeans already have achieved CFA status and approximately another 500 persons are in various phases of the program.

Additional information concerning training and certification of investment professionals by ASAC member societies can be obtained by contacting these organizations at the following addresses:

The Securities Institute of Australia
Exchange Centre, Level 10
20 Bond Street
Sydney, NSW 2000, Australia
Tel: 61–2–232–5144
Fax: 61–2–223–5158

The Hong Kong Society of Security Analysts Limited
c/o Glass Radcliffe & Co.
806 Yu Yuet Lai Building
43 Wyndham Street, Hong Kong
Tel: 852–250171
Fax: 852–8101417

The Institute of Chartered Financial Analysts of India
Road No. 3, Banjara Hills
Hyderabad 500 034, India
Tel: 91–842–229062
Fax: 91–842–229107

The Security Analysts Association of Japan
Daini Shokenkaikan Building
2–1–1, Nihonbashi-Kayabacho
Chuo-ku, Tokyo 103, Japan
Tel: 813–3–666–1411
Fax: 813–3–666–5843

The Korea Securities Analysts Association
12th Floor, Securities Building
34, Youido-dong, Yongdungpo-gu
Seoul, Korea
Tel: 82–2–784–1865
Fax: 82–2–784–9125

Research Institute of Investment Analysts Malaysia
4th Floor, Exchange Square
Off Jalan Semantan, Damansara Heights
50490 Kuala Lumpur, Malaysia
Tel: 60–3–254–6662, 254–6433
Fax: 60–3–255–7463

The New Zealand Society of Investment Analysts Incorporated
P.O. Box 11–579
Manners Street
Wellington, New Zealand
Tel: 64–4–499–1870
Fax: 64–4–710–439 (c/o Mr. G. A. Paterson, Doyle Paterson Brown Ltd.)

The Security Analysts Association, R.O.C., Taipei
6th Floor, No. 20
Nan Hai Road
Taipei, Taiwan, R.O.C.
Tel: 886–2–321–9730
Fax: 886–2–391–7134

The Indonesian Society of Securities Analysts
Flat Danareksa
III Floor (P.P.U.E.)
Jln. Kebon Sirih No. 48
Jakarta Pusat, Indonesia
Tel: 62–21–376989

The Association of Members of the Securities Exchange—Thailand
Unico House Building, 11th Floor
29/1 Soi Lungsuan, Ploenchit Road
Patumwan
Bangkok, 10330, Thailand
Tel: 66–2–254–9396
Fax: 66–2–254–9397

The Singapore Society of Financial Analysts
10 Shenton Way #10–01
MAS Building
Singapore 0207
Tel: 65–220–8566
Fax: 65–224–4947

EFFAS

EFFAS was organized in 1962 to bring together under a federation structure societies located throughout Europe, with the objectives of raising the standards of financial analysis, improving the quality and quantity of financial information given to investors, and supporting the unification of analytical methods throughout the area. The constituent societies of EFFAS are located in Austria, Belgium, Denmark, Finland, France, Germany, Great Britain, Ireland, Italy, Luxembourg, Netherlands, Norway, Portugal, Spain, Sweden, and Switzerland. Membership in these 16 societies is in excess of 9,000 persons. In addition to each of the 16 constituent societies conducting educational and program meetings on a regular basis, EFFAS itself holds a congress every other year to provide attendees the opportunity of hearing innovations and developments of interest to the global investment community. Among the initiatives sponsored by EFFAS are the Commission on Stock Markets, which studies and publishes the characteristics of stock markets in Europe; the Bond Commission, which documents information on bond markets in Europe; the Commission on Financial Accounting, which evaluates accounting differences and urges greater harmonization of accounting practices throughout Europe; and the Commission on Training and Qualification, which is in the process of harmonizing training and professional certification programs throughout the area.

Only a limited number of formalized training and qualification programs leading to a professional designation are now in place among the 16 constituent societies of EFFAS. Efforts now are underway by the EFFAS Commission on Training and Qualification to develop a certification program with reasonably common standards for all of the societies, in concert with the many other harmonization initiatives being carried out in preparation for the formation of the European Community at the end of 1992. The modules for the proposed program include bond analysis and evaluation; stock analysis and evaluation; futures, options, swaps, and other investment vehicles; portfolio management; market structure, regulations and practice; analysis of financial reports and accounts; and corporate finance. Candidates for certification would be expected to attend more than 200 hours of classroom lectures and other formal preparation, at the conclusion of which an examination would be given. Successful passage of the examination would lead to a country-specific designation, with an EFFAS endorsement. Language, cultural, and other differences among the countries in which the 16 EFFAS societies are located constitute a burden in designing the program, but this has not prevented the Swiss society from implementing one starting in January 1991. It seems inevitable that the differences can gradually be overcome and that EFFAS will eventually have a program reasonably common to all of its constituent societies. In designing the program, EFFAS has sought technical and other assistance from the

ICFA, with the hope of cross-recognition of designations at an appropriate time in the future.

As previously stated, the Society of Investment Analysts (SIA) in London, one of the constituent societies of EFFAS, has an arrangement with the ICFA whereby those SIA members who attain the Associate designation under its new curriculum can pursue the CFA designation by taking only the equivalent of the ICFA Level III examination. Likewise, a CFA can become an Associate of the SIA by taking only part of its examination.

Additional information concerning training and certification of investment professionals by EFFAS and its constituent societies can be obtained at the following address:

Mrs. Martine d'Herbecourt   Telephone: 33–1–42–61–90–93
   FEAAF/EFFAS   Facsimile: 33–1–47–03–98–34
   11, Rue Saint-Augustin
   75002 Paris, France

AIMR/ICFA/FAF

AIMR was organized in January 1990 through a merger of the Financial Analysts Federation, formed in 1947, and the Institute of Chartered Financial Analysts, established in 1962. In view of an increasing overlap of membership and objectives of the two entities, the merger was effected to provide for a more efficient management and operating structure, to combine programming and education activities, and to be able to speak with one voice on behalf of the combined membership on regulatory, legislative, and other issues affecting investment professionals and the capital markets. While all financial and other resources now are centered in AIMR, both the FAF and ICFA continue as subsidiary entities, carrying out specific functions under their respective names, utilizing AIMR resources.

While AIMR/ICFA/FAF are headquartered in North America and the bulk of their 18,000 members reside in the United States and Canada, the organizations conduct some of their activities on a global basis. One of the 65 constituent societies of the FAF is the International Society of Financial Analysts (ISFA), formed in 1985 to provide an organizational entity with which qualified investment professionals can identify for the purpose of sharing international experiences. The ISFA has more than 800 members, including those of affiliates in Singapore, Bermuda, the Bahamas, and Mexico. In addition, a group in Puerto Rico has expressed an interest in becoming a chapter of ISFA.

The ICFA has also extended its reach beyond North America. Since its inception, more than 14,000 persons have earned the coveted CFA designation, and nearly another 14,000 are currently enrolled to take the examinations. Of the latter, almost 15 percent are located outside of North America, compared to 2 percent of 5,500 candidates only 6 years ago. As pointed out in other sections of this chapter, the ICFA is working closely with other world investment professional organizations toward a common cause, namely, to enhance the professional and ethical standards of practice of those involved in the investment process.

Additional information concerning the activities of AIMR/ICFA/FAF can be obtained by contacting these organizations at the following address:

Association for Investment Management   Telephone: 804–977–6600
and Research (comprising the ICFA   Facsimile: 804–977–1103
and FAF)
5 Boar's Head Lane
Post Office Box 3668
Charlottesville, VA 22903

South Africa and Brazil

The Investment Society of Southern Africa (P.O. Box 454, Johannesburg 2000, Republic of South Africa) and ABAMEC (Rua São Bento, 545, 8° Andar, CEP 01001 Sao Paulo, Brazil) are evaluating training and certification programs in conjunction with ongoing development of their capital markets.

Regulation

Legislated rules and regulations pertaining to the practice of security analysts, portfolio managers, and others involved in various aspects of the investment decision-making process range from complex and comprehensive in some parts of the world to virtually nonexistent in others. However, those countries with little or no endorsement and/or enforcement procedures are gradually recognizing that high ethical principles are as important, if not more so, than professionalism in the investment process itself, and many are beginning to adopt more stringent standards of professional conduct. Among the primary areas of focus of new and established regulatory programs are insider trading, price manipulation, misrepresentation, frontrunning, and general fiduciary responsibilities.

Several countries implementing new rules and regulations are adopting in whole or in part the AIMR/ICFA/FAF Code of Ethics and Standards of Professional Conduct, which apply to all members of these organizations as well as CFA candidates, a universe of more than 25,000 persons. The code and the standards are stated in Exhibit 17.1.

Endorsement and adoption of high ethical standards of practice for investment professionals is an obvious first step in promoting the image that the business of the capital markets of a given country is conducted

ASSOCIATION FOR INVESTMENT MANAGEMENT AND RESEARCH

CODE OF ETHICS AND STANDARDS OF PROFESSIONAL CONDUCT

Effective January 1, 1990

THE AIMR RESOLUTION

WHEREAS, the profession of securities analysis and investment management has evolved because of the increasing public need for competent, objective and trustworthy advice with regard to investments and financial management; and

WHEREAS, the Financial Analysts Federation (FAF) and the Institute of Chartered Financial Analysts (ICFA) were organized to advance the profession and its members and for benefit of the investing and general public; and

WHEREAS, the members of the FAF and the ICFA have engaged in the profession of securities analysis and investment management, and the term financial analysis has historically been applied to this profession by the FAF, the ICFA and others; and

WHEREAS, both the FAF and the ICFA adopted in the early 1960s a Code of Ethics and Standards of Professional Conduct governing the conduct of their members and the holders of and candidates for the professional designation Chartered Financial Analyst; and

WHEREAS, the FAF and ICFA combined, effective January 1, 1990, and all members of the FAF and ICFA became members of the Association for Investment Management and Research (AIMR) as well as continuing to be members of the FAF and ICFA respectively; and

WHEREAS, effective January 1, 1990, members of AIMR are obligated to comply with the AIMR Code of Ethics and Standards of Professional Conduct.

NOW, THEREFORE, The Association for Investment Management and Research hereby adopts the Code of Ethics and Standards of Professional Conduct set forth below.

All members of the Association for Investment Management and Research, the Financial Analysts Federation and the Institute of Chartered Financial Analysts and the holders of and candidates for the professional designation Chartered Financial Analyst are obligated to conduct their activities in accordance with the following Code of Ethics and Standards of Professional Conduct. Disciplinary sanctions may be imposed for violations of the Code or Standards.

CODE OF ETHICS

A financial analyst should conduct himself* with integrity and dignity and act in an ethical manner in his dealings with the public, clients, customers, employers, employees, and fellow analysts.

A financial analyst should conduct himself and should encourage others to practice financial analysis in a professional and ethical manner that will reflect credit on himself and his profession.

A financial analyst should act with competence and should strive to maintain and improve his competence and that of others in the profession.

A financial analyst should use proper care and exercise independent professional judgment.

THE STANDARDS OF PROFESSIONAL CONDUCT

I. Obligation to Inform Employer of Code and Standards

The financial analyst shall inform his employer, through his direct supervisor, that the analyst is obligated to comply with the Code of Ethics and Standards of Professional Conduct, and is subject to disciplinary sanctions for violations thereof. He shall deliver a copy of the Code and Standards to his employer if the employer does not have a copy.

---

*Masculine personal pronouns, used throughout the Code and Standards to simplify sentence structure, shall apply to all persons, regardless of sex.

II. Compliance with Governing Laws and Regulations and the Code and Standards

A. Required Knowledge and Compliance

The financial analyst shall maintain knowledge of and shall comply with all applicable laws, rules, and regulations of any government, governmental agency, and regulatory organization governing his professional, financial, or business activities, as well as with these Standards of Professional Conduct and the accompanying Code of Ethics.

B. Prohibition Against Assisting Legal and Ethical Violations

The financial analyst shall not knowingly participate in, or assist, any acts in violation of any applicable law, rule, or regulation of any government, governmental agency, or regulatory organization governing his professional, financial, or business activities, nor any act which would violate any provision of these Standards of Professional Conduct or the accompanying Code of Ethics.

C. Prohibition Against Use of Material Nonpublic Information

The financial analyst shall comply with all laws and regulations relating to the use and communication of material nonpublic information. The financial analyst's duty is generally defined as to not trade while in possession of, nor

---

Exhibit 17.1.   Association for Investment Management and Research

communicate, material nonpublic information in breach of a duty, or if the information is misappropriated.

Duties under the Standard include the following: (1) If the analyst acquires such information as a result of a special or confidential relationship with the issuer or others, he shall not communicate the information (other than within the relationship), or take investment action on the basis of such information, if it violates that relationship. (2) If the analyst is not in a special or confidential relationship with the issuer or others, he shall not communicate or act on material nonpublic information if he knows, or should have known, that such information (a) was disclosed to him, or would result in a breach of a duty, or (b) was misappropriated.

If such a breach of duty exists, the analyst shall make reasonable efforts to achieve public dissemination of such information.

D. Responsibilities of Supervisors

A financial analyst with supervisory responsibility shall exercise reasonable supervision over those subordinate employees subject to his control, to prevent any violation by such persons of applicable statutes, regulations, or provisions of the Code of Ethics or Standards of Professional Conduct. In so doing the analyst is entitled to rely upon reasonable procedures established by his employer.

III. Research Reports, Investment Recommendations and Actions

A. Reasonable Basis and Representations

1. The financial analyst shall exercise diligence and thoroughness in making an investment recommendation to others or in taking an investment action for others.
2. The financial analyst shall have a reasonable and adequate basis for such recommendations and actions, supported by appropriate research and investigation.
3. The financial analyst shall make reasonable and diligent efforts to avoid any material misrepresentation in any research report or investment recommendation.
4. The financial analyst shall maintain appropriate records to support the reasonableness of such recommendations and actions.

B. Research Reports

1. The financial analyst shall use reasonable judgment as to the inclusion of relevant factors in research reports.
2. The financial analyst shall distinguish between facts and opinions in research reports.
3. The financial analyst shall indicate the basic characteristics of the investment involved when preparing for general public distribution a research report that is not directly related to a specific portfolio or client.

C. Portfolio Investment Recommendations and Actions

The financial analyst shall, when making an investment recommendation or taking an investment action for a spe-

cific portfolio or client, consider its appropriateness and suitability for such portfolio or client. In considering such matters, the financial analyst shall take into account (1) the needs and circumstances of the client, (2) the basic characteristics of the investment involved, and (3) the basic characteristics of the total portfolio. The financial analyst shall use reasonable judgment to determine the applicable relevant factors. The financial analyst shall distinguish between facts and opinions in the presentation of investment recommendations.

D. Prohibition Against Plagiarism

The financial analyst shall not, when presenting material to his employer, associates, customers, clients, or the general public, copy or use in substantially the same form material prepared by other persons without acknowledging its use and identifying the name of the author or publisher of such material. The analyst may, however, use without acknowledgement factual information published by recognized financial and statistical reporting services or similar sources.

E. Prohibition Against Misrepresentation of Services

The financial analyst shall not make any statements, orally or in writing, which misrepresent (1) the services that the analyst or his firm is capable of performing for the client, (2) the qualifications of such analyst or his firm, (3) the investment performance that the analyst or his firm has accomplished or can reasonably be expected to achieve for the client, or (4) the expected performance of any investment.

The financial analyst shall not make, orally or in writing, explicitly or implicitly, any assurances about or guarantees of any investment or its return except communication of accurate information as to the terms of the investment instrument and the issuer's obligations under the instrument.

F. Fair Dealing with Customers and Clients

The financial analyst shall act in a manner consistent with his obligation to deal fairly with all customers and clients when (1) disseminating investment recommendations, (2) disseminating material changes in prior investment advice, and (3) taking investment action.

IV. Priority of Transactions

The financial analyst shall conduct himself in such a manner that transactions for his customers, clients, and employer have priority over personal transactions, and so that his personal transactions do not operate adversely to their interests. If an analyst decides to make a recommendation about the purchase or sale of a security or other investment, he shall give his customers, clients, and employer adequate opportunity to act on this recommendation before acting on his own behalf.

V. Disclosure of Conflicts

The financial analyst, when making investment recommendations, or taking investment actions, shall disclose to

Exhibit 17.1. *(continued)*

his customers and clients any material conflict of interest relating to him and any material beneficial ownership of the securities or other investments involved that could reasonably be expected to impair his ability to render unbiased and objective advice.

The financial analyst shall disclose to his employer all matters that could reasonably be expected to interfere with his duty to the employer, or with his ability to render unbiased and objective advice.

The financial analyst shall also comply with all requirements as to disclosure of conflicts of interest imposed by law and by rules and regulations of organizations governing his activities and shall comply with any prohibitions on his activities if a conflict of interest exists.

VI.   Compensation

A.   Disclosure of Additional Compensation Arrangements

The financial analyst shall inform his customers, clients, and employer of compensation or other benefit arrangements in connection with his services to them which are in addition to compensation from them for such services.

B.   Disclosure of Referral Fees

The financial analyst shall make appropriate disclosure to a prospective client or customer of any consideration paid or other benefit delivered to others for recommending his services to that prospective client or customer.

C.   Duty to Employer

The financial analyst shall not undertake independent practice for compensation or other benefit in competition with his employer unless he has received written consent from both his employer and the person for whom he undertakes independent employment.

VII.   Relationships with Others

A.   Preservation of Confidentiality

A financial analyst shall preserve the confidentiality of information communicated by the client concerning matters within the scope of the confidential relationship, unless the financial analyst receives information concerning illegal activities on the part of the client.

B.   Maintenance of Independence and Objectivity

The financial analyst, in relationships and contacts with an issuer of securities, whether individually or as a member of a group, shall use particular care and good judgment to achieve and maintain independence and objectivity.

C.   Fiduciary Duties

The financial analyst, in relationships with clients, shall use particular care in determining applicable fiduciary duty and shall comply with such duty as to those persons and interests to whom it is owed.

VIII.   Use of Professional Designation

The qualified financial analyst may use, as applicable, the professional designation "Member of the Association for Investment Management and Research", "Member of the Financial Analysts Federation", and "Member of the Institute of Chartered Financial Analysts", and is encouraged to do so, but only in a dignified and judicious manner. The use of the designations may be accompanied by an accurate explanation (1) of the requirements that have been met to obtain the designation, and (2) of the Association for Investment Management and Research, the Financial Analysts Federation, and the Institute of Chartered Financial Analysts, as applicable.

The Chartered Financial Analyst may use the professional designation "Chartered Financial Analyst", or the abbreviation "CFA", and is encouraged to do so, but only in a dignified and judicious manner. The use of the designation may be accompanied by an accurate explanation (1) of the requirements that have been met to obtain the designation, and (2) of the Association for Investment Management and Research, and the Institute of Chartered Financial Analysts.

IX.   Professional Misconduct

The financial analyst shall not (1) commit a criminal act that upon conviction materially reflects adversely on his honesty, trustworthiness or fitness as a financial analyst in other respects, or (2) engage in conduct involving dishonesty, fraud, deceit or misrepresentation.

Exhibit 17.1.   (*continued*)

in a fair and orderly way and otherwise protects the best interests of the customer. Turning that image into reality requires *enforcement* of those high ethical standards of practice. Enforcement entails the combination of appropriate legal procedures and an "ethical culture" within the investment firm that is effectively communicated by top officials to all staff members. The question can be posed that if an investment firm does not have an acceptable and appropriate culture, how can it reasonably be expected for the personnel within that firm to practice the highest levels of morality and ethics? It is heartening to note that with the urging and guidance of global investment professional associations, executives of a growing number of investment firms around the world are adopting a "culture" which is designed to improve and enforce higher ethical standards of conduct.

INVESTING IN EMERGING MARKETS

18

Emerging Markets: An Overview

Sumner N. Levine
Nortech Associates
and
State University of New York
Stony Brook

Though emerging markets account for only about 5 percent of world market capitalization, interest in these countries has grown substantially in recent years. The next chapters survey two important regions: Southeast Asia (Malaysia, Indonesia, Singapore, and Thailand) and Latin America. South Korea is, at this writing, closed to foreign investors (except through mutual funds), though restrictions, we are informed, will gradually be lifted starting in 1992. Matters in Eastern Europe are still too much in a state of flux to warrant inclusion at this time. However, since Germany will probably be the major supplier of goods and financing to the Eastern European countries, it will, in all likelihood, be the major beneficiary of the region's development. Because of this, investment in German firms has been proposed as the best way to profit from Eastern European opportunities.

Table 18.1 provides total equity returns for selected markets for 1990. As shown, there is a very substantial range in performance; results vary from a gain of 603 percent for Venezuela to disastrous collapses of the markets in Brazil (−65 percent) and Taiwan (−50.5 percent). The negative correlation between various markets would, of course, contribute to reduction of the portfolio risk.

From Table 18.1, it is apparent that country selection is a matter of some importance in realizing return. The choice of a country is governed by a number of considerations, some of a general nature, others unique to the country. Generally applicable considerations favorable toward investment in a country include: a stable political climate favoring policies that encourage foreign investments, a relatively high GNP growth rate, a

Table 18.1.* Total Equity Returns for 1990 (in percent)

Venezuela....................	603.2
Chile........................	40.2
Mexico......................	30.1
Indonesia....................	.2
United States................	−3.1
Germany.....................	−8.9
France......................	−13.4
Taiwan......................	−50.5
Brazil.......................	−65.4

*Based on data from *Emerging Stock Market Fact Book 1991*, International Finance Corporation, Washington, D.C.

low inflation rate (or the implementation of policies designed to reduce inflation), a strong work ethic, a high rate of literacy, a substantial infrastructure (power, transportation, and communication facilities), a growing manufacturing base, and a trade surplus (or at least a contracting trade deficit).

Desirable investment-oriented criteria include market liquidity, the absence of restrictions on currency repatriation, low transaction costs and taxes, public availability of timely and reliable investment and market information, and high standards for reporting company financial information. Exchange rate considerations are, of course, important, as discussed elsewhere in this book.

Technical market indicators favoring foreign investments include a relatively low P/E, or cash flow to price ratios; and a high-dividend yield on an *intracountry* comparison basis. Crosscountry comparisons are often misleading because of differences in accounting practices and business customs.

In addition, attention must also be given to developments that are specific to a country. For example, free trade negotiations between the United States and Mexico were a major factor in the recent appreciation of the Mexican securities market. Thailand and Malaysia have benefited from Japanese investments, motivated by the availability of a cheap but relatively well-educated labor force. The collapse of the Brazilian markets in 1990 resulted from the introduction of a plan by President Collor to fight the very high inflation rate. The Collor plan involved, among other things, the freezing of all assets, the imposition of a high tax on stock transactions, and the introduction of a new currency. Sources of information helpful in following country developments are provided in Chapter 15.

Further details concerning the preceding considerations are provided in the tables included here. An overview of emerging equity markets is given in Table 18.2, which provides data on market capitalization, daily vol-

Table 18.2. Overview of Emerging Stock Markets, End 1990

Market	Market capitalization (US$ millions)	Average daily value traded (US$ millions)	Number of listed companies	Market P-E ratio	Percent change from the end of 1989		
					Change in IFC total return index (in US$)	Change in IFC total return index (in local currency)	Change in currency exchange rate
Latin America							
Argentina	3,268	3.53	179	3.11	−36.25	165.79	−76.01
Brazil	16,354[a]	23.23	581	5.34	−65.39	393.24	−92.98
Chile	13,645	3.17	215	8.86	40.19	60.56	−12.69
Colombia	1,416	0.29	80	10.66	38.06	70.66	−19.10
Mexico	32,725	49.05	199	13.20	30.08	42.91	−8.97
Venezuela	8,361	9.07	66	29.31	603.17	704.03	12.55
East Asia							
Korea	110,594	260.10	669	21.48	−25.55	−21.47	−5.19
Philippines	5,927	4.86	153	24.51	−50.62	−38.30	−19.96
Taiwan, China	100,710	2,544.50	199	44.41	−50.48	−49.38	−2.18
South Asia							
India[b]	38,567	113.57	2,435	20.59	18.30	27.51	−7.22
Indonesia	8,081	16.43	125	30.84	0.15	5.27	−4.87
Malaysia	48,611	44.37	282	23.01	−4.99	−4.99	0.01
Pakistan	2,985	1.01	487	8.53	11.39	13.85	−2.16
Thailand	23,896	92.69	214	10.90	−19.47	−20.44	1.23
Europe/Mideast/Africa							
Greece	15,228	16.70	145	26.23	97.81	101.85	−2.01
Jordan	2,001	1.63	105	8.15	4.44	4.98	−0.51
Nigeria	1,372	0.04	131	7.01	40.86	64.50	−14.37
Portugal	9,201	6.86	181	15.47	−27.85	−34.10	9.48
Turkey	19,065	23.65	110	22.50	27.09	60.62	−20.88
Zimbabwe	2,395	0.21	57	12.01	95.18	131.36	−15.64

a. Sao Paulo only.
b. Bombay only.
Source: *Emerging Stock Market Factbook 1991*, International Finance Corporation, Washington, D.C., p. 46.

**Table 18.3.   Withholding Tax for U.S.-based Institutional Investors
(Percentage Rates in Effect at the End of 1990)**

	Interest	Dividends	Long-term capital gains on listed shares
Latin America & the Caribbean			
Argentina[a]	16.8	17.5	36.0
Barbados	15.0	15.0	0.0
Brazil[b]	25.0	25.0	25.0
Chile[b]	10.0	10.0	10.0
Columbia	15.0	0.0	30.0
Costa Rica[c]	15.0	5.0	0.0
Jamaica	12.5	15.0	0.0
Mexico	15.0	0.0	0.0
Trinidad & Tobago	30.0	10.0	0.0
Venézuela[d]	20.0	20.0	0.0
Asia			
India	25.0	25.0	40.0
Indonesia	20.0	20.0	20.0
Korea	15.0	25.0	0.0
Malaysia	20.0	0.0	0.0
Pakistan	0.0	15.0	0.0
Philippines[e]	15.0	15.0	0.3
Sri Lanka	0.0	15.0	0.0
Taiwan, China[a,f]	20.0	20.0	0.0
Thailand[g]	0.0	20.0	25.0
Europe/Mideast/Africa			
Botswana	15.0	15.0	0.0
Greece[h]	0.0	42.0/45.0	0.0
Jordan	0.0	0.0	0.0
Kenya	12.5	15.0	0.0
Nigeria	15.0	15.0	20.0
Portugal[j]	25.0	25.0	0.0
Turkey	0.0	0.0	0.0
Yugoslavia	0.0	0.0	20.0
Zimbabwe	10.0	20.0	30.0

a. Capital gains tax applies to gains above inflation.

b. No dividend withholding tax in reinvested.

c. Capital gains tax of 52 million colones.

d. No withholding taxes apply to shares of publicly controlled companies (SAICA).

e. Transaction tax on gross transaction value.

f. Available only to investors in approved investment vehicles.

g. Rates for funds registered in Thailand are half of rates shown.

h. Unlike other countries, Greece has no corporate profit tax on distributed earnings. Registered shares' rate is 42%, bearer shares' rate is 45%, after exemptions.

j. On 80% of the total dividend.

Source: *Emerging Stock Market Factbook 1991*, International Finance Corporation, Washington, D.C., p. 70.

ume, number of listed companies, and representative P/E ratios. Table 18.3 summarizes information about withholding taxes on interest, dividends, and capital gains. A summary of market protection available to investors and the quality of information is given in Table 18.4. Allocation of investments among emerging countries by quantitative methods, as outlined in Chapter 2, requires a knowledge of correlation coefficients and standard deviations given in Tables 18.5 and 18.6.

REFERENCES

The data set in this chapter is provided by the annual *Emerging Stock Market Fact Book*, International Finance Corporation, Washington, D.C. This publication is currently the best source of data concerning the emerging markets. Needless to say, the information given here applies to 1990 and is subject to change.

Table 18.4. Market Information and Investor Protection

	Share price index (1)	Securities exchange publications (2)	International electronic coverage (3)	Regular publication of P-E, yield (4)
Latin America				
Argentina	X	AQMWD	X	P
Brazil	X	AMWD	X	C
Chile	X	AMWD	X	C
Columbia	X	AMWD	X	P
Mexico	X	AMWD	X	C
Venezuela	X	AMWD	X	P
Asia				
India	X	AMWD	X	C
Indonesia	X	AMD	X	C
Korea	X	AMWD	X	C
Malaysia	X	A(M/2)WD	X	C
Pakistan	X	AD	—	P
Philippines	X	AMWD	X	C
Taiwan, China	X	AMWD	X	C
Thailand	X	AQMWD	X	C
Europe/Mideast/Africa				
Greece	X	AMWD	X	C
Jordan	X	AMWD	X	P
Nigeria	X	AWD	X	P
Portugal	X	AMWD	X	C
Turkey	X	AMWD	X	C
Zimbabwe	X	AWD	—	P

Market commentaries in English (5)	Financial disclosure requirements — timing			Accounting standards (9)	Investor protection (10)
	Company brokerage reports (6)	Consolidated annual audited (7)	Interim statements (8)		
LR	LR	X	Q	A	AS
LR,IR	LR,IR	X	Q	G	GS
LR	LR,IR	X	Q	G	GS
—	LR	X	Q	A	AS
LR,IR	LR,IR	X	Q	G	GS
—	LR	X	S (banks only)	A	AS
LR	LR	X	S	G	GS
LR,IR	LR,IR	X	S	P	AS
LR,IR	LR,IR	X	S	G	GS
LR,IR	LR,IR	X	S	G	G–
LR	—	X	S	A	AS
LR,IR	LR,IR	X	S	G	AS
LR,IR	IR	X	Q	P	PS
LR,IR	LR,IR	X	Q	A	AS
LR,IR	LR,IR	X	S	P	P–
LR,IR	LR	X	–	P	AS
LR,IR	LR	X	Q	A	AS
LR,IR	LR,IR	X	S	A	AS
LR,IR	LR,IR	X	Q	A	PS
LR	LR	X	S	A	AS

Key:

Column	Symbols	
(1)	X	= At least one share price index is calculated; most have several, and many have sectoral indexes as well.
(2)	A	= Annual; Q = Quarterly; M = Monthly; (M/2) = Biweekly; W = Weekly; D = Daily.
(3)	X	= Daily coverage of stock market on an international wire service.
(4)	P	= Published; C = Comprehensive and published internationally.
(5) & (6)	LB	= Prepared by local brokers or analysts; IR = Prepared by international brokers or analysts.
(7)	X	= Consolidated audited annual accounts required.
(8)	Q	= Quarterly results must be published; S = Semiannual results must be published.
(9) & (10)	G	= Good, of internationally acceptable quality; A = Adequate; P = Poor, requires reform.
	S	= Functioning securities commission or similar government agency concentrating on regulating market activity.

Source: *Emerging Stock Market Factbook 1991*, International Finance Corporation, Washington, D.C., p. 68.

Table 18.5.   Correlation Coefficient Matrix of Total Return Indexes (Five Years Ending December 1990)

	USA	EAFE	FTEP	IFCC	IFCL	IFCA	Arg	Bra	Chi	Col	Gre	Ind
USA	1.00											
EAFE	0.45	1.00										
FTEP	0.45	1.00	1.00									
IFCC	0.37	0.26	0.27	1.00								
IFCL	0.31	0.20	0.21	0.67	1.00							
IFCA	0.36	0.26	0.27	0.89	0.33	1.00						
Arg	0.03	−0.14	−0.14	0.00	−0.04	−0.03	1.00					
Bra	0.03	0.10	0.11	0.40	0.81	0.11	−0.21	1.00				
Chi	0.34	0.07	0.08	0.44	0.36	0.37	−0.08	0.09	1.00			
Col	0.16	0.12	0.12	0.09	0.06	0.06	−0.14	0.04	0.42	1.00		
Gre	0.13	0.08	0.07	0.00	0.03	−0.04	0.10	0.01	0.14	0.33	1.00	
Ind	−0.11	−0.18	−0.18	−0.05	−0.02	−0.16	0.31	−0.03	−0.07	−0.08	−0.03	1.00
Idn	0.20	−0.11	−0.11	0.22	−0.15	0.19	−0.07	−0.16	0.42	0.23	0.20	−0.07
Jor	0.02	0.14	0.13	0.01	−0.19	0.03	−0.13	−0.14	−0.01	0.12	0.16	−0.08
Kor	0.30	0.34	0.36	0.20	0.17	0.21	−0.17	0.06	0.06	0.00	−0.27	−0.11
Mal	0.66	0.37	0.37	0.44	0.29	0.50	0.00	0.07	0.25	0.01	0.02	−0.03
Mex	0.46	0.20	0.20	0.48	0.37	0.48	0.11	−0.08	0.35	0.07	0.16	0.04
Nig	0.07	0.04	0.05	−0.14	−0.02	−0.23	0.11	0.03	0.05	0.08	0.13	0.03
Pak	−0.17	0.10	0.10	0.01	−0.03	0.01	0.10	−0.04	0.06	0.18	−0.11	0.22
Phi	0.28	0.32	0.32	0.13	0.07	0.15	−0.15	0.11	0.23	0.11	0.05	−0.10
Por	0.17	0.38	0.37	0.37	0.28	0.32	−0.01	0.09	0.21	0.33	0.42	−0.12
Tai	0.18	0.19	0.19	0.82	0.27	0.91	−0.01	0.09	0.36	0.14	0.04	−0.14
Tha	0.43	0.39	0.39	0.46	0.27	0.49	0.15	0.07	0.29	0.15	0.28	−0.03
Tur	0.01	0.03	0.03	0.25	0.26	0.14	0.20	0.18	0.09	0.07	0.14	0.27
Ven	−0.10	−0.23	−0.23	−0.35	−0.30	−0.30	0.03	−0.31	−0.20	−0.14	−0.10	0.17
Zim	−0.32	−0.05	−0.04	−0.23	−0.19	−0.20	−0.24	−0.06	0.00	0.20	0.05	0.12

Notes:

•S&P 500 for USA, MSCI for EAFE (Europe, Australia and Far East), and FT-Actuaries for FTEP (FT EuroPacific).

•Portugal starts January 1986, Turkey starts December 1986, and Indonesia starts December 1989.

Source: *Emerging Stock Market Factbook 1991*, International Finance Corporation, Washington, D.C., p. 93.

1.00													
0.24	1.00												
−0.16	−0.20	1.00											
0.37	0.03	0.19	1.00										
0.18	−0.07	0.22	0.45	1.00									
0.09	−0.10	0.03	−0.21	−0.14	1.00								
−0.03	0.07	0.12	−0.10	0.04	0.01	1.00							
0.63	0.15	0.26	0.26	0.07	0.07	0.01	1.00						
0.16	−0.02	0.05	0.22	0.39	−0.23	0.09	0.04	1.00					
0.19	0.09	−0.03	0.24	0.38	−0.23	0.02	0.02	0.39	1.00				
0.45	0.09	0.01	0.52	0.46	−0.10	0.14	0.23	0.40	0.43	1.00			
0.06	−0.11	−0.07	0.24	0.20	0.14	0.05	−0.04	0.17	0.09	0.18	1.00		
0.13	−0.05	−0.18	−0.13	−0.12	−0.01	0.06	−0.24	−0.08	−0.27	−0.25	−0.17	1.00	
0.05	0.12	−0.17	−0.11	−0.11	−0.02	0.17	−0.01	0.15	−0.08	−0.11	0.00	0.02	1.00
Idn	Jor	Kor	Mal	Mex	Nig	Pak	Phi	Por	Tai	Tha	Tur	Ven	Zim

Table 18.6.   Standard Deviations of Total Return Indexes (Five Years Ending December 1990)

Market	Number of months	Standard deviation
Latin America		
Argentina	60	31.68
Brazil	60	22.94
Chile	60	8.20
Colombia	60	6.45
Mexico	60	15.79
Venezuela	60	13.68
East Asia		
Korea	60	8.80
Philippines	60	12.66
Taiwan, China	60	17.94
South Asia		
India	60	8.87
Indonesia[a]	12	10.81
Malaysia	60	8.49
Pakistan	60	3.06
Thailand	60	9.45
Europe/Mideast/Africa		
Greece	60	15.29
Jordan	60	5.06
Nigeria	60	11.40
Portugal[b]	59	16.52
Turkey[c]	48	32.58
Zimbabwe	60	5.72
IFC Regional Indexes		
Composite	60	8.08
Latin America	60	13.43
Asia	60	9.90
Developed Matrix		
U.S.A. (S&P 500)	60	5.43
EAFE (MSCI)	60	6.58
EuroPac (FT-Act)	60	6.71

a. Since December 1989.

b. Since January 1986.

c. Since December 1986.

Source: *Emerging Stock Market Factbook 1991*, International Finance Corporation, Washington, D.C.

19

Stock Markets of Singapore, Malaysia, Thailand, and Indonesia

Kie Ann Wong
National University
of Singapore

W. Scott Bauman
Northern Illinois University
DeKalb, IL

This chapter describes the evolution, structure, and operations of the stock markets of Singapore, Malaysia, Thailand, and Indonesia. It also deals with the regulation of the securities industries, activities in these stock markets, stock market trends, sources of investment information, transaction costs, pattern of shareownership, restrictions on foreign investors, and income taxes.

Development of the Stock Exchange of Singapore (SES)

Singapore was formed as a trading post by Sir Stamford Raffles in 1819. Because of its deep, well-sheltered harbor and its free port status, Singapore developed rapidly. As trade flourished, joint-stock companies were formed to pool risks and rewards. These companies introduced the concepts of limited liability for shareholders and free transferability of shares. The capital of these companies was divided into shares, which subscribers could sell for cash.

To facilitate the transfer of interest in these joint-stock companies before the 20th century, stockbrokers gathered informally in a little room in the Arcade at Raffles Place to buy and sell shares for their clients (Tan, 1978). The shares transacted were mostly those of British rubber and tin companies in peninsular Malaysia. The rubber boom in 1910 and the growth of tin mining, which resulted in the flotation of a number of new companies, had contributed to the growth of share-trading activities in Singapore.

The transaction of business by stockbrokers at informal gatherings in the Arcade continued for many years. It was only in June 1930 that 15 firms formed the Singapore Stockbrokers Association in order to protect the investing public by regulating the conduct of its own members and stock trading activities (*Fact Book*, 1989). In 1938, the Association was reconstituted as the Malayan Stockbrokers Association to reflect the Pan-Malayan character of its membership and to admit new member firms from peninsular Malaysia, which had witnessed a fairly rapid growth of share-trading activities. After the Second World War, the Malayan Stockbrokers Association continued to supervise the stock market until March 1960, when it was reconstituted as the Malayan Stock Exchange.

The Malayan Stock Exchange initially had ten member firms in Singapore, four in Kuala Lumpur, three in Penang, and two in Ipoh. It adopted the scoreboard system of trading in November 1960. All the stocks were posted on boards in a trading hall that was like an auction market. When a bid and offer matched for a particular stock, a transaction was executed. All the stocks were considered simultaneously. With the introduction of the scoreboard system of trading and the linking of the Singapore and Kuala Lumpur trading rooms by direct telephone lines in 1962, a single stock market for Singapore and Malaya was formed.

When Singapore joined the Federation of Malaysia in August 1963, the exchange changed its name to the Stock Exchange of Malaysia. Even when Singapore left the Federation in August 1965, the exchange continued to function as a single market, except that the name became the Stock Exchange of Malaysia and Singapore. This reflected the close ties between the business communities of the two countries.

The decision by the Malaysian government to discontinue the currency interchangeability between Malaysia and Singapore brought about the split of the exchange into two separate, independent exchanges on May 8, 1973: the Stock Exchange of Singapore (SES) and the Kuala Lumpur Stock Exchange (KLSE). The Stock Exchange of Singapore Limited was incorporated on May 24, 1973 under the Companies Act as a company limited by shares and commenced full operation as an independent exchange on June 4, 1973. In many respects, the separate existence of the SES has provided Singapore with the opportunity to transform itself into a financial center.

The SES developed rapidly. Efforts were made to list more local and internationally known companies. A stock exchange library was set up, followed by the establishment of the Singapore Securities Research Institute in December 1974. As part of the modernization process, a new trading system was implemented and computer services introduced in early 1975. A Dealers' Representative Examination was established and member firms switched over from sole proprietorships and partnerships to incorporated companies. On February 1, 1977, the SES introduced a pilot scheme for trading in share options, thereby making Singapore the first financial center in Asia to have an organized options trading market (*Fact Book*, 1989). As part of the computerization of the exchange trading and information system, the Stock Exchange of Singapore Order Processing System (SESOPS) was introduced in mid-1988. The SESOPS provides instantly available data to brokers and their associates, who may in turn relay the stock trading information to their clients through telephones. The SES also introduced the STOCKWATCH system, which updates banking and other financial institutions with immediate stock transaction data.

Structure and Operations of the Stock Exchange of Singapore

The SES is a not-for-profit company limited by shares, with an authorized capital of 2,000 S$1 par value shares. (S$ denotes *Singapore dollars*.) Each member of the SES owns one of these shares. The income and property of the SES are used solely for the SES's objectives, which are to be a channel for government agencies and business companies to raise capital funds from the public and to be an efficient marketplace for investors to buy and sell listed securities.

The SES has two types of members, individual and corporate. A corporate member is owned by one or more individual members of the exchange. An individual who holds a membership seat of the exchange must be at least 21 years old, be either a Singaporean citizen or have resided in Singapore for not less than five years, and possess qualifications and experience acceptable to the SES. In addition, the individual must be of good character and sound financial standing. A member firm may be a limited liability company or an unlimited company.

In the case of a limited liability company, two or more individual members of the exchange are to hold not less than 51 percent of its paid-up capital. In the move toward expanding corporate membership, the "Big Four" local banks received approval to join the SES as full trading members in 1986 through their wholly owned subsidiaries: DBS Securities Singapore Pte. Ltd., OCBC Securities Pte. Ltd., OUB Securities Pte. Ltd., and UOB Securities Pte. Ltd.

Trading in the SES is handled not only by stockbrokers, but also by dealers and remisiers attached to member firms. Dealers are employees of member firms. They buy and sell securities for both their own and their firm's clients. Remisiers are not employees of the firms to which they are attached, but rather, they share the brokerage fees for buying and selling securities on behalf of their own clients. Persons who wish to become dealers or remisiers have to pass the relevant examination of the SES.

Table 19.1 shows the composition of firms and people associated with the SES. By the end of 1989, there were 26 member firms to which 99 indi-

Table 19.1.   SES: Members, Dealers, Remisiers, and Employees as of December 31, 1989

Category	1975	1981	1983	1986	1989
Member firms	19	24	25	29	26
Member firms' staff	1081	1612	1574	1234	1791
SES staff	57	62	98	119	193
Individual members	80	104	109	102	99
Dealers	21	58	72	100	346
Remisiers	282	558	641	539	771

Source: Stock Exchange of Singapore, *Fact Book,* various issues.

vidual members, 346 dealers, and 771 remisiers were attached. Comparing these figures with those in 1975, it is evident that there was a significant growth in the stock exchange community over the period, particularly in the number of dealers. An additional 1,791 staff members were employed by member firms in 1989, an increase from 1,612 during the stock market boom in 1981.

Currently, the management of the SES is entrusted to a committee of nine members, known as the Committee of the Stock Exchange of Singapore (the Committee). Five members of the Committee are non-elected, nonbroker members representing listed companies, banks, merchant banks, investors, and professionals, while the remaining four are elected at the annual general meeting of the members of the SES. The Committee has extensive policy-making authority in carrying out the objectives of the SES, including enforcing the rules and bylaws of the SES and initiating improvements in its operational efficiency. The day-to-day running of the SES is left to a full-time staff headed by a chief executive who has complete control over its employees and activities. As shown in Table 19.1, the staff of the SES grew from 57 to 193 during the period 1975–1989.

Listed stocks are classified into six sectors: industrial and commercial, finance, hotel, property, plantation, and mining. Table 19.2 shows the details of the listed companies as at December 31, 1989. Of the total 333 listed companies, 191 were in the industrial and commercial sector. A majority of these industrial and commercial companies were incorporated in Malaysia, as were almost all plantation and mining companies. Malaysian-incorporated companies constituted about 55 percent of the total number of listed companies on the SES.

As of January 1, 1975, all listed companies are assigned either to the First Trading Section or to the Second Trading Section. Companies assigned to the first section must meet certain criteria determined by the

Table 19.2.   Companies Listed on the SES By Industry Sector and Country of Incorporation in 1989

Sector	Singapore	Malaysia	Overseas	Total
Industrial and Commercial	83	98	10	191
Finance	21	12	2	35
Hotel	17	1	—	18
Property	15	23	2	40
Plantation	—	35	1	36
Mining	—	13	—	13
TOTAL	136	182	15	333

Source: Stock Exchange of Singapore, *Fact Book*, 1990.

Committee. These criteria include a minimum requirement in terms of paid-up capital, number of shareholders, volume of shares traded, and annual dividends. However, the Committee has absolute discretion to exempt a company from any of the criteria on the basis of the overall performance of the company. The listed companies which cannot meet the criteria for the first section are assigned to the second section. About two-thirds of the companies listed on the SES are assigned to the first section. From January 1990, the trading of cross-listed Malaysian companies (incorporated in Malaysia) on the SES have been moved to the OTC market, called CLOB International, in Singapore.

Stocks traded on a "ready contract basis" are due for delivery on the same day in the following week, with payments due the next day after delivery. An investor who buys shares must take delivery of the shares and pay for them within one and a half days following the due date of the contract. Investors who wish to receive the proceeds of their sales on the next market day following the date of the sale can make use of the "immediate market." A seller must deliver the shares on the date of sale and the buyer must take delivery on the following day.

The SES does not use a jobber system. The stockbrokers trade directly with one another on the trading floor of the SES. The trading floor resembles an auction market with bid and offer prices of securities posted onto the computerized SESOPS system. When a bid and an offer match, a transaction is made. Trading is usually done in lots of 1,000 and 2,000 shares. For stocks with a unit price of above S$10, trading may also be done in lots of 500 or 100 shares. The scale for minimum spread of bids is:

$\frac{1}{2}$ cent for prices up to $1
1 cent for prices up to $3
2 cents for prices up to $5

5 cents for prices up to $10
10 cents for prices up to $25
50 cents for prices up to $100
S$1 for prices exceeding $100

Development of the Kuala Lumpur Stock Exchange (KLSE)

The KLSE was founded in May 1973, when the Malaysian government decided to terminate the interchangeability of currencies between Malaysia and Singapore and split the joint Stock Exchange of Malaysia and Singapore into two separate and independent exchanges: the KLSE and the SES. Although the KLSE and the SES were thus divided, many of their "Siamese-twin" characteristics persisted, particularly in the regulatory systems and the legislative frameworks. Most notable was the cross-listing of all stocks quoted on both exchanges at that time, though in January 1990 the cross-listed Singapore companies were delisted by the KLSE. However, because Singapore is a more developed and efficient financial center, most Malaysian stocks are traded on the Singaporean market and a good deal of the orders for Malaysian stocks have been channeled to Singapore. While Malaysian authorities have discouraged the listing of foreign-incorporated companies on the KLSE, Singapore authorities have continued to allow them to be traded in the Singaporean stock market, subject to certain requirements.

Changes in Malaysian economic policies have affected the listing of foreign companies on the KLSE. The New Economic Policy (NEP) aims to distribute the country's wealth more equally among the different ethnic groups of the country. Thus, companies wishing to list their shares on the KLSE must be incorporated in Malaysia and comply with the requirements of the NEP, which requires at least 30 percent ownership of the companies by Bumiputra (native Malaysian citizens).

After the delisting of the 53 Singapore-incorporated companies, 280 companies remained listed on the KLSE by the end of 1990. Of the total MR131,239.4 (MR denotes *Malaysian ringgit*, the monetary unit) million market capitalization, 99.6 percent was accounted for by Malaysian-incorporated companies. In 1989, the 53 Singapore-incorporated companies accounted for 31.2 percent of the total market value. Detailed statistics are given in Table 19.3.

In 1989, the KLSE had 53 member stockbrokers throughout Malaysia. However, there are weaknesses in the structure of the brokerage industry, including undercapitalization and overtrading by brokerage firms. Brokers in Malaysia are not permitted to have a branch network, preventing brokerage firms from growing to a size appropriate for the stock market. Brokers are, however, encouraged to merge. The system of remisiers or dealer representatives is another factor that militates against size among the securities houses. In Malaysia, about 3,000 remisiers are employed to

Table 19.3. Market Capitalization of KLSE Listed Companies (MR million)

By Sector

	1990		1989		1985	
Industrial	89,929.8	68.5%	85,431.4	54.9%	28,193	49.0%
Finance	12,838.6	9.8%	31,384.5	20.2%	12,894	22.4%
Hotel	1,276.4	1.0%	3,933.5	2.5%	2,356	4.1%
Property	9,497.2	7.3%	18,007.4	11.6%	3,536	6.1%
Oil Palm	9,685.4	7.5%	8,624.3	5.5%	4,358	7.6%
Tin	1,743.5	1.3%	2,295.9	1.5%	1,298	2.3%
Rubber	5,827.7	4.5%	6,011.5	3.9%	4,875	8.5%
TOTAL	131,239.4	100.0%	155,688.4	100.0%	57,510	100.0%

By Country

Malaysia	130,714.3	99.6%	107,101.9	68.7%	N/A	N/A
Singapore	—	—	48,456.1	31.2%	N/A	N/A
U.K.	525.1	0.4%	130.4	0.1%	N/A	N/A

Source: KLSE, *Fact Sheets.*

bring share-trading business from friends and other contacts to the brokers. They share the commission on any deal they take to the brokers.

Because the brokers in Malaysia are highly dependent on the remisiers and their contacts for business, they often fail to build up their own sales force and are not directly responsible for monitoring their client base. Remisiers take a KLSE examination and pay a deposit to the brokers they are linked to. However, the deposit paid may not be enough to cover the risks involved in dealing with largely unknown clients.

With the country's NEP, the KLSE was, for some years, preoccupied with the establishment of a special Bumiputra Stock Exchange. This special exchange was originally set up under the auspices of the Council of Trust for Indigenous People (MARA). However, the supervision of this special exchange was later transferred to Kompleks Kawangan (Financial Complex Berhad). The special exchange was intended for use by unsophisticated small Bumiputra investors who would be able to trade their shares free from the threat of the bigger market operators on the KLSE. It has only nine companies listed (each with a minimum paid-up capital of MR250,000), and because it has no marketing network, Bumiputra investors in rural areas must go to Kuala Lumpur if they wish to buy or sell shares. The special exchange has no trading floor, and the market is not big enough to be subject to the provisions of the Securities Industry Act.

In recent years, the KLSE has improved its market structure and increased its activities by adopting a corporatization policy, setting up an interbroker fidelity fund, introducing real-time price dissemination and the KLSE Composite Index, and amending its listing requirements.

Corporatization entails existing stockbrokerage firms taking in corporate partners such as merchant banks, commercial banks, and international brokerage houses by giving them equity shares. This move could strengthen the financial position of stockbrokerage firms, transform the KLSE into a more sophisticated entity, and improve the professional skill of stockbrokers. In October 1987, the KLSE had three corporate members, namely: Arab-Malaysian Securities Holding Sendirian Berhad, WI Carr (Malaysia) Sendirian Berhad, and Public Consolidated Holdings Sendirian Berhad. The KLSE is looking into the possibility of setting up an interbroker fidelity fund that will serve as a "fall-back" security for brokers who need to use it. The computerization undertaken by the KLSE has given information on real-time stock prices and other information more rapidly to brokers and subscribers. Moreover, the amendments made to the listing requirements have enhanced the corporate disclosure policy. Listed companies are required to make immediate disclosure to the KLSE of all matters that may affect stock prices.

Development of the Securities Exchange of Thailand (SET)

The Securities Exchange of Thailand (SET) was founded in April 1975, though the market was not active until early 1977. During this period, the SET Index moved between a level of 80 and 85, and the average daily volume traded was less than 4 million Baht (the monetary unit of Thailand). The SET experienced its first bull market in November 1978 when the index reached a peak of 266 and crashed one year later when the index dropped to 146 in November 1979. The crash was caused in part by higher interest rates, the political situation in Indochina, and the collapse of the Raja Finance and Securities Company.

During the crash, the government was forced to intervene with damage control measures such as setting up a fund to stem the panicked sale of stocks and alleviating the liquidity problem. Moreover, the SET Act (1974) was amended, effective 1984, to lift some restrictive regulations and establish greater control over stock manipulation.

The market picked up significantly from mid-1986, when the SET Index rose from 135 to a record high of 472. Following the "Black Monday" in October 1987, the index plummeted to 244 in December 1987. A fund called "Ruam Pattana" was inaugurated to stabilize the market.

Since 1988, the SET has been in an almost continuous bull market, with only some minor interruptions. Good economic and corporate performances have stimulated the market, which has begun to gain notice from foreign investors. The rise of foreign interest has increased the trading activity on "the alien board," established in September 1987 for overseas investors to trade in foreign registered stocks where the foreign holding limit had been reached.

The number of stocks traded on the SET has increased dramatically from 16 listed companies and 5 authorized companies in 1975 to about 147 listed companies and 30 authorized companies in 1990. The requirements for authorization on the SET are not as stringent as for a listed status. Listed stocks also receive a reduction in corporate income tax from 35 percent to 30 percent.

Market capitalization is distributed among the 5 major sectors approximately as follows: industrials, 50 percent; finance, 26 percent; service, 7 percent; commerce, 6 percent; and others, 11 percent. The top 10 companies in terms of volume of shares traded account for about 40 percent of the total market volume, while the 10 largest companies in terms of capitalization account for about 39 percent of the total market capitalization.

Stock trading is limited exclusively to members of the SET and must take place on the trading floor during the regular hours of trading. Most of the members of the exchange are securities and finance houses. There are 35 member seats occupied on the SET. The SET's "share depository" acts as a clearing house for all transactions. The exchange is currently preparing to shift to a computerized trading system.

The Indonesian Stock Market

In the early 1900s, the Dutch developed a stock market in Indonesia for the listing of Dutch-owned companies in Indonesia. The market was closed during the 1940s and, despite an attempt to reopen it in the 1950s, effectively remained closed until 1977, when it was formally reopened by presidential decree. The reopening of the Indonesian Stock Exchange (ISE) was facilitated by the requirement that foreign joint-venture companies fulfill local ownership regulations and by new tax concessions given to public companies. Between 1977 and 1983, 19 companies listed their shares.

Following the reform of the securities market in 1977, the government created the Capital Market Policy Council to provide guidance to the Ministry of Finance and established the Capital Market Executive Agency (BAPEPAM) to institute, regulate, and operate the ISE. In 1987, the government introduced a series of fundamental deregulation measures as follows:

1. Imposition of a 15 percent tax on interest earned on deposits.
2. Simplification of the process of issuing shares.
3. Participation of foreign investors in the capital market.
4. Introduction of bearer shares.
5. Establishment of the over-the-counter (OTC) market.

The main objective of these measures was to promote the role of capital markets as alternative sources of financing. A new OTC market (currently called the Parallel Market) was created in early 1989 with simpler listing requirements than those of the Jakarta Stock Exchange (JSE). The BAPEPAM administers the JSE and generally regulates these securities markets in Indonesia.

As part of the deregulation measures, the government introduced a new policy for the capital market in December 1988. The development included the following three steps:

1. A private stock exchange was established in addition to the existing government-operated stock exchange and OTC market. It is required that all shares of the privately operated stock exchange must be owned by Indonesian citizens or national corporations.
2. Stock exchanges were opened in other cities in addition to Jakarta.
3. Companies listed on other stock exchanges could register their shares for trading on the JSE. Moreover, insider trading activities were prohibited. Members of the board of directors of any listed company were restricted to holding a maximum of 10 percent of its listed shares.

Regulation of the Securities Industry

Singapore

In order to protect the interests of the investing public and to ensure that savings are made available to corporations to finance new investments through the stock market, it is necessary to have laws and regulations to prevent undesirable practices in share trading. Initially, the SES was registered under the Societies Ordinance, which had only minimal control of the stockbrokerage business. Provisions for the control of the stockbrokerage business are now contained in the Companies Act. The act includes provisions on disclosure of the following: substantial shareholdings, directors' share dealings, beneficial interest in the company's voting shares and loans to persons connected with directors of the lending company, and insider trading of shares.

By the late 1960s, there was widespread concern over the inadequacy of the provisions in the Companies Act and the ease with which a person could enter the securities profession. This concern, coupled with the desire to improve the image of Singapore as a financial center, led to the introduction of the Securities Industry Act on December 30, 1970. The act was largely based on the recommendations submitted by George M. Ferris, a governor of the New York Stock Exchange, who was appointed by the Singapore government to lead a study of the securities market in Singapore and Malaysia. However, the enforcement of the act was postponed and many changes and improvements were introduced as a result of the subsequent decision to split the joint stock exchange in 1973.

The improved act that came into force on May 23, 1973 was known as the Securities Industry Act 1973. This act, together with many provisions in the Companies Act, aimed to protect the interests of investors. Since September 1984, the act has been administered by the Monetary Authority of Singapore (MAS). The act broadly covers the following areas:

1. Establishment and operation of stock markets.
2. Licensing of dealers, dealers' representatives, investment advisers, and investment representatives.
3. Keeping of reports by dealers, dealers' representatives, investment advisers, investment representatives, and financial analysts.
4. Conduct of securities business.
5. Investment of stockbrokers' trust funds.
6. Keeping of accounts by dealers.
7. Auditing of dealers' accounts.
8. Establishment of the fidelity fund.
9. Trading in securities.

The need for a tighter legal framework for the securities industry was highlighted when Pan-Electric Industries Ltd., a Singapore-incorporated company listed on the SES, collapsed in December 1985. Through its relationship with other listed companies and stockbrokerage firms, the Pan-Electric incident exposed a number of weaknesses in the Singapore stockbrokerage industry and led to the collapse of five stockbrokerage firms. In order to restore confidence in the stock market trading system and to give the MAS tighter control over management of the securities industry, the Securities Industry Act 1986 and the complementary Securities Industry Regulations 1986 were passed. The act and the regulations took effect on August 15, 1986.

The 1986 act and regulations spelled out new capital adequacy requirements for member firms of the SES, new limits on lending to directors of stockbrokerage firms, new limits on a firm's exposure to a single client and a single security, requirements for maintenance of reserve funds by firms, and margin requirements for firms. The regulations explained in detail how the act took effect and defined who is affected by and who is exempted from the specific requirements. This legal package was intended to strengthen the securities industry in Singapore.

The Securities Industry Council was established under the Securities Industries Act in 1973 essentially as an advisory and consultative body. The council, in guiding the SES and coordinating its activities, is to protect the interests of the investing public, the corporate sector, and the Singapore government. It administers the Singapore Code on Takeovers and Mergers and approves applications by companies wishing to raise capital funds by a public issue. It advises, among other things, the Minister for Finance and the SES on matters affecting the securities industry and the listing of companies.

The Singapore Code on Takeovers and Mergers gives guidance on the principles of conduct and the procedure to be observed in takeover and merger transactions. It is modeled on the U.K. City Code on Takeovers and Mergers. In addition, the listing manual and the corporate disclosure policy of the SES sets out various prerequisites for admission to the "Official List" of companies traded on the SES and specific guidelines for the timely disclosure of corporate information by listed companies.

Malaysia

The Malaysian securities industry is basically governed by the Securities Industry Act 1983 and the Securities Industry Act (Amendments) 1987, and regulated by three different bodies, namely: the Foreign Investment Committee (FIC), the Capital Issues Committee (CIC), and the Takeover Panel. The Registrar of Companies is the authority empowered to enforce the 1983 and 1987 acts. The KLSE is required to work closely with the office of the registrar but has no authority to enforce the provisions of the acts.

The function of the CIC is to determine, in the national interest, the viability and suitability of all new listings, whereas that of the KLSE is to ensure a minimum number of outside stockholders (not less than 500 persons) in listed companies and other criteria for the protection of investors. The KLSE does not have the authority to approve applications for new listings. That role and the formulation of policies relating to the securities industry are assumed by the CIC.

The principal function of the FIC, formed in 1974, is to ensure that all matters relating to the restructuring of equity ownership, including takeovers, mergers, and acquisitions, comply with the objectives of the NEP. Furthermore, all investments exceeding MR one million must be approved by the FIC. The Takeover Panel was instituted to take charge of corporate acquisitions. The Malaysian Code on Takeovers and Mergers was published in March 1987.

Thailand

The SET is a nonprofit organization under the jurisdiction of the Ministry of Finance pursuant to the SET Act 1974, amended by the SET Act 1984. The Ministry of Finance is also responsible for the control and supervision of the SET. It has the power to regulate the SET on matters of insider trading and stock manipulation and to set up an ad hoc committee, in case of any violation, to identify and penalize the offender.

To assist the Minister of Finance on matters of the securities business, there is an advisory board of not more than seven persons appointed by the Council of Ministers. The board advises the minister about listing requirements, rules, and regulations of the SET, the setup of the second board (for trading smaller companies), the listing of new instruments, and the suspension and delisting of existing securities.

Certain supervisory and control powers are entrusted with the SET's Board of Directors, which is comprised of nine members: four appointed by the Council of Ministers, four elected by SET members, and one ex-officio member who is the president of the SET. The Board of Directors is responsible for the formulation of policies; for prescribing rules and regulations concerning the number of members, qualifications, discipline and punishment, margin requirements, brokerage commission rates, actions taken against listed companies, and accounting standards and disclosure; and for the management of the SET.

The offering of new issues of companies is under the jurisdiction of the Ministry of Commerce, pursuant to the Civil and Commercial Code and the Public Company Act. An increase of capital by issuing new shares requires a special resolution at a general meeting of a company's stockholders. The issuing price of the new share must not be lower than the par value.

Indonesia

As mentioned earlier, the BAPEPAM administers the JSE and regulates the securities markets generally. Since the formal reopening of the exchange in 1977, the Capital Market Policy Council has provided guidance to the Ministry of Finance, and the BAPEPAM has regulated and operated the stock exchange. The National Investment Trust (PT Danareksa) was established to promote the distribution of ownership of listed stocks to small investors through underwriting and issuing mutual fund certificates in small denominations to the public.

The BAPEPAM has the power to suspend trading in stocks of listed companies and to delist companies in order to protect the interests of public investors. Insider trading and other forms of market manipulation are addressed in provisions of the December 1987 Ministerial Decrees concerning the supervisory and control powers of BAPEPAM. Fraud and default by members of the exchange are also monitored by BAPEPAM through the implementation of various measures.

Functions of the New Issue Market and the Secondary Market

The main function of a new issue market is to provide an efficient means for corporations and government agencies to raise new capital funds. However, the performance of the new issue market depends on the liquidity of the secondary market to enable newly issued securities to be subsequently bought and sold readily. Table 19.4 shows the number and the market

Table 19.4.   Number and Market Value (S$million) of Listed Companies on the SES New Listings vs. Total Listings

| | New Listings | | Total Listings | | |
| | | Market Value | | Market Value | |
Year	Number	(a)	Number	(b)	(a)/(b)
1974	8	209.1	263	7,965.4	2.6%
1975	12	2,237.2	269	13,710.1	16.3%
1977	4	494.8	258	18,250.2	2.7%
1980	4	791.5	261	51,118.9	1.5%
1983	13	2,836.4	301	91,446.1	3.1%
1986	1	1,097.3	317	85,288.7	1.3%
1989	6	242.6	333	136,338.4	0.1%

Source: Stock Exchange of Singapore, *Fact Book,* various issues.

value of new listings compared with the total listed companies and the total market value on the SES in Singapore. The number of companies seeking listing tends to increase to some extent during boom periods. In terms of percentage, the market value of new listings compared to that of total listings was relatively low except for 1975.

Table 19.5 shows the number of listed companies on the SES by their country of incorporation. Due to a significant number of delistings in earlier years, the total number of listed companies did not increase in the 1970s. Over the period 1974–1980, the listing of companies incorporated outside Singapore and Malaysia actually declined from 28 to 8. This fall was largely offset by the increase of Singapore-incorporated companies

Table 19.5.   Number of Listed Companies on the SES by Country of Incorporation

Year	Singapore	Malaysia	Others	Total
1974	82	153	28	263
1975	90	154	25	269
1977	85	159	16	258
1980	97	156	8	261
1983	118	172	11	301
1986	122	183	12	317
1989	136	182	15	333

Source: Stock Exchange of Singapore, *Fact Book,* various issues.

from 82 to 97. The total number of listings of companies incorporated in Singapore and Malaysia has increased significantly since 1980. The strong representation of Malaysian-incorporated companies on the SES is a reflection of the close economic ties between the two countries and of the historical link of the SES and the KLSE.

Liquidity in a secondary market means that participants can buy and sell securities readily without unduly disturbing the state of the market. Thus, a liquid stock market is a fully informed, competitive market where trading activities provide appropriate signals for effective allocation of capital funds to the most profitable investment opportunities. The liquidity of a secondary market may be measured by the ratio of the number of shares traded to total number of shares outstanding, or by the ratio of the market value of shares traded to the total market capitalization.

Table 19.6 gives the total market value of securities traded, the number of shares outstanding and units of these traded on the SES, and the turnover rate of shares traded. The turnover percentage is somewhat overestimated, as the total number of shares outstanding does not include securities other than ordinary shares, while the turnover units include other securities traded. The annual number of shares traded and the value of securities traded fluctuated considerably over the period 1974–1989. In general, the level of turnover was much higher in the 1980s than in the 1970s. The turnover percentage shows that the high figures usually occur in the boom years, particularly in 1980 and 1989.

In Malaysia, 95 new companies were listed on the KLSE during the period 1974–1986. About 70 companies were delisted during the same period to facilitate the restructuring of foreign companies. Table 19.7 shows the

Table 19.6. Turnover and Value of Securities Traded on the SES

Year	(1) Value of Securities Traded S$ (Million)	(2) Number of Units Traded (Million)	(3) Total Shares Oustanding (Million)	(4) Turnover Percentage (2) ÷ (3)
1974	1,093.5	534.4	4,744.5	11.3
1975	1,839.5	810.3	6,041.8	13.4
1977	1,161.6	643.8	6,620.6	9.7
1980	7,824.7	2,222.2	10,303.4	21.6
1983	11,807.1	3,605.2	23,618.9	15.3
1986	8,000.5	3,951.4	33,913.8	11.7
1989	29,149.9	21,646.1	45,832.3	47.2

Source: Stock Exchange of Singapore, *Fact Book,* various issues.

Table 19.7.   Number of Existing and Newly-Listed Companies on the KLSE

Year	Malaysian Companies	Foreign Companies	Total	Newly Listed
1974	163	101	264	9
1975	167	101	268	7
1977	177	79	256	5
1980	182	68	250	4
1983	204	67	271	10
1986	227	61	288	4
1989	251	56	307	12*
1990	255	3	258	4*

* Estimate

Source: Kuala Lumpur Stock Exchange, *Fact Sheets.*

total number of listed companies and newly-listed companies as well as the distribution between Malaysian- and foreign-incorporated companies since 1974. There was a net increase of 43 listed companies over the period 1974–1986. However, the total number decreased to 258 listed companies after the delisting of 53 Singapore companies in 1990.

Since its inception in 1973, the KLSE has grown rapidly in market capitalization and annual turnover volume. As can be seen from Table 19.8, the market value of securities outstanding grew about 19 times over the period 1974–1989.

Similarly, the volume of securities traded in terms of units on the KLSE in 1989 was about 26 times that in 1974. The corresponding number for turnover of securities in terms of market value in 1989 was about 25 times that in 1974. However, the annual average turnover percentage over the period 1974–1989 was only about 10 percent of the total market value outstanding.

Table 19.9 compares the basic new listing requirements of the SES, KLSE, SET, and the JSE. It can be seen that the requirements are quite similar except for the restriction concerning the prospective P/E ratio and the specific requirement of net tangible assets per share imposed only by the SES.

Major Stock Market Indicators and Trends

A stock market index measures the overall movement of a group of stock prices in the market in order to indicate the performance of the market as a

Table 19.8. Turnover and Value of Securities on the KLSE

Year	(1) Number of Companies	(2) Volume of Shares Traded (Million)	(3) Market Value of Securities Traded (MR Million)	(4) Market Value of Securities Outstanding (MR Million)	(5) Turnover Percentage (3) ÷ (4)
1974	264	391	723	8,085	8.9
1975	268	617	1,306	11,748	11.1
1977	256	598	1,048	13,376	7.6
1980	250	1,482	5,600	43,095	13.0
1983	271	2,276	7,934	80,346	9.9
1986	288	2,289	3,369	64,504	5.2
1989	307	10,162	18,535	156,100	11.9

Source: Kuala Lumpur Stock Exchange.

whole over a time period. In Singapore, there are a number of stock price indices prepared by various organizations. Among the major indices are the SES All-Share Indices prepared by the SES, the Straits Times Indices provided by the *Straits Times,* and the OCBC Index produced by the Oversea-Chinese Banking Corporation.

The SES All-Share Indices are based on the prices of all the listed companies in each of the six industry sectors (industrial and commercial, finance, hotel, property, plantation, and mining) and one overall index that covers all the stocks traded on the SES. The six sector indices measure the price movement of all the stocks in each sector, and all seven indices are market-weighted, similar to the New York Stock Exchange Index. The index number is expressed as a percentage of the current aggregate market value relative to the aggregate market value in the base period. The index takes into consideration the relative importance of the various stocks as reflected by their total market value. The index is adjusted for changes in capital structure, new listings, and delistings.

The Straits Times Indices are unweighted indices first introduced in 1948. Since then, this series has undergone many changes. Presently, the series also consists of six sectoral indices: industrial, finance, hotel, property, plantation, and mining. Only the industrial index is widely used and well known. The industrial index is made up of 30 blue-chip stocks selected from the industrial and commercial sector. Over the years the composition of the 30 stocks has changed to take into account delistings and new listings.

Table 19.9.   Criteria for New Listing

Require-ments	Stock Exchange of Singapore	Kuala Lumpur Stock Exchange	Stock Exchange of Thailand	Jakarta Stock Exchange
Minumim Paid-up Capital	S$4 million	MR5 million	20 million Baht	Rp 200 million
Propor-tion of Paid-up Capital to be Held by Public	S$1.5m or 25% of paid-up capital, which-ever is greater	MR1.25m or 25% of paid-up capital, which-ever is greater	30% of paid-up capital	N/A
Profit Record	5 years	3 years	Sound financial status and good prospects	2 years, net profits at least 10% of the equity for the latest year
Net Tan-gible As-sets Per Share	Not less than the par value of the share	—	—	—
Pricing of New Issue	Should justify projected pro-spective P/E indicated in prospectus	Prospective gross P/E of 3.5 to 8 times	Must not be lower than the par value	N/A

Source: Vickers da Costa and others.

The OCBC Index is a composite index with 55 stocks selected from the six sectors. The index was developed in cooperation with Capital International SA, Geneva, Switzerland. When the index was first introduced in 1973, it consisted of only 40 stocks. But on April 1,1982, the coverage was enlarged to 55 stocks that constitute about 60% of the total stock market capitalization. The OCBC Index is a market-weighted index similar to the SES All-Share Index.

In Malaysia, the KLSE publishes a composite index and five sectoral indices. The KLSE Composite Index is widely followed by investors. The base year of the index is 1977 and the weighting system used is the number of shares listed of each of the 82 stocks. The KLSE Composite Index is also a market-weighted index similar to the OCBC Index.

In Thailand, two stock market indices are widely used by investors, the SET Index and the Book Club Index. Both indices incorporate all quoted stocks, are market-weighted, and are adjusted for capital changes and fluctuations in the number of stocks. However, certain differences exist in the methods the SET and Book Club indices use to measure prices for untraded stocks and adjust for capital changes. Sectoral indices are also available for the banking, financial, commercial, construction, and textiles sectors.

In Indonesia, the main stock market indexes are the Jakarta Composite Index and the BT Index, which cover all of the listed stocks. In March 1990, there were 92 stocks listed on the Jakarta Stock Exchange.

Table 19.10 shows the stock market size and performance of the four countries over the past five years. This table should be read together with Table 19.11, which shows the stock market valuation and some economic indicators over the same five years. We can see that the Singapore market is the largest of the four markets in terms of the amount of market capitalization and number of listed companies. The Malaysian market is the second largest followed by the Thai market and then the Indonesian market.

Table 19.10 also indicates that the small markets are more speculative than the large markets in terms of the fluctuation of stock market indices and the turnover rate of shares traded. In general, the Singaporean and Malaysian markets are relatively more mature and stable than the Thai and Indonesian markets. The Indonesian market has been growing dramatically only since 1988. The recent rapid growth of the Indonesian and Thai stock markets has caused their price earnings (P/E) ratios to be higher than those of the Singapore and Malaysian markets. This is especially true for Indonesia in 1989 when the average stock was unrealistically expensive, with a P/E ratio of 198.7 and a dividend yield of only 1 percent. As shown in Table 19.11, the Singapore stocks were cheaper than the stocks of the other three markets in terms of both P/E ratio and dividend yield in 1990. The argument for the greater stability of the Singapore market is further supported by the lower percentage change of the Consumer Price Index in Singapore in the same year.

Table 19.12 gives the average annual returns of the four stock markets. It shows that over the period 1980–1989, the average returns were the highest for the Indonesian market and the lowest for the Malaysian market. However, the Indonesian market also has the highest risk in terms of standard deviation. When we computed the average returns per unit of risk (standard deviation), the Thai stock market had the highest return over the period, followed by Singapore as the second highest.

Table 19.10. Market Size and Performance

Country/Indicator	1986	1987	1988	1989	1990
Singapore					
ST Industrial Index	891	824	1,038	1,481	1,154
Market Capital (S$Bil.)	85.3	85.3	103.6	136.3	249.0
Trading Volume (S$Bil.)	8.0	22.5	12.7	39.2	36.8
Number of Listed Companies	317	321	327	333	316
Exchange Rate (per US$)	2.18	2.00	1.95	1.90	1.76
Malaysia					
KLSE Composite Index	252	261	357	562	506
Market Capital (MRBil.)	64.5	73.8	99.1	156.0	131.7
Trading Volume (MRBil.)	3.4	10.1	6.9	18.5	29.5
Number of Listed Companies	289	291	295	307	280
Exchange Rate (per US$)	2.60	2.49	2.72	2.70	2.70
Thailand					
SET Index	207	285	387	879	642
Market Capital (BtBil.)	75.2	138.2	223.7	666.3	N/A
Trading Volume (BtBil.)	25.0	122.1	156.5	381.5	N/A
Number of Listed Companies	92	102	122	145	177*
Exchange Rate (per US$)	26.3	25.7	25.3	25.7	25.3
Indonesia					
BT Index	70	82	285	623	754
Market Capital (RpBil.)	N/A	531	1,839	1,729.5	N/A
Trading Volume (RpBil.)	1.8	5.2	30.6	1,189.8	N/A
Number of Listed Companies	24	24	24	61	93*
Exchange Rate (per US$)	1,644	1,653	1,732	1,803	1,845

* Estimate.

Source: Bankers Trust Securities, *Asia Pacific Markets Quarterly Statistical Bulletin,* Autumn 1990; *KLSE Fact Sheet.*

The Indonesian market ranked the third and the Malaysian market the lowest.

Corporate Disclosure Practices

A company which lists its stocks on a stock exchange is, in fact, inviting the public to invest. Therefore, the company has an obligation to disclose to the public on a timely basis adequate information enabling investors to make informed investment decisions. In Singapore, a listed company is required to make immediate public disclosure of all material

Table 19.11. Valuation and Economic Indicators

Country/Indicator	1986	1987	1988	1989	1990
Singapore					
P/E Ratio (Times)	35.2	21.3	20.9	23.1	15.8
Dividend Yield (%)	3.0	3.2	2.7	2.3	2.4
Consumer Price Index Change (%)	−1.4	0.5	1.6	2.4	3.4
GDP Growth Rate (%)	1.8	8.8	11.1	9.2	8.3
Per Capita Income (US$)	6,005	7,259	8,470	9,456	N/A
Malaysia					
P/E Ratio (Times)	26.4	30.6	21.0	36.2	25.5
Dividend Yield (%)	3.5	3.0	3.4	2.0	2.3
Consumer Price Index Change (%)	0.7	1.1	2.5	2.8	3.1
GDP Growth Rate (%)	1.2	5.4	8.9	8.8	9.2
Per Capita Income (US$)	1,571	1,829	1,867	2,032	N/A
Thailand					
P/E Ratio (Times)	12.3	9.3	14.0	26.4	28.0*
Dividend Yield (%)	4.3	3.7	3.8	2.1	1.8*
Consumer Price Index Change (%)	1.9	2.5	3.8	5.4	6.5
GNP Growth Rate (%)	4.9	9.5	13.2	12.3	10.0
Per Capita Income (US$)	776	893	1,076	1,241	N/A
Indonesia					
P/E Ratio (Times)	5.6*	5.0	29.6	198.7	30.0*
Dividend Yield (%)	11.5*	14.1	5.1	1.0	1.7*
Consumer Price Index Change (%)	5.8	9.2	8.6	6.4	8.5*
GDP Growth Rate (%)	6.0	4.6	5.7	7.4	6.0
Per Capita Income (US$)	430	388	420	445	N/A

* Estimate.

Source: Bankers Trust Securities, *Asia Pacific Markets Quarterly Statistical Bulletin*, Autumn 1990, and other stock exchange sources.

Table 19.12. Annual Average Performance of Major Southeast Asia Stock Markets, 1980–1989

Market	Mean Return %	Median Return %	Standard Deviation %	Standard Deviation Rank	Mean Return/ Standard Deviation %	Mean Return/ Standard Deviation Rank
Indonesia	52.61	5.00	109.69	1	0.48	3
Malaysia	13.24	9.00	31.90	2	0.42	4
Singapore	15.30	12.00	27.86	3	0.55	2
Thailand	17.11	11.00	24.47	4	0.70	1

Source: Compiled from M. Ariff and L. W. Johnson, *Securities Markets and Stock Pricing*, Longman Singapore Publishers, 1990, Table 4.

information concerning its financial condition and prospects, mergers and acquisitions; dealings with employees and other business partners, and significant changes in insiders' ownership of the company. The material information is required to be released by the fullest public dissemination. Insiders must not trade on the basis of material information that has not been publicly disclosed. Even after material information has been released, insiders should refrain from trading for a period sufficient to permit thorough public dissemination. An interim (half year) report must be released by the company within three months after the first six months of each fiscal year, and an annual audited report must be released within three months after each fiscal year.

As in Singapore, companies in Malaysia must release an interim report within three months after the completion of the first six months of each fiscal year. This report concerns the company's activities and profits, as well as group activities where applicable. It should also state any material factors and circumstances affecting the earning capacity and profits of the company. Listed companies are required to report immediately to the KLSE after their boards of directors approve the financial statements for the preceding fiscal year, including the net profit or loss of the company and of its subsidiaries for the year. Subsequent to any announcement made in the interim report or final annual results, the KLSE may request such explanations or clarifications as may seem necessary regarding any ambiguities appearing in the statements. At the time of any securities rights issues, bonus issues (stock dividends), or return of capital, the company is required to indicate any expected change in profitability and cash dividends from that of the previous fiscal year.

In Thailand, the SET places great importance on the ready availability to public investors of any material information that may influence the stock price of a listed company. Such information must be disclosed promptly, accurately, and impartially. Within 45 days from the end of each fiscal quarter, a listed company must disclose its financial statements. A company must disclose its annual financial report within three months if the fourth quarter statements were released within 45 days after the end of the fiscal year; otherwise the annual report must be disclosed within 60 days after the fiscal year. All information on operation and financial structure that may affect stock prices and shareholders' interests must be disclosed promptly.

Listed companies in Indonesia must submit financial statements to BAPEPAM no later than 120 days after the close of each fiscal year. Moreover, listed companies are obliged to notify BAPEPAM within 30 days of any event that may materially affect their operations. They must also provide any additional reports that may be requested by BAPEPAM and publish audited financial statements in at least two Indonesian-language newspapers within 120 days after the close of the fiscal year.

Major Sources of Investment Research Information

Of the stock markets in the world, those in Southeast Asia, especially in Singapore, Malaysia, and Thailand, are among the most rapidly developing ones. Because these markets have emerged in international importance in only the past two decades or so, investment research information is not yet available in the same volume as for the older, established Western stock markets. However, with the rapid growth of economies in this region and the concomitant growth of investment interest in their corporations, the quantity and quality of investment research information is also rapidly expanding.

Because commerce and trade have historically played a major role in the development of Singaporean society, this country has led the way in becoming a major center for financial and securities markets in Southeast Asia. Its path could be considered a model that the other emerging countries in the region will seek to follow. The sources of investment research in Singapore are more highly developed than those of other countries in the region. The research information gathered in Singapore pertains not only to stocks of Singaporean and Malaysian corporations, but also of those that trade in the neighboring countries. Likewise, research is conducted on Southeast Asian stocks by organizations headquartered in Hong Kong, London, and elsewhere.

Nevertheless, if investors become familiar with the sources of investment information in Singapore, they will understand how stocks are researched in Southeast Asia and anticipate how this type of research will become more fully developed in the future in the neighboring stock markets of Southeast Asia.

We will now examine the available investment research information in Singapore that pertains to stocks in terms of five major sources: corporations, securities dealer research, institutional investor research, publishing media, and other sources.

Corporations as a Source of Information

The most important information publicly disclosed by corporations is considered to be the financial statements that are published twice a year. One peculiar accounting practice in Singapore is that companies publish financial statements only twice a year, a *half year* report covering the first half of the fiscal year and an annual report for the total year. Corporate officials generally believe that more frequent quarterly statements are not necessary and that quarterly reports would erroneously focus too much investor attention on short-term results rather than on a more proper longer-term perspective.

In order to understand the past performance and current financial position of corporations, an analysis of the financial statements is essential because managements do not otherwise publicly disclose much detailed information about past and current conditions. The annual financial statements are audited, mostly by the American Big Six public accounting firms, and are usually published within three months after the end of the fiscal year. The statements tend to conform to the requirements of the Singapore Society of Public Accountants and to international accounting standards that reflect a combination of American FASB and British standards. The accounting practices used by Singaporean corporations are considered to be among the best in Asia, but they are not up to American standards. Although the practices are improving, they need further work, especially in terms of more disclosure and greater comparability. The standards of disclosure are excellent among several corporations, including Singapore Airlines, Straits Steamship Company, and Development Bank of Singapore (DBS), while other companies, such as the major banks, disclose the bare minimum.

A second important source of information is management comments in corporate reports. These comments are generally less informative than those made by managements of Western corporations. Although the comments are useful, they tend to be too general or vague regarding explanations of past performance and especially about expectations for corporate sales and earnings over the next year or two. Although managements are beginning to furnish more information, they usually do not discuss corporate financial objectives, plans, or strategies.

Managements have been reluctant to disclose information beyond what is legally required for several reasons:

1. The majority of the stocks of some companies are owned by a closeknit family or by one or more holding companies, so management perceives no incentive to inform outside minority stockholders.
2. Some companies anticipate no need to issue new shares of stocks but will borrow funds, and therefore, are unconcerned about whether their market price reflects informed expectations.
3. Some managements believe that disclosures may give competitors an advantage.
4. Some families sold a minority portion of the family corporation in order to establish a public market price for special purposes such as being able to pledge family shares as collateral for bank loans.
5. Some companies lack an understanding of what information investors want to know, and managements consider making disclosures an unnecessary chore.
6. The Asian culture, by nature, is more secretive or less open.

Many analysts believe that managements will gradually become more open as the corporate economy grows and as Singapore society becomes more cosmopolitan. In reviewing the chairman's statement in the annual reports of 249 listed companies over the four years 1979–1982, it was found that the number of statements that made no prediction about future corporate profitability tended to decrease over the years, from 51 in 1979 to 39 in 1982 (Meng, 1987).

Corporate public announcements and news releases vary widely in informativeness. Some announcements are considered to be of little importance, pertaining to trivial matters, company propaganda, or matters already widely known, and many companies issue very few announcements. Under insider information rules, corporations are required to report on any significant developments. Therefore, when major rumors circulate or a major stock price fluctuation occurs, a listed corporation is expected by the SES to issue a news release. Such announcements are considered important. The SES provides a timely news release service that research analysts monitor two or more times a day.

Corporate management speeches are considered the least useful of any source mainly because managements rarely give speeches or presentations, and when they do, the presentations seldom reveal any new information. Notable exceptions are Singapore Airlines, Straits Steamship, and companies planning a public offering, when they put on "road shows" in Singapore and in international financial centers. Explanations offered for the rarity of speeches are the absence of such a custom here, managements fear of being misunderstood or misquoted by journalists, and managements apprehension about being asked difficult or embarrassing questions. Some executives, however, have expressed an open-mindedness to considering an invitation to speak before analysts.

The fifth corporate source is management comments reflected in financial publications. Most managements are not particularly open to revealing useful information to financial publishers, but on those few occasions when they do, this source can be quite helpful.

By far the most crucial corporate source is the information gathered by investment research analysts through their contacts with corporate management. A skilled analyst who develops a rapport with managements and gains their respect and trust is able to gather valuable information. This channel ranks very high for two reasons. First, research analysts depend heavily on this source because of a perceived shortage of corporate information available from other sources. Second, managements appear to be quite open and cooperative with professional investors on the telephone or on visits when they are dealing with only one or a few knowledgeable people at a time. Corporate officials in Singapore are frequently just as informative and cooperative in direct contacts as those in Western companies.

Research Information from Securities Dealer Firms

Investment research sources from securities dealer firms are considered to be very important, second only to corporate financial statements and analyst contacts with corporate managements.

Printed research reports published by securities dealers are quite useful. These reports are generally obtainable only by institutional investors and large individual investors; they are not advertised or otherwise made available to the investing public. Telephone conversations and other oral communications between investors and dealers are also important sources.

Research information is furnished by Singaporean dealer firms and foreign-owned dealers located in Singapore. Although the research from both types of dealers is important, the quality of dealer research varies among Singapore dealers and among foreign dealers. Analysts try to make their reports as reliable, objective, and accurate as possible, but they vary widely in terms of adequacy. Some of the reports tend to be overly factual, with insufficient rigorous, in-depth analysis of a qualitative and quantitative nature. Some analysts need to better understand their assigned industries and companies, become better skilled in determining the outlook for their companies, and become better at forecasting company sales and earnings. Analysts are frequently hampered by company managements that are less cooperative in furnishing information than Western corporations. However, this barrier may be reduced in the future as experienced analysts build close relations with managements and learn how to ask them probing questions. Singaporean research reports are of better quality than those in other emerging markets but do not yet meet the standards of those in mature Western financial markets. The belief that the quality of research has improved significantly in recent years and will be a great deal better in the future is widespread.

In the aftermath of the recession and the Pan Electric stock market crisis in 1985, the SES took steps to strengthen the capitalization of stock-brokerage firms. In 1986, the big four Singaporean banks were permitted to establish securities dealer subsidiaries, and in 1987 the SES allowed one-third of its 24 member firms to be owned, up to 49 percent, by foreign brokerage firms. As a result of the infusion of new capital into the securities dealer industry, competition is keener, research departments have larger budgets, and more research analysts have been hired. In the past, analysts were paid low salaries and turnover was high. At present, the average analyst is young with a few years of experience. Because Singapore wants to serve as a major financial center in Asia, the number of trained research analysts has expanded significantly. In 1987, Singapore established a local chapter of the International Society of Financial Analysts, a constituent society of The Financial Analysts Federation. The Institute of Banking and Finance in Singapore conducts a Chartered Financial Analysts (CFA) candidate study program, and in 1991, 478 candidates took the CFA examinations in Singapore, the largest number of candidates in any country outside of the United States and Canada. The number of CFA candidates who took the examinations has increased in each of the past six years; 19 took the examinations in 1985, 48 in 1986, 74 in 1987, 183 in 1988, 263 in 1989, and 318 in 1990.

Institutional Investor In-House Research

Research information generated internally by institutional investors is a useful source, though less important than research from securities dealers. A greater reliance appears to be placed on the research conducted by Singaporean institutional investors than that of foreign-owned institutions. This practice is based on a belief that Singaporean institutions devote a greater effort to researching Singaporean and Malaysian companies.

Publishing Media

Publications constitute another source of information, though once again not as important as information originating from corporations and investment analysts. Many analysts believe that financial news coverage in Singapore is inadequate and incomplete. Singapore has two leading daily news periodicals, both owned by the same company: the *Straits Times* and the *Business Times*. The *Straits Times*, which includes a business section, is intended for a broad readership, while the *Business Times* specializes in news intended for a business readership.

Business news reporting is usually reliable and accurate, but not always. A prevailing view is that reporting standards have been low; though slowly improving, they still have far to go. Some journalists are underpaid, lack an understanding of business and finance, are unable to critically analyze or correctly interpret news events, lack the ability to check out rumors and engage in penetrating investigative reporting, or are unable to place a news development within its larger context. Some analysts believe too much of the news coverage is factually descriptive, a transmission of corporate management platitudes and mundane corporate current events, or a rehash of outdated information. On the other hand, journalists encounter difficulties in trying to gather information from sometimes inaccessible corporate managements and analyzing an event under the time pressures of a daily publication deadline.

Other pertinent business media include local publications such as *Singapore Business* (monthly), the SES (Stock Exchange of Singapore) *Journal* (monthly), *Malaysian Business*, and SES daily company news announcements. Several foreign publications are considered important in reporting on economic, political, and business developments in the world and in Southeast Asia, and on developments in Singapore and Malaysia. Foreign publications frequently used by analysts are the *Far Eastern Economic Review* (FEER), the *Asian Wall Street Journal* (AWSJ), the *Economist*, and specialized industry journals. The FEER and AWSJ are examples of good journalistic reporting in which developments are covered with comprehensive, penetrating analyses, whereby the events are placed in the perspective of the larger context.

Other published financial services are not available for Singaporean and Malaysian stocks, with the main exception of technical stock price chart services that are used for selecting stocks and for timing transactions. Consequently, an acute need currently exists for publishing services that regularly cover fundamental financial research on regional industries and stocks.

Other Sources

Other potential sources of information used by analysts to research a stock include a company's competitors, customers, and vendors, although most analysts find these sources are reluctant to furnish information.

The value of another source, industry trade associations, varies widely depending on the particular association. Some of the associations that provide useful industry information represent manufacturing, shipbuilding, hotels, real estate, palm oil, banking, and motor vehicle sales.

Government agencies and officials provide extensive, good quality information, much of which consists of statistical data regarding the economy, business conditions, and industry sectors such as manufacturing, tourist trade, and shipping, or pertains to the money supply, bank loans, government budgets, government economic policy pronouncements, production, and trade. Such information is quite important because government actions have a major impact on domestic industries. Government agencies that provide useful information are the Monetary Authority of Singapore (MAS), the Ministry of Trade and Industry, the Economic Development Board, and the Tourist Promotion Board.

Some analysts make use of gossip, rumors, leaks, or tips gathered through a network consisting of friends, company managers, board members, bankers, accountants, market traders, and other personal contacts. This source of information plays a larger role in the Singaporean and Malaysian markets than in other Western markets for several reasons. First, corporations publicly disclose less information. Second, brokerage research reports are given only limited distribution. Third, other publishing services that cover corporations are limited or nonexistent. Finally, Singapore tends to be a small, close-knit community, so that gossip circulates quickly and easily. Due to a lack of other sources of information, rumors, whether true or false, can have a great impact on market prices. However, it can be dangerous to act on rumors because they are frequently false.

The use of insider information is legally prohibited in Singapore, and the MAS and SES act to enforce this law. Some analysts believe that insider information is not used much and is of less importance than in other Asian markets such as Hong Kong. Other analysts insist that it is difficult to determine what information is actually insider or not and thus to know the extent to which insider information is used. Others claim that insider information is used no more than it is in every other country. Some think that insider information is definitely being used, at least to some degree. Occasionally rumors circulate about important company developments, such as the possible declaration of a stock dividend (called bonus shares). Although the rumors may be publicly denied by a company's management, they are accompanied by noticeable market price fluctuations, and the actual development is nonetheless confirmed at a later date.

Based on a review of the stock markets in Southeast Asia, it is clear that the characteristics investment research information are similar in some respects to but different in other ways from the information available in developed Western stock markets. The recent improvement in the quantity and quality of investment research information is expected to continue in the years ahead, driven by increased competition. The standards of disclosure and investment analysis of corporations are higher in the Singaporean and Malaysian markets than in many other Asian financial markets, but has not attained the standards of Western markets. As public stock ownership broadens, more corporate managements are expected to recognize the benefits of opening the channels of communication to both professional and individual investors. As the public gains greater affluence, opportunities will possibly develop for securities dealers and publishing services to make available fundamental investment research to the investing public in Singapore, Malaysia, elsewhere in Southeast Asia, and in the West. Institutional and large individual investors currently appear to have reasonably adequate access to important and useful sources of information in order to make common stock investment decisions.

Transaction Costs

In Singapore, stockbrokers charge their clients a commission for trading securities. For orders at prices of S$1.00 and above per share, the commission rates are as follows:

On the first S$250,000:	1.0%
On the next S$250,000:	0.9%
On the next S$250,000:	0.8%
On the next S$250,000:	0.7%
On amounts above S$1 million:	Negotiable, but subject to a minimum of 0.5%

For orders at prices below S$1.00 per share, the commission rates are as follows:

Under S$0.50	½ ¢ per share
S$0.50–0.99	1 ¢ per share

In all cases, the commission rate is subject to a minimum charge of S$5.00 per order. In addition, there is a clearing fee of 0.05 percent on the market value of the transaction, subject to a maximum of S$100. There are also contract stamp and transfer stamp duties. The former is S$1 per S$1,000 or part thereof, and the latter is 0.2 percent of the value of the transaction payable when stocks are sent for registration.

Brokerage commission rates in Malaysia according to price per share are as follows:

Price Per Share	Commission Rate
Under MR 0.50	MR 0.005
MR 0.50–1.00	MR 0.015
Above MR 1.00	1%

A clearing fee of 0.05 percent of the transacted value is payable for services provided by the clearing house. A stamp duty is also payable on contract notes, transfer, and share certificates. The rates per contract notes and transfer are MR 1 per MR 1,000 of value and MR 3 per MR 1,000 of value or fraction thereof respectively. The stamp duty per share certificate is MR 2 per certificate.

Standard brokerage charges for buying or selling securities in Thailand are 0.5 percent of market value traded for stocks and unit trusts and 0.1 percent for government bonds and debentures. In all cases, there is a minimum brokerage charge of 50 Baht. Transfers of stocks, bonds, and debentures, must pay stamp duty according to the value of the paid-up shares or the market value of the instrument transferred, whichever is greater, at the rate of 1 Baht for every 1,000 Baht or fraction thereof, with the exceptions of the transfers of unit trusts and government bonds.

In Indonesia, the brokerage commission rate is 1 percent on gross proceeds, or Rp 50,000 (Rp denotes *rupiah*, the monetary unit of Indonesia), whichever is larger. In addition, there is a transaction levy by the stock exchange which is 0.1 percent on the gross proceeds. There is also a contract stamp duty of Rp 1,000 (US$0.55) per transaction.

Patterns of Share Ownership

The Singapore Securities Research Institute conducted three surveys, in 1975, 1980, and 1985, on the pattern and changes in ownership of stocks listed on the SES. The surveys revealed the distribution of shareholdings by class of shareholders. Individuals were clearly dominant among shareholders in 1975 and 1980, comprising about 93 percent of the total number of shareholders. However, in terms of the percentage of shareholdings, individuals collectively owned only about 25 percent of the total shares of listed stocks in 1980, and this was a drop of 5 percent from the 30 percent figure in 1975. At the same time, institutions owned 12.2 percent in 1980, an increase of 3 percent from 9.3 percent in 1975, indicating the rise of their importance in terms of shareholdings.

Over 60 percent of the shareowners of Singapore companies resided in Singapore, with about one-third residing in Malaysia and the rest residing elsewhere. The amount of shares owned by holders in Singapore increased from 72.6 percent in 1975 to 80.4 percent in 1980, while that held by owners in Malaysia dropped from 13.3 percent to 10.4 percent. Although there were some changes in the distribution of shareholders and shareholdings among sectors between 1975 and 1980, the largest proportion of shareholders and shareholdings was in the industrial and commercial sector.

The third shareownership survey was taken in 1985. Individuals continued to form the bulk of the total number of shareholders, comprising 92.5 percent. Nominees were next with 3.5 percent, followed by corporations at 3.0 percent. Though individuals were the largest group of shareowners, they held only 21.1 percent of shareholdings compared with corporations, which held 43.2 percent, and nominees, which absorbed 27.5 percent. This pattern did not hold in 1975 where individuals absorbed 37.4%, corporations 34.2%, and institutions 14.6%.

Rowley (1987), quoting a little-publicized survey by the KLSE, indicated that by the end of 1984 institutional holdings of Malaysian shares had reached about 48 percent of total market shares issued, while individual holdings represented about 24 percent and nominee holdings about 26 percent. This high institutional concentration was not expected, as it had been previously thought that private holders accounted for over 60 percent of total holdings, with only about 20 percent of total holdings in the hands of investment companies, pension funds, and state economic development corporations. Merchant banks and insurance companies were thought to hold another 10 percent to 15 percent, with the remaining held by foreigners.

In the SET, the ten largest stockholders of each of the listed companies owned about 58 percent of the total market capitalization. This can be broken down as 42 percent domestic stockholders and 16 percent foreign stockholders. The domestic stockholders can be further divided into 68 percent Thai institutions, 28 percent individuals, and 4 percent Thai funds. Of the figure for total foreign major stockholders, foreign institutions make up about 66 percent, while foreign individuals account for about 34 percent.

In Indonesia, the share trading volume is very small by world standards. The average turnover per day in 1988 was less than US$70,000. It was estimated that PT Danareksa, the national investment trust, held about 35 percent to 40 percent of the shares quoted on the JSE. PT Danareksa issues mutual fund certificates sold to the public to stimulate stock ownership among small investors and to assist in the development of the exchange.

Restrictions on Foreign Investors

In Singapore, the Banking Act and the Newspaper Act, which specifically indicate a restriction on foreign ownership in banks and newspaper publishing companies, constitute the only legislation governing foreign investors. However, some companies in "sensitive" industries can incorporate a foreign ownership restriction clause in their memorandums. As part of the corporation scheme of stockbrokerage firms introduced in 1987, foreign firms have contributed up to 49 percent of the paid-up capital of some of the SES member stockbrokerage firms. There are no foreign exchange controls on the trading of securities by nonresidents and no limitations on the repatriation of income, capital gains, or capital.

In Malaysia, under the NEP, Bumiputras (natives of Malaysia) must own at least 30 percent of corporate equity, with 40 percent held by other Malaysians, and not more than 30 percent by foreigners. Moreover, Malaysian regulations deny foreign investors access to subscriptions for new listings. The FIC must approve any transactions which result in: the transfer of control to foreign ownership through a joint venture; 15 percent of company voting power held by any single foreign interest, or 30 percent in aggregate; or assets or interests exceeding MR 5 million in value. There are no exchange controls preventing foreign investors from freely repatriating principal, capital gains, dividends, or interest received. However, approval from Bank Negara (the Central Bank of Malaysia) is required when making remittances exceeding MR 2 million in a single transaction.

Thai companies, as permitted by law, can be 49 percent foreign owned. However, companies can, and do, choose to restrict ownership by foreign investors. Therefore, shares permitted to be held by foreign investors are scarce and expensive. An "alien board" for trading securities on the SET was created in 1987 to facilitate trading in the shares alloted to foreign investors, though often at a considerable premium in prices. Inward remittances of foreign exchange are documented by means of the Bank of Thailand's E.C. 71 form. To repatriate proceeds from sales or dividend payments, this form must be produced to prove that stocks were purchased with legally imported foreign exchange. Repatriation of funds is effected by means of an E.C. 31 form.

In Indonesia, there are both legal and company limitations on foreign shareholdings for all companies. Foreigners can invest directly in securities issued only by certain corporations. For most companies, foreign ownership of equity is limited to a maximum of 49 percent. A number of the listed companies are off-limits to new investors because they are foreign joint-venture companies in which the foreign partner already holds more than 49 percent. The rest are open to foreign investors. Indonesia imposes no controls on the flow of capital or income into or out of the country, with the exception of loans from non-Indonesian lenders with a maturity of more than one year. Such loans are required to be reported on a regular basis. There are also no restrictions on the repatriation of sale proceeds or dividend income by foreign investors.

Income Taxes

The profits of companies incorporated in Singapore are subject to a 31 percent corporate tax, except those "pioneer" companies that have been granted a tax exemption or concession status. The cash dividends that a shareholder receives from listed companies are not subject to further tax. To avoid double taxation on their income, shareholders are entitled to a rebate on the portion of the dividend paid as corporate tax if their personal income tax bracket is below the 31 percent corporate tax rate. Capital gains from share transactions are not taxed, and capital losses are not deductible. However, investment holding companies and unit trusts are required to pay tax on capital gains on a graduated basis according to the length of the investment holding period.

There is no tax on capital gains derived from transactions of securities in Malaysia. Dividend income is, however, subject to income tax. Only dividends paid by companies granted "pioneer status" are tax-exempt. Nonresident shareholders are subject to an income tax of 35 percent on cash dividends. Resident shareholders are refunded the amount of income tax deducted through a tax credit when they file their personal tax returns.

In Thailand, dividends are subject to a withholding tax of 15 percent in the case of foreign individual investors and 20 percent for foreign corporations. There is no tax on capital gains for foreign individual investors. For foreign corporations, capital gains are subject to a withholding tax of 25 percent. Those countries that have a double taxation treaty with Thailand will benefit from exemption of the capital gains tax.

For foreign investors in Indonesia, dividend income is subject to a 20 percent withholding tax deducted by the company. For domestic investors, the withholding tax on dividends is 15 percent. There is no tax on capital gains arising from transactions of securities in Indonesia by funds or foreign individuals unless they carry on the business of dealing in securities through a permanent establishment there. For domestic investors, capital gains are treated as income and taxed at progressive personal tax rates.

REFERENCES

Ariff, M., and L. W. Johnson. *Securities Markets and Stock Pricing*. Singapore: Longman Singapore Publishers, 1990.

George, R. L. *A Guide to Asian Stock Markets*. Hong Kong: Longman Group, 1989.

Kuala Lumpur Stock Exchange. *Listing Requirements*.

Meng, Tan Teck. "Reliability of Chairmen's Statements in Annual Reports of Listed Companies for Forecasting Company Profitability." *The Singapore Stock Exchange Journal* (December 1987) pp. 8–19.

Rowley, A. *Asian Stockmarkets: The Inside Story*. Hong Kong: Far Eastern Economic Review, 1987.

Singapore Securities Research Institute. "Shareownership Survey 1985." *Securities Industry Review*, 14, No. 1 (April 1988).

Singapore Securities Research Institute. "Pattern of Shareownership 1980." *Securities Industry Review*, 8, No. 2 (October 1982).

Stock Exchange of Singapore. *Fact Book*. 1989.

Stock Exchange of Singapore. *Listing Manual Corporate Disclosure Policy*. undated.

Tan, P. T. "The Development of the Securities Industry." *Securities Industry Review*, 4, No. 1 (April 1978).

Tan, C. H. *Financial Markets and Institutions in Singapore*. Singapore: Singapore University Press, 1989.

Tan, C. H., and K. C. Kwan, eds. *Handbook of Singapore-Malaysian Corporate Finance*. Singapore: Buterworths, 1988.

CHAPTER
20

Investing in Latin America

Jayant S. Tata
International Finance
Corporation
Washington, DC

Sophisticated global investors increasingly recognize that investments in emerging markets add important new dimensions of competitive returns and diversification to their portfolios. In each of the last five years, over half of the top ten performing stock markets were represented by emerging market bourses, and they significantly outperformed the S&P 500 Index. According to International Finance Corporation (IFC), the private sector development affiliate of the World Bank, over the past decade the top 20 emerging markets experienced phenomenal growth: total capitalization increased seven-fold, total value traded increased 39 times, and the number of listed companies doubled. During 1990, more than 1,200 companies raised over US $22 billion through equity offerings in these markets. Yet, as of the end of 1990, the total emerging market capitalization of US $470 billion was only 5 percent of world equity market capitalization even though emerging market economies represented 12 percent of 1989 world GDP. The primary means of including emerging markets in international portfolios has been emerging market country funds, which at the end of 1990 numbered over 140 and had an aggregate net asset value of over US $12 billion. The global investor simply can no longer afford to overlook emerging markets, of which Latin America represents a significant example (see Table 20.1).

Political and economic reform—the foundation for rapid and sustained growth—is sweeping through the region. The five major Latin American countries of Argentina, Brazil, Chile, Mexico, and Venezuela have successfully made the transition to democracy with popularly-elected governments. This democratic political process gives the initially painful policies of economic structural reform and liberalization a crucial, and indeed necessary, legitimacy.

Table 20.1. Overview of Major Latin American Stock Markets

	1989			1990				
	Gross Domestic Product US% bil	External Debt (Est) US$ bil	Market Cap US$ mil	Avg Daily Value Traded US$ mil	Number of Listed Companies	Price/ Earnings Ratio	Price/ Book Value Ratio	% Change[b] in Local Market Index
Argentina	59.25	56.5	3,268	3.5	179	3.1	0.37	1.0
Brazil	479.90	112.1	16,354[a]	23.2	581	5.3	0.75	−73.1
Chile	25.25	16.9	13,645	3.2	215	8.9	1.42	45.7
Mexico	195.07	90.8	32,725	49.1	199	13.2	1.29	36.7
Venezuela	43.83	33.2	8,361	9.1	66	29.3	5.94	511.2

a. Sao Paolo.

b. In US $ terms.

Sources: IFC Emerging Markets Database, Word Bank World Debt Tables 89–90.

All of the five major Latin American countries are implementing extensive market-oriented reforms in key areas: anti-inflation fiscal and monetary policies, privatization, trade liberalization, realistic exchange rate policies, and external debt restructuring. Curbing inflation—the bane of Latin America—is a central objective with top priority. Monetary expansion and government budget deficits have been rejected as policy instruments to stimulate growth. The governments are rapidly withdrawing from their role of controlling operating enterprises and are shifting this function to the private sector. Privatization has become a major means of accomplishing several objectives: reducing budget deficits by generating revenues while also shrinking the bureaucracy, decreasing external indebtedness through debt/equity swaps in financing a number of privatizations, and promoting continuing foreign financial and technological investment to modernize and expand these enterprises. Chile, Mexico, and, more recently, Argentina, have been notable in this regard. The five major Latin American economies have been opened up to foreign investment and foreign goods. Trade barriers in terms of both quotas and duties are being systematically dismantled. The currencies are floating against the dollar and realistic exchange rates increasingly prevail. The overhang of external debt is being addressed. Debt-to-equity conversion programs, pioneered by Chile, are being adopted by Argentina, Mexico, Venezuela, and, most recently, Brazil. As a practical matter, Chile has emerged from its debt problem. Debt restructurings on a more orderly basis, involving elements of debt forgiveness, have been successfully concluded by Mexico and Venezuela. Argentina and Brazil are now beginning to address the issue constructively.

These political and economic changes help reinforce the role of Latin America's resilient and entrepreneurial private sector as an engine of growth and provide a crucial common denominator for perhaps the most important development in the long run, the creation of a "free-trade" zone in the Americas. There is growing recognition of the mutual benefits of such a free-trade zone: U.S. capital; Latin American resources and cheaper labor and operating costs; huge North-South trade flows. The tripartite "fast track" negotiations for a free-trade agreement among Mexico, the United States, and Canada will be the "defining development" in this regard.

In the decade of the nineties, Latin America is being rediscovered by global investors. The five major Latin American markets of Argentina, Brazil, Chile, Mexico, and Venezuela have more than doubled in size from US $35 billion in 1984 to US $74 billion in 1990 (Figure 20.1). These five Latin American markets represent about 16 percent of total emerging market capitalization and 38 percent of the total GDP of emerging markets (Figure 20.2). This low ratio of market capitalization to GDP indicates that there is significant growth potential as the current low ratio comes closer to the higher market-capitalization-to-GDP relationship prevailing in developed countries (Figure 20.3).

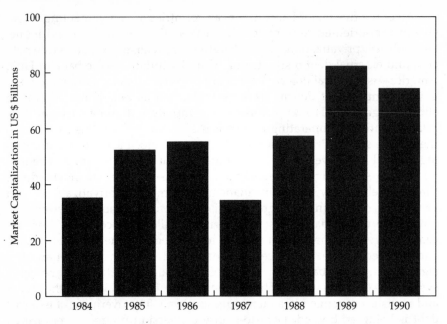

Figure 20.1. Six-Year Growth of Major Latin American Markets: Argentina, Brazil, Chile, Mexico, and Venezuela (Source: IFC Emerging Markets Database)

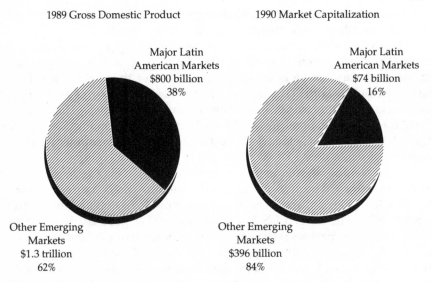

Figure 20.2. Major Latin American Markets: Argentina, Brazil, Chile, Mexico, and Venezuela (Source: IFC Emerging Markets Database)

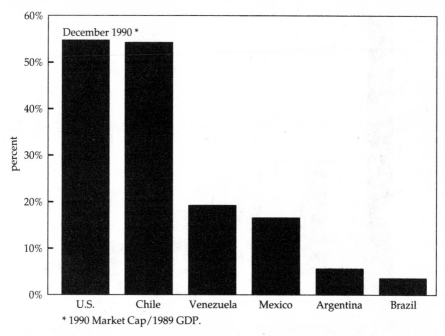

Figure 20.3. Market Capitalization as a Percent of GDP (Source: IFC Emerging Markets Database)

In addition, Latin American markets are undervalued, with low price/earnings ratios (Figure 20.4) and price/book value ratios (Figure 20.5), and have excellent portfolio diversification characteristics: low to negative correlations relative to developed markets as well as among themselves (Table 20.2). In each of the five major Latin American countries there are successful, well-managed, "world class" companies that are significantly undervalued simply because their local markets are undervalued.

Over the last five years, Latin American equities have provided high, albeit volatile, returns. For example, in U.S. dollar terms, Brazil's stock markets fell 73 percent in 1990 but rose 82 percent in the first quarter of 1991; Venezuela's stock market soared slightly more than 500 percent in 1990 compared to the nearly 40 percent decline experienced in the prior year (Figures 20.6 through 20.11). Over the past five years, the volatility of Latin American markets, as measured by the standard deviation of local price indices in U.S. dollar terms has been about twice that of developed markets (Table 20.3).

Although Latin American markets are relatively thin, liquidity is improving. For example, the average daily value traded in U.S. dollar terms for Mexico doubled from about US $25 million in 1989 to about US $52 million in 1990 (Figures 20.12 through 20.16).

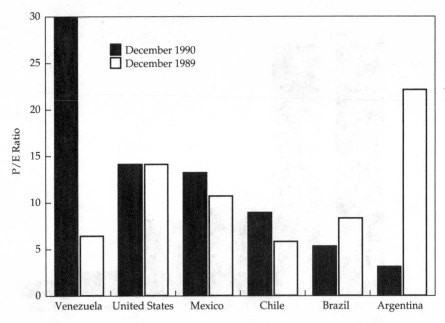

Figure 20.4.   Price/Earnings Ratios (Source: IFC Emerging Markets Database)

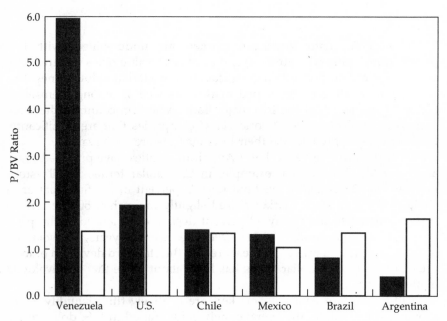

Figure 20.5.   Price/Book Value Ratios (Source: IFC Emerging Markets Database)

Table 20.2. Correlation Coefficient Matrix of Major Latin American Price
Indexes for Five Years Ending December 1990

	S&P 500	Argentina	Brazil	Chile	Mexico	Venezuela
S&P 500	1.00					
Argentina	0.02	1.00				
Brazil	0.04	−0.19	1.00			
Chile	0.29	−0.08	0.08	1.00		
Mexico	0.43	0.11	−0.10	0.35	1.00	
Venezuela	−0.10	0.04	−0.30	−0.19	−0.12	1.00

Source: IFC Emerging Markets Database.

Trading and settlement procedures are being improved and streamlined, and in Brazil and Mexico are already computerized. The securities
regulatory framework, accounting standards, and company information
and disclosure requirements are steadily improving as Latin American
countries focus on the development of their capital markets.

During 1990 Latin American companies raised over US$1 billion
through debt and equity issues in the international markets. In 1991,
Telmex's international offering alone was about US$2 billion. It is quite

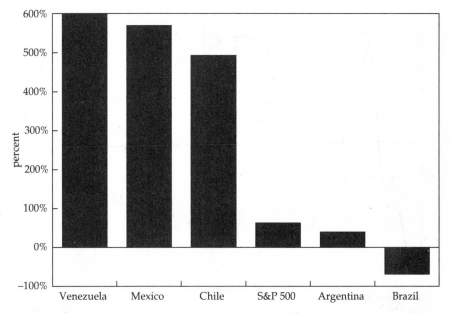

Figure 20.6. Market Index Returns in U.S. Dollars for Five Years Ending
December 1990 (Source: IFC Emerging Markets Database [IFC Price Indexes])

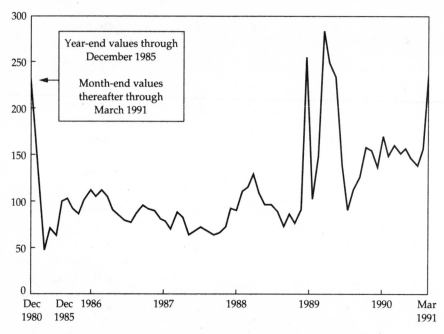

Figure 20.7.   Movement of Argentina's *Indice General* (December 1985 = 100, Index Values US$ Adjusted) (Source: Batterymarch Financial Management)

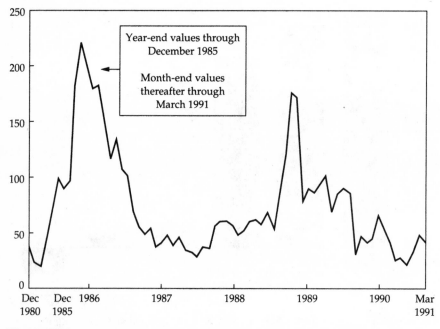

Figure 20.8.   Movement of Brazil's *BOVESPA* Index (December 1985 = 100, Index Values US$ Adjusted) (Source: Batterymarch Financial Management)

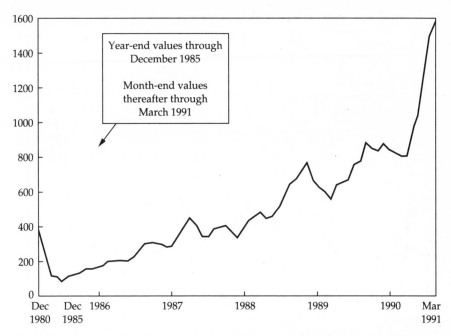

Figure 20.9. Movement of Chile's *IPSA* Index (December 1985 = 100, Index Values US$ Adjusted)

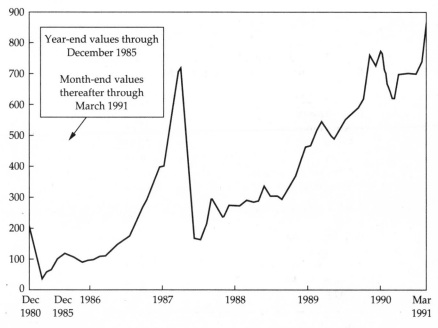

Figure 20.10. Movement of Mexico's *Indice de Precios* (December 1985 = 100, Index Values US$ Adjusted)

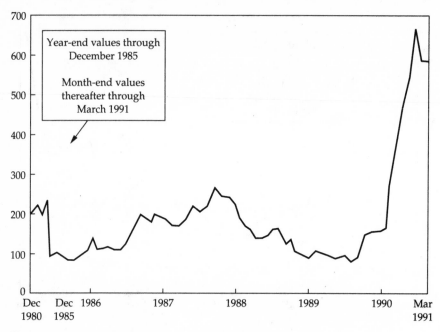

Figure 20.11. Movement of Venezuela's *Bolsa* Index (December 1985 = 100, Index Values US$ Adjusted)

Table 20.3. Standard Deviation of Price Indexes for Five Years Ending December 1990

Market	Standard Deviation
Latin America	
Argentina	31.69
Brazil	22.81
Chile	8.34
Mexico	15.83
Venezuela	13.67
IFC Latin America Index	13.34
Developed Markets	
U.S. (S&P 500)	5.47
U.K. (FT-100)	6.19
Japan (Nikkei)	6.73
EAFE (MSCI)	6.57

Source: *IFC Emerging Markets Factbook,* 1990.

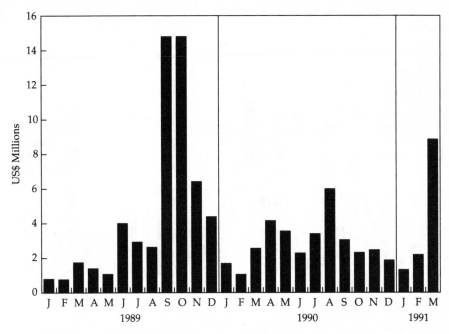

Figure 20.12. Average Daily Value Traded: Argentina, January 1989 to March 1991 (Source: IFC Emerging Markets Database)

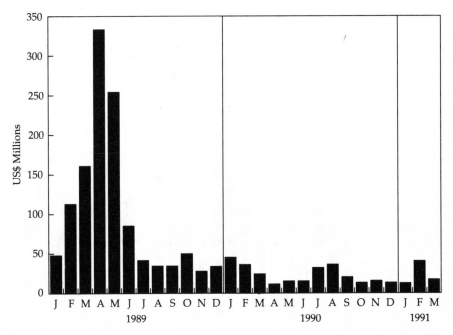

Figure 20.13. Average Daily Value Traded: Brazil, January 1989 to March 1991 (Source: IFC Emerging Markets Database)

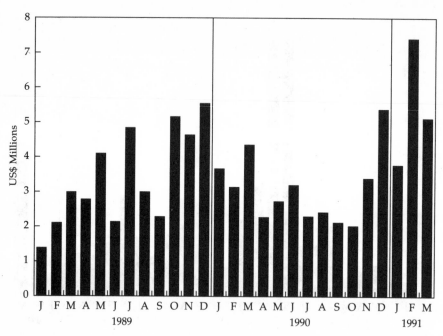

Figure 20.14.   Average Daily Value Traded: Chile, January 1989 to March 1991 (Source: IFC Emerging Markets Database)

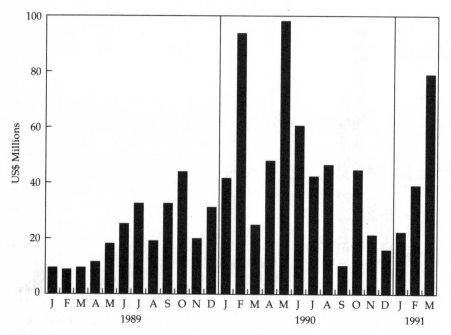

Figure 20.15.   Average Daily Value Traded: Mexico, January 1989 to March 1991 (Source: IFC Emerging Markets Database)

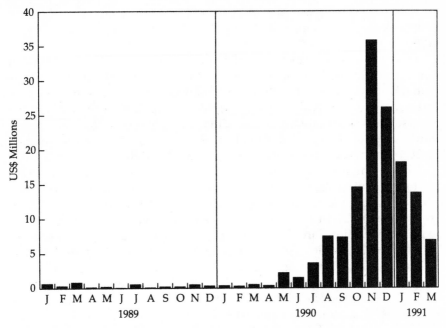

Figure 20.16. Average Daily Value Traded: Venezuela, January 1989 to March 1991 (Source: IFC Emerging Markets Database)

likely that during 1991, and future years, a number of major issuers from emerging markets will be offering their securities in the international markets. These emerging global companies will be coming to the home markets of international investors, complementing the trend of international investors going to emerging markets for investment opportunities on local bourses. The net result will be greater breadth and depth for Latin American securities.

In terms of access for foreign investors, all five of the major Latin American markets permit investment through "country funds" and "regional funds." Argentina, Mexico, and, most recently, Brazil permit institutional investors to invest directly in their local stock markets. (There are now only relatively minor restrictions in the types of listed securities that can be owned by foreigners; the principal restriction relates to the ownership of bank stocks in Venezuela and Mexico.) A number of the Latin American country and regional funds are listed in New York and London. These are probably the best way for investors to get an initial exposure to Latin American investments. However, it should be noted that these country funds are typically closed-end funds that can often trade at a discount to the underlying net asset value (although it should be pointed out that these funds can trade at a premium as well). A major new development that will likely accelerate during this decade is the listing of major Latin American companies on the principal international stock exchanges.

For example, *Telefonos* of Chile and *Telmex* of Mexico are now traded on the New York Stock Exchange in the form of American Depository Receipts (ADRs).

In opening up their markets to foreign investment, the five major Latin American countries have made great efforts to ensure that entry and exit is relatively easy in both procedural and financial terms. Investment income (interest, dividends, and capital gains) is freely repatriable, though in some cases subject to withholding taxes. Chile has a five year "lock-in" period with respect to the original capital invested. A summary of the taxation for U.S. institutional investors is provided in Table 20.4.

The essential source book for accurate and reliable basic information on emerging markets, including Latin America, is the *Emerging Stock Markets Fact Book,* which is published annually by the International Finance Corporation (IFC). In addition, IFC has an extensive database that is used by major institutional investors. Other emerging markets database sources include Morgan Stanley Capital International (MSCI) and Center for International Financial Analysis and Reporting (CIFAR). A number of major international brokerage firms as well as local brokerage firms now provide excellent research on Latin American companies. Of course, there are various magazines and newspapers such as the *Economist, Latin Finance,* the *Financial Times,* and the *Wall Street Journal* that provide good topical coverage of Latin America. Information in quality, quantity, and form is expanding and improving rapidly.

Investing in Latin America is not a "sure bet." The risks of investing in Latin America are the usual risks associated with emerging market

Table 20.4.   Withholding Tax for U.S.-Based Institutional Investors, as of Year-End 1990

Country	Interest	Dividends	Long-Term Capital Gains on Listed Shares
Argentina[a]	16.8%	17.5%	36.0%
Brazil[b]	25.0	25.0	25.0
Chile[b]	10.0	10.0	10.0
Mexico	15.0	0.0	0.0
Venezuela[c]	20.0	20.0	0.0

a. Capital gains tax applies to gains above inflation.

b. No dividend withholding tax if reinvested.

c. No withholding taxes apply to shares of publicly controlled companies (SAICA).

Source: *IFC Emerging Stock Markets Factbook 1990.*

investments: political risk, in terms of government instability; attitudes toward foreign investments (turning from negative to cautious); economic risks, particularly inflation; government intervention, particularly in pricing and operations of enterprises; financial risks, in terms of volatility and thinness of markets; and currency risks, in terms of devaluation versus major currencies as well as in limited availability of foreign exchange, which could result in exit restrictions. However, the clear trend in Latin America today is a rapid reduction of these risks, both in relative and absolute terms.

If the decade of the eighties was Latin America's "lost decade," the decade of the nineties is likely to be Latin America's "take-off" decade. For the informed investor, Latin America is an opportunity well worth considering.

GUIDE TO MAJOR WORLD SECURITIES EXCHANGES

21

Guide to Major World Securities Exchanges

Gideon Pell, Editor
KPMG Peat Marwick
New York
(In collaboration with the
International Staff of KPMG)

Introduction*

Dramatic changes have occurred in recent years in the structure and operations of the international capital markets, and further developments in this sphere are continuing apace. Increasing competition for business between the major financial centers, together with the approach of a European Single Market in 1992, are forcing stock exchanges to improve the environment for securities trading and enhance their attractiveness to corporations and investors alike. Current trends include:

- Integration of regional exchanges into a national exchange.
- Gradual replacement of trading on the exchange floor with a continuous electronic market and screen-based system.
- Introduction of computerized price information systems to enhance transparency of the market.
- Development of markets in derivative instruments, particularly options, futures, warrants and convertible bonds, which are increasingly used by investors for hedging and speculative purposes.

*The information contained in this chapter has been compiled with the assistance of the KPMG offices and partners in the respective locations worldwide. Certain data were obtained from the local stock exchanges, whose assistance we acknowledge and greatly appreciate. The chapter has been compiled based on data available as of April 1991 and has not been updated for developments since that date.

• Harmonization of national regulations dealing with admission and listing procedures, takeover bids, and investor protection.

With the spread of technology and the increasing sophistication of clearance and settlement systems, the continuing reforms of the stock markets are aimed at attracting additional business from domestic and international investors, drawn by the more secure and direct form of access to securities trading. Greater harmonization and integration of regulation and settlement practices between national stock exchanges is also contemplated, leading to the development of a European cross-border share-trading system.

This chapter provides an overview of the organization and trading features of the stock exchanges in eleven of the major financial centers around the world. The dynamism of the changes taking place in each of these markets will soon render some information out of date; we have therefore indicated wherever possible the direction in which the exchanges are currently believed to be headed in terms of further development of existing trading structures or practices.

AUSTRALIA (ASX)

General Background

The Australian Stock Exchange (ASX) was formed in April 1987 through the amalgamation of the six former state stock exchanges and aims to provide the most internationally competitive market for the fair trading of Australian financial securities and derivatives for the benefit of all market participants. The ASX equities market operates entirely through a national computerized order display and execution system known as SEATS (Stock Exchange Automated Trading System). The ASX also comprises the Australian Options Market (which is the eighth largest options market in the world) and a small equity futures market.

In contrast with many overseas exchanges that provide "quote-driven" markets where market makers stand continuously in the market quoting buy and sell prices, the ASX equities market is an "order-driven," or auction, system where buy and sell orders are directly displayed to the market and a trade results when there is a match.

Main Board Market:
The Australian Stock Exchange Limited (ASX)
Location: Secretariat's Office
              Level 9
              Plaza Building
              Australia Square
              Sydney, NSW 2000 Australia
              Telephone: (02) 227–0000
              Facsimile: (02) 235–0056

Trading hours:	10:00–16:00 (Sydney is ten hours ahead of Greenwich Mean Time)	

Number of
listed companies:
(December 31, 1990)

Main Board

Domestic companies	1,089
Overseas-based companies	33
	1, 122

Second Board: 238 companies (with a market capitalization of A $0.4 billion)

Market capitalization:
(December 31, 1990)

Ordinary Shares

Domestic companies	A $136.1 billion
Overseas based companies	56.9 billion

Securities convertible to ordinary shares

Convertible Notes	A $ 2.2 billion
Warrants	0.4 billion

Total value of listed equities   **A $195.6 billion**

Share turnover:
(year ended
December 31, 1990)

Ordinary shares

Mining (8.6 billion shares)	A $ 11.4 billion
Oil (2.2 billion shares)	3.9 billion
Industrial (22.9 billion shares)	36.1 billion

Total Main Board   **A $51.4 billion**

Market index: All Ordinaries Share Price Index

Regulatory Framework:

On January 1, 1991 the Australian Securities Commission was formed to provide a uniform national regulatory organization for corporations and securities in Australia. Corporation and securities law is now standardized across all Australian states. The statutory provisions that govern the securities industry are defined in the Corporations Law.

The ASX enforces its own listing rules and trading regulations, which are designed to provide a fair, orderly, and informed marketplace and to ensure adequate protection is afforded for investors.

Market Trading Information

Main Types of Securities Traded

The following types of securities are traded on the ASX: common and preferred stocks, rights, warrants, options on equities, convertible notes, fixed interest securities, and Treasury bonds.

Types of Markets

Main Board Market.   The Main Board Market is the principal market in Australian- and overseas-based equities. Since September 1990 *all* listed securities are traded using SEATS. The minimum number of shareholders required for listing on the Main Board is 300 persons (and $A300,000 paid-in capital).

Second Board Markets.   Second Board Markets were established to provide a market for smaller industrial companies that would not otherwise be eligible for admission to the official lists of the ASX. The key features of the Second Board Markets are as follows:

- The minimum number of shareholders required for listing is reduced from 300 persons (and $A300,000 paid-up capital) on the Main Board to 100 persons (and $A200,000 paid-up capital) on Second Board Markets.
- Different classes of shares are permitted with differential voting rights.
- Listing fees are approximately half those of the Main Board.
- Restrictions may be imposed on the payment of cash as vendor consideration and on the sale, assignment, or transfer of shares issues as vendor consideration.

Australian Options Market (AOM).   The basic function of the options market is to permit the transfer of risks and opportunities between investors through a secondary market in listed options contracts. The Australian Options Market is conducted by the ASX in Sydney. It primarily provides trading facilities in stock options for 26 leading securities. The stock options are cleared by Options Clearing House Pty. Ltd. (OCH), a wholly owned subsidiary of the ASX. For the year ended December 31, 1990, 7.8 million call contracts and 2.7 million put contracts were traded in various classes of stock options with an aggregate premium value of A$2.8 billion. Automation of the board broker's order book has followed the introduction of Options Automated Trading System (OATS). It may be that OATS will be further extended if such automation can be justified by market efficiency and user demand.

Australian Futures Market.   In September 1985 the ASX established a new futures market based in Melbourne, ASX Futures. The unique aspect of this market is that the futures contracts (Australian futures contracts [AFCs]) are based on the specific individual listed shares, and all contracts are settled in cash. The AFCs are based on 10,000 ordinary shares.

Sydney Futures Exchange (SFE)

Grosvenor Street
  Sydney, NSW 2000
  Australia
  Telephone: (02) 256–0555
  Facsimile: (02) 256–0666

Although established originally to provide a market in futures contracts for rural commodities (wool, cattle, etc.), the SFE in recent years has been dominated by futures and option trading in financial instruments, particularly 90-day bank-accepted bills, 3-year and 10-year Commonwealth Treasury bonds, All Ordinaries Share Price Index, Eurodollar interest rates, COMEX gold, and Australian dollars.

The Sydney Futures Exchange is the ninth largest in the world, based on the number of contracts traded. Membership is divided into (1) floor members that can deal for themselves or for clients, (2) local members that can deal for their own account or for floor members, but not on behalf of clients, and (3) associate members that must deal through a floor member but may be members of the clearing house. As of December 31, 1990, there were 29 floor members and approximately 350 local and associate members.

Market Trading Systems

Orders are placed through brokers in their capacity as agents for their clients. Prior to the inception of SEATS, brokers dealt directly with each other at trading posts on the floor of the exchange.

SEATS (Stock Exchange Automated Trading System) was introduced on October 19, 1987, and was tested on twenty typical stocks. Since September 1990 SEATS has been extended to allow all stocks to be traded through computer screens in the broker's office rather than on the trading floor. SEATS is a fully automated, on-line, real-time, order-driven execution system that does not require the intervention of a specialist or market maker. Brokers enter client order details, prices, and volumes onto screens in each office, and overlapping bids and offers are automatically executed. The status of unfilled orders can be monitored and execution is effected by means of an "electronic handshake"; no voice or other communication is required between traders. Contract notes are issued to clients immediately following execution.

"Core Computing Systems" have been introduced involving a major refurbishment of both computer hardware, to achieve uniformity, and software systems, to allow development of new applications with maximum efficiency. This system replaces the previous BSS (Broker-to-Broker System).

SFE. In November 1989, the SFE introduced the Sydney Computerized Overnight Market (Sycom), an automated trading system that allows after-hours access to SFE contracts by London and European traders. Sycom is available to all floor members via personal computer or dial-up telephone line. Local members may use Sycom for their own trading, using the trading screen of their nominating floor member. Contracts traded on Sycom since its inception include the 3-year and 10-year Treasury bonds, 90-day bank-accepted bills, and Share Price Index. As of October 1990, Sycom trading represented 2.3 percent of all floor trading. Plans to extend Sycom to all futures and options contracts are currently being developed.

Contracts traded under link with overseas exchanges include COMEX gold contract specifications, traded under link with the Commodity Exchange, Inc. (COMEX) in New York; and U.S. Treasury bond futures contracts and three-month Eurodollar interest rate futures, traded under link with the London International Financial Futures Exchange (LIFFE).

Clearance and Settlement Procedures

In practice, there is no fixed settlement period, although settlement of larger transactions in major stocks usually occurs within five days. Transactions are settled with cash against physical delivery.

ASX's most pressing priority is the continued reform of Australia's securities delivery, settlement, and registration system. FAST (Flexible Accelerated Security Transfer System), introduced in July 1989, allows the rapid settlement of trades by enabling securities to be held in uncertificated form, thereby reducing the costs of administration and funding for market participants. By June 30, 1990, FAST was being used for securities of 26 companies, with significant support from the participants. The current objective is to extend FAST to the top 100 listed companies and to achieve settlement of five business days after the trade date. CHESS (Clearing House Electronic Sub-register System), an extension of FAST still under development, will involve the electronic linking of records of uncertificated holdings and transfers to registries. This will expedite the transmission of uncertified holdings data and the reconciliation with total issued capital of the companies involved. An infrastructure will be established to enable settlement of trades to occur within three days of the trade date. It is anticipated to be in operation by the end of 1992.

There are buying-in procedures to provide monetary penalties to selling brokers who fail to deliver sold securities within a specified period. Securities may be borrowed from other brokers to effect delivery. Securities are predominantly registered in the client's name. Most brokers and banks provide nominee facilities enabling securities to be held and settled on behalf of clients. Safe custody of client securities is normally provided by brokers or banks. There is no central safe custody depository.

The clearing function for the Sydney Futures Exchange is performed by the International Commodities Clearing House Limited (ICCH), a branch of the London company of the same name, which is wholly owned by a consortium of six London clearing banks. The exceptions are gold futures contracts, which are cleared in New York by the COMEX Clearing Association, and U.S. Treasury bond and Eurodollar interest rate contracts, which are cleared by ICCH in London. All floor members of the SFE must also be members of the ICCH. The SFE is in the process of establishing its own mechanism for the clearing of member trades. This will be done through a new company, Sydney Futures Exchange Clearing House, which is planned to be operational by December 1991.

Procedures for Market Price Publication

A wide range of computer-based market information services that carry price and trading data derived from SEATS activity are provided by the ASX. The ASX Data Service (ADS) is a series of electronic data transmissions provided by ASX to meet the needs of the investing public. The ADS contains a variety of "signals" that are made available to various sectors of the marketplace to satisfy the wide-ranging requirements of brokers, merchant bankers, institutions, third party data vendors, and others. These signals contain real-time data transmissions, providing instant trading information from SEATS; course-of-sales data; and an end of day "snapshot" for those parties requiring the closing picture of the stock market rather than real-time data. The signals extend to overnight trading summary and official market close statistics, including all securities data and diary adjustments. A new information service called Beacon is expected to be introduced to replace the aging Jecnet system. Beacon is being developed and marketed by Citibank and the Australian Broadcasting Corporation.

Taxes, Commissions, and Other Trading Costs

Taxes

Domestic Investors: Capital gains tax applies to profits arising on disposal of securities. If the securities have been held for more than 12 months the original cost is inflation-adjusted for capital gains tax purposes. Dividends received by individuals are subject to dividend imputation credits that effectively pass on to shareholders the benefit of tax paid by the company.

Foreign Investors: Capital gains tax is applicable only if more than 10 percent of the issued capital of a publicly listed company is held by the investor. Dividends paid to nonresidents are subject to withholding tax except where the dividend has been paid out of income that has borne company tax under the imputation system. Withholding tax rates are subject to the provisions of any double tax treaty in existence between the countries involved.

Commissions

Trading commissions are freely negotiable between broker and client. Typical commission rates for institutional clients range between 0.25 percent and 0.75 percent of contract value. Minimum commissions are rarely imposed for such clients providing they generate reasonable levels of trading activity. For private investors, commissions typically range up to 2.5 percent of contract value with minimum commissions normally between A\$50 and A\$100 per contract note.

Procedures for Issuing and Listing New Securities

Conditions for admission to the official list for a domestic company include:

- All ordinary shares must have the same nominal value.
- Paid-up value of the shares must be at least A$300,000.
- At least 300 holders of marketable parcels of shares, and members of the public must hold at least 200,000 of the company's shares.
- The company must show operating profits from ordinary activities for the last three years of at least A$500,000 in aggregate.
- The company must have net tangible assets of at least A$5,000,000.

A foreign company must be able to present net tangible assets of at least A$500 million, and operating profits from ordinary activities in each of the last three years of at least A$100 million. The company must also be listed on a recognized stock exchange and agree to keep the market informed on circumstances that would be likely to materially affect the price of those securities so as to avoid the establishment of a false market in the company's securities.

Takeover and Merger Transactions

Takeovers are regulated by the Australian Securities Commission (formerly the National Companies and Securities Commission). There are two principal approaches to a public company takeover:

- A formal Part A offer for shares in a listed company. This is often conditional and may be for consideration of cash and/or shares. If 90 percent of the company's shares are acquired, the offeror may be able to proceed to compulsory acquisition of the remaining shares, subject to certain other conditions.
- An on-market Part C announcement must be unconditional and must be for cash.

Foreign Investors

Foreign brokers are generally encouraged, but are subject to ASX approval.
   Foreign companies may be listed on the exchange if the following conditions are met:

- Compliance with local listing requirements.
- Maintenance of an Australian share register.
- Distribution of 200,000 shares to 200 Australian residents.
- Full disclosure of all relevant information to the Australian market.

The Australian government places few restrictions on Australians who wish to purchase foreign securities. Foreign holdings of 15 percent or more in Australian listed stocks must be reported to the authorities.

Exchange Membership Requirements

Nonmembers are permitted to hold up to 100 percent of voting shares in a member corporation.

One quarter of the directors, or two of the directors, whichever is greater, of a member corporation must be members of the exchange. Also, the majority of the directors of a member firm must be Australian residents.

Member organizations may be partnerships provided three-fourths of the partners are members, or where there are three or fewer partners, at least two are members.

Costs of membership are currently $A25,000 for a natural person and $A250,000 for a member corporation.

Member firms must maintain minimum liquid capital equal to the greater of 5 percent of aggregate indebtedness or $A250,000 for corporations and $A50,000 for partnerships.

Annual audited financial statements must be filed by all firms, together with quarterly unaudited financial statements.

Futures brokers are required to segregate client funds into specially designated accounts and monitor client positions against margin requirements.

Investor Protection

The Australian Stock Exchange, in conjunction with the Australian Securities Commission, is committed to the maintenance of a fair and orderly market in the trading of Australian securities.

Australian quoted companies are required to lodge audited accounts annually and to provide unaudited semiannual reports. They must also disclose to the ASX all information that would have a material impact on the price of the company's securities or would, if not disclosed, create a false market in those securities.

The ASX maintains a separate division responsible for market surveillance. Its role is to monitor market trading to detect possible instances of market manipulation, insider trading, or similar practices. The ASX has developed specialized computer systems to detect unusual movements in prices and volumes.

The National Securities Exchange Guarantee Corporation Limited (NSEGC) has been established to complete unsettled transactions in the event of a failure of a broker intermediary. Surplus funds accumulated by the NSEGC are reinvested into the development of the industry generally, particularly for the improvement in the speed and efficiency of trading and settlement of securities dealings.

Trading on insider information (information not available to the public) is prohibited by securities legislation.

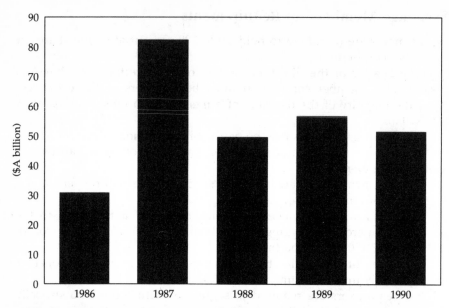

Figure 21.1.   Shares Turnover—Australian Stock Exchange (1986–1990) ($A billion)

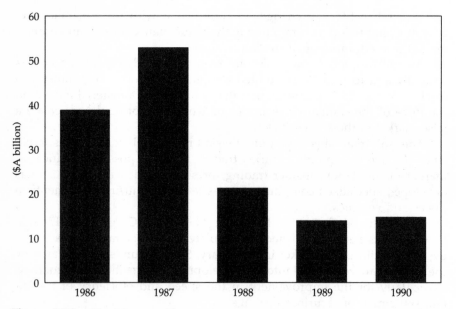

Figure 21.2.   Fixed-Income Turnover—Australian Stock Exchange (1986–1990) ($A billion)

CANADA

General Background

Canada has five stock exchanges and a futures exchange. The principal exchange is the Toronto Stock Exchange.

Toronto Stock Exchange (TSE)
The Exchange Tower
2 First Canada Place
Toronto, Ontario
M5X 1J2
Telephone: (416) 947–4700
Telefax: (416) 947–4466

Toronto Futures Exchange (TFE)
The Exchange Tower
2 First Canadian Place
Toronto, Ontario
M5X 1J2
Telephone: (416) 947–4700
Telefax: (416) 947–4466

Alberta Stock Exchange
300 5th Avenue South West
3rd Floor
Calgary, Alberta
T2P 3C4
Telephone: (403) 262–7791
Telefax: (403) 237–0450

Vancouver Stock Exchange
609 Granville Street
P.O. Box 10333
Vancouver, British Columbia
V7Y 1H1
Telephone: (604) 689–3334
Telefax: (604) 688–5041

Montreal Exchange
800 Victoria Square
Montreal, Quebec
H4Z 1A9
Telephone: (514) 871–2424
Telefax: (514) 871–3533

Winnipeg Stock Exchange
955-167 Lombard Avenue
Winnipeg, Manitoba
R3B 0V3
Telephone: (204) 942–8431
Telefax: (204) 947–9536

The Toronto Stock Exchange (As of December 1990)

Trading hours:	9:30–16:00 (Toronto is five hours behind Greenwich Mean Time)
Number of listed securities:	1,593 (representing 1,193 companies)
Market capitalization:	C$703 billion, of which C$281 billion is of Canadian-based companies
Average daily share turnover:	C$260 million (1990)
Market index:	TSE 300 Composite Index

Regulatory framework:

The securities industry in Canada is regulated in each province by a securities commission. Many of the responsibilities of the securities commissions are carried out through five self-regulatory organizations: The Toronto, Montreal, Vancouver, and Alberta Stock Exchanges, and the Investment Dealers Association of Canada.

In Ontario, the Ontario Securities Commission administers the Ontario Securities Act and Regulation and oversees the Toronto Stock Exchange.

The TSE regulates compliance of its members with capital requirements and trading rules.

Market Trading Information

Main Types of Securities Traded

Securities traded on the TSE include: common and preferred shares, rights and warrants, options, Toronto 35 Index Options, and Toronto 35 Index Participation units (TIPS).

Common and preferred shares, rights, warrants, and options are also traded on the Montreal and Vancouver exchanges. Financial and commodity futures are traded on the Montreal Exchange and certain IOCC options are traded in Vancouver.

The Toronto 35 Index was developed by the Toronto Stock Exchange (TSE) in 1987 for the purpose of trading derivative products specifically designed to meet the trading and hedging needs of investors and fund managers. This index is composed of 35 Canadian stocks chosen for the liquidity, size of publicly held float, and option eligibility. The value of the Index is updated every 15 seconds.

TIPS were first distributed in 1989 as an affordable way for small investors to diversify their portfolios without incurring portfolio management fees. Each TIPS unit represents an interest in a trust that holds a basket of the stocks in the Toronto 35 Index.

TSE membership is held by 73 firms, which may act in either in-agency or principal capacity, or both.

Other Markets

Futures.   The Toronto Futures Exchange (TFE) shares a trading floor with the Toronto Stock Exchange. TFE seats are held by approximately 200 members, including dealers from all over the world, banks, and other financial institutions. There are no citizenship or residency requirements for membership. Commodities traded include Toronto 35 Index Futures (TSF), Toronto 35 Index Options (TXO), TSE 300 Spot Index Futures (TSE), Government of Canada Bond Options, and silver options.

Over-the-Counter.   The COATS (Canadian Over-the-Counter Automated Trading System) is an electronic quotation and regulated trade reporting system for unlisted securities trading in Ontario. The COATS computer system is provided by the TSE. The Ontario Securities Commission is responsible for COATS operation and regulation.

Exchange Links.   To establish cross-border trading, the TSE has established two-way electronic links with the American Stock Exchange (AMEX) in New York and the Midwest Stock Exchange (MSE) in Chicago. These links apply at present to a limited number of interlisted Canadian and U.S. issues, but are expected to eventually cover many other stocks listed on the three exchanges. The system is also supported by automated links between the Canadian Depository for Securities and the respective clearing corporations in New York and Chicago. Canadian and U.S. currency conversions are handled by a TSE-developed automatic foreign exchange facility. It allows Canadian and U.S. investors to settle completed trades in the currency of their choice.

Market Trading Systems

Orders to buy or sell shares are handled either by a trader on the exchange floor or by the Computer-Assisted Trading System and a trader. Orders are sent back from the brokerage office to the firm's telephone clerk stationed on the exchange floor. On the floor, the clerk passes the order to the firm's floor trader, who takes it to the area where the stock is traded. The buying trader shouts out the order to attract the attention of a trader wanting to sell the same stock. The trade is completed when the buying and selling traders meet and establish a price for the order. The trade information is entered into the exchange's computer.

The trading floor has two automated trading systems that deliver orders to the floor and assist traders in maintaining an efficient marketplace, the Limited Order Trading System (LOTS) and the Market Order System of Trading (MOST). The MOST system routes small market orders directly from the member's office to the post where the stock is traded. These trades are guaranteed by the market-maker who is responsible for the stock. Most active issues have a guarantee of 1,099 shares. The LOTS trading system files limit orders that come to the floor until market prices move to the specified price so that the order can be filled. LOTS ensures that members' orders are either displayed, if on the market, or traded, if the market moves.

Clearance and Settlement Procedures

Government of Canada Treasury bills	Same clearing day as the transaction date
Other Government of Canada issues and guarantees maturing in less than one year	Second clearing day following the transaction date
Government of Canada issues and guarantees with terms of one to three years	Second clearing day following the transaction date
Other securities	Fifth clearing day following the transaction date

Securities may be borrowed from other brokers or from the clearing house to effect delivery. A broker may initiate a "buy-in" for failed trades. Transactions may settle directly between members; however most settlements in equities are effected through Canadian Depository for Securities Ltd. (CDS). Options settle through Trans Canada Options Inc. (TCO), as do TFE contracts. Members of the TFE are required to make a daily net settlement of the required margin and deposits.

CDS has two daily cycles for settlement. Delivery through CDS may be physical delivery of net position or through the book-based system.

Physical certificates may be registered in the name of clients and delivered to them or held by the broker in safekeeping. Alternatively, fully paid securities may be held by brokers in "street name" (registered in the name of the broker). These securities must be segregated.

Procedures for Market Price Publication

Bid, ask, last-trade prices, and trade-by-trade statistics for listed securities are maintained by the Toronto and other stock exchanges. Price and volume data for over-the-counter securities is maintained through the COATS system.

This information for both listed and unlisted securities is immediately available to the public through on-line computer services provided by companies such as Reuters, Dataline, and Canadian Market Quotes (CMQ). The stock exchanges publish daily quote sheets with volumes and closing prices.

Major newspapers and financial newspapers electronically obtain price and value information for listed and unlisted securities, including bonds, and print it daily.

Taxes, Commissions, and Other Trading Costs

Income Taxes

Canadian resident corporations are taxed on their world income from all sources, computed in accordance with Canadian tax law. Only 75 percent of capital gains are subject to tax with 75 percent of any capital losses being deductible, but only against capital gains. Further, individuals may qualify for a C$100,000 lifetime capital gains deduction (C$500,000 for "small business shares"). In general, gains or losses on securities purchased for the purpose of resale or by a trader/dealer in securities are considered income in nature (i.e., fully taxable), whereas securities held as long-term investments to generate interest and dividend income may be considered capital in nature (i.e., 75 percent taxable). Interest income and business income are subject to tax at the individual's or corporation's marginal rate of tax. Dividends received by individuals from Canadian securities are subject to tax at a preferential tax rate. Canadian dividends (and certain foreign affiliate dividends) received by Canadian corporations are received tax-free but may be subject to a special tax that is 25 percent refundable when distributed out to shareholders.

Nonresident corporations and individuals are taxed on their income from conducting business in Canada and are subject to a nonresident withholding tax of 25 percent on any dividends, rents, royalties, or interest paid to them. There are a number of exemptions or reductions in withholding tax, particularly under Canada's various tax treaties.

Brokers' Commissions

Bond trades generally are principal transactions in which dealers earn a spread. Other transactions are subject to negotiated commission rates. Full-service brokers usually charge full standard commission for small retail trades and will negotiate on larger trades. Discount brokers charge lower commissions but provide no research or investment advice. Institutions usually pay the lowest commission, quoted in cents per share. Two to five cents per share is typical for institutional orders.

There are generally no other trading costs incurred by customers, other than for additional services such as custodial or portfolio management services.

Procedures for Issuing and Listing New Securities

An offering of securities to the public generally requires the issuer to file a prospectus with the securities commission of each Canadian province in which the securities are to be offered. There are exemptions for large transactions with a limited number of purchasers or with "sophisticated" purchasers.

The prospectus will contain extensive disclosure about the issuer, its business, the offering, and financial matters in accordance with regulations of the securities commissions. A preliminary prospectus must be filed and pre-cleared by the securities commissions before a final prospectus is filed.

Companies intending to list on a stock exchange must complete the appropriate listing application and provide any additional information deemed necessary by the exchange. For example, the Toronto Stock Exchange (TSE) requires net tangible assets of at least C$1,000,000, adequate working capital and capitalization to carry on the business, and a reasonable likelihood of future profitability. The exchange also considers the management of a company and the sponsorship of the listing application by an existing member to be important factors in determining whether to approve the application. Minimum requirements are also imposed with respect to the market value of outstanding shares, the number of shares outstanding, and the number of shareholders. Generally, the Exchange requires four to eight weeks to review and approve a listing application. Fees for an approved original listing on the TSE are C$4,000 to C$50,000 with annual fees of C$2,500 to C$11,500.

Takeover and Merger Transactions

The securities commissions have complex rules and policies in place applicable to acquisitions of 20 percent or more of any class of the securities of an issuer (10 percent in the case of corporations incorporated under the Canada Business Corporation Act). The rules do not apply to bids made through the stock exchanges, which govern such transactions.

Generally, the offeror must make a press release of his intentions, and an offering circular must be prepared and filed with the securities commission(s) setting out details of the offer and all information available to the offeror concerning the offeree. The offeree must also issue a press release and a directors' circular must be sent to shareholders.

Purchases by the offeror of securities subject to a takeover bid may not exceed 5 percent.

Foreign Ownership

Foreign acquisition of Canadian businesses may be subject to review and approval by Investment Canada (a federal government department) or may simply require notification to be filed.

The following investments by non-Canadians are reviewable under the *Investment Canada Act:*

- direct acquisition of control of a Canadian business with assets of C$5 million or more through acquisition of voting shares, voting interests (in the case of partnerships, trusts, or joint ventures), or of all or substantially all of the assets of the business.
- indirect acquisition of control of a Canadian business with assets of C$50 million or more (an indirect acquisition occurs where control of the Canadian business results from the acquisition of control of its foreign parent).
- indirect acquisition of control of a Canadian business with assets between C$5 million and C$50 million if the value of the assets of the Canadian business amounts to more than 50 percent of the value of the total international transaction.
- acquisition of control of a business below the asset thresholds set out above and establishment of a new business (regardless of size) in culturally sensitive industries if the federal Cabinet decides a review is required in the public interest.

Under the Canada-U.S. Free Trade Agreement, Canada has agreed to phase in new rules governing the acquisition of control of a Canadian business by an American. For a **direct acquisition** of control of a Canadian business, the threshold for review is C$100 million in 1991 and

C$150 million in 1992. For an *indirect acquisition* of control of a Canadian business by an American, where the Canadian business assets are less than half of the total assets acquired in the international transaction, the limit is C$500 million for 1991 with no review required in 1992 and thereafter.

Exemption from the *Investment Canada Act* applies to transactions involving securities dealers, venture capitalists, realization of security granted for a loan, financing, corporate reorganizations, Canadian government businesses, banks (see the following), involuntary acquisitions, and insurance company portfolios.

Specific Industries

Foreign banks may operate subsidiaries in Canada (called Schedule II banks); however no person may hold more than 10 percent of any class of shares of Schedule I banks (Canadian-owned banks). The aggregate foreign ownership of Schedule I banks may not exceed 25 percent.

In addition, there are restrictions on the degree of foreign ownership in several other industries, including broadcasting, life insurance, loan and trust businesses, commercial fishing, mining, oil and gas, and uranium.

Exchange Membership Requirements

In order to trade on any one of the Canadian stock exchanges, a broker must own a seat on that exchange.

As of February 1991, a TSE seat costs approximately C$200,000.

Requirements to Become a TSE Member

In order to be accepted as a TSE member, the applicant must:

- Be principally engaged in the securities business.
- Not be a partner or shareholder in another securities firm.
- Have 40 percent of the partners or directors approved by the TSE, each of which should have the following qualifications:
  - Be actively involved in the member's business.
  - Five years securities business experience.
  - Complete certain courses required by TSE.
- Have other directors accepted by the exchange.

Foreign Ownership Restrictions

Memberships may be foreign-owned except for restrictions on ownership, by foreign-owned federally regulated financial institutions, including banks; loan, trust, and insurance companies; and cooperative credit associations.

Continuing Requirements

Exchange members must maintain several types of insurance, including fidelity bonds, mail insurance, and a financial institution bond covering trading losses, securities, forgery, alterations, and the like. Members must pay premiums based on their capital to the Canadian Investor Protection Fund.

Minimum capital requirements start at C$250,000, depending upon the size of firm and type and volume of activity. Net free capital must be maintained at all times and is reported to the stock exchanges in a two-page Monthly Financial Report. Other periodic reporting includes:

- Annual audited financial statements.
- Annual audited Joint Regulatory Financial Questionnaire and Report (JRFQR).
- Interim unaudited JRFQR.

An annual audited statement of financial condition must be made available to customers upon request.

Investor Protection

The securities commissions, stock exchanges, and the Investment Dealers Association of Canada (IDA) set numerous standards to promote fair trading practices and protection of investors. Compliance with these is checked by compliance audits performed by staff of the exchanges or IDA as well as the audit of capital requirements.

Insider Trading

Local and federal regulations require insiders of a public company or issuer to file reports of their holdings of securities in the company. Trading on insider information (information not available to the public) is prohibited.

Canadian Investor Protection Fund

The CIPF is funded by assessments to members of the stock exchanges and the IDA. It provides investor protection to all customers in the event of insolvency of a member, other than those not dealing at arm's length with the insolvent member. Coverage is limited to C$250,000 per investor, including cash balances up to C$60,000.

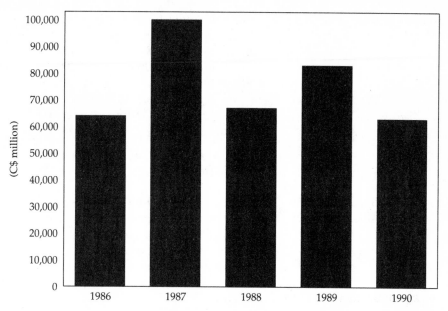

Figure 21.3. Shares Turnover—Toronto Stock Exchange (1986–1990) (C$ million)

FRANCE

General Background

The French bourses are located in Paris, Bordeaux, Lille, Lyon, Marseilles, Nancy, and Nantes. Effective the beginning of February 1991, the six regional bourses were merged with the Paris Bourse to form the national bourse. All securities are now quoted on the on-line computer system, Cotation Assistée en Continu (CAC), to which all seven bourses have direct access. Each of the seven bourses can trade in all securities quoted by CAC regardless of the bourse of the original listing. The following commentary will concentrate on the Paris Bourse, being the largest and most important.

In addition to the stock exchange there are two other separate markets in France, the Marché des Options Négociables de Paris (MONEP), the French options market; and the Marché à Terme d'Instruments Financiers (MATIF), the French financial futures market.

Bourse de Paris—Paris Bourse
Location: Palais de la Bourse
75002 Paris
France
Telephone: (1) 40–41–10–00
Facsimile: (1) 40–26–31–40

Trading hours:	Private bonds: 10:00–17:00
	Public bonds: 10:00–16:00
	Equities and bonds traded on the continuous market: 10:00–17:00
	Securities traded on the over-the-counter-market: 12:30–14:30
	Stock options (MONEP): 10:00–17:00
	Financial futures (MATIF): 10:00–16:00
	(Paris is one hour ahead of Greenwich Mean Time)

Number of listed securities: (as of December 31, 1990)	Stocks: 1,133 (of which 268 are foreign companies)
	Bonds: 2,828 (of which 214 are foreign bond issues)
	Options: 27 classes

Market capitalization (1990):	Shares: FF 1,467 billion
	Bonds: FF 2,467 billion

Average daily turnover (1990):	Shares: FF 1.05 billion
	Bonds: FF 11.90 billion

Market indices:	Indice Générale CAC Actions Françaises
	CAC–40 (Top 40 shares)

Regulatory authorities:

The Conseil des Bourses de Valeurs (COB) [French Stock Exchange Council] is the market's supervisory and regulatory authority. The Conseil des Bourses de Valeurs, defines the rules governing market operations. These rules, collectively known as the Règlement Général du Conseil des Bourses de Valeurs, set forth terms and conditions for the creation of new brokerage houses, security listings, removals from listing and suspension, and takeover bids; and establishes a professional code of conduct for bourse members, their subsidiaries, directors, and employees.

The Société des Bourses Françaises (SBF) implements decisions taken by the Conseil des Bourses de Valeurs; handles day-to-day administration, security, development, and promotion; and provides investors and the general public with comprehensive information on market activities. In addition, it monitors and supervises the market and bourse member firms, is authorized to temporarily suspend trading in any stock, and is in charge of procedures for takeover bids. It also acts as the clearing house for transactions between *sociétés de bourse* (licensed stockbrokerage firms), guaranteeing settlement and delivery of securities and cash.

The COB is the market watchdog and holds the status of an autonomous administrative body, patterned on the U.S. Securities and Exchange Commission. The COB's main functions are:

- Verifying information published by companies (on stock or bond issues, offers to the public, takeovers, and in quarterly, semiannual, and annual publications).
- Authorizing the creation of mutual funds (SICAVs and FCPs).
- Monitoring of financial markets (equities and bonds, MONEP-traded options, and MATIF financial futures and commodities).
- Supervising transactions for infringement of French law, which prohibits insider dealings and price manipulation.
- Investigating complaints filed by the public.
- Using its right of veto over listing or removal of a company ordered by the Conseil des Bourses de Valeurs if it feels that it is necessary to protect investors.

The SCMC is a 100 percent subsidiary of the SBF and operates on behalf of the SBF in relation to operations on the MONEP. Its primary responsibilities in this regard are to manage and promote MONEP; to act as a clearing house for all transactions in traded options, guaranteeing settlement between clearing members; and to monitor operations and participants on the market.

The Conseil du Marché à Terme is the regulatory body for the MATIF, the French financial futures and commodities market. It investigates and approves new products to be traded on the market and monitors operations and participants on the market.

Market Trading Information

Main Types of Securities Traded

The main types of securities traded on the Paris Bourse are common and preferred stocks, bonds, and warrants.

Options are traded on the Marché des Options Négociables de Paris (MONEP), the stock options market, which is part of the Paris Bourse and is placed under its regulatory body, the Conseil des Bourses de Valeurs. Options are American-style; thus they can be exercised at any time before maturity and are based either on stocks or on the CAC-40 index.

Financial futures and commodities are traded on the Marché à Terme d'Instruments Financiers (MATIF). Trading is located in the Palais de la Bourse, but the MATIF is an independent market and is regulated by the Conseil du Marché à Terme International de France. The main financial futures contracts traded on the MATIF are based on the three-month Paris

Interbank Offer Rate (PIBOR), the long-term notional bond, the CAC–40 Stock Index, the long-term ECU, and the three-month Euromark contract. The MATIF also offers contracts on white sugar, sugar options, potatoes, cocoa beans, and Robusta coffee.

Types of Markets

The Marché Officiel (Official Market) is the market for the largest French and foreign companies. To be listed on the Marché Officiel, at least 25 percent of the company's shares must be available for distribution to the public. The Marché Officiel is composed of the Marché au Comptant (Cash Market) and the Marché à Règlement Mensuel (Monthly Settlement Market).

On the Marché au Comptant, orders may be placed for any quantity of securities, starting with a single unit. This market requires immediate cash settlement and delivery of traded securities.

Securities are traded on the Marché à Règlement Mensuel, generally in round lots of 5, 10, 25, 50, and 100, as set by the Société des Bourses Françaises, depending on their unit price. While transactions are firm in both price and quantity, cash settlement and delivery of securities does not take place until the end of the account or the trading month. Investors must pay an initial margin call representing a percentage of the total amount of their order. The percentages required are 20 percent in liquid assets, 25 percent in French Treasury notes or bills, or 40 percent in other securities. Investors may request immediate settlement on condition that they have available the corresponding cash (for a purchase) or securities (for a sale). Trading in odd lots must be settled immediately.

The Second Marché (Second Market) was established for medium-sized companies with at least 10 percent of their capital available for distribution to the public. Trading requires immediate cash settlement and delivery.

All other companies not listed on the Marché Officiel or on the Second Marché are traded, without formalities or conditions, on the Marché Hors-cote (Over-the-Counter Market). In practice most stocks on the Marché Hors-cote represent small companies with low share turnover. Any quantity of stocks may be negotiated for immediate settlement and delivery and all transactions are in cash.

The MONEP is the stock options market where, as of December 1990, options were being traded on 27 French securities. Trading requires immediate cash settlement.

The MATIF (Financial Futures Market) operates a market-maker system providing for the leading market makers to continuously display their prices.

There are no special rules governing the private placement of foreign currency denominated bonds and stocks for residents of the European Community. For residents outside the European Community, permission must be obtained from the Conseil des Bourses de Valeurs and from the

French Minister of Finance. Permission will more likely be given if the security is quoted on the exchange in the country of origin.

Market Trading Systems

Stock Exchange. Trading takes place on a centralized order-driven market through member firms acting as brokers. With the exception of the limited number of securities still traded on the floor by open outcry (including certain state bonds), transactions are handled by CAC, an electronic trading system, via terminals installed by brokerage firms and linked to the central computers of the Société des Bourses Françaises. CAC is derived from the CATS system used on the Toronto Stock Exchange, and is very similar to the CORES system used in Tokyo. *Sociétés de bourse,* acting on behalf of clients or for their own account, enter all orders into the CAC system. Orders are automatically ranked by price limit and within each limit are queued to reflect order of arrival.

This system has recently been enhanced by the introduction of a new component dubbed COCA. COCA is directly linked to member firms' order books and automatically sorts and feeds orders into the CAC computers. It issues to the sender a timestamped receipt for each order, indicating the exact time at which it was logged into the central computer, and sends confirmations back to member firms' order books as soon as trades are executed. It also sends updates on current market conditions to member firms. COCA allows all odd lot orders to be executed by member firms acting as principals at prices identical to those quoted simultaneously on the central market, where COCA then accumulates and clears those orders.

From 9:00 to 10:00 orders are fed into the centralized order book, without any transactions taking place. At 10:00, when the market opens, the central computer automatically calculates, depending on the limit orders received, the opening price at which the largest number of bids and asks can be matched. At the same time, the system transforms orders at market price into limit orders at the opening price. This results in all limit-buy orders at higher prices and all limit-sell orders at lower prices being executed in full. Limit orders at the opening price are executed to the extent that matches are available. For the rest of the day trading takes place on a continuous basis. The arrival of a new order immediately triggers one (or several) transactions if a matching order (or orders) exists on the centralized book. Assuming identical price limits, orders are executed as they arrive: first entered, first matched.

The Conseil des Bourses de Valeurs is responsible for ensuring price controls. On the Marché au Comptant, the Conseil des Bourses de Valeurs does not allow opening prices to differ from the previous day's closing prices by more than 2 percent to 3 percent for French bonds or by more than 4 percent to 5 percent for French equities. If market factors indicate that an opening price will exceed the limit, the Conseil will set a fixed price for that day, with a spread of about 2 percent for bonds and about 4 percent for shares. If less than 20 percent of the orders can be fulfilled at the set price, trading is suspended for the day. On the Marché à Règlement Mensuel, the opening price of securities may vary from the prior day's closing price by a maximum of 8 percent. If the price movement exceeds this limit, trading is stopped. Trading is then resumed later in the same session.

The prices of foreign securities are not controlled by the Conseil des Bourses de Valeurs, but are free to move in accordance with the prices of their home market. Data dissemination is part of the CAC network. Client subscribers to the network receive in real time the five latest transactions completed (price, number of shares traded, time), along with the five best bids and asks in price and quantity. This information is disseminated as it appears on traders' screens inside the sociétés de bourse. CAC also gives traders an in-depth display of data on a given security at any time.

MONEP. Stock and index options are currently traded on the floor of the Paris Bourse. Trading members (French brokerage firms, credit institutions, and insurance companies who are required to meet specific conditions for entry) have two means of access to the market. The first is through traditional phoning or routing to their representatives on the floor, where the orders can be executed in open outcry trading. The second, for retail orders from clients, is through terminal screens in their own trading rooms. In this case, orders are keyed into the central system of the public order book and the data is displayed and disseminated to users. Such orders are either matched automatically inside the book, if those correspond to the market's best prices, or are routed to SCMC officials for priority execution on the floor, if better prices are available there. The MONEP automated trading system, with the automated public order book, is dubbed STAMP, for Système de Transactions Automatisées du MONEP.

Trading members can act as brokers or market makers. As brokers they trade orders received from clients or issued for brokerage houses' own accounts. These orders are executed among brokers, with order book officials at SCMC, or with market makers. As market makers, members help to ensure that the market runs smoothly and is sufficiently liquid. Market makers must be able to provide a spread of buy/sell prices at any time for each series of classes attributed to them. Within this spread they must be able to execute a minimum number of contracts in accordance with clearly defined rules.

MATIF. The members on the futures market are split roughly equally between the sociétés de bourse, banks, and insurance companies. The banks and insurance companies must be credit institutions and must meet certain specific requirements with regards to share capital, etc.

In November 1989 the MATIF joined the GLOBEX system, set up by the Chicago Mercantile Exchange and Reuters. This system enables participants in the market to trade in futures outside normal trading hours with the aid of electronic information systems. At present only the long-term notional bond and the three-month PIBOR contracts are traded on GLOBEX, but the other products will follow in the near future. During 1991 a new system named CBOT will be implemented following its introduction to the United States marketplace.

Members of the market operating as *mainteneurs de marché* (market makers) must ensure that their dealers remain on the floor of the exchange throughout trading hours and that the market remains sufficiently liquid. They must be able to quote a spread of buy/sell prices for each contract attributed to them and have a minimum monthly activity. The only requirements for being a mainteneur de marché are to be a trading member, or a representative of one, and to agree to meet the stated conditions for trading. In this case a certificate will be issued by MATIF S.A., the market clearing house.

Ordering and Settlement Procedures

All orders into the market must be placed by a société de bourse. Orders must include specific information on the period of validity and the execution price.

Clients may specify a date beyond which unexecuted orders are no longer valid. When no limit is set, orders are deemed to be a *révocation* or *good till cancelled* (GTC). For securities traded on the Marché au Comptant, GTC orders remain valid until the last day of the current month. On the Marché à Règlement Mensuel, they are valid until the next settlement date.

Clients may specify if orders are limit orders or market orders. Limit orders specify either a maximum (in the case of a purchase) or a minimum (in the case of a sale) price. Market orders placed before the market opens are executed at the opening price. Orders placed during trading will be executed at the best price available at the time. Special instructions may also be given. For example, "all or none" orders must be executed fully or not at all.

A new clearing system was introduced during 1990 based on delivery five days after the initial transaction (or at the end of the month for securities traded on the Marché à Règlement Mensuel). This system encompasses new issues, secondary market trading, and all types of transactions, both on the market and over-the-counter.

On the last day of the current account, operators who have not closed their positions and cannot deliver securities sold or present payment for securities purchased may carry their positions over to the next account period through a special market organized once each month. This *contango market* determines the rate at which buyers can obtain the cash, and sellers can buy the securities, they need until the next settlement day.

Both shares (bearer and registered) and bonds exist only as book entries in a computerized system and are transferred between intermediaries' accounts. Each authorized intermediary (banks, sociétés de bourse, etc.) has an account with the central depository, Société Interprofessionnelle de Compensation des Valeurs Mobilières (SICOVAM).

Different clearing houses function with respect to the various market segments. For stocks, bonds, and warrants, the clearing house is the Société des Bourses Françaises, which has delegated the clearing of traded options to the Société de Compensation des Marchés Conditionnels (a specialized subsidiary charged with clearing, general administration, and market surveillance), but remains the financial guarantor of last resort. MATIF S.A. is the clearing house for the financial futures and commodities market.

Procedures for Market Price Publication

Various sources of market price information exist. Real-time information is provided by various companies through subscription or otherwise. These companies are directly linked to the CAC system. The Société des Bourses Françaises also publishes daily the data concerning the day's trading. Other sources of information include the daily press.

On-line systems provide the same information that is made available to the member firms. The daily press provides the opening and closing position and movement for the day, number of shares quoted, highest and lowest price both for the day and since issue, and net dividend. The closing position and movement for the day for the CAC–40 are also disclosed.

Both stocks and convertible bonds traded are priced in francs and centimes. With only a few exceptions, other bonds are quoted as a percentage of their nominal value, excluding accrued interest.

Taxes, Commissions, and Other Trading Costs

The *impôt de bourse* (stock exchange tax) is payable at 3 percent on the first FF 1 million of all sales and purchases of shares and bonds, and at 1.5 percent on the portion of all transactions over FF 1 million. There are certain exemptions from this tax.

On July 1, 1989 fixed commissions were abolished in France. Commissions are now freely negotiated between clients and the société de bourse, although most sociétés de bourse have standard commission rates.

The only transaction fee on shares (excluding commissions) is a stamp duty of 0.3 percent per transaction. Option trades are levied a fee of FF 12.50 per contract (payable to the clearing house) and a negotiable brokerage fee (payable to the intermediary handling the contract).

Futures trades attract a transaction fee of FF 8 per contract, payable to MATIF S.A. In addition, a deposit must be made at the beginning of each day, based on a percentage of the trader's closing position at the end of the previous day.

Capital gains tax is payable by French residents on profits made from transactions on the bourse.

Procedures for Issuing and Listing New Securities

The rules relating to the listing of securities on the French bourse can be summarized as follows.

- A company issuing and listing securities on the French bourse must agree to comply with certain regulations laid down by the Conseil des Bourses de Valeurs. The company must inform the conseil of any changes to its articles and memorandum of association, any events that could affect the price of its shares, and any items published by the company. If the shares are also quoted on a foreign stock exchange, then the company must provide information to the conseil in at least as much detail as that required by the local authorities.
- Applications for admission onto the bourse must be addressed to the Conseil des Bourses de Valeurs by the intermediary (normally a credit institution) charged by the company with overseeing the admission. The granting of an application lasts for three months, within which time the shares must be issued. The conseil decides upon the conditions for the quotation of new shares and how they can be traded. The granting of an application is published by the conseil, detailing the market on which the shares are to be quoted, the procedures for dealing, the date of the first quotation, and the method of introduction.
- The company must have published or filed its accounts for the three years (two years for the Second Marché) prior to the application, the last two years to be accompanied by an auditor's report. If the year-end was more than nine months prior to the application, a set of semi-annual audited accounts must be prepared. The financial statements must be translated into French, where applicable, and the translation reviewed by a firm of French auditors.
- For admission onto the Marché Officiel, a minimum of 25 percent of the share capital of the company must be on offer to the public by the day of the introduction of the shares onto the market. For the Second Marché the requirement is 10 percent.
- Three methods exist by which shares can be issued onto the market: the *procédure ordinaire* (ordinary procedure), the *procédure de mise en vente* (placement for sale), or the *procédure d'offre publique de vente* (public offer). The procédure ordinaire means that the shares are quoted and traded in the ordinary way for that market or that group of shares. For the procédure de mise en vente the number of shares available to the market and the minimum price is disclosed. The information is published at least one week before the date of the first quotation. For the procédure d'offre publique de vente the number of shares available to the market and a fixed price is disclosed. The information is published at least one week before the date of the first quotation. If the offer is declared successful, the price at which the shares are first quoted is the same as the offer price.

Takeover and Merger Transactions

The regulations of the Conseil des Bourses de Valeurs cover the public offer to purchase or exchange shares and the acquisition of a controlling interest.

The public offer has to be notified to the conseil, which will suspend trading in those shares and publish the fact in the official bulletin, the *Bulletin Officiel de la Côte*. The offerors must prepare a document, addressed to the conseil, disclosing the number of shares to which the offer relates, the price, and their intentions at the date of the offer. The conseil announces its decision within five days, giving the details of the offer, which has to stay open for at least 20 working days.

When a person acquires more than one-third of the voting rights or one-third of the shares of a company quoted on the Marché Officiel or the Second Marché they must inform the conseil and initiate a public offer to purchase. The public offer must enable this person to acquire two-thirds of the voting rights, including those already owned.

When persons contract to buy a block of shares of a company quoted on the Marché Officiel or the Second Marché, with the aim of obtaining majority control of the company, they must obtain permission from the Conseil des Bourses de Valeurs. The request must include, among other things, details of the names of the sellers, the date, the price, the consideration, and the number of shares concerned. The buyers must commit themselves to buying all the shares offered to them by the minority shareholders at the same price and with the same conditions as the contract giving them majority control. This offer must stay open for at least fifteen working days from the date of the announcement by the conseil.

All operations (purchases, sales, subscriptions, exercise of options, etc.) which result in a shareholder's stake moving above or below thresholds of 5 percent, 10 percent, 20 percent, 33.3 percent, and 50 percent of a French company's total equity must be declared to the company itself within two weeks. If the company is quoted on the Marché Officiel or the Second Marché the operation must be disclosed to the Société des Bourses Françaises within five days. The Société des Bourses Françaises will make the operation public in their daily official list.

Disclosure is obligatory, whether operations take place on or off the market. Off-market trading occurs when individuals (not firms) trade privately off the bourse without an intermediary.

Foreign Investors

Nonresidents are free to buy or sell French and foreign securities traded on French markets. Their operations must be financed either by the sale of foreign currency on the French currency market, in which case the French franc equivalent is credited to the foreign resident's account in francs, or by francs already credited to a foreign account.

Securities purchased by nonresidents are held in the buyer's name by the bourse member firm or another authorized institution. These shares or bonds may be transferred overseas at any time. French francs credited to an account of a foreign resident in France may be used to purchase other securities or financial instruments, cover expenses in France, or buy foreign currencies on the French market with a view to repatriation.

A non-European Community resident's stake in a company listed on the Marché Officiel or Second Marché may not exceed 20 percent without previous authorization from the Ministry of Economy and Finance. Residency is determined according to French law.

Nonresidents are not subject to capital gains tax.

Exchange Membership Requirements

Members of the bourse, sociétés de bourse, have to be authorized by the Conseil des Bourses de Valeurs. The number of Sociétés de Bourse is limited to 58, the number as of January 22, 1988. No new sociétés de bourse will be authorized before December 31, 1992. After that date access to the bourse will be open to other firms, provided the Conseils des Bourses de Valeurs agrees to increase the number of seats.

No fees are incurred in becoming a member of the bourse. However, a tax is levied on member firms based on annual profits. At present discussions are being held as to whether to charge fees to any new sociétés de bourse authorized for admission after December 31, 1992.

Member firms are empowered to act as principals and fill orders for blocks of shares at prices freely negotiated with their clients, whether or not such prices fall within the market spread. Trading of this type is subject to the following conditions:

- The shares involved must be among those approved for block trading by the Conseil des Bourses de Valeurs. Approval is conditional on high trading volumes. Such stocks are those underlying options or included in an index underlying options or in a futures contract.
- The conseil establishes a separate minimum volume for trades in each approved stock.
- To act as principals, member firms are required to individually obtain approval from the conseil and undertake to respect the conditions it sets down. The firms must meet specific levels of financial assets.
- If a trade is concluded at a price outside the market spread, the member firm must satisfy the central market within five minutes. This means it must fill buy orders with higher price limits, and sell orders with lower limits, than the price negotiated for the block trade.

Foreign access to the Bourse is allowed through direct investment in a société de bourse.

Investor Protection

Each société de bourse is responsible to its clients for completing their transactions. This initial guarantee is augmented by the Règlement Général du Conseil des Bourses de Valeurs, which defines minimum capital bases for member firms and sets prudential ratios for:

- Risk cover, based on total commitments in proportion to total assets.
- Risk spread, to avoid excessive risk on a single issuer and/or counter-party.
- Liquidity, to ensure that short-term commitments are covered by liquid assets.

The same regulations require sociétés de bourse to maintain strictly separate accounts for client funds and their own funds, to ensure that they do not use client funds for business for their own account.

The Conseil des Bourses de Valeurs establishes the rules governing the management of a guarantee fund set up and funded by the sociétés de bourse to protect the interests of investors on the stock market. Should the fund prove insufficient, the conseil can require the Sociétés des Bourses Françaises to make an additional contribution.

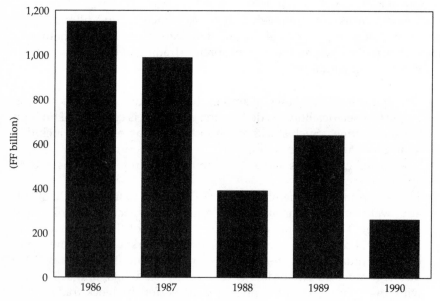

Figure 21.4. Shares Turnover (Marché Officiel)—Paris Stock Exchange (1986–1990) (FF billion)

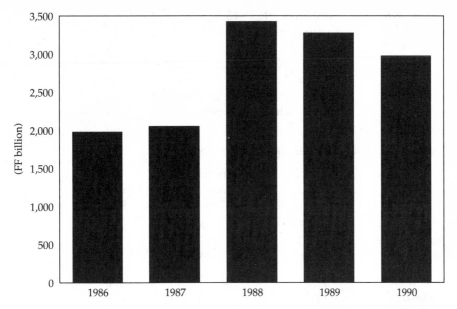

Figure 21.5. Bonds Turnover—Paris Stock Exchange (1986–1990) (FF billion)

GERMANY

General Background

Germany has eight stock exchanges, located in Frankfurt, Dusseldorf, Munich, Hamburg, Berlin, Stuttgart, Hannover, and Bremen. In 1986, the eight stock exchanges united to form the Federation of the German Stock Exchanges. Frankfurt is the leading stock exchange, accounting for approximately 75 percent of bond and share transactions. The German domestic bond market is the biggest in Europe, and the stock market is the fourth largest in the world in terms of market capitalization, behind Tokyo, New York, and London.

Frankfurter Wertpapierborse—Frankfurt Stock Exchange
Location: Frankfurt Stock Exchange Limited
            Borsenplatz 6
            P.O. Box 10 08 11
            D-6000 Frankfurt am Main
            Telephone: (069) 21–97–0
            Telefax: (069) 21–97–4–55

Trading hours: Securities: 11:30–13:30
                        Currencies: 13:00–14:00
                        Gold: 12:00–12:05
                        Trading hours can be extended if
                        the need arises
                        (Frankfurt is one hour ahead of
                        Greenwich Mean Time)

Number of listed securities: (as of May 1990)

	Amtlicher Handel (1st Segment)	Geregelter Markt (2nd Segment)	Freiverkehr (3rd Segment)	Total
Total Shares	**795**	**158**	**463**	**1,416**
Domestic	530	153	115	798
Foreign	265	5	348	618
Total Bonds	**12,328**	**2,748**	**100**	**15,176**
Domestic	11,313	2,695	71	14,079
International	1,015	53	29	1,097
Total Warrants	**200**	**70**	**205**	**475**
Domestic	110	70	197	377
Foreign	90	0	8	98
TOTAL	13,323	2,976	768	17,067

As of December 1990, 490 companies were listed on the Official Market, of which 233 were foreign, and 1,163 corporations were listed on the exchange, 628 domestic and 535 foreign. Many Frankfurt-listed securities are also listed on the other German exchanges.

Market capitalization: Domestic shares: DM 487.5 billion
                            (nominal value: DM 59.3 billion)

Stock exchange turnover: *Official Market (DM million)*
                            Shares and warrants: DM 1,104,872
                            (foreign: DM 39,628)
                            Fixed-income: DM 1,257,376
                            (foreign: DM 1,177,615)

Market index:

The primary market index for Germany is known as DAX. DAX is based on 30 blue-chip stocks that account for approximately 80 percent of the total share transactions in Germany. The unique characteristic of DAX is that it is adjusted for dividends under the assumption that dividends are reinvested in equities. This practice avoids distortions on dividend due days. The success of the DAX system has led to the exploration of a uniform bond pricing index.

Regulatory framework

Germany's system of supervision consists of three elements: public law, legal supervision of the "land" or state in which it is located, and the self-regulation of market participants. There is no regulatory body similar to the SEC in the United States. The law prohibits anyone who is not a representative of a bank or a broker from participating on the exchange. Banks are supervised by the Federal Banking Supervisory Office, whereas brokers' activities are governed by the Stock Exchange Act of 1989, which places great emphasis on the self-administration of the exchanges.

Supported by the State Commissioner, the Lander Government is responsible for supervising the financial standing of the stock exchanges and ensuring the propriety of activities. The stock exchange Board of Governors, as the senior body, ensures the smooth running of the stock exchange. On a day-to-day basis, stock exchange management is responsible for managing the exchange's affairs. The Federation of the German Stock Exchanges was established for the purpose of dealing with and coordinating trading, organizational, and technical problems on the national level.

Membership Categories

Trading is usually conducted between representatives of the banks, with the involvement of a *Kursmakler* (official broker) or a *freie Makler* (free broker). Official brokers are appointed by the Lander Government to act as intermediaries between members on the stock exchange floor and to determine the official prices of individual securities. Outside the stock exchange hours, they are permitted to act as free brokers. Free brokers are admitted by the Board of Governors and act as intermediaries as well as trade for their own accounts. They are not allowed to take part in the official fixing of market prices in the top market segment. The presence of both types of brokers guarantees a fair and orderly market.

At December 1990, there were 3,169 individual members of the exchange, consisting of 363 bank representatives, 38 Kursmakler, 64 freie Makler, and 2,704 others (primarily dealers and technical employees).

Market Trading Information

Main Types of Securities Traded

The main types of securities traded on the German Stock Exchange are common and preferred stocks, bonds, warrants, and futures and securities options.

Exchange trading is heavily concentrated in fixed-income securities, primarily debt issued by the government, financial institutions, and foreign companies. Germany's domestic bond market is now considered the largest in Europe.

Domestic shareholders are thinly spread among both private and institutional investors. To stimulate investment in the private sector, the government is proposing a promotion of equity purchases via savings bonuses and tax breaks. Tax concessions also exist for the purchase of company shares by employees below the market price, and consideration is being given to the issuance of non-par-value shares at lower prices to the small investor in Germany.

Types of Markets

The German Stock Exchange currently has three segments, which encourages wider participation by corporations:

Official Trading (Amtlicher Handel) consists mostly of trades in highly active blue-chip securities. Disclosure requirements for this segment include the filing of annual and interim reports and a market value of newly listed shares of at least DM 2.5 million (for nonshare securities, total par value must be at least DM 500,000). Also, at the time of admission or soon after, at least 25 percent of the total nominal amount of the shares offered must be spread widely among the general public.

The admission requirements for the **Regulated Market** (Geregelter Markt) are less stringent in order to allow more small and medium-size enterprises to go public. There is no minimum percentage of shares that have to be spread among the general public, and interim reports do not have to be filed. Application for admission to the exchange can be lodged not only by a bank but also by other qualified financial institutions.

Although the **Free Market** (Freiverkehr) operates on the trading floor of the exchange, it is organized under private law and its admission and trading practices are regulated by a special free market committee or association of security dealers. Listing can be obtained by any corporation that provides the minimum disclosures required under stock corporation law and can demonstrate that its shares will be regularly traded by virtue of their wide distribution among the general public.

DTB.   The Deutsche Termiborse (DTB), one of the few screen-based computerized exchanges in the world, began trading in January 1990 with options on 14 German blue-chip stocks. The stock options comprise 50 equities and are offered with a maturity of 1, 2, 3, and 6 months. They can be exercised at any time during the term of the contract.

DTB has since expanded its product range to include two types of financial futures: the Bond Futures, which represent contracts on a National Federal bond with a maturity of 8 to 10 years and a coupon of 6 percent; and a futures contract based on the basket of stocks that make up the DAX index. The par value of the interest rate contract on federal bonds is DM 250,000. The listing is in DM with two figures after the decimal point and is based on a par of 100. The contract value of the DAX future is at 100 per DAX point. Delivery for both futures contracts are March, June, September, and December, with a term of three, six, or nine months. Further index contracts are planned for the future.

There are 59 members of the exchange, including 13 foreign banks. Membership is divided into (1) general clearing members, which can clear for other financial institutions belonging to the exchange, themselves, and their clients; (2) direct clearing members, which can clear for themselves and their clients; and (3) nonclearing members.

Market Trading Systems

Trade prices are determined on the exchange floor on a bid-and-offer basis using the open outcry trading system. For all shares with a narrow market, the price is fixed by the official Kursmakler once per day. Shares that are traded more frequently are subject to continuous trading throughout the session, using variable prices. Once the transaction price has been determined, the official broker enters the price via an input terminal into the electronic, realtime price information system, the Kurs Information und Service System (KISS). This is complemented by the Borsen Order Service System (BOSS), an electronic order routing system that forwards purchase and sales orders placed by banks to the brokers in electronic form, whether via screen, data medium, or computer network.

Far-reaching developments are currently taking place in the various off-exchange systems that are competing with each other and with the official exchange for the business in shares of German-listed companies. The Inter-Banken-Information System (IBIS) was launched by seven leading banks in 1989 as a screen-based price information system. Its features have since been expanded to serve as a stock exchange trading system through which comparatively large lots of blue-chip stocks can be traded throughout the day. The system is a "free" market-making operation; there is no obligation for market makers to quote two-way prices. In practice, firm bid and offer prices are quoted by only a few market makers, even for some of the largest companies which make up the DAX index. As a result of the transfer of IBIS's ownership to the Frankfurt Stock Exchange, it is now under the supervision of the exchange, also allowing official brokers to become members for the first time. This may eventually lead to an integration of the broker and screen-based systems. In fact, IBIS recently commenced trading blocks of the stocks making up the DAX 30 index under the auspices of the exchange.

In response to the establishment of IBIS, a number of Kursmakler launched the Makler Tele-Information System (Matis), which carries prices on six pages of Reuters. Since the Kursmakler can now participate in IBIS, much of the basis for maintaining Matis as a separate system has been eliminated.

The third screen-based system in operation is the Market-maker Information and Trading System (Midas). This system was developed by a number of the country's *freie Makler* to compete with the other systems from which they were excluded. Midas claims to have technically superior features compared with the other electronic systems. Prices for 200 securities are available on Midas, with the capacity to increase this number to 600. The system maintains knowledge of participants' settlement instructions and counterparty limits, facilitating the immediate settlement and confirmation of trades. Midas is expected to introduce later in 1991 full execution of trades conducted on the screens. Cross-border trades can be cleared through Citibank, which is also responsible for maintaining custody of participants' securities at the central clearing house, *Kassenverein*. Midas has applied to various state authorities for permission to act as an official exchange, an act that would increase competition with the IBIS system.

In 1988, continuous quotes for trading in high-turnover bonds began at all German stock exchanges, enabling uninterrupted trading throughout each session. The service comprises certain securities of the federal government, railways and post office.

Trades on DTB are processed through a computerized trading and clearing system that market participants can access irrespective of their geographic location. Orders and bids from exchange members are automatically collated in the central computer, matched, and processed. Market makers are obliged to quote binding bid and offer prices for those options and futures in which they make markets. Trading takes place from 10:30 A.M. to 3:00 P.M. Backed by 17 banks, the private company running DTB guarantees performance of the contractual obligations.

Clearance and Settlement Procedures

Clearance and settlement occur on the second business day following the day of contract. The short settlement cycle serves as a competitive advantage for the Frankfurt Stock Exchange compared to the exchanges in other European countries. To strengthen this advantage, the six securities deposit associations and securities collective banks merged to form the German Central Securities Depositories (Deutscher Kassenverein), which acts as a central clearing house. Given the centralization of safe custody deposit bookkeeping, it may be possible in the future to process transactions in real time.

Procedures for Market Price Publication

In 1988, Frankfurt and Dusseldorf (the second largest German exchange) centralized their two data processing systems relating to stock trading, after-hours trading, back office operations, and pricing information. This made it possible to display current prices from all exchanges simultaneously on one screen. The new system, known as Deutsche Wertpapier-daten-Zentrale (DWZ), is based in Frankfurt.

Since 1989, banks and institutional investors have had access to a nationwide computer-assisted information system (IBIS) that takes indicative prices for German blue chips and the frequently traded federal bonds. These are the prices at which banks are prepared to conclude securities transactions over the telephone with other market players. IBIS simultaneously displays prices and, at given time intervals, the volumes at which transactions have been concluded.

The pricing information service system, KISS, records and transmits in real time the prices of all shares, convertibles, bonds with warrants, warrants, and continuously traded federal bonds. This system also provides the daily movements in the DAX and selected prices from the CAC system of the Paris Stock Exchange.

Prices in the official market are also published in the daily official list of the exchange, and prices in the regulated market appear in the *Borsen-Zeitung*.

Taxes, Commissions, and Other Trading Costs

Taxes

Domestic Investors: All dividends are subject to a withholding tax of 25 percent of gross dividends. Domestic investors also receive a tax credit of $\frac{9}{16}$ (on receipts before withholding tax) for the income tax paid by the corporation. Interest is taxable as personal income.

Foreign Investors: Dividends are subject to a withholding tax of 25 percent of gross dividends. Tax treaties provide reductions to rates varying between 5 percent and 15 percent. Foreign investors receive a tax credit only to the extent that the distributed profits of the corporation were received by a branch office in Germany. There is no taxation of interest on straight bonds when a tax treaty exists. Participation certificates, convertible bonds, and income bonds are subject to a withholding tax at a flat rate of 25 percent.

Transaction Charges: Commissions and Fees

Commission on share trades is charged at .08 percent of the total amount. With warrants, convertibles, and participation certificates, commissions range from .075 percent of nominal value for an issue of less than DM50,000 to .0075 percent for an issue exceeding DM5 million. The minimum commission is DM500. All other issues incur commissions which range from .075 percent for less than DM50,000 to .006 percent for an issue exceeding DM5 million. The minimum commission is DM400.

The securities turnover tax was recently abolished.

Procedures for Issuing and Listing New Securities

Requirements for admission to the official market include the filing of an application by the issuer and the underwriting bank. The application must be accompanied by a corporate report containing the last annual audited accounts, an interim report providing information on the condition of the company, and other information relating to the organization and operation of the company. Shares or other securities being admitted to listing must have a nominal amount of at least DM 2.5 million, and the company must have a trading history of three years or more. At least 25 percent of the shares being offered must be distributed to the general public.

The requirements for admission to the regulated markets are similar to those above, with the exception that an abridged report can be submitted and interim reports are not required. Entrants to the regulated markets must have shares with a nominal amount of at least DM500,000 available to the market, and are not subject to any requirement with respect to minimum period of operation.

Takeover and Merger Transactions

Takeover bids involving German companies are not frequent occurrences. The various stock exchanges have established voluntary guidelines regulating takeovers and mergers.

Foreign Investors

There are no restrictions on foreign holdings in German companies, although stakes of more than 25 percent must be disclosed. A foreign broker or dealer may become a member of the Frankfurt Stock Exchange by establishing a branch or subsidiary that is recognized as a bank by German banking authorities.

Exchange Membership Requirements

The Frankfurt Stock Exchange has no residency or citizenship requirements for membership of the exchange. However, to be considered a bank as defined by German banking law, the firm must have an office in or near Frankfurt. Member firms are subject to an initial admission fee and subsequent annual fees that are based partly upon the number of employees. Membership cannot be purchased; therefore, there is no trading of seats.

The Stock Exchange Act provides a uniform statutory basis for the monitoring of brokers. The Lander Government is responsible for supervising their financial standing and for ensuring that business done is in due order. The authorities supervising the stock exchanges are required to carry out at least two audits per year to review compliance with stock exchange regulations and financial requirements. In addition, brokers' annual accounts are subject to audit.

Investor Protection

On June 19, 1989, the Council of EC Finance Ministers formulated its joint stance on the draft directive submitted by the EC Commission prohibiting insider trading. After it has passed the European Parliament, this will be written into German law and will have a great effect on Germany and its voluntary code of conduct. In Germany the definition of insider refers to those who have a particularly close relationship to the company in whose equities they are dealing. It also defines information as only that information relating to capital changes, mergers and takeovers, changes in dividends, and significant changes in profits or liquidity. Inspection commissions monitor these rules at each exchange.

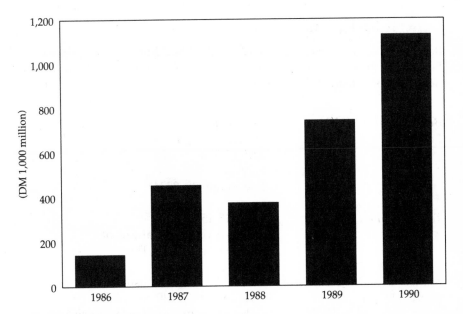

Figure 21.6. Shares and Warrants Turnover—Frankfurt Stock Exchange (1986–1990) (DM 1,000 million)

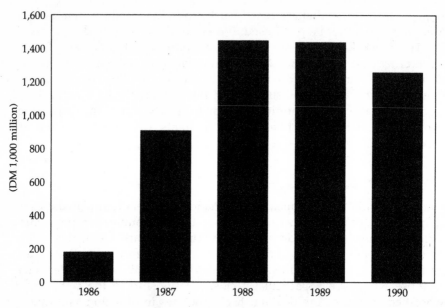

Figure 21.7.   Fixed-Income Securities Turnover—Frankfurt Stock Exchange (1986–1990) (DM 1,000 million)

ITALY

General Background

Italy has five stock exchanges located in Milan, Rome, Turin, Venice, and Florence. The Milan Stock Exchange accounts for the majority of the business and is considered the main point of reference for international investors.

Borsa Valori Di Milano—Milan Exchange
Location: Piazza Affari, 4
                                20100 Milan
                                Italy
                                Telephone: 02–85341

Trading hours: 10:00–13:45
                                (Milan is one hour ahead of
                                  Greenwich Mean Time)

Number of listed securities: Official Market: 334 listed securities
(April 1991)   representing 220 companies
                                Unlisted Securities Market: 39 securities
                                  representing 37 companies
                                Over-the-counter market: 34 securities

Market capitalization: *(April 1991)*	Official Market: Lit 203,588 billion Unlisted Securities Market: Lit 12,275 billion
Annual share turnover: *(1990)*	Official Market: Lit 168,134 billion Unlisted Securities Market: Lit 14,520 billion
Market indices:	BCI Index MIB Index
Regulatory authority:	Commissione Nazionale per la Societa e la Borsa (CONSOB) Via Isonzo 16 00100 Rome, Italy

This regulatory body is made up of five commissioners, appointed by the president of the republic, whose responsibilities cover the disclosure requirements of listed companies and the functioning of the stock exchange, including new listings and the filing of interim and annual balance sheets by listed companies. CONSOB also oversees the regulations governing public offerings.

An executive committee representing the stockbrokers in each stock exchange is responsible for the daily operations of the exchange. The committee in Milan consists of eight people who hold two-year terms.

Categories of Membership:

Membership of the stock exchanges is restricted to *agenti di cambio* (stockbrokers) who thus have a monopoly on the transactions carried out on the exchanges. They act solely in an agency capacity and conduct their business as individuals with unlimited liability.

Other intermediaries in the market include *commissionarie di borsa* (commission broking houses) and banks. The commissionarie are generally owned by major financial and industrial organizations and can trade for their own account. Foreign institutional investors generally trade through the commissionarie who can offer more confidentiality and liquidity of trading, as well as research material. The banks, meanwhile, handle the largest proportion of all trade orders through their branch networks and, for the most part, match orders internally. In December 1990, there were 113 agenti di cambio and 110 commissionarie di borsa in the Milan marketplace.

In January 1991, legislation that radically overhauled existing market practices was passed by the Italian Parliament. A new designation of firm, *Societa di Intermediazione Mobiliare* (SIMs), was created to function as the only type of financial institution permitted to deal in securities.

Agenti di cambio may continue to act in a capacity purely as agents, but all trades must be passed on to the exchange floor for execution. Trades may be conducted off the exchange only if agreed to by both parties.

SIMs will be able to perform a wide range of stockbroking, fund management, and financial consultancy services, and may be owned by Italian banks and foreign institutions. As corporations or limited partnerships, their minimum capital requirements will be Lit 600 million, although this may vary according to the type of activities that they propose to undertake. To deal on the exchange during the first 18 months, an SIM must have an agenti di cambio as a significant shareholder. Implementation of these new rules will be phased in over a two-year period. Detailed regulations governing the new framework will be drawn by CONSOB, which will be responsible for supervising the SIMs' activities. The Bank of Italy will monitor the financial position of SIMs for compliance with the capital requirements.

Market Trading Information

Main Types of Securities Traded

Securities traded on the Milan Stock Exchange include ordinary and preference shares, saving shares, convertible bonds, straight bonds and government stocks, and securities issued by medium-term credit institutes and other public bodies.

Types of Markets

There are two types of regulated markets operating on the exchange:

Official Stock Exchange (Borsa Valori): Admission to the Official Stock Exchange requires industrial companies to have shareholders' equity of at least Lit 10 billion and banks and insurance companies to have shareholders' equity of at least Lit 50 billion. The financial statements of the last three years must indicate a profit, and the most recent balance sheet and profit-and-loss account must be audited.

Unlisted Securities Market (Mercato Ristretto): For admission to the Unlisted Securities Market, a company must be an Italian joint-stock company with its head office located within domestic boundaries. It must have shareholders' equity of at least Lit 1 billion and the financial statements for the most recent period must show a profit.

Over-the-counter trading in listed Italian stocks occurs extensively in an unregulated third market. Approximately 70 percent of trading in listed stocks may be taking place off the exchange floor.

Market Trading Systems

At present, most securities are traded at a set time each day, whereby daily prices are fixed at the end of the security trading period. This auction-based system is known as trading in *corbeille* (ring). Corbeille is the place where such trading physically takes place. Prices for the top 30 to 40 Italian-listed stocks that make up the majority of the daily trading volume may, however, be fixed throughout the day. In fact, it is estimated that more than two-thirds of the exchange's market capitalization is accounted for by 10 industrial conglomerates.

In conjunction with the changes taking place in the status of intermediaries, it has been proposed that the auction system be replaced by the middle of 1992 with a continuous electronic market and screen-based trading system. The cost of these reforms will be shared by the agenti, commissionarie, and banks.

Clearance and Settlement Procedures

Stocks and warrants are traded on an account system similar to that of the International Stock Exchange in London, with the account closing on the 16th of the month and clearance occurring at the end of the month. The settlement period currently averages about six weeks. Bonds generally have three days between trade and settlement. Implementation of a rolling settlement system is planned in the next few years.

Most listed companies have deposited their shares at the central securities depository, Monte Titoli, a limited company owned by a number of banks. Monte Titoli is also authorized to effect securities settlement on behalf of commissionarie di borsa, mutual funds, and other financial institutions. The majority of bond transactions are recorded in book entry form by Gestione Centralizzata, a company owned by the Bank of Italy. All shares must be registered in the customer's name, while bonds may be registered in the customer's name or to the bearer. Monte Titoli is also authorized to handle foreign securities and, where appropriate, deposit them with the central depository authority of the country in which the issuing entity is located.

The clearing house (Stanza di Compensazione) of the Bank of Italy currently provides clearing and settlement functions for those certificates that are still handled in physical form and have to be endorsed in the name of the new shareholder.

Procedures for Market Price Publication

Current market prices are available on the electronic board of the exchange and on broker screens through the Reuters service.

Taxes, Commissions, and Other Trading Costs

Taxation

Capital gains arising from securities transactions are taxed at a rate of 15 percent to 25 percent, depending whether realized losses are reflected in the computation. Nonresidents are subject to tax only on securities dealt on the financial markets for which no double tax treaty exists with the country of residence.

Dividend income is taxable to shareholders resident in Italy at a rate of 10 percent. Nonresident shareholders are taxed at rates varying between 0 percent and 32.4 percent, depending on the terms of the tax treaties between Italy and the country of residence. Resident shareholders must include dividends in their taxable income but can deduct withholding tax and the underlying tax paid by the distributing company.

Corporations or banking institutions must withhold tax on interest paid to Italian corporations at the following rates:

- Italian government securities
  issued before September 20, 1986   no withholding tax
  issued between September 20, 1986
  and before August 24, 1987   6.25%
  issued after August 24, 1987   12.25%

- Interest on current and deposit accounts   30%

- Interest on debenture bonds
  issued on or before December 31, 1983   10.8%
  issued on or after January 1, 1984   12.5%

Interest on loan agreements paid to individuals resident in Italy or to nonresident companies is subject to a withholding tax of 15 percent. Resident companies do not suffer withholding on such interest.

Commissions

Trading commissions are currently set by custom at 0.7 percent (0.25 percent for institutional clients) plus stamp duty for stocks, 0.3 percent plus stamp duty for bonds, and 0.15 percent plus stamp duty for Treasury bonds. Stamp duties range from 0.065 percent to 0.1 percent according to the security type.

Procedures for Issuing and Listing New Securities

Industrial companies seeking an official listing for their shares must have net assets of at least Lit 10 billion. Banks and insurance companies must have minimum net assets of Lit 50 billion. Financial statements for three years must be submitted with the application, with the latest balance sheet and income statement audited by an auditing firm approved and included in the registry of authorized auditors of the CONSOB.

Takeover and Merger Transactions

Mergers

Effective February 1991, new legislation came into force which reflected EEC Directives III and IV.

At least one month prior to a merger, the board of directors of each company involved in a merger must file a merger plan with its registered office and publish it in the *Gazzetta Ufficiale*. A report must also be prepared describing the merger plan and financial arrangements. The fairness of the share exchange must be assessed by an expert appointed by the president of the court or, for listed companies, by a public accounting firm.

Listed companies must submit the merger plan together with the report from the directors to the CONSOB. During the 30 days preceding the shareholders' meeting, the merger plan, directors' and experts' reports, and the last three years' financial statements must be deposited with the company's registered office. Debtors of the company can oppose the merger decision within two months following the recording of the merger agreement in the company's register or its publication in the *Gazzetta Ufficiale*.

All individuals or companies that invest, directly or indirectly, in at least 2 percent of the shares of a listed company must communicate with the CONSOB. Listed companies must similarly inform the CONSOB of any investments of 10 percent or more in the shares of an unlisted company.

Public Purchase Offer

A holder of 25 percent to 50 percent of the ordinary issued share capital (including convertible warrants) of a listed company can purchase 5 percent or more of the ordinary shares of the company only by a public purchase offer. These percentages may be changed by the CONSOB in instances where voting control of the company rests in the holders of a smaller proportion of the issued shares due to a high diffusion of the shares. Any shares exceeding 5 percent that are not purchased by public offer must be sold within one year. CONSOB regulations prescribe the nature of information that must be published in connection with the public offer, the duration of the offer, and other formalities.

Foreign Investors

Currently, exchange membership is restricted to Italian citizens. Foreign broker/dealers may establish subsidiaries but they must use intermediary brokers to purchase securities. Commissions charged for such trading range from 0.8 percent to 1 percent inclusive of stamp duty. As described above, the securities reforms have introduced a new category of intermediary, SIMs, which may be foreign-owned.

There are no restrictions on share ownership by foreigners, although holdings of more than 2 percent must be disclosed.

Exchange Membership Requirements

Stockbrokers, or agenti di cambio, are Treasury-appointed public officials of Italian citizenship who have passed a competitive examination. Seats are not transferable. Commissionarie di borsa status may be purchased from the Commissione di Borse.

Agenti di cambio are not subject to minimum capital or periodic reporting requirements. In contrast, commissionarie di borsa must maintain capital in excess of Lit 600 million and submit annual audited financial statements and interim unaudited financial statements that are available for public inspection.

Investor Protection

Legislation was passed in May 1991 implementing the European Commission Directive to ban trading on insider information.

Stockbrokers are required to make deposits at the Bank of Italy and with the Executive Committee of stockbrokers of the relevant exchange. These deposits are required in order to guarantee any transactions in the event of broker default. A voluntary guarantee fund has also been established by the National Association of Stockbrokers as a means of affording additional security to investors.

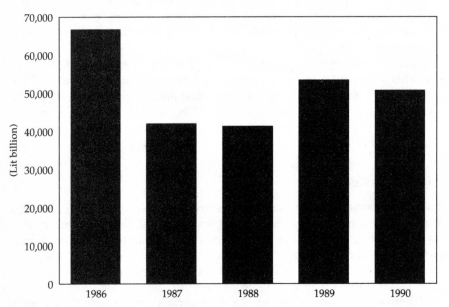

Figure 21.8.   Shares Turnover—Milan Stock Exchange (1986–1990) (Lit billion)

JAPAN

General Background

Japan has eight stock exchanges located in Tokyo, Osaka, Nagoya, Kyoto, Hiroshima, Fukuoka, Niigata, and Sapporo. Also in Tokyo is the International Financial Futures Exchange, which began operations in 1990. The Tokyo Stock Exchange generates approximately 80 percent of the value of all trades conducted in Japan.

Tokyo Stock Exchange (TSE)

Location:	2-1-1 Nihonbashi Kayaba-cho Chiyo-ku, Tokyo 102 Japan Telephone: 813–3666–0141 Facsimile: 813–3663–0625
Trading hours:	9:00–11:00 13:00–15:00 (Tokyo is nine hours ahead of Greenwich Mean Time)
Listed securities:	Stocks (first and second sections, including foreign stocks), bonds, warrants, futures, and options
Market capitalization: *(Dec 1990)*	Stocks: ¥379,231 billion Fixed-income: ¥118,702 billion
Average daily *turnover: (1990)*	Stocks: ¥747 billion Fixed-income: ¥131 billion
Market indices:	Nikkei Average TOPIX (Tokyo Stock Price Index)

Regulatory framework:

The Securities Bureau of the Ministry of Finance (MOF) is the primary regulatory authority for matters relating to the securities markets. The Securities Bureau consists of six sections: General, Capital Markets, Corporate Finance, Trading Markets, Securities Business, and Inspection. The Securities and Exchange Council is an advisory body to MOF with the purpose of investigating and deliberating matters relating to the issuance and trading of securities. The Financial Accounting Deliberation Council is also an advisory body to MOF that issues opinions setting financial accounting and auditing standards.

The Finance Bureau of MOF and their branch offices are responsible for local securities administration under the guidance and supervision of the Securities Bureau. The Stock Exchange Comptroller, under the control of the local Finance Bureau manager, supervises the business and trading in the eight stock exchanges.

The significant laws administered by the Securities Bureau are: the Securities and Exchange Law, the Law Concerning Foreign Securities Firms, the Securities Investment Trust Law, the Certified Public Accountant Law, the Law Concerning Depository and Book Entry for Share Certificates, and the Law Concerning the Regulation of Securities Investment Advisory Business.

Market Trading Information

Main Types of Securities Traded

	Issues
Stocks: first section	1,197
Stocks: second section	437
Foreign stocks	125
Warrants	47
Bonds	281
Convertible bonds	1,159
Bonds with warrants	14
Futures	4
Options	2

Approximately 28 percent of the total number of companies listed on the Tokyo Stock Exchange are also listed on at least one of the other stock exchanges in Japan. Many Japanese stocks are also listed on the New York, London, and other international stock exchanges.

Currently, stock transactions on the first section are generated by the following groups: 29% by securities companies, 17% by financial institutions, 10% by investment trusts, 9% by corporate companies, 25% by individuals, and 10% by foreigners.

The Tokyo Stock Exchange trades futures contracts based on TOPIX (Tokyo Stock Price Index, the average price index of all stocks listed on the first section), Japanese government bonds, and U.S. Treasury bonds. Most recently it has begun trading options based on TOPIX and on Japanese government bond futures.

The Osaka Stock Exchange (OSE), Japan's second largest stock exchange, trades many of the same types of securities as the TSE, except no foreign stocks are listed on the OSE. One popular product unique to the OSE is a futures contract on the Nikkei 225, the index of the leading 225 stocks listed on the TSE.

During 1990, the Tokyo International Financial Futures Exchange was opened to trade three-month Euroyen and Eurodollar interest rate futures, and yen/dollar currency futures.

Types of Markets

Securities are traded on the eight exchanges of Japan, with the Tokyo Stock Exchange representing the most significant volume of shares traded. Shares are also traded in the over-the-counter (OTC) market.

Settlements of traded securities are primarily "regular way," settled on the third business day following the transaction. Over 99% of trading is settled regular way. Other methods of settlement include: *cash*, settled on the day of or the day following the transaction; *special agreement*, settled fourteen days after the transaction (or an agreed upon future date); and *when issued*, settled upon the issuance of new shares.

Foreign investors may be able to issue a portion of their foreign currency denominated securities on a private placement basis to prudent financial institution investors in Japanese markets. Currently there is no system to facilitate trading or enhance the liquidity of private placement issues because investors are required to make these purchases for investment, not resale, purposes and a minimum-two year holding period is necessary.

It is believed, however, that reform of certain aspects of the securities market is being considered by the Ministry of Finance. Changes would include greater flexibility on the issuance of private placements (placements could be made with nonfinancial institutions, and the required two-year holding period would be eliminated), and the institution of certain disclosure requirements for private placements.

Market Trading Systems

The TSE market is a two-way, auction market in which *regular members* place buy and sell orders through *satori members*, who match orders based on a "price priority and time precedent" policy. For the 150 most actively traded stocks, buy and sell orders are matched on the trading floor.

For all listed stocks that are not traded on the floor, the TSE has developed the Computer-Assisted Order Routing and Execution System (CORES), which allows a regular member to enter orders and a saitori member to match them, both through the computer, and provides each with a printed confirmation of the transaction. CORES will automatically execute any orders within a specified narrow price range of the last sales price. When a transaction is completed, the trade price is automatically transmitted from CORES to the Market Information System on the exchange. The TSE has developed similar computer trading systems for trading futures and options.

To maintain a stable market, saitori members of TSE will post a special bid/ask quote at a price slightly higher or lower than the last sale price in situations where there is a major order imbalance in a listed stock. The exchange also imposes a limit on the daily price fluctuation of a particular stock.

Bonds are traded on the floor or through CORES in a manner similar to the trading of stocks. Large blocks of Japanese government bonds are also traded by telephone directly through saitori members in the Government Bond Block Trading Room.

Ordering and Settlement Procedures

For the 150 most actively traded stocks, regular members communicate customer orders to their clerks on the TSE trading floor, who in turn place the orders verbally with the saitori members who match the buy and sell orders and effect the trades. When the trade is made, the regular members are notified electronically through the Trade Report Output Device. For listed securities traded through the CORES system, customers' orders are placed with the saitori members electronically through the system; however the process is essentially the same.

Margin transactions in Japan are permissible in accordance with the Securities and Exchange Law. Currently, the margin requirements include a minimum deposit of 30 percent of the transaction or ¥300,000, whichever is greater.

Failed trades may be borrowed by the broker from other securities companies to effect delivery to their customers.

Clearing on the TSE is by book entry rather than physical delivery of securities. The Japan Securities Clearing Corporation (JSCC), a wholly owned subsidiary of the TSE, clears all transactions. The JSCC is in the process of registering share certificates in their nominee names. Most certificates are currently registered in the customer's name.

Transactions can take place between brokers without clearing through the JSCC. These transactions, which are called *baikai* transactions, are made between brokers off the floor of the exchange. Securities companies are required to report details of baikai transactions when they take place.

While the JSCC acts as a central depository for stocks, there is no central depository for bonds and other instruments.

Procedures for Market Price Publication

Current market prices and trading volumes of all listed securities are available through the real-time Market Information System of the TSE. The prices and volumes of the 150 most actively traded stocks of the first section are input into the Market Information System by exchange clerks when the trades are completed on the floor. The prices and volumes of the securities that are traded through the CORES system are automatically updated on the Market Information System when they are matched on the computer.

For the over-the-counter market (OTC), the Japan Securities Dealers Association (JSDA) collects the information from securities companies and other financial institutions and publishes the bid/ask price of registered OTC stocks, selected bond issues, and the high/low yields of bond repurchase or resale contracts (*gensaki*) on a daily basis. The JSDA also accumulates and publishes the market prices of 248 bond issues on a weekly basis.

Taxes, Commissions, and Other Trading Costs

The following is a general description of the taxes that apply to corporations, individuals, and foreign investors holding investments in Japanese securities. Investors should obtain more detailed tax information from their tax advisors prior to investing in Japanese securities.

Corporate Taxes

Capital gains and losses are regular components of the taxable income of a corporation. Eighty percent of dividends received are excluded from taxable income of a corporation unless the corporation owns 25 percent or more of another corporation, in which case 100 percent of the dividends are tax-free. Interest expense on funds borrowed to purchase the stocks on which the dividends are received may be deducted only up to the amount of dividends received; excess amounts are not deductible. Interest income is included in taxable income.

Individual Taxes

Capital gains taxes for individuals on sales of securities are generally as follows: a 0.5 percent to 1.0 percent withholding tax on gross proceeds from sales or a 26 percent tax on the gains from sales. An additional 13 percent tax applies to gains on shares of newly listed securities sold within one year of issuance. Dividends on shares or investment trusts generally have taxes withheld at 20 percent. Taxes on bond interest are withheld at 20 percent. On a discounted bond, an 18 percent tax on redemption profit is withheld at the time of issuance.

Foreign Investor Taxes

Capital gains are taxed at 37.5 percent for nonresident corporations. Taxes are withheld on dividends at a rate of 10 percent to 15 percent to nonresident foreign investors from countries that have treaties with Japan. There is a 20 percent withholding tax on dividends to nonresident foreign investors from countries that do not have treaties with Japan. Taxes on interest on bonds and bank deposits are withheld at a rate between 10 percent and 15 percent depending on the nonresident foreign investor's country and the terms of its treaty with Japan. A nonresident foreign investor comprises individuals and corporations having no permanent establishment in Japan. Those foreign investors having permanent establishments in Japan will be taxed as either corporations or individuals.

Other Taxes

A securities transfer tax is applicable to all sellers of securities. The tax, based on sales price, ranges from .03 percent on the sale of bonds to .30 percent on the sale of stocks (for a securities company the tax ranges from .01 percent to .12 percent). There is a .001 percent tax, to both the buyer and seller, on the trading value of futures, and a .01 percent tax on the trading value of options.

Commissions

The following are the maximum and minimum marginal commission rates that are applicable based on trading, par, or contract values:

Type of Security	Maximum	Minimum	On trades greater than
Stocks, warrants, and sub-scription rights	1.20%	.15%	¥1 billion
Nonconvertible bonds	.80%	.05%	¥1 billion
Convertible bonds and bonds with warrant	1.00%	.15%	¥1 billion
Japanese government bond futures	.015%	.0025%	¥5 billion
Options on Japanese government bond futures	1.30%	.25%	¥50 million
U.S. T-Bond futures	.03%	.004%	$10 million
TOPIX futures	.04%	.005%	¥1 billion
TOPIX options	2.00%	.30%	¥50 million

These rates are also applicable to sales and purchases of over-the-counter stocks that are registered with Japan Securities Dealers Association. For other securities traded in the over-the-counter market (a majority of bonds and certain unregistered stocks), the price of the trade is determined through negotiations between the dealers and investors, and no separate commission is applied. The minimum rate charged on the Tokyo International Financial Futures Exchange is ¥1,030 per contract for trades involving 50 futures contracts or more.

Other fees that are applicable to investors are annual custodial fees charged by securities companies for holding stocks and other certificates, and a fee for a change of title to the stock certificate, which must be registered with the stock issuing corporation through a stock transfer agent.

Procedures for Issuing and Listing New Securities

The criteria for eligibilty for listing securites on the Tokyo Stock Exchange include: minimum number of shares to be listed, maximum number of shares to be held by certain related parties, a minimum of five years of incorporation, and minimum shareholders' equity, income and dividend levels in prior years. The procedures for listing include filing a "Securities Report for Listing" with the TSE, an examination and evaluation by the TSE, and approval of the TSE and Ministry of Finance prior to listing. For new securities issues, a prospectus is required that includes detailed disclosures about the operations of the company, including management's analysis, and three years of audited financial statements.

For foreign companies, the "Securities Report for Listing" must include the company's audited financial statements translated into Japanese, although these financial statements may be prepared according to the rules and regulations of the home country of the applicant. The eligibility criteria generally requires that the securities of foreign companies have good liquidity in their home market and that the company has 1,000 or more shareholders in Japan. The foreign company must also have at least ¥10 billion or more in equity and at least ¥2 billion of income before taxes in each of the last three years. Also, cash dividends must have been paid in each of the last three years, with the prospect of continued dividends in the future.

The fees of an original issue listing include a ¥5 million fixed listing fee and a ¥.045 per share fee payable to the TSE, as well as certain annual listing fees are also applicable. For a foreign issue listing, the fees include a fixed listing fee of ¥2.5 million plus per share fees ranging from ¥.0045 to ¥.0225, based upon the percentage of shares held in Japan. The ¥1 million examination fee and the annual listing fees are also applicable to foreign issuers.

Takeover and Merger Transactions

Current requirements call for the disclosure of substantial shareholdings (5 percent or more) of a company that may affect the price of its shares. An investor who owns 5 percent or more of the issued and outstanding shares in a company that is listed on an exchange or is dealt over-the-counter is required to file a report stating the amount and purpose of ownership and the amount and source of funding for the purchase with the Ministry of Finance within five days of purchase. Copies of the Substantial Shareholding Report must also be filed with the appropriate stock exchange, or the Japan Securities Dealers Association, and the issuing company. Any subsequent material changes in ownership or facts to the Substantial Shareholdings Report must also be filed within five days.

The Antimonopoly Act prohibits the formation of holding companies in Japan. This act prohibits holdings in corporations by individuals or other corporations that would result in substantial harm to competition in any particular market or market sector. The Antimonopoly Act also places restrictions on the shareholdings of financial institutions to prevent them from controlling industrial corporations. The act prohibits financial institutions from holding more than 5 percent of the outstanding shares of other Japanese corporations.

Foreign Investors

There are no specific restrictions on the acquisition of shares of a Japanese company by foreign investors for portfolio investment purposes. However, acquiring the stock of a Japanese company in order to own the company or to actively participate in its management is restricted by the Foreign Exchange and Foreign Trade Control Act (FEFTC Act). When a foreign investor intends to purchase up to 10 percent of a publicly held Japanese company, the investor must file prior written notification with the Ministry of Finance stating the purpose of the acquisition, the purchase price, and the expected date of acquisition. The investor is precluded from completing the proposed acquisition for 30 days after the notification to the Ministry of Finance.

Because holding companies are prohibited, foreign investors cannot organize or own stock of a Japanese company for the purpose of using it as a holding company for owning stock in another Japanese company. However, it is possible for a foreign investor to organize or own a Japanese company and use it as a vehicle for merging with or acquiring another Japanese company, as long as the company acting as the vehicle remains as an operating entity for a certain period of time.

Furthermore, no foreign corporation can merge with or be merged into a Japanese corporation. Therefore, a foreign corporation seeking to acquire a Japanese corporation through merger must establish a subsidiary in Japan to act as a vehicle for the merger. When a subsidiary merges with a Japanese company, it becomes subject to the restrictions on mergers provided for in the Antimonopoly Act. Under the Antimonopoly Act, all foreign corporations (except financial institutions) holding stock in Japanese companies are required to file annual shareholding reports with the Fair Trade Commission. The restriction that prevents domestic financial institutions from having no more than a 5 percent holding of stock in another Japanese company also applies to foreign financial institutions.

Exchange Membership Requirements

The TSE has regular members and saitori members. Regular members buy and sell securities through the TSE as either agent or principal. Saitori members are specialists, acting as intermediaries for securities transactions between regular members. Saitori members are not allowed to trade for their own accounts and are prohibited from having public customers. In December 1990, there were 128 members of the TSE.

TSE membership is available to both domestic and foreign companies that are licensed by the Ministry of Finance in accordance with the Securities and Exchange Law. There are four types of licenses that are issued by the Ministry of Finance: to trade as a dealer, to act as a broker, to underwrite new securities or secondary offerings, and to engage in the retail distribution of securities. Securities firms generally have more than one license. Securities companies are also prohibited from acting as principal and agent in the same transaction.

Approximately 45 percent of all of the securities companies in Japan are TSE member firms, and approximately 20 percent of TSE member firms are foreign securities companies.

The minimum capital requirements for TSE member firms varies from ¥300 million to ¥3 billion depending upon the type of license held.

New members of TSE are required to pay an initial fee of approximately ¥1.3 billion, which represents capital contribution, admission fees, initiation fee, default compensation reserve, and certain other fees, some of which are refundable if there is a sale or resignation of membership. Other fees include a monthly fee based upon the capital of the member firm, percentage fees based upon the trading or nominal values of securities turnover, and a fee of ¥.03 per share of stock traded. No specific insurance coverage is required.

Investor Protection

The Securities and Exchange Law provides the overall regulation for the securities issuing and trading markets. Two of the provisions of the Securities and Exchange Law are to ensure adequate disclosure of business conditions, in order to provide investors with accurate information necessary to make investment decisions, and to ensure an orderly securities market. It accomplishes these objectives through the regulation and supervision of the securities companies, the Japan Securities Dealers Association, the stock exchanges, and other principal institutions carrying out the functions of the securities market.

Trading on insider information is prohibited by the Securities and Exchange Law. Any officers or major shareholders that trade in their own company's securities are required to file a report disclosing such purchase or sale to the Ministry of Finance. Also, insider trading control regulations have been instituted by Japan Securities Dealers Association, establishing a functional separation between the brokerage and underwriting departments (the so-called *Chinese Wall*) of securities companies operating in Japan.

Also, in accordance with the Securities and Exchange Law, all publicly traded companies are required to file audited financial statements annually.

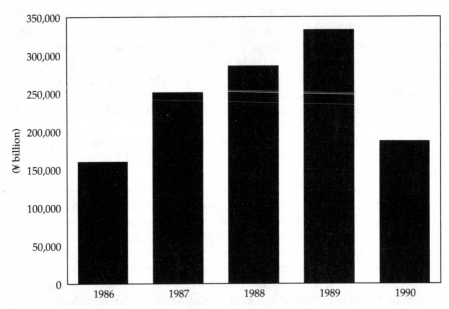

Figure 21.9. Shares Turnover—Tokyo Stock Exchange (1986–1990) (¥ billion)

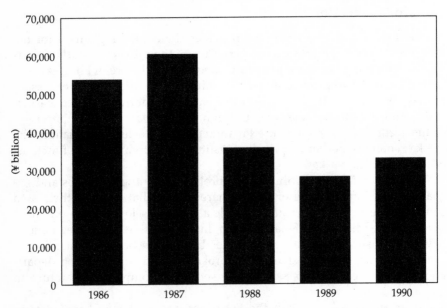

Figure 21.10. Fixed-Income Securities Turnover—Tokyo Stock Exchange (1986–1990) (¥ billion)

THE NETHERLANDS

General Background

There is one stock exchange in the Netherlands, located in Amsterdam. It ranks second worldwide, after London, in number of foreign listings. Also located in Amsterdam are the European Options Exchange (EOE) and the Financial Futures Market Amsterdam (FTA).

Amsterdam Effectensbeurs—Amsterdam Stock Exchange (ASE)

Location:	Beursplein 5
	1012 JW Amsterdam
	Netherlands
	Telephone: 020–52–34–567
	Telex: 12–302 EFBEU NL
	Telefax: 020–24–80–62
Trading hours:	10:00–16:30
	Trading in international Dutch shares is possible until closing time of the New York Stock Exchange
	Government bonds are traded from 9:00–17:00
	(Amsterdam is one hour ahead of Greenwich Mean Time)
Number of listed securities: *(1990)*	Stocks: 683 (297 of which are foreign) Bonds: 1,168 (168 of which are foreign)
Market capitalization: *(1990)*	Official Market: Dfl 573 billion Parallel Market: Dfl 3 billion
Average daily turnover: *(1990)*	Shares: Dfl 600 million Bonds: Dfl 755 million
Market indices:	CBS General market index (*CBS stemmingsindex*) CBS price-indicator for shares (*CBS-koersindex voor aandelen*)

Regulatory framework:

The regulatory structure has three levels: the Ministry of Finance, the Securities Trading Surveillance Board (*Stichting Toezicht Effectenverkeer*), and the Amsterdam Stock Exchange. In the near future, regulations for nonexchange trading will be brought in line with exchange trading.

The Ministry of Finance approves the listing of stocks on the ASE and supervises the self-regulating exchanges, although the supervisory function is delegated to the Securities Trading Board. In 1992, the Stock Exchange will be granted the responsibility of issuing listing permits, and the supervisory role will be directly assumed by the Securities Trading Board.

Market Trading Information

Main Types of Securities Traded

The Official Market listing includes government and mortgage bonds, shares, Eurobonds, and warrants and claims of domestic and foreign companies. The majority of shares, in terms of market capitalization, are also traded on other foreign markets. Institutional investors account for approximately 70 percent of stock trading activity, with private investors representing the other 30 percent.

Types of Markets

In addition to the Official Market, the ASE operates an Official Parallel Market. This market offers the advantages of an official regulated secondary market to smaller capitalized companies. The trading rules are equivalent to those of the Official Market, although the listing requirements are less stringent.

Unlisted securities are traded over-the-counter by members of the ASE subject to the trading rules of the exchange.

Shares of foreign companies may be listed and traded in their domestic currency at the ASE via the Amsterdam Security Account System (ASAS).

European Options Exchange (EOE)

Rokin 65
  1012 KK Amsterdam
  Netherlands
  Telephone: 020-55-04-550
  Telex: 14596 eoepr nl
  Telefax: 020-23-00-12

In cooperation with the American Stock Exchange (AMEX) in New York, the EOE trades options on the Major Market Index (XMI), which are then cleared by the Options Clearing Corporation (OCC) in Chicago. As of December 1990, options were being traded on 44 contracts based on listed equities, bonds, stock indices (EOE Dutch Stock index, Dutch Top 5 index, European Top 100 index), currencies, and precious metals. The option terms range in three-, six-, and nine-month cycles and three- and five-year cycles.

Financial Futures Market Amsterdam (FTA)

Nes 49
  1012 KD Amsterdam
  The Netherlands
  Telephone: 020–55–04–555
  Telefax: 020–6–24–54–16

The FTA currently lists three futures: a Notional Guilder Bond Future (FTO), a future on the Dutch Top 5 Index (FT5), and a future on the EOE Dutch Stock Index (FTI).

Expiration months range in one-, two-, three-, six-, nine-, and twelve-month cycles. Contract specifications are as follows:

FTI Dfl 200 × the EOE Dutch Stock index
FT5 On points; one point is Dfl 200 per contract
FTO A notional Dutch government bond with a nominal value of Dfl 250,000, an interest rate of 7 percent, in points Dfl 100

Market Trading Systems

The Official Market is currently an order-driven market without designated market makers. Banks and brokers submit client orders directly to one of the *hoekmannen* (specialists) assigned the responsibility to ensure an orderly market in that security. At least two specialists compete in each security. The *hoekmannen*, in consultation and also in competition with other *hoekmannen* dealing in the same securities, seek to find a balance between supply and demand by establishing the price at which as many orders as possible can be executed. As brokers and banks take their orders to buy or sell a specific security to the corner, *hoekmannen* are continuously updating price quotations and the number of securities that can be traded at a particular price. A *hoekman* can also decide to take a position in a security in order to bridge a gap between supply and demand.

The *hoekman* firms are not allowed to maintain relations with investors, and in turn, banks and brokers are not allowed to have an interest in the operating results of *hoekman* firms.

Floor trading is computer-assisted, with automated back-office processing and transfer of information between the specialists and the banks and brokers. The Trading Support System is a data processing system through which brokers and banks can communicate directly with the stock exchange. Some of the functions of the TSS are (1) the electronic processing of buy and sell orders; (2) automatic processing of transactions; (3) continuous information overview on members' order books or positions; (4) written confirmations; (5) support system for pricing (in addition, banks and brokers receive continuous information on prices at which *hoekmannen* propose to execute particular orders, their own position and order books, and their own transaction reviews); (6) analysis of *hoekmannens'* positions in a particular security; and (7) automatic routing of all transactions to the clearing and settlement systems.

No restrictions exist as to the size of trades or odd or round lots. Post-trade information is almost instantaneously available on the electronic trading board of the floor, as well as worldwide through data communications systems. The quotation officer, an official of the exchange, supervises both trading and compliance with trading rules. The officer may stop trading in particular securities for a period of time and may declare trades null and void.

The Amsterdam Interprofessional Market (AIM) provides block-trading by banks and brokers directly with institutional investors, without the intervention of a specialist and with no commissions. All AIM transactions involve shares and bonds traded on the Official Market and are reported to the central market data system within 15 minutes. Transactions are dealt net of mandatory commissions because they are not handled by the specialists. AIM handles equity transactions over Dfl 1 million in value and bond transactions over Dfl 2.5 million. The *hoekmannen* can act as interbroker dealers in cases where banks handling large deals cannot match the bargains themselves.

Further integration of the official or central market with AIM has been proposed and is being implemented in phases. The objective is to create a fully automated open-order book held by the *hoekmannen* that will be fed by retail orders of less than Dfl 2.5 million and AIM orders of up to Dfl 5 million, as at present, together with current wholesale quotes from AIM dealers for sizes above Dfl 5 million. The best bid and offer prices would be displayed publicly by the *hoekmannen*, and therefore could be accessed by all exchange members.

To date, the new system has been used only for Dutch government bond trading, which is exchange-based in Amsterdam. It is expected that this facility will shortly be extended to other debt securities.

EOE.   Each option has at least one active market maker. Market makers trade directly with the public order members (pom) and floor brokers (fb) in an open outcry market. The quotation officer surveys the trade. Post-trade information is immediately available.

FTA.   Since February 1991, market makers in the futures market are no longer required to quote bid and ask prices for all sizes of futures contracts.

Clearance and Settlement Procedures

Orders are entered in the electronic order books by the banks and brokers at their stations on the floor, or are passed on to the order books of the *hoekmannen* concerned. When an order has been executed, the transaction is confirmed and the order is removed from the order book. Settlement occurs on the seventh business day following trade date. Securities may be borrowed to effect delivery of a short sale. All transactions are settled through the *Effectenclearing* (Securities Clearing Corporation), a subsidiary of the stock exchange. As soon as it has processed the trades and given confirmation to the stock exchange parties, *Effectenclearing* interposes itself between the buyer and seller, and guarantees delivery and payment. Purchases and sales in the same security are balanced daily by the clearing corporation for each member firm, and settlement takes place on a net basis by participant. All deliveries and receipts of securities are also handled by *Effectenclearing* via Necigef (see below).

Traded securities are in bearer form and are generally deposited at the central security depository, the *Nederlands Centraal Instituut voor Givaal Effectenverkeer BV* (Necigef), where transfer is effected by book entry. Participants in Necigef include banks, brokers, and Effectenclearing, which guarantees delivery versus payment by effecting delivery of securities via Necigef and payment of funds through Kas-Associatie, a subsidiary of the stock exchange. Each of the members of the stock exchange has a cash account at Kas-Associatie. Preparations are being made to extend the functions of the central securities depository through the use of a nominee. For this purpose, the Netherlands Interprofessional Securities Center (NIEC) has been established.

Settlement of transactions on ASAS are handled through a nominee company, a subsidiary of the stock exchange, which holds the original shares for the Amsterdam system. Delivery is achieved by book transfer within the nominee company, and the associated money settlement is effected through the Kas-Associatie. The current registration system allows implementation of a settlement period of three business days at short notice.

The EOE clearing organization settles expired option contracts with a clearing member of the exchange. Such contracts are settled by the clearing member with the client, via the pom. The EOE and FTA clearing organizations ensure the performance of each contract traded on their respective exchanges. To protect the clearing organizations from financial loss in the event of defaults, clearing members with open positions on the exchange are required to deposit margins with the clearing organizations.

The settlement intervals between the EOE clearing organization and the clearing members are as follows:

Equities and Bonds:
    Exercises resulting from expiration: Next Friday
    All other exercises: Seventh calendar day
Indexes: Next trading day
Currencies: Fourth trading day
Gold: Fourth trading day

The last trading day is the third Friday of the contract month, provided that is a business day. Actual expiration is the day after, normally

Saturday. All options of the EOE, except index and jumbo dollar options, are American-style. American-style options, contrary to European-style, can be exercised before expiration.

Brokers and banks are allowed to accept one-day orders only on the futures exchange. Settlement months and last business day for FTA's contracts are, respectively:

FTI	January, April, July, and October
FT5	January, April, July, and October
FT0	March, June, September, and December

FTI, FT5	Third Friday of the settlement month, or if this is not a business day, the fourth Friday
FT0	Seventh calendar day or next business day

FTI and FT5 futures that are still outstanding after the last business day are settled in cash. The Guilder Bond Future (FTO) is a physical delivery contract of the closest equivalent underlying bond.

The clearing organization on the FTA is the European Futures Clearing Corporation B.V.

Procedures for Market Price Publication

Market prices are published daily in the Official Price List of the stock exchange. The information is also distributed on a real-time basis via data exchanges based on information reported by the *hoekmannen*. The Trade Support System is used to inform the market on a large variety of news items via *Beursnieuws* (Stock Exchange News), a specific publications service.

Post-trade information about market prices on the EOE and FTA is distributed through the Official Price List of the exchange market every day. Each exchange has developed a real-time information feed for automatic data capture by a computer on the premises of information vendors or other interested parties.

Taxes, Commissions, and Other Trading Costs

Taxation

Capital gains, dividends, and interest income arising from securities transactions are subject a corporation tax. Shareholders owning 5 percent or more of the share capital of the issuer are generally exempt from the corporation tax. Private individuals are normally not subject to taxation on capital gains.

Withholding tax applies to all dividends paid at a rate of 25 percent. The Netherlands has tax treaties with a number of countries to minimize the double taxation of income.

The exchange tax, or tax on transactions, was recently abolished.

Commissions

Fees and commissions related to securities transactions are freely negotiable and vary from bank/broker to bank/broker. No minimum commissions are imposed.

Procedures for Issuing and Listing New Securities

The major requirements for introduction to the ASE, which must be sponsored by a member of the exchange, are as follows:

- Issuance of a prospectus that incorporates financial information, articles of incorporation, and a description of management.
- Application for all outstanding securities to be listed (minimum of 10 percent on the Official Parallel Market).
- Initial market capitalization of at least Dfl 30 million (Official Parallel Market Dfl 2.5 million).

Recently authorized prospectuses in other EC countries comply with ASE requirements. Exchange fees payable upon introduction are limited to Dfl 6,000. Annual fees vary from Dfl 2,500 to Dfl 30,000.

Listed companies must provide the same information to the exchange and shareholders alike. Price-sensitive information must be published immediately. Companies must prepare unaudited interim financial statements and audited annual financial statements.

Takeover and Merger Transactions

Takeovers and mergers do not require regulatory approval but must be conducted in accordance with rules established by the committee for merger affairs of the Social and Economic Council. The major requirements are:

- Timely information and involvement of unions.
- Timely and complete information to shareholders.
- Equal treatment of all shareholders.

Tender offers and partial offers (limited to 30 percent) are permitted.

The merger prospectuses of listed companies must be approved by the ASE.

Exchange Membership Requirements

ASE

The ASE comprises three categories of membership: banks, brokers, and specialists *(hoekmannen)*. In December 1990, the Stock Exchange Association was made up of over 100 banks and stockbrokers and almost 40 specialist *(hoekman)* firms.

Membership is represented by corporate and private members. Directors of corporate members must have a minimum of two years of experience. Annual membership fees amount to Dfl 10,000 for corporate members and Dfl 2,500 for personal members. Admission fees amount to Dfl 300,000 for corporate members and Dfl 10,000 for private members.

Members may act in either an agent or principal capacity, or both.

No restrictions apply to the ownership of member firms. Non-EC companies can be members of the ASE through a local branch office.

Brokers supervised by the Central Bank and banking institutions must comply with rules, including capital adequacy rules, imposed by the Central Bank. Reporting to the Central Bank is required on a monthly basis. Members may handle money and securities received from customers.

Nonsupervised brokers and specialists are monitored by the ASE. Minimum net capital requirements amount to Dfl 1 million. These members must report financial information to the ASE on a monthly basis, and their portfolio positions more regularly. The mutual compensation fund managed by the ASE serves as a protection to investors in the event of member firms' financial difficulties.

Audited annual financial statements must be filed with the compliance office of the ASE by all members.

EOE

Membership of the EOE is classified as follows: clearing member, public order member, public order correspondent member, off-floor trader, market maker, and floor broker. In December 1990, there were 256 members in total.

Foreign membership is not restricted. There are no specific citizenship or residency requirements except for clearing members. Clearing members must be limited companies, and foreign companies must have an office in Amsterdam.

Members and market makers are "shareholders" in the EOE. Each share entitles the holder to one seat. The last transfer of an exchange seat occurred in December 1990 for approximately Dfl 500,000. The annual membership fee amounts to Dfl 3,000.

FTA

Membership of the FTA is classified as follows: market maker, trader, broker, and clearing member.

A clearing member must have at least one managing director who is a natural person resident of the Netherlands. It must satisfy the clearing organization that it has the capability and facilities in Amsterdam necessary to service all of its potential customers.

To be admitted as a seat holder, the applicant must be in possession of a subordinated bond issued by the FTA, normally valued at Dfl 25,000, for each seat applied for. There is also an application membership fee of Dfl 2,000.

Investor Protection

Foreign investors are accorded the same rights and protections as domestic investors.

Investor protection consists of the following:

- In the event that a member firm defaults on its obligations, Effecten-clearing can implement a compensation scheme that was established to protect participants as well as investors.
- Member firms are not permitted to trade on behalf of clients unless authorized to do so.
- Insider trading is prohibited by law. Management of listed companies must comply with a model code prescribed by the ASE.
- Business ethics rules must be adhered to by all members.
- Complaint procedures have been established.
- Chinese Wall procedures have been implemented by banks and brokers.

A new law has been proposed that provides that shareholders with a 10 percent interest or any change in ownership of a 10 percent or higher interest must be disclosed.

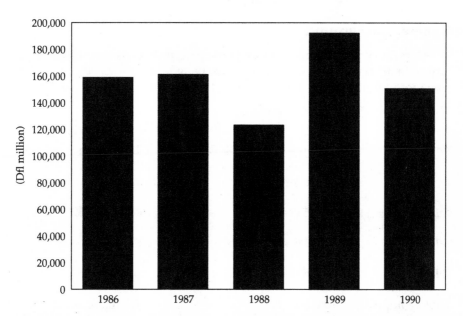

Figure 21.11.   Shares Turnover—Amsterdam Stock Exchange (1986–1990) (Dfl million)

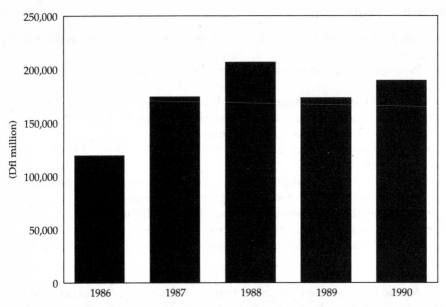

Figure 21.12.   Bonds Turnover—Amsterdam Stock Exchange (1986–1990)
(Dfl million)

SINGAPORE

General Background

Investors in Singapore are able to participate in both the securities and futures markets under two principal exchanges, the Stock Exchange of Singapore Limited (SES) and Singapore International Monetary Exchange Ltd. (SIMEX) respectively.

	SES	**SIMEX**
Address:	1 Raffles Place #24–00 OUB Center Singapore 0104	1 Raffles Place #07–00 OUB Center Singapore 0104
Telephone:	(65)–535–3788	(65)–535–7382
Telex:	RS 21853 SEMS	RS 38000 SIMEX
Telefax:	(65)–532–4476	(65)–535–7282
Trading hours:	10:00–12:30 14:30–16:00 (8 hours ahead of GMT)	7:45–18:30, actual time varying with respective contracts (8 hours ahead of GMT)

Listings:	Main Board: 172 companies SESDAQ: 13 companies Bonds: 144 companies Clob International: 144 companies	Futures: 6 contracts Futures & Options: 4 contracts
Membership:	26 full members 1 approved overseas representative office 40 clearing members	41 nonclearing members 11 commercial associate members
Market indices:	SES All Singapore Straits Times Industrial DBS—CPF Trustee Stocks Business Times Composite and Morgan Grenfell Asia OCBC 30 Index UOB SESDAQ Index	
Market capitalization: (1990)	S$84,035 million	
Average daily turnover: (1990)	S$135 million	23,000 contracts
Regulations:	The Securities Industry Act The Securities Industry Regulations SES Rules & Bylaws Singapore Code on Takeovers & Mergers	The Futures Trading Act The Futures Trading Regulations SIMEX Consolidated Rules
Regulators:	The Monetary Authority of Singapore (MAS) SES	MAS SIMEX

Market Trading Information

Main Types of Securities Traded

SES. Securities traded on the SES comprise ordinary and preferred stocks, bonds, transferable subscription rights, warrants, loan stocks, and floating rate notes. Trading in stock options is expected to be operational in 1992.

Securities listed on foreign exchanges recognized by the SES can either seek a listing on the Main Board on a quotation on Clob International. Currently six Hong Kong companies and one Japanese company are listed on the Main Board, whereas Clob International, which is an over-the-counter

(OTC) market for international securities listed on foreign stock exchanges, currently provides quotation on selected regional stocks, principally Hong Kong and Malaysian. It is intended that shares from other countries in the region will be included in the future. The SES is also linked to the National Association of Securities Dealers (NASD) for trading in selected NASDAQ stocks and to the Luxembourg Stock Exchange (LSE) for trading in Eurodollar and Asian dollar bonds as well as stocks.

SIMEX.   The futures contracts traded on SIMEX are Nikkei Stock Average, three-month Euromark, British pound, gold, high-sulphur fuel oil, and Dubai crude oil. The options on futures contracts traded are three-month Eurodollar, three-month Euroyen, Japanese yen, and Deutsch mark. Four contracts, three-month Eurodollar, Deutsch mark, Japanese yen, and British pound futures are traded on the SIMEX-CME (Chicago Mercantile Exchange) Mutual Offset System whereby trades initiated at one exchange may be liquidated at the other. In addition, after the June 1991 contract is put into effect, SIMEX will align the final settlement price of its Euroyen futures contract with the identical Euroyen contract on the Tokyo International Financial Futures Exchange (TIFFE). SIMEX will also introduce interexchange spread margin, thus reducing margin requirements for accounts with open positions in SIMEX with opposite positions in TIFFE.

Types of Markets

Securities are traded on: the SES Main Board, the primary market for locally listed securities; the SESDAQ, the second tier market for smaller companies not eligible for the Main Board; and Clob International, the OTC market for foreign listed securities (currently regional stocks). SES is also linked to foreign exchanges for common listing of selected securities, including the National Association of Securities Dealers (NASD) for NASDAQ stocks, and the Luxembourg Stock Exchange (LSE) for Eurodollar and Asian dollar bonds and stocks.

Trading on Main Board shares is currently enacted on both a scrip and a scripless basis. Scripless trading requires delivery of scrips within seven days of the transaction date. This also applies to trading of Clob International shares. Settlement takes place on the eighth day after the transaction date. Settlement of scripless trading on the Main Board, SESDAQ, and NASD Link takes place through a central clearing house run by the Central Depository (Pte.) Ltd. (CDP). Investors and participants in these markets maintain global securities accounts with the CDP or subaccounts with approved depository agents. These accounts are updated with book entries by the CDP on clearance and settlement of trades.

The cash market is available for Main Board and Malaysian stocks quoted on Clob International. Delivery is due by 17:00 on the contract date. Sellers are paid against delivery or on the next day. Delivery to buyers occurs after 15:00 the day after contract date.

The SES will institute compulsory buying-in procedures against selling brokers who fail to deliver on due date. Correspondingly, member companies can buy in against clients who fail to deliver.

Market Trading Systems

SES. Trading on the SES is off-the-exchange floor in board lots of 1,000 shares per lot, based on an order routing system dubbed the Central Limit Order Book (CLOB). Orders are keyed into the terminal of the Singapore Order Processing System (SESOPS) for a match by CLOB. A confirmation is obtained through the terminal when a match exists. Unmatched orders are held in the CLOB according to price and time priorities. An order book is maintained for every traded stock, and each order in the book has a limit price at which the order can be executed depending on whether it is a buy or sell order. Stockbrokers are able, through the screen, to see the aggregate order book for each stock in real time and advise their clients accordingly. Investors are also assured of the best deal, since orders are executed at the best possible prices.

Off-the-floor transactions or married deals are limited to a minimum of 50,000 shares or U.S.$150,000 per transaction. The volume of such deals are added to each day's trade done but not reflected in the high, low, or last-done prices to avoid distortion.

Traders in the odd lot market can trade in odd-sized blocks of shares. Settlement rules are the same as for the ready market.

SIMEX. All trades must be done on the SIMEX floor and are executed by open outcry, in which all prices bid, offered, and traded are shouted out loud by traders. These prices are disseminated through established information networks such as Reuters, Telerate, Quick, ADP Comtrend, Unicom, IDM Compak, and SBC Text.

Once a trade is done, a trader in the pits must record the price, quantity bought or sold, the opposite broker/trader, and the clearing member through whom the counterparty clears the trade. At half-hourly intervals the trades recorded are submitted to the SIMEX Clearing House for trade matching. Hourly out-trade reports are posted for verification by the traders. Contract sizes vary with the type of futures and option contract. Trades are settled on a daily basis.

All open positions are revalued on a daily basis using SIMEX's end-of-day settlement prices. This is to ensure that all debts are cleared before trading begins the next day. The Gross Margins System of SIMEX requires all SIMEX clearing members to maintain margins with the clearing house for house positions separately from customers' positions. In addition margins for customers' positions are computed on a gross basis; thus, one customer's long position cannot be used to offset another's short position.

SIMEX will undertake delivery of failed contracts.

Ordering and Settlement Procedures

Orders received from investors by the stockbrokers are keyed into the SESOPS terminal, specifying the client account code and the price and quantity of shares. Each accepted order entry is assigned a unique order number. Orders for odd lots must be matched completely or not at all, whereas orders for board lots may be matched partially. Confirmation of a match is given to the dealer through the terminal.

The seller delivers the physical scrips together with the transfer document duly signed by the shareholder named on the certificate via the broking member to the clearing house, Securities Clearing and Computer Services (Pte.) Ltd. (SCCS), a subsidiary of the SES. Buyers do not register their interest unless they intend to hold the shares for the long term or want to register their claim for entitlements. Upon registration, the scrips may be registered in the investor's name or in a nominee company's name for the benefit of the investor.

Under scripless trading, investors open accounts either with the CDP directly or sub-accounts with depository agents. The latter are either SES member companies, banks, merchant banks, or trust companies who have approved depository agent status with the CDP. There are presently approximately 80 agents. Trades are cleared and settled by the CDP via book entries into the accounts of the respective investors. Securities purchased are credited to the "available" balance on the day following the due date, until settlement has been effected by the investor. On payment to the broker, the securities will be moved to the "free" balance. Sales are also debited on the day following the due date.

Stockbrokers are held responsible for ensuring that their clients are able to deliver the shares sold on the due date. The SES has the right to institute buy-in procedures against short sale positions, even if the company has squared its net delivery position. Buying-in against member companies will be done at progressively increasing prices throughout the market day and, if necessary, the following market days, until the shares are bought in.

Member companies are allowed to extend credit facilities to approved clients subject to margin account requirements of the SES. Margin deposited by clients can take the form of cash, government securities, marginable securities, and such other instruments as prescribed from time to time by the SES. The equity in a client's account must initially not fall below 150 percent of the debit balance in the margin account, and if it subsequently falls below 140 percent, additional margin calls must be made. If it falls below 130 percent of the debit balance, the member company has the discretion to liquidate the margin account to bring it to not less than 140 percent of the debit balance.

Procedures for Market Price Publication

As a result of the CLOB system, market prices can be disseminated by the SES in real time via brokers' screens. In addition, the following are available on screens approximately 15 seconds behind real time: SBC Text, run for subscribers by Singapore Broadcasting Corporation; Teleview, run for subscribers by Singapore Telecoms; and Reuters, for subscribers on selected counters.

In addition, market prices for Main Board, SESDAQ, NASDAQ, Clob International and Unit Trusts are published daily in the local newspapers such as *Straits Times* and *Business Times*. The SES publishes a monthly journal containing information on securities. Most broking firms also have research units that publish research information to their clients.

Taxes, Commissions, and Other Trading Costs

Taxation

As there is no capital gains tax in Singapore, investment gains arising from the disposal of investment assets are free of tax. When the securities transactions constitute a trade carried on by investors or their representatives in Singapore, the trading gains therefrom are subject to tax. The gains or profits from the disposal of securities derived by an offshore fund (when the investors are neither residents nor citizens of Singapore) managed by an approved fund manager in Singapore are specifically exempted from income tax.

Dividends and interest income are subject to tax in Singapore. Under the full imputation system of taxation, the corporate tax paid by companies resident in Singapore is deemed paid by the shareholders on receipt of the dividends, other than tax-exempt dividends paid by companies enjoying tax incentives. A foreign investor is not required to pay further tax on dividend income since the tax would be equivalent to the corporate tax deemed paid by the shareholders. A resident investor whose effective tax rate is less than the corporate tax deemed paid on the dividend will receive a tax refund. Dividends are not subject to Singapore withholding tax.

Interest arising in Singapore and paid to nonresidents is subject to withholding tax at the rate of 31 percent. The interest withholding tax can be reduced in accordance with treaty provisions when the interest is paid to residents in a country with which Singapore has a tax treaty.

Commissions

Commissions are payable by both buyers and sellers. For stocks and shares, the rates, based on contract values, are graduated starting with 1.0 percent on the first S$250,000 and reduced by 0.1 percent on each succeeding S$250,000, up to S$1,000,000. Commissions on amounts exceeding S$1,000,000 are negotiable, subject to a minimum of 0.5 percent. For contracts at prices below S$1.00 per share or stock unit, the commission rates, subject to a minimum brokerage of S$5.00 per contract, are:

Under 50 cents	$\frac{1}{2}$ cent per share
50 to 99 cents	1 cent per share

The above schedule also applies to Malaysian stocks quoted on Clob International. Brokerage on Hong Kong stocks is 0.25 percent to 0.5 percent subject to a minimum of HK$25 per transaction. All banks and merchant banks are entitled to rebates of 0.25 percent on the brokerage payable. All transactions are subject to a clearing fee of 0.05 percent subject to a maximum of S$100 per transaction, with the exception of Hong Kong stocks transactions, which carry a maximum of HK$400 per transaction. A contract stamp duty is also payable equivalent to S$1 per S$1,000.

For Singapore and other government securities as well as nonconvertible Asian currency bonds, the transactions are on a net contract basis. Brokerage for registered corporate loan securities and debentures are at 1 percent on the first S$50,000, reduced to 0.5 percent on the next S$50,000 and 0.25 percent on values in excess of S$100,000, with a minimum brokerage of S$5.00.

Rates of brokerage for dealings in overseas shares that are not quoted on the SES are chargeable at members' discretion.

Procedures for Issuing and Listing New Securities

The criteria to be met by companies seeking a listing on the Main Board of the SES are as follows:

- 5-year operating record, the last 3 years of which must be profitable.
- Cumulative profit before tax in the last 3 years must be at least S$7.5 million.
- Shareholders' funds must be at least S$15 million before submission is made to the SES for listing.
- Market capitalization must be at least S$50 million at the time of listing.
- At least 25 percent of the issued and paid-up capital must be held by not less than 500 shareholders at the time of listing.
- A minimum percentage of the issued and paid-up share capital must be in the hands of shareholders each holding between 500 to 10,000 shares:

Nominal value of issued and paid-up capital:	Minimum percentage:
Less than S$50 million	20%
Between S$50 and S$100 million	greater of 15% or S$10 million
Greater than S$100 million	greater of 10% of S$15 million

Foreign companies seeking a listing on the SES must already be listed on their home exchange or traded in an over-the-counter market. The number of stockholders of 100 or more shares must be 2,000 worldwide and the number of shares publicly held 2 million worldwide. The net tangible assets value of the entity must be S$50 million worldwide, with a pre-tax income of S$50 million cumulative for the past 3 years or S$20 million minimum for any 1 of the 3 years. This requirement also applies to listing applicants for foreign bonds, which in addition must have at least 200 bondholders. An applicant not meeting the criteria may be guaranteed by another corporation that is able to meet the criteria, or by a government.

The application for listing must be accompanied by the appropriate listing fee and various relevant documents, including the draft prospectus. The contents of the prospectus must comply with the requirements of the Fifth Schedule of the Companies Act, Chapter 50; principally, it must include details of the minimum amount of capital required to be raised, the background of the company and related companies, the accountants' report, profit forecast with the auditors' report thereon, a report from the directors, details of material contracts outside the normal course of business including the details of the underwriting agreement relating to the public issue, valuation report on any properties of the company, and the net tangible assets per share of the company.

Approval is normally given within six weeks of the date of submission. Upon approval, the company files the final copy of the prospectus with the Registrar of Companies and the SES. The prospectus is issued to the public and the offer period opens, usually for about seven to ten market days. When the public offering is oversubscribed, allotment of shares is by public balloting held on the day after the close of the offer, on the basis of the allotment decided by the board of directors of the company with the approval of the SES. Unsuccessful applicants have their applications returned within three days and successful applicants are informed within one to three weeks of balloting. The securities are traded three days after certificates have been dispatched.

The initial listing fee is S$500 per million dollars or part thereof of the issued capital of the company, with a minimum fee of S$2,000 and a maximum of S$20,000. The annual listing fee is S$100 per million dollars or part thereof of the issued capital of the company, with a minimum of S$400 and a maximum of S$2,000.

Foreign companies seeking a listing on the SES are required to meet similar criteria and comply with the same procedures for application. The SES requires the trading of such shares to be in a foreign currency, have a minimum lot size of 1,000 units, and have an issue price equivalent to a minimum of US$2 per share.

Listed companies have the duty of promptly informing shareholders of any significant events and making public disclosure of material information. At the half-year, listed companies must publish interim financial information in the format prescribed by the SES.

Takeover and Merger Transactions

Companies are bound by the provisions of the Companies Act and the Code of Takeovers and Mergers. A takeover scheme involves an offer to acquire all or sufficient shares in a public company, resulting in effective control, defined as at least 25 percent of the voting shares of the company. An offer becomes mandatory when any person, together with persons acting in concert, acquires shares carrying 25 percent or more of the voting rights of a company or, if these parties hold between 25 percent and 50 percent of the voting rights, they acquire in any period of 12 months an additional 3 percent of voting rights.

The offer must be presented in the first instance to the board of directors of the offeree company. The code imposes a mandatory obligation of the offeree board to obtain competent independent advice on any offer and to make known to the shareholders the substance of the advice. The shareholders must be informed of the offer without delay. The offeree board must circulate its views of the offer by way of a circular that must contain a wide range of information, including information on the directors' shareholdings in the offeree and offeror companies as well as details of service contracts. The Companies Act requires the offeror to give notice of the offer not earlier than 28 days and not later than 14 days before the offer document is dispatched to the shareholders. This gives the directors of the offeree company time to advise the shareholders.

Before making a takeover bid the offeror must ensure that it is able to obtain all necessary consents and has the necessary resources to offer a cash alternative. In the announcement of the bid, the offeror must not impose any conditions that will create uncertainty as to whether or not the offer will be made. The only condition that may accompany a mandatory offer relates to acceptance, whereby an offer will only be declared unconditional after the offeror has secured acceptances that, together with its own holdings, bring its aggregate total to more than 50 percent of the company's capital. Government approval must be obtained before an announcement of a mandatory bid. The Securities Industry Council (SIC), which administers the code, must give its approval before an offer can be withdrawn. The offer must be in cash or be accompanied by a cash alternative.

Foreign Investors

There are no foreign exchange controls on remittances and repatriation of capital or restrictions on the remittance of income, trading profits, and capital gains. Foreigners are allowed to own shares in local companies. Their holdings in companies in strategic industries are, however, limited to 40 percent for banks, 25 percent for the national airline, and 49 percent for both the national press and shipping companies. When the foreign limit has been reached, foreign investors may register their shares only if they are already foreign-owned or the foreign limits have fallen. Some companies have adopted a queueing system for the registration of foreign-owned shares. Local investors may trade in foreign-held shares provided they are traded under the scripless system.

Exchange Membership Requirements

SES

The SES has three classes of membership: individual, corporate, and international. Individual members must be Singaporean citizens or residents of at least five years who meet the professional requirements of the Committee of the Stock Exchange. Individual members are known as stockbroking members. Corporate members must be Singapore-incorporated stockbroking companies whose shareholders (or executive directors, in the case of subsidiaries of local banks) have been approved as stockbroking members by the Committee of the Stock Exchange.

Currently, foreign participation is limited to 49 percent of the equity of the existing local corporate member. Preference is given to joint-venture proposals from regional securities firms. Foreign participation in joint ventures existing prior to October 1990 are permitted to increase their participation up to a maximum of 70 percent if they meet the conditions stipulated in the previous guidelines. In October 1990, the SES introduced a new category of membership, the international member, whereby foreign securities houses are able to become full members of the SES without entering into joint ventures with local entities. International members are, however, restricted to dealing with nonresidents and their affiliates in transactions of not less than S\$5 million. Furthermore, international members are not eligible for election to the SES Committee nor may they vote on a resolution for election of the committee.

Cost of Membership. On the basis of the last transaction, a seat for a local corporate member is currently valued at S\$3.8 million. The cost of membership in the clearing house is S\$200,000. No international members have yet been admitted to the SES.

Minimum Capital Requirements. All member companies are required to have a paid-in capital of at least S\$10 million, but there is a proposal to increase this to S\$15 million. In addition, their adjusted net capital must not fall below S\$250,000, and their aggregate indebtedness must not exceed 1,200 percent of their adjusted net capital. Adjusted net capital comprises shareholders' funds after adjustment for certain prescribed deductions, principally including deficits in clients' accounts and shortfalls in the value of securities held by the company. Furthermore, the member companies must maintain a statutory reserve fund out of their net profits, as prescribed by the Securities Industry Act.

SIMEX

SIMEX has five classes of members, three corporate and two individual. The corporate class consists of clearing, nonclearing, and commercial associate members. The individual class comprises nonclearing members and trading permit holders. Corporate clearing members are companies incorporated in Singapore or a branch of a foreign company. Each member owns three seats, exercises full trading rights on the floor, clears trades, and accepts customer business. Corporate nonclearing members must be companies incorporated in Singapore. Each member owns three seats, exercises full trading rights on the floor, and accepts customer business. All trades must, however, be qualified and cleared through a clearing member. Commercial associate members comprise reputable oil trading companies that trade strictly in energy futures for their own companies' accounts or that of their related or associated companies. They hold one seat on SIMEX. Individual nonclearing members are individuals who have full trading rights but trade only for their own account. Trading permit holders are individuals who trade only in energy futures and for their own account.

A clearing member is required to have a minimum capital of S$2 million and an adjusted net capital of S$4 million or 10 percent of customer funds. There must also be a security deposit placed with SIMEX of US$250,000 cash or a standing letter of credit. A nonclearing corporate member's minimum paid-up capital is S$1 million with adjusted net capital of S$1 million or 10 percent of customer funds. Commercial associate members must have minimum net adjusted capital of S$25,000 and standing letter of credit of S$1 million.

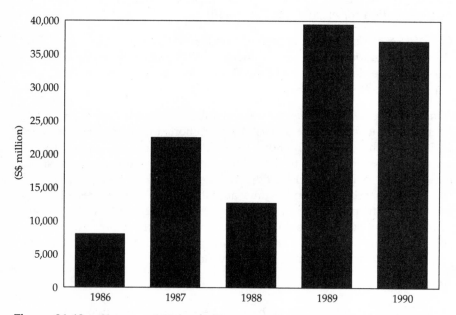

Figure 21.13. Shares and Warrants Turnover—Singapore Stock Exchange (1986–1990) (S$ million)

SWITZERLAND

General Background

Switzerland has five stock exchanges, located in Zurich, Geneva, Basle, Bern, and St. Gallen. St. Gallen is expected to close soon, as did Lausanne and Neuchâtel recently. In the short- to medium-term, only three stock exchanges, Zurich, Geneva, and Basle, representing about 90 percent of the total trading volume, will remain. It is anticipated that ultimately these three floor-based exchanges will be replaced by an electronic trading system, dubbed EBS. Additionally, the Swiss Options and Financial Futures Exchange (SOFFEX) provides for the trading of financial futures and options contracts. This review will focus primarily on the Zurich Stock Exchange as it commands approximately 65 percent of the Swiss securities market.

Zurich Stock Exchange

Location: Address until June 1992:
Bleicherweg 5
CH-8001 Zurich, Switzerland

New address as of June 1992:
Selnaustrasse 30
CH-8009 Zurich, Switzerland

Mailing address:
P.O. Box, 8021 Zurich
Telephone: 41 (1) 229–21–11

Trading hours:

Domestic and foreign bonds,
   domestic stocks:
8:15   Opening of pre-bourse trading
9:00   Opening of official trading in
              listed bonds

Continuous trading until 17:00 (14:00 to 15:00 break)

Foreign stocks: 8:45–14:30

Options: 9:00–17:00

Zurich has no official fixed closing time except for continuously-traded stocks. Regular securities trading continues as long as deals are being made, which can vary substantially depending upon trading volumes. Zurich is one hour ahead of Greenwich Mean Time.

Number of securities listed:	**Bonds**	
	Domestic:	1,483
	Foreign:	895
	Stocks	
	Domestic:	330
	Foreign:	236
	Total	2,944

Market capitalization:	**Bonds**	
(Dec 1990)	Domestic:	SFr bn. 113
	Foreign:	93
	Stocks	
	Domestic:	217
	Foreign:	N/A

Average daily share and bond turnover (1990):   SFr 2bn.

Market indices: Association Tripartite Bourses
(ATB) Swiss Index including:
  ▪ Swiss Performance Index (SPI)
  ▪ Swiss Market Index (SMI)
Swiss Bank Corporation
(SBC) Price Index
Credit Suisse (SKA) Index

Regulatory framework:

The Swiss stock exchanges are subject to the laws of the individual cantons. The Zurich Stock Exchange is a private-sector organization established by the banks and supervised by the Canton of Zurich.

The framework for securities trading in the Canton of Zurich is the "Law on Professional Dealings in Securities." This law sets out the conditions for the granting of the state's license for the professional securities business. Since stock brokers are normally banks, they are additionally subject to the "Federal Law on Banks and Savings Banks." They are supervised in their business activity by the Federal Banking Commission. Membership in the Stock Exchange Association, the institution operating the Zurich Stock Exchange, is prescribed by law.

The highest supervisory authority for the stock exchange is the Department of Economic Affairs of the Canton of Zurich. Immediate state control is delegated to the stock exchange commissioner's office. The purpose of state supervision is to protect the public from abuses in securities trading. The most important duty of the stock exchange commissioner's office therefore comprises supervision of the orderly establishment of prices at the trading rings of the exchange.

The government is also assisted by the Stock Exchange Committee as an expert advisory body. It is headed by the director of the Department of Economic Affairs. It has six members, two of whom are representatives of the Stock Exchange Association. The stock exchange commissioner also attends its meetings in an advisory capacity.

Market Trading Information

Main Types of Securities Traded

The following securities are traded on all stock exchanges in Switzerland.

Equities

- Bearer shares.
- Registered shares:
  Registered shares are frequently restricted to Swiss nationals. Most companies issue more registered shares than bearer shares. However, price differentials have been reduced in recent years due to some banks offering *Stillhalter* options on registered shares (see below). Recently, a number of Swiss companies have increased the availability of their registered shares.
- Restricted transferable shares:
  These registered shares cannot be transferred without prior approval by the Board of Directors of the company.
- Participation certificates; profit-sharing certificates; preference shares, and co-operative shares.

Debt Instruments

- Straight bonds:
  Double currency bonds, multiple currency clause bonds, Swiss franc bonds, bonds with variable interest rates (floaters), zero coupon bonds, discount bonds, and premium bonds.
- Other bonds, including convertible bonds, option bonds, warrant bonds, and mortgage bonds.

Hybrid Forms

- Trust units, covered options, options, warrants, and *Stillhalter* (silent holder) options, which are negotiable options on registered shares permitting foreign investors to invest in registered shares but with the issuing bank retaining the dividend on the shares it holds as securities.

In the course of 1989 a new trading ring was built in order to provide more space and capacity, especially for trading in derivative instruments, particularly warrants and options. At the end of the year, 71 issues were traded.

Types of Markets

Cash or Spot Market.   Approximately 80 percent of all transactions on the Zurich Stock Exchange are concluded as cash bargains. In practice, a period of between three and ten banking days is allowed for performance of the contract, though three days is standard (except for notes). Securities are delivered through the Swiss depository and clearing organization, SEGA, and payments are settled simultaneously via the Swiss Interbank Clearing (SIC) system.

Forward Market.   Forward transactions are traded like spot transactions, but with later delivery and payment. Settlement day is the fourth from last trading day of each month and value date is the last day of the month. Forward contracts can be settled within one to three months in Zurich, and in Basle and Geneva up to nine months. Securities bought and sold by forward transactions are settled at the end of the month among stock exchange banks via SEGA.

The following markets handle cash and forward trades:

Main Stock Exchange.   Only listed securities are traded on the main stock exchange (official market). The official list of securities is split into groups and organized alphabetically. A security can be traded once it has been called by the stock exchange clerk, and the trading period finishes once the next group has been called. Trading is performed *à la criée*, which means that the dealers at the ring trade directly with one another by shouting bid and offer prices.

Continuing Trading.   The shares of approximately 49 of the most important domestic and foreign companies (37 Swiss, 12 European) are considered continuously traded securities. These securities are opened for trading first, and can be traded at any time throughout the entire stock exchange session. Continuously traded securities are part of the main stock exchange. Only seven registered shares are traded on this basis, the rest being bearer shares and participation certificates.

Nebenbourse Market (lesser exchange). On the Nebenbourse market (formerly the pre-bourse market), or the semi-official market, shares of companies which fail to meet the listing terms for official trading are traded. Trading can take place at all times without restriction and is outside the scope of supervision of the cantonal stock exchange commissioner. The market mechanism closely parallels that of the main stock exchange.

Over-the-Counter Market.   The over-the-counter market facilitates the trading of securities at nonofficial prices. The market has no official rules, and dealing is mostly performed by phone. The majority of trading in private placements, or notes (see the following), is conducted on this market.

Private Placements. Private placements are generally traded by telephone off the exchange floor. Most private placements are denominated in Swiss francs, though some dual currency issues have appeared. Private placements, or notes, are generally aimed at institutional investors, with a minimum denomination of SFr50,000. The certificates must be deposited with the lead manager or with SEGA. These are usually medium-term instruments with four- to seven-year maturities.

The main borrowers in this market are Japanese companies (currently estimated at about 60 percent of the market), supranational organizations, and governments.

SOFFEX. The Swiss Options and Financial Futures Exchange is a purely electronic exchange based on a market-maker system. At the SOFFEX, options on 13 Swiss blue chips and on the Swiss Market Index (SMI) are traded, as well as SMI futures. The options and futures are contracts each involving up to five basic securities. All contracts can be established for a maturity of either one, two, three, or six months. Options and futures on interest rates and currencies are currently under consideration. All options traded at SOFFEX are American-style options.

Market Trading Systems

The trading system at Swiss stock exchanges is *à la criée*. Unique to the Swiss markets, trading is concluded directly between the representatives of the stock exchange member banks, without using brokers, intermediaries, or specialists.

Stock exchange orders can be used by the client at any bank, by phone, or in writing. If the client does not determine a maximum or minimum price, the order is executed "at best." With a stop-loss order the client requests that the security be sold if it drops below a certain level (there is no floor price guarantee). With an *ordre lié* a purchase will be performed only if a related selling order is executed.

Each transaction is executed in full view of the other stock exchange dealers. Prices are immediately listed individually in the quotations list, so that in the course of a session several different prices are listed for the same security. This is known as continuous quotation or variable prices.

Minimum price graduations are prescribed, depending on the market price. Only round lots can attract the official price. As a general rule, a round lot for shares has a value of about SFr10,000, and bonds are traded in units of at least SFr5,000. If a price differs by more than 10 percent from the previous trade, trading in that security will be stopped for about half an hour, giving the dealers the opportunity to contact their clients. This mechanism also serves to prevent extreme volatility.

The Association Tripartite des Bourses (ATB), an association jointly managed by representatives from the Basle, Geneva, and Zurich exchanges, coordinates the transmission of price information between the exchanges.

Major changes are expected to occur in the near-term, leading to the unification of the three major exchanges and a gradual shift of trading from the exchange floor to an electronic system. A new electronic system, Elektronische Borse Schweiz (EBS), is in the development phase for application to the trading of straight bonds. Other bonds, notes, warrants, and equities may be transferred to the system at a later date. To promote further liquidity and transparency, banks will be obliged to execute all trades not exceeding a predetermined size through the system. Orders above this limit may be executed outside of the system, but with immediate reporting of price and volume.

According to the ATB, an important feature of EBS will be its order-driven trading capability with a continuously updated order book. Trades will be determined by an automatic matching process or by an electronically supported acceptance system. The opening procedure will follow the principle of maximum tradeable volume, which means that a security will only be opened if all orders "at best" can be executed. After opening a security, it will be traded continuously. The automated system will prevent extreme volatility by suspending trading automatically if larger deviations from the last price paid occur.

SOFFEX operates via a nationwide electronic network, with designated market makers. The host computer is located in Zurich. Members request and receive market information electronically, enter orders and quotes, and obtain automatic execution as soon as buy and sell orders are matched by the central computer.

Clearance and Settlement Procedures

The various aspects of the settlement process, including delivery, payment, recording, and confirmations, are increasingly carried out with the aid of electronic data processing. All stock exchange member banks are linked to the stock exchange's automatic processing system. During the trading session, the banks continuously enter their contracts via terminals into a central computer that performs matching and confirmation procedures. The banks receive all data relating to the transaction in computer-readable form, so that the back offices can complete the confirmation and recording process the same day.

Stock market transactions are generally settled for value three days ahead (i.e., the calculation of interest begins on the third day after trade date). Buy and sell orders are matched, and only the differences are traded between dealers. After the stock exchange session, the dealers allocate the number of securities and price to their clients.

Most clients maintain a securities deposit account at a bank. Schweizerische Effekten-Giro AG (SEGA), the Swiss depository and clearing organization, established to eliminate delivery of securities from bank to bank, maintains collective custody of securities. On value date, traded securities are transferred from one bank's account to the other with a corresponding cash movement. In order to participate in the SEGA network banks must have an account with the Swiss National Bank. At present, only banks can be full members of SEGA.

Securities clearing and settlement via SEGA is normally "delivery against payment" (DAP). Certain companies no longer print share certificates, instead utilizing a new SEGA facility for recording the holders of registered shares. Certificates are not issued unless requested by the shareholder. The registered shares of foreign companies traded in Switzerland are registered with the Swiss Nominee Company (SNOC), run by SEGA, and are traded in the form of certificates in Swiss Francs.

Short sales are, in general, not permitted by SEGA (although individual clients may go short as long as their bank has adequate shares deposited), and borrowing of stock is not an accepted practice. However, recent moves by two banks indicate that borrowing of securities may become accepted in the near future, in particular to allow traders to exploit arbitrage situations between futures and the underlying securities.

The Swiss Interbank Clearing (SIC) is an on-line Swiss Interbank clearing system whose objectives are to speed up clearing, reduce paperwork, improve liquidity, and increase the level of unconditional payments (i.e., without Swiss National Bank margin control).

Intersettle is an organization formed under the auspices of the Swiss Bankers Association as an international securities clearing organization that processes transactions against payment in customary market currencies. Brokers and finance companies resident in Switzerland can join Intersettle, clearing securities handed by SEGA and other major clearing organizations against payment in Swiss francs. Non-banks need to have an account with a bank, as they themselves cannot be members of SIC or SEGA.

SOFFEX. Orders and quotes on SOFFEX are recorded, sorted, and matched automatically by the computer network. Matched trades are posted immediately to the integrated clearing system. The actual clearing process is handled overnight through electronic interfaces with the Swiss Securities Clearing Corporation, a computerized book-entry system, and the Swiss National Bank, where all members maintain accounts.

Procedures for Market Price Publication

Stock exchange member banks report daily all transactions in Swiss shares to the ATB, which transmits price information between the exchanges and to the bank's own computers.

Price information is disseminated worldwide through the services of Telekurs AG (Investdata). Prices also appear in the daily stock exchange bulletin, *Kursblatt*, and in the major newspapers.

Taxes, Commissions, and Other Trading Costs

Taxation

In most Swiss cantons, capital gains are not taxable in the hands of private investors. A withholding tax of 35 percent is applied to dividends and interest income from Swiss-resident companies. Foreign investors can claim this credit if a tax treaty between Switzerland and their country exists.

A Swiss federal stamp duty is levied on new issues and on the transfer of securities. In most cantons there is also a cantonal tax or stock exchange fee levied on the transfer of securities.

Tax on new issues of domestic securities ranges from 0.9 percent to 3 percent of the contract value, according to the nature of the issue. Tax on the transfer of securities varies from zero on warrants, futures, and options to 0.3 percent on securities issued by foreign residents. Cantonal tax for transfers is typically 0.015 percent. A Swiss national stamp duty charged to securities dealers is divided equally between the two parties to the transaction.

Commissions

Since the removal of fixed commissions on January 1, 1991, the broker is free to negotiate commission rates with the banks. In practice, the banks follow, more or less, the commission structure defined by the Brokerage Convention of the Association of Stock Exchanges, which provides for commission rates on share transactions of 0.2 percent to 1.1 percent depending on the size of the transaction, and rates on Swiss franc bond transactions of 0.1 percent to 0.8 percent.

For each trade in shares or bonds, a minimum brokerage fee of about SFr80 is required. As a general rule, the brokerage rate is about 1 percent of the trade value. The brokerage fee for trust units is significantly lower.

Procedures for Issuing and Listing New Securities

Generally, securities are admitted for listing provided that distribution among the public is large enough to facilitate an active market and that sufficient information regarding the issuer and the securities is available to the public. The Stock Exchange Association reviews and approves applications for listing. Additionally, the Swiss Administration Board, made up of representatives of the banks, stock exchanges, large industrial companies, and the Swiss Federal Department of Finance must approve listings for foreign securities. The listing requirements, which are set forth in the listing regulations of the Zurich Stock Exchange, include the following:

- Financial statements for five years.
- Minimum paid-up capital of 5 million Swiss francs for Swiss issuers and 10 million Swiss francs for foreign issuers.

- Total par value of at least 10 million Swiss francs or a market value of at least 25 million Swiss francs for shares of Swiss issuers; 20 million and 50 million Swiss francs, respectively, for foreign issuers.
- Publication of a detailed prospectus.
- Applications for listing submitted through a member of the stock exchange to the secretariat of the Stock Exchange Association.
- Securities of foreign issuers must be included in at least 250 portfolios of major Swiss banks and the market value of these securities located in Switzerland must not be less than 10 million Swiss francs.

Takeover and Merger Transactions

On September 1, 1989, the Swiss Takeover Code became effective. A voluntary agreement between the banks, this code applies to all public offers relating to the acquisition of shares of Swiss public companies traded on the stock exchange or of other securities giving the holder a right to acquire such shares; for example, convertible bonds and options. There is no percentage holding that would automatically trigger a formal takeover offer.

A takeover offer can be valid for between one and two months and must be published in certain newspapers. The offer can be subject only to conditions that the offeror cannot influence, such as the acquisition of a minimum percentage of shares or the registration of the offeror. The offer can be neither withdrawn nor revised, except to increase the consideration or to extend it within the two-month limit. If a counter-offer is published, the offer may be withdrawn or revised, but the shareholders also have the right to withdraw their acceptances. If the offer is successful, it has to be extended for at least ten banking days after publication of the offer's result. An offeror who has more than 50 percent of the voting rights must buy all securities presented for sale, even if the offer is already closed.

The following information must be included in the offer:

- Identity of the offeror and any persons acting in concert.
- Special agreements with the offeree company's officials or shareholders.
- Minimum and maximum of shares to be acquired.
- Details of any shares or voting rights the offeror holds and the number of shares the offeror has acquired and sold in the preceding year.
- Details of the financing for the offer with a confirmation from the accounting firm that is supervising the offer.
- Offer price per share and closing date of the offer.

The offeror has the following additional obligations:

- Confirm that the persons acting in concert with the offeror are respecting the code.

- Communicate the terms of the offer to the Commission for Regulation of the Association of Swiss Exchanges and to the offeree company as soon as it is made public.
- Appoint a firm of accountants to ensure that the offeror discharges required duties during the offer period.
- Not manipulate the market, for example, by selling securities after the publication of the offer.

Foreign Investors

There is no government prohibition against foreigners buying stocks. However, Swiss companies may choose to refuse registration of their registered shares by foreigners (residents or nonresidents).

Article 8 of the Bank Law defines the types of capital export transactions made by banks and finance companies that are subject to advance approval of the Swiss National Bank. The bank has published a circular giving a detailed technical explanation of the transactions subject to its approval. This circular is regularly updated to reflect the ever-changing situation of the capital and money markets. The last amendment to this circular was dated March 1, 1990.

A wide range of Swiss franc transactions covered by a general permit only require reporting after the event. The transactions subject to advance approval include bond issues, loans, and share sales to nonresidents in excess of SFr10 million or its equivalent unless specifically excluded by the current circular.

The purchase of foreign notes and private placements in amounts exceeding SFr3 million is also subject to prior Swiss National Bank approval.

Exchange Membership Requirements

Under securities law, licenses are granted to: (1) stock exchange dealers (i.e., stock exchange member banks) or "ring banks"; and (2) securities dealers outside the stock exchange (i.e., other banks, finance companies, trust companies, etc.).

The simplistic designations *A-License*, in the case of the stock exchange member banks, and *B-License*, in the case of the securities dealers outside the stock exchange, are commonly used.

The license for stock brokers entitles the holders to buy and sell securities as agents in their own name for the account of third parties, or for their own account. If the license is issued to a stock exchange member bank, the bank must designate a person as its representative. Both bank and representative are equally subject to the provisions of the securities law. Furthermore, trading on the stock exchange requires the nomination of deputies who also require a federal or cantonal license. A representative who leaves the bank automatically loses the authority to conclude transactions on the stock exchange. The bank must make a new application for the successor.

Holders of licenses for professional securities trading must comply with the following:

- Possession of civil rights and a good reputation (in practice this includes possession of Swiss citizenship).
- Proof of the necessary specialized knowledge.
- Residence or business domicile in the canton of Zurich.
- Conduct of business according to recognized commercial principles.

Securities dealers must pay the canton an annual charge, calculated according to turnover. In addition, a guarantee (in cash or securities) must be paid to the cantonal treasury.

Investor Protection

Insider trading is prohibited by the Swiss criminal code and is punishable with imprisonment or a fine. By convention between the banks, securities dealers are precluded from taking a mark-up on the price of the securities in addition to their commission.

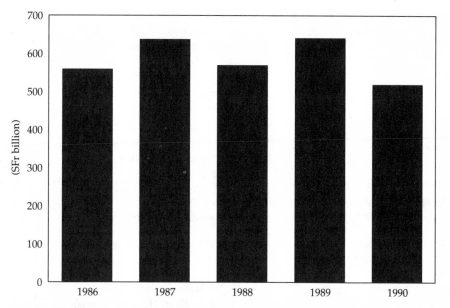

Figure 21.14. Shares and Fixed Income Securities Turnover—Zurich Stock Exchange (1986–1990) (SFr billion)

THE UNITED KINGDOM

General Background

The London Stock Exchange (LSE)
Old Broad Street
London EC2N 1HP
Telephone: 071–588–2355
Telefax: 071–588–3504 (secretariat)

The London International Financial Futures Exchange
Royal Exchange
London EC3V 3PJ
Telephone: 071–623–0444

London Stock Exchange

Trading hours:	U.K. equities: 8:00–16:45 (mandatory quote period: 8:30–16:30)
	International equities: 9:30–15:30 for most countries (U.S. and Canada to 13:00)
	Gilts and fixed-interest securities: 9:00–17:00
	Traded options: 8:35–16:10
	(These times are Greenwich Mean Time, except during the summer, when U.K. time is one hour later than GMT)
Number of securities listed: *(As of September 30, 1990)*	Official List: U.K. and Irish equities: 2,086 U.K. and Irish fixed-interest securities: 2,028 Foreign: 552 Unlisted Securities Market: 428 Third Market (ceased operation 1/1/91): 55 U.K. and Irish government: 170 Other public securities: 1,899 Traded options: 71
Number of exchange members: *(September 1990)*	409 member firms 5,124 individual members
Market capitalization: *(September 1990)*	£1,448,718 million (equities) £315,062 million (fixed income)
Annual share turnover: *(1990)*	£499,273 million (equities) £510,580 million (fixed income)

Market indices:	FTSE 100 Share Index
	European equities: FT-SE Eurotrack 100 Index (started October 1990 and calculated in Deutsche marks)
	The LSE also plans to introduce the FTSE Eurotrack 200, which will combine the FT-SE 100 and the FT-SE Eurotrack 100 (calculated in ECU)

Regulatory framework:

The regulatory framework is set out in the Financial Services Act 1986. This act put into law a structure of self-regulation within a statutory framework, combining the speed and flexibility of self-regulation with statutory protection for the investor.

The regulatory framework is overseen by a central agency, the Securities and Investments Board (SIB), which has certain powers under the act and is answerable to the Secretary of State for Trade and Industry.

The SIB has delegated its powers of regulating most authorized investment businesses to four self-regulating organizations (SROs). The SRO that regulates members of the LSE is principally the Securities and Futures Authority (SFA), which was formed by the recent merger of The Securities Association (TSA) and the Association of Futures Brokers and Dealers. Transitional arrangements have been made pending full harmonization of their respective rulebooks. Commentary provided below on regulatory matters is based upon TSA's current rulebook. The SRO rulebooks basically comprise two elements: conduct of business rules, which place various requirements on how a firm can deal; and financial regulations, which place capital and record-keeping requirements on each firm.

The LSE has been designated a Recognized Investment Exchange. Its primary functions are to ensure that adequate information is provided to potential investors about securities that are to be listed, and to ensure that an orderly secondary market is maintained in those securities that are traded on the exchange. It has been authorized to regulate dealing in the following four markets:

- domestic equities
- foreign equities
- U.K. government stock (gilts), public sector, debt, and company fixed-interest securities
- options

Market Trading Information

Main Types of Securities Traded

The main types of securities traded are: U.K. equities; foreign equities; U.K. government securities (gilts) and other public sector and Commonwealth securities; U.K. and foreign company fixed-interest securities (including Eurobonds); and traded options on approximately 70 alpha securities, the FT-SE 100 Index, and currencies.

U.K. securities are quoted overseas following individual applications by companies for listings on overseas exchanges. A popular means of trading U.K. securities in the United States is in American Depository Receipt (ADR) form, as this avoids the full SEC listing requirements.

Private investors account for approximately 18 percent of trading by value, but nearly 75 percent by number of bargains. There has been a steady decline in the private investor's share of the U.K. market over the last three decades as pension funds and insurance companies have increasingly been used as the investment medium.

Types of Markets

Market Tiers.　The market is divided into the Official List and the Unlisted Securities Market (USM). These categories are distinguished by different initial and ongoing obligations on the companies seeking a quotation, as discussed in the later section on the procedures for listing new securities.

Options are quoted on the London Traded Options Market.

The LSE also permit dealings under Rule 535.2 in a number of smaller companies, and under Rule 535.4a in foreign equity securities quoted or traded on specified stock exchanges, financial marketplaces, and associations.

For dealing purposes the market is subdivided into U.K. equities, foreign equities, fixed-interest securities, gilts, and traded options.

Trading Periods and Settlements.　Equities are settled by reference to trading periods known as accounts. Accounts are normally ten business days in duration. Customers then either settle the net balance due on transactions dealt within the account on "Account Day," which is the second Monday following the end of the account, or settle each transaction when the stock is delivered, which is, at the earliest, Account Day. This settlement practice allows investors to buy and sell shares during the account in volumes greater than they are able to settle without any form of margin requirement. Members are allowed to settle equities for cash; settlement in these cases takes place on the second business day following dealing.

The gilts, new corporate issues, and traded options markets are cash markets, being settled on the next business day after dealing.

Certain sterling issues by non-U.K. residents and certain fixed-interest nonconvertible debt issued by U.K. companies are settled seven calendar days after dealing.

Private Placements of Foreign-Currency Denominated Securities. Issuers wishing to obtain a listing for their securities are obliged to comply with the requirements outlined in the following "Procedures for Issuing and Listing New Securities" section. Private placements of unlisted securities will be subject to rules expected to be issued by the Secretary of State for Trade and Industry in mid-1991 once agreement has been reached on a common set of rules for the European Community (EC). These rules will identify the circumstances under which public documents will have to be prepared, the necessary contents, and other requirements.

Market Trading Systems

The Stock Exchange Automated Quotations system (SEAQ) is the LSE's real-time system for the display of market makers' quotations in over 2,000 U.K. securities. The screens are installed in the market makers' offices. Only traded options are traded by open outcry on the floor of the exchange.

Securities are classified on SEAQ according to their *normal market size*. This is an average based on the level of customer business in each security over the previous 12 months, and it is reviewed quarterly. To avoid odd lots, 12 normal market size levels have been established, ranging from 500 shares to 200,000. Market makers are obliged to quote firm prices in minimum sizes set equal to the current normal market size.

As of October 2, 1990, there were 25 market makers in U.K. equity securities, down from 36 in 1987. The average number of market makers for each of the most liquid securities was 12; there were 2 for the least liquid securities quoted on SEAQ.

The LSE also maintains a parallel system to SEAQ for foreign securities, known as SEAQ International. On December 31, 1989 there were 787 foreign companies quoted on SEAQ International.

Market makers are obliged to deal at the prices and sizes they quote. Odd lots may be dealt at negotiated prices. Market makers are not obliged to quote prices outside the mandatory quote periods, but if they do they must quote firm, two-way prices in at least the minimum sizes.

Market makers can anonymously display block order information to institutions and other market participants in deal sizes above the maximum permitted on SEAQ through the LSE's Block Order Exposure System (BLOX).

Interdealer brokers, whose function it is to provide liquidity to the market by matching deals between market makers on an anonymous basis, place their own terminals in market makers' offices.

The LSE is also responsible for the Company News Service, an electronic system that captures and distributes information to subscribers, giving market makers and brokers who use screen-based trading systems rapid access to the latest company news.

Real-time prices are now being shared with the New York Stock Exchange, and NASDAQ prices of certain American OTC shares are now displayed in London. Members also typically use the services of a number of commercial information systems such as Reuters, Telerate, and Datastream, particularly for Eurobonds and non-SEAQ International securities.

Ordering and Settlement Procedures

Ordering.   Customers contact their brokers in writing, or more commonly by telephone. Their orders can then be satisfied in one of three ways:

- Directly by broker/dealers (as they are permitted to deal as both principals and agents).
- Executed by the broker/dealer with a market maker by telephone.
- Executed by the broker/dealer through SAEF (SEAQ Automatic Execution Facility).

SAEF is only used for agency retail business in U.K. equities and it only operates during the SEAQ mandatory quote period. SAEF routes orders up to a maximum size (currently set at 10 percent of the normal market size for the relevant security) into SEAQ for automatic execution at the best price quoted. Market makers not offering best prices can nevertheless elect to execute SAEF orders at best prices. The broker/dealer receives instant confirmation of the execution of the trade.

Member firms are required to direct all orders in up to the relevant maximum SAEF size for that security only to market makers who are either displaying best prices or are indicating that they will deal at best prices.

Trade Reporting and Confirmation.   All transactions must be reported to the exchange, with the exception of foreign equities for which the rules of the principal exchange on which they are quoted require trades to be reported to that other exchange. The reporting deadlines vary between the markets: for instance, all trades executed in the mandatory quote period in SEAQ securities must be reported with real-time stamps within 3 minutes. Gilt transactions over £100,000 dealt between 9:00 and 17:00 must be reported within 5 minutes. In many cases it will be the market maker's responsibility to report the trade, through the SEAQ service.

All bargains, excluding traded options, futures, and Eurobonds, must be submitted to the Central Checking Service for matching with the counterparty's input, unless the parties agree to check the bargains themselves. Matched bargains in Talisman-eligible securities are then automatically passed into Talisman for settlement.

The LSE has recently developed SEQUAL, which is a trade confirmation system for international securities designed for use on a worldwide basis.

Settlement.   Settlement takes place by reference to the settlement cycles described in the earlier section on Types of Markets.

Most securities in the U.K. market are registered securities. Share certificates are issued by the individual company's registrar. Security settlements involve the delivery of the share certificate by the customer to the selling broker, who, for the majority of U.K. equities, forwards the certificate to the LSE for central settlement. Certain equities that are either not eligible for central settlement or that the members wish to settle outside the central systems, pass from selling member to buying member according to the registration details provided by the buying member on a *ticket*.

The clearing organizations currently operating are:

Talisman: The LSE's central computerized settlement system which coordinates the delivery of certificates between buying and selling brokers and the company registrars. Intramarket transactions only are settled by book-entry, the securities being held by the LSE in the name of SEPON. Talisman debits or credits the consideration for settled securities, rights, and dividends to cash memorandum accounts, which are cleared by check payments between the LSE and the member on the following day. INS (Institutional Net Settlement) is a service offered as part of the Talisman system, offering positive acceptance of trades, net payment, and direct deposit of certificates facilities for nonmembers of the LSE.

Central Gilts Office (CGO): A settlement service for gilt-edged securities. This system includes a facility allowing book-entry transfer of stock against a system of assured payments, provided through agreement with the clearing banks. The securities are immobilized at the Bank of England and transferred between CGO members on a book-entry basis. Nonmembers either effect settlement by delivery or receipt of securities in physical form or use the nominee services of a CGO member. The system also handles stock borrowing and lending between gilt-edged market makers and money brokers (see subsequent section).

Central Moneymarkets Office (CMO): A settlement service for sterling money market instruments run by the Bank of England. The service operates in a similar way to the CGO. The Bank of England is considering enhancing the system in the future to handle dematerialized securities.

London Options Clearing House (LOCH): The clearing house for the settlement of traded options. This is another book-entry system. Firms that are not direct clearers use the services of a clearing member firm. It has a facility for the automatic exercise of in-the-money equity options, removing the burden from the broker and client.

Eurobonds are normally cleared through either EUROCLEAR, an organization based in Brussels, Belgium; or CEDEL, based in Luxembourg. Both of these organizations are owned by banks and provide facilities for trade confirmation and book-entry settlements.

Dematerialization of Securities. Plans for the dematerialization of U.K. securities are well advanced. The LSE's book-entry system TAURUS (Transfer and Automatic Registration of Uncertified Stock) will be used. Details of shareholdings in dematerialized form will be maintained by account controllers linked through a network to the TAURUS central control system.

TAURUS will be fully integrated with Talisman, which will remain the means by which share transactions are reported, confirmed, and settled. The two systems will together provide the U.K. equity market with a central settlement and depository organization, as recommended by the Group of Thirty.

Account controllers will typically be stockbrokers, banks, institutions, or other accredited intermediaries and will act as liaisons between the investor, the market, and the company registrar. The total shareholding maintained by each account controller in each listed company will be recorded and controlled within the central TAURUS system. The company's registrar will consolidate the investors' details reported by the various account controllers into a register of membership.

TAURUS is due to be implemented initially in October 1991 for a limited number of equities, registrars, and account controllers. Once the system has been proven, further equities and organizations will be permitted to use it. The basic book-entry system is intended to be fully operational by October 1992. The LSE then plans to switch to a five-day rolling settlement policy for all U.K. equities in 1992 and offer guaranteed payment versus delivery services in 1993.

Stock Borrowing.   Securities may be borrowed by market makers from money brokers to effect delivery. The Bank of England supervises stock borrowings of gilts and directly authorizes money brokers. Equity-only money brokers require authorization from the Inland Revenue and are permitted to lend securities to member firms registered as market makers in the securities borrowed.

Fails.   There are buy-in rules that allow a member to apply to the LSE for a buy-in against another member who is failing to deliver securities. Securities bought for account day or rolling settlement may be bought in ten calendar days after the settlement due date has passed. Securities bought for cash settlement may be bought in immediately. Sell-outs are permitted after the settlement due date.

Exchange Links.   Settlement links have been established with Midwest Securities Clearing Corporation (MSCC) in Chicago, allowing member firms to settle U.S. securities; and with the International Securities Clearing Corporation (ISCC) in New York, permitting U.S. firms to settle U.K. securities via Talisman. Talisman can additionally handle the settlement of both South African and Australian securities.

Safe Custody Depositories.   Allowable safe custody depositories for private customers' securities are as follows:

- Nominee companies controlled by the member.
- Nominee companies owned by a Recognized Investment Exchange (RIE) or a Designated Investment Exchange (DIE) authorized by the SIB.

- Eligible custodians or their nominees; eligible custodians include approved banks, approved depositories, and members of a RIE/DIE.
- Any other person specifically nominated for particular securities by the client concerned.

The institutions with which the LSE has established safe custody links include:

- Japanese Securities Clearing Corporation (JSCC), Tokyo.
- Deutsche Auslandskassenverein (AKV), Frankfurt.
- Société Interprofessionnelle de Compensation des Valeurs Mobilières (SICOVAM), Paris.
- Canadian Depositary for Securities Ltd (CDS), Toronto.
- Madrid Stock Exchange/Telefonica.

Procedures for Market Price Publication

TOPIC is the LSE's own videotex network used for disseminating information on SEAQ and SEAQ International. Bargains in SEAQ securities with a consideration of up to the *maximum publication level* (which is currently three times the normal market size) are published immediately on SEAQ by the LSE. Details of trades in excess of this level are published on SEAQ after 90 minutes. In addition, details of all trades in securities involved in takeover bids and *agency crosses* will be published immediately irrespective of size. Agency crosses are client orders matched in-house by a member firm.

MARKET-EYE is an LSE system that captures and distributes share prices for use by the retail end of the market, such as branch banks.

SEDOL (Stock Exchange Daily Official List) places in printed form the closing price of each security quoted on the exchange together with the price range within which the security was traded on the previous day.

Taxes, Commissions, and Other Trading Costs

General Scheme of Direct Taxation

Income from securities held by individuals is subject to income taxes, currently at 40 percent or 25 percent, depending on the level of total income earned by the individual. Corporations are subject to a corporate tax on income, currently at a rate of 35 percent. In general, all income received on securities will be subject to taxation, although income on certain gilts (U.K. government securities) is exempt for persons not ordinarily resident in the United Kingdom. U.K. tax legislation contains extensive anti-avoidance provisions to counter investors converting income into capital gains to obtain a tax advantage.

The profit on the sale of a security is subject to capital gains taxes, currently at the same rate as income taxes. Certain securities are exempt from capital gains taxes; these particularly include gilts and qualifying corporate bonds (broadly speaking, nonconvertible sterling bonds).

For capital gains tax purposes, the acquisition cost of an asset increases over time by an indexation allowance, thereby removing the general inflationary element of the gain from the charge to tax. The second feature is the concept of *pooling*. The idea of pooling is to provide a simple set of rules for calculating the tax payable on the disposal of securities. A holding of similar securities is pooled, or grouped together, in order to match the disposal of securities out of the pool with an acquisition for the purposes of identifying the base cost of the particular securities sold. Despite the objective of simplicity, the rules relating to pooling are extremely complicated.

The above capital gains rules will not apply to a person trading in the securities concerned in such cases where any profit or loss on disposal is to be treated as part of trading income. Indeed, most traders will have unrealized gains and losses brought into their tax computations. Indexation relief is not available where the profit on a sale is taxed as income.

Territorial Scope of Taxation

Nonresidents will be liable for U.K. tax only on U.K. source income or if they carry on a trade in the United Kingdom through a branch or agency. In the latter situation they are assessed a tax according to all the profits of that branch or agency's trade. Similarly, nonresidents will not be liable to capital gains tax unless they carry on a trade in the United Kingdom through a branch or agency. If they do, they will be assessed a tax according to gains accruing on the disposal of U.K. assets connected with the trade in the United Kingdom.

By concession, the liability for tax on certain types of U.K. source income, such as interest, is not pursued by the U.K. tax authorities if the nonresident has received payment of the income gross and has no other connection with the United Kingdom.

Withholding Taxes and Double Tax Treaties

In the United Kingdom a withholding tax is applied to payments of interest on debts that are capable of being outstanding for greater than one year. There is no withholding tax on dividends as such, although a U.K. company paying a dividend must account for a prepayment of its corporation tax to the Inland Revenue. This prepayment, known as Advance Corporation Tax (ACT), is not technically a tax on the shareholder but a tax on the company itself. However, U.K. resident individual shareholders are given a credit with respect to the ACT to offset any basic rate tax liability that they would otherwise have had in connection with the dividend. U.K. corporate shareholders are exempt from taxes resulting from dividends from other U.K. companies, and the tax credit can be recovered against payments of tax due by the recipient company associated with the payment of its own dividends. Some tax treaties enable a nonresident shareholder to claim a refund on part of the ACT. In the absence of a double tax treaty the domestic rate of withholding tax is currently 25 percent. The United Kingdom, however, has an extensive network of treaties that often significantly reduce or eliminate any withholding.

Commissions and Other Transaction Costs

Commissions are negotiated where charged; alternatively dealers quote net prices, profiting by the spread between bid and offer prices. Approximately 65 percent of all U.K. equity bargains, but only 25 percent of overseas equities, are traded with commission. Most brokers quote minimum commissions per bargain and apply a sliding scale of charges expressed as a percentage of the bargain consideration; average commission rates are approximately 0.39 percent for U.K. equities, 0.32 percent for foreign equities, 0.13 percent for gilts, 0.37 percent for other fixed-income securities, and 1.25 percent for traded options.

Other dealing costs are stamp duty, VAT on commission (nonresidents are exempt), and a nominal levy on most transactions, used to fund the Panel for Takeovers and Mergers (see later section on "Takeover and Merger Transactions").

Transaction Taxes

Stamp duty is a tax on documents, and stamp duty reserve tax (SDRT) is its equivalent for certain paperless transactions. A stamp duty or SDRT is levied on the transfer of U.K. equities, for which the tax of 0.5 percent is payable by the purchaser. In general, debt securities are exempt from such duty. The territorial scope of the stamp duty depends upon whether the instrument is executed in the United Kingdom or relates to any U.K. property. If it does, it is subject to stamp duty. The territorial scope of SDRT depends on the securities being "chargeable" (generally speaking securities of a non-U.K. company will not be) and on there being one party to the agreement in the United Kingdom. Both of these taxes are to be abolished when the LSE's new paperless share transfer system TAURUS is introduced.

Procedures for Issuing and Listing New Securities

Basic Requirements

Companies seeking admission to the Official List must satisfy a number of basic requirements:

- The expected market value of the securities to be listed must initially be at least £700,000 for equities and £200,000 for debt securities, although the LSE may admit smaller issues if they are satisfied that adequate marketability can be expected.

- The securities must be freely transferable.
- The company must have published or filed accounts covering a period of three years preceding application; in exceptional circumstances a shorter period may be accepted.
- At least 25 percent of any class of shares must be in the hands of the public (i.e., persons not associated with the directors or major share-holders) no later than the time of admission; again, a lower percentage may be accepted in exceptional circumstances where the LSE is satis-fied that a secondary market can operate properly with less.
- Issues having an equity element must, in the absence of exceptional circumstances, be offered in the first place to the existing shareholders in proportion to their holdings (preemption rights) unless the share-holders have approved other specific proposals.

Those seeking admission to the Unlisted Securities Market (USM) must have a two-year trading record, although carefully researched *greenfield* projects may also be accommodated. Such greenfield applicants will be expected to demonstrate that management has already committed signifi-cant time and resources to the project, that the research and development stage has been completed, and that funds are now required to commence commercial production of the developed product or service. Qualifying projects are likely to involve new technology or be unique in some other material respects. The greenfield category is not intended to cover start-up ventures that have simply completed market research and prepared a business plan.

Listing Procedures

Applicants must appoint a member firm of the LSE to sponsor its applica-tion. The role of the sponsor is to ensure that all of the listing procedures are complied with and in particular that all of the necessary documents are filed with the Quotations Department.

A company must have published or filed accounts covering the three years preceding application (or lesser period if incorporated less than three years), drawn up in accordance with the company's national law and pre-pared and independently audited in accordance with standards appropri-ate for U.K. and other companies of international standards and repute. In particular, it is expected that accounts will be drawn up to comply in all material respects with international accounting standards or account-ing standards as applied in the United Kingdom or United States, and the auditors must have reported on the accounts without any qualification considered material for the purposes of admission. In addition, applicants are required to lodge with the LSE a letter from the issuer's auditors or re-porting accountants as to whether, in their opinion, the company's annual accounts, and financial information included in listing particulars based on such accounts, have been prepared and audited in accordance with stan-dards appropriate for companies of international standing and repute.

It is a basic condition of admission to the Official List or USM that the sponsoring member firm or issuing house must advise the LSE by letter that it has received confirmation from the directors of the issuer that the working capital available to the group is sufficient. In addition, the reporting accountants and the sponsoring member firm or issuing house must report to the LSE on any relevant profit forecast. This applies to any profit forecast already published or included in the listing particulars for any period for which audited accounts have not yet been published. If the profit forecast is included in the listing particulars, then these reports must also be set out therein.

Listing Fees

Initial charges for a listing vary in proportion to the value of the securities to be listed and the type of security concerned. Some examples of the charges currently applied are:

Type of security	Size of issue	Initial charge
Equity	£1,000,000	£1,260
Equity	£1,000,000,000	£53,300
Fixed-income	£1,000,000	£640
Fixed-income	£1,000,000,000	£21,120
Eurocurrency debt		6p per £1,000 (maximum £4,000)

Annual charges vary with the nominal value of listed equity for the company concerned. For example, the annual charge for a company with a nominal value of listed equity of £1,000,000,000 is £17,600. A fixed charge of £1,120 applies when only fixed-income securities are listed. There are no annual charges for the listing of Eurocurrency debt securities.

Concessions Available to Listed Non-U.K. Companies

Rather than require a specially commissioned accountants' report, the LSE permits the more common practice outside the United Kingdom of reproducing financial information extracted from the past audited accounts. In addition, the requirement for the latest audited financial period to have ended not more than six months prior to the date of the listing particulars is relaxed to twelve months, a modified form of indebtedness statement is acceptable, and the directors (rather than the sponsor) can provide the letter confirming adequacy of working capital. In addition, foreign companies pay only one-half of the initial and annual listing charges quoted above.

Mutual Recognition of Listing Particulars

Mutual recognition of listing particulars is now required within the EC. This means that listing particulars produced for the sale of securities in one member state of the EC must, subject to translation, be accepted by other member states when the listing of the same securities at the same time (or within six weeks) in another member state. It should be noted that for listing particulars to qualify for mutual recognition, the issuer must have its registered office in another member state or, if not, it must either be a listed company or the LSE must be satisfied that it can properly be regarded as a company of international standing and repute. Mutual recognition applies only to listing particulars. Thus conditions of admission may vary from country to country in the EC, as may the continuing obligations.

Listing particulars should include the following:

- Information on the company, its directors, and professional advisers.
- Information on the company's securities and on the terms and conditions of any marketing of securities being, or recently, carried out.
- General information about the company and its share and loan capital.
- Information on the company's activities.
- The financial record of the company or group.
- Information on the company's management.
- Information on recent developments in the company's business and on its future prospects.
- Any other information necessary for a proper understanding of the company and its securities.

Continuing Obligations for Non-U.K. Listed Foreign Companies

Continuing obligations have been streamlined for non-U.K. listed foreign companies, so that they are, in general, less onerous, and greater regard is now paid to the requirements of the domestic exchange. Thus, for example, the required level of information about acquisitions has been reduced, and other conditions found burdensome by non-U.K. listed companies, such as rules on preemption rights of existing shareholders, have been modified.

Takeover and Merger Transactions

Merger Legislation

Under the Fair Trading Act of 1973, "merger situations qualifying for investigations" may be referred to the Monopolies and Mergers Commission (the Commission). Such a reference can be made only by the Secretary of State, who usually acts on the advice of the director general of the Office of Fair Trading.

The Commission's function is to determine whether merger situations referred to it qualify for investigation and, if so, whether they operate or may be expected to operate against the public interest. The Commission makes a report of its findings to the Secretary of State, who has the power to take a variety of actions to prevent damage to the public interest in the event of adverse findings.

LSE Rules Regarding Takeovers and Mergers

Takeovers and mergers are expected to comply with the City Code on Takeovers and Mergers and the Rules Governing Substantial Acquisitions of Shares, codes of conduct issued by the Panel on Takeovers and Mergers, whose board is appointed by the governor of the Bank of England. These rules operate to ensure fair and equal treatment of all shareholders in relation to takeovers and mergers, providing an orderly framework for conducting such transactions. The rules do not carry the force of law but are accepted by the LSE and the regulatory bodies. The ultimate sanction for failure to comply with the rules is the withdrawal of listing privileges for companies and the withdrawal of authorization for firms conducting investment business.

Before a company with securities traded on the LSE acquires or realizes a significant asset, a document must be sent to shareholders providing details of the proposed transaction. Larger deals involving listed companies, in which the size of the transaction relative to the offeror or offeree is at least 25 percent, require shareholder approval before they can be completed. For USM companies, a document must be sent to shareholders in cases when the size of the transaction relative to the offeror or offeree is at least 35 percent, and shareholder approval is required if the 75 percent threshold is breached. Except when a listed company takes over another listed company, an accountants' report must be filed on the company or business and assets being acquired in the larger deals.

Foreign Investors

In general, there are no restrictions upon foreign investment in the United Kingdom. However, the government has placed limits on the extent to which shares in companies privatized in recent years may be held by foreign investors.

Exchange Membership Requirements

Membership Requirements and Costs

Membership is open to all parties; there are no citizenship or residency requirements. Corporate applications are evaluated on the experience of the directors and the financial strength of the firm. Individual membership is granted according to professional experience and examinations. Entrance fees and annual subscriptions for U.K. corporate members are based on the number of TSA *registered persons*. The entrance fees for 1990–1991, for instance, ranged from £5,000 for less than five registered persons to £50,000 for more than 150 registered persons. Annual subscriptions are approximately £150 per registered person. Overseas members pay £10,000 in entrance fees and £10,000 for annual subscriptions.

In order to conduct investment business in the United Kingdom, member firms must also become members of an SRO, for which there are no citizenship or residency requirements. A firm's membership in TSA, for example, is granted when TSA is satisfied that the firm is "fit and proper" to conduct investment business. In addition to the firm's membership, each trader, salesman, director, and manager is required to be individually registered. Here also, the "fit and proper" test is applied.

TSA's subscriptions are charged by reference to the number of registered persons. Including an element designed to recover SIB's levy on TSA, the 1990–1991 charges vary from £780 for one registered person to £161,096 for 800–1,000 registered persons.

Minimum Capital Requirements

A member firm shall not permit its total capital requirement to exceed its qualifying capital. The total capital requirement comprises the aggregate of the following three components:

- A base requirement that is the higher of an absolute minimum requirement and 25 percent of annual expenditure.
- A position risk requirement that quantifies the risks associated with holding securities positions.
- A counterparty risk requirement that quantifies the risk of default by counterparties.

Compliance with these capital requirements is monitored through review of unaudited monthly and quarterly capital calculations, which must be submitted to TSA within 10 and 20 business days of the end of the month, respectively. The quarterly reporting statements contain a profit and loss account and balance sheet, both in specified formats, in addition to the capital calculations. Because of the potential volatility of securities positions, however, TSA also requires the submission of biweekly position risk summary reporting statements within 5 business days and a detailed monthly position risk reporting statement within 10 or 20 business days (depending on whether it is a month or quarter end).

Annual audited financial statements must be submitted to TSA within three months of the year end.

Insurance Coverage

The LSE stipulates that all members based in the Isle of Man, Channel Islands, and the Republic of Ireland must maintain insurance policies against losses caused by fraud, theft, and forgery. There are no insurance requirements for other members because investors are covered by the SIB's Investors' Compensation Scheme arrangements (see "Investor Protection"). TSA has no insurance requirements for the same reasons.

Dealing Capacity

Members are permitted to act in a dual capacity as both principals and agents. They may also make markets in one or more securities upon approval by LSE. Interdealer brokers, however, are not permitted to take positions.

Restrictions on Ownership of Member Firms

There are no restrictions on domestic or foreign ownership of member firms, although, in practice, the LSE and TSA discuss the situation with proposed new owners and the member firm to ensure that there are no circumstances suggesting that the member firm should cease to meet the "fit and proper" test. Many overseas banks have taken significant stakes in stockbrokerages, and others have set up their own securities dealing operations.

Investor Protection

Investor protection depends largely on the compliance of investment businesses with extensive rules covering financial records, minimum capital adequacy, conduct of business, and protection of client assets and money. The rules regarding conduct of business require the member firm to enter into a written agreement with every customer to whom they wish to provide advisory or discretionary management services. This ensures that the private individual is aware of the member's services and their respective charges. Private clients have the protection of "best execution" rules requiring broker/dealers to obtain the best price available in the market. Other categories of customers, such as expert investors and business customers, are entitled to best execution upon request. In addition, risk warnings must be issued for derivative products and disclosures made about any material interests the member firm or a connected party may have in certain transactions.

Strict provisions that apply to both prospective and existing customers exist for unsolicited calls. The rules state that calls, whether by telephone or visit, must not be made other than at the express request of the customer. For existing customers the effects of this rule can be reduced by including the appropriate contact name in the customer agreement.

Compensation Funds

In the event of default by a member firm, compensation funds provide limited sums to reimburse customers who have suffered financial loss. The SIB has set up an Investors' Compensation Scheme (ICS), funded by the SROs. TSA's scheme currently is paid for by members in proportion to the number of registered representatives. This scheme compensates members of the public in the event of default by an SRO member as follows: 100 percent of the claim up to £30,000 and 90 percent of the claim for the next £20,000.

Insider Dealing

Trading on insider information (unpublished price-sensitive information) is prohibited according to the Companies Securities (Insider Dealing) Act 1985. It is also an offense for such individuals to advise or procure any other person to deal in the securities in which they are prevented from dealing on their own account. The mere passing of insider information is also an offense if the individual knows or has reasonable cause to believe that the recipient of the information will make use of it for the purpose of dealing in those securities.

Exemptions are available to liquidators, receivers, and market makers, and to price stabilization activities under the Financial Services Act 1986.

The LSE requires listed companies to adopt a model code for securities dealings to help secure compliance with the law. Also TSA requires its members to monitor all dealings by their staff and to endeavor to ensure employees do not contravene the act.

Restrictions on the Use of Clients' Money and Assets

Each SRO has published detailed rules on customer assets and monies. TSA, for example, requires that assets be held with approved institutions, that two physical counts or external confirmations of customer assets are made per annum, and that annual statements of holdings are sent to the customer.

TSA has also published a detailed list of client money rules. *Free money,* client money not intended to be applied in a pending bargain settlement, must be segregated in a trust account with an approved financial institution and may not be commingled with the member firm's money. A reasonable rate of interest must be paid to customers on such free money.

Funds in the course of settlement are also segregated according to a complex formula that can involve the netting of funds due from one customer with funds owed to another customer.

Audit and Accounting Requirements

All member firms of the SROs must prepare and submit annual audited financial statements. The auditors appointed must be members of one of a list of approved bodies. The Financial Services Act 1986 requires auditors to communicate directly with the regulator in certain circumstances. In addition, TSA reserves the right to appoint accountants of its choosing to conduct an investigation into a member firm's affairs.

Other Compliance Procedures

TSA visits member firms on roughly an annual basis to review the member's compliance with TSA rules and regulations. In the course of its visit the TSA will typically evaluate the results of the annual compliance review that the member firm's compliance officer is required to perform.

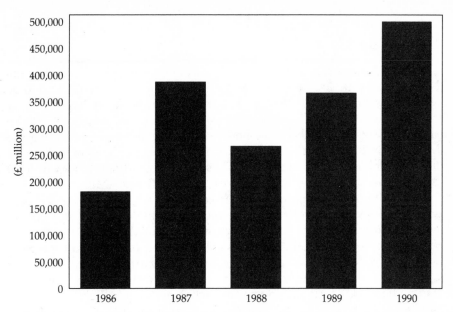

Figure 21.15. Shares Turnover—London Stock Exchange (1986–1990) (£ million)

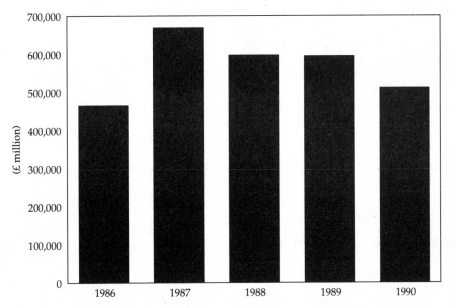

Figure 21.16. Fixed-Income Securities Turnover—London Stock Exchange (1986–1990) (£ million)

UNITED STATES

General Background

The United States has several stock exchanges. The best known are the New York Stock Exchange (NYSE) and the American Stock Exchange (AMEX), both located in New York. Generally, the stocks of larger companies trade on the NYSE, whereas companies traded on AMEX tend to be smaller in size. A number of regional exchanges also exist, including the Midwest Exchange in Chicago, the Pacific Exchange in San Francisco, and the Philadelphia Stock Exchange. These exchanges trade stocks of local corporations as well as stocks listed on the NYSE and AMEX.

In addition, there is the over-the-counter-market (OTC), which consists of a network of brokers and dealers linked by telephone and private wires. Smaller or relatively new companies are traded on the OTC. Trading information for many OTC stocks is collected and displayed on the computerized system, the National Association of Security Dealers Automatic Quote System (NASDAQ). Unlike the exchanges, there is no centralized trading floor. U.S. futures and options exchanges include the Chicago Mercantile Exchange (CME), the Chicago Board of Trade (CBOT), the Chicago Options Exchange (CBOE), and the Philadelphia Stock Exchange's foreign currency options market. Together, the CME and CBOT trade 10 of the industry's 12 most active futures contracts, while the CBOE's trading activity represents over half of the total U.S. options market.

This section will focus on the three largest stock markets in the United States by volume and market capitalization, the NYSE, NASDAQ, and AMEX.

New York Stock Exchange
Location:

111 Wall Street
New York, NY 10005
Telephone: 212–656–3000
Facsimile: 212–656–5557

Trading hours:

9:30–16:00
(New York is five hours behind Greenwich Mean Time)

(All data as of December 31, 1990)

Number of securities listed:

Stocks: 1,774 (of which 96 are
   foreign companies)
Bonds: 2,912 (of which 36 are
   foreign bond issues)

Market capitalization:

Shares: US$2.8 trillion
Bonds: US$1.6 trillion ·

Average daily turnover:

Shares: US$5.2 billion
(160 million shares)
Bonds: US$43.0 million

Market indices:

Dow Jones Common Stock Index
(which includes the Industrial
Average and the Composite Index)
NYSE Composite Stock Index
Standard & Poor's 100 Stock Index
Standard & Poor's 500 Stock Index

*American Stock Exchange
Location:*

86 Trinity Place
New York, NY 10006–1881
Telephone: 212–306–1000
Facsimile: 212–306–1488

Trading hours:

9:30–16:10

Number of securities listed:

Stocks: 1,063 (of which 77 are
issued by foreign companies)
Bonds: 949 (of which 689 are
government bond issues)

Market capitalization:

Shares: US$102 billion
Bonds: US$3.4 billion

Average daily turnover:

Shares: US$404 million
(13.2 million shares)
Bonds: US$13.8 million

Market indices:

Market Value Index with 16
Geographical and Industrial
subindices

*The NASDAQ Stock Market
Location:*

National Association of
Securities Dealers, Inc.
1735 K Street, NW
Washington, DC 20006–1506
Telephone: 202–728–8000

Annual share volume: 33.4 billion
Average daily share volume: 132 million
Annual dollar volume: US$452.4 billion
Companies listed (1989): 4,293
Number of issues (1989): 4,963
Foreign securities issues/
   ADRs (1989): 194/92

ADR share volume/dollar value: 2,219 million/US$22 billion
Market indices: NASDAQ Composite and
                                          related subindices

Regulatory Authorities:

The Securities and Exchange Commission has regulatory responsibility over U.S. securities markets, the self-regulatory organizations within the securities industry, and those conducting a business in securities. Persons who execute transactions in securities generally are required to register with the commission as broker-dealers. The commission is required to approve most proposed rules of the self-regulatory organizations. The Securities Exchange Act also requires the filing of registration applications and annual and other reports with national securities exchanges and the commission by companies whose securities are listed on the exchanges.

Futures trading is regulated by the Commodity Futures Trading Commission (CFTC), the federal agency created under the Commodity Exchange Act of 1974.

The NYSE and AMEX regulate their member firms, including examining the books and records of the firms, to help ensure their compliance with financial and operational requirements.

The National Association of Securities Dealers, Inc. (NASD), is the self-regulatory organization of the securities industry responsible for the regulation of NASDAQ and the over-the-counter markets. NASD's members comprise virtually all the broker-dealers in the country who do securities business with the public.

Market Trading Information

Main Types of Securities Traded

The main types of securities traded on the NYSE are common and preferred stocks, bonds, options, and futures. The NYSE market lists nearly 83 billion shares issued by more than 1,700 companies. The total value of these shares is more than US$3 trillion. The NYSE bond market includes trading in close to 3,000 bonds issued by the U.S. government, U.S. corporations, foreign governments, foreign corporations, and international banks. Options are traded in some 45 stocks, including several OTC securities. A NYSE subsidiary, the New York Futures Exchange (NYFE), trades in five financial futures contracts, based on the NYSE Composite Index, the Commodity Research Bureau's Futures Price Index, and U.S. Treasury bonds. Larger futures and options markets operate, however, on the Chicago Mercantile Exchange (CME), the Chicago Board of Trade (CBOT), and the Chicago Board Options Exchange (CBOE).

The CME currently trades futures, and options in many cases, on agricultural commodities, foreign currencies, interest rates, and stock market indices. Daily average trading volumes on the exchange exceed 400,000 contracts. The CME comprises three divisions: the Chicago Mercantile Exchange, the International Monetary Market (IMM) Division, and the Index and Options (IOM) division. Principal financial futures and futures options contracts traded on the exchange are based on the Eurodollar, S&P 500 Index, Nikkei 225 Stock Average, Libor, Treasury Bills, and the major currencies.

The CBOT trades futures and options on futures based on agricultural commodities, U.S. Treasury bonds and notes, Major Market and the Municipal Bond indices, 30 day interest rate, 5-Year Interest Rate Swaps, and gold and silver. The CBOE trades options on the Standard & Poor's 100 and 500 market indices, and U.S. Treasury bonds and notes.

The main types of securities traded on the American Stock Exchange (AMEX) are equities, options on listed and over-the-counter stocks, index and currency warrants, contingent value rights, commodity trust units, and Americus trusts. In 1990, AMEX became the first U.S. exchange to list put and call warrants on foreign stock indices. Trading in the Nikkei Stock Average of Japan, the FT-SE 100 Share Index of the United Kingdom, and the CAC 40 index on the Paris Bourse accounts for approximately 15 percent of equity volume. AMEX has formed a partnership with the Chicago Board Options Exchange to develop a worldwide after-hours electronic system for the trading of options and listed equities. It has also entered into an exclusive licensing agreement with the European Options Exchange in Amsterdam that enables it to trade derivative products on the new EURO TOP-100 index of the highest capitalized stocks in nine European countries. Long-term options on 10 individual blue-chip stocks and on the Major Market Index (XMI) of 20 blue chips (LT-20 options) are also traded.

NASDAQ trades primarily stocks, including ADRs, which are foreign equity issues traded in the form of American Depository Receipts.

Types of Markets

The NYSE and AMEX markets are made up of a broad spectrum of participants, including listed companies, individual investors, institutional investors, securities firms, and dealers with assigned responsibility. Member firms, also known as securities firms or brokerage companies, represent customers' orders to buy and sell securities. They also trade on behalf of their own accounts.

The NASD operates and regulates three distinct securities markets: the NASDAQ Stock Market, the PORTAL Market, and the OTC Bulletin Board. Each uses electronic screen-based systems that collect and disseminate online, real-time information.

The NASDAQ System receives, stores, and transmits price and volume data and market statistics for more than 4,900 domestic and foreign equity securities to the financial services industry in the United States and 48 other countries, to individual and institutional investors, and to the print and broadcast media. More than 4,200 companies list their securities on NASDAQ. The upper tier of the market consists of almost 2,700 NASDAQ National Market securities. These securities are traded under real-time price and volume reporting and account for more than 90 percent of total NASDAQ dollar volume and market value. Institutional investors held approximately 40 percent of the market value of NASDAQ/NMS common stocks at the end of 1989, although only 29 percent of the outstanding shares.

NASDAQ International, a U.K.-based version of the NASDAQ stock market, is scheduled to commence operations in 1992, providing NASD members with the opportunity to make markets in NASDAQ securities, as well as U.S. exchange-listed securities, during European trading hours.

In 1990, the NASD, taking advantage of the expanded opportunities for trading private placements under SEC Rule 144a, launched PORTAL, a real-time electronic market that brings together qualified buyers and sellers of securities in the private placement market. Participation is limited to brokers, dealers, and large institutional investors. SEC Rule 144a provides safe harbor protections by exempting the private placements of certain issuers from the SEC's registration and disclosure requirements and by allowing eligible institutions to freely trade these securities among themselves.

The NASD introduced the OTC Bulletin Board in June 1990 to provide issuers of securities not eligible for listing on NASDAQ with a more visible, liquid, and easily regulated market. By the end of 1990, the number of market-making positions exceeded 10,000 in more than 4,200 securities.

Market Trading Systems

NYSE. NYSE-assigned dealers, also known as specialists, are required to maintain a fair and orderly market in the securities assigned to them. The interaction of buyers and sellers determines the price of a NYSE-listed stock. In contrast, in the over-the-counter market, the price is determined by a dealer who comes between buyer and seller on every trade.

Assigned dealers on the NYSE perform four functions. First, they electronically quote and record current bid and ask prices for the stocks assigned to them. This enables current price information to be transmitted worldwide, keeping all market participants informed of the total supply and demand for any particular NYSE-listed stock. Second, they act as agents, executing orders entrusted to them by a trading floor broker if and when a stock reaches a price specified by a customer. Third, on those occasional instances when there is a temporary shortage of either buyers or sellers, NYSE-assigned dealers will buy or sell for their own account, against the trend of the market. Fourth, they act as catalysts, bringing buyers and sellers together, ensuring that all offers to buy are matched with all offers to sell.

SuperDot. SuperDot is an electronic order-routing system that enables member firms to quickly and efficiently transmit market and limit orders in all NYSE-listed securities directly to the specialist post where the securities are traded or to the member firm's booth. After the order has been executed in the auction market, a report of execution is returned directly to the member firm office over the same electronic circuit that brought the order to the trading floor, and the execution is submitted directly to the comparison systems. The components of the SuperDot system are described in the following:

Opening Automated Report Service (OARS): OARS, the opening feature of the SuperDot system, is designed to accept preopening market orders of up to 30,099 shares per member firm for rapid, systematic execution and immediate reporting. OARS automatically and continuously pairs buy and sell orders and presents the imbalance to each specialist up to the opening of a stock, thus assisting the specialist in determining the opening price. OARS is floorwide in all issues.

Market Order Processing: All SuperDot service features apply to post-opening market orders of up to 2,099 shares. However, SuperDot's market order system is designed to process member firm's market orders of up to 30,099 shares. The system provides for rapid execution and reporting of market orders.

Limit Order Processing: The limit order system electronically files orders that are to be executed when and if the specific limit price is reached. The system accepts limit orders up to 99,999 shares, appends a turnaround number, and either electronically updates the specialist's electronic book or delivers printed orders to the member firm's booth. Good-'til-cancelled orders not executed on the day of submission are automatically stored until executed or canceled.

Electronic Book: The electronic book is a tool which greatly increases the assigned dealer's volume handling and processing capabilities. The data-base system facilitates the recording, reporting, and researching of limit and market orders, and in the process helps eliminate paperwork and processing errors. At the end of 1990, there were more than 2,000 stocks on electronic books on the NYSE trading floor.

Post-Trade Processing: After a trade is executed, SuperDot automatically submits it to the comparison cycle on a locked-in basis. This guarantees that each member firm's systematized orders are processed error-free with a complete audit trail prior to settlement and delivery of securities.

The Consolidated Tape prints all transactions in NYSE-listed stock on participating markets, consisting of seven stock exchanges and two over-the-counter markets. Consolidated Reported Trades consists of a count of every sale in a NYSE-listed issue as it was reported to the Consolidated Tape. Reported trades may involve the execution of two or more separate orders of transactions, particularly at the opening of the market and for small orders on the NYSE.

Block trading by institutions amounted to over 50 percent of NYSE reported volume in 1990. Program trading volume accounted for approximately 10 percent of total NYSE volume.

Intermarket Trading System (ITS).   ITS is an electronic communications network that links eight markets, the New York, American, Boston, Cincinnati, Midwest, Pacific, and Philadelphia stock exchanges, and the NASD. The system enables brokers representing public customers, as well as specialists and market makers trading for their own accounts, to interact with their counterparts in other markets whenever the nationwide Composite Quotation System shows a better price. The over 2,000 issues eligible for trading on ITS at the end of 1990 represented most of the stocks traded on more than one exchange.

AMEX.   Members of the AMEX perform functions similar to those of members of the NYSE. There are three functions performed by AMEX specialists: (1) Brokers who hold orders for other brokers on behalf of customers. These orders are to be executed when the market for that issue reaches a specified value; (2) Facilitators who use their knowledge of the market in order to bring together potential buyers and sellers; and (3) Dealers who buy and sell from their own accounts in order to affect a change on the market when there is insufficient activity or to close the gap between buy and sell orders.

The AMEX clearance systems are Post Execution Reporting (PER), which is similar to the NYSE DOT system; the Opening Automated Report System (OARS), which is similar to the NYSE OARS system; and the Specialist Electronic Book (SEB), an electronic file used to control market, limit, and opening orders.

AMEX member firms communicate with their employees on the floor using hand signals; there is no verbal or written communication. Also, the procedure for awarding trades is *priority prorata*. This means that although one broker may have priority, as is the case with the NYSE, after priority, shares are allocated in round lots among the other participants.

NASDAQ.   The computer and communications facility for the NASDAQ market is connected to over 3,500 trading terminals over which a composite display of quotations in each NASDAQ security is provided to securities firms and financial institutions. Market data vendors also connected to the facility distribute best bid and ask prices and volume information on all NASDAQ securities to stockbrokers and others over desktop terminals.

The broker of an investor who places a buy or sell order for a NASDAQ security routes that order to the firm's trading room. If the firm makes a market in the security, it will normally execute the order internally, as principal, at a price equal to or better than the best price being quoted in NASDAQ by all of the competing market makers. Depending on whether the customer is a buyer or a seller, the firm will charge a markdown or markup, which is required to be disclosed.

If the firm is not a market maker in the security, it will handle the order as agent for the customer. Trading room personnel will check their NASDAQ terminal screens to determine which market maker has the best price and then execute the order on behalf of the customer, with a commission charge.

Nearly 500 securities firms compete for order flow in NASDAQ securities. Very active securities have 50 or more market makers; the average security in the NASDAQ National Market has 11.

For trades of 1,000 shares or less, the firm may complete the transaction through the NASD's Small Order Execution System (SOES). This system permits automatic execution of a customer's order and guarantees that the customer will receive the best price available in NASDAQ at the time the order is entered. SOES directs orders to the market maker displaying the best bid or offer. This system eliminates the need for direct voice contact with a market maker and executes an order in seconds. The limit order match feature enables public customers to receive automatic execution of matching limit orders priced within the best bid and ask. The Computer-Assisted Execution Service (CAES) allows the submitter acting as principal to lock in a trade of up to 20,000 shares.

Same-day comparison capability is provided by the Automated Confirmation Transaction (ACT) service, which issues reports to the clearing agency concerning previously negotiated two-party trades on the evening of trade date.

The firm also may use the Order Confirmation Transaction (OCT) to route and execute orders electronically. Through the use of OCT, a firm can send an order of any size and for any account to a specific market maker over the computer, without personal telephone contact. The market-making firm responds electronically by accepting, rejecting, or countering the order with new terms.

Through The Advanced Computerized Execution System (ACES), market makers execute the orders of their broker-dealer customers automatically in certain securities up to specified amounts at the best prices available in NASDAQ at the time such orders are entered into ACES.

Large institutional traders, including mutual and pension funds, insurance companies, and investment managers, often trade blocks of stocks directly with each other. This information is collected and displayed on the Instinet System.

Futures and Options Markets

Trading on the various futures and options exchanges is generally done using the *open-outcry* system. Each trader or broker openly declares a particular bid and offer price. Most traders or brokers do not normally take actual delivery of a commodity; rather they will usually opt to close out a contract with an offsetting transaction or, alternatively, contracts will be "cash-settled" based on the prevailing cash price.

The marketplace encompasses floor traders and floor brokers. Floor brokers execute orders for the accounts of the Exchange's member firms, either for the firms themselves or for their individual and institutional customers.

The respective exchange's clearinghouse, which deals only with its clearing member firms, settles all transactions at the end of each day's trading. By interposing itself between the two transacting parties, it guarantees the contractual obligations of the transaction. It allows each party to offset the transaction without having to reach a new agreement with the same party. Every account holding futures positions is adjusted in cash daily when it is marked-to-market. Each day, the clearinghouse checks margin on deposit for each clearing member to ensure that they meet or exceed required levels. If a clearing-member firm's margin-account balance falls below a certain maintenance margin level, an additional deposit, or margin call, is collected to restore it to the necessary level. The clearing member would then repeat that process with its customer accounts for collection of original margin.

Membership of the futures and options exchanges consists of independent traders as well as representatives of major brokerage firms, banks, and investment houses. Also included are Futures Commissions Merchants (FCMs) which execute trades for others. A non-exchange-member individual or firm must direct its orders through a clearing member of the exchange.

Ordering and Settlement Procedures

When investors buy or sell shares of a listed company, they contact a retail broker (also known as a registered representative or account executive) who is an employee of a member firm.

The registered representative can handle the customer's order in two ways. In some cases, the account executive notifies a broker on the NYSE trading floor, who executes the trade on behalf of the customer. Information about this transaction is then made available to investors worldwide and the trade is confirmed in seconds. Customer orders can also be executed and processed electronically through SuperDot, the computerized order-routing and reporting system that completes the trading loop within seconds. This includes transmission of an order to the NYSE for execution and communication to the participants that the trade has been completed.

In all instances where orders are sent electronically into the NYSE market, the same electronic system that reports the transaction to the firm also creates electronic bookkeeping entries, comparing the details of the trade and updating the records of the brokerage firms for both the buyer and seller, enabling the NYSE to reconstruct the specifics of the trade if any questions about it should arise in the future.

With respect to those orders that are not entered electronically into the NYSE market, the member firms representing the buyer and seller must submit details of the trade to a clearing corporation for comparison.

Ownership of the shares is immediate upon completion of the transaction. The buyer's account is debited in the appropriate dollar amount, and another entry removes 100 shares from the account of the seller, whose account is credited in the appropriate dollar amount. The transfer of shares, a complex procedure involving several steps, is almost completely automated. Virtually the only piece of paper involved will be the stock certificate, and then only if the buyer insists on holding it instead of having it registered and held in the brokerage firm's name to facilitate the rapid sale of the shares if and when the buyer so desires.

Various types of orders are commonly used. A *market* order must be executed by a broker at the best price available at the time of purchase. *Limit, stop,* and *stop limit* orders can be placed to meet different conditions, using standby instructions that are activated if the price of a stock moves up or down to a specified level.

Trading on margin allows a customer to make only a partial payment for the securities, borrowing the rest from the broker. The Federal Reserve's initial margin requirement on qualified stocks currently stands at 50 percent. Thus, an investor wishing to purchase US$10,000 worth of stocks has to put up at least US$5,000 either in cash or in securities having a loan value of US$5,000; the investor can obtain, at most, US$5,000 in credit.

In addition to federal regulation of credit, the NYSE has certain credit requirements. No person may open a margin account with a member firm without depositing at least US$2,000 or its equivalent in securities. The NYSE also sets requirements for the maintenance of margins, as distinguished from the initial margin requirements of the Federal Reserve Board. Generally, a customer's margin account equity may at no time be less than 25 percent of the current market value of the stocks or marginal convertible bonds carried. Should a customer's margin account equity fall below these levels, the customer is required to put up more margin or the securities are sold either by the customer or by the broker.

Transactions in exchange-listed or OTC stocks are generally cleared through the National Stock Clearing Corporation (NSCC) with custody and book-entry arrangements through the Depository Trust Company (DTC). The NASD, NYSE, and AMEX are each one-third owners of NSCC. Buy and sell orders are routed to NSCC via a computer-to-computer linkage and the majority of trades on the NYSE and AMEX are *locked-in,* meaning trade details are already matched between the buyer and seller. NSCC clears and settles trades through Continuous Net Settlement (CNS), an automated clearance accounting system. The CNS system accumulates a net long or short securities position in each eligible issue that a participant has traded and then receives or delivers the net quantities (versus a net payment) each day within DTC book-entry accounts. As the positions are netted, NSCC becomes the contraside to each participant's requirements and guarantees the settlement obligation. CNS applies only to depository-eligible securities. Among the services provided by DTC are accepting deposits of securities for custody and making computerized book-entry deliveries of securities that are immobilized in its custody.

The Institutional Delivery (ID) system facilitates the reporting, affirming, and settling of trades between brokers, dealers, and financial institutions. It essentially provides an automated process to coordinate the clearance and settlement activities between brokers and dealers, financial institutions and investors, and custodian banks.

Buy and sell orders on the futures and options exchanges are transmitted directly to member firms on the exchange floor by means of telephone or data transmission lines. The order is signaled to the appropiate trading pit by a runner who gives it to a broker for execution. If it is a market order, the broker attempts to fill it immediately. Otherwise, the order is held in a stack awaiting execution.

When the customer's order is executed, the floor broker endorses its time, price, and quantity. The price is relayed by mobile phone for immediate entry into the exchange's computerized price reporting system. Price information is displayed on the price quotation boards on the floor and transmitted to investors and brokers around the world via wire services and quotations vendors.

Procedures for Market Price Publication

Share prices are fixed on the NYSE and AMEX using the auction system, with the specialist acting to ensure an orderly market. Upon execution of a trade, the transaction is recorded and processed into the exchange's market data system, which flashes it onto the electronic ticker tape, and to electronic displays and market information inquiry systems worldwide.

Video screens now make current, detailed market data available to financial institutions and professional and nonprofessional investors around the world. This information may come directly from exchanges or through vendors who subscribe to exchange market data services.

The information on a screen usually consists of the price and volume of a stock's latest trade and the current bid and ask prices, as well as additional data supplied by vendors, such as dividends and yields on individual securities. In addition, significant administrative announcements, such as a delayed opening or a temporary trading halt in a stock pending the release of important news, will be displayed along with other information regarding general market conditions and trends.

In 1975, the NYSE helped inaugurate the Consolidated Tape Association. The term *tape*, a carryover from the days of the ticker tape, is still used to describe today's high-speed electronic transmission of the stock symbol, price, and volume of the individual transactions in each stock.

Reports of transactions in NYSE-listed stock executed on the NYSE and other domestic markets are consolidated into a continuous stream of real-time price information, otherwise known as Network A of the Consolidated Tape. Reports of transactions in any non-NYSE-listed stocks listed on the American Stock Exchange and in other local issues listed in regional markets throughout the United States make up Network B of the Consolidated Tape.

NASDAQ market makers display the number of shares they will buy and sell at their quoted prices in amounts no less than their trading obligations in the Small Order Execution System.

National, regional, and international daily newspapers carry NYSE, AMEX, and NASDAQ price and volume information.

Taxes, Commissions, and Other Trading Costs

Taxation of Domestic Investors

Income from securities held by individuals arising from the sale of securities is subject to federal income tax, currently at the effective rates of 15 percent, 28 percent, or 33 percent depending on the level of income earned. Corporations are subject to federal tax on taxable income currently at a rate of 34 percent. State taxes at various rates may also be payable on such income.

The profit on the sale of a security is subject to capital gains tax currently at the same rate as income tax. Any capital losses incurred in a tax year are deductible only to the extent of any capital gains made during the year plus, in the case of noncorporate taxpayers, ordinary income of up to US$3,000. Individuals and other noncorporate taxpayers may carry over a net capital loss for an unlimited time, whereas a corporation may carry back a capital loss to each of the three tax years preceding the loss and carry forward an excess for five years following the loss year. Securities held for sale to customers in the ordinary course of a dealer's business are not capital assets and are therefore not subject to the limitations described above.

Generally, all interest income received or accrued is fully taxable except interest on tax-exempt state or municipal bonds or certain loans by banks to employees.

Dividends (cash and other distributions) and interest received must be included fully in gross income. A deduction, ranging from 70 percent to 100 percent of the dividend depending on the size of the holding, is available to distributions from domestic corporations received by corporate shareholders.

Taxation of Foreign Investors

A foreign corporation engaged in a trade or business in the United States is taxed on certain U.S.-source investments and passive income, and on income that is effectively connected with the conduct of a trade or business in the United States. A foreign corporation not engaged in the business of trading in securities will only be taxed on U.S.-source passive or investment income.

U.S.-source fixed or determinable annual or periodic income (for example, dividends and interest) are taxed at a flat 30 percent rate. The following nonbusiness income is not taxable to a foreign corporation or individual if it has a U.S. source:

- Interest received on portfolio debt investments. (Portfolio interest does not include interest received by a foreign investor that also owns 10 percent or more of the voting stock of the U.S. corporation.)
- Interest on certain obligations issued by U.S. state and local governments.
- Original issue discount on debt obligations that mature within 183 days or less after issuance or on certain debt obligations that pay tax-exempt interest.

Withholding Tax

U.S.-source interest and dividends paid to nonresident alien individuals and foreign corporations is subject to a withholding tax of 30 percent of the gross amount of the payment, provided that the income is not effectively connected to the conduct of trade or business within the United States. However, the United States has an extensive network of treaties that significantly reduce or eliminate any withholding.

Transaction Taxes

There is no stamp duty payable or equivalent tax on the transfer of securities in the United States.

Commissions and Other Trading Costs

Commissions are freely negotiated between broker and client. Typical commission rates for institutional investors range between 3 and 6 cents per share, depending on the volume of business generated by that client and the size of the transaction. For private investors, commission rates will generally be higher, ranging up to 2.5 percent of contract value subject to minimum commissions.

For all transactions on the NYSE, a fee of 1 cent for each US$300 or fraction thereof is charged by the SEC. The fee is payable by the seller.

Procedures for Issuing and Listing New Securities

Admission to Listing

To qualify for admission to the exchanges, according to corporate governance standards, a company must: have a minimum of two independent directors on its board, maintain an audit committee composed of a majority of independent directors, provide shareholders with annual reports and make quarterly and other reports available to them, examine all related-party trades for potential conflicts of interest, hold an annual meeting of shareholders, solicit proxies and provide statements for all meetings of shareholders, and secure shareholder approval for certain transactions and increases in the amount of stock outstanding.

The NYSE also requires the company's adherence to the following quantitative standards:

1. Income before taxes of at least US$2.5 million for the most recent year and US$2 million for each of the preceding two years or, alternatively, pretax income for the last three fiscal years aggregating US$6.5 million or more together with a minimum in the most recent fiscal year of US$4.5 million. (All three years must be profitable.)
2. Net tangible assets of US$18 million. (Greater emphasis is, however, placed on the aggregate market value of the common stock.)
3. Market value of publicly held shares, subject to adjustment depending on market conditions, of at least US$18 million. (December 1990).
4. A total of 1,100,000 common shares publicly held. (If the unit of trading is less than 100 shares, the requirement relating to number of publicly held shares is reduced proportionately.)
5. Either 2,000 holders of 100 shares or more, or 2,200 total stockholders, together with an average monthly trading volume for the most recent six months of 100,000 shares.

To qualify for admission to the NASDAQ National Market System, a company must have either (a) net tangible assets of US$4 million, net income and pretax income in the last fiscal year or two of the last three fiscal years of at least US$400,000 and US$750,000, respectively, and a minimum of 500,000 public shares with a market value of at least US$3 million, or (b) net tangible assets of US$12 million, an operating history of at least 3 years, and a minimum of 1 million public shares with a market value of at least US$15 million.

In evaluating candidates for listing, the AMEX has established the following financial guidelines:

1. Pretax income of US$750,000 in the latest fiscal year or in two of the latest three years.
2. Market value of the publicly held shares of at least US$3 million.
3. Market price per share of at least US$3.
4. Stockholders' equity of at least US$4 million.

Alternatively, the market value of the public float must be US$15 million or higher, and the company must have an operating history of at least 3 years and shareholders' equity of at least US$4 million.

Certain companies that are unable to meet these criteria for a variety of reasons may qualify if they possess the financial resources to continue operations for an extended period of time, meet the alternative financial criteria outlined above, and are otherwise regarded as suitable for exchange listing.

Foreign Companies

To provide an alternative set of listing standards for companies organized outside the United States that meet the normal size and earnings yardsticks for NYSE listings, the NYSE will consider the acceptability of such companies' shares and shareholders on a worldwide basis, with regard to the liquidity and depth of the market for the company's shares in its home market.

Continued Listing

The exchanges may at any time suspend or delist a security when continued dealings in the security are not considered advisable, regardless of whether a security meets any specified criteria. For example, the NYSE would normally give consideration to suspending or removing from the list a security of a company having (1) fewer than 1,200 round lot holders, (2) 600,000 shares or fewer in public hands, or (3) aggregate market value of publicly held shares, subject to adjustment depending on market conditions, below US$5 million (December 1990).

Continued inclusion in the NASDAQ/NMS requires net tangible assets exceeding US$2 million if the issuer has sustained losses from continuing operations and/or net losses in 2 of its 3 most recent fiscal years or US$4 million if the issuer has sustained losses from continuing operations and/or net losses in 3 of its 4 most recent fiscal years. The market value of the shares traded must exceed US$1 million, with publicly held shares of at least 200,000.

Takeover and Merger Transactions

Beneficial Ownership Reporting

Section 13(d) of the Securities Exchange Act of 1934 requires the reporting of certain information on Schedule 13D when a person acquires beneficial ownership of more than 5 percent of publicly traded securities. Schedule 13D is usually the first report filed by a bidder in tender offer. This schedule must then be amended for material changes, such as buying and selling more than 1 percent of the company's shares.

Tender Offers

Anyone making a tender offer that could result in owning more than 5 percent of a class of securities registered under the 1934 Act must file

Schedule 14D-1 with the SEC on the day the offer begins. Disclosure under Schedule 14D-1 covers the following matters:

- Information about the offer, such as the expiration date, offering price, withdrawal rights, and proration.
- Trading history of the security.
- Information about the offeror and its officers, directors, partners, and controlling persons, including their employment history and any criminal violations.
- Past contracts, transactions, and negotiations between the offeror and the target.
- Sources and amounts of funds or other consideration to purchase the tendered shares.
- Purpose of the offer and the offeror's plans after buying the securities, such as selling off assets or going private.
- Bidder's (and its principal's) shareholdings in the target and recent transactions in its stocks.
- Terms of any contracts, understandings, or relationships between the bidder and other persons with respect to the target's securities.
- Advisors the bidder is using on the offer.
- Financial information about the offeror if material to the shareholder's tender decision.
- Applicability of any regulatory, antitrust, and margin requirements that must be satisfied, and any legal proceedings related to the offer.

Most of the information required by Schedule 14D-1 must be disseminated to the shareholders of the target company. For certain tender offers, an advertisement published in a widely read newspaper will meet the requirements. Copies must also be sent to the target company, any other bidder for the same securities, and each national securities exchange that lists the securities. A bidder publicly announcing a planned tender offer must make these filings within five days after the announcement.

Tender offers must remain open for no less than 20 days after they begin, but can have an unlimited duration. Should there be a change in the offer price or amount of securities sought, the offer must be extended at least 10 days. Tender offers must be made to all holders of a securities class, and the consideration offered cannot vary between shareholders. Bidders do not need to extend their offer when a competing one is made. During the period in which the offer remains open, any tendering shareholder can withdraw the deposited shares. Should the tender offer be oversubscribed, the bidder must buy from all tendering shareholders on a pro rata basis.

The SEC has also adopted the 1934 Act rules that provide disclosure requirements and antifraud provisions with respect to going-private transactions. Such transactions eliminate or substantially reduce the public equity interests in a corporation, thereby resulting in the corporation or its successor becoming a privately held corporation. Similar to the tender offer rules, the rules governing private transactions are designed to enable securities holders to obtain the material information concerning the proposed transactions necessary to make informed investment decisions.

In addition to the federal securities laws, each state has established a layer of rules and regulations governing takeovers and mergers involving corporations incorporated or doing business in that state.

Exchange Membership Requirements

Before a securities firm is admitted to membership of an exchange, it must select an appropriate firm name, possess adequate net capital, prepare written supervisory procedures, obtain fidelity- and surety-bond coverage, and meet various personnel qualification requirements.

To be accepted for NYSE, AMEX, and NASD membership, firms must meet the provisions of the SEC Net Capital Rule 15c3-1. Generally, the net capital rule requires minimum amounts of US$2,500, US$5,000, US$25,000, or US$100,000. The types of securities products and the activities engaged in by the firm dictate the minimum category required.

Virtually all firms that conduct securities business with the public are members of NASD (in addition to being members of the local exchange), giving the firm the right to participate in the investment banking and the over-the-counter securities businesses on a preferential basis and to distribute new issues and the various kinds of securities that are underwritten and sponsored by NASD members.

A firm must establish, maintain, and enforce written procedures that will enable it to properly supervise its employees' activities and that are designed to assist in achieving compliance with all applicable securities laws, rules, and regulations to which it is subject.

All members must carry a fidelity bond in the amount equal to at least 120 percent of their required minimum net capital, with a minimum bond of US$2,500. In addition, a number of states require broker-dealers to meet surety bonding requirements.

Before admission to NYSE, AMEX, or NASD membership:

- A broker-dealer must have at least two officers, partners, or directors qualified and registered as principals in the category(ies) of registration equivalent to the types of business in which the firm is engaged.
- A firm must designate, qualify, and register one officer, partner, or director as its chief financial and operations principal.
- All security firms that will engage in put and call options activity are required to qualify and maintain registration of at least one registered

options principal. They also must designate a senior registered options principal (SROP) and a compliance registered options principal (CROP).

- All members must designate one employee to represent, vote, and act on behalf of the member in all actions with the NYSE, AMEX, and/or NASD.

Certain broker-dealers will be subject to federal statutory provisions requiring them to become members of the Securities Investor Protection Corporation, which manages an insurance fund for the protection of other member firms and investors should any firm default on its obligations. A firm is also generally subject to the requirements of the securities laws and registration requirements of any or all states where it conducts securities business.

Membership is sold by the seat. The last sale price of a NYSE seat as of December 31, 1990 was US$295,000. Memberships may also be leased.

There are four types of memberships on the AMEX: (1) regular members (661) who transact business in equities and options; (2) options principal members (203) who may only perform transactions in options; (3) associate members who have wire access to the floor, but whose orders are actually executed by a regular member and (4) allied members who are general partners and principal executive officers of member companies. On December 31, 1990, 25 specialist units operated on the floor of the AMEX, representing a total of 215 specialists. The last sale price of an AMEX seat as of December 31, 1990 was US$60,000.

Investor Protection

Member Firm Regulation

The exchanges and NASD, together with the SEC, regulate their member firms, including examining the books and records of firms, to help ensure compliance with financial and operating requirements. Using automated financial surveillance systems, the exchanges conduct continuous evaluation of financial and operations reports of member firms.

Market Surveillance

The exchanges and the NASD maintain continuous surveillance of the markets for manipulation in order to ensure compliance with rules governing member firm trading, such as those relating to conflicts between trading for customers and trading for their own account, and to watch for evidence of insider trading. A technical tool at the disposal of the NYSE, for example, is Stock Watch, an electronic monitoring system that flags unusual prices and volume activity in NYSE-listed securities, permitting surveillance personnel to seek an immediate explanation of unusual activity. NYSE surveillance personnel are also able to utilize the Intermarket Surveillance Information System (ISIS), a database of trading information from major U.S. securities markets. Exchange and NASD analysts can instantly reconstruct unusual trading patterns and create a complete audit trail of quotation activity for all member firms or market makers.

Enforcement

Cases investigated and prosecuted by the enforcement division of the exchanges include: sales practice violations; violations of the financial responsibility and operational requirements of member firms; and marketplace integrity matters, such as instances of market manipulation and insider trading.

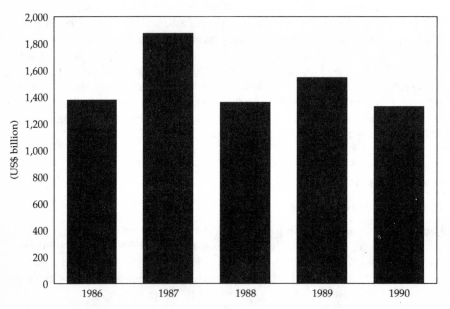

Figure 21.17. Shares Turnover—New York Stock Exchange (1986–1990) (US$ billion)

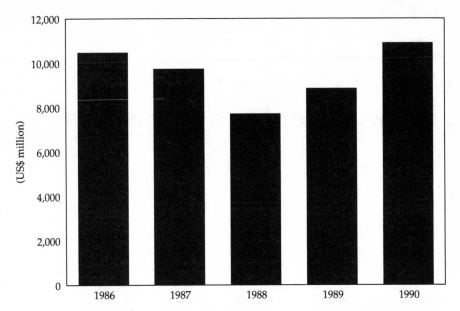

Figure 21.18. Bonds Turnover—New York Stock Exchange (1986–1990) (US$ million)

CHAPTER
22

Guide to Comparative Financial Reporting Practices*

This section compares financial reporting practices of the following countries: Australia, Belgium, Finland, France, Germany, Italy, Japan, Netherlands, Spain, Sweden, Switzerland, U.K., and United States.

AUSTRALIA

Highlights

Consolidation

Companies must present group accounts, normally in the form of consolidated financial statements. All overseas subsidiaries must be taken into consideration. Due to the requirement to present the balance sheet and P&L in a standard format, a greater volume of information is now disclosed in the notes to the accounts.

Earnings Per Share

This is calculated by dividing earnings (profit after tax, minority interest, preference dividends, and abnormal items, but before extraordinary items) by the weighted average number of shares in existence during the period.

Goodwill

Goodwill must now be amortised through the P&L over a period not exceeding 20 years. Goodwill should not be taken through the reserves.

Business Combinations

Acquisition accounting must be used at all times, as the pooling of interests is not permitted.

*Source: USB Phillips & Drew, London.

Deferred Taxation

This is provided on all timing differences which will reverse. The tax rate used is that in existence at the current year end.

Practical Considerations

Background

British traditions and practices characterize Australia to a significant extent. Companies law governs business affairs. The Companies Acts of the States and Commonwealth Territories comprise the "Uniform" Act of 1961, which, with subsequent amendments, constitutes the underlying legislation presently in effect. In order to achieve uniformity, the territories and States agreed upon a scheme whereby they would adopt the company law applicable to the Australian Capital Territory. The resultant law (The Companies Act and Code) came into effect in 1982, with further important amendments in 1984. The code is very similar to previous Australian company law and continues to bear basic similarities to British law.

In 1965, the Australian Accountancy Research Foundation was established with the task of developing statements of accounting principles. This body is directly comparable to the "ASC" in the U.K. and has issued standards on a wide variety of topics. However, although Australian company legislation leans heavily on Britain, the development of accounting standards also draws from American experience, where financial reporting standards in a geographically large and politically federated nation appear relevant.

Consolidated Financial Statements

Group accounts are compulsory for all companies. In practice, this is achieved by way of the consolidated financial statements, including all overseas subsidiaries. Associate companies are defined in exactly the same way as in the U.K. and are equity accounted (AAS 14). Investments of less than 20 percent voting shares, or where significant influence is not maintained, are put in the balance sheet at cost, though they can be subsequently revalued. Joint ventures, for example in mining projects, are commonly accounted for on a proportional consolidation basis.

Following a recent change in regulations, Australian companies now have to present their balance sheet and profit and loss account in a standard format. There is no scope for a different presentation. This change in format has led to a greater volume of information being disclosed via the notes to the accounts. In order to get a 'true and fair' view of the financial statements, investors will have to read the notes extremely thoroughly. Australian companies are also required (AAS 12) to disclose a statement of sources and applications of funds. These are extremely detailed and provide a lot of useful information for readers. In contrast to the balance sheet and profit and loss account, there is flexibility in the format of the statement.

Earnings Per Share (EPS)

As in the U.K., EPS is calculated by dividing earnings (profit after tax, minority interests, abnormal items, and preference dividends, but before extraordinary items) by the weighted average numbers of shares in issue during the period. As explained above, readers will have to scan the notes to the accounts in order to find any specific items for which they may need to adjust.

Goodwill

The standard on goodwill has recently been updated, following the controversy which arose from its original recommendations. Goodwill now must be amortised over its useful economic life. This period must not exceed 20 years. Goodwill must not be taken through the reserves. This practice is different from the U.K., where companies can either amortise goodwill or write it off against reserves. This difference in policy may be significant, especially with regard to EPS calculations.

Business Combinations

Companies must use the acquisition method of accounting at all times. Assets are revalued at the date of acquisition and any positive or negative goodwill calculated. The pooling of interest method must not be used.

Deferred Taxation

Australian companies have to account for deferred tax. They provide for all timing differences in existence at the year end. However, the rate used is that operating at the year end. In contrast to the U.K., it is not unusual to see a deferred tax asset in the balance sheet of an Australian company. This arises principally from losses carried forward (where there is a virtual certainty that the benefit will be realised) and also from the legal requirement to give employees long-service leave after a set period of time. The company accrues for the long-service leave annually, but is only given the tax benefit in the year in which the employee takes this statutory holiday.

Other Features

The following are more theoretical comments about Australian accounting practice.

Depreciation

Fixed assets must be written off by means of a systematic charge to the P&L over its useful economic life. If an asset is revalued, then depreciation must be based on the revalued amount. There is a requirement for companies to reassess the economic useful life on an annual basis. As in the U.K., land is not depreciated.

Leasing

Australian accounting always tries to recognize the substance rather than the form of any transaction. Consequently, under AAS 17 if an asset is categorized as a finance lease, the asset and liability must be capitalized. However, if the asset is defined as an operating lease, it must not be capitalized and the company must debit the rental expense to the P&L.

The standard also requires a comprehensive disclosure in the notes to the accounts, identifying its leasing commitments (for example, liabilities which fall due within one year, between one and two years, between two and five years, and after five years).

Stock

Stock must be valued at the lower of cost or net realizable value. There are a number of methods which are acceptable under AAS 2—for example, FIFO, or weighted average. Although the standard specifically prohibits the use of LIFO in the vast majority of cases, it does recognize that Australian subsidiaries of parent companies incorporated in the United States may be required to use the *last in/first out* valuation method.

Segmental Reporting

Under AAS 16, a company must give detailed segmental information. This information should be given both on an industrial and geographic basis.

Reserves

Reserves are divided between *capital reserves* and *revenue reserves*. The former may arise from premiums received upon the issue of capital stock, revaluations of fixed assets, or other capital transactions. These reserves are generally unavailable for distribution to shareholders. Revenue reserves, on the other hand, are typically unappropriated net income. They are available for general company purposes and not created in accordance with any statutory requirements.

Fixed Assets

Fixed assets are generally stated at historic cost less accumulated depreciation. Real estate, machinery, and other equipment can be revalued, following a *director's* or an *independent* valuation. Such a revaluation would normally trigger higher depreciation charges to the P&L.

Extraordinary Items and Abnormal Items

Extraordinary items are defined in exactly the same way as in the U.K. (i.e., items which are material, nonrecurring, and occur outside the normal course of business). In contrast, abnormal items (equivalent to exceptional items in the U.K.) are material and nonrecurring, but within the normal course of business. Abnormal items should be included in EPS calculations.

Foreign Exchange

Australia uses the *immediate recognition method* for foreign exchange transactions. Exchange differences resulting from monetary items are recognised in the P&L account in the period in which they arise. This occurs in all cases except for those where the monetary item can be reasonably attributed to a qualifying asset (i.e., an asset ready for productive use) or to hedged transactions regarding goods and services. In these cases, exchange differences will be included in the cost of acquiring the asset or included in the measurement of the purchase or sale respectively.

Australia follows the U.K., when translating the P&L and balance sheet in order to produce consolidated accounts, by distinguishing between those foreign operations which are self-sustaining and those which are integrated with the reporting entity. In the former case, the financial statements are translated at the balance sheet date using the current rate method, and exchange differences are taken to the "Foreign Currency Translation Reserve." In the latter case, the temporal method is used. The key features of this method are outlined in the U.K. section.

BELGIUM

Highlights

Consolidated Financial Statements

Consolidated financial statements are only required for holding companies. General Belgian practice is to consolidate fully all undertaking in a group. However, proportional consolidation is also accepted.

Accounting for Associated Companies

Current Belgian practice allows either the cost or equity method of accounting to be used.

Earnings Per Share Calculations

Adjustments may have to be made to published earnings figures. These will be specific to the particular company, rather than the result of general accounting adjustments which should be made to all Belgian companies.

Practical Considerations

Background

In Belgium, no real accounting legislation existed until the adoption of the Accounting Law of July 17, 1975. This law provides general rules and principles in respect of the official accounting books to be used and sets forth a general framework that has been further amplified by a set of subsequent Royal Decrees, the most important of which are those of October 8, 1976 and September 12, 1983. These two are outlined below:

1. *The Royal Decree of October 8, 1976* regulates the form and content of the annual financial statements, in compliance with the requirements of the Fourth EEC Directive. The principal issues dealt with by the decree are the standard format and the basic accounting concepts to be used.
2. *The Royal Decree of September 12, 1983* updates previous regulations and further requires the use of a minimum standardized chart of accounts by all companies which are already subject to the Decree of October 8, 1976. Belgian financial statements are closest in philosophy to those produced in France, Italy, and Spain. Certainly, the quality of disclosure in public companies' financial statements is reasonable, so that investors can generally use the figures published for their analysis without major reservations.

Consolidated Financial Statements

Consolidated financial statements are required only for holding companies and should be drawn up in accordance with International Accounting Standards and similar standards issued by the Belgian Institut des Reviseurs d'Entreprises.

As in the rest of the EEC, the Seventh EEC Directive will eventually be implemented in Belgium and will lead to the regular preparation of the consolidated financial statements. General Belgian practice is to consolidate fully all undertakings in a group, although proportional consolidation is also acceptable. The Directive requires full consolidation, permitting proportional consolidation only when one undertaking included in the consolidation manages another undertaking jointly with other undertakings outside the group, and the requirements for full consolidation (e.g., control of at least 50 percent voting rights) are not met.

The Seventh Directive requires the use of the equity method of accounting (see Glossary in Appendix A) for investments in undertakings that are subject to the significant influence (greater than 20 percent voting rights) of one of the companies included in the consolidation. Belgian accounting practice agrees with the Directive's definition of significant influence but allows accounting for associated undertakings by either the cost or the equity method. In cases where associated undertakings meeting the equity method requirements of the Directive are at present being accounted for by the cost method, a change to the equity method will be required.

Earnings Per Share (EPS)

Belgium earnings per share calculations are based on the profit after tax and minority interests, but before extraordinary items. This is then divided by the weighted average number of shares that were in issue during the year.

The investor may need to make adjustments to the published earnings figure, but these will depend on the individual circumstances of the company, and as such no general rules can be given.

Other Features

The following are more theoretical comments on Belgian accounting practice.

Fixed Assets

Fixed assets must normally be stated at cost less accumulated depreciation. Fixed assets may under certain conditions be revalued, in which case the amount of the revaluation must be recorded in an undistributable revaluation reserve account. However, general revaluation for inflation is not permitted. Purchase type leases must be capitalized and the related liability recorded in long-term debts.

Goodwill, Deferred Charges, and Intangible Assets

Goodwill and intangible assets are shown at the lower of acquisition cost or valuation and are written off over their useful economic lives. Start-up costs and formation expenses must, however, be written off over a maximum period of five years.

Inventories

Stock values must not exceed the lower of cost or market value (cost being defined as purchase price of raw materials plus direct and indirect production costs). Accepted valuation methods are FIFO, LIFO, and weighted average, applied on an item-by-item basis.

Liabilities

Long-term liabilities must be shown separately from short-term liabilities. Details of secured liabilities are provided in the notes.

Provisions for losses and contingencies must be made when necessary, even if the loss or contingency is only known after the balance sheet date. Such provisions must, however, be specific. "General" reserves and provisions are not tax-allowable.

Capital and Reserves

The disclosures required in respect of capital and reserves are as follows:

Capital

1. The number of shares issued and nominal value.
2. Subscribed and unpaid amount of capital.

3. Number of convertible bonds issued and conditions of conversion thereof.
4. Share premiums and reserves must be disclosed separately. Reserves must disclose the amounts of undistributable reserves and reserves available for distribution.

Reserves

1. **Legal reserve**. Five percent of the net profit after taxes of each year must be set aside to a legal reserve not available for distribution. This allocation is no longer necessary when the legal reserve reaches 10 percent of the capital.
2. **Untaxed reserves**. Proceeds from fixed asset sales can be credited to an untaxed reserve. This reserve can only be used for reinvesting in fixed assets. If the company wants to pay out this reserve, the amount to be released then becomes eligible for tax.

FINLAND

Highlights

EEC

Finland is not a member of the EEC and its companies' financial statements are thus not influenced by the EEC Fourth and Seventh Directives.

Influence of Taxation

As in its neighbor, Sweden, accounting practices in Finland are heavily influenced by tax considerations.

Deferred Taxation

The tax effect of timing differences is not recognized in Finnish financial statements.

Inventories and the Inventory Reserves

Inventories manufactured by the company are valued excluding overheads. Companies are permitted to write down the value of inventories to the inventory reserve.

Earnings Per Share

Published earnings figures must be adjusted for the "Change in Adjustment Items" and the "Change in Reserves."

Depreciation

Changes in the depreciation method and the consequent effects on earnings are not disclosed.

Practical Considerations

Background

Most Finnish companies gear their accounting system and the annual financial statements to the provisions of the tax laws, because tax concessions are generally available only if recorded in the accounts and thus in the financial statements.

Accounting practices are thus heavily affected by tax considerations as they are, for example, in Sweden. In addition, because of the lack of a developed stock market, managements generally do not attach great importance to making financial statements particularly informative, although the larger companies tend to be more forthcoming.

There are a number of points of which the investor should be aware. These are dealt with below, and are followed by a more theoretical discussion on Finnish accounting procedures.

Inventories

Inventories are carried at the lower of variable cost or market value. For goods purchased, the determination of the variable costs included in the stock value is easily calculated. It is simply purchase price plus freight. **Goods manufactured by the company are valued at variable production costs, but overheads are excluded.** The value may thus be considerably lower than it would be using international accounting principles which include overheads.

The FIFO method is generally accepted in Finland, It is possible to write down the value of the stocks by a maximum of 40 percent, except if the company has an operational reserve (see reserves), in which case the reserve is limited to 35 percent. **Larger companies must now indicate the stock reserve.**

Earnings Per Share (EPS) and the P&L

The profit and loss statement is very easy to read as it starts with the turnover (net sales) and ends with the net published profit. As disclosure of the stock reserve is becoming generally more common and has been compulsory in larger limited companies since 1982, the profit and loss statement gives a fairly good picture of the company's performance. If the change in stock reserve is not given, the profit figures must be adjusted by this change in the reserve. Similarly, the investor must adjust for the changes in other reserves, such as the investment reserves (see below), as the worked example on Nokia below shows.

Depreciation is divided into depreciation on buildings, machinery and equipment, intangible assets, and other. In their profit and loss statements, large companies often separate depreciations according to planned and extraordinary depreciations, but most companies do not. However, as the amount written off on each group of assets is shown separately, it is possible to compare actual depreciations with, for instance, maximum depreciations allowed by tax laws. This may give an indication of true, underlying profitability. On the rare occasions when planned depreciation is separated from extraordinary depreciation, the investor can make an adjustment by adding the extraordinary depreciation back to profit.

Among other income and expenses, the major problem is to choose which items may be considered extraordinary, such as profit on sales of fixed assets. Such sales may, especially if they are tax-free, also be entered directly into an equity account, not affecting the result at all.

A new rule introduced in the Accounting Act requires more complete information about the cost-of-debt financing than before. Beginning in 1986, the profit and loss statement has to show interest expense and other cost of debt separately.

The net published profit is not the true profit, but the profit the company wishes to publish for dividend and other reasons. To arrive at the true profit, all pre-tax allocations, such as "Change in Adjustment Items" and "Change in Reserves" and the other profit-adjusting items mentioned above, should be adjusted for.

NOKIA-EPS example	Published accounts FMm	Adjusted accounts FMm
Operating profit	1,251	1,251
Adjustment for inventory valuation		26
Adjustment for goodwill		(8)
	1,251	1,269
Adjustment for foreign exchange	100	44
Profit before appropriations	1,151	1,225
Appropriations–Untaxed reserves	(582)	
Taxations	(193)	(193)
Minorities	(188)	(188)
Net profit	188	844
Number of shares	63.0	63.0
EPS FM	3.0	13.4

Analyst: D. Exton.

Fixed Asset Revaluations

Fixed assets can be revalued if the current value significantly and permanently exceeds the book value. The revaluation should be shown on the liability side of the balance sheet as a valuation item. **As revaluation is voluntary, hidden reserves may result from undervaluation of some companies' fixed assets.**

Depreciation

Unlike the U.K., changes in the depreciation method and the effects on earnings are not disclosed. This presents investors with an almost impossible task in making an adjustment, unless they have an intimate knowledge of the company.

Deferred Taxation

The tax effect of timing differences is not recognized in Finnish financial statements. However, it would be very difficult for investors to make any compensating adjustments without being given additional information by the company.

Special Reserves

Investment Reserves. These give companies the possibility of allocating untaxed reserves for future investments in fixed assets. The allocation may not normally exceed 50 percent of the net profit before the allocation, but the government may allow allocations of up to 80 percent in certain years. A deposit of at least 50 percent of the allocation must be made in an interest-bearing blocked account with the Bank of Finland. When an investment fulfilling the government's requirements is made, the amount may be withdrawn. When used, the investment reserve is booked against assets acquired, decreasing the depreciation base.

Procurement Reserve. This is another kind of investment fund which applies to investments in developing areas.

Counter-Cyclical Reserves. In some years the government has also enforced various counter-cyclical reserves. While transfers to reserves in general are voluntary, some transfers to counter-cyclical reserves have been compulsory and a 100 percent deposit may be requested.

Operational Reserve. To give companies with no stocks or limited stocks some compensation for being unable to benefit from the stock valuation rules, this reserve was created in 1978. The operational reserve may amount to a maximum 30 percent of the amount of salaries and wages paid during the preceding 12 months.

Other Features

The following comments are of a more theoretical nature.

Consolidated Financial Statements

The new Companies Act, effective from January 1, 1980, requires the preparation of consolidated accounts by a company if it:

1. Owns at least 50 percent of the share capital in another company.
2. For some other reason has a decisive influence or a material interest in the profit of the other company.

The 1980 act also requires that more information be given about certain balance sheet items as well as the profitability of the company. The most important requirement is, as previously mentioned, the stating of the stock reserve. More specific information on company shareholdings and other interests in affiliated companies is also required.

Fixed Assets

Fixed assets are generally carried at net book value, although if the value of an asset is permanently reduced, it must be reflected in the accounts. As mentioned above, depreciation in Finnish accounts is very much determined by tax laws. Depreciation allowed under the tax laws is quite liberal by international comparison. Finnish tax laws have, with a few exceptions, accepted accelerated depreciation, with the greatest benefit from this system being obtained by capital-intensive companies.

Intangible Assets

Intangible assets, such as goodwill, patents, and trademarks may be shown at cost in the balance sheet, but they must be amortized over their effective lives or for tax purposes, in any case, within ten years.

Liquid (Financial) Assets

Receivables in foreign currency are converted into Finnish marks at a rate not exceeding the foreign currency purchase rate of the Bank of Finland on the closing day of the financial year.

Liabilities

Liabilities are divided into current liabilities and long-term debt:

1. *Current liabilities* are those maturing in less than one year. A noticeable item in this category is deferred liabilities (accrued expenses, transitory items). In accordance with the *matching principle* all accrued costs not yet paid are booked as deferred/accrued liabilities. The large deferred items are usually holiday wages and salaries, interest, and taxes.
2. *Long-term debt* is usually divided into loans from financial institutions, pension loans, and other long-term debt.

Provisions

Under the Accounting Act, provisions may be made to cover any possible specific expense or loss in the future. The tax laws do not, however, admit any general provisions other than provision for bad debts and guarantee reserves.

Notes to the Accounts

As Finnish balance sheets and profit and loss statements are quite detailed, they can often be read without reference to notes. However, some companies do give very detailed explanations in their notes, although only a few notes are compulsory. The most important compulsory notes are changes in equity, contingent liabilities, and securities pledged.

FRANCE

Highlights

Foreign Currency Translation

Unrealized gains are deferred whereas unrealized losses are taken to the profit and loss account.

Leasing

Leased assets are not capitalized.

Depreciation

The decline in fixed-asset values must be recognized. In order to claim tax deductions, it is necessary to put *excess* depreciation through the accounts.

Earnings Per Share

This is calculated as in the United Kingdom. However, no distribution is made in France between exceptional and extraordinary items, and *provisions réglementées* may contain items that require adjustments to be made.

Deferred Tax

It is a rare, though increasing, practice for deferred taxation to be recognized in the financial statements.

Income Statements

Despite the EEC Fourth Directive, the typical French income statement is not very similar in appearance to the typical British profit and loss account.

Practical Considerations

Background

The popular belief about French financial statements is that they are standardized and presented in a uniform format almost to the exclusion of all other considerations. This is based on the existence of the General Accounting Plan (Plan Comptable Général), which is a very detailed accounting guide, containing among other items, definitions of accounting terms, valuation and measurement rules, and model financial statements.

In recent years, however, and more immediately with the introduction of the provisions of the EEC Fourth Directive, an increasing number of large public companies are producing financial statements more in keeping with Anglo-American practices.

Under the EEC Fourth Directive the financial statements must show a true and fair view. In the past, the objectives could have been interpreted to mean conformity with the substance of the rules and procedures in force.

Despite the EEC harmonization process, some important differences with U.K. accounting practices still exist, and there are also other factors of which the investor should be aware. These are dealt with below:

Foreign Currency Translation

Assets and liabilities denominated in foreign currencies should be translated at year-end rates of exchange for the preparation of financial statements. Exchange differences should be accounted for in a suspense account in the balance sheet. **As a general rule, unrealized gains are then deferred, whereas unrealized losses are taken to the profit and loss account by way of a provision for exchange losses. This contrasts with the standard U.K. practice, where both unrealized gains and losses are taken to the profit and loss account.**

Leasing

Leased assets are not capitalized in France. (This contrasts directly with the policy recommended in SAAP 21 in the United Kingdom for the treatment of finance leases.) Disclosure of the original cost of the asset is required in the notes, however, as well as the depreciation charge and accumulated depreciation as if it has been purchased.

Depreciation

The decline in value of fixed assets must be recognized either by systematic depreciation or by way of provision for loss. Systematic depreciation is defined as the recognition in the accounts of the reduction in the value of the asset resulting from usage, the passage of time, or changes in technical considerations, the effects of which are irreversible. Depreciation should be spread over the estimated economic life of the assets.

Whatever the depreciation method used, in order for the charge to be deductible for tax purposes it must be recorded in the accounting records. The minimum depreciation (obligatory if the accounts are to show a true and fair view) is the equivalent of the charge obtained by applying the straight-line method, although the declining balance method may be used for certain types of assets, such as tools and machines. In France the depreciation charged to the profit and loss account may be in excess of what would be debited if the straight line method was used. In order to gain a tax deduction, the charge must be recorded in the accounting records. This system is known as *amortissement dérogatoire,* or derogatory depreciation.

Example of Derogatory Depreciation

The following example aims to clarify how derogatory depreciation works, and where the various components are to be found in the balance sheet and the profit and loss account:

Asset costs	100

Asset costs   100
Economic life   5 years (i.e. 20% depreciation per year)
Coefficient   2
(This is given to assets by the tax authorities)

Year one

	FF
Brought forward value	100
Total depreciation (60 × 20% × 2)	(40)
Carried forward value	60

(Asset value × straight line depreciation rate × coefficient)

The depreciation will be split between its straight line depreciation (20 percent, found under *charges d'exploitation*) and the extra depreciation (20 percent, found under *charges exceptionnelles*) charged in order to gain the relevant tax benefits.

In the balance sheet, the asset will be reduced by the straight line depreciation and a special reserve (*provisions réglementée*) will be credited with the extra depreciation.

Year two

	FF
Brought forward value	60
Total depreciation (60 × 20% × 2)	(24)
	36
Profit and loss:	
Charges d'exploitation—debit	20
Charges exceptionnelles—debit	4
	24
Balance sheet:	
Assets—credit	20
Reserves—credit	4
	24

Year three	
	FF
Profit and loss account:	
Charges d'exploitation—debit	20
Produits exceptionnels—debit	(8)
	12
Balance sheet:	
Fixed asset—credit	20
Reserves—a release	(8)
	12

As the derogatory depreciation ($36 \times 20\% \times 2 = 14.4$) is less than the straight line depreciation, the brought forward value is divided by the number of years remaining according to straight line depreciation. This figure is treated as follows, with a release from the reserve being effected:

$$\text{Depreciation: } 36 \text{ divided by } 3 = 12$$

Year Four and Year Five.   The figures for years four and five are exactly the same as for year three.

Implications.

1. The investor may wish to adjust the figures for the *exceptionnel* items. This would smooth the results. However, in practice this adjustment is not put through.
2. If there are large exceptional credits to the profit and loss account, the company may be reducing its level of capital expenditure. This might impact on future results.

Earnings Per Share (EPS)

Earnings per share calculations are commonly performed by dividing the net profit figure by the weighted average number of ordinary shares in issue. There are, however, a number of adjustments that can be made depending on the extent of the financial information available.

Extraordinary items are not distinguished from exceptional items in France, in contrast to U.K. practice. An investor should try to establish the amounts applicable to each category, and exclude the extraordinary profits or losses from the earnings per share calculations (see example of Remy Martin, below).

Remy Martin: Calculation of earnings per share

	1987 Actual	1988 Actual
Published earnings (FF mil)		
Sales	2,994	3,318
Other revenues	149	148
Cost of sales	−1,750	−1,967
Operating expenses	−1,251	−1,324
Depreciation	−72	−83
Operating profit	69	92
Net interest	−73	−82
Other income (a)	104	94
Pre-tax profit	100	104
Tax	−55	−28
Associates	0	2
Minorities	10	−18
Total profit	55	60
Number of shares in issue (mil)	6.05	6.05
Published EPS (FF)	9.1	9.9
Adjusted earnings (FF mil)		
Sales	2,994	3,318
Other revenues	149	148
Cost of sales	−1,750	−1,967
Operating expenses	−1,251	−1,324
Depreciation	−72	−83
Operating profit	69	92
Net interest	−73	−82
Pre-tax profit	−4	10
Tax	−24	−18
Associates	0	2
Minorities	10	22
Total profit	−18	15
Number of shares in issue (mil)	6.05	6.05
Adjusted EPS (FF)	−3.0	2.5

Analyst: S. Massot.

Note: Other income comprises extraordinary items and therefore must be excluded from the EPS calculation. The full impact for 1988 is:

	FF
Other income	−94
Tax	9
Minority interest	40
	−45

It is common in France for companies to hold their own shares. In calculating EPS these shares should be excluded, and only the number owned by outside shareholders used. The example below, featuring Pernod Ricard, should clarify this.

Pernod Ricard: Calculation of earnings per share

	1987 Actual	Forecast 1988	Forecast 1989
Net attributable profit (FF mil)	607	720	800
Shares ranking (mil) (adjusted)	9.1	8.7	8.7
Fully diluted EPS (FF mil)	66	83	92

Analyst: S. Massot.

Notes:

(1) Pernod Ricard cancelled 0.4 million shares in early 1988.

(2) Pernod Ricard now has 9.8 million shares in issue, of which 1.1 million (1987: 1.1 million) are owned by the company. For the purposes of calculating EPS the total number of shares owned by outside shareholders is used; i.e., 8.7 million (1987: 9.1 million).

Where provisions réglementées appears in consolidated financial statements, the investor should try to establish its components and nature. This category may consist of some of the following:

- Fluctuation des cours.
- Fluctuation hausse des prix.
- Provisions pour investissement.

If investors can find out what makes up provisions réglementées, they can make net of tax adjustments. However, it may be difficult to obtain the necessary information.

Deferred Tax

A major difference between the U.K. and French accounting practices arises with the treatment of deferred tax.

In France, deferred tax is increasingly being recognized in the consolidated financial statements, particularly where companies are listed on the Bourse. If no provision is made in the accounts, disclosure is normally made in the notes (*annexe*).

The major reason for this potential difference with the United Kingdom is that there is little difference between the profit/loss for accounting and tax purposes, as the section on depreciation has already explained.

There are, however, a few occasions where timing differences will occur. The most common of these arise from reserves that are not tax deductible until actually paid and from unrealized translation gains which are not recognized in book income but must be included in taxable income.

Income Statements

Although it is in conformity with the Fourth Directive, the typical French income statement is not very similar in appearance to the typical British profit and loss account. There are three main reasons for this:

1. French companies are not permitted to use the format from the Fourth Directive most frequently adopted by U.K. companies (i.e., the format which discloses cost of sales, distribution costs, and administration expenses).
2. French companies often show more detail on the face of the statement than in the notes. However, the trend is for increasing disclosure in the notes in order to give a "true and fair view."
3. The greater emphasis, in France, is on the mandatory formats on goods produced as well as sold. Revenues and expenses are classified by origin and are systematically analyzed into three overall categories:
   a. Operating revenues and expenses (including prior year items).
   b. Financial revenues and expenses (including write-downs of securities).
   c. Exceptional revenues and expenses (including items of a nonoperating and nonfinancial nature and accounting entries booked for tax purposes).

Provisions for Risks and Charges

The increase or decrease in the value of an asset or a liability is accounted for as a change in value if it is considered to be irreversible. When the change is not considered definitive, it is accounted for as a provision. Provisions for risks and charges are designed to cover losses or expenses that events in progress at the balance sheet date render probable, and that have a well-defined nature, but the realization of which is not certain. A "cushion" can easily be built into this category, but it will be very difficult for an analyst to find out enough information to adjust accurately.

Regulated Provisions (provisions réglementées)

Regulated provisions are classified in the balance sheet as part of shareholders' equity. These provisions may relate to certain risk areas but in most cases they are portions of profits which are temporarily not taxable (for example, provision for increases in inventory prices). Often an element of deferred tax is attached to these provisions which is generally not recorded in the accounts.

Consolidated Financial Statements

Consolidated financial statements are required from relevant groups of companies for accounting periods beginning on and after January 1, 1986.

Although the full consolidation method is used predominantly, the proportional consolidation (intégration proportionelle) technique is allowable where an operation is conducted jointly by two companies.

The *annexe* (notes to the financial statements) may not be as informative in consolidated accounts as it is in the single entity's statements. However, as companies start producing consolidated financial statements on a regular basis, this shortcoming should be removed.

Other Features

The following are more general, theoretical comments on French accounting practice.

Balance Sheet

Headings are classified by function rather than by degree of liquidity of cash categories, as in the United Kingdom. The distinction between long- and short-term is only provided in the notes.

Notes to the Financial Statements

Before the implementation of the Fourth Directive, French financial statements were accompanied by very few notes as understood in the United Kingdom and United States. They are now much more detailed and represent a substantial increase compared to previous amounts of disclosure in French financial statements, so as to provide a true and fair presentation. These notes consist of accounting rules and methods used in preparing the financial statements, supplementary information relative to the balance sheet and income statements, and other information.

Funds Statements

Publication of a funds statement (*tableau de financement*) was obligatory for accounting periods beginning on and after January 1, 1986, although it had already become common practice for large companies. The statement is divided into two parts. The first part states the long-term sources of funds (*stables*) and the long-term uses of funds (*durables*). The balance represents the change in working capital (*fonds de roulement*), which is analyzed in the second part of the statement. The analysis distinguishes between operating funds (stocks, trade debtors, trade creditors) and nonoperating funds (other debtors and creditors) with a subtotal. The balance then represents changes in net liquid funds (*trésorerie*). The statement is normally constructed before profit distribution, so that uses of funds include dividends paid during the accounting period. The sources side is headed by *autofinancement* (essentially, net profit after adding back depreciation) and is in contrast with the United Kingdom, where the starting point is profit on ordinary activities before taxation.

Company Formation and Similar Expenses (frais d'établissement)

This category includes not only formation costs, but also the cost of issuing shares or debentures. All must be amortized over a period not exceeding five years.

Fixed Assets

Fixed assets are to be shown in the accounts at their historic cost, which is represented either by their acquisition cost or their cost of construction. Acquisition costs are those costs related directly or indirectly to the purchase. Interest charges incurred for the acquisition of the assets should be charged to the profit and loss account and not capitalized. The 1982 General Accounting Plan states that the costs of construction can include the interest charge relating to loans incurred to finance the construction, but only to the extent that interest expense was incurred during the construction period.

The revaluation of fixed assets is not forbidden and it can be made either in accordance with a legal revaluation or by decision of management. In the latter case, the revaluation surplus is taxable as if it were ordinary income. There has been no legal revaluation since 1975.

Investments

The 1982 chart of accounts defines three types of investments, with distinct valuation methods.

1. *Investments in affiliated companies.* These are investments which enable a company to exercise control over an affiliated company. Investments fall into this category if a company owns at least 20 percent of the share capital of the affiliate. Investments in affiliated companies should be valued in the financial statements under the equity method (see Glossary).
2. *Other investments.* These are investments, excluding those in affiliated companies, that the company intends to keep over a long period of time or cannot resell in the near future.
3. *Marketable securities investments.* These are acquired with the objective of making a short-term capital gain and are to be valued at the lower of cost or market value at year end.

Stocks and Work-in-Progress

Stocks and work-in-progress are shown in the accounts at their cost of acquisition or their production cost. In some circumstances, the added costs of warehousing may also be included. Overheads are allocated to costs on the basis of normal production capacity. The costs of acquiring or manufacturing stocks are allocated between costs of sales and stocks using a weighted average cost method or the FIFO method. At the end of the year, stocks are valued at the lower of cost or market value.

Pension Costs

Pension expenses are generally excluded from the profit and loss account. However, the amount is normally disclosed in the annexe. Although the investor should make an adjustment for this, the sums involved are unlikely to be material.

Reserves

Legal Reserve (réserve légale).   A legal reserve of at least 10 percent of the par value of the share capital has to be maintained and, until it reaches this proportion, 5 percent of the net profits must be appropriated annually. This reserve is not distributable during the life of the company, although it may be used to offset losses.

*Share Premium (**Primes d'émission, de fusion, d'apport**).*   The item translated as share premium is made up of primes d'émission arising from an issue of shares for cash, of primes d'apport arising from an issue of shares for a consideration other than cash, and of primes de fusion arising on the issue of shares when absorbing another company.

Regulated Reserves.   These are required in some cases to benefit from certain fiscal dispensations, such as the reserve for long-term capital gains. The distribution of such a reserve attracts the payment of the difference between the tax calculated at the normal company tax rate and the tax paid at the reduced rate when the reserve was constituted.

Disclosure.   As a result of the recent changes in French accounting regulations, **the profit and loss for the accounting period can now be shown as part of capital and reserves**. Previously it was disclosed either at the foot of the capital and liabilities side (if a profit) or the assets side (if a loss).

GERMANY

Highlights

Earnings Adjustments

The DVFA (Institute of German Analysts) have devised a formula for adjusting the published figures to allow intercompany comparisons to be made.

Consolidated Financial Statements

German practice differs significantly from British and American procedures. Overseas subsidiaries need not be consolidated. A *consolidation difference* is calculated annually. Full consolidation will only be mandatory after 1990.

Reserves

It is possible to create hidden reserves, for example, by ultraconservative valuation. All movements on reserves in the balance sheet must be passed through the income statement.

EEC Directives

Compliance with the Fourth Directive is required for accounting periods beginning on or after January 1, 1987. The Seventh Directive on Consolidated Financial Statements must be applied for accounting periods beginning on and after January 1, 1990.

Fixed Assets

German accounting rigidly follows the principle of an historical cost presentation. Revaluations are not permitted even where supported by certified valuations.

Depreciation

Accelerated depreciation is allowable for tax purposes on certain types of capital investment.

Practical Considerations

Background

Published accounts in Germany tend to be guided more by compliance with legal requirements and by fiscal considerations than by the desire to present a true and fair view of the company's earnings, as understood by the accountancy profession in Great Britain and the United States.

The financial statements generally include a balance sheet and a profit and loss account. As most of the information required by law is incorporated on the face of the financial statements, a comprehensive set of explanatory footnotes is not published. In addition to these statements, corporations must publish a report on the company's operations to the management board.

For the investor, German published financial statements can be somewhat obscure, due to the lack of information given and to the not unusual reticence of the companies to be more forthcoming.

The impact of the EEC Fourth and Seventh Directives will be considerable, and this is commented on below together with the following important points:

- German accounts and the DVFA method of adjustment
- Consolidated financial statements
- Reserves
- Fixed assets

The Impact of the Fourth and Seventh EEC Directives on Germany

The introduction of the requirements of the EEC's Fourth and Seventh Directives into German law should give rise to a number of important changes. These will be discussed below, and should result in some narrowing of the area of difference between German and Anglo-American accounting.

The two Directives were introduced into Germany with the passing of the Law of December 1985 (Bilanzrichtinien-Gesetz). **Compliance with** the Fourth Directive is required for accounting periods beginning on and after January 1, 1987. The Seventh Directive must be applied to accounting periods beginning on and after January 1, 1990, although it can be adopted earlier should companies wish to do so.

The EEC Fourth Directive. The essential areas of possible change arising from the Fourth Directive, as they relate to the accounts and reports of public corporations (*Aktiengesellschaften*), may be summarized by the following comments:

1. *True and fair view.* **The requirement for a true and fair view replaces the view of the German Stock Companies Act that annual accounts shall give "within the limits of the valuation rules, as accurate a picture as possible of the assets and liabilities, financial position, and results of the company."**
2. *Write down.* If the reason for a write-down in the valuation of an item no longer exists, the entry will have to be reversed, unless the write-down has been accepted for tax purposes.
3. *Equity method of valuation.* **The equity method of valuation can now be used.** However, it is not clear as yet whether it will be widely taken up by German companies. It will be mandatory after 1990.
4. *Provisions.* Member states have the option to authorize the creation of provisions intended to cover charges which have their origin in the financial year or in a previous period.
5. *Profit distributions.* Profit distributions will be prohibited where formation expenses which have been capitalized have not been written off. This will not be applicable, however, where the revenue reserves are greater than the unamortized expenses.
6. *Notes to the accounts.* **The present *company's report* will, in future, be replaced by *notes on the accounts* and an *annual report.* The notes are** comparable to that part of the company report which gives explanations on the annual financial statements, but go beyond the present requirements. The annual report corresponds to the general business section of the company report and, as a supplement to the annual financial statements, should help to provide an overall economic assessment of the company.
7. *Publication requirements.* Publication requirements will increase the volume of information to be included in the notes on the accounts and in the annual report.

EEC Seventh Directive. German law currently requires public corporations to prepare and publish consolidated accounts and a management report. Adoption of the Directive will modify the undertakings included in the consolidation. German law does not require consolidation of foreign subsidiaries of the operating companies and generally, they are not consolidated. **As stated, the Seventh Directive requires such consolidation.**

German Accounts and the DVFA (Institute of German Analysts)

Investment analysts in Germany have long been unhappy with published net profit figures as an indication of a company's "true" earnings. They have therefore devised a formula for adjusting the published figures. This method seeks to arrive at adjusted profit figures which allow comparisons between companies to be made on a basis which approximates to Anglo-American principles. A company's published net profit for the year represents the legally disposable surplus that may be distributed and/or transferred to reserves. It takes into account all items, irrespective of whether they are current or outside the period under review, whether they arise from normal trading, or are extraordinary. It is normally declared after certain provisions, which may be made for purely fiscal reasons or determined by the level of profitability.

It is important to know to what extent the published figures have been influenced by special factors. **Only an earnings figure which has been adjusted to allow for such items and which includes the attributable earnings of nonconsolidated subsidiaries and associates can be used for realistic earnings comparisons and for share price evaluation.**

Hence, the German Association of Investment Analysts (the DVFA) was encouraged to recommend a workable scheme that could be used by both companies and investment analysts to make uniform adjustments to published net earnings in order to arrive at an earnings figure which eliminates extraordinary items and includes the attributable earnings of nonconsolidated associates.

With the adoption of the EEC Fourth and Seventh Directives, new accounting principles have been introduced into Germany. The DVFA method of restatement was revised, and its new statement of adjustments was published in March 1987.

These new recommendations for the calculation of *DVFA earnings* had to be applied for the first time to companies whose financial periods end on and after June 30, 1987.

The principal adjustments recommended by the DVFA are as follows:

1. *Extraordinary items.* **The exclusion of all items of an extraordinary or prior-year nature.** The former will include all income and expenditures that are considered to have been incurred outside the company's normal trading—for example, the cost of a new issue of shares or the profit or loss owing on the disposal of any fixed assets. However, in contrast to U.K. practice, no distinction is made between the disposal of any fixed assets such as plant and machinery that are due to be replaced and the disposal of a major part of the business. Profits or losses arising from either type of disposal are excluded.

2. *Accelerated depreciation.* **The elimination of any unnecessarily rapid depreciation of fixed assets, deductions from the valuation of stocks, or transfers to special reserve accounts.** These items arise solely for

tax reasons and are considered to have no effect on "real" profits. One example is special or accelerated depreciation, which is allowable for tax purposes on certain types of capital investment.

3. *Provisions.* **The writing back of any transfers to medium- and long-term provisions.** The principal reason for doing this is that although such transfers are within the letter of the law, companies tend to make larger provisions in good times and smaller in bad. Due to their subjective nature the DVFA add back the medium- and long-term provisions.

Pensions provisions is one of the most important categories, and has been affected by the new accounting principles which have resulted in two important changes:

   a. Companies must capitalize pension commitments entered into after December 31, 1986. However, companies are still able to choose between capitalizing pension payments or charging them directly to the profit and loss account for commitments made before this date.

   b. Companies who have not fully capitalized their pension provisions must report the amount of the deficit in the notes to the financial statements.

Consequently, the DVFA have had to change their treatment of pension provisions in computing earnings.

Up to now, the total net increase of pension provisions in one year has been included in the calculations of DVFA earnings.

In future, the amount representing a normal allocation for the financial period (based on the standard 6 percent tax allowable discount factor) will be regarded as an ordinary expense. However, adjustments will have to be made for extraordinary allocations to pension provisions.

4. *Nontrading items.* **The elimination of any currency gains or losses incurred outside normal trading business.**

5. *Associates.* **Although the equity method of accounting is allowed, it is still not widely used. Therefore, the inclusion of the attributable earnings of nonconsolidated associates is necessary, and one of the primary DVFA adjustments.**

6. *Inventory valuation reserves.* The creation or realization of inventory and work-in-progress valuation reserves is included in the calculation of the new DVFA earnings as it was under the previous method. However, this procedure has gained additional significance owing to the new accounting principles, since the companies' inventories are now more likely to be valued at direct costs (i.e., overhead costs need no longer be taken into account). It is possible that a significant once-off write-down in stock valuation will occur that will depress DVFA earnings per share.

The adjustment of profits in accordance with the DVFA principles may lead to results which differ substantially, either in a positive or a negative direction, from the published net disposable profits calculated on a legal accounting basis. **As a rule, the adjusted earnings figures are greater than published profits.** In addition, there does not appear to be a fixed relationship between adjusted earnings and published profits, with the former being more volatile than the latter, presumably because the adjusted earnings give a better indication of the effects of changing trading conditions on profitability.

There are, however, a number of limitations to the DVFA method:

1. *The method is only applicable to the published profits of industrial companies.* No satisfactory formula has been devised for the adjustments necessary for either banks or insurance companies.
2. *It is very difficult to evaluate the performance of a company during the course of the year.* DVFA-adjusted figures are usually only available after the annual accounts have been published. Any announcements made, be they interim or final, are, of course, unadjusted for DVFA purposes. Hence it is possible that share price may not react to published earnings in the same way as in the U.K. or United States.
3. *Because there is a judgmental element involved, adjusted figures can vary from one analyst to another.* While the DVFA method has its limitations and may not produce earnings figures that are on a truly comparable basis with those in the United States or the United Kingdom, it is nevertheless accepted on the whole by investors as providing the basis of useful international comparison. Adjusted earnings figures, however, should always be seen in the context of figures published by companies, as not only are these more readily available throughout the business year, but also they have a greater influence on the level of dividend distribution.
4. *Comparative figures.* Despite introducing a new method of earnings restatement, the DVFA has declined to adjust companies' previous year earnings. This will undoubtedly lead to significant difficulties for analysts at the outset in making valid year-to-year comparisons, unless companies are more forthcoming with information than they have previously been.

In order to bring these DVFA adjustments to life, two worked examples are given below:

Discussion of Schering DVFA Earnings Calculation

Extraordinary Gain from Disposal of Fixed Assets. This profit is extraordinary in nature and in this case resulted from the disposal of an administrative building. These extraordinary profits are deducted from published earnings on a gross = net basis.

Extraordinary Investment Grants. Investment bonuses, which are a form of government subsidy for capital investment in Germany, are deducted

Calculation of earnings according to the DVFA method, Schering 1987

	Gross (DM mil)	Net of Tax (DM mil)	Source
Published net profit for the year		144.4	P&L
Extraordinary gain from disposal of fixed assets	−15.3	−15.3	P&L, notes
Extraordinary investment bonuses and/or grants (estimated)	−13.0	−13.0	Co. notes
Currency exchange losses from consolidation	10.5	10.5	Notes
Amortization of goodwill additional accumulated amortization	13.4	13.4	P&L
Depreciation of financial assets	25.2	11.3	P&L
Exceptional transfers to pension provisions	15.0	6.8	Notes, co.
Earnings according to DVFA		158.1	
Net minority interests		1.0	P&L
DVFA net profit		157.1	
Average number of shares in issue (mil)		5.66	Notes
DVFA earnings per share		28	
Unadjusted Earnings per Share:			
Published net profit for the year		144.4	
Average number of shears in issue (mil)		5.66	
EPS		26	

Analyst: M. Sears/D. Foyll.

from published net profit on a gross = net basis. In the case of Schering, this amount was estimated—based on talking with the company—and is briefly mentioned in the notes regarding "other operating income."

If the investment bonus is of a persistent nature as a result of a special legal situation, then the bonus is not treated as an extraordinary item, however, it must be capitalized according to the effective life of the investment. An example of a situation where this might apply is the Berlin Promotion Law.

Currency Exchange Losses from Consolidation. The DVFA policy regarding uniform currency presentation is that this consolidation does not involve a valuation as defined by accounting principles and, as a result, the foreign exchange gains or losses should not therefore influence net profit. Since the currency translation does not incur income tax, deducted gains and added back losses (as in Schering's case) are done on a gross = net basis. The exchange loss arising from consolidation was disclosed in the "other operating expenses" section of the notes to the financial statements.

Additional Accumulated Amortisation of Goodwill.   Schering has chosen to use the capitalization option in offsetting goodwill against equity capital. This amortization is assessed at gross = net as increasing earnings. The specific amount was obtained from the "changes in fixed assets" schedule.

Depreciation of Financial Assets.   This item is added back to earnings after the appropriate tax has been deducted. The German corporate rate is 56 percent, however the effective tax will vary as it does in this case. This data was obtained from the "changes in fixed assets" schedule.

Exceptional Transfers to Pension Provisions.   This item, which is referred to in the "other operating expenses" note to the financial statements, is combined with various other miscellaneous items and the actual figure is only available from the company. This exceptional transfer was the result of Schering using a more conservative discount factor (the standard tax allowable discount factor is 6 percent) to determine its future pension liabilities. This difference is considered extraordinary.

Calculation of earnings according to the DVFA method, Karstadt 1987

	Gross (DM mil)	Net of Tax (DM mil)	Source
Published net profit		171.6	P&L
Additional tax credits		28.5	Co.
		143.1	
Disposal of fixed assets	−50.4		Notes
Elimination of reserves	−6.8		Co.
	57.2	−21.0	
Special depreciation	37.5		Notes
Depreciation of investments	6.1		Co.
Losses from disposal	6.7		Notes
Value adjustments to current assets	21.7		Co.
	72.0	26.7	
DVFA net profit before minorities		148.8	
Minorities		—	
DVFA net earnings		148.8	
DVFA EPS		20.7	
Unadjusted Earnings per Share:			
Published net profit for the year		171.6	
Average number of shares in issue (m)		7.2	
DVFA earnings per share		23.8	

Analyst: M. MacLachlan.

Net Minority Interests. This was the net of minority interests in gains and losses.

Discussion of Karstadt DVFA Earnings Calculations

Additional Tax Credits. These were brought forward because Neckermann (100-percent owned subsidiary) was loss-making for 10 years previous to this account.

Extraordinary Gain from Disposal of Fixed Assets. This item consists mainly of book profits on the sale of Karstadt's 50 percent share in a department store in Lyon, France to Jelmoli SA of Switzerland.

Special Depreciation. This arose from profits from sale of fixed assets which under German tax law can be used for tax-efficient reinvestment if put into a special reserve.

Losses from Disposals. This occurs in retailers as they dispose of small usually loss-making subsidiaries.

Value Adjustments to Current Assets. Results mainly from bad debts incurred by Neckermann mail order.

Consolidated Financial Statements

Despite the adoption of the EEC Seventh Directive, consolidated financial statements will still not be mandatory in Germany until 1990. Until then, companies need not consolidate their overseas subsidiaries. This can be a very significant exclusion, for example, in the case of BMW, two-thirds of whose sales come from abroad. If it were not for the DVFA adjustments, analysis of the company's accounts would be rendered meaningless.

Consolidation difference is a term more common to continental European accountants than their Anglo-American counterparts. It refers to the difference that arises on consolidation because the amount paid by the investor company is greater or less than its proportionate share of the tangible and identifiable intangible net assets of the acquired business or investee. In the United Kingdom and the United States (except where merger accounting or pooling of interests is used), it is standard practice to make this calculation at the date of acquisition, to take the net assets at their current value at that date, and to refer to the resulting balancing figure as *goodwill on consolidation*.

German practice is quite different. A consolidation difference is calculated at the date of each balance sheet. The book value of the investee is defined to include share capital and reserve but not the *Bilanzgewinn* or *Bilanzverlust* (profit or loss for the year before dividends, but after transfers to and from reserves). This means that the size of the consolidation difference changes every year. This method of treating consolidation differences is not, however, a statutory requirement, and some German companies, such as Siemens, have adopted the Anglo-American method.

Reserves

All movements on reserves in the balance sheet must be passed through the income statement. In German financial statements the following reserves can be found:

1. *Legal reserve.* Every corporation must create a legal reserve by allocating 5 percent of its annual profit to the reserve until 10 percent of the share capital has been accumulated. The amount of the legal reserve, up to 10 percent of the share capital, may only be used to offset an accumulated loss.
2. *Free reserves.* Out of the remaining profit for the period, the board of management may, with the approval of the supervisory board, appropriate a share of up to 50 percent of the period's net profit to the so-called *free reserves*. These are available for distribution to shareholders at the discretion of the board of management and are similar to retained earnings. Allocations greater than 50 percent may be made, although they must be ratified by the shareholders.
3. *Creditors reserve.* Since July 1, 1979, as a result of the inclusion of the Second EEC Directive into German company legislation, there is a requirement to maintain a reserve of a company's own shares equivalent to the value of such shares in the assets section. This provision is for creditors' protection.
4. *Secret reserves.* It is possible to criticize continental European accounting practice for creating secret reserves by undervaluing assets and overvaluing liabilities. The most common ways to create hidden reserves are:
   a. By taking advantage of certain options in valuation regulations and accounting requirements (e.g., by simply following a conservative valuation principle).
   b. By legal requirements with respect to accounting and valuation (e.g., the historical cost rule or the exclusion of intangibles other than those purchased).

   The possibility of creating secret reserves by ultraconservative valuation is compensated, to a certain extent, by the requirement to disclose valuation and depreciation methods in the management report. Moreover, the so-called *fixed value* principle in company laws, which involves a constant valuation policy for certain items over time, is a useful barrier against creating secret reserves. On the other hand, conservatism is legally enforced in some cases. This is a particular handicap when trying to present a true and fair view of the company's financial position, for example, in the cases of land and buildings and long-term investments.

Thus, a complication in arriving at shareholders' equity is the tax-allowed reserves. These are partly deferred taxation and partly shareholders' funds. The difficulty is that the rate of tax which will have to be paid when the reserves are released is not known. The reserves can, in certain circumstances, be deducted from nondepreciable assets such as land or investments, leading to an almost permanent postponement of taxation. Even where this is not the case, the amount of taxes payable depends on the company's future dividend policy. Clearly, therefore, the investment analyst's practice of splitting the tax-allowed reserves equally between shareholders' funds and taxation liabilities will rarely be correct.

Fixed Assets

1. Fixed assets must be stated at purchased or manufacturers cost-less depreciation. Revaluations are not permitted even where supported by certified valuations. **German accounting, therefore, rigidly follows the principle of an historical cost presentation.**
2. Depreciation must be provided in accordance with a consistent plan designed to write off assets over their useful lines. Both declining-balance and straight-line depreciation are permitted. Accelerated depreciation is allowed, however, as it must be recorded in "the books" in order to obtain a tax deduction.

Other Features

The following are more theoretical comments on German accounting practice.

Consolidation Principles

Existing German consolidation procedures in many cases do not coincide with those contained in the EEC Directive. However, German law does coincide with the directive in the area of eliminating intercompany results, transactions and balances, the dates of the financial statements included in the consolidation, and the disclosure of minority interests in equity and profit or loss.

Changes in existing consolidation practices will be required in the following areas:

1. *Valuation of assets and liabilities.* The directive requires uniform valuation of assets and liabilities included in the consolidation on the same basis applied by the entity preparing the consolidation. The directive also requires that subsidiaries' assets and liabilities that have been valued by methods differing from those used in the consolidation be revalued in accordance with the methods used in consolidation.
2. *Consolidation.* German practice is to consolidate all domestic undertakings without changing the valuation methods used in the individual accounts. Foreign subsidiaries' financial statements, if consolidated, are normally adjusted to comply with German accounting principles. Adoption of the directive will impose the need to make adjustments in consolidation for consistent valuation of assets and liabilities.

The directive requires goodwill to be calculated at the date of acquisition of the shares, at the date the undertaking is first included in the consolidation or the date the directive is first applied. Any resultant positive goodwill must be either amortized to the profit and loss account or immediately written off to reserves.

ITALY

Highlights

EEC Fourth and Seventh Directives

Neither the EEC Fourth nor Seventh Directive has been enacted into Italian legislation. However, the spirit of the Fourth Directive is already largely respected in Italian financial statements, particularly by the larger companies.

Consolidated Financial Statements

Consolidated financial statements, as understood in the United Kingdom and the United States, are still rarely published in Italy.

Earnings Per Share

Adjustments to earnings should be made for accelerated depreciation and excess additions to provisions.

Deferred Taxation

Deferred taxation is not recognized in the financial statements.

Foreign Exchange and Foreign Currency Translation

Transactions in foreign currency are converted into Italian lire at the rate prevailing on the transaction date. Disclosure of the policy used is **NOT** required.

Practical Considerations

Background

Increased foreign interest in the Italian bourse and the spectre of "1992" with its liberalized Community market have focused attention on Italian companies as never before. Many sectors, such as insurance, are seen as underdeveloped, and this has resulted in a wave of corporate activity. However, those principally accustomed to Anglo-American accounting conventions and disclosure requirements often have difficulty in understanding Italian financial statements and in making accurate comparisons with U.K. or U.S. companies. Many of the problems confronting the reader of Italian company accounts are common to continental Europe as a whole—consolidation, delays in and infrequent reporting, classification of balance sheet and profit and loss items, and the lack of segmented data.

However, over the past ten years there have been considerable advances on the Italian accounting scene as the local profession has adapted to the changing economic, fiscal, and political climate, culminating in the enactment in 1980, of the Presidential Decree of March 1975. This laid down the audit and reporting requirements for listed companies and is overseen by CONSOB (the Stock Exchange Control Committee). There has also been an increasing Anglo-American influence on the style and content of Italian financial statements.

Although they must be aware of the pitfalls, the foreign readers can now feel more at home with the information given in the financial statements of listed companies and those under CONSOB supervision.

Which Set of Accounts Do I Use?

The old joke about the financial statements of Italian companies was that different sets were maintained for the management, the tax authorities, and the shareholders. Nowadays those under CONSOB supervision probably maintain just two sets of accounts—one for the management and one for the tax authorities and shareholders.

Fiscal laws continue to have a very significant impact on the content of the balance sheet of Italian companies. In order for items to be tax deductible, they must be recorded in the published profit and loss account. Two of the most obvious methods in which the accounts may be altered, in order to ensure the tax breaks, are as follows:

1. The charging of accelerated depreciation, which writes off the cost of the asset over a shortened economic life.
2. The setting up of reserves to cover bad and doubtful debts. These reserves will be larger than would be made if a purely commercial view was taken.

Shareholders obviously receive the published tax-oriented financial statements. In order for them to gain a true picture of the earnings, they must make several adjustments to the stated profit figure (see "Earnings per Share" below). Management on the other hand will review the "true" P&L in order to be able to make accurate commercial decisions.

EEC Directives

As yet, Italy has not implemented either the Fourth or the Seventh EEC Directive. The introduction of the Fourth Directive must inevitably have a significant impact. It is fair to say that many of the specific requirements of the Directive have no present parallel in Italian legislation and the formal differences between provisions of the Directive and the Civil Code are therefore numerous. **On the other hand, the spirit behind most of these requirements is already largely respected in Italian financial reporting, though perhaps not explicitly.**

Whilst the enactment into Italian law of the Fourth Directive will clearly give rise to changes, the substance (as reflected, for example, in the net profits or loss account) may well not be significantly different. One of the most important changes is that the financial statement will need to give a *true and fair* view rather than giving a *clear and precise* view. Similarly, the Seventh Directive will have a considerable impact as companies are made to consolidate. Additional disclosures, such as the basis of foreign currency translation, will also be necessary.

Earnings Per Share (EPS)

In contrast to the United Kingdom, there is no requirement for Italian companies to calculate and disclose EPS. Even now, the major quoted companies do not do this as a matter of course. Despite this, certain companies have taken the lead. Olivetti, for example, publishes an extremely detailed analysis of how it calculates its earnings per share. This analysis only deals, however, with the calculation of the numbers of shares to be used.

EPS Example–MONDADORI Spa

Published Figures (L mil)	1987	1986
Pre-tax profits	153,187	107,058
Extraordinary items[1]	(13,546)	(13,430)
Income taxes	(33,845)	(18,273)
Minority interest	(4,486)	(175)
Net earnings	101,310	75,180
Number of shares (mil)	79,687	73,125
EPS	1,271	1,028
Adjusted figures (L mil)		
Pre-tax profit	153,187	107,058
Income taxes	(33,845)	(18,273)
Accelerated depreciation[2]	8,000	8,300
Minority interests	(4,486)	(175)
Net earnings	122,856	96,910
Number of shares (mil)	79,687	73,125
EPS	1,541	1,325

Analyst: P. Lardera.

[1]For comparison with UK companies, extraordinary items have to be excluded from EPS calculations.

[2]The add back of accelerated depreciation is calculated by the company's auditor, and is the amount in excess of the normal depreciation charge.

The main adjustments are made in order to convert the fiscal nature of the accounts to a truer accounting basis. However, it is very difficult to adjust accurately for accelerated depreciation, overzealous bad debt provisioning, or to assess whether the categories *other costs* or *other provisions* are hiding profits.

Foreign Exchange and Foreign Currency Translation

The principal reference to foreign exchange translation is found in tax law. **Transactions in foreign currency are converted into Italian lire at the rate prevailing on the date of settlement when the transaction is made. Disclosure of the policy used in translation is not required.**

Unrealized losses are calculated and added to the provision to cover losses on exchange rate fluctuations in the liabilities side of the accounts. However, unrealized profits are often excluded from the balance sheet as they would be liable to taxation.

Deferred Taxation

As mentioned above, there is a close relationship between taxation and entries made in the financial statements. It is not therefore very surprising that deferred taxation is not recognized in the accounts. Although timing differences may arise, it will not be possible for the analyst to identify the extent of the amount to adjust.

Extraordinary Profits and Losses

There is no analysis of exceptional and extraordinary items. It is thus necessary to try and work out the split in order to calculate the EPS. However, this task may not be easy, and without help from the company an arbitrary breakdown may have to be made.

Distributable Profits

In accordance with current laws, Italian companies analyze distributable reserves and any related tax implications in a statement which is attached to the financial statements.

Other Features

The following are more theoretical comments on the content of Italian financial statements.

Capital and Reserves

Capital.   Capital is to be shown at par value, distinguishing between ordinary shares and shares of other classes.

Reserves.

1. *Share premium reserve.* Any excess paid in for capital over par value is credited to a share premium account and may not be distributed until

the legal reserve has reached the stipulated level of 20 percent of share capital.

2. *Legal reserve.* The Civil Code provides that an amount of not less than 5 percent of the profits of each year shall be appropriated to a legal reserve until the reserve is equal to the 20 percent of share capital mentioned above. It is generally understood that the legal reserve may be applied only in reduction of a deficit and then only after all the disclosed free reserves have been utilized.

3. *Revaluation reserve.* In addition, most Italian companies carry in their balance sheet a revaluation reserve resulting from the provision of the 1952, 1975, and 1983 laws authorizing revaluation of fixed assets.

Inventories

Inventories should be stated at the lower of cost and market value. For tax purposes, inventories must be valued at cost including all attributable expenses but excluding interest and general expenses. The tax code provides a pricing method for inventories which is basically a LIFO method or the average cost method. However, other methods can be used with the approval of the tax authorities.

Consolidation

The CONSOB requires the preparation and publication of consolidated accounts for all holding companies whose shares are listed on the stock exchange. However, such accounts do not, as yet, have to be audited, although in practice the majority are. These accounts generally follow IASC criteria. However, there are some significant differences:

1. Many groups consolidate financial statements drawn up in accordance with the Italian Civil Code and, as a result, the valuation criteria are not necessarily uniform within the group.
2. Due to the strong fiscal influence, it is not surprising that deferred taxation is not recognized in the accounts.
3. Minority interest balances are often not classified under liabilities or accounted for in the profit and loss account.
4. An analysis of revenues, profits, and other data by division of geographical breakdown is not often provided.

However, for nonquoted companies, consolidated financial statements are still the exception as opposed to the rule.

Asset Valuation

The use of cost rather than the market valuation of assets leads to the existence of hidden reserves in a company's balance sheet. These can often be extremely large and would significantly affect the asset valuation of a company. The following areas are the most important and need adjusting:

1. Investments are valued at the lower of cost and market value. Disclosure of the market value of the investments is not required if it is in excess of the cost, and it is almost impossible for an interested party to calculate accurately.
2. Fixed assets cannot be shown at a value above cost. The impact of the tax rules, as mentioned above, means that the fixed assets are always written down as quickly as possible. The true value will be impossible to determine, but will usually be vastly different to the balance sheet value, particularly for example, where there is a sizeable real estate portfolio.
3. Inventories are valued at the lower of cost or market value. For tax purposes, inventories must be valued at cost, including all attributable expenses, but excluding interest and general expenses. The LIFO method is most generally used in order to comply with the tax authorities' requirements. Although the LIFO method tends to understate the value of stock in the balance sheet, the cost of replacement must be disclosed in the explanatory notes.

An accurate evaluation of a company's assets is virtually impossible without the help of the company's management.

Intangibles

Intangibles should be carried in the balance sheet at cost and must be amortized in proportion to their usage or economic value, which is generally considered not to exceed five years.

Goodwill can be carried in the balance sheet only when it results from the acquisition of a company. It, too, can be amortized over a period not greater than five years.

Leasing

At present there is no accounting standard for lease transactions in contrast to the United Kingdom. In practice, leased assets are not shown in the balance of the lessee and the leasing expenses are charged to the profit and loss account as incurred.

JAPAN

Highlights

Taxation

Japanese tax law and practice shape accounting principles and exercise a very considerable influence over Japanese financial statements.

Hidden Reserves

Japanese accounts often contain hidden reserves via the understatement of assets and the dispensations granted by the tax authorities.

Group Structure

Although large conglomerates may not legally exist, companies do still exist under a group "umbrella." This gives advantages in areas such as financing and the ability to operate a long-term plan.

Debt

Despite exposure to more sophisticated capital markets, Japanese companies still use bank borrowing as their major form of finance.

Consolidation

Companies quoted on the Japanese Stock Exchange must consolidate where appropriate. Associates must be equity-accounted.

Philosophy

Shareholders take a long-term attitude toward profit growth and consequently are willing to accept their return in the form of capital appreciation as opposed to dividend income.

Practical Considerations

Investor Philosophy

Japanese shareholders do not expect a high return on their investment in the form of dividends (see below), and companies are therefore given the opportunity to operate a long-term plan. Management emphasis is focused on consistent sales growth and expanding the balance sheet total, with a high level of liquidity in cash and short-term securities. Shareholders will not necessarily view a decrease in profitability due to substantial interest and research and development charges as being a weakness. Indeed, they will positively approve if this results in the company expanding. The emphasis is very much on long-term growth.

Although investors do not expect significant dividend income, they do expect capital appreciation. Clearly, investors in Japanese stocks should have been satisfied with their total return over the last decade.

Influence of Taxation

The tax laws have a great influence on accounting practices in Japan. The Corporation Tax Law and its related regulations specify the accounting methods to be used in recording transactions and balances. Detailed schedules of useful lives determine tax-allowable depreciation charges by class of asset. Frequently these schedules determine the treatment in the financial statements. Similarly, provisions for bad debts are often made on the basis of the tax law and not for commercial reasons. In more extreme cases, companies won't provide for known liabilities if not tax deductible. As a result of this, companies' pension liabilities are frequently understated. Since the effect of recording these allowances permitted under tax laws and regulations is a deferral of otherwise currently payable income taxes, most Japanese companies follow tax accounting when applicable in preparing their financial statements.

Dividends

Although, as mentioned above, shareholders do not seek high yields, a dividend is required in order to maintain a quotation of the stock exchange. A standard rate is 10 percent of the par value. However, investors would be alarmed if a dividend payment were passed; the company management therefore endeavors to maintain a stable, if low, dividend policy.

Earnings Per Share (EPS)

EPS is calculated by dividing a company's net profit by the number of shares in issue. This treatment differs significantly from U.K. practice:

- Net profit includes extraordinary items.
- The net profit used is frequently that of the parent company and not that of the consolidated group.

Parent company profits are used primarily for the following reason: The parent results must be lodged with the stock exchange within two months of the end of the period, whereas consolidated figures have generally been significantly delayed. However, from April 1989 quoted companies will have to publish consolidated accounts at the same time as their parent results. The idea is that investors and analysts will begin to focus on the group's profits instead of the parent's, which can be misleading because nonperforming subsidiaries can be hidden from view. However, there is considerable doubt whether or not this switch in emphasis will be followed by the investing community, particularly as the quantity of information disclosed by consolidated accounts will remain poor and as no interim results will be reported. During the 1980s, quoted companies have issued a proliferation of convertibles and warrants which has led to significant dilution. Nevertheless, investors still tend to view the EPS trend on an unadjusted basis. Further, instead of concentrating on EPS and P/E multiples, the investment yardsticks still tend to be the parent company's sales performance and growth of current (i.e., before extraordinary items and tax) profit.

Hidden Reserves

In common with many European countries, Japanese accounting practices can lead to hidden reserves in the balance sheet. Investors should be particularly wary of the following:

1. Revaluation of real estate is not permitted in Japan, unless the company is subject to amalgamation, in which case revaluation is mandatory. Given the low rate of corporate activity, revaluation has taken place

infrequently. Substantial hidden reserves therefore arise, referred to as *fukumi shisan,* or latent assets.

2. Investments are always stated at the lower of cost and market value. Given the phenomenal rise of the Japanese stock market and the very substantial number of cross-holdings between companies, significant latent assets arise.

3. The tax authorities have permitted many special provisions, which are tax-exempt, to be set up as part of industrial policy. The reader of the accounts will usually not be given any indication of the extent of the over-provisioning. The following are examples of tax-deductible reserves:

   • Reserve for inventory price fluctuation.
   • Reserve for development of overseas markets.
   • Reserve for loss on overseas investment.

4. Companies can make use of accelerated depreciation in order to claim special tax allowances. As the depreciation rate for tax purposes is greater than that used to write off the asset over its useful economic life, the fixed assets will be understated.

Group Structure

During the occupation, the large Japanese cartels (*zaibatsu*) such as Mitsui, Mitsubishi, and Sumitomo were broken up. The leading zaibatsu have been reconstituted by cross-holdings and now operate in concert, trading with each other wherever possible, for mutual benefit. The Antimonopoly Act specifically prohibits holding companies.

The companies within a "group" support each other, so an investor should not look at a company's financial position in isolation from that of its group. Intragroup debt, for example, is usually semipermanent in nature.

A further aspect of the group system relates to dividends and earnings growth. Group members will usually take a longer-term view and may be content to receive their investment return via trading opportunities, instead of through dividends or capital appreciation.

Balance Sheet Debt

A Japanese company will have a very close relationship with its bank, which will act as an advisor and consultant. Indeed, senior banking staff are often assigned to a company, sometimes for a period of years.

Bank loans generally appear as current debt in a company's balance sheet, which although technically true, often disguises the fact that the loan may be automatically rolled over year after year.

Over the last two decades, the nature of the Japanese economy has changed and the capital markets have developed substantially. The heavy reliance on bank borrowing has been replaced by a reliance on other capital instruments. Despite this, bank borrowing is still a major form of finance for most companies and is particularly efficient when tax rates are high. Investors should therefore not be unduly alarmed when they find large bank borrowings on a company's balance sheet, and consequently high-gearing ratios.

Consolidation

Under Japanese Securities Exchange Law, firms are required to present audited consolidated financial statements (balance sheet, profits and loss statement) and supporting notes as supplementary information according to certain guidelines concerning the size of the stake and materiality.

The pressure for consolidated financial statements has grown substantially in the 1980s as companies have diversified and as pressure has grown to adopt reporting standards closer to the Anglo-Saxon norms. Currently all public companies must lodge parent accounts (both interim and final) with the stock exchange within two months of the balance sheet date and with the Ministry of Finance within three months. It is expected that companies will also be required to present consolidated accounts with their parent accounts from March 1989. Even so, it is not unusual now for the leading companies, who have overseas interests, to present consolidated statements in accordance with GAAP. However, this consolidated information is usually only presented a considerable time after the balance sheet date.

Accounting for Associate Companies

In the preparation of consolidated financial statements, the equity method of accounting must be applied. However, because of the complex company groupings (see group structure), holdings can be reduced to below 20 percent in and can be used, for example, to avoid including the results of a problematic group company.

Compensating Balances

The practice of compensating balances still exists in the Japanese business environment. Under this system, companies are persuaded to borrow more than they need and to deposit the surplus funds back with the lending bank. This benefits the bank by increasing the effective interest rate on the net borrowings in homes when interest rates have been controlled by the government.

Companies accept this because they want to maintain a close relationship with their bankers. By keeping the bank happy by overborrowing, the company is assured of having access to funds in times of need. However, companies are now no longer so reliant on the banks and increasingly resist bank pressure.

The existence of these balances, which are not offset on balance sheets, must be taken into consideration when analyzing a company's financial situation.

Other Features

The following paragraphs deal with the more theoretical aspects of Japanese accounting practice.

Stock

Inventories are generally accounted for at the lower of cost or market value. The method of determining inventory cost must be disclosed—weighted average cost is the predominant method and, consequently, LIFO and FIFO are not extensively used.

Research and Development

R&D costs are written off as they are incurred. Companies are required to disclose the amount of costs charged to income in the notes to the accounts.

Finance Leases

There is no specific requirement in Japan with respect to accounting for leases. In a minority of forms, leases are accounted for by the lessee as an installment purchase, when the substance of the lease transfers the risks and rewards of ownership from the lessor to the lessee.

Deferred Tax

As a result of the influence of taxation (see above) on the financial statements, Japanese companies do not make any provision for deferred taxation.

Severance Pay

Japanese taxation law allows companies to deduct 40 percent of severance costs against its P&L account. This is open to misuse, and frequently companies will make a provision just to obtain a tax deduction. Japan Airlines, for example, set aside $65 million in 1987 with no explanation in the notes.

Discounts on Bonds

In Japan the discount on bonds issued is written off to the P&L account. Elsewhere in the world such costs are part of a company's financing costs and are spread over a number of years. Japanese practice results in profits being understated.

NETHERLANDS

Highlights

Goodwill

Goodwill can be amortized over a period not exceeding five years.

Foreign Currency Translation

Exchange gains arising on monetary items are deferred as unrealized gains.

Current Cost Accounting

Historic cost accounting is used more than current cost accounting. The provision of current cost information is much more widespread in the Netherlands than in the United Kingdom.

Deferred Taxation

Deferred taxes are provided in full for all timing differences in the year in which they originate.

Earnings Per Share Calculations

Earnings figures are taken after extraordinary items but before preference dividends. This is in direct contrast to the United Kingdom.

Merger Accounting

Merger accounting is not permissible in the Netherlands.

Consolidated Financial Statements

Consolidation is a well-established practice. Therefore the effects of the EEC Seventh Directive will not be significant.

Practical Considerations

Background

As in the United Kingdom, the main direct influences on Dutch financial reporting are company law and the accountancy profession. Taxation is relatively unimportant; there is no national accounting plan and there is no equivalent of the American SEC or the French COB. However, the similarities with the United Kingdom must not be pressed too hard—**there are important differences**. These arise in the following areas:

- Goodwill
- Foreign currency translation
- Current cost accounting
- Deferred taxation
- Earnings-per-share calculations
- Accounting for acquisitions and mergers
- Consolidated financial statements.

Goodwill

In the Netherlands goodwill should be amortized over a period not exceeding five years unless the directors of the company can justify a longer

period, which cannot be longer than ten years. Under U.K. accounting standards goodwill is amortized over the estimated useful life. However, in both countries it is acceptable to charge goodwill directly to retained earnings.

Foreign Currency Translation

In the United Kingdom, exchange gains arising on monetary items can be included in the profit and loss account for the period, unless there are doubts as to the convertibility or marketability of the currency in question. In contrast, the Dutch pronouncements allow the result to be deferred as an unrealized gain.

As under accounting principles in the United Kingdom, translation of the financial statements of foreign subsidiaries (which operate as separate, quasi-independent entities rather than as a direct extension of the investing company) is performed using the exchange rate ruling at the balance sheet date. The results of translating the opening retained earnings, net income at average rates, and balances of an investment nature with the subsidiary are taken directly to reserves. Under Dutch accounting principles these translation reserves are not available for distribution.

Current Cost Accounting

The EEC's directives on company law are bringing financial reporting practices closer together in all member states. This harmonization, however, does not extend to inflation accounting, and Dutch theory and practices in this area are likely to remain rather distinct, although as a result of the Fourth Directive the minority of Dutch companies which previously reported only current cost data must now report some historical cost information as well.

Before the 1983 company law amendments, consequent upon the EEC Fourth Directive, there were no legislative requirements or guidance as regards current values or historical costs. The guidelines, however, recommended that net operating income be shown on both a historical and a current cost basis, the company choosing which basis to use in the main statements and which in the supplementary statements.

The Civil Code, as amended in 1983, permits, but does not require, the use of current cost accounting (CCA), companies being required to choose between CCA and historical cost accounting (HCA). Contrary to widespread belief, HCA is in fact more common than CCA in Dutch external financial reporting. It is not permissible to use CCA in the balance sheet and HCA in the profit and loss account, but HCA in the balance sheet is not regarded as incompatible with current cost depreciation in the profit and loss account.

The substance, scope, and method of application of CCA are regulated by the asset valuation decree of December 22, 1983 which applies only if a company chooses to use CCA. The decree provides, in effect, for the use of deprival values. Tangible fixed assets, fixed-asset investments, and stocks may be valued at replacement value, recoverable amount, or realizable value, and estimates may be used if necessary. Increases in current cost have to be credited to a revaluation reserve and decreases debited thereto. Irrespective of whether HCA or CCA is chosen, intangible assets and current assests other than inventories are not permitted to be valued at current cost. Akzo, the chemical/speciality chemical and consumer company, is typical of most Dutch-listed companies in that it follows the historical cost convention but also provides supplementary current value information. In contrast, the best-known company that uses the replacement value approach is Philips.

The Dutch practice is therefore in contrast to that used in the United Kingdom, where the provision of current cost information is no longer required.

Deferred Taxation

The objective of deferred tax accounting in the United Kingdom is to provide for future taxes that will be payable due to current timing differences. To accomplish this, deferred taxes are provided for timing differences only to the extent that future tax liabilities are expected to arise in years in which the timing differences reverse. This partial allocation approach requires an assessment of the probability of future taxes becoming payable or recoverable because of the reversal of these timing differences. The allocation approach also involves consideration of past and future patterns of capital expenditure and forecasts of future operations and cash flows.

Under existing Dutch requirements, deferred taxes are provided in full for all timing differences in the year in which they originate. The objective is to defer the tax effect of a transaction and reflect it in the income statement in the year in which the transaction giving rise to that timing difference is reported in book income.

The U.K. partial liability approach has resulted in earnings reported by U.K. companies that are substantially higher than would be the case if the Dutch practices were used. Although this tendency will continue, it will be of decreasing significance due to changes in tax allowances set out in the U.K. 1984 Finance Act. These will decrease the size of future timing differences and, as a result, the difference between partial and comprehensive deferred tax accounting.

U.K. financial statements do disclose what the balance sheet reserve would be if deferred taxes had been provided in full on all timing differences. Thus it is possible to adjust for the effects of the differing practices. However, the adjustment will not be perfect as U.K. deferred taxes are based on current tax rates rather than rates in effect in the year in which the timing difference arose.

Earnings Per Share (EPS)

Earnings per share appear to be calculated after extraordinary items and before charging any preference dividend, which is treated as an appropriation of net earnings.

To conform with U.K. accounting standards, both extraordinary items and preference dividends should be reversed, so that EPS is calculated on earnings after preference dividends but before extraordinary items.

The example below, taken from the Dutch publisher VNU, should help to clarify this process.

VNU–EPS calculations

	Thousands of guilders	
Stated EPS	**1987**	**1986**
Pre-tax profits	179,450	129,659
Income taxes	−70,332	−31,885
	109,118	97,774
Extraordinary loss	(12,831)	(6,713)
3 Tax benefit	5,056	4,158
Net earnings	101,343	95,219
Weighted number of shares (m)	11.7	11.7
Earnings per share	7.88	6.41

	Thousands of guilders	
Adjusted EPS	**1985**	**1984**
Pre-tax profits	170,450	129,659
Income taxes	(70,332)	51,885
Preference dividends	(210)	(210)
Net earnings	99,908	77,564
Weighted number of shares (m)	11.7	11.7
Earnings per share	8.54	6.63

Analyst: D. Terrington.

Accounting for Acquisitions and Mergers

Merger accounting as opposed to acquisition accounting (or pooling of interests) can be used in certain circumstances in the U.K.. **As yet, the Dutch Council for Annual Reporting has not yet issued pronouncements on the accounting for acquisitions and mergers.**

Consolidated Financial Statements

The main legal requirements relating to consolidation in the Netherlands are set out in the Civil Code. This provides that financial data concerning the subsidiaries must be included in group annual accounts drawn up in accordance with the full consolidation method.

Participating interests (i.e., affiliated companies in which a stake between 20 percent and 50 percent of the share capital is owned) are usually valued by the net asset method of equity accounting, which is used in both the group accounts and, in contrast to the United Kingdom, in the accounts of the parent company.

The EEC Seventh Directive on consolidated accounts, adopted in 1983, is unlikely to be implemented in practice in the Netherlands before the early 1990s. Since consolidation is already a well-established practice, its effects will not be great, but Dutch law will have to define in more detail the requirements relating to consolidated accounts, especially with respect to the definition of a subsidiary and consolidation techniques. There will also be some minor changes in disclosure requirements.

Other Features

The following paragraphs deal in detail with the more theoretical aspects of Dutch accounting practice.

The Dutch Civil Code requires that the management of a company prepare and present to shareholders, within five months after the close of the financial year, the following:

1. Balance sheet and income statement accompanied by explanatory notes disclosing the bases of stating assets and liabilities and of determining results.
2. Annual (directors') report including comments on specified subjects.
3. Other information giving supplementary data including the auditors' report, certain legal matters, and significant subsequent events not reflected in the financial statements. In addition, a funds statement is given by larger quoted companies and an increasing number of other companies.

Income Statement

Certain items have to be disclosed. These include sales (by lines of business and by geographical area), salaries and wages, social charges, the operating result, and details of financial income and expense. Results before and after tax are to be shown for both ordinary operations and extraordinary items.

Fixed Assets

Assets (intangible, tangible, and financial fixed assets) with a limited useful life should be depreciated over that life. Additional reductions in the value of fixed assets of a lasting nature should be accounted for. The tax authorities will usually accept any reasonable commercial basis for depreciation and do not, therefore, prescribe specific rates.

Current Assets

These must be stated at the lower of cost and market value. Exceptional value reductions expected to take place shortly after the balance sheet date may be taken into account.

Inventories and Bonds and Shares

Inventories may be stated at weighted average prices using FIFO, LIFO, or similar rules. Bonds and shares held by investment companies may be stated at market value.

Capitalization of Interest

Interest may only be added to the production cost of an asset if it is paid to third parties.

Capital and Reserves

Share Premium Reserve.   Capital in excess of par or stated value is to be shown as a contributed surplus/share premium.

Free Reserves.   Legal reserves that are nondistributable and created by charge to free reserves or profit appropriation are required for:

1. Undistributed profits of subsidiaries and other related companies recorded by the reporting company.
2. Carrying value of share issue expenses and research and development expenses.
3. Under certain circumstances, noncash consideration given by the reporting company for shares in a public company (*Naamloze Vennootschap,* or NV).

Revaluation Reserve.   All revaluations of assets must be credited to a revaluation account. The revaluation account may be used for the issue of capital and reduced to the extent that it is no longer required under the accounting system used or for the purpose for which it was created. The minimum balance must represent the amount of the revaluations of assets still held at the balance sheet date.

Accounting for Leases

In the United Kingdom, under SSAP 21, a finance lease is defined as a lease which transfers substantially the risks and rewards of ownership of an asset to the lessee. It is presumed that such a transfer occurs if, at the inception of the lease, the present value of the minimum lease payments amounts to substantially all of the fair value of the asset. Although similar in nature, the Dutch pronouncements assume a lease to a finance lease if any one of the following conditions are met:

- At the end of the lease the asset can be acquired at a bargain price.
- The term of the lease covers a substantial part of the economic useful life of the asset concerned.
- The term of the lease is less than the economic useful life of the asset concerned, but the contract gives the lessee an option to extend the term of the contract to the economic useful life at significantly lower lease installments.

Notes to the Financial Statements

As in the United Kingdom and the United States, a great deal of information is provided by Dutch companies in the notes to the financial statements. Disclosure of the following items, amongst others, as notes, is specially required by the Civil Code:

- Movements in capital and reserves.
- Interests in other corporate bodies.
- Analysis of net turnover by class of business and geographical area.
- Important long-term financial commitments and contingent liabilities under guarantees, pending litigation, and other claims.
- Employee information.
- Remuneration of, and loans and advances to, supervisory and managerial directors.

SPAIN

Highlights

EEC

Spain has just joined the EEC. The Fourth and Seventh Directives have not yet been implemented. When the necessary legislation is enacted, Spanish financial statements will become much more comparable with other European countries.

Earnings Per Share Calculations

Investors must adjust for accelerated depreciation and any extraordinary charges.

Deferred Taxation

Deferred taxation is not recognized due to the close links between tax values and book values.

Foreign Exchange

Unrealized exchange gains or losses are not always accounted for. Best practice, however, is to carry the unrealized gain or loss in an exchange fluctuation account until realized.

Practical Considerations

Background

Spanish accounting and reporting practices are closely allied to those of countries such as Italy, Greece, and France. For example, the Spanish have a General Accounting Plan as the French do. **Similarly, Spanish accounting practice is heavily influenced by taxation laws.**

The Plan General de Contabiladad sets out a standardized form of financial statements. These tend to be less informative than the United Kingdom or U.K. equivalents, particularly in the area of the income statement, and the notes will generally contain less detailed disclosures.

There are several notable features of which the readers of Spanish financial statements should be aware.

Consolidated Financial Statements

To date, the presentation of consolidated financial statements is relatively rare in Spain (a notable exception being banks, who, by the Royal Decree of August 1, 1985 must submit consolidated statements to the Bank of Spain). The method used is full (Anglo-American) consolidation although the Instituto de Planificacion Contable (Accounting Planning Institute) has issued guidelines for consolidation. The text, which is modeled on the EEC's Seventh Directive, does not impose the obligation to prepare and present consolidated financial statements until 1990.

The consolidation decree incorporating the guidelines envisages full and proportional consolidation (i.e., the Anglo-American and French methods respectively) as well as equity accounting.

Income Statements

The income statement normally consists of four separate accounts:

1. *A trading account (Cuenta De Explotacion)* which includes income from normal trading or commercial operations and the associated indirect costs.
2. *An account of nontrading operations (Cuenta de resultados extraordinarios)* reflecting the income and expenses other than those related to normal trading or commercial operations, and extraordinary items.
3. *An investment portfolio account (Cuenta de resultados de la cartero de valores)* showing the net gains or losses resulting from sales of investments and subscription rights, as well as dividend and interest income.

4. *A profit and loss account (Cuenta de perdidas y Ganacias)* summarizing the results of the previously mentioned accounts and reflecting the corporate tax charge where applicable, the amounts allocated to certain provisions, and the appropriations to reserves and dividends.

Earnings Per Share (EPS)

As the financial statements are considerably influenced by the taxation laws in Spain, excess depreciation is charged in the income statement. The investor must try to establish the extent of this charge and adjust accordingly by adding the amount back to profit. There are two main ways of doing this.

1. If the company discloses a *provision for accelerated depreciation* the difference between two consecutive years can be taken as the amount to add back.
2. The analyst can try to establish a depreciation trend relative to the asset level and mix. Spanish companies may also make an extraordinary charge to the income statement for inventories. This arises because companies are permitted to charge depreciation on stocks. An adjustment should be made for this, and the most common method is to try and establish a year-to-year trend and adjust accordingly.

Other adjustments may need to be made.

- *Extraordinary items.* Unlike U.K. practice, Spanish accounting does not differentiate between extraordinary and exceptional items. Investors should try to establish the split and adjust EPS calculations accordingly. However, the willingness of the company to part with the information is open to doubt.
- *Capitalization of costs.* This problem is particularly prevalent in the electrical industry, which accounts for over 20 percent of the stock exchange by market capitalization.

While a power station is under construction, all costs related to it (including interest on the loans financing the works) are capitalized and are not, therefore, charged to the profit and loss account. On completion and at the end of the testing period, capitalization of the expenses stops and these are then charged to results, while depreciation of the power station starts simultaneously. Consequently, every time a new power station enters into service the costs of the company concerned rise strongly, then subsequently tail off over the useful life on the facility. In contrast, revenue derived from the additional electricity produced by the new plant is a function of the electricity tariff, which in turn grows steadily. This means that in the first few years of operations of each power station the revenue produced is out of step with the related recorded costs thereof, which the utility will be able to offset over the useful life of the power station.

Spanish companies are allowed to defer costs in excess of the depreciation in order to maintain profitability and to enable payment of a dividend. The analyst should adjust, by subtracting the excess deferrals from profit. This may well have a material difference to the valuation of the company.

Investors should also consider net income and price/cash flow issues in any analysis of the company. However, information may be difficult to glean, particularly as source and application of funds statements are not provided.

Reporting Requirements

Companies listed on the Spanish Stock Exchange (Bolsa) have to report their annual financial results within six months of the year end. In addition, every listed company must report quarterly to the Bolsa, within 30 days of the end of the period. However, it is not mandatory to send out quarterly results to shareholders.

Deferred Taxation

Deferred taxation is not recognized in Spain, as the book and tax values of assets are so interlinked. It is not feasible for investors to make any meaningful adjustments because of the impossibility of obtaining the necessary information.

Foreign Currency Liabilities

Foreign currency liabilities are translated at the exchange-rate ruling at the time of incurring the debt. The local currency equivalent of the debt remains unchanged unless the parity of the peseta to the respective foreign currency changes, in which case the liability should be restated at the year-end exchange rate. Exchange differences arising from currency fluctuations should be recorded when the related debt is paid. **Companies can choose to defer currency gains and losses rather than take them through the income statement in the year that they are incurred.**

Foreign Exchange

Accounts receivable and payable in foreign currency must be stated at the exchange rate prevailing on the date the underlying contract is formalized. This carrying value must be maintained, unless a formal devaluation occurs. **Unrealized exchange gains or losses are not always accounted for. However, best practice, followed by a few quoted companies, is to restate the peseta equivalents of foreign currency amounts, carrying the unrealized gain or loss in an exchange fluctuation account until realized.**

Other Features

The following comments are more theoretical and concern Spanish accounting practices.

Inventories

Inventories are valued at the lower of cost or market value. Cost includes invoiced amounts plus all additional expenses arising up to the point of arrival at the warehouse. The cost of manufactured products should include raw and indirect materials, labor, and direct production costs in accordance with the normal costing system used by the company. Market value is defined as the lower of replacement cost or realizable value.

The average cost valuation method is recommended, although the FIFO and LIFO methods are used in circumstances where this is held to be appropriate.

Fixed Assets

Fixed assets must be stated at cost less accumulated depreciation, which is calculated on the basis of the estimated useful lives of the assets. Fixed assets may be revalued in accordance with statutory coefficients. However, because of the tax consequences relating to unrealized capital gain, this treatment is rarely adopted.

Intangible Assets

Spanish accounting allows the classification of research and development costs as an intangible asset which can be amortized over 25 years.

Capital

Capital paid up in excess of par value is segregated in a share premium reserve that is not freely distributable. Uncalled or called and unpaid capital are shown as assets in the balance sheet. Spanish companies often issue new shares of way-of-rights issue at less than par value. This is permitted provided that the difference can be capitalized from capital reserves.

Reserves

The following are the reserves most commonly found in the balance sheets of Spanish companies.

Legal Reserve *(reserva legal).* If the profit of a corporation after tax exceeds 6 percent of the capital, a minimum of 10 percent of net income must be transferred to a legal reserve until it equals 20 percent of the paid-up capital. This reserve may only be used to offset future losses and, if so used, must be reinstated by subsequent transfers from net income.

Voluntary Reserve *(reserva voluntaria).* The voluntary reserve is the balance of retained earnings after allocating to the legal reserve. The total amount is available for distribution, provided the capital of the company is intact. This provision is necessary because it is Spanish practice, attributable partly to tax rules, to book losses in a separate "intangible asset" account and not to deduct them automatically from retained earnings.

Losses so booked can be covered by all or any of the reserves linked here before restricting the distribution of the voluntary reserve.

Share Premium Reserve *(prima de emision de acciones)*.   Premiums received on the issue of the company's own shares may be distributed once the legal reserve has reached the statutory 20 percent of the paid-up capital.

Regularization Reserves *(reservas de regularizacion)*.   The regularization reserves arise generally from the revaluation of fixed assets on the basis of statutory coefficients. Reference should be made to the specific legislation in each case to determine the purpose for which these reserves may be used.

Short- and Long-Term Debt

For balance sheet purposes, Spanish accounting allows the classification of short-term debt as those liabilities with maturities up to 18 months and long-term as those over 18 months.

SWEDEN

Highlights

EEC

Sweden is not a member of the EEC. Thus the EEC Fourth and Seventh Directives do not apply to Swedish financial statements.

Taxation

Swedish tax law and practice exercise a very considerable influence over Swedish financial statements. The government is committed to reforming the tax system. The previous corporation tax rate of 56 percent was expected to be reduced to 30 percent by 1991. At the same time, opportunities to transfer profits to untaxed reserves will be removed.

Deferred Taxation

Deferred taxation is not recognized. The financial statements do not reveal the enormous deferred tax liabilities relating to the untaxed reserves found in almost every balance sheet.

Untaxed Reserves

These reserves represent the accumulation of charges which are allowed for tax purposes. Although not required for fair presentation purposes, Swedish tax law requires that they be recorded in the books in order to qualify for deduction.

Depreciation

Accelerated depreciation is shown in the financial statements as a transfer to reserves.

Earnings Per Share

There is no legal requirement to disclose EPS, but over 90 percent of Swedish listed companies do. Adjustments must be made for appropriation to reserves and taxes.

Consolidated Financial Statements

All parent companies are required to prepare consolidated financial statements. Equity accounting, although not mandatory, can now be applied to associate companies.

Practical Considerations

Background

The primary aim of Swedish financial statements is conformity with the law. This formal approach has overshadowed the desirability of a fair presentation of net income and stockholders' equity.

However, developments in company legislation over the past decade (a new Companies Act and a modernizing Accounting Law), increased activity by FAR (the Swedish Institute of Authorized Public Accountants), and a widespread movement toward information disclosure have all contributed to revolutionizing the form and content of and information given in Swedish financial statements.

The Companies Act requires a company's annual financial statements to include an administration report, a balance sheet, income statement, statement of changes in financial position, and notes to the financial statements. The last four items are required both for the company alone and, where appropriate, on a consolidated basis.

There are a number of features in the content and presentation of Swedish financial statements that require explanation as they are significantly different from U.S. and U.K. practice. These are:

- The taxation system and the absence of deferred taxation
- Untaxed reserves
- Foreign currency translation
- Depreciation
- Earnings per share

The Taxation System

The single biggest factor in distorting Swedish financial statements is the unique stranglehold which Swedish tax law and practice have on the country's accounting and reporting practices. The basic rule of Swedish taxation that taxable income is principally based on book income has been carried to extremes. **Companies who wish to claim several of the more important tax incentives available in Sweden must record charges in their**

books equivalent to the pre-tax amount of these incentives. Thus, from a financial statement viewpoint the unique feature of these incentives is that their taxes are reflected as expense items in income statements and not, as in most other countries, as adjustments in the tax return. Thus, by excluding accelerated depreciation, for example, net profit will be adjusted upwards.

Deferred Taxation

Swedish law and practice do not recognize deferred tax accounting except in the case of untaxed reserves in subsidiaries (see below). **Hence Swedish financial statements do not reveal the enormous deferred tax liabilities relating to the untaxed reserves which are found in practically every balance sheet.** Most domestic and some U.S. analysts will apply a 50 percent tax rate. However, many international analysts take the view that, as the reserving was done for specific purposes, the tax is unlikely ever to be paid. In such a case, one may consider these reserves as part of shareholders' funds.

Untaxed Reserves

There are a number of untaxed reserves which appear in Swedish accounts, immediately preceding the shareholders' equity category:

- Inventory reserves
- Payroll reserves
- Reserves for future investment
- Compulsory investment reserves
- Accelerated depreciation
- Development reserves

All of them represent the accumulation of charges which are allowed for tax purposes but are not required for fair presentation purposes. Swedish tax law nonetheless requires that they be recorded in the books in order to qualify for deduction.

Inventory and Payroll Reserves.   Inventory reserves have existed for many years as a means whereby manufacturing industry could defer taxes and/or smooth taxable income. Payroll reserves extend the same sort of possibility to labor-intensive companies with little or no inventory.

Reserves for Future Investments.   Reserves for future investments are in effect advance additional depreciation relating to unspecified fixed assets yet to be acquired.

Compulsory Investment Reserves.   Compulsory investment reserves were introduced in 1980 as a means of mopping up excess corporate liquidity through compulsory deposits with the Bank of Sweden (these appear in the accounts as "blocked accounts with the Bank of Sweden").

Development Reserves. Development reserves are compulsory appropriations of pre-tax profits. They can be used for employee training or research and development purposes. International analysts may choose to treat them as shareholders' funds as the deferred tax liability is never likely to be paid.

Investors must make an adjustment for these untaxed reserves in calculating, for example, asset value per share or the debt/equity ratio. This is done by applying an approximate tax rate of 50 percent to the reserves. Clearly the ratio will increase as the equity denominator is reduced as a result of this adjustment.

Depreciation

Swedish companies show depreciation charges at two levels in their income statements, in arriving at operating income and as a transfer to/from special reserves.

The charge to operating income is normally computed on a straight-line basis over the estimated useful lives of the various classes of asset. **The difference between the charge to operating income and the total amount claimed for tax purposes is shown as a transfer to/from untaxed reserves.** As mentioned above, normally the reserve itself is shown as a separate item in the balance sheet in the section immediately preceding shareholders' equity, but sometimes it is included in the total amount of accumulated depreciation deducted from the related asset captions.

Swedish tax depreciation on building and land improvement is broadly in line with normal straight-line, useful-life, original cost depreciation. However, in the case of machinery and equipment the methods allowed for tax purposes in effect permit such assets to be written off over five years. In addition to the annual depreciation charges under the tax regulations, companies can also utilize reserves for future investments to achieve significant accelerated depreciation benefits.

Foreign Currency Translation

Neither the Accounting Law nor the Companies Act deals with the question of how items in foreign currencies or foreign subsidiaries' financial statements should be translated. Where significant amounts are involved most companies do disclose the principles applied. The general practice is as follows:

1. *Receivables and payable in foreign currencies.* **Receivables are translated at the lower of the transaction-date rate and the current rate. Payables are converted at the higher of the transaction rate and the current rate.** Losses on long-term debt are frequently spread over the remaining term of the loan. In rare cases, current rates are used.
2. *Financial statements of foreign subsidiaries.* **Foreign subsidiaries' financial statements are translated mainly at current rates, although almost as many companies use the monetary/nonmonetary method, frequently**

treating inventories as a monetary item. FAR is now recommending the current method for independently operating subsidiaries and the current/noncurrent basis for "extended-arm" operations such as pure marketing subsidiaries.

3. *Accounting for exchange gains and losses.* This is usually a significant item. There is a wide variety in the classification of the translation effect in financial statements. In the income statement it can be shown as an operating item, a financial item, or an extraordinary item. The latest thinking is that the differences should be reported as financial items because they essentially arise from financial exposure. As the general rule is not to credit unrealized gains net of unrealized losses to the income statement, a deferred income item often arises in the balance sheet. This is most usually included among other current liabilities, but in some instances it appears as an untaxed reserve under some such heading as "Reserve against consolidated assets."

Developments in other countries, such as the experience gained from the application of FAS 52 in the United States, will naturally influence Swedish practice in the future.

Earnings Per Share

There is no legal requirement to disclose earnings per share, but almost 90 percent of Swedish listed companies do present this information. As the method of computing earnings per share is not regulated by the accounting, company, or tax laws, the amounts reported in some ways represent the nearest approach to fair presentation to be found in the income/equity area of Swedish annual reports. The most commonly used starting point for computing earnings per share is to apply a standard tax rate (usually 50 percent) to the reported figure of earnings before special adjustments and taxes.

The following example, taking figures from the 1987 financial statements of Volvo, shows clearly the adjustments that need to be made when analyzing Swedish accounts.

Consolidated Financial Statements

All parent companies are required to prepare consolidated financial statements. Only in very special circumstances may a subsidiary not be included in the consolidated financial statements (for example, a foreign subsidiary may be compelled to apply special local accounting principles, and it may be difficult to obtain enough information for a restatement to Swedish accounting principles or exchange rates, and differences may affect a subsidiary's accounts in such a way that inclusion would result in accounts that would not be true and fair).

Consolidated financial statements should consist of a statement of consolidated income, a consolidated balance sheet, and, for large groups, a

VOLVO–Earnings per share

(Sk mil)	Swedish GAAP Income Statement	Swedish GAAP EPS			
		Actual tax EPS	Full tax EPS	Standard 50% tax EPS	US GAAP EPS
Operating income	6,722				6,928
Net interest income	802				743
Foreign exchange gain	561				0
Gain on disposals	1,186				1,170
Equity in associates	0				401
Profit after financials	9,271				9,242
Employee bonus	−260				−260
Profit before tax and allocations	9,011	9,011	9,011	9,011	8,982
Allocations to untaxed reserves	−3,426	0	0	0	0
	5,585	9,011	9,011	9,011	8,982
Taxes (actual)	−2,220	−2,220	−2,220	−4,408	−4,266
Taxes on untaxed reserves at 50%	0	0	−1,713	0	0
Minority interest	−74	−74	−74	−119	−80
Income before extraordinary items	3,291	6,717	5,004	4,484	4,636
Extraordinary inc./(exp)	0	0	0	0	0
Net income after extraordinaries	3,291	6,717	5,004	4,484	4,636
EPS Skr	42.4	86.6	64.5	57.8	59.7
Average shares in issue	77.6	77.6	77.6	77.6	77.6

Analyst: P. Dupont.

Notes to the EPS example:

(1) (a) Actual tax earnings are based on appropriations to reserves (and, sometimes, extraordinary items) but without making any adjustment to the tax charge.

 (b) Full tax earnings increase the tax charge to take account of the deferred tax liability represented by the transfer to reserves.

 (c) Standard tax earnings adjust the tax charge by replacing it by 50% of the profit before appropriations (and in this case before extraordinary items as well).

(2) Some companies will give full or standard tax earnings with the share in income from associates (less dividends received) added in at the pre-tax level.

(3) The standard and full tax methods correspond more closely than the actual tax method to the German DVFA method of adjusting earnings—Germany being the other major country where large discretionary transfers to reserves can be made. The actual tax method corresponds more closely to UK accounting practice.

consolidated statement of changes in financial position. These statements should have the same form and contain the same information as parent company statements.

As regards the methods to be used for preparation of the consolidated financial statements and, in particular, the elimination of internal shareholdings, the legislation only states that this should be done in accordance with generally accepted accounting principles. **The great majority of Swedish consolidations are based on the purchase accounting method, which is FAR's preferred method, although pooling of interests is used in a few cases.**

Equity Accounting

In February 1986 FAR issued an exposure draft of a recommendation dealing with investments in associated companies. This represents a major step forward in harmonizing Swedish practice with International Accounting Standards. **Features of the draft are that equity accounting may only be applied in consolidated financial statements and that the equity in an associated company's undistributed earnings must be classified as a nondistributable consolidated equity.** Equity accounting may not be applied in parent company or single company financial statements. In these cases a form of note disclosure on the face of the income statement is proposed.

Stock Exchange Investments

Companies are required to list their balance sheet date holdings with book values. This allows a more accurate assessment of the organization's asset value to be made.

Other Features

The following paragraphs deal with the more theoretical aspects of Swedish accounting practice.

Income Statement

The income statement must reflect all business income and expense during the financial year and must clearly indicate how the net result for the year was arrived at.

Capital and Reserves

Share Capital.   Share capital must be shown at par value.

Legal Reserve.   Any excess over par value paid for shares must be allocated to the legal reserve, even though the reserve may already amount to the minimum stipulated level (20 percent of share capital, otherwise funded by retaining 10 percent of annual profit until the relevant level is reached). The legal reserve may not be distributed in whole or in part.

Leasing

Accounting for leases is governed only by a brief FAR recommendation which requires lessees to capitalize assets subject to leases including an obligation to purchase.

Inventories

Inventories are normally stated at the lower of FIFO cost and market value. In some instances average cost is used when it approximates FIFO. Market value is usually interpreted as net realizable value, but replacement cost, if lower, is permissible in the case of raw materials and semi-finished products. In the absence of a need for higher provision, Swedish companies normally set aside 5 percent for inventory obsolescence, the standard amount permitted by the tax law.

Property, Plant, and Equipment

These assets are normally stated at original cost, but the Companies Act allows them to be revalued, subject to certain restrictions. The amount of a fixed asset revaluation can either be used to provide for required write-downs of other fixed assets, or to finance a bonus issue of capital stock, or be transferred to a revaluation reserve which can later be used for either of the preceding two purposes.

It is permissible, but not mandatory, to capitalize as part of the asset cost interest expense incurred during the period of construction of fixed assets.

Income Taxes Payable

This is one area where there is a need for more informative disclosure. The accounting principles on which taxes payable are reported are rarely disclosed and only a minority disclose the reasons for abnormal effective tax rates. These usually include research and development allowances, investment allowances, the effect of double taxation treaties on foreign earnings and deduction for dividends on new capital stock issues.

Pension Provision

Swedish company law and current practice do not require that all pension commitments are provided for in the financial statements. It is an acceptable alternative to disclose the actuarially computed amount of such commitments as a contingent liability, the charges to income being made on a cash basis. This alternative treatment is frequently used, mainly in connection with older commitments, often in respect of former owners. The amounts involved are usually relatively insignificant.

SWITZERLAND

Highlights

EEC

Switzerland is not a member of the EEC. Its companies' financial statements are not bound by the EEC Fourth and Seventh Directives. However, there is increasing pressure from Brussels for Swiss companies to adopt similar procedures.

Deferred Taxation

There is no obligation for companies to provide for deferred taxes.

Undisclosed Reserves

The undervaluation of assets in the balance sheet and/or the creation of undisclosed reserves is permissible. Neither the existence and amounts of undisclosed reserves nor any changes in such reserves made during the year are required to be disclosed.

Income Taxes

Only income taxes that are due in the current year need to be accrued in the accounts.

Consolidated Financial Statements

There are no legal requirements governing consolidated accounts. Associated companies may not be valued in excess of cost.

Earnings Per Share

There is no requirement to disclose earnings per share. Calculation of a company's EPS may be very difficult due to the lack of information given in the financial statements.

Foreign Currency Translation

Unrealized translation gains may not be credited to income, and provision must be made for unrealized losses.

Practical Considerations

Background

It is often believed that Swiss financial statements are not as useful as those prepared in other European countries. This belief stems from the fact that Switzerland has not joined the EEC and therefore is not bound to implement EEC Company Law Directives. There is, however, a trend for the larger corporations, particularly those operating internationally, to present more information and this is expected to continue.

In Switzerland, the legal requirements governing the accounting and reporting practices of corporations are contained in the Code of Obligations.

The Code requires the preparation of financial statements, which must be true and fair, to be made in accordance with generally recognized commercial principles. There is no prescribed format for these financial statements except for corporations subject to special legislation (banks, mutual funds and their management companies, insurance companies, pension funds, and railways).

Inevitably, there are significant accounting differences between Switzerland and the United Kingdom of which the investor must be aware. The important divergent areas are as follows:

- Deferred taxation
- Reserves
- Income/corporation taxation
- Consolidated financial statements
- Earnings per share

Deferred Taxation

In the United Kingdom, a partial-liability approach to deferred taxation is used. **Switzerland, however, lays down no obligation for companies to provide for deferred taxes.** The investor is not able to make a satisfactory adjustment for this difference due to the absence of any information in the Swiss financial statements.

Undisclosed Reserves

For Swiss companies the undervaluation of assets in the balance sheet and/or the creation of undisclosed reserves by other means is permissible to the extent that it is deemed necessary for a corporation's continued prosperity or in order to distribute as normal a dividend as possible. Neither the existence and amounts of undisclosed reserves nor any changes in such reserves made during the year are required to be disclosed in a corporation's financial statements or in its director's business report. (Such practices are not permitted in U.K. financial statements.) One possible way to gauge asset values is via the disclosure of the insurance value of fixed assets (excluding land). This is found in the notes to the accounts. Although this is not perfect, the reader of the accounts should be able to get a reasonable idea of the company's true asset value.

Income Tax

In Switzerland, taxes due in a particular year are normally determined on the basis of income earned in one or more prior years. **Under Swiss accounting practices, only income taxes that are due in the current year need to be accrued in the accounts. The amounts of future income taxes**

on income earned during the period covered by the company's financial statements are not commonly recorded.

This is different from the U.K. practice, which would disclose all tax liabilities in the accounts. It is extremely difficult to adjust for this discrepancy in methods.

Consolidated Financial Statements

In contrast to the United Kingdom, there are no legal requirements in Switzerland governing the preparation of consolidated accounts. However, if group accounts are compiled, it is common practice for the accounting principles used to be disclosed and for statements to be prepared on a consistent basis.

Permanent investments in associated companies may not be valued at an amount in excess of the lower of their cost or their intrinsic value (this includes consideration of future earnings and net asset values on a going concern basis). This is clearly a difference in practice between Swiss and the United Kingdom, where the equity method of accounting is used.

For the investor, nonconsolidated accounts provide major problems as regards investment decisions. **However, it is to be hoped that the growing tendency toward producing group financial statements will continue and that this will lead to a more complete and accurate picture of the group being given.**

Earnings Per Share (EPS)

There is no requirement in Switzerland to disclose earnings per share. Further, any meaningful calculation of a company's EPS is extremely difficult because of the notorious unreliability of published earnings figures. For the investor, it may be more useful to base investment decisions on the following factors:

1. *General*
   - Market sentiment
   - Market trends
   - Sector trends
2. *Specific*
   - Company growth in terms of sales.
   - Cash flow—this could be worked out approximately by taking profit and adding back provisions and depreciation.
   - As many factors, such as provisions and depreciation are obscure, company and local broker guidance may provide the only significant insight into the company's performance.

Foreign-Currency Translation

In principle, all internationally recognized translation methods are acceptable (for example the temporal method and the closing rate method). Unrealized translation gains may not be credited to income (in contrast to the United Kingdom) and provision must be made for unrealized losses. Translation gains and losses on cash, marketable securities included in current assets, or bank overdrafts are considered to be realized.

Other Features

The following section deals in more detail with the theoretical side of Swiss accounting practice.

Income Statement

There is no uniformity in the presentation of the profit and loss account. For example, sales and cost of sales are often shown separately, but sometimes only the gross profit on sales is disclosed.

Asset Valuation

In general, corporations are required to value their assets at amounts not in excess of the lower of cost or current value. In the balance sheet of a Swiss corporation, assets are generally not stated in excess of what their valuation would be in accordance with International Accounting Standards (IAS). Accounts payable are normally stated at the face amount, and accrued expenses are generally recorded at least to the extent required by IAS. There may, however, be additional accruals and reserves for losses and expenses not yet incurred, either included in accrued expenses or shown separately.

Fixed Assets

Real estate, property, buildings, machinery, equipment, and vehicles must be carried at not more than cost less appropriate provision for depreciation and obsolescence.

Intangible Assets

Intangible assets may not be stated at amounts in excess of their cost less appropriate amortization. There is a specific provision in the law permitting the capitalization of organization costs and of stamp duty paid in connection with the issue of capital stock. Deferred organization cost and deferred stamp duty must be amortized over a period not exceeding five years. Research and development expenses can be deferred only if their recovery through future operations appears to be certain. Purchased goodwill may not be stated in excess of cost less appropriate amortization.

Depreciation

The Code of Obligations provides that fixed assets may not be stated at amounts in excess of their cost less appropriate depreciation. Fixed assets may, however, be stated net of the accumulated depreciation, and there is no requirement that cost and depreciation be disclosed separately in the balance sheet. Depreciation reserves, which may include accumulated depreciation and replacement reserves, may also be shown on the liability side of the balance sheet. The law does not prescribe any rules for depreciation accounting, and different methods are used in practice. As a general rule, the net value placed on fixed assets is not permitted to exceed the lower of cost or the amount that is deemed to be recoverable through future operations. Depreciation is frequently taken in excess of a company's economic requirements, and therefore hidden reserves created as the value of fixed assets are greatly in excess of their stated amount.

Inventories

The valuation of inventories (raw materials, supplies, work-in-progress, and finished goods) may not exceed the lower of their cost or current market value. Cost is based on FIFO or an average cost basis.

Long-Term Contracts

Profits on long-term contracts are accounted for under the *percentage-of-completion* method or under the *completed-contract* method. Losses are recorded as soon as they become apparent.

Legal Reserve

Corporations must make the following appropriations to a legal reserve out of the balance of profit:

1. Five percent of annual profit until the reserve equals 20 percent of the paid-in capital.
2. The equivalent of 10 percent of the dividend or other profit distributions which exceed 5 percent of the paid-in capital.

In addition, amounts received in excess of the par value of shares, to the extent that they are not used for depreciation or amortization of assets, must also be incorporated in the legal reserve.

To the extent that the legal reserve does not exceed one half of the authorized and issued capital, it can be used to cover losses or maintain the corporation in times of adverse business conditions. It is generally held that no further appropriations out of earnings are required once the legal reserve amounts to one half of the authorized and issued capital.

Contingent Liabilities Guarantees

The Code of Obligations requires information to be disclosed on contingent liabilities, guarantees, and charges on accounts in respect of liabilities of their parties. Provisions for all anticipated losses must be made. Post-balance sheet events must be commented on, if material, in the management report.

Leases

The operating method, in which the lease is treated as a rental arrangement and income is charged based on the amount of the lease payment, is used by most lessors. Lessees' assets, less appropriate depreciation, are normally shown in the lessor's accounts, and income is recognized as lease payments are received. Lessees are not required to disclose lease commitments. If the economic ownership of an asset is transferred to the lessor under a finance lease, the lessee may either capitalize the lease or use the operating method. In practice, the operating method is most commonly used.

United Kingdom

Highlights

Earnings Per Share

This is calculated by dividing earnings (calculated as profits after taxation, minority interest, exceptional items, and preference dividends, but before extraordinary items) by the weighted average number of shares in issue during the period.

Goodwill

Goodwill can either be written off immediately by a charge against share-holders' funds or be capitalized and amortized over a period not to exceed 40 years. There is no requirement to adopt either approach on a consistent basis. The controversial decision by companies such as Rank Hovis McDougall to give a value to product brands is likely to hasten the current review of the treatment of intangibles.

Foreign Currency Translation

Exchange gains and losses resulting from balance sheet translation are recorded as a movement on reserves, and are never reflected in the profit and loss account.

Deferred Taxation

Deferred tax is provided on those timing differences that are expected to reverse in the foreseeable future. The tax rate applied is based on the rate expected to apply when the timing difference reverses.

Acquisition and Merger Accounting

Merger accounting is permissible but not mandatory when shares are issued to finance an acquisition and other specified criteria are met. Acquisition accounting must be used in all other situations.

Leasing

Since leasing an asset under a finance lease is similar to ownership, finance leases must be capitalized in the lessee's balance sheet. The profit and loss account is charged with depreciation on the asset and an amount representing the finance charges inherent in the lease payments.

Consolidation

Consolidated financial statements are mandatory for all companies that have subsidiaries.

Practical Considerations

Background

The statutory requirements governing U.K. annual financial reporting are contained in the Companies Act 1985. This act, which applies to all limited-liability entities, gives the form and content of the annual financial statements, together with mandatory footnotes and other financial disclosures. This is supplemented by Statements of Standard Accounting Practice (SSAP) issued by the Institute of Chartered Accountants via the Accounting Standards Committee that enable specific guidance on areas of accounting practice to be given.

Earnings Per Share (EPS)

Earnings per share (EPS) should be calculated by apportioning the earnings (i.e., the consolidated profit of the period after taxation, minority interests, exceptional items, and preference dividends, but before extraordinary items) over the weighted average number of equity shares in issue during the period.

Where a listed company has any of the following outstanding:

- A separate class of equity shares which do not rank for dividend in the period but will do so in the future;
- Debentures or loan stock convertible into equity shares of the company; or
- Options or warrants to subscribe for equity shares of the company;

the company has entered into obligations which may dilute the EPS in the future. In these circumstances the fully diluted EPS should be calculated and shown on the face of the profit and loss account. In addition, full information as to the rights of the holders (existing shareholders, convertible shareholders, preference shareholders, or holders of options or warrants) should be provided.

If the difference between the fully diluted EPS and the ordinary EPS calculation is material (i.e., greater than 5 percent), both figures must be shown.

Beazer–consolidated profit & loss account

	1988 £ mil	1987 £ mil
Turnover	1,343.3	1,033.0
Cost of sales	−1,135.2	881.1
Gross profit	208.1	151.9
Distribution costs	−29.3	−19.8
Administrative costs	−55.9	−47.3
Operating profit	122.9	84.8
Net interest payable	−20.6	−18.4
Other income and expenses	3.8	5.9
Profit before exceptional items	106.1	72.3
Exceptional item	8.6	0
Profit on ordinary activities before taxation	114.7	72.3
Taxation	−37.8	−24.7
Profit on ordinary activities after taxation	76.9	47.6
Minority interests	−1.3	−1.6
Profit before extraordinary items	75.6	46.0
Extraordinary items after taxation	16.5	5.4
Profit attributable to members of the holding company	92.1	51.4
Dividends: ordinary practice	−17.6	−14.7
	−3.4	0
Retained profit for the year	71.7	36.7

Analyst: G. Foster.

Calculation of earnings per share:

Undiluted.

	Earnings	
	1988	**1987**
Profit after tax	76.9	47.6
Minorities	−1.3	−1.6
Preference dividend	−3.4	0
	£72.2m	£46.0m
No. of shares in issue	276.5	228.8
EPS	26.1	20.1

Fully Diluted.   In this instance we need access to the balance sheet and associated notes to determine the full number of shares in issue after the exercise of share options and after allowing for full conversion rights attaching to Beazer's 8.5 percent convertible loan stock (essentially we need to take into account all cases where fixed coupon securities are convertible at some future date into shares). After allowing for full conversion, the weighted average becomes 300.5 million for 1988 and 250.7 million for 1987.

Also, upon conversion there will be an interest saving from the redemption of the 8.5 percent convertible loan stock, and an interest benefit from the proceeds derived from the exercise of share options. Net taxation of these adds £2.0m and £1.7m to earnings in 1988 and 1987.

	1988	**1987**
Published earnings	72.2	46.0
Interest saving	2.0	46.0
Fully diluted earnings	£74.2m	£47.7m
Adjusted no. of shares in issue	300.5	250.7
Fully diluted EPS	24.7	19.0

Acquisition and Merger Accounting

Before discussing merger accounting **it will be useful to define the key features of acquisition (purchase) accounting** so that a clear comparison can be made:

1. Shares purchased in a subsidiary company are valued in the balance sheet of the acquiring company at cost, that is at the fair market value of the consideration given to acquire them (less any dividends out of preacquisition profits).
2. There is no problem when shares are purchased for cash. However, on a share exchange, that is where the acquiring company gives shares in itself in exchange for the shares in the subsidiary, it is necessary to place a value on the consideration given. If this fair value exceeds the nominal value of the shares issued, a share premium account is required.
3. **Preacquisition profits of the subsidiary company are no longer available for distribution.** They are "frozen" at the date of acquisition and only postacquisition profits of the subsidiary are consolidated with the distributable profits of the acquiring company.
4. **Assets and liabilities of the subsidiary are required to be revalued to their market value at the date of acquisition.** The difference between the consideration and the sum of the net assets is treated as **goodwill or capital reserve on consolidation**.

The use of merger accounting in the United Kingdom has been increasingly prevalent in the 1980s and has attracted considerable criticism that it is being abused. Although it is extremely likely that revisions will be made, currently merger accounting may be applied if *all* of the following conditions are met:

1. The business combination results from an offer to the holders of all equity shares and the holders of all voting shares that are not already held by the offeror.
2. The offeror has secured, as a result of the offer, a holding of at least 90 percent of all the equity shares (taking each class of equity separately) and the shares carrying at least 90 percent of the votes of the offeree.
3. Immediately prior to the offer, the offeror does not hold either 20 percent or more of equity shares of the offeree (taking each class of equity separately), or shares carrying 20 percent or more of the votes of the offeree.
4. Not less than 90 percent of the fair value of the total consideration given for the equity share capital (including that given for shares already held) is in the form of equity share capital; not less than 90 percent of the fair value of the consideration given for voting nonequity share capital (including that given for shares already held) is in the form of equity and/or voting nonequity share capital.

The main features of merger accounting are:

1. Shares issued by the holding company in exchange for shares in a subsidiary are valued at nominal value, not at fair market value.

2. The consolidated balance sheet includes the retained profits of both companies as being distributable.
3. Assets and liabilities may be retained at their book value in the consolidated accounts. The only adjustment which may be made is that necessary to bring the accounting policies of the two companies into line with one another.
4. The profit and loss account includes the full year's results of both companies, even though the merger may have taken place toward the end of the financial year.

Proponents of merger accounting see several advantages of the method:

1. The acquisition method does not appear to be suitable in the case where two companies come together and neither has absorbed the other.
2. The merger method usually results in higher distributable reserves as the consolidated figures include the preacquisition profits of both companies.
3. The merger method usually uses historical values for assets, and there is no goodwill which means that the capital employed is lower. The profits under this method will be higher as the depreciation charge is based on lower fixed-asset values and there is no charge for amortization of goodwill. This will lead to higher earnings per share and higher return on capital employed.

It is important to stress that, in contrast to the United States, merger accounting is not obligatory if the necessary conditions are met.

Intangible Assets

The valuation of intangible assets (see Glossary) is an extremely hot topic. Recently, a number of well-known companies have stretched the boundaries of credibility with their accounting treatment of such items. They are allowed to do this because of the latitude given by the current accounting standards and guidelines. Rank Hovis McDougall, for example, has decided to give an asset value to each brand it owns, thereby grossing up its balance sheet considerably. The problems are even greater with service companies whose balance sheets are likely to be dominated by intangibles.

In a separate development, Saatchi & Saatchi and Hanson have also put the presence of intangibles to the fore in determining their borrowing limits. Both companies decided to include all goodwill previously written off for the purpose of calculating these limits. The use or misuse of intangibles is gaining pace, but no concrete, relevant guidelines have been issued by the accountancy profession to standardize practice.

The most significant intangible is usually goodwill.

Goodwill

The predominant practice in the United Kingdom is to write off goodwill against reserves directly upon acquisition. Where it is capitalized, the company is required to amortize the goodwill over its estimated useful economic life. Rarely will this exceed 20 years.

The treatment of goodwill has provoked considerable debate, with reference to merger accounting. A recent Exposure Draft has supplemented the existing accounting statement and requires additional disclosure requirements to be made.

The main proposals laid down were as follows:

1. The full amount of purchased goodwill should be shown in all cases, including, for example, where merger relief is applied.
2. The following disclosures should be made for each material acquisition:
   a. A table showing the book values and fair values of each major category of assets and liabilities acquired.
   b. An analysis of the *fair value* adjustments made, indicating the amount attributable to conforming with accounting policies, to revaluations, to provisions (separating out provisions for anticipated future losses), and to any other major item.
   c. A brief explanation of the reasons for the fair value adjustments.
3. Subsequent movements on acquisition-related provisions should be disclosed.
4. The following disclosures should be made for each significant disposal of a previously acquired business/business segment:
   a. Profit or loss arising.
   b. Where it occurs within three years of acquisition, the amount of attributable purchased goodwill written off to reserves.
   c. Details where the proceeds of disposal are accounted for as a reduction in acquisition cost.
   d. Where goodwill is amortized, the earnings per share before, as well as after, amortization.

These disclosures should present a much clearer view of the accounts, and will certainly help the reader.

Foreign Exchange

Until comparatively recently, companies with overseas subsidiaries had little difficulty in producing group accounts. Most exchange rates were fixed and translation was simple except where major devaluations occurred. With the advent of floating exchange rates, the treatment of overseas accounts has become fraught with major problems, in particular over the rate of exchange to be used in translating the P&L account and balance sheet items of foreign subsidiaries and associates into sterling when producing consolidated accounts.

U.K. practice mirrors that of the United States. **Under SSAP 20 the** *closing rate/net investment method* **should normally be used. The main features of this method are:**

1. *Balance sheet* items should be translated into the currency of the holding company at the *closing rate*. Differences arising from the retranslation of the opening net investment, the holding company's proportion of the subsidiary, or the associated company's share capital and reserves at the closing rate should be taken to reserves.
2. *Profit and loss account* items should be translated using either the average rate for the accounting period or the closing rate. Any differences between translation at the average rate and the closing rate should be taken to reserves.

In rare circumstances the *temporal method* may be used. Where the trade of a subsidiary is a direct extension of the trade of a holding company, this method should be used. **Its key features are:**

1. All transactions should be translated at the rate ruling on the transaction date or at an average rate for the period if this is not materially different.
2. Nonmonetary assets should normally be translated at a historic rate.
3. Monetary assets and liabilities should be retranslated at the closing rate.
4. All exchange gains and losses should be taken to the P&L account as part of the profit and loss from ordinary activities.

Deferred Taxation

The aim of deferred taxation accounting is to recognize differences in the timing of revenues and expenditure for accounting and tax purposes. Companies in the United Kingdom only provide to the extent that future tax liabilities are expected to arise in the future (partial allocation), and not on all timing differences (full allocation). Partial allocation requires an assessment of the probability of future taxes being payable or recoverable and involves consideration of past and future patterns of capital expenditures, as well as forecasts of future operations and cash flows. Tax provisions are based on rates expected to apply in the periods in which timing differences are expected to reverse.

Following the fundamental changes to corporation tax brought in by the 1984 Finance Act the importance of deferred taxation has diminished. The act introduced the phased reduction of the rate of corporation tax down to 35 percent, together with the phased elimination of First Year Capital Allowances. This has the effect of reducing the timing differences originating in a period but not necessarily eliminating them.

Extraordinary and Exceptional Items

Unlike many European countries, the United Kingdom makes a clear distinction between extraordinary and exceptional items.

1. *Extraordinary items* are those which are:
   a. Not expected to recur
   b. Outside the ordinary activities of the business
   c. Material
   Examples of extraordinary items are the discontinuance of a significant part of a business and the sale of an investment which was not acquired with the intention of being resold. The significance of these items is that they are not included in the calculation of earnings per share.
2. *Exceptional items,* such as abnormally high bad debt write offs or abnormal provisions for losses on long-term contracts, **differ from extraordinary items in that they are within the ordinary activities of the business. As such, they have to be included in EPS calculations.**

Leasing and Off-Balance Sheet Financing

Accounting practices always try to reflect the commercial substance of the transaction involved, and not merely the strict legal form. Since leasing an asset under a finance lease is similar to ownership, lessee companies are required to capitalize them.

If finance leases were not capitalized in the company's financial statements, the company would be guilty of understating their economic resources and level of future obligations. In other words, the company would have off-balance sheet financing. There is general agreement that additional information should be disclosed for special transactions involving off-balance sheet finance so that the accounts will show a true and fair view of a company's financial position and the results of its operations. This was reinforced by a **recent pronouncement from the accountancy profession, which recognized the need to make a full disclosure of all off-balance sheet financing, for example via controlled nonsubsidiaries and securitizing receivables**. The existence and extent of off-balance sheet financing will be progressively reduced as companies are obliged to follow these accounting requirements. However, until then, readers of the accounts will have to rely on the company disclosing the information voluntarily.

Other Features

The following are more theoretical comments on U.K. accounting practice.

Consolidated Financial Statements

Group Accounts. These are mandatory for those companies that have subsidiaries. Group accounts for this purpose normally comprise:

1. A consolidated balance sheet dealing with the state of affairs of the company and all the subsidiaries to be dealt with in group accounts; and
2. A consolidated profit and loss account dealing with the profit or loss of the company and its subsidiaries.

However, **it is possible to exclude a subsidiary from consolidation in the following circumstances:**

1. Where the activities of the companies are dissimilar (e.g., a bank in the same group as a manufacturing company).
2. Where the group does not control more than half the voting rights or is restricted in its ability to appoint the majority of the directors.
3. Where a subsidiary operates under severe restrictions, for example, where there are restraints on the amount of profit remitted from an overseas subsidiary.
4. Where control over the subsidiary is intended to be temporary.

If a subsidiary is excluded because of dissimilar activities, the group accounts should include separate financial statements for that subsidiary, with a note of the holding company's interest, particulars of intragroup balances, the nature of transactions with the rest of the group, and a reconciliation of the amount included in the consolidated financial statements for the group's investment in the subsidiary which should be stated under the equity method of accounting.

Associate Companies. The treatment of associate companies is often referred to as the *equity method of accounting.* Associated companies are generally those in which the investing group has an interest of between 20 percent and 50 percent and is in a position to exercise a significant influence. In addition, the investing company should hold its stake for the long-term with no intention of resale.

The treatment of associates in the consolidated profit and loss account and the balance sheet is as follows:

1. **Profit and loss account.** The relevant share of the associate's profits (or losses) before taxation is included usually under the heading "Share of profits less losses of Associated Companies." The taxation on the profits is shown separately within the group tax charge. Similarly the group's share of the associate's extraordinary items (net of tax) is also disclosed separately.
2. **Balance sheet.** The amount included in the consolidated balance sheet is the total of:
   a. The investing group's share of the associate's net assets other than goodwill.
   b. The investing group's share of goodwill.
   c. The premium paid (or discount) on the acquisition of the interest in the associate.

Statement of Source and Application of Funds

This is a very important tool for investors and helps to explain differences in balance sheet figures from one year to the next. The funds statement gives a view on a company's performance which is not readily available from either the profit and loss account or the balance sheet and aims to provide the following information:

1. The manner in which funds generated by the business have been applied.
2. The proportion of profit taken up by tax and dividends.
3. The investment or disinvestment in subsidiaries, associated companies, fixed assets, and working capital.
4. The extent to which the company has been financed by internally generated funds and externally generated funds.
5. The form external finance has taken—equity, long- or short-term loans.
6. The effect the company's operations and investment program have had upon its solvency, particularly its net liquid funds.

Current Cost Accounting

With the stabilization of inflation at a low level, current cost accounting (CCA) is no longer mandatory. This is probably a great relief to the accounting profession as it never came out with a standard that was universally accepted. Although companies can still disclose current cost information in the notes to be accounts, few do.

However, CCA is still used by utilities such as British Gas and the electric companies. In these cases, the companies have an enormous quantity of fixed assets, most of which are very old. Clearly, CCA is necessary to give a true and fair view of the company's operations.

Revaluation of Fixed Assets

Unlike practice in the United States and several European countries, companies in the United Kingdom are allowed to revalue their fixed assets. However, the notes to the accounts must describe the valuation bases and methods adopted for fixed assets and depreciation. Surplus or deficits arising on the revaluation of fixed assets must be reflected in a revaluation reserve.

Depreciation

Fixed assets must be depreciated down to their residual value over their useful economic life. This applies to freehold buildings as well as both long and short leasehold properties. However, freehold land is never depreciated.

Investment Properties

Property investment companies objected most strongly to the requirements regarding depreciation, arguing that their land and buildings were held for investment potential and that depreciation was inappropriate. The companies won their case and now, with the exception of leases less than 20 years, depreciation is not charged. Instead, investment properties must be revalued annually at their open market value and any surplus or deficit has to be reported as a movement on an "Investment Revaluation Reserve."

Research and Development Expenditure

U.K. companies can capitalize R&D where there is a clearly defined project, the related expenditure is identifiable, and the outcome can be assessed with reasonable certainty. **In all other circumstances it must be expensed.** In addition, following the EEC Fourth Directive and in attempt to satisfy international accounting standards, companies are now required to disclose R&D costs charged to the profit and loss account in the notes to the accounts.

Stock Valuation

Inventories are valued at the lower of cost and net realizable value. **The predominant practice in the United Kingdom is to value the stock on a first in and first out (FIFO) basis.** Cost is defined as being that expenditure that has been incurred in the normal course of business in bringing the product or service to its present location and condition. Cost includes the cost of conversion, which comprises not only the direct expenses of production, but also production overheads. Net realizable value is the actual or estimated selling price less all further costs to completion and all costs to be incurred in marketing, selling, and distributing the product. The LIFO (last in first out) method, which is predominant practice in the United States, is generally not accepted under U.K. accounting guidelines.

Reserves

Share Premium Account (SPA). When shares are issued at a premium to their nominal value, the premium must be transferred to the SPA. The account is disclosed separately on the balance sheet and may not be used to pay out dividends to shareholders, except on liquidation or under a capital reduction scheme authorized by the court. It is permissible, however, to charge the SPA with:

- The preliminary expenses of forming a company.
- The expenses and commissions incurred in any issue of shares of debentures.
- Any discount on the issue of loan capital.
- Any premium paid on the redemption of debentures.

Revaluation Reserve. Any surplus or deficit on a revaluation of assets must be taken to this reserve.

Capital Redemption Reserve (CRR). Shares may only be redeemed or purchased by the company out of distributable profits or out of the proceeds of a new issue of shares. Where redemption or purchase is out of distributable profits, an amount equal to the amount by which the company's issued share capital is diminished must be transferred to the CRR. This is a nondistributable reserve, except upon liquidation or a capital reduction scheme, and aims to prevent a company's overall share capital plus nondistributable reserves from being reduced when share capital is repaid.

Retained Profit and Loss Reserve. At the end of each financial year, the retained profit or loss is transferred to this reserve. This reserve is distributable and can be used to pay out dividends to shareholders.

United States

Highlights

Deferred Tax

Comprehensive accounting for deferred tax is mandatory, using the deferred tax method.

Goodwill

Goodwill must be capitalized and amortized over a period not exceeding 40 years.

Inventory Valuation

LIFO is used extensively in practice.

Fixed Assets

Fixed assets are included in the balance sheet at historical cost less depreciation. No upwards revaluation of these assets is allowed.

Earnings Per Share

Earnings per share (EPS) calculations are required for both income before extraordinary items and net income. Common stock equivalents are included as part of the EPS information.

Business Combinations

Pooling of interests accounting is mandatory when there is a combining of shareholder interests through an exchange of shares and specified criteria are met. If the criteria are not met, purchase accounting must be used.

Practical Considerations

Background

The power to determine the financial accounting policies that are used in the United States is divided between the public sector (for example, the SEC) and the private sector (bodies such as the FASB). Financial accounting has developed primarily in the private sector via the Financial Accounting Standards Board (FASB), which is part of the American Institute of Certified Public Accountants. The FASB standards are accounting rules that govern the preparation of financial statements in the United States and are considered to be more detailed and industry-specific than the U.K. equivalents. The primary influence of government on the establishment of U.S. GAAP is through the Securities and Exchange Commission (SEC), which was created via an Act of U.S. Congress in 1934. It was set up to perform quasi-judicial, quasi-legislative, and administrative functions, regulating the selling and trading of securities to the public. The general purpose of the SEC is to ensure full and fair disclosure to the investors. The SEC officially recognizes the FASB's standards as authoritative.

As a general rule, the financial statements of U.S. corporations require more extensive disclosure than their counterparts around the world. The disclosures required by the accounting profession and the SEC are extremely stringent. For example, in addition to the annual report, a publicly quoted corporation must file a statement with the SEC (the 10K statement, certified by its auditors) containing additional information about the company and its performance. These corporations must also file quarterly reports, together with a 10Q statement (the quarterly equivalent to a 10K) within 45 days of the end of the period.

Deferred Taxation

Deferred taxes are provided in full for all timing differences in the year in which they originate. The objective is to defer the tax effect of a transaction and to reflect it in the income statement in the year in which the transaction giving rise to that timing difference is reported in book income. The deferred taxes are provided at the rates in effect in the period in which the timing difference originates. Under the deferral method no adjustment is made to amounts for deferred tax in the balance sheet for subsequent tax rate changes.

Goodwill

Goodwill arising on a purchase acquisition should be amortized over the useful life of the goodwill. This period must not be longer than 40 years. Amortization of goodwill acquired before November 1, 1970 is not required, unless that amount has been permanently impaired, in which case it should be immediately written down. Negative goodwill is allocated pro-rata against the fair values of property and other nonmonetary assets. If this allocation reduces the nonmonetary assets to a value of zero, the remainder of the excess over cost is classified as a deferred credit and amortized to the P&L over a period not exceeding 40 years.

Research and Development

In the United States most research and development costs are expensed as incurred. The only exceptions are R&D performed for others and certain computer software development costs which are considered inventory.

Stocks (Inventories)

In sharp contrast to U.K. accounting practice, the LIFO (last-in first-out) method of stock valuation is extensively used in the United States. During periods of rising prices, a U.S. company's cost of sales will be higher than it would be for a U.K. company using FIFO. However, its balance sheet entry for inventories will be lower.

Fixed Assets

Fixed assets are carried at historical cost in the balance sheet, and no revaluation is permitted. Again, this is in contrast to practice in the United Kingdom, where companies are allowed to revalue.

Leases

Leases that meet specified criteria and are, in substance, acquisitions of assets (i.e., capital leases) must be capitalized, and the consequent obligation recorded as a long-term debt in the balance sheet of the lessee. Payments on other leases, known as *operating leases,* are charged straight to the P&L account.

Earnings Per Share (EPS)

If a company's securities (debt or equity) are publicly traded and if the company is not a wholly owned subsidiary, its EPS must be disclosed. EPS should be disclosed for both income before extraordinary items and net income for all periods presented. It is recommended, but not required, that EPS amounts be presented for extraordinary items.

The average number of shares should include not only the shares actually issued, but also stock options and other securities that are equivalent in substance to common stock (i.e., *common stock equivalents*) and also are dilutive in their effect.

Purchase Accounting or the Pooling of Interests

Business combinations are accounted for either as purchases or pooling of interests. However, these two methods are not alternatives for the same business combination. If certain criteria are met, the pooling of interests must be used; if not, the purchase method applies.

Under the purchase method, the assets and liabilities of the acquired company are adjusted to reflect fair values, and goodwill (based on the purchase price paid) is recognized where appropriate. The financial statements of the companies are combined at the date of acquisition. They are not restated to include the results of the operations of the acquired company for periods prior to acquisition, although for public companies proforma results of operations should be disclosed in a note for the period immediately preceding, as though the companies had been combined at the beginning of that period.

The rationale behind this method is that the combining shareholders neither withdraw nor invest assets. Instead, they exchange voting shares in a ratio that determines their respective interests in the combined company. In order for pooling of interests to be used, specific criteria have to be met. If these criteria are met, pooling of interests is mandatory.

The major test is that at least 90 percent of the voting common shares must be exchanged. In addition, the following points must also be satisfied:

1. The shares issued must be voting shares and must all have the same rights.
2. Neither combining company can have been a subsidiary for two years prior to the merger.
3. The terms of the offer must be the issue of voting shares only. However, payment of dissenters in cash, up to 10 percent of the issued shares, is permissible.
4. Neither of the combining companies can have owned more than 10 percent of the share capital of the other prior to the merger.

Extraordinary Items and Discontinued Operations

Extraordinary items are limits to those events and transactions that are both unusual and that occur infrequently. In practice, many more items are classified as extraordinary in the United Kingdom than in the United States. In contrast to the United Kingdom, U.S. GAAP does not differentiate between extraordinary and exceptional costs.

Under U.S. GAAP, the costs associated with discontinued operations are reported as part of the results of discontinued operations and not as an extraordinary item, as they would be in the United Kingdom. Further, the results of the operations applicable to a discontinued segment are reported separately in the income statement, after income from continuing operations and before extraordinary items.

Other Features

The following are more theoretical comments about accounting practices in the United States.

Consolidated Financial Statements

The consolidation should only include those subsidiaries (both domestic and foreign) over which the company has effective and permanent control. Subsidiaries in business that are completely dissimilar to that of the parent company (for example, the insurance subsidiary of a manufacturing company) are often excluded from consolidation and instead are stated on an equity basis. Unlike the United Kingdom, there is no requirement for uniform accounting policies for all companies which are included in the consolidation.

The financial statements consist of a balance sheet, an income statement, supplementary notes, and a statement of changes in the financial position (known as a *statement of source and application of funds* in the United Kingdom). Balance sheets prepared under U.S. GAAP generally show assets and liabilities in decreasing order of liquidity, and the equity section appears after liabilities. In contrast, U.K. balance sheets usually show assets in the reverse order of liquidity. U.S. income statements are more detailed than their U.K. equivalents and can contain up to 24 line items, together with extensive note disclosure. Under U.S. rules, a statement of changes in financial position is required for all profit-oriented organizations. Its context and format does not differ markedly from that in the United Kingdom. However, the U.S. statement begins with post tax net income (or loss) instead of the pre-tax result as in the United Kingdom, and more emphasis is placed in the United States on showing the investing and financing activities separately.

Foreign Currency Translation

In December 1981, FASB 52 was issued, superseding FASB 8. The standard aims to reflect the diversity of circumstances surrounding foreign operations. Because of this diversity, FASB 52 recognizes that no single method of translation is appropriate in all circumstances.

The standard introduced a new concept, the *functional currency*. Companies must identify the functional currency of each foreign operation. The functional currency of a particular operation is the currency of the primary economic environment in which it operates. For example, the functional currency of an operation that is relatively self-contained and integrated within a foreign country would ordinarily be its local currency. But the U.S. dollar would normally be the functional currency of a foreign entity that is a direct extension of the company's U.S. operations, such as a branch. The functional currency is important because under the new rules the method of translation used for a particular foreign operation depends on that entity's functional currency.

- Where the local currency is designated as the functional currency, translation will be accomplished through the use of the current rate method.
- Where the U.S. dollar is designated as the functional currency, the temporal method (outlined in FASB 8) will continue to be used, with certain exceptions.
- The temporal method is also required in translating the results of operations in highly inflationary economies. This requirement has been included in the statement in order to prevent the "evaporation" of long-term assets that would occur if the current rate method were to be applied under highly inflationary conditions. The standard provides that the designated functional currency should be used con-

sistently, unless significant alterations in economic facts and circumstances clearly indicate a need to change the functional currency.

The two methods of translation—the current rate and the temporal method—are to be used as follows:

1. *The current rate method of translation.* The current rate method applies where the local currency is the functional currency. Under this method, all assets and liabilities are translated at the exchange rate ruling at the balance sheet date. Translation gains and losses are accumulated in a reserve and are only transferred to income on sale or liquidation of a foreign subsidiary. Exchange gains and losses on foreign currency transactions are, however, included in income.
2. *Temporal method.* This is essentially the FASB 8 method and, under the new rules, applies to operations where the U.S. dollar is designated as the functional currency. Under this method, nonmonetary accounts (e.g., fixed assets and depreciation, inventory, and cost of sales) are translated at historical exchange rates while monetary items (such as cash, receivables, and payables) are translated at the current rate. Moreover, under this method all translation and transaction gains and losses are included in determining net income.

In order to give the reader of the accounts a true and fair view, certain disclosures must be made.

1. The transaction gain or loss included in income for the period.
2. An analysis of changes in the reserves due to exchange movements.
3. Any exchange rate changes that occur after the balance sheet date and their effect on unsettled foreign currency balances, if material.

Investment Properties

Investment properties, like properties held for the company's own use, should be stated at the historical cost and depreciation over its useful economic life.

Changes in Accounting Principles

When a company changes its accounting policies (e.g., inventory valuation is changed from LIFO to FIFO) it has to perform a retroactive computation and work out the cumulative effect. This amount is then reported as a separate item in the profit and loss account. In contrast to the U.K., prior-year financial statements should not be restated.

Business Segment Reporting

The annual financial statements of companies whose debt or equity securities are *publicly traded* must provide an analysis of certain information (such as sales and profits) for the company's operations in different industries and in foreign countries. In addition, the company must also give details of revenues from major customers, and both depreciation and capital expenditure by segment. These requirements are much more far-reaching than those applying to U.K. companies.

"Treasury Shares"

In common with the United Kingdom, U.S. corporations are permitted to buy their own shares. However, whereas the U.K. companies are required to cancel those shares it had acquired, the American companies can hold the stock in its balance sheet. This amount should be netted off when calculating shareholders' funds.

Pension Costs

The aim of U.S. pension accounting requirements (FASB 87) is to recognize the cost of an employee's pension benefits on a systematic basis over the employee's period of service. These requirements include, for example, that pension expenses be determined according to a prescribed actuarial cost method, that these calculations are made annually, and that past service costs are amortized. Actuarial gains and losses are recognized as part of total pension costs.

Comparison of international accounting principles

Accounting principles

1. **Consistency**—accounting principles and methods are applied on the same basis from period to period.
2. **Realization**—revenue is recognized when its realization is reasonably assured.
3. **Fair presentation** of the financial statements is required.
4. **Historical cost convention**—departures from the historical cost convention are disclosed.
5. **Accounting policies**—a change in accounting principles or methods without a change in circumstances is accounted for by a prior-year adjustment.
6. **Fixed assets–revaluations**—in historical cost statements, fixed assets are stated at an amount in excess of cost which is determined at irregular intervals.
7. **Fixed assets—revaluations**—when fixed assets are stated, in historical cost statements, at an amount in excess of cost, depreciation based on the revaluation amount is charged to income.
8. **Goodwill**—amortized.
9. **Finance leases capitalized.**
10. **Short-term marketable securities**—at the lower cost or market value.
11. **Inventory** valued at the lower cost or market value.
12. **Manufacturing overhead** allocated to year-end inventory.
13. **Inventory costed** using FIFO
14. **Long-term debt** includes maturities longer than one year.

15. **Deferred tax**—recognized where accounting income and taxable income arise at different times.
16. Total **pension fund** assets and liabilities excluded from a company's financial statements.
17. **Research and development** expensed (note 4).
18. **General purpose** (purely discretionary) **reserves** allowed.
19. **Offsetting**—assets and liabilities are offset against each other in the balance sheet only when a legal right of offset exists.
20. **Unusual and extraordinary gains and losses** are taken to the income statement.
21. **Closing rate method** of foreign translation employed.
22. **Currency translation** gains or losses arising from trading are reflected in current income.
23. **Excess depreciation** permitted.
24. **Basic statements reflect a historical cost valuation** (no price level adjustments).
25. **Supplementary inflation-adjusted** financial statements provided.
26. **Accounting for long-term investments:**
    (i) less than 20% ownership cost method.

    (ii) 20%–50% ownership—equity method.

    (iii) More than 50%—full consolidation.
27. Both **domestic and foreign subsidaries consolidated.**
28. **Acquisitions accounted for under the purchase cost method.**
29. **Minority interest excluded from consolidated income.**
30. **Minority interest excluded from consolidated owners' equity.**

UK	USA	France	Germany	Netherlands	Sweden	Switzerland	Japan
YES	YES	YES	YES	YES	PP	PP	YES
YES	YES	YES	YES	YES	YES	PP	YES
YES	YES	YES	YES	YES	YES	YES	YES
YES	YES	YES	YES	YES	YES	RF	RF
YES	NO	YES	MP	RF	MP	MP	NO
MP	NO	YES	NO	RF	PP	NO	NO
YES	NO	YES	NO	YES	YES	NO	NO
MP	YES	YES	YES	M	YES	MP	YES
YES	YES	NO	NO	NO	YES	RF	NO
YES	YES	YES	YES	YES	YES	YES	YES
YES	YES	YES	YES	YES	YES	YES	Mixed
YES	YES	YES	YES	YES	YES	YES	YES
PP	M	M	M	M	PP	PP	MP
YES (note 1)	YES	YES	NO	YES	YES	YES	YES
YES	YES	YES (note 2)	NO (note 3)	YES (note 3)	NO	NO	NO
YES	NO	YES	NO	YES	YES	YES	YES
YES	YES	YES	YES	YES	YES	YES	PP
NO	NO	YES	YES	YES	YES	YES	YES
YES	YES	YES	YES	YES	YES	PP	YES
YES	YES	YES	YES	YES	YES	YES	YES
YES note 5a	YES note 5a	YES	YES	YES	YES note 5b	YES	YES
YES	YES	MP	MP	MP	MP	MP	MP
YES	NO	YES	YES	YES	YES	YES	YES
YES	YES	YES	YES	M	YES	YES	YES
MP	MP	NO	NO	MP	YES	NO	NO
YES	YES (note 6)	YES (note 7)	YES	NO	YES	YES	YES
YES (note 6)	YES	YES	NO	YES	MP	M	YES
YES	YES	YES	YES	YES	YES	YES	YES
YES	YES	YES	M	YES	YES	MP	YES
PP	PP	YES	YES	YES	PP	YES	YES
YES	YES	YES	YES	YES	YES	YES	YES
YES	YES	YES	YES	YES	YES	YES	YES

(continued)

Key to accounting principles table
PP—Predominant practice
MP—Minority practice
M—Mixed practice
RF—Rarely or not found

Notes to accounting principles table
Note 1
Long-term debt includes maturities longer than four years.

Note 2
Deferred tax most commonly seen in conjunction with:

(1) Provisions reglementées
(2) Amortisement exceptionnel
(3) Provisions pour payées congées

Note 3
Commercial accounts oriented towards the tax calculations. Commercial and tax statements should agree, as in order to obtain the maximum benefit from tax allowances, the most favourable tax-oriented valuations have to be taken up in the financial statements.

Note 4
Under certain circumstances research and development expenses can be capitalized.

Note 5
(a) In certain cases the temporal method is acceptable.
(b) Monetary/nonmonetary method of foreign currency translation used.

Note 6
Proportional consolidation can also be used.

Note 7
Equity/net asset value method used.

APPENDIX

A

Glossary

Accountancy Concepts

There are four basic accounting assumptions:

Going Concern. The enterprise will continue in operational existence for the forseeable future.

Accruals. Revenue and costs are accrued (that is, recognized as they are earned or incurred, not as money is received or paid), matched with one another so far as their relationship can be established or justifiably assumed, and dealt with in the profit and loss account of the period to which they relate.

Consistency. There should be consistency in accounting treatment of like items within each accounting period and from one period to the next.

Prudence. Revenue and profits are not anticipated, but are recognized by inclusion in the profit and loss account only when their realization can be assessed with reasonable certainty. Provision is made for all known liabilities (expenses or losses) whether the amount of these is known with certainty or is a best estimate in the light of the information available.

Acquisition (Purchase) Accounting

The assets and liabilities of the subsidiary are revalued to their fair market value at the date of acquisition. The difference between the consideration and the sum of the revalued net assets is treated as positive or negative goodwill.

The preacquisition profits of the acquired company are not available for distribution.

Book Value

Book value is the value that an asset or liability is given in the financial statements (i.e., its historical value). An asset, such as freehold land, may have a market value in excess of its book value. A liability should not be understated in the financial statements.

Source: USB Phillips & Drew, London.

Consolidation

Full Consolidation.   The results of the subsidiary (i.e., where the parent has over 50 percent voting rights) are taken into the consolidated accounts in full. An appropriate deduction is made for the shares not owned by the parent (i.e., *minority interests*) after "profit on ordinary activities before taxation."

Partial Consolidation.   This method is used mostly for joint ventures. The company will take into its consolidated results its share in the joint venture (if the company owns 60 percent of the joint venture it will take 60 percent sales, cost of sales, etc.).

Equity Accounting.   Equity accounting is used where a company has between 20 percent and 50 percent equity stake in another enterprise, and exercises significant influence. The relevant percentage is taken into the profit and loss account under "share of profits/losses of associated companies." In the balance sheet, the investment is valued at cost plus the relevant share of postacquisition retained reserves.

Deferred Taxation

1. Deferred taxation is the tax attributable to timing differences.
2. Timing differences result from inconsistencies between profits and losses as computed for tax purposes and profits and losses as presented in financial statements. These arise from the inclusion of items of income and expenditure in tax computations in periods different from those which are included in the financial statements. Timing differences originate in one period and are capable of reversal in one or more subsequent periods.

Depreciation

Depreciation is the measure of the wearing out, consumption, or other loss of value of a fixed asset, whether arising from use, passage of time, or obsolescence through technology and market changes.

Earnings Per Share

Earnings per share in the United Kingdom is defined as the profit in pence attributable to each equity share, based on the consolidated profit of the period after tax and after deducting minority interests and preference dividends, but before taking into account extraordinary items, divided by the number of equity shares in issue and ranking for dividend in respect of the period.

Exceptional and Extraordinary Items

Exceptional Items.   Exceptional items are material items which derive from events or transactions that fall within the ordinary activities of the company, and which need to be disclosed separately by virtue of the size or incidence if the financial statements are to give a true and fair view.

Extraordinary Items. Extraordinary items are material items which derive from events or transactions that fall outside the ordinary activities of the company and which are therefore not expected to recur frequently or regularly.

The distinction between extraordinary items and exceptional items is very important in the UK. Earnings in the earnings-per-share calculation includes exceptional items but excludes extraordinary items. In Europe, it is often difficult to distinguish between the two types of items through lack of information.

Goodwill

Goodwill is the difference between the purchase consideration and the aggregate of the fair values (market value) of its separable net assets (those assets and liabilities which can be identified and sold separately, without necessarily disposing of the business as a whole).

Holding Company

A company which exercises control over another company, its subsidiary company, and is referred to as the parent company.

Investment Properties

Investment properties are properties which are held as disposable investments rather than for use in a manufacturing or commercial process.

Leases

1. A *finance lease* is a lease that transfers substantially all the risks and rewards of ownership of an asset to the lessee.
2. An *operating lease* is a lease other than a finance lease.
3. A *hire purchase contract* is the contract for the hire of an asset which contains a provision giving the hirer an option to acquire legal title to the asset upon the fulfillment of certain conditions stated in the contract.

Merger Accounting (Pooling of Interests)

The main features of merger accounting are as follows:

1. Shares issued by the holding company in exchange for shares in a subsidiary are valued at nominal value, not at fair market value.
2. The consolidated balance sheet includes the retained profits of both companies as being distributable.
3. Assets and liabilities may be retained at their book value in the consolidated accounts. The only adjustment which may be made is that

necessary to bring the accounting policies of the two companies into line with each other.

Net Realizable Value

The actual or estimated selling price less all further costs to completion and all costs to be incurred in marketing, selling, and distribution.

Prior Year Adjustments

These are material adjustments applicable to prior years arising from changes in accounting policies or from the correction of fundamental errors.

Share Capital.

1. *Share capital* in the balance sheet is the nominal value of the shares in issue.
2. *Share premium* is the amount paid for a share, on its issue, in excess of the nominal value.
3. *Called-up share capital*
   a. *Fully-paid called-up share capital*—Share capital that is authorized, issued, and fully "paid up."
   b. *Partly-paid called-up share capital*—Share capital that is authorized, issued, and only partly "paid up."

Subsidiary

A company is a subsidiary of another if, but only if, that other either is a member of it and controls the composition of its Board of Directors, or holds more than half the nominal value of its equity share capital.

True and Fair View

In the United Kingdom there is no definition of *true and fair* provided by statute. However, it is generally accepted that to give such a view, accounts must:

1. Be prepared on the basis of the four fundamental accounting policies concepts (see Accounting Concepts).
2. Present an overall picture that is not in any way misleading.
3. Disclose all information material to a proper understanding of the accounts.
4. Describe the amounts in the accounts in such a way that their true nature is described unambiguously.

Useful Economic Life

The best estimate of the life of the asset from the date of purchase.

Withholding Tax

Withholding tax is tax that is withheld at source on dividend payments.

B

International Accounting Organizations

International Accounting Standards
  Committee (IASC)
  41 Kingsway
  London WC 28 6 YU
  United Kingdom

International Federation of Accountants
  (IFAC)
  540 Madison Avenue
  New York, NY 10020
  U.S.A.

European Accounting Association (EAA)
  c/o EFMD
  40 Rue Washington
  B-1050 Brussels
  Belgium

Index